PETROTYRANNY

Praise for *Petrotyranny*

"John Bacher's carefully researched book opens the reader's eyes to the evil role crude oil has come to play in the modern world, creating dictatorial regimes, stirring up civil strife, generating wars among nations, and guiding empires in their policies of domination. Focusing on oil reveals the inner connections between the politics of injustice and oppression as it is variously practiced on all continents of the world. Moving from country to country, John Bacher shows how oil interests have helped to shape the structures of inequality and exclusion. At the same time, the author offers a hopeful picture of the social movements in support of human rights and ecological responsibility. Petrotyranny is not an ineluctable condition. If all of us participate in a cultural revolution, justice and peace may still prevail."

Gregory Baum

"For understanding our present human situation few subjects are of such urgency as that of Petroleum. Our food, clothing, energy, transportation and plastics are more dependent on petroleum than on any other of our natural resources. So too our economic-political structures and functioning are largely determined by this resource. For these reasons the study of petroleum in the life of our society is of overwhelming significance. Others have written on petroleum and its geographical location in the Earth, its volume, its role in contemporary economics. This book by an accomplished scholar does something different. It gives us, for the first time, a thorough overview of the influence of petroleum on the political-social structures and functioning of the various nations of the world. Even more it identifies movements already in progress for shifting from a polluting non-renewable petroleum basis of our economy to an ecologically sound renewable source for all our basic needs. The American people, especially those still in their younger years, should read this book if they are to make wise decisions in these perilous moments as we enter the 21st century."

Thomas Berry
Author of The Great Work:
Our Way Into the Future

"If society allows the pillage of Mother Earth to continue, our children's future will be blacker than the oil extracted. John Bacher brings the concerns and wisdom of the Sacredness of our Mother Earth's body in his new book about greed, war, pollution and survival."

Ronkwetason, Spirit Man (Danny Beaton),
Turtle Clan Kahniakehaka (Mohawk)

PETROTYRANNY

JOHN BACHER

SCIENCE FOR PEACE

DUNDURN PRESS
TORONTO · OXFORD

Editors: Shirley Farlinger and Derek Paul
Design: Jennifer Scott
Printer: Transcontinental

Canadian Cataloguing in Publication Data

Bacher, John C. (John Christopher), 1954-
   Petrotyranny

ISBN 0-88866-956-9

1. Petroleum industry and trade — Political aspects. 2. Renewable energy sources. I. Title.

HD9560.5B23 2000   333.8'232   C00-931871-2

1 2 3 4 5   04 03 02 01 00

THE CANADA COUNCIL | LE CONSEIL DES ARTS
FOR THE ARTS | DU CANADA
SINCE 1957 | DEPUIS 1957

Canadä

ONTARIO ARTS COUNCIL
CONSEIL DES ARTS DE L'ONTARIO

We acknowledge the support of the **Canada Council for the Arts** and the **Ontario Arts Council** for our publishing program. We also acknowledge the financial support of the **Government of Canada** through the **Book Publishing Industry Development Program, The Association for the Export of Canadian Books**, and the **Government of Ontario** through the **Ontario Book Publishers Tax Credit** program.

Care has been taken to trace the ownership of copyright material used in this book. The author and the publisher welcome any information enabling them to rectify any references or credit in subsequent editions.

J. Kirk Howard, President

Printed and bound in Canada.
Printed on recycled paper.

Science for Peace
University College
University of Toronto
Toronto, Ontario M5S 1A1

www.dundurn.com

Dundurn Press	Dundurn Press	Dundurn Press
8 Market Street	73 Lime Walk	2250 Military Road
Suite 200	Headington, Oxford,	Tonawanda NY
Toronto, Ontario, Canada	England	U.S.A. 14150
M5E 1M6	OX3 7AD	

Dedication

This book is dedicated to my mother
Mary Bacher and to two other friends
who helped and encouraged me with the draft manuscript
Metta Spencer and Gracia Janes and to my friend
Danny Beaton who put me in touch with many
Native American spiritual elders

John Bacher

CONTENTS

PREFACE

Books submitted for publication in our Dundurn series are accepted on their merits, compatibility with the goals of Science for Peace and timeliness of subject matter. Generally a typescript is submitted to a process of peer review prior to acceptance. Authors wishing to publish through Science for Peace should write in the first instance to the Publications Committee, Science for Peace, H2, University College, University of Toronto, Toronto, Ontario M5S 1A1.

Notes: Throughout this book the word *oil* is used as a general term to include petroleum and the derivatives of oil. Only when natural gas is specifically to be included do we use the more cumbersome word *petroleum*. Dollar values given in this book are in US dollars unless otherwise stated. Several key words occur so frequently that they have been omitted from the Index; for example: automobile, car, democracy, dictatorship, environment, Europe, Latin America, Middle East, natural gas, oil, United States, US.

— The editors

ACKNOWLEDGEMENTS

The preparation of this book has been greatly assisted by the most useful comments of Professor Simon Dalby and Professor Mel Watkins, which we acknowledge with gratitude. Special thanks to Tom Lane for his reading. In addition we have received useful comments or help from Bruce Allen, Bev and Rob Carruthers, Phyllis Creighton, Stephen Dankovich, Barbara and Terry Doran, David Dorey, Janet and Bob Gouinlouck, James Lemon, Julia Morton-Marr and Douglas Woodward. Lastly, we received some useful data from Lise Christofferson of the Royal Danish Consulate General, for which we are grateful. To all of these people we express our thanks.

The author and the editors

FOREWORD
BY DAVID SUZUKI

The media continue to portray climate change as a scientific "controversy." Thus, an expert warning of the need to reduce greenhouse gas emissions is invariably "balanced" by another expert discounting the evidence of global warming and warning of the prematurity of taking action to reduce emissions. The reality is that all but a handful of climatologists are convinced climate change induced by human activity is occurring.

In countries like the United States and Canada, the fossil fuel industry has enormous political clout by virtue of its role in the economy. In advertising alone, tens of millions are expended by the industry to counter any attempt to reduce greenhouse gas emissions. Most political candidates face increasingly expensive campaigns for office and depend on financial support from corporations. Thus, industries acquire considerable political access and lobbying influence. The industry constantly warns of the economic devastation that would result from imposition of targets for reducing greenhouse gas emission.

This book is a shocking documentation that the influence of the fossil fuel industry extends far beyond the political corridors of North America. Those who call for less and less government action in setting reduction targets and enforcing emission standards are dooming future generations to problems that will be far more expensive and much more intractable. If knowledge is power, then any reader of this book should be loaded for action.

CHAPTER ONE
INTRODUCTION

Oil consumption is seen by most citizens of affluent democracies as an innocent, almost wholesome activity. Although oil sometimes receives negative attention, as it did in the Gulf War and following the Exxon Valdez disaster, burning oil as fuel is seldom viewed as one of the deadly sins. Smoking, littering and illegal drug use all receive much more public censure than filling up the tank. Although movements for the smoke-free workplace are growing, few have lobbied for the creation of analogous oil-free zones.

Many of the reasons for the apparent innocence of oil are understandable, even admirable. In the densely populated areas of prosperous and democratic Japan, Europe and North America, forest cover increased as oil replaced wood-burning stoves. Even the familiar horrors of oil, such as tarred sea birds and blazing oil wells, are commonly viewed as mild compared to older dangers of coal and the newer hazards of nuclear power.

US theorist Lewis Mumford spoke eloquently and passionately of the horrors of the "Paleotechnic age" when coal was the world's dominant energy source. The perils of coal were and remain quite real. Coal is the most objectionable fossil fuel contributing to global warming. Burning coal causes acid rain and mining it poisons streams. Coal creates a deadly nightmare of dangers for workers and their communities. These include collapsing mineshafts and landslides that can bury schools and villages.

The use of oil is generally associated with progress and comfort. Despite traffic jams, breakdowns or risky incidents, driving is commonly viewed as a pleasurable activity. Even the luxurious carriages of the Victorian elite fail to inspire a similar promise of satisfaction. The days of the horse and buggy, although within the lifespan of most of our grandparents, appear as remote as the Middle Ages. The idea of being met by a carriage at a train station, for a week-end trip to the summer cottage, seems equally remote.

Nearly every person who owns a private means of oil-assisted transport treasures the sense of freedom that comes from these powerful possessions. The humblest motor scooter gives options that surpass the fastest chariot or stagecoach of days gone by.

Few appreciate that the most wasteful forms of oil consumption, such as driving a massive sports utility vehicle to fetch a carton of milk during a smog alert, do harm comparable to smoking in a crowded public place. Letting car engines idle or using petroleum-powered lawnmowers can contribute to fatal illnesses in heavily polluted cities, yet they are not viewed as crimes comparable to assault. Such offensive actions could be ended by using a hand-powered lawnmower, or walking to the nearest store.

This book highlights the remarkable success in curbing oil consumption in democracies such as Taiwan, Japan, Costa Rica, Denmark and the Netherlands. These examples illustrate how reducing oil consumption can be relatively painless. Restrictions that would push society backward into an unacceptable past mode of living are unnecessary.

The popular association of oil consumption with comfort has been greatly reinforced by land-use planning in North America, which has long been based on the assumption that private transport is an inevitable and dominant fact of life. Even the great iconoclast Lewis Mumford boasted that his model town was designed for the car. The most harmful manner in which incentives have been built into urban form to encourage cars and motorcycles is single-purpose land-use zoning. Zoning to keep polluting, coal-burning factories away from residential neighbourhoods assists the goals of public health and safety. However, the public good is not served by keeping apart retail services and housing. With suburban tracts segregated from shopping centres, the task of getting a loaf of bread becomes an athletic challenge for those without private transport, particularly the elderly. As several chapters illustrate, this is not the way that land-use planning and transportation issues are handled in Copenhagen, Bologna, Amsterdam, or Curitiba, Brazil.

In dictatorships, oil's environmental impacts cannot be effectively regulated by legislated standards. For example, traffic safety is difficult to achieve. Tyrannies invariably have high accident and death rates. This is a theme of Chapter Three, which shows how oil consumption presents most of humanity with a cruel illusion.

Laws to protect forests and wildlife and to prevent pollution may exist in dictatorships, but they are less well enforced than in democracies. Attempts to circumvent these laws by corruption are less subject to public sanctions in dictatorships. Here there are not the pressures of a free press and possible governmental defeat in multi-party elections. Thus, environmental problems associated with oil, such as gas flaring and leaking pipelines, are especially severe in countries whose citizens are denied basic human rights.

Oil has its most tragic consequences in connection with dictatorships. Oil wealth is the biggest single factor sustaining these tyrannies. Oil profits' aid to repression also makes them a principal cause of war. This book shows how, by sustaining dictatorship, oil wealth goes hand in hand with forest destruction and the loss of biodiversity in much of the world.

Most of the planning and expenditure for wars involves internal conflict within oil-rich states, or possible wars between dictatorships over disputed oil resources. This problem is examined for a number of countries, including Mexico, Colombia, Peru, Indonesia, the two Congos, Chad, Cameroon, Angola and every petroleum-producing state in the Middle East.

This book illustrates how the deadly trinity of oil, war and dictatorship presents the greatest challenge to humanity at the start of the new millennium. Fortunately, with conservation, and by replacing fossil fuels and nuclear energy with renewables, it is possible to foster instead a holy trinity of peace, human rights and environmental sustainability.

Security threats to democracies have been the subject of considerable debate, although not the focus of writers on the petroleum industry, such as Daniel Yergin, author of the provocative history of that industry, *The Prize*. The debates have tended to be grouped into two camps of influential writers: the strategic studies analysts dominated by the towering figure of Samuel Huntington through his book, *The Clash of Civilizations*; and the other group stressing the destabilizing effects of environmental scarcity, highlighted in the innovative writings of University of Toronto Peace Studies Professor Tad Homer-Dixon, and the controversial American journalist Robert Kaplan.

Both the writings on the clash of civilizations and those on resource scarcity tend to overlook the great magnitude of the problems caused by petrotyranny. In particular, Huntington's stress on Islam as a barrier to democracy ignores how oil wealth in these same states has been a buttress to dictatorship. Most writings on resource depletion ignore the role of dictatorships in degrading the environment.

Today nearly all environmental groups that are concerned about climate change and promote sustainable energy recognize the need to stop coal and oil burning in the long term. Since these fuels pollute in the short and medium term, society must without delay begin the change to dependence on renewables.

The urgency of dealing with climate change has brought about a renewed interest in nuclear energy in some circles. However, the hazards of nuclear power, linked to weaponry that has the potential to destroy all human life with a push of a button, are ominous. The catastrophe of Chernobyl dwarfs the worst disasters connected with petroleum.

This book highlights a new urgency to move away from fossil fuels by clarifying the threats of petrotyranny and war. The challenge of achieving a democratic peace is thus connected to global energy policies everywhere, which are detailed in all the chapters dealing with dictatorship.

The transition to an oil-free, democratic world is required to prevent a holocaust of species extinctions, horrific military expenditures and prolonged wars. Dictatorships can be challenged through courageous nonviolent actions. Such action saw the Berlin Wall come down and stopped a coup by communist hardliners against the freedom movement in the USSR. Similar nonviolent democratic oppositions have toppled tyrannies from South Africa to the Philippines.

In the world's remaining dictatorships and semi-democracies, nonviolent human rights activists continue bravely to advance the cause of freedom. We can help these heroic efforts by reducing the flow of oil income to their oppressors.

CHAPTER TWO
How Oil Sustains Dictatorship

Oil is critical to the support of dictatorships since it provides the most abundant form of wealth for a repressive government — income that does not have to be obtained through taxation. The collection of taxes generally compels a higher degree of consent from citizens than a misappropriation of oil rents when big money is needed for the repressive apparatus of despotism.

While repression is in retreat in the post-Cold-War world, the remaining havens of dictatorship are concentrated in oil-rich states, many of which export war and repression beyond their borders. Such mischief is encouraged by the two Congos, the tiny but oil-rich Sultanate of Brunei, Angola and almost every oil-producing state in the Middle East.

Semi-democracies such as Mexico, Colombia, Russia and Peru are helped in their repressive power by their oil exports. Russia can support allies such as Yugoslavia through its revenues from oil exports. Mexico's role as a reliable oil producer causes it to receive billions in bailouts from the United States in place of the economic sanctions that are imposed on other human-rights abusers.

The Superoil Dictatorships

The US superpower is frequently challenged by the phenomenon of the superoil dictatorships — the five Persian Gulf states each having more than 70 billion barrels of oil. They are: The United Arab Emirates, Iran, Iraq, Kuwait and Saudi Arabia. Of these only Kuwait is rated by the US human-rights group Freedom House as partially free. The rest are ranked as "not free", the designation given by Freedom House for absolute dictatorships.

The impartiality of Freedom House, an American human-rights organization, is shown by its consistently low ranking for Saudi Arabia despite its being a close US ally. The Saudi reserves of 258 billion barrels amount to more than double those of any other superoil dictatorship, or of any other country.

Since Freedom House began its annual national rankings for political rights and civil liberties in 1955, Saudi Arabia has consistently been given the worst ratings. One of its closest allies in the pro-US Gulf Co-operation Council, The United Arab Emirates, another oil superpower, is also rated by Freedom House as not free [1].

Freedom House recognizes that there are different degrees of repression among dictatorships. It has a ranking scale of freedom for the world's states, with separate categories for both political rights and civil liberties. Full democracies are ranked at one to three, partially free states at four to five, and dictatorships or not-free states at six to seven.

There are 16 states currently ranked as the worst dictatorships, with ratings of seven in both civil liberties and political rights. Among these 16 are some of the world's biggest oil producers including Saudi Arabia and Iraq.

Significant oil producers in the rogue's gallery of despotic states include Equatorial Guinea, China, Turkmenistan, Sudan, Syria, Libya, and Myanmar (formerly Burma). Several other states without exploited petroleum reserves that are among the most repressive dictatorships, most notably North Korea and Afghanistan, receive substantial economic assistance from oil-rich states. Out of the said 16 worst countries only four are not tied to the vortex of oil-financed oppression.

The human-rights situation is disastrous in Iraq. Its oil reserves, like those of its enemy, Iran, are estimated to be 100 billion barrels [2].

The superoil dictatorships are sharply divided on issues of religion, alliance, language and ideology. A common feature is the absence of any independent labour movement.

Free labour movements have been critical in crushing despotism from Poland to South Africa. Oil wealth now keeps such movements out of the Persian Gulf, where labour organizing died out in the late 1970s. At that time a flood of money was obtained from the sudden price increases achieved by the Organization of Petroleum Exporting Countries (OPEC). This made it possible for the superoil states to buy off labour demands without recognizing the democratizing principles of free collective bargaining [3].

In addition to providing a carrot, oil wealth gives the superoil states a big stick, used with special severity against groups in the state not represented in their country's ruling elite. These states have maintained the most wide-ranging religious persecution of the post-Cold-War period, except for Myanmar. All these tyrannies continue to practise capital punishment and use torture. Some make mutilations part of normal sentencing.

Saudi Arabia's religious intolerance is a product of the dictatorship's historic roots in an alliance between the ruling Saud dynasty and the Wahhabi sect of Sunni Islam. This has resulted in religious persecution that falls harshly on Christians and Shiite Muslims. Christians are forbidden to wear crosses, read a Bible in public, or utter non-Islamic prayers. *Religious police* search for clandestine church services. In December 1992 two Christian Filipino nationals were arrested for preaching on Christmas Day. Because of their foreign nationality, their deaths sentences were commuted, and they were deported [4].

Iraq's secular Arab nationalist government has brutally relocated many Shiite civilians and driven thousands into exile. Bans on Shiite ceremonies and books have been imposed. Authorities have desecrated the faith's most holy shrines [5].

Since its revolution in 1978, Iran's Shiite theocracy has exhibited extreme repression against religious minorities. Amnesty International estimates that 200 Baha'is have been executed. Authorities rarely grant approval for the publication of Christian texts. Islamic knowledge is required for admission to universities and the civil service [6].

Dissidents in the superoil states are threatened by the world's most ruthless security services. In Iran, executions of 100 to 200 persons per year for political reasons have been the norm since the revolution. Saudi Arabia employs one of the most blood-stained judicial systems. In 1997, it executed 123 persons. Police routinely torture detainees to extract confessions. The UN has documented the disappearance of 16,000 Iraqi civilians in recent years. Iraqi women are subjected to the worst terror in the world: men are granted immunity for killing female relations involved in alleged acts of vice [7].

OIL, NOT SPIRITUAL CULTURE, HAS BLOCKED THE SPREAD OF FREEDOM

Many of the religious faiths have been blamed for delays in the advance of liberty since the end of the Cold War. American strategic studies analyst, Samuel Huntington, has vilified Islam, while Robert Kaplan described animism as the curse of Africa.

Islamic states suffer not from their ancient and honourable spiritual cultures but from the curse of oil. Only Mali is now recognized by

Freedom House as fully democratic among Islamic majority states. It is a country that lacks oil. Except for Kuwait, all the Islamic states that export oil are rated as not free.

There are also several Islamic majority semi-democracies that lack oil — Albania, Bosnia, Bangladesh, the Kyrgyz Republic and Turkey. They all have better democratic ratings than Kuwait, the most liberal Islamic-majority state that exports oil. In Albania and Bangladesh, governments have been peacefully changed through free elections.

In the vanguard of freedom in many Islamic nations there have been many heroic champions of democracy. Freedom, for instance, came to oilless Bangladesh in 1990. This democratic restoration took place after a 15-year old military dictatorship was overthrown through massive demonstrations and strikes.

Since the return of democratic government Bangladesh has made considerable progress. One step was signing on December 2, 1997, an accord which successfully ended its long civil war in the Chittagong Hills District. This tolerantly granted regional autonomy for a district largely composed of Buddhist hill tribes [8].

Prior to India's independence, many Islamic supporters of freedom were committed democrats in the Congress Party. Most of these democratically minded Muslims stayed in India following independence. However, many others stayed in newly formed Pakistan. The most deeply committed to the cause of freedom was a close supporter of Gandhi, the remarkable statesman, Badshah Khan.

Badshah Khan was colonial India's bravest champion of nonviolent tactics in situations of extreme danger. He organized his Congress Party followers in the North West Frontier Province, bordering Afghanistan. Here his Khudai Khidmatagar movement was able in the early 1930s to face down gunfire from British troops as part of a successful campaign for an elected provincial government.

Following the establishment of Pakistan, Badshah Khan spent 15 years in and out of prison and seven in exile. In 1962, he was honoured by Amnesty International as their prisoner of the year. In 1956, Badshah Khan founded the Awami League. This was Pakistan's first social democratic party and is now the dominant political force in Bangladesh. His heroic story is typical of many brave crusades for freedom in the Islamic world [9].

With his finger pointing at animism, Kaplan is as off the mark as Huntington is in his castigation of Islam. The progress of democracy in Africa, as in the rest of the world, has been swiftest when there is no oil to hinder it. Benin is the only predominantly African animist state, but it is one of a handful of fully democratic democracies on the continent. Apart from the strength of its democratic movement, its absence of oil made it easier for outside lenders to encourage a democratic transition when the country was essentially bankrupt during the worldwide democracy wave of 1989 [10].

Huntington's witch-hunting of the world's religions for demons who oppose democracy leaves few corners in the world untouched. He attributes much of the authoritarianism in Latin America to Catholicism. Likewise the difficulties of democratic transitions in the USSR and much of Eastern Europe are blamed on Orthodox Christianity. He stresses antidemocratic elements in Hinduism and ancient Chinese civilization.

Huntington's varied attacks on diverse faith traditions ignore the deadly mix of oil and fundamentalism that undermines democracy in much of the world. Blaming European influences for most of the authoritarian elements in Latin-American culture, Huntington ignores the role played by American oil companies and their allied Protestant fundamentalist sects. His suspicions about the incompatibility of Orthodox Christianity and democracy have recently been challenged by the success of freedom movements in Romania and Bulgaria. While these countries have the same faith as Russia, they lack its great oil wealth [11].

The antidemocratic outrages of Belarus, Serbia and Russia are more the result of the totalitarian toxic residue from atheistic Communism than holy Eastern Christian spiritual traditions. The embrace of the ruthless Russian military actions in Chechnya by the atheistic leadership of the Chinese Communists on the eve of Christmas 1999 illustrates how tyrants still unite against the free world.

The divisions between Western and Eastern Christianity are not based on profound doctrinal concepts. They emerged largely from linguistic differences between Greek and Latin and an ancient administrative division of the Roman Empire.

The Orthodox clergy of Serbia are playing a major role in their country's brave democracy movement. It is a small part of this ancient faith's crusade for ecological healing in the new millennium. Guided by its visionary Patriarch, Bartholomew, the Eastern Orthodox Church is now engaged in a remarkable effort that unites the quest for peace, freedom and environmental restoration.

The core leader of Orthodox civilization is in profound disagreement with Samuel Huntington. Patriarch Bartholomew supports the entry of more countries into the European Union and has refuted Huntington's notion "that Europe ends where Orthodoxy begins."

Bartholomew's quest for a united free Europe is based on the notion of a Christian faith revitalized by a reverence for nature. He has termed pollution a "sin" and "sacrilege". The Eastern Patriarch has passionately declared that it is "morally unacceptable to burden others with our waste."

The spiritual passion for nature of the Orthodox Patriarch emerged in his blessing the Danube River, in early December 1999. Here he lamented, "The Danube is a life-giving river. Yet it is in danger of becoming a river of death, carrying pollutants and toxic substances."

The Reverend John Chyssargis, an important adviser to the Patriarch, has stressed that "part of worshipping God is to respect nature. In modernity we have separated the soul from nature. We are saying that we can bring them back together again."

The religious seminaries of the Orthodox faith have become training centres and forums in democratic environmental green activism. Such strategies are intended to eventually transfer the environmental concerns of the church's leadership into grass roots actions at the parish level [11].

Huntington correctly identifies a tendency for an affluent minority to take part in fundamentalist movements that weaken democracy and threaten war. However, he disregards how lower income groups tend to have a non-fundamentalist religion, frequently based on reverence for nature. Examples of a democratic green faith include the Sufi of Sudan, the Catholic base communities of Latin America and the popular Hinduism of rural India. While oil, authoritarianism and fundamentalism mix, so do Earth-respecting movements for ecology and freedom.

In India, both secular authoritarians and Hindu fundamentalists tend to have contempt for concerns of environmental preservation. The *Emergency* was a two-year period of martial law from 1975 to 1977. It was spearheaded by secular authoritarians such as auto enthusiast Sanjay Gandhi, the black sheep of the democratically minded Nehru family.

The *Emergency* was catastrophic for the environment. During this time the enormous Kudremukh iron ore mining and smelting complex was begun in the South Indian State of Karnatakata. It turned formerly lush tropical rainforests of the mountainous Western Ghats into sterile bare rock for subsidized steel and automotive production. This scheme was pushed by the suspension of normal democratic debate and controls [12].

Secular assaults on Indian democracy have been replaced by attacks based on religious fundamentalism. Much of folk Hinduism is expressed in defence of forests threatened by the oil-based luxuries loved by India's fundamentalist minority. One of these popular democratic actions is the defence of sacred groves of trees. The most revered is the grove of Karikanamma, mother goddess of a dark forest perched on a hill overlooking the Arabian Sea [13].

Late-Victorian notions of progress, coupled uncomfortably with notions of the sacredness of nature, further stimulated conflicts between Muslims and Hindus in India. British university-educated founders of the Muslim League, which created the notion of a separate Islamic state of Pakistan, had contempt for Sufi rites intended to secure an emotional bond with the Earth. They despised ancient Sufi seers and poets who stressed religious tolerance and love of nature. Likewise imperially trained high-caste Hindus ridiculed popular elements of their own traditional veneration of nature, such as the pacifist and literally tree-hugging Bishnoi.

Reverence for sacred trees is a common part of popular religion among both Hindus and Muslims in India. This has taken on a new ecological significance. The sacred neem tree is now appreciated as a non-toxic insecticide, a vital ingredient to organic-farming movements around the world. The pipal tree is popularly considered as the dwelling place for the Hindu sacred Trinity of Brahman, Vishnu and Shiva. It is also revered as the tree where Buddha obtained enlightenment. The pipal tree is a common feature around the shrines of many sacred sites of different faith traditions. The sandalwood tree of southern India has long been venerated by rural communities of both Hindus and Muslims. The sacred banyan tree cannot be used for firewood or fuel, and is also planted near shrines.

The coconut palm, a central element of the economy of the green democratic oasis of Kerala, is widely viewed as a sacred species throughout the tropics. Coconuts are used ceremonially in blessing the bridegroom at weddings.

Nowadays these trees are threatened with destruction to provide luxuries for affluent fundamentalists. Muslim and Hindu villagers protect trees at the risk of their lives. Such humble passion for the Earth is incomprehensible to the haughty strategists of India and Pakistan who develop mad scenarios for nuclear war between the two states [13].

OIL, NOT RELIGION, FUELS DICTATORSHIP AND WAR

Huntington's warnings of a possible third world war between a combination of Islamic and Chinese civilizations, versus "the west", popularize the earlier work of another American strategic studies expert,

Kent Calder, author of *Pacific Defense*. However, many of Calder's facts, as opposed to the analysis he draws from them, actually support the notion of building democracy through devaluing oil.

TABLE 1

LIBERTY AND DICTATORSHIP IN ASIA

AMONG OIL HAVES AND HAVE NOTS IN 1992

Oil Haves	+ Export / - Import (1000s of barrels/day)	Freedom Rating
Indonesia	+ 840	not free
Malaysia	+ 450	partly free
China	+ 450	not free
Brunei	+ 165	not free
Vietnam	+ 75	not free

Oil Have Nots		
Japan	-5,282	free
South Korea	-1,185	free
Taiwan	- 570	free
Thailand	- 440	partly free
Singapore	- 380	partly free
Philippines	- 225	free

When combined with Freedom House's human rights rankings, a different threat to security emerges from Calder's energy data. His illustration of Asia's oil "haves and have nots" reveals Asia's oil exporters to be repressive, while those that import oil were in 1992, or have since become, full democracies except for Singapore.

Calder's data show all four Asian full democracies on Freedom House's 1998 list as oil importers, while every "not free" country was an oil exporter in 1992. Japan has been a democracy since 1947, whereas lack of oil made the former dictatorships of Taiwan, South Korea and the Philippines more vulnerable to their freedom movements. All listed countries that were oil exporters in 1992 had failed to democratize by the beginning of 1998.

Indonesia has subsequently begun a democratization process but the human rights situation in every other 1992 Asian oil exporter — Brunei, Vietnam, Malaysia and China — has still not improved.

There are many other ways in which the relationship between oil and dictatorship can be quantified and studied. This is evident in tables 2 and 3, which compare nations' freedom ratings and their oil reserves.

TABLE 2

NUMBERS AND PERCENTAGES OF COUNTRIES HAVING OIL WEALTH
ABOVE VARIOUS MINIMA

The wealth is given in billions of barrels (bbl) of reserves

Rating	Total Countries	Reserves more than 1 bbl	Percent of countries	Reserves more than 0.2 bbl	Percent of countries	Reserves more than 0.095 bbl	Percent of countries
Free	81	7	8.6	11	13.6	17	21.0
Partly Free	57	10	17.5	15	26.3	19	33.3
Not Free	53	18	34.0	25	47.1	27	50.9

TABLE 3

TOTAL RESERVES AND RESERVES PER COUNTRY BY FREEDOM RATING

Rating	Number of Countries	Total Reserves bbl	Reserves (bbl) per country
Free	81	122	1.51
Partly Free	57	204	3.58
Not Free	53	783	14.77

Clearly these data show that oil is a storehouse of revenues for dictatorships. The data are even more striking when it is considered that only two countries ranked by Freedom House as full democracies for every year of the post-Cold-War era, Norway and Trinidad & Tobago, are net oil exporters. In every one of the repressive countries with oil exports, such revenues help sustain a repressive military and security apparatus [14].

ROYALTIES: THE BIGGEST BARRIER TO FREEDOM

Petroleum exports are simply the most lucrative form of wealth stemming from locational advantage, rather than hard work and creativity. Royalties from oil extraction, often called rents by writers on the oil industry, do not dominate the economies of the world's successful capitalist countries.

Royalties are not the basis for new technologies such as the microchip, solar power and the *information highway*. Nor do they characterize the entertainment industry, art, fashion, repair and maintenance, crafts, sports, family farms and electronics.

While not found in the commanding heights of Hollywood, Wall Street, the Olympics, or the City of London, royalties dominate the economies of the most repressive tyrannies of the world. Not one of the 16 countries rated worst by Freedom House is an engine of new science, or of technology, a centre of banking or of motion pictures, insurance or stock exchanges. Oil does not drive the capitalist dream machine, protect it from risk, or lubricate its liquidity. Freedom, more than oil, serves to make the world go round.

Oil is powerful since its supporters are better organized than their more diffuse opponents. Oil interests dominate dictatorships and have considerable influence in the democratic world. Their foes have failed to exhibit comparable skills in coalition building. Environmentalists are just getting used to the idea of appealing to capitalist self-interest. Oil companies benefit from long experience in painting their opponents as extremists.

Insurance revenues are four times greater than oil and their stability is important for the long-term success of the global capitalist economy. In many ways insurance's requirements are similar to the predictable rule of law which is important for democratic capitalist prosperity.

Despite the fact it is strongly in their own interest, the global insurance industry has failed to lobby in a cohesive fashion so as to discourage the consumption of fossil fuel. Insurance companies have never mounted, for instance, anything comparable to the $13 million TV and print campaign waged in the United States by oil industry opponents of the Kyoto Treaty. American insurance companies are particularly timid, being unwilling to co-operate with the European and Japanese company initiatives to build support for environmental protection. On the issue of global warming the fossil-fuel industries of the United States, Australia and Canada are able to have their views prevail in Chambers of Commerce and other business coalitions [15].

The notion of rent extraction, with its concept of unfairly exploiting a locational advantage for unusually high profits, was evident in the barons of the feudal era who exacted tolls from travellers along a river. After feudalism was abolished the concept of rentierism evolved to describe the "unearned increments" from real property, denounced by the foe of land speculation, economist Henry George. Profits from land speculation are not enough to finance a repressive army and security apparatus. This is one of the reasons both Adam Smith and George liked the idea of restricting government revenues to this source, since there would not be enough money to pay for expensive, militarist adventures.

What can pay for repression is the control of resources in the ground, such as petroleum, diamonds and other minerals. Repressive regimes also benefit from other sources of rentier wealth such as the narcotics trade and gambling. Angola is plagued by both oil and diamond wealth. Although the former Belgian Congo is a small but growing oil producer, most of its repressive apparatus has been paid for by its mineral wealth. Some repressive states such as Colombia and Nigeria combine narcotics and oil exports. During its last years as an oil-rich, military dictatorship, Nigeria was cut off from US government foreign aid because of its role in the narcotics trade [16].

Several factors make oil the preferred source of rentier wealth to prop up dictatorships. Its uneven distribution causes most industrialized nations to import oil. More evenly distributed coal and natural gas have never been the basis of a successful cartel such as OPEC.

Russia is unusual in getting a major rentier advantage from natural gas. It is the world's largest producer and can export to European markets via pipelines. Minerals aid repression in a number of nations, notably Sierra Leone, and even Papua New Guinea is guilty of flagrant human rights abuses in favouring mining development on offshore Bougainville island.

There are only a few petroleum- and mineral-poor dictatorships. What is critical to maintaining the repressive, resource-poor regimes in Afghanistan, Burundi and Somalia is foreign aid flowing in from Saudi Arabia, France and Iran respectively. Unlike the United States, since the end of the Cold War, these countries are not inclined to impose "donor democracy."

HOW DEMOCRATIC CULTURE KEEPS TWO OIL RICH STATES FREE

There are currently 57 free states in the world, among them only three net oil exporters. One, Venezuela, has a shaky democracy, being recently ranked by Freedom House as only partly free. Its President, Hugo Chavez, is a convicted coup plotter and has dismissed the country's elected legislature. The only two stable, full democracies are Norway and Trinidad & Tobago.

Norway's ability to combine democracy and oil exports has been helped by fortunate timing. Here oil wealth was never used by an oligarchic elite to cling to power. When Norway became a full democracy in 1919, and the king's last prerogatives over defence and foreign policy passed to the elected government, the country imported all its oil. Democracy in Norway was a product of a long struggle by the country's peasant, labour and co-operative movements, which could not be bought off by a share in oil wealth. Norway, with Sweden, leads the world in the high percentage of parliamentary seats held by women.

Since 1919, Norway has been one of the world's most prosperous and successful constitutional monarchies. Its only interruption of democratic government took place when the country was invaded by Nazi Germany. Norway's North Sea oil boom in the 1970s could not corrupt a democratic culture that was a half-century old.

Although it is a far smaller oil exporter than Norway, Trinidad & Tobago faced the danger of dictatorship when it achieved independence from Great Britain in 1962. The country's political elite could have used its position as an oil exporter to orchestrate a coup and cling to power by oil revenues funding a repressive security apparatus. That the country's elite did not succumb to this temptation is a sign of their commitment to democracy.

A requirement for democracy is that political leaders believe in it. This was the case in Trinidad. The remarkable statesman that guided the new nation in its formative years of independence, Eric Williams, was quite familiar with the authoritarian excesses of rentierism. Before becoming Prime Minister, Williams wrote a well received book, *Capitalism and Slavery*. It exposed the horrors of the 17th century slave trade and provided excellent preparation for avoiding the 20th century curse of oil and dictatorship.

Williams steered Trinidad away from dictatorship, helping to make it a harmonious place for four great civilizations. Here Christianity, Islam, Hinduism and the Earth-respecting culture of native Americans are able to live together in a democratic peace.

Trinidad's political leaders are a representative sampling of the country's diverse races and faith communities. Following Williams' death, political power peacefully passed through elections away from his heavily black People's National Movement, to a multiracial coalition government. It is headed by Basedo Panday, an East Indian, who is widely respected for efforts to curb the narcotics trade through the creation of a regional witness-protection program [17].

Trinidad's democratic success is shared broadly by all the British Commonwealth Caribbean island nations. None of these 12 states is currently ranked as not free. Each one, with the exception of Antigua and Barbuda, is currently regarded by Freedom House as a full democracy. Most have retained the form of constitutional monarchy headed by a crown shared with Great Britain.

Great Britain exported its democratic political culture to the Caribbean. This was encouraged by the British trade union movement in which many of its independence leaders were schooled to democratic norms. The pageantry of British *civic religion*, the mace, crown and the rites of the Gentleman Usher of the Black Rod, form part of the democratic political culture of these free states. This is not the situation where the profitability of empire was enhanced by great pools of oil, far in excess of the limited reserves of Trinidad.

HOW OIL TAINTED THE TWILIGHT OF EUROPEAN COLONIALISM

In his book warning of the dangers of a third world war, Samuel Huntington stresses that Third-World democracy was a product of European colonialism. The most striking failure in his analysis is to ignore how the presence of oil wealth commonly caused Europeans to cling to empire through authoritarian means rather than prepare for an orderly democratic transition to independence.

The parliamentary ritual of Westminster provides the civic religion for Barbados, its symbolism celebrating the limiting and division of power that are quite alien to the oil-rich successor states of the British Empire. Nothing could be conceived that is so different in spirit from the militaristic rituals of government in Iraq, which had been the heart of the Anglo-Arabian empire. While oilless Jordan and Morocco have succeeded in adopting the style of a British parliamentary monarchy, their Hashemite cousins in Iraq were beheaded for such attempts in 1958.

Unless there was substantial oil or mineral wealth, a colony was a drain on the budget of its European government. In most cases the small profits of imperialism would be overwhelmed by administrative expenses.

31

The difference that mineral wealth caused is exemplified by the contrasting British departures from Iran and India.

At the end of empire both Iran and India had strong nationalist-minded, democratic movements. Apart from the turmoil caused by partition, the British peacefully handed over power in India to P.J. Nehru, a committed democrat. During the discussions over the transfer of power, there were no clashes over the nationalization of any significant mineral resource in India. The most prickly point proved to be who would pay the pensions of the Indian civil service. Similarly minded democrats in Iran, led by Mohammad Mossadeq, were prepared to assume power as imperial power waned. However, these democrats were regarded as unacceptable by the British because of conflict over oil, with the more business-minded attempting to acquire the entire Anglo-Iranian Corporation, including its British retail outlets [18].

The end of the Spanish, Portuguese, French and Dutch empires became human-rights disasters wherever oil was found. One of Spain's last 20th century colonies, Equatorial Guinea, is a tiny country that is one of the most repressive nations in the world. The one Portuguese colony with major oil resources is Angola, the only one to be ranked by Freedom House as not free. The human rights records of the oilless Portuguese colonies of Sao Tomé, Cabo Verde, Mozambique and Guinea-Bissau are far better [19].

The one area of France's black African empire that enjoyed a partially free character following independence was Senegal. It kept a constitutional, multiparty system with extensive civil liberties. The bulk of the French empire, which retained more valuable oil, mineral and forest resources, became dictatorships following independence.

The Senegalese were given French citizenship and extensive civil liberties, such as a free press. Freedom and literacy could be given to the Senegalese intelligentsia and peasantry, whose subsistence farming was supplemented by exporting peanuts to France. Democratic culture was not exported to Gabon where oil workers could challenge French economic interests [20].

One of the greatest disasters in the imperial twilight took place in the Dutch East Indies. Since World War I the Dutch record of colonization was the most brutal of any European democracy. During the last half century of colonial rule, its oil wells were controlled by Royal Dutch which, following the merger with Shell, became the world's largest oil company. Unilaterally proclaimed independence was only accepted by the Netherlands after three years of war as a last minute alternative to massive conscription. The lack of a Dutch democratic legacy caused Indonesia's independence to be plagued with massacres and genocide [21].

Democratic Civilization Versus Oil

The great threat at the dawn of the new millennium is not a clash of civilizations based on ancient religious teachings that stress humility in face of the awesome powers of the universe. The uppermost dangers are posed by dictatorships kept alive by vast oil wealth.

Among varied cultures of human civilizations, respect for the sacredness of the Earth is clashing with a militaristic and toxic oil culture. This finds its most obsessive form in the remaining dictatorships. The strongest foe of these tyrannies is the global environmental movement, the leading force in the recent wave of freedom.

Notes

1. Freedom House Survey Team, "Freedom in the World, 1997-1998" (New York: Freedom House, 1998) pp.445-447.

2. Jim West ed., "The International Petroleum Encyclopaedia, 1992" (Tulsa: Penn Well, 1997) p.260.

3. F. Gregory Gause III, "Oil Monarchies" (New York: Council on Foreign Relations Press, 1995) pp.130-160.

4. Ralph Kinney Bennett, "The Global War on Christians" in Bernard Schechterman and Martin Slann, ed., "Violence and Terrorism, 1999/00" (Guilford: Dushkin/McGraw Hill, 1999) pp.27-29.

5. Freedom House Survey Team, *loc. cit.*, pp.288-291.

6. *Ibid.*, pp.285-288.

7. *Ibid.*, pp.285-291, pp.445-447.

8. *Ibid.*, pp.137-139.

9. Eknath Easwaran, "A Man to Match His Mountains: Badshah Khan, Nonviolent Soldier of Islam" (Pealuma: Nilgri Press, 1984) *passim.*

10. Freedom House Survey Team, *loc. cit.*, pp.147-149.

11. *Ibid.*, pp.165-167, 425-428; *New York Times*, December 6, 1999, p.A10.

12. Madhav Gadgil and Ramachandra Guha, "Ecology and Equity" (London: Routledge, 1995) pp.44, 45.

13. *Ibid.*, pp.91, 93, 185; Nathaniel Altman, "Sacred Trees" (San Francisco: Sierra Club Books, 1994) *passim.*

14. Kent Calder, "Pacific Defense" (New York: William Morrow, 1996) pp.4361; Freedom House Survey Team, *loc. cit.*, pp.605, 606.

15. Lydia Dotto, "Storm Warning" (Toronto: Doubleday, 1999) pp.59-63.

16. Freedom House Survey Team, *loc. cit.*, pp.394-396.

17. *Ibid.*, pp.502, 503.

18. Manucher Farmanfarmaian and Roxane Farmanfarmaian, "Blood and Oil" (New York: The Modern Library, 1997) pp.234-262.

19. Freedom House Survey Team, *loc. cit.*, pp.605, 606.

20. *Ibid.*, pp.447-449.

21. *Ibid.*, p.282.

CHAPTER THREE
OIL POWER'S CRUEL PROJECTION OF LUXURY

Oil power projects a cruel illusion of luxury. Its deadly elixir of unrealisable fantasy falls heavily on the great majority of the world's families. Most will never obtain the comforts it promises, not even the cheapest form of private motor transport, the motor scooter or motorized bicycle. Widespread Third-World poverty causes many to toil and pay taxes for cars they will never own but which may bring death or injury to their families through road accidents.

Entire cultures of motorless people are threatened with extinction by oil, for example, the Huorani people of Ecuador and the pygmy people of Cameroon. Inhabitants of the last tropical rainforests, these peoples have lived sustainably with their environments for thousands of years, and are now threatened with oil access roads as a prelude for massive ecocidal invasion of their ancient homelands. In a different context, but similarly involving oil, death has been meted out to the ancient, motorless Buddhist culture of Tibet. This was brutally carried out by communist China, employing slave labour to build roads in a region that had not a single gas tank prior to its invasion by their army in 1949.

UNIVERSAL MOTORIZATION — THE UNATTAINABLE AMERICAN DREAM

The universalization of motorized luxuries is the most destructive aspect of what has been termed the American dream. It is a Utopian image because it is not attainable — the capitalist equivalent to the Communist dreams of *pie in the sky come the revolution.*

Universal access to motorized vehicles is the ultimate form of destructive private consumption in conflict with the public good. What John Kenneth Galbraith mocked as the affluent society, rich in private goods but poor in public wealth, is most disagreeably symbolized by the fact that it is the United States which has come closest to the dream of universal car ownership. It is also the only affluent industrial democracy to be without universal health insurance. Cars are subsidized by American taxpayers at the huge rate of $300 billion annually.

One of the most notorious covert operations of the US Central Intelligence Agency (CIA) was its involvement in the Chilean truckers' strike against the democratic socialist government of President Salvador Allende. It resulted in the imposition of the fascistic dictatorship of Augusto Pinochet. The coup illustrates the reactionary nature of elements in the working class tied to the fossil-fuel economy. While Chile's peasants, copper miners, and service workers remained loyal to a government that improved health care and basic living conditions, its truckers' union was dazzled by the motorized American dream.

One of Allende's most profound observations was: "Socialism can only be achieved on a bicycle [1]." His assassination by army generals in a brutal coup assisted by the American military, set the stage for a general massacre of opponents of the American automotive dream in Latin America.

Following the assassination of the liberal Democratic President John F. Kennedy in 1963, right up until the 1976 election of the human rights crusader Jimmy Carter, several American governments, most ruthlessly Richard M. Nixon's, brought about military dictatorships in Latin America. These served, *inter alia*, to impose the agenda of American corporations in the oil and automotive industries, in order to weaken environmental regulations and entrench the car culture.

Before the American-assisted coup, Chile had over 50 years of effective and continuous democratic government, with South America's strongest system of environmental regulations. These were quickly gutted by the Pinochet dictatorship. Prior to the coup the country's temperate rainforest was largely intact. As with Brazil's tropical rainforest under military rule during the same period, logging concessions were granted to supporters and relatives of the army brass, resulting in environmental devastation.

One of the characteristics of the war on the poor during Pinochet's dictatorship was the favouring of the country's motorized elite in the central city at the expense of lower income families living in suburban shack towns, and dependent on walking, cycling and transit. Americans from the "Chicago school" of economics (influenced by Milton Friedman) achieved the complete deregulation of the bus system. This resulted in poor bus maintenance, higher pollution and more hazards for riders.

The restoration of democracy in Chile during the freedom wave that broke down the Berlin Wall in Europe meant many gains for environmentalists. The country's buses were reregulated, resulting in cleaner and safer transit, and lower fares. New environmental controls also hit middle class car owners. Bans were imposed restricting certain vehicles from entering Santiago and vehicle inspections were instituted to curb pollution [2].

Efforts to impose the American motorized dream in most of South America resulted in a nightmare of militarily imposed torture, supported by the US Republican Nixon and Ford administrations. A case was initiated in Spain two years ago by some of the relatives of an estimated 600 Spanish autoworkers who disappeared in Argentina during the military repression [3].

AUTHORITARIAN IDEOLOGIES AND THIRD-WORLD MOTORIZATION

While in North America car ownership and democracy have happily coexisted, in lower income nations it has been much more associated with exclusionary ideologies. The silence of Iranian families losing loved ones in its war with Iraq was purchased by the gift of a car. Cars have been similarly used to secure popular support for oil-rich and despotic Libya.

Cows in India have been sacred because they have served as holy waste disposal machines, cleaning the streets by their digestive tracts, and creating milk in the process. Once protected by the zeal of priestly high-caste Brahmins, this revered animal is sacrificed on a massive scale to the higher god of motorization.

Now the sacred cow's street scourings result in its death from the ingestion of plastic bags. This cow slaughter takes place on a massive scale. Despite the concerns of Gandhian ecologists, no substantial protests have erupted from these wholesale deaths due to plastic trash. The Hindu fundamentalists of India, led by a tiny car- and motorcycle-riding high-caste minority, are more committed to the glories of oil power than to the ancient nature-revering traditions of their faith. They will denounce the few Muslims who kill cows near a temple, while ignoring the more grotesque bloodshed from oil technology.

The fundamentalist versions of Hindu and Muslim civilizations frequently clash, but not over their common worship of petroleum wealth. Both the semidemocratic governments of India and Pakistan are committed to universalizing such petroleum-based machines as tractors and motorcycles. Following their recent electoral victory in Pakistan, Muslim extremists have championed a tractor for every farmer, while

India's ruling Hindu fundamentalists have displayed contempt for the country's ecological movement.

In the Persian Gulf oil states Hindu and Muslim fundamentalist workers employed in petroleum refineries have rioted against each other. Despite their mutual hatreds, the aristocracy of Indian labour is blinded by the cruel and illusionary elixir of oil. The male-dominated Indian labour movement, in stark contrast to the country's Gandhian influenced peasants and feminists, has studiously avoided environmental issues. Indian men are usually the first to try their luck in the big city, frequently to earn income for a scooter or motorcycle. Women and children tend to stay involved in subsistence farming [4].

The everyday life of the vast majority of pedestrians, transit riders and cyclists in India subjects them to hazards arising from the country's motorized elite. Indian buses are among the most crowded and dangerous in the world. Many deaths take place when passengers are forced to ride on running boards or hang onto the outsides of buses. Passengers are also frequently run over when boarding or leaving buses. Requests for safer, separate facilities for nonmotorized transport are ridiculed in arrogant replies that money cannot be wasted on transportation modes that will be doomed by progress.

Highway traffic accidents continue to soar as motorization advances. In 1993, an estimated 885,000 people died in traffic accidents, largely in the world's less affluent countries. Such a scale of annual fatalities has not been seen on the battlefield since the end of the Cold War. According to the International Federation of Red Cross and Red Crescent Societies, within 20 years cars will be killing and maiming more people than wars, tuberculosis or AIDS. Cars already have become the leading source of death worldwide for males between 15 and 44. Thirty million people have perished in automotive accidents since 1898. The Red Cross estimates that the annual economic cost of automotive devastation is $53 billion [5].

THE DEADLY MIX OF OIL, PLASTICS AND CHEMICALS

The disturbing dance of "progress" includes increasing consumption of a variety of risky products of the oil industry, notably plastics. The full consequences of plastics for human health are disturbing, but not yet fully understood. Current research has already linked their use to cancer, and reproductive disorders.

Oil-based endocrine-disrupting plastics represent one of the most serious threats to the human species. Chemicals used in their production have been linked to decreasing human sperm counts. Similar hormone-disrupting agents have been found in oil-based pesticides.

Chemicals leached from plastics have been linked to cancer because of increased estrogen exposure. The breakdown of chemicals found in pesticides can give rise to estrogenic nonylphenol. Synthetic chemical fungicides have been found to interfere with the action of male hormones. Mounting evidence from research shows connections from petrochemical inputs to cancer, sterility, increased propensity to violence, and loss of intelligence. Uncritical use of oil-based products, such as cooking in microwave ovens with plastic wrappers, can result in serious illness.

One of the most deadly residues of oil dictatorships is higher concentrations of persistent chemicals in human tissues. These have fallen in democracies where pesticides, most notably DDT, are banned. High levels continue to be found in oil dictatorships and semidemocracies where use of such chemicals is still permitted. This blights the human body in Latin America, Africa and Asia. In Egypt high residues of 15 pesticides have been found in milk samples. Dictatorships use over 18 million kg of chemicals annually that are banned in democracies [6].

HOW OIL DICTATORSHIPS HELP SUSTAIN
OIL CONSUMPTION

The Persian Gulf oil dictatorships have taken the most aggressive stance against efforts to curb greenhouse gas emissions. At the centre of their strategies is a denial of the reality of global warming. A particularly active role in this has been played by the Kuwait Foundation for the Advancement of Science. It funded the work of American geographer Robert Balling, which was later translated into Arabic and distributed to all the OPEC governments [7].

Already at the Rio Earth Summit of 1992, Canadian diplomat and Conference organizer Maurice Strong found OPEC more opposed to conservation and alternative fuels than they had been in the 1970s [8]. In these changes one can detect the influence of lobbying by the Global Climate Council (GCC) [9], a private, nonprofit organization whose membership and sources of funding are secret [10]. GCC's purpose is to represent energy companies "whose business could be affected by laws related to potential climate change" [11]. It has status in the US as a nongovernment organization, which gives it the opportunity to participate in meetings of the International Panel on Climate Change (IPCC), which it regularly has done. The GCC employs a Washington lawyer, Donald Pearlman, who has successfully influenced delegates from oil-rich Arab countries to IPCC. Arab delegates have even been seen entering meetings with notes in Pearlman's own handwriting and referring to these during sessions [12].

Pearlman works also for the Washington law firm of Patton, Boggs and Blow, which has represented clients such as Abu Dhabi, an oil-rich province of the United Arab Emirates, and a brutal dictatorship.

How the American Democratic Model
of Car Ownership Will Be Difficult to Export

The United States is the only nation that has achieved car ownership for the majority of its households. This has been sustained for less than 50 years. In the process, the transition drove most competing forms of transportation — notably bicycles, draft animals and slow moving street cars — off the streets.

America's lead in establishing the place of the car and truck on the road had the fringe benefit of introducing some safety measures for pedestrians and vehicle drivers. This took place during the creation — opposed by motorists — of a complex automotive regulatory system. Speed limits, driver testing, and safety regulations all had to be democratically lobbied for by people concerned for road safety. Car owners resisted the passage of such legislation. They are still fighting such effective controls in most dictatorships and semidemocracies.

The complex regulation of automobiles in western democracies is a tribute to the power of political lobbying by the victims of car accidents. These people have less influence in dictatorships. No photo-radar will democratically track down and issue tickets to speeders in the streets of the absolute monarchies of the Persian Gulf.

Despite considerable improvements from the situation in 1898, when the first unsuspecting street car passenger was killed by a passing motorist, deaths and injuries on the roadways of the developed world still retain a strong element of class conflict and discrimination. Pedestrian victims of automotive accidents, especially children, continue to be lower on the social scale than the drivers of vehicles [13].

In pursuit of an unobtainable Utopia, oil oligarchies and their followers accept the heavy mortality on the roads of lesser developed nations which is similar to the slaughter experienced in New York or Chicago around 1912. They must thus possess a sense that the sacrifice of lives is justified for the attainment of First-World levels of progress [14].

The early days of the automobile saw a great massacre on the roads. Henry Ford boasted that cars did not scare wellbred horses, but with the advent of motorization, horse-related fatalities in New York City doubled from 1899 to 1907. Over a thousand children were killed in New York City during the first decade of motorization [15].

Automotive casualty rates remain high in big Third-World cities. Unlike affluent America, most citizens of Delhi, Shanghai and Cairo can only afford an oxcart or a bicycle. Deaths caused by an elite of car owners and truck drivers are excused by a belief that such losses are sacrifices to the god of progress. Demands by environmentalists for pedestrian zones have gone nowhere outside of Europe, Japan, and the Western Hemisphere.

Part of the difficulty in determining the impact of the automobile in the oil dictatorships lies in the lack of records of automotive injuries and fatalities. One of the few Third-World countries that attempts to keep track of automotive deaths is democratic India.

India's capital, Delhi, experienced the world's highest rate of road fatalities. Its 12.5 deaths per annum per 10,000 vehicles is far worse than the corresponding 1.7 in Washington, and the 2.7 of Los Angeles. Delhi also has the highest accident rate in the world: 75.5 per 10,000 vehicles annually.

Delhi's death toll from cars is akin to class warfare of the most brutal kind. Most victims of automotive violence are lower class and caste — pedestrians and cyclists. In 1980, 246 pedestrians and 137 cyclists were killed in accidents with motorized vehicles.

Intercity travel in India is particularly dangerous. Between cities, motor cars frequently collide with buses. This contributes to India's accident rate of 57 deaths per 10,000 vehicles, the highest in the world. Trucks are also a major cause of fatalities, made worse by drivers' widespread use of drugs such as speed. In Delhi trucks cause 10 times as many accidents as cars [16].

In the 1990s, with the increased use of motorcycles and scooters, pollution has grown. In Delhi such vehicles emit 400 tonnes of pollutants a day. Emissions from trucks add to this. Delhi's carbon monoxide damages brain tissue and its diesel fumes are laced with carcinogenic oxides of nitrogen.

Delhi gets 400 kg of lead per day in its atmosphere from motorized exhaust. It has proven especially harmful to road and construction workers and traffic police. Although legislation has been passed against leaded gasoline in India, it has not yet been enforced [17].

The average resident of Mumbai (formerly Bombay) and New Delhi has the lung capacity of a two-pack-a-day smoker. According to the Tata Institute, air pollution in India caused 2.5 million deaths in 1997, equivalent to the entire population of Jamaica or Singapore. Diesel fumes' sooty emissions also aggravate asthma and bronchitis [18].

What the peddlers of oil fail to realize is that the global attainment of even the modest Japanese level of car ownership is an impossible and unworthy dream. The automobile in the United States resulted in the paving over of 155,000 km^2 (15.5 million hectares) of land — two percent of the country's land base. Parking a car in an average suburban shopping mall requires 4,000 square feet of asphalt. In Los Angeles two thirds of the urban space is used to accommodate the car. Most American cities use close to half their land base for such infrastructure [19].

Heavy population densities in major Third-World cities make automotive use typical of western cities impossible to attain. To universalize even Taiwan's 10 percent of car ownership — which has resulted in serious environmental problems — would be to invite widespread ecological catastrophe. Taiwan has experienced disastrous impacts of motorization. This is most evident in its capital of Taipei, where only one in 10 families owns a car [20].

Taiwan's democratization has encouraged the gradual development of car restraint and inspection programs. In more repressive countries, transportation policies are shaped heavily by the motorized minority. This is part of a misguided effort to promote motorization by reducing its immediate costs through the absence of environmental controls.

Two-stroke engines are banned in some countries of the free world. The two-stroke engines commonly employed on motorcycles in such petrotyrannies as Vietnam emit 10 times more hydrocarbons and smoke per kilometre than much heavier cars [21].

A POTENTIAL NIGHTMARE: CHINESE ADOPTION
OF THE AMERICAN DREAM

The Utopian basis of automotive universality is most evident when its impact on China is considered. China's and India's still largely carless populations are now among the most ecologically efficient in the world. They require only about 1.7 hectares of land per person. In contrast the United States has the highest ecological footprint, some 8.7 hectares of land per person. This gives the average American car owner the impact of six Indian or Chinese subsistence farmers.

China's planned increase in car consumption over the next 13 years is equal in its ecological impact to a population rise of 132 million people. The expected 22 million increase in numbers of cars more than cancels out the land savings from China's draconian one-child-per-family policy. Some zealous Communist cadres advocate 100 million cars for China, which would mean the loss of 24 million hectares of farmland. In 1994 the total cultivated land base in China was only 34.7 million hectares.

Already China's ambitious car strategy has paved over some of its best ricelands through developing a new superhighway between Hong Kong and Guandong [22].

POLITICAL DEBATE SHAPED ACCEPTANCE OF MOTORIZATION IN THE DEVELOPED WORLD

Even in the industrialized world mass motoring did not win acceptance without extensive political debate. It did not come about, as is commonly thought, through an inevitable force of nature. The late-Victorian British red-flag law long delayed mass motoring. The bill's provisions for red-flag escorts for automobiles arose from well justified concerns for safety and also from the strength of the train industry.

The car was initially hated by the working class of Europe and North America as a rich man's murderous toy. The terror tactics of automotive road hogs, who vigorously fought against the complex regulatory system that was eventually developed, sparked riots in low-income neighbourhoods in major cities. Such angry working class protests took place in both London and New York. Stonings of cars by children were common. Working class children resented how they could no longer play cricket or baseball in the streets. Riots became especially violent after reckless motorists killed children.

Automobiles at the turn of the century were widely called the "devil's wagons". One American social reformer, Dr. Charles Parkhurst, maintained that in a democracy the elite five percent of car owners had no right to tyrannize and run over the majority of the population that did not drive an automobile. In 1905, Woodrow Wilson, then President of Princeton College, called car owners the worst menace facing America [23]. On a world scale today, if not in America, auto users are in the same small minority position denounced by Wilson during the Progressive Era.

How Dictatorship Shapes Third-World Motorization

Dictatorships ultimately have shaped the distorted priorities that put the luxury motorized toys of a tiny elite above the welfare of most citizens. The elite of dictatorships in these countries zoom by in luxury, even while millions experience hunger.

The autocratic Ivory Coast exceeds the Third-World average in car ownership. At 15 per thousand, the rate is much higher than democratic India's. Ignoring the needs of the vast majority of their citizens, African dictators concentrated on an Africar — which they dreamed would be manufactured in Africa. Haiti is another example where a country's limited resources are wasted in the motorized toys of the dictatorial elite. Only one out of every two hundred people owns a car in Haiti. Nevertheless, a third of its import budget goes towards automotive fuel and transportation. Such attention to elite pleasures diverts resources from dealing with Haiti's crisis of deforestation and soil erosion [24].

While Haiti and most of the Third World have subsequently experienced varied degrees of democratization, transportation planning remains distorted by the authoritarian control of motorized masters. Planning studies — even in China — have overlooked the bicycle. This machine is widely ignored despite the fact that increased access to it can rapidly improve the quality of life of its users. Bicycles provide an alternative to harmful methods of moving goods still common in the Third World, such as head loading.

Given war on the poor by the cronies of rich dictators, it is predictable that, in times of weakness of repressive regimes, revolt is expressed through widespread destruction of cars. These periodic orgies of smashing the symbols of class oppression have been depicted as signs of a coming "Dark Age" of anarchy [25].

Anticar protests of West Africa have more of the character of a festival of the carless oppressed than aimless anarchy. Hopefully, this jacquerie of exploited pedestrians against the feudal road hogs will be followed by democratic regulations such as pedestrian zones and bicycle paths.

Notes

1. Pryor Dodge, "The Bicycle" (New York: Flammarion, 1995) p.200.

2. John Terborgh, "Requiem for Nature" (Washington: Island Press, 1999) p.180; The World Resources Institute, "World Resources, 1995-96" (Oxford: Oxford University Press, 1997) pp.82-110.

3. "Where Torture is Job One", *Earth Island Journal*, Spring 1998, p.14.

4. Geoffrey Kemp and Robert Harkavy, "Strategic Geography and the Changing Middle East" (New York: Carnegie Endowment for International Peace and the Brookings Institute, 1997) pp.7, 87-88, 100, 108, 189, 332, 333, 425. Presentation by Vandana Shiva on the Chipko Movement, made at the 1987 European Nuclear Disarmament Conference.

5. World Resources Institute, *loc. cit.*, pp.87, 90-91; *Earth Island Journal*, fall, 1998, p.20.

6. Theo Colborn, Dianne Dumanoski and John Peterson Myers "Our Stolen Future: Are We Threatening Our Fertility, Intelligence and Survival? A Scientific Detective Story" (New York: Dutton Books, 1996) pp.67, 80-90, 198-200, 233.

7. Ross Gelbspan, "The Heat is On" (New York: Addison Wesley, 1997), pp.44-45.

8. Maurice Strong, "Where on Earth Are We Going?" (Toronto: Alfred A.Knopf, 2000) p.222.

9. The Global Climate Council, which employs Donald Pearlman, should not be confused with the Global Climate Coalition, which was founded by Donald Pearlman in 1989. To avoid confusion we do not abbreviate Global Climate Coalition in this book! This latter organization is required by law to have open membership, because of its legal status. Oil companies have recently been leaving the Coalition to incorporate mitigation of climate change into their business strategies. United Nations Environment Program reported in *Our Planet*, 11, no.1, 2000, "its final dissolution as a membership coalition open to individual companies."

10. Jeremy Leggett, "The Carbon War" (London: Penguin, 1999) p.11.

11. Ross Gelbspan, *loc. cit.,* p.120.

12. Further accounts of Pearlman's influence are given by Leggett, loc. cit., pp. 15, 195-203, 243; and Ross Gelbspan, *loc. cit.,* p.119.

13. Peter Freund and George Martin "The Ecology of the Automobile" (Montreal: Black Rose Books, 1993) p.49.

14. Clay McShane, "Down the Asphalt Path" (New York: Columbia University Press, 1994), pp.174-177.

15. Clay McShane, *loc. cit.,* p.176.

16. "The State of India's Environment" (New Delhi: Centre for Science and Environment, 1982) p.102.

17. Malcolm Adiseshiah, "Natural Resource Environment of India", in "The Emerging Challenges", ed. M.V. Nadkarni, A.S. Seetharamu and Abdul Aziz (New Delhi: Sage Publications, 1991) p.210.

18. Payal Sampat, "What Does India Want?" *World Watch*, July/August, 1998, p.36.

19. Michael Renner, "Rethinking the Role of the Automobile" (Washington: World Watch Institute, 1988) p.46.

20. Marcie Lowe, "The Bicycle: Vehicle for a Small Planet" (New York: World Watch, 1989) p.17.

21. Robert Cervero, "The Transit Metropolis" (Washington: Island Press, 1995) pp.40-60.

22. Lester Brown, "Who Will Feed China?" (New York, W.W. Norton, 1995) pp.26, 58-60.

23. McShane, *loc.cit.*, pp.174-200.

24. Wolfgang Zuckerman, "The End of the Road" (Cambridge: Lutterworth Press, 1991) p.253.

25. Robert Kaplan, "The Coming Anarchy", *The Atlantic Monthly*, February, 1994, *passim.*

CHAPTER FOUR
THE MIDDLE EAST AND NORTH AFRICA

The Middle East, which in this chapter will be a term that includes North Africa, is trapped in a cycle of war and death technologies; power comes not from ballots but bullets. Oil and its toxic fumes are a deadly incense for death-worshipping cults based on the denial of basic human rights. Nowhere else in the world have war, dictatorship and militarism been as pervasive since the end of World War II. Almost half of the world's remaining dictatorships and three quarters of its proven oil reserves are in the Middle East.

There are 29 states in the Middle East if one adds in the contiguous, predominantly Islamic states that broke away from the USSR in 1991. Of these 23 are currently ranked by Freedom House as not free. These oil-rich dictatorships include Algeria, Libya, Syria, Iran, Iraq, Yemen, Oman, the United Arab Emirates and Saudi Arabia. Only Israel is ranked as a full democracy. It has no oil reserves. Kuwait is the only partially free major petroleum producer. Four out of five semidemocratic states in the Middle East — Turkey, Morocco, the Kyrgyz Republic and Jordan — lack significant proven oil reserves. The only two states in the region where citizens are able to use the ballot box to change governments are Turkey and Israel. Both states lack oil [1].

Oil and dictatorship make the Middle East a deadly magnet for arms, expenditures on weapons having soared to $100 billion annually during the 1970s and 1990s. Over 13 million people have been killed, wounded, disabled or displaced by various armed conflicts since the Arab-Israeli war of 1948.

Four of the five remaining full-scale civil wars in the world with more than a thousand people being killed annually are in the Middle East. These conflicts plague Afghanistan, Iran, Turkey, Sudan and Algeria. The threat of war in the region tends to set the pace for the development of new military technologies around the world [2].

HOW OIL INVIGORATED THE SICK MAN OF EUROPE

Although some scoffed at the Ottoman Empire as the sick man of Europe, oil wealth gave it excellent life support. The Empire continued to dominate the Middle East until both it and its ally Germany were defeated in World War I. The Ottoman Empire did not go softly into the historic night.

The allure of oil wealth was the basis for the Berlin-Baghdad railway. The Ottoman-German alliance helped the Empire resist democratization efforts attempted by Great Britain and France. German-built rail lines would remove a million Armenians to death camps in World War I. The alliance reinforced authoritarian attitudes on both sides. Hitler's concept of genocide against European Jews would be based on the success of Turkey's actions against Armenians in World War I [3].

OIL AND THE FAILURE OF THE SUCCESSOR STATES OF THE OTTOMAN EMPIRE TO DEMOCRATIZE

Having earlier helped the Ottoman Empire to resist pressures for democratization, oil wealth gave a similar curse of tyranny to the Empire's successor states. It also plagued the bordering Persian Empire. The prospect of losing control over oil wealth dissuaded the British and French from repudiating the secret Sykes-Picot agreement, which divided the Ottoman Empire outside of Turkey between Great Britain and France. France was given Lebanon and Syria, while the rest was allotted to Great Britain.

The Allies took control over all the Middle East's known petroleum deposits, many of which were seeping out of the ground. Broad-minded statesmen such as Winston Churchill viewed the Sykes-Picot agreement as outdated but did not prevail in this view. The agreement, however, was modified by turning its claims into temporary French and British mandates under the League of Nations, which facilitated a fairly rapid transition to independence for the countries of the region.

The Allies refused to accept demands for a united Arab Kingdom based in Damascus under the leadership of Sharif Hussein, head of the Hashemite dynasty and a direct descendant of the prophet Mohammed.

Sharif Hussein was the ruler of Hejaz, an Arabian province of the Ottoman Empire that included the holy city of Mecca. Although Great Britain refused the demand for a united Arab Kingdom, it did create Jordan and Iraq as Arab states for two of Sharif Hussein's sons. Hejaz, however, lost its British support, resulting in its conquest in 1926 by Ibn

Saud. It was incorporated into the new state of Saudi Arabia, which was consolidated by 1932.

The downfall of Hejaz made the spread of democracy in the Middle East more difficult. The Hashemites, given their role as keepers of the keys of Mecca, tended to have more liberal interpretations of Islam. This was influenced by pilgrims from diverse cultures around the world. Until the Hashemites' alliance with the Ottomans was shaken by the emergence of Turkish nationalism the powerful Mecca dynasty supported the empire in preference to the sect of Wahhabi, an 18th century Muslim prophet. King Ibn Saud's triumph in consolidating Saudi Arabia was thus a major victory for his supporters of the authoritarian Wahhabi sect [4].

Wahhabi's followers clashed not only with the Ottoman Caliphs but also with the Sufi who favoured a more liberal Islamic practice and tended to venerate nature. Early clashes with Sufis intensified over the Wahhabi's destruction of sacred trees. Following their victories in Saudi Arabia the Wahhabi imposed a harsh version of Shari'a law. This featured punishments such as lashings, public beatings and wider application of capital punishment. Women were banned from the streets. Laws against public laughing and singing were also imposed [4].

The fractured Hashemite kingdoms of Jordan and Iraq did evolve under British guidance into semiconstitutional monarchies, in contrast to the British Trucial States where only Kuwait was left with a democratic system upon independence in 1964.

British behaviour in the oil-rich Middle East did not favour the development of a liberal democratic system of government, in vivid contrast with other parts of its empire, such as the predominantly black West Indies and India, which were developing systems of self-government based on transitions to democratic rule. British influence was most disastrous in the Persian Empire in fostering autocracy that was vital to naval oil supplies — a major source of revenue for the British government.

Although Persia was never part of the British Empire, being able to retain a nominal independence, the Anglo-Iranian Corporation, later named British Petroleum, interfered bluntly in its internal affairs. This resulted in the overthrow of the constitutional monarchy of the Qajar dynasty in favour of the absolutism of Reza Khan in 1925.

The British government preferred the absolutism of the newly installed Pahlavi dynasty because its centralization of power made it easier for the oil industry. Under the Qajar's efforts to establish constitutional rule British proposals for the oil industry were rejected by the Persian parliament, the Majlies. This increased the distrust by British authorities for liberal constitutional government in the oil-rich Middle East [5].

Kuwait's liberal constitutional evolution was frozen in time after oil was discovered in 1933. Previously its monarch had made concessions to the country's merchants, but all this stopped when oil was discovered and the crown no longer needed to impose taxation. The British protectorate of Bahrain had a liberal constitutional system after independence briefly from 1972 to 1975. Elections were never held, however, in independent Arab states that were once part of the British Empire such as the United Arab Emirates, Oman and South Yemen.

Jordan and Iraq under the Hashemites did prove to be important allies of the democratic world in World War II. Jordan's Arab Legion evicted pro-Vichy French from Syria. Iraq successfully withstood an attempted coup backed by pro-Nazi officers headed by Rashid al Gailani. The perpetrators ruled Baghdad for a month, during which time there were some anti-Semitic outrages. Although short-lived, these outrages were ominous precursors of the Nazi-style human-rights violations that would plague Iraq later — after the explosive situation created by the birth of Israel. Army officers who supported the brief pro-Nazi regime in Iraq would return to power with the overthrow of the Hashemite dynasty in 1958 [6].

THE VIOLENT BIRTH OF ISRAEL AND THE SEEDS OF WAR FOR OIL

The greatest fiasco in the successor states of the Ottoman Empire took place in Palestine, governed until 1947 by Great Britain under a League of Nations mandate. The disaster was exacerbated by failure to build the tools of democracy throughout the oil-rich Middle East.

Palestine was blighted by Nazi manipulation of Arab discontent. This was a problem throughout the Middle East but it was especially deadly in Palestine. It fostered an extremist, anti-Semitic basis for Arab conflicts with Zionist settlers. Until the creation of the state of Israel, all purchases of Arab land were agreed to voluntarily; thus conflict over land might have been avoided, had it not been for the extremism.

To the problem of Nazi intrigue was added British incompetence. There were no elective institutions common to Arabs and Jews, even at the municipal level. Instead, the political institutions such as the Jewish Agency and Arab High Command of the Palestine Mandate were separate, setting the stage for future war.

There were not even any common charities or other forms of civil society that involved both Arabs and Jews. The new Palestinian identity became forged in competition with Zionism. A Palestinian National Fund for instance, would be created to mimic the purposes of the Jewish National Fund. Later the organizations of Palestinians, such as their various political parties, would come to imitate the state of being of the Zionist movement.

Prodded by extremists, both sides refused to accept the United Nations partition plan of 1947 for Palestine. Israel, under the fiercely anti-Arab leadership of David Ben-Gurion, successfully used the conflict to expand its borders beyond those fixed by the UN. This was the main reason 700,000 Palestinians became refugees.

EXTREMISTS COMPOUND THE PROBLEMS OF THE BIRTH OF ISRAEL

The problems created by the violent birth of Israel would be compounded by further extremist behaviour that set the stage for the disastrous *third world war for oil* by 1958. Critical would be two charismatic leaders that would polarize their societies. These were Egypt's Abdel Gamel Nasser and Israel's David Ben-Gurion.

Moderates on both sides attempted to turn the armistice of 1948 into a lasting peace. This was helped by the functioning until 1958 of a parliamentary monarchy in Jordan. Lebanon in this period was also a stable democracy that sought peace with Israel.

Critical in peacemaking efforts was the Israeli Prime Minister Moshe Sharett. He attempted to secure a lasting peace based on the admission of some Palestinian refugees and the payment of compensation for those who remained outside Israel. There was also to be a program of economic development for mutual benefits between Jordan and Israel.

A peace between the democratically allied nations of Israel, Jordan, Iraq, Lebanon, and the Palestinian refugees threatened extremists in Israel and in the Arab world. In Israel, it threatened the expansionist dreams of Ben-Gurion's supporters for more land and for more Jewish immigration from minorities in other Middle Eastern states. It also clashed with Nasserist and Baathist ideologists who sought, through an alliance with the Soviet Union, to exploit the Palestinian issue to create a powerful pan-Arab state controlling most of the world's oil wealth.

Extremists sabotaged peace in the strangest ways. Israeli secret agents, without the knowledge of Prime Minister Sharett, set fires in Cairo movie cinemas. Rather than attempt to assist Sharett through a muted response to the unauthorized actions, Nasser exploited it to its fullest potential, executing some of the agents. Nasser likewise provoked Israel by allowing the Gaza strip to be used to assist terrorists infiltrating Israel. The resulting Israeli retaliatory actions helped to foment the Suez War. Such inflammatory deeds would be used with great propaganda effect to undermine moderate anti-Nasserist governments in the Arab world.

Even more bizarre were Israeli actions towards Iraq, the most powerful Arab state and one that was inclined to favour a compromise peace. Its Jewish community played an important part in the moderate Hashemite monarchy's civil service. Desiring to have its 100,000 citizens move to Israel, extremist elements in the Israeli secret police launched a wave of terrorist bombings, blaming the actions on the Iraqi government. The exodus of Jews who had loyally staffed Iraq's civil service left the government fatally vulnerable in 1958 to a Nasserist coup [7].

The outbreak of war in the Suez crisis in 1956, although a military defeat, was a great triumph for Nasser and his extremist antidemocratic allies in the Arab world, many of whom had previously supported Hitler, especially in oil-rich Iraq. The outrage over the alliance between Israel, Great Britain and France over the colonial relic of the Suez Canal Company would contribute greatly to anti-NATO Arab nationalist triumphs in Syria, South Yemen, Iraq, Algeria and Libya. This shift in power would disastrously abet war between these states and the remaining Islamic countries in the region allied to the free world. What was particularly disastrous was the creation of a pro-Soviet government in oil-rich Iraq. This completely destroyed American efforts to create the Baghdad Pact as an extension of NATO for regional security in the Middle East [8].

THE *THIRD WORLD WAR FOR OIL* BEGINS IN 1958

The tragic pattern of the Middle East being polarized between pro-Soviet and pro-NATO dictatorships became solidified by 1958. This would establish the pattern of the *third world war for oil*, which overshadowed and continued past the Cold War. Outside of oilless Turkey, which began a difficult path to semidemocracy in 1945 and Israel, havens of freedom shrank. This set the stage for chronic war between dictatorships for the control of oil wealth.

Lebanon's previously successful democratic system became disrupted by the explosion of extreme pro-Nasserist pan-Arabism. The country was only rescued from civil war by US military intervention.

After the overthrow of its family allies in Iraq, Jordan ended its liberal constitutional monarchy and became ruled by martial law. The removal of precautionary checks and balances in its political system would contribute to its disastrous participation in the Six Day War of 1967. This further exacerbated the problem of Palestinian refugees with Israel's conquest of the West Bank. The new refugee exodus eventually resulted in the destruction of democracy in Lebanon with the emergence of private armies from the exodus of Palestinians expelled from Jordan. Lebanon is now dominated by oil-rich, authoritarian Syria.

NATO unity in the Cold War was most seriously threatened by the allure of oil wealth in the Middle East. The Suez disaster illustrated this most effectively and was a time bomb waiting to happen as European powers had difficulty in adjusting to postcolonial realities. In 1951, under the leadership of Harry Truman, the United States had to dissuade Great Britain from plans to invade Iran in response to its nationalization of the oil industry. This would have created a similar explosive outrage as the Suez invasion throughout the Middle East. Aggression was nevertheless contemplated despite the World Court affirming Iran's right to nationalize its oil wells, using legislation based on Great Britain's own legislation to acquire its coal mines [9].

International pressure on Iran included an astonishingly leak-proof boycott of Iranian oil. This began from the time of the nationalization in 1951 and lasted almost three years until a CIA-inspired coup during the Eisenhower Republican administration imposed a more favourable government in Teheran. The coup deposed the architect of nationalization, Prime Minister Mohammad Mossadeq.

The coup also had the unfortunate impact of weakening democracy in Iran. Mossadeq had been the first popularly elected Prime Minister. He was able to build a political party that secured a parliamentary majority against the wishes of the country's ruling dynasty for the first time in Iranian history. His nationalist, social-democratic followers were also undermined. This benefited greatly Iran's authoritarian Shiite clergy who much later triumphed under Ayatollah Khomeini.

Despite the CIA coup and increased American involvement in the Iranian oil industry, Mossadeq's nationalization law was not repealed. It eventually became the model for every state in the Persian Gulf, including the staunch pro-American allies of the Gulf Co-operation Council. Widespread nationalizations followed the OPEC price hike of 1973. The result is that the oil economies of the Middle East are among the most state-controlled in the world. The fabled "seven sisters", which were so powerful in 1949-53, being able to orchestrate a boycott of Iran's oil, now are forced to share power with the nationalized petroleum industries of the Persian Gulf states. The most important of these, Saudi Arabia's Aramco, is also an important shareholder and business partner in powerful American oil corporations.

Oil power since 1973 has at least lost its old trappings of anti-Arab racism and colonialism. The American allies in the Gulf Co-operation Council which controls most of the world oil are no mere pawns of global capitalism. They are significant players, often making it difficult to distinguish between American oil companies and the Arab dictatorships that invest heavily in their operations. Gulf state investors such as Aramco and the Kuwaiti investment office are more important as shareholders than the old American oil families of the past such as the Rockefellers.

In 1956, the future partnerships between Arab oil wealth and the western petroleum industry were still unclear, as colonialist attitudes continued to prevail. American diplomats in Baghdad were shocked at how Arabs would not be permitted into British clubs in the core of their neocolonial oil empire. The British and French governments kept the US in the dark about their invasion schemes against Egypt. The resulting fiasco dangerously affected the entire Cold War since it prevented any western response to the crushing of the democratic Hungarian revolution.

The allure of oil contributed to the only significant defection of a major power during the Cold War, France. It left the joint military command of NATO at a time when France sought to curry favour with the Soviet-allied oil dictatorships. In 1972, during an Iraqi confiscation of western oil companies, France was exempted because of what Iraq's then Vice-President, Saddam Hussein, praised as its "privileged position." It later took the lead in developing diplomacy favourable to Middle-Eastern dictatorships as the best defence to counter the use of the "oil weapon." France also developed close ties to Islamic extremist groups in Iran. It continues to oppose US government efforts to impose economic sanctions that seek to restrict investment by French oil companies — even in Syria, the sponsor of the most determined extremist groups which seek to destroy the Palestinian-Israeli peace process [10].

Despite racist stereotypes of its people as somehow prone to violence war has not always been a chronic condition in the Middle East. Before the explosive polarization unleashed by the Suez debacle the region was one of relative peace. Even the Arab-Israeli war of 1947-48 was a minor scale conflict in which the troops of Israel outnumbered those of the entire Arabic-speaking world. This situation of relative peace soon changed after the emergence of oil-rich dictatorships allied with the Soviet Union, starting in 1958. The situation would be made even more volatile with the emergence in Iran in 1979 of an authoritarian and messianic government bent on the export of its own distinctive brand of exclusionary ideology.

The conflicts between Israel and its Arab neighbours after 1958 have involved 200,000 deaths. This bloodshed was only a small part of the millions of casualties caused by wars financed by oil wealth and dictatorship in the Middle East. Typical in its brutality was war between North and South Yemen. Soviet-allied Egypt backed South Yemen, while American-allied Saudi Arabia supported North Yemen. From 1962 to 1972 100,000 people were killed in the conflict [11].

After moving into the Soviet bloc Iraq found itself in continuing armed conflict with Iran, over a border dispute that had been previously resolved peacefully through a 1937 League of Nations mediation. This border became one of the hottest frontiers of the Cold War resulting in bloody skirmishes. Iraq retaliated by providing a haven to the Shah of Iran's leading critic, Ayatollah Khomeini. Iran fought back by financing a Kurdish armed insurgency against the Sunni dominated Arab government of Iraq.

The short-lived peace accord between Iran and Iraq in 1975 is illustrative of the deadly synergistic combinations among war, oil and dictatorship. The cynical accord between the two dictatorships on opposite sides of the Cold War was encouraged by the *Realpolitik* of Henry Kissinger and the Nixon-Ford Republican administration. The accord sought to achieve interstate peace so as to facilitate internal repression. Iran imposed border terms on Iraq harsher than those agreed to by the Hashemite monarchy and the earlier Ottoman Empire. In exchange, Iran withdrew its support for Iraqi Kurds. Now vulnerable, Iraq's Kurds were soon being massacred in large numbers. Iraq withdrew support for Iran's political opposition. This allowed the Iranian government to end the liberal, democratic constitutional features of its monarchy, making it a more repressive one-party state.

Cynical efforts by the two divergent petrotyrannies to mutually reinforce their dictatorships eventually exploded by events beyond the control of the two countries' despotic rulers. This resulted in the bloodiest war in the history of the Middle East, between Iraq and Iran, in 1980.

Increased repression in Iran with the banning of all political parties encouraged the opposition to gravitate towards the extremist Shiite clergy, hostile to democracy. The resulting Shiite revolution, which saw the mass executions of the core leadership of the Iranian army, prompted Iraq to reverse the peace terms imposed by the Shah. Iraq also used the war to seize control of oil fields in the Arabic-speaking region of Khuzistan, Iran, seeking to exploit the potential grievances of their eroded minority rights under the Iranian revolution [12].

From 1980 to 1986 the war between Iran and Iraq resulted in 800,000 deaths. One million people were displaced. Oil facilities were deliberately targeted, as was Iran's uncompleted nuclear reactor. The worst damage was caused by an Iraqi attack on an Iranian well in the Nowruz and Ardeshir offshore fields, resulting in the spillage of two million barrels of oil into the Persian Gulf [13]. The border between the two countries became a desolate wasteland, resembling the devastated trench lands of the end of World War I in Europe.

After the war with Iran ended, Iraq persecuted ruthlessly its Marsh Arab minority, largely Shiite Muslims. Earthen dams were built to stop the Tigris waters from entering the marshes. Canals were dug to drain them and toxic chemicals dumped into lakes and ponds. Satellite photographs reveal that previously lush wetlands have been transformed into arid desert [14].

Civil war has plagued the Middle East since 1958, greatly intensifying previous conflicts. Civil wars in Iraq since the Nasserist overthrow of the Hashemite dynasty have brought about 400,000 deaths. Civil wars in Syria in the same period killed 30,000 people [15].

About half of the deaths in Iraq's civil wars have been associated with attempted genocide against its Kurdish minority. Throughout the Middle East the Kurds have been despised as a backward peasant class for clinging to traditional ways — ones that are not dependent on oil technology. The assault on this nation is worst in Iraq where, since the 1980s, 1.5 million Kurds have been deported from mountain villages to fortified towns. Near the end of the Iraq-Iran war in the 1980s, Kurdish villages were bombed by poison gas, resulting in 180,000 deaths. Following the Gulf War, 250,000 Kurds were forcibly evacuated to other parts of Iraq [16].

Civil war in Lebanon since 1958 has resulted in 180,000 deaths. While this is a minor theatre in *the third world war for oil*, its centrepiece, the Gulf War, experienced fewer casualties, about 120,000 [17].

The Gulf War was a third world war in a new sense because of the widespread nature of the environmental contamination it unleashed. The level of soot in the stratosphere jumped to between 10 and 100 times the normal level as a result of the conflict. A Japanese ski expedition found a layer of crude oil on glaciers in the Himalayas. Mountain peaks in Germany were also oiled. The war's burning oil wells caused a 1,500 mile long smoke plume extending from Kuwait to Pakistan. Kerosene falling on an Indian village sparked a massive algae bloom in Kashmir's Lake Dal. Black acid rain fell from the Persian Gulf to the southern former USSR. Blizzards hit Israel, Lebanon, Jordan and Syria for the first time in the experience of most residents of these states.

Desertification was brought about by the Gulf War. Acid rain from oil fires killed vegetation. In the western province of Iraq, one-third of the trees were killed. Sulphuric soot-oil, characteristic of Kuwaiti crude, dropped in heavy amounts over Oman and Turkey. Oil lakes were created, one of them eight kilometres in length, and these killed thousands of birds for years after the war. Some 20,000 sea birds, including the endangered Socotra cormorant, died from oil slicks. The Iraqi army deliberately butchered most of the animals in the Kuwait zoo. Sea grasses deep in the Persian Gulf were covered by oil. It took nine months to stop the oil fires set by Iraq, a process made more difficult by the mining of the wells. Two years after the war, one-third of Kuwait was covered by plant-choking soot and tarcrete. The war pulverized topsoil and wiped out vegetation causing sand dunes to advance [18].

How Oil Revenues Sustain War and Dictatorship in the Middle East

All dictatorships in the Middle East are helped in some way by oil revenues. States that are relatively small-scale petroleum producers, such as Tunisia, which receives only 15 percent of its budget from oil, are still buffeted from pressures by free states and international aid agencies to democratize. Egypt receives a third of its budget from oil. Syria, a significant oil producer in its own right, is further helped by oil superpower Iran in its sponsorship of terrorism to derail the peace process between Israel and the Palestinians.

Corruption and the funding of secret instruments of repression are facilitated by central command control over oil wealth. Morocco is an oilless semi-democratic state, the only predominantly Arabic-speaking nation that has developed a modern fiscal system with transparent accounting of public revenues. It is also unique in having constitutional government and multiparty elections for a period longer than the post-Cold-War years [19].

Warrior dictators in the Middle East need not fear taxpayer revolt. Their military schemes are funded on their control over oil.

CURRENT WARS IN ALGERIA, SUDAN, KURDISTAN AND AFGHANISTAN

The Middle East is home to most of the world's remaining full-scale wars. Here oil-rich powers intervene on behalf of various factions in conflicts which are conducted on a quite ruthless basis. Both sides of Afghanistan's civil war are supported by oil-rich powers. Iran assists the armed Kurdish rebels in Turkey and the repressive government of Sudan. In both Sudan and Algeria, the misuse of oil wealth helps prolong two of the worst civil wars.

ALGERIA'S CIVIL WAR

Since 1991, Algeria's civil war has resulted in 80,000 deaths. It reveals the tragic pattern of most of the Middle East and of oil dictatorships in general. Some $4 billion annually in Algeria's $10 billion in oil revenues goes towards funding its civil war [20].

Following independence in 1962, Algeria was for more than 30 years a one-party dictatorship under the rule of the Front Liberation Nationale (FLN). The FLN favoured heavy military spending and costly efforts to develop nuclear reactors, which contributed to widespread poverty following the collapse in oil prices in the 1980s. Large sums were invested in money-losing steel mills. Agriculture languished from efforts to impose collective farming. Massive industrial investments meant little new residential construction took place creating a serious housing shortage. Huge sums in oil revenues were lost through corruption.

Algeria's failure to use oil wealth to advance human welfare was exploited effectively by its Islamic fundamentalist opposition during a democratic transition launched by the FLN in 1989. This followed seven days of rioting after the removal of food subsidies and the imposition of health care user fees [Appendix I].

Although a sudden political liberalization resulted in the creation of 30 political parties, only the Islamists had much popular appeal. At the time of the military coup in January 1992, it appeared that the Islamic Salvation Front (FIS) was about to be elected on an antidemocratic platform to impose Shari'a law.

Algeria's hope in ending civil war lies in its civil society which is growing despite the dual authority of the military and fundamentalists. One sign of hope is its growing labour movement, despite the assassination of several hundred activists by Islamic extremists. Another is the work of the Algerian League for the Defence of Human Rights which investigates abuses on both sides of the civil war.

The now moderate FIS is encouraging a democratic peace process. Armed militants formerly associated with it have splintered off to form the more extreme Armed Islamic Group (GIA) which has publicly declared Christians and Jews to be targets for assassination [21].

While moderates work for peace in Algeria one of their greatest difficulties is that hard-line extremists on both sides of the war have access to great oil wealth. Algeria funds the army from its own petroleum revenues, while its armed opposition is helped by oil-rich Iran and its ally Sudan.

ECONOMIC DOMINATION BY GUNS AND OIL

The Middle East's former subsistence peasantry is increasingly integrated into the dominant oil economy. It has largely vanished except in very isolated areas and among persecuted minorities such as the Kurds. Even the peasantry of rural Iran was replaced by workers on Soviet-style state farms. The transition came with the mania for tractor farming and massive irrigation schemes created by the OPEC oil boom.

The welfare of Egypt's farming sector depends largely on the state of Middle-East oil. This was the most important agricultural area in the Middle East, but now agriculture has been reduced to a hobby activity here. Income from oil, either seasonal or from relatives, is responsible for improving living standards in the fertile Nile delta as well as in less favoured rural areas throughout the Arabic-speaking Middle East. After 1973, Tunisia, Syria and Egypt were no longer able to export food. Only oilless Morocco increased agricultural production [22].

Peasant and nomadic dry agriculture is geared to arid climatic limitations which evolved in the Middle East over thousands of years. Such traditional methods have been replaced by heavier irrigation and the use of oil-based inputs.

Libya has embarked on a massive irrigation scheme called the "Great Man Made River Project", based on the rapid depletion of groundwater aquifers. This threatens traditional oasis farming as wells are projected to run dry in 68 years, depleting aquifers that took 30,000 years to fill. Similar groundwater stripping policies are pursued in Saudi Arabia which has become self-sufficient in wheat through massive irrigation, although such grains could be purchased at one-quarter the price on the world market. The aquifers of Arabia are projected to be empty in less than 50 years [23].

The Middle East's economy is locked into a polluted time warp; that is, it is cut off from green technologies of the past and future. It is unable to move into the newer technologies of the microchip era. The Persian Gulf's industrial sector remains geared to oil by-products, along with some energy-intensive aluminum refineries, steel mills and cement production [24].

The limited financial services industry of the Persian Gulf is concentrated in Bahrain and Kuwait. However, the Gulf War stimulated capital flight from the region. This sector has become an accessory to the marketing of weapons and the financing of war. Its stock exchanges, brokerage houses and insurance corporations are of no significance to the global economy [25].

MIDDLE-EAST PETRODICTATORSHIPS SUSTAINING MILITARISM AND DICTATORSHIP ELSEWHERE

Hawkish strategic studies experts have tended to repackage the former Cold-War threat to the world's democracies into a "western" clash with authoritarian Han and Islamic civilizations. The repackaging does express the reality of arms deals and repression in China, the oil-rich states of the Middle East and Russia, but it ignores the antidemocratic behaviour that was characteristic of western oil corporations in the past, notably the infamous Anglo-Iranian Corporation. Rather than a clash of civilizations there is a tawdry pursuit of oil-based profits at the expense of fundamental human rights.

China's emerging oil companies are intended to function as those of the gigantic capitalist world, sharing their indifference for human rights. China's oil strategies have tended to be in the vanguard of corporate efforts to remove economic sanctions from human rights abusers in the Middle East.

Rather than embarking on aggressive war schemes for oil, China is interested in securing oil through the normal capitalist methods. War and instability in the Persian Gulf are as much a threat to China's rising oil companies as to the directors of the Chase Manhattan Bank. China lost $2 billion as a result of Iraq's invasion of Kuwait, but has become the biggest market for the petrochemical fertilizers produced in Kuwait and Saudi Arabia. Kuwait is involved in expanding China's capacity to produce such fertilizers, investing in oil development in China. Kuwait has struck a deal to construct a pipeline that serves Chinese refineries on the condition that it carries exclusively Kuwaiti crude [26].

China is aggressively pursuing oil deals in rich pariah states targeted for sanctions by the United States because of their human rights abuses and aid to civil wars. China's national oil companies are making major investments in Sudan, Iraq, Iran and the oil-rich dictatorships of the former USSR. In June 1997, the Chinese National Petroleum Company gave a huge windfall to the besieged Iraqi state. It purchased 50 percent of Iraq's Al Ahadab field for $1.2 billion. It is holding talks with Iran's national oil company for joint ventures to explore oil in Iranian waters. Major investments by China in petroleum development in Turkmenistan, Uzbekistan and Kazakhstan are premised on the construction of pipelines between these countries and Iran. These and further investments by Gazprom, Petronas, and the French Total corporation, are creating major pressures for the United States to lift sanctions on Iran [27].

China's bold entry into the Middle East petroleum market has already caused the US Clinton administration to relent and allow US companies to participate in the construction of one gas pipeline across Iran. This concession has further increased business pressure for US participation in the construction of more pipelines so that, in the words of a business journalist, American companies will not "have to watch from the counter, while European and Asian companies do all the feasting [28]."

China's efforts to buy influence in the Middle East through investments in the petroleum industry are coupled with arms sales to Iraq and Iran that are barred to US companies. That Russia and China have pursued arms sales with such vigour conjures up Lenin's warning about capitalist greed going as far as to sell the rope for its own execution. Their nuclear assistance to Middle East dictatorships, North Korea's marketing of missiles and China's sales of missile guidance systems to Iran, increasingly take on the role of commercial ambition. China is more interested in having its oil companies enter the ranks of the Fortune 500 than in exporting socialism. However, it wants to restrict the growth of human rights and multiparty democracy.

Along with policies of commercial opportunism, a consistent thread in Russian, Chinese, Malaysian and North Korean policy is an absence of concern for human rights. This tends to nullify the modest efforts by full democracies to improve human rights in the region [29].

IRAQ'S PEOPLE: PRISONERS OF REGIONAL HUMAN-RIGHTS ABUSES

Concerted action against oil dictatorships are rare, no matter how outrageous their behaviour. One exception to this rule is the continual siege of Iraq, involving UN imposed sanctions and 1998-9 prolonged bombing.

Heated debates over the causes of starvation in Iraq frequently ignore how such hardships are common in dictatorships which prefer to give higher resources to their military than necessities for their powerless civil population. International relief organizations have assumed the costs of public health in Iraq. This needed humanitarian intervention does, however, allow the regime to divert even more resources to its military. Thus, the people of Iraq have become hostages to their dictatorship [30].

The UN sanctions have made the enclave of Kurdistan a relative zone of prosperity in Iraq. Here humanitarian assistance under the UN food-for-oil program actually prevents hunger. The contrast with the rest of the country is caused by the fact that in Kurdistan the program is administered by the UN. Its relief agencies clear mine fields, hand out food rations and deliver medical supplies. Only here do Iraq's limited oil sales serve human welfare instead of adding to military might [31].

Freedom for Iraq is not attractive to the dictatorships surrounding it. This harsh reality further discourages the US Congress from approving substantial assistance to the democratic Iraqi National Congress, since many see its cause as doomed because of regional hostility to human rights. Iran in particular is threatened by the emergence of a democratic Iraq because of the many non-Farsi speaking minorities in Iran that would be encouraged to assert their rights given a neighbouring free state. These include Kurds, Arabs and Turks. Despite ideological differences, Iran has assisted Iraq greatly in smuggling oil.

The best hope for a state that would assist the removal of Saddam Hussein's regime is semidemocratic Turkey which, however, it is not a full democracy largely because of its ongoing repression, involving a civil war against its Kurdish minority. This has made Turkey quite ambivalent toward efforts to promote democracy in Iraq.

Turkey's scorched-earth policies discourage dissident Iraqis from fleeing their country. It has displaced two million Kurds near its southern border with Iraq and has razed 3,000 villages. The Turkish army and the ultra nationalist anti-Kurdish Special Operations Team deliberately set forest fires in this campaign of ethnic cleansing. Rather than a frontier of freedom, as in Europe, NATO's borders on the Middle East are a zone of state terror.

By recently daring to call for autonomy, rather than independence, the abducted and arrested Kurdish leader, Abudullah Ocalan, has risked becoming peacemaker in the fashion of Yasser Arafat. The embrace of the peace process by the Palestine Liberation Organization (PLO) has provided a model for moderate Kurds. One of the difficulties they face is media censorship in Turkey. By its continual anti-Kurdish propaganda, the press increases the difficulties faced by the country's political leaders to make the federalist concessions necessary for peace [32]. Press censorship in Turkey has the perverse effect of encouraging the survival of Saddam Hussein. Turkish voters, much like those of Serbia in their prejudices against Albanians, are misinformed by media that project simplistic and untrue stories based on hatred.

Turkey's award of candidate membership in the European Union (EU) in December 1999 strengthened democratic currents throughout the Middle East by making it impossible to execute Ocalan and increase repression. Turkey's EU membership application compels it to develop conciliatory federalist solutions for its conflict with its Kurdish minority. One of the immediate democratizing impacts of Euro-candidacy was a decision to allow Kurdish-language broadcasting, despite protests by authoritarian Turkish nationalists. Turkey's EU application is also expected to bring its military under elected civilian control.

Kept alive by a surrounding belt of repressive states and continuing Israeli conflicts with Palestinians that serve to legitimate the dictatorship, Iraq's defiance epitomizes the dangers of the hard energy path warned against by Amory Lovins. It has sacrificed $100 billion in potential oil revenues in order to continue its development of weapons of mass destruction. This has persisted despite concerted efforts by the United Nations Special Commission (UNSCOM) and later British and US bombing. Critical to this situation are continued delays in the Palestinian-Israeli peace process, since progress tends to isolate the Iraqi regime further from the Arab world.

Nowhere else do the dangers of oil and dictatorship appear more ominous than in the epics of UNSCOM which far exceed, in their drama, the fictional spy thriller genre. The most serious exposés by the UN mission came after investigators in June 1991 made a departure from their normal six hours advance notice at a military site that was suspected of housing uranium enrichment equipment. After a prolonged standoff, inspectors were permitted to climb on top of a water tower that stood outside of the facility. This allowed them to spot dozens of trucks loaded with cargo driving through the back gate. Other inspectors chased down the convoy, while Iraqi soldiers fired over their heads.

Although the inspectors were stopped and searched, they were able to photograph giant twelve-ton magnets lashed to the trucks. These were calutron devices, used for enriching uranium for nuclear weapons. This was followed up by a raid on the Nuclear Design Centre in downtown

Baghdad. Here four boxes of the program's records were recovered. Subsequently, after the inspectors visited Petro Chemical-3, the code name for Iraq's nuclear program, they were trapped by Iraqi soldiers in a parking lot. Fortunately, satellite phone connections allowed the UN inspectors to give interviews to the media during the standoff. International pressure resulted after eight days of tension in Iraq allowing the inspectors to leave with 50,000 pages of documents, including a top-secret report proving that Iraq had been working on a design for an atomic bomb. Such cloak-and-dagger episodes are part of the constant state of terror the world is placed in by the continuing power of oil-financed dictatorship [33].

GUNS FOR OIL IN THE PERSIAN GULF

One of the most perverse aspects of a petroleum-influenced world economy is the extent that it encourages a pattern of trade based on guns for oil in the Persian Gulf. Petrodollars are recycled in the worst way possible for bigger and better weapons systems to abet the complex conflicts among the varied dictatorships of the Middle East.

Heavy military expenses force the wealthy pro-NATO members of the Gulf Co-operation Council into chronic conditions of budget deficits despite considerable wealth from their state-owned oil industries. The survival strategy of these countries against a possible invasion from Iraq, Iran, Syria, or theoretical combinations of these dictatorships is based on the command of the skies. Under this assumption the best high-tech weapons must be purchased from NATO member states. In the advent of war, air supremacy would give more time for the arrival of foreign ground forces.

A close relationship exists between the Gulf Co-operation Council states and the US aerospace industry. Only US-made commercial aircraft are purchased by Saudi Arabia. This helped McDonnell-Douglas through difficult times when it was completing its C17 military transport program.

Co-operation between the Gulf states and the US has raised the stature of the US as the world's only superpower. Other arms producers in the democratic world are going out of business, unable to match the combined strength of Saudi oil money and American technology.

The Gulf War gave excellent advertising for US weapons, resulting in such contracts as $500 million from Saudi Arabia for Patriot missiles capable of shooting down Iraqi Scuds. The $30.4 billion in US arms purchases by Saudi Arabia from 1990 to 1993 amounted to more than half of all US arms contracts. In addition Saudi Arabia continues to pay for the Gulf War and the ongoing costs of US forces in the Persian Gulf. Current defence spending of the Gulf-Co-operation states is around $40 billion. States such as the United Arab Emirates spend annually around $5 to $6 billion on new arms procurement [34].

Since the Iran-Iraq war began in 1980, the Persian Gulf has been the scene of continual recycling of petrodollars for wars and arms. In 1980, when it began its invasion of Iran, Iraq had foreign cash reserves of $30 billion. When it gave up its efforts to annex Iran's oil fields in the compromise truce of 1986, it had $100 billion in debts. During the war Iraq received $119 billion from oil sales. This means the pursuit of Iraq's designs on Iran's oil cost $295 billion. Adding on the heavy damage caused by the fighting, the war cost Iraq about $495 billion. This is a colossal sum. Its waste was made possible only by Iraq's ability to receive huge sums through the sale of oil. No normal economies, where public revenues depend on taxation, could have sustained the costs of such a war [35].

In order to recover from the economic mess of its war with Iran, Iraq became an enforcer of the demands for higher prices and limited sales by the OPEC cartel. This policy clashed with the interests of Kuwait and the United Arab Emirates, which had major investments in oil-consuming states. Iraq received the support of Saudi Arabia, Iran and the Republican administration of George Bush, closely allied to US oil interests in its conflicts with Kuwait over oil. Iraq's desire for more oil revenue, however, got out of hand. Instead of occupying contested border areas, for which it had tacit approval from the US government, it greedily sought to annex the entire country [36].

After the world's economy had been distorted by the flows of billions from the Iran-Iraq war it soon received a similar jolt from the Gulf War. Reversing Iraq's invasion of Kuwait cost about $70 billion. Japan and Germany each came up with $3 billion. The bulk of the expense, however, $52 billion, came from Arab countries, predominantly Saudi Arabia [37].

For the relatively modest share of the cost of the Gulf War, Japan and Germany reinforced their pursuit of an oilless strategic economic policy. Despite the protests of their Arab allies, the European and Japanese contributions to the Gulf war were paid through taxes on their domestic oil consumption. This was done to discourage the need for such rescue operations for oil producers in the future [38].

SAUDI ARABIA AS REGIONAL DEFENDER OF DICTATORSHIP

Pressure from Saudi Arabia resulted in the suspension of Kuwait's liberal constitution in 1986. Popular outrage and protests over this decision gave Iraq the misleading signal that its occupation would be welcomed [39]. Also, the restrictions on civil liberties in Kuwait made it harder to influence change on the oil issues on which Iraq clashed with Kuwait. During the regime that ended in 1986 issues such as the rate at which Kuwait exploited the joint Romailia oil field and oil production quotas were openly debated in the press and parliament. Such avenues were closed on the eve of the invasion [40].

Restoration of Kuwait's constitution after the Gulf crisis was not easy. At the end of the crisis it, like Saudi Arabia and many other Gulf states, experienced heightened repression, brutally expelling residents whose nations did not support them during the Gulf War. Particularly harsh treatment was given to the Palestinians. Many died from arbitrary punishment in a fashion similar to what Kuwaitis experienced during Iraq's occupation [41].

Victory in the Gulf War was not simply created by American high-tech weapons and Saudi money. Important to Iraq's defeat and the eventual restoration of Kuwait's semidemocracy was Kuwait's strong civil society. Its co-operative movement covertly provided food free of charge to families in need. It also proved a means of communication. This underground resistance subsequently led the movement for the restoration of Kuwait's constitution. It received US support, despite the denunciation by Saudi King Fahad of elections being inimical to Arab tradition [42].

Kuwait has the Arabic press which is the least subjected to government censorship. Its message is viewed with hostility by states within the region that want to legitimate repression [43].

Saudi Arabia has not experienced any improvement in human rights in the past decade. For a 10-month period during the Gulf crisis, Saudi Arabia stopped public beheadings, flogging and amputations. After most Americans were gone these traditions were renewed. In "Chop Square" in its capital city of Riyadh, in a three-week period in June 1991 some 16 people were beheaded [44].

With the smallest oil reserves of any state bordering the Persian Gulf, Bahrain is in many ways an excellent candidate for freedom. It is a small island state of 590,000 people, where fishing is still an important industry. This is threatened by oil pollution in the Persian Gulf. With annual spills of 150,000 tonnes being common, fishmongers in Bahrain's market joke that their products are already freshly oiled [45].

Saudi Arabia has been quite outspoken in opposing the spread of liberal constitutionalism among its allies in the Gulf Co-operation Council. This pressure has been most successful in Bahrain, despite its strong democracy movement. Bahrain had previously been ruled from 1972 to 1976 under a liberal constitution. The present democracy movement not only receives support from the country's oppressed majority Shiite Muslims but also from the privileged Sunni minority. Its democratic opposition has endured severe repression. Since 1990, over 40 people have died as a result of government crackdowns against democratic activists. Riot police have attacked Shiite mosques [46]. Nevertheless, the post-Cold-War wave of democratization has impacted favourably on the other four of the smaller states, Kuwait, Qatar, Oman and Yemen, the last three being relatively small oil producers.

In Qatar, Sheikh Hamad has played an enlightened role. Since coming to power in 1995 he has gradually increased voting rights and civil liberties. This rapidly democratizing state is running out of oil, but has significant reserves of natural gas. It is supportive of the Arab-Israeli peace process and hopes to sell liquefied natural gas to Israel. Qatar recently helped the peace process by televised interviews that discredited its critics. Qatar's all-news satellite television channel, al-Jazeera is an inspiring voice for a democratic peace throughout the Arabic-speaking world. Its interviews with dissidents and exiles from throughout the Middle East and lively debates have inspired furious protests from neighbouring petrodictators. They feel threatened by the Qatar's most deadly weapon — well informed ridicule.

Oman has also increased popular participation in government; but the greatest improvement has been made in Yemen, now able to conduct regular and generally fair multiparty elections. The Yemeni Human Rights Association is able to operate openly. In an unusual sign of the advance of liberty in the Arabian Peninsula, the Yemeni national airline in 1997 was able to experience a legal strike [47].

Among the Gulf Co-operation Council states there is a clear and growing division between the two most powerful superoil dictatorships and the smaller five on issues concerning terrorism, Islamic fundamentalism and human rights. At the same time Saudi Arabia has improved relations with Iran. It has also clashed with Kuwait over its support of American actions against Iraq.

The five smaller nations tend to be more reliable allies to the United States and the free world than the other two. Their press is less controlled by censorship and is open to a wider range of ideas. They are also more inclined to embark on a process of gradual democratization and support the Arab-Israeli peace process. They also have real democratic oppositions, such as the Bahrain Freedom Movement. These nonviolent oppositions are in sharp contrast to the authoritarian Islamic fundamentalisms that confront the stronger oil monarchies. The fundamentalists have employed terrorism, including the bombing of US military bases in Saudi Arabia.

Women in the smaller Gulf states also have more rights. The women of Qatar are entitled to vote, and recently won the right to decline marriage proposals. They were allowed, in May 1998, to both watch and compete in an international track meet.

Unlike Saudi Arabia and the United Arab Emirates, the smaller five are not interested in helping the Taliban, and have denied it diplomatic recognition. Nor do they aid Pakistan in its conflict with India.

Militarily vulnerable Kuwait has not allowed itself to be used as a base for Islamic fundamentalists engaged in terrorism and civil war in other countries. There has been no evidence within Kuwait of attempts to pay out protection money to Osama bin Laden, whereas bin Laden is known to have had much support from Saudi Arabia.

The five smaller states, far from being the manipulators of petrotyranny, are to some extent its victims [48].

EXTREMISM AND THE PALESTINIAN GRIEVANCE

While Saudi Arabia's oil wealth has encouraged authoritarian rule within the Arabian peninsula, a far more destructive role has been played by the intrigues of the anti-NATO Middle Eastern and North African oil-rich states — Syria, Libya, Algeria, Iraq, Tunisia, Iran and Sudan. What all the these states have in common, despite their frequently bloody internecine conflicts, is opposition to the peace process between Israel, Jordan, Egypt and the new Palestinian authority. Critical is Syria, which has the backing of Iran and also supports armed extremists in Lebanon.

Syria is enriched by oil in several ways. Although not an oil superpower on the scale of the Persian Gulf, it is a significant oil producer, with 1.7 bbl in proven reserves. It has 964 producing wells. Oil accounts for about 40 percent of Syria's economy. Although Syria was previously able to offset drops in price by rising production, this is no longer possible. Given the absence of new discoveries it is expected that Syria's oil production has peaked and will decline steadily over the next few years. Predictions that Syria will have to import oil in five or ten years put additional pressure on the regime to make a peace deal with the new Labour government in Israel.

Syria benefits from transit fees from the pipelines that cross its territory and has investments in the Persian Gulf oil industry. It also benefits by smuggling oil from Iraq. Moreover, Syria receives assistance from other oil-rich nations because of its status as a "front line" state in the war with Israel. Syria also benefits from considerable investment by non-American multinational oil companies. Shell and the German-owned Deminex have major investments in Syrian oil fields and are currently engaged in major exploration projects.

Syria is one of the most repressive states towards Kurds in the Middle East. Its 200,000 Kurds have been stripped of their citizenship and cannot own property. Their former lands were confiscated under the pretext of land reform. It is illegal to teach or publish in Kurdish. Kurds are distrusted because they are part of the country's Sunni Muslim majority in a state which, despite official secular Arab nationalism, is dominated by the minority Islamic Alawite sect.

Syria recently eased its past hostilities with Iraq by reopening a border that had been sealed since the Gulf War. It has contracted with China and North Korea for improved weapons [49].

The intervention of antidemocratic, oil-rich powers was critical to Lebanon's inability to function as a successful democracy following its civil war which ended in the Tarif Accords of 1990. Syrian intervention has frustrated the democratic intention of a compromise constitutional settlement. Its armed presence caused most Christians to boycott the 1992 elections. Electoral boundaries were redrawn to favour pro-Syrian candidates. Permits for demonstrations are frequently denied to Christian groups. The Syrian-backed government blamed the Maronite Christians for the bombing of one their own churches, an incident subsequently used as a pretext to limit press freedoms and arrest 100 persons. The continuing civil war in southern Lebanon between the Iranian- and Syrian-backed Hezbollah and the Israeli-supported South Lebanon Army has for the past two years resulted in about a hundred deaths annually [50].

THE EMERGING DEMOCRATIC PEACE IN THE OILLESS *BENELUX* OF THE MIDDLE EAST

The evolving peace process was vividly captured by former Israeli Prime

Minister Shimon Peres by his recognition of the emergence of a co-operative Benelux-style federation between Israel, Jordan and the new Palestinian authority. This is an imaginative application of the peaceful and successful customs union between Belgium, Luxembourg and the Netherlands. It has already accelerated following the 1999 formation of a Labour Party government in Israel [51].

A quite mainstream Israeli politician, in fact the heir of his hawkish mentor and patron, David Ben-Gurion, Peres was a relative newcomer to the Arab-Israeli peace process. His initiation into this process had tragic origins. It was begun by the Norwegian government during a Lisbon meeting of the Socialist International when its early brave prophet, Issam al-Sartawi was assassinated by Syrian-backed extremists hostile to the notion of a democratic Arab-Israeli peace. Before his tragic death, al-Sartawi was able to convert many Arabs and Jews to the path of peace. One of his more remarkable converts was the Hashemite King of Morocco, King Hassan II. While transforming Morocco into a parliamentary semidemocracy, the King ended discrimination against Jews at al-Sartawi's prompting.

The oil-free havens of freedom in the Middle East are all pioneering on the paths of green technology. This is especially true for the region's only full democracy, Israel. From its early years it has been one of the world's pioneers in solar power. Israel's founder, David Ben-Gurion, installed a solar water heater in his home. He supported a pioneering couple, the Yissars, who made use of the power of the Sun by painting an old tank black and using it as a bath tub. After the end of the 1948 war, Rani Yissar encouraged her husband Levi to do further research on solar power. He built the first prototype Israeli solar water heater in his home and soon set up 25 such heaters among his neighbours. By 1953, Yissar created the NerYah Company which became Israel's first commercial producer of solar water heaters. Some 50,000 solar water heaters were sold in Israel from 1957 until the Six-Day War of June, 1967 [52].

Israel's victory in the 1967 war briefly made it a self-sufficient oil power through its seizure of Egypt's Sinai oil fields. The conquest devastated its solar industry which, however, revived after the Camp David Accords, brokered by US President Jimmy Carter, returned these oil fields to Egypt. Oil and gas prices in Israel escalated and public policy encouraged solar power. Building codes required that solar water heaters be installed in most buildings, including any apartments more than eight stories high. Now two-thirds of households in Israel have solar water heaters, the highest percentage of any country. Annually 50,000 solar water heaters are installed in Israel [53].

The boom in solar water heaters has also extended into Jordan which uses the Sun for most of its hot water. The peaceful Benelux of the Middle East is being constructed on several avenues of solar technology. One is a cascade of solar fields which supply hot water and steam to hospitals, hotels and industry. In the township of Kalil all homes are equipped with photovoltaic panels and solar water heaters [54].

GREEN AND DEMOCRATIC PEACE EMERGING IN THE MIDDLE EAST

A green and democratic peace is evolving rapidly in parts of the Middle East that lack major oil reserves. This includes Israel, Jordan, Morocco, the Palestinian Authority and Turkey. All these countries are becoming allied against the anti-NATO oil dictatorships that are attempting to destroy the peace process. They are encouraging a democratization process among many of the oil monarchies in the Gulf Co-operation Council which, apart from the United Arab Emirates and Saudi Arabia, are showing growing signs of success. This democratic peace process is now being encouraged by the powerful American Jewish community which increasingly understands that Israel's security depends not only on its military strength, but on good relations with democratically minded Arab neighbours. Suspicious of oil companies, it has been a major force behind the American economic sanctions against oil producers such as Iran.

Morocco and Turkey are both oilless semi-democracies. They have achieved the most progress outside the *Benelux* states towards the application of renewable energy technologies. In June 1998, Orguz Capan, then President of Turkey's small ROC oil company, visited the offices of the World Watch Institute in Washington, an American environmental group. Capan's visit was to announce that low oil prices had persuaded him to sell his oil company and invest the proceeds in wind and solar energy. Morocco is also pioneering solar power. Here the International Finance Corporation is preparing a $5 million plan to boost sales of photovoltaic systems [55]. Danish manufacturers have succeeded in establishing a beachhead in the Middle East for wind power — in Morocco. It now leads the region with an installed capacity of 50 megawatts.

Their lack of oil wealth has made both Morocco and Turkey vulnerable to international pressures for a democratic peace. Morocco submitted to a UN-brokered process to achieve peace in the former Spanish Sahara which it invaded in 1975. A peace pact in 1991 ended 15 years of guerrilla war and has been kept in force by the United Nations Mission for a Referendum in the Western Sahara (MINUSRSO).

The considerable international pressure on Turkey to negotiate with its Kurdish minority will speed its democratization process. Oilless Turkey has had considerable experience with democracy since 1945, although it has been fractured by two military coups. Its growing human rights movement has investigated repression against Turkey's Kurdish minority and has established rehabilitation centres for the victims of torture. Despite state persecution, the Turkish Democratic People's Party champions Kurdish minority rights [56].

Environmental groups in the Middle East do not yet have a mass membership base. Despite challenging circumstances, small independent groups have emerged. Encouraging progress has been evident in Jordan. Its Environment Society is the largest green organization in the Middle East and has 5,000 members. Jordan has developed environmental education programs for youth.

Jordan's pioneering greens are having an impact. It is the country in the Middle East that has achieved the most progress in eliminating lead from gasoline. Its 1995 multiparty elections resulted in legislation that defined and enforced public policies towards the environment [57].

In the emerging oilless *Benelux* there is growing co-operation in environmental conservation efforts between Arabs and Jews. With the exception of Saudi Arabia, all states bordering the Gulf of Aqaba are now engaged in efforts to cleanse it of oil pollution. Shortly following the signing of peace between Israel and Jordan in October 1994, an ecological restoration treaty for the Gulf of Aqaba was developed between these states and Egypt. On September 17, 1995, thousands of Israelis, Jordanians and Egyptians co-operatively cleaned up beaches. Israel and Jordan in 1994 inaugurated a project to capture runoff from the Yarmouk river, where decades ago their troops exchanged gunfire over the same water source. In the October 1998 peace accords signed by Israel and the Palestinian National Authority, it was agreed that three percent of the land ceded to Palestine would become a nature protection area [58].

The most formidable barriers to the spread of a green and democratic peace in the Middle East are the anti-NATO dictatorships of Libya, Iraq, Syria, Afghanistan, Sudan and Iran. They have not established nature reserves meeting the standards set by the International Union for the Conservation of Nature. Unlike even the repressive oil monarchies, they have failed to make limited experiments in solar power.

Outside the anti-NATO dictatorships the region's rich wind and solar resources are slowly replacing oil. The glacial pace of change will turn into an avalanche with continual improvements in alternative-energy technologies that lower production costs. It will then become increasingly difficult to disguise nuclear bomb making schemes under the guise of electrical power generation.

Although cursed with oil, the Middle East will be blessed by its devaluation. This will end the tragic trade of guns and oil which characterizes the post-Cold-War world of strategic thinking obsessed with the potential closure of the Strait of Hormuz to oil tankers. As in the rest of the world, coping with the difficult transition to environmental sustainability within democratic societies will replace the megalomaniac competition between dictatorships over the control of oil wealth.

NOTES

1. Freedom House Survey Team, "Freedom in the World" (New York: Freedom House, 1998) *passim*. Jim West ed. "International Petroleum Encyclopedia" (Tulsa, Penn Well, 1998) pp.274-275.

2. Saad Eddin Ibrahim, "Civil Society and the Promise of Democratization in the Arab World", in Augustus Richard Norton, ed. "Civil Society in the Middle East" (New York: EJ Brill, 1995) p.35.

3. Richard Rubenstein, "The Age of Triage" (Boston: Beacon Press, 1983) pp.10-20.

4. Dilip Hero, "Holy Wars: The Rise of Islamic Fundamentalism" (New York: Routledge, 1989) p.41.

5. Manucher Farmanfarmaian and Roxane Farmanfarmaian, "Blood & Oil" (New York: The Modern Library, 1997) p.61.

6. Leonard Mosley, "Power Play" (London: Weidenfeld and Nicholson, 1973) pp.40-43.

7. Wilbur Crane Eveland, "Ropes of Sand" (New York: W.W. Norton, 1980) pp.47-49.

8. Daniel Yergin, "The Prize" (New York: Simon & Schuster, 1991) pp.400-490.

9. Farmanfarmaian, *loc. cit.*, p.259.

10. Mosley, *loc. cit.*, p.338; M.A. Adelman, "The Genie out of the Bottle" (Cambridge: MIT Press, 1995) pp.113, 114.

11. Ibrahim, *loc. cit.*, p.46.

12. Martin Malin, "Is Autocracy an Obstacle to Peace? Iran and Iraq, 1975-80" in Miriam Fendius Elman ed. "Paths to Peace" (Cambridge: MIT Press, 1997) pp.373-404.

13. Frank Barnaby, "The Environmental Impact of the Gulf War", *The Ecologist*, July/August 1991, p.170; William Thomas, "Scorched Earth" (Gabriola Island: New Society, 1995) p.119.

14. Thomas, *loc. cit.*, p.129.

15. Ibrahim, *loc. cit.*, p.46.

16. "The Kurds: An Ancient Tragedy", *The Economist*, Feb. 20, 1999, p.51.

17. Ibrahim, *loc. cit.*, p.46.

18. Susan Lanier-Graham "The Ecology of War" (New York: Walker, 1993) pp.43-51.

19. Giacomo Luciani, "The Oil Rent, the Fiscal Crisis of the State and Democratization", in Ghassan Salame, "Democracy Without Democrats?" (London: IB Taruis, 1994) pp. 130-155.

20. "Algeria's Army Picks Its Man", *The Economist*, March 20, 1999, p.49.

21. Freedom House Survey Team, *loc. cit.*, pp.112, 113.

22. Hamid Ait Amara, "The State, Social Classes and Agricultural Policies in the Arab World", in Hazem Bellawi and Giacomo Luciani eds. "The Rentier State" (New York: Croom Helm, 1997) pp.139-179.

23. Sandra Postel, "Last Oasis: Facing Water Scarcity" (New York: Norton, 1992) pp.30-33.

24. Michael Chatelus, "Policies for Development" in Bellawi and Luciani, *loc. cit.*, pp.120-125.

25. F. Gregory Gause III, "Oil Monarchies" (New York: Council on Foreign Relations Press, 1995) p.169.

26. John Calabrese, "China and the Persian Gulf: Energy and Security", *Middle East Journal*, Summer 1998, pp.351-366.

27. Ahmed Rashid and Trisha Saywell, "Beijing Gusher" *Far Eastern Economic Review*, February 26, 1998, pp.47-49.

28. Ahmed Rashid, "This Way Out", *Far Eastern Economic Review*, September 18, 1997, pp.60, 61.

29. Calabrese, *loc. cit.*, p.364.

30. John Walker, "Orphans of the Storm: Peacebuilding for the Children of War" (Toronto: Between the Lines, 1993) p.64.

31. "The UN's own little Kurdish state", *The Economist*, February 20, 1999 p.51.

32. "Army Arsonists and Land Mafias Torch Turkey", *Earth Island Quarterly*, Winter 1999, p.23.

33. Jessica Stern, "The Ultimate Terrorist" (Cambridge: Harvard University Press, 1999) pp.107-127.

34. Janice Stein and Geoffrey Kemp, "Powderkeg in the Middle East" (New York: Rowan & Littlefield, 1995) *passim*; Francis Tusa, "The Money Mirage", *Armed Forces Journal*, November 1993, pp.20-23.

35. Kanan Makiya, "Cruelty and Silence" (New York: W.W. Norton, 1993) pp.274-278.

36. Adelman, *loc. cit.*, pp.289-293.

37. Makiya, *loc. cit.*, pp.274-278.

38. Adelman, *loc. cit.*, pp.291-293.

39. Ghassan Salame, "Small is Pluralistic: Democracy as An Instrument of Civil Peace", in Salame, *loc. cit.*, pp.90-95.

40. Neil Hicke and Ghaim alNailar, "The Utility of Traditional Civil Society in Kuwait", in Richard Augustus Norton, ed. *loc. cit.*, pp.186-193.

41. Luciani, *loc. cit.*, p.144; Freedom House Survey Team, *loc. cit.*, p.219.

42. Salame, *loc. cit.*, p.108.

43. Thomas, *loc. cit.*, p.119.

44. Makiya, *loc. cit.*, p.303.

45. Salame, *loc. cit.*, pp.102108; Freedom House Survey Team, *loc. cit.*, pp.135, 136.

46. Freedom House Survey Team, *loc. cit.*, pp.399, 400, 423, 424, 545, 546.

47. *Ibid.*, pp.485-487; Jim West, "Syria", "International Petroleum Encyclopedia, 1995" (Tulsa: Penn Well, 1995) p.94; "Syria: Gathering Clouds" *The Economist*, April 24, 1999, p.44.

48. Freedom House Survey Team, "Freedom in the World, 1998-99" (New York, Freedom House, 1999) pp. 378-390; Yossef Bodansky, "Bin Laden: The Man Who Declared War on America" (Rocklin: Prima, 1999) *passim*; "Arabian Gulf", *Earth Island Journal*, Spring 2000, p.14.

49. *Ibid.*, pp.327-329; Christopher Flavin and Nicholas Lenseen, "Power Surge" (Norton: New York, 1994) p.97.

50. Shimon Peres and Robert Little, "For the Future of Israel" (Baltimore: John Hopkins University Press, 1999) p.123.

51. Ken Buti and John Perlin, "A Golden Thread: 2,000 Years of Solar Architecture and Technology" (Palo Alto: Cheshire Books, 1980) pp.235-238.

52. David Berman and John T.O. O'Connor, "Who Owns the Sun?" (Chelsa Green: White River, 1996) pp.14, 15.

53. Madanjeet Singh, "The Timeless Energy of the Sun" (San Francisco: Sierra Club Books, 1998) pp.133, 150.

54. Christopher Flavin and Molly O'Meara "Solar Power Markets Boom", *World Watch*, September/October, 1998, p.35.

55. Binnaz Topark, "Civil Society in Turkey", in Richard Augustus Norton, *loc. cit.*, pp.87-118; Birger T. Madsen, "Energy's Wind of Change", *The UNESCO Courier*, March, 2000, p.10.

56. Joseph G. Jabbra and Nancy Jabbra, "Challenging Environmental Issues: Middle Eastern Perspective" (New York: Brill, 1997) pp.19-30.

57. Aaron Sachs, "The Aqaba Paradigm Revisited", *World Watch*, February, 1996, p.36.

58. "Make Parks Not War", *International Wildlife*, June, 1999, p.38.

CHAPTER FIVE
NIGERIAN OIL AND DICTATORSHIP

Nigeria's post-independence history is characterized by a strong democratic movement, facing complex barriers built by competing authoritarian ideologies and elites, mainly financed by oil. The strength of its democratic civil society is evident from the eventual triumph of its freedom movement.

HOW OIL CONTAMINATED NIGERIA'S BIRTH

Like many former British colonies, Nigeria benefited from a political leadership committed to democratic rule. Such blessings, however, could not steer the country away from the temptations of oil and dictatorship.

Oil was discovered in Nigeria in 1957 during the sunset of colonial rule. The prospect of oil wealth increased tension among Nigeria's political elite although, until independence, actual revenues from petroleum remained quite marginal [1]. Arguments over how oil revenues should be divided among the states of federal Nigeria were critical to the breakdown of democracy. The war was sparked by the first military coup and subsequent eruption of civil war following the failed secession of Biafra. The rebellious, Ibo-dominated south-eastern state attempted to cut off the flow of oil to the rest of the country. The government retaliated by dividing up the State to the advantage of non-Ibo minorities, such as the Ogoni, who received no benefits from petroleum wealth [2].

Nigeria's civil war of the 1960s was one of the bloodiest conflicts over the control of oil in human history. It resulted in over two million casualties. Most were war-related civilian deaths caused by famine.

The war also included battles over the country's oil industry. Targets were oil fields, pipelines, refineries and ports. Key oil flow stations were bombed and the resulting fires forced widespread evacuations [3]. Casualties were heaviest in oil-producing regions such as Ogoniland. Ten percent of this linguistic group was killed in the fighting in the Niger delta, the source of Nigeria's oil wealth [4].

NIGERIA'S OIL WEALTH WASTED BY DICTATORSHIP

After the civil war ended, the flood of oil revenue to Nigeria helped with national reconciliation, but major headaches, compounded by continuing dictatorship, soon emerged. The sudden influx of petroleum wealth resulted in corruption and inequitable economic development. Much of Nigeria's oil windfall was wasted on ill-considered schemes for giant industrialization projects based on heavily subsidized steel and automobile industries. Neglected were the small-scale farmers who remained the majority of Nigeria's population. Until the oil boom took off in 1969 these farmers produced most of Nigeria's foreign exchange. Farming became overly dependent on women and children as many men moved to the cities.

The industrialization of the 1970s, assisted by higher oil prices, resulted in massive land speculation as cities rapidly tripled in size. Traffic chaos resulted from a sudden 700 percent increase in car ownership in such booming cities as the historic Islamic centre, Kano. Automobile trips and jet travel became symbols of the wealth of the small elite that benefited from the oil boom.

Nigeria did make some investments in agriculture from its oil boom, but these were poorly conceived. Inefficient mechanized state farms, such as national companies for livestock, grains and root-stocks, were encouraged [5]. Irrigation schemes also resulted in harmful environmental consequences resulting in both peasant revolts and ruthless repression.

Considerable sums were wasted in money-losing Soviet-designed steel mills, intended for an African automotive industry. In 1975 the production of Volkswagens began in Lagos and continued until 1983 when it faced fatal competition from the fact that the elite who could afford cars preferred to smuggle in Mercedes-Benz [6].

Nigeria's steel and auto industries require massive subsidies from the state made possible only through petroleum wealth. The country lacks coal and iron and therefore must import these commodities crucial to steel at considerable expense. This makes Nigeria's steel twice the world's price. Investing huge sums in failing factories left little room for more profitable investments in foreign securities [7].

NIGERIA'S RESTORED DEMOCRACY HIT BY FALLING OIL PRICES

Under dictatorship much of Nigeria's oil wealth was lost through graft and corruption. Many construction projects financed through the oil boom were ruined by the use of inferior cement, causing buildings to collapse and roads to wash away. Imported pharmaceutical drugs were useless since they were purchased long after their expiry date.

Aided by corruption scandals, Nigeria's democracy movement triumphed in 1979 by the return to civilian rule and the creation of the Second Republic. Unfortunately the restoration of democracy took place when the country suddenly experienced falling oil prices, as the OPEC cartel began to lose its clout [Appendix I]. This helped cause democracy to die in Nigeria in 1983 at a time when the country's per capita income was lower than when the OPEC price hike came into effect a decade earlier [8].

ISLAMIC FUNDAMENTALISM HELPS DESTROY DEMOCRACY IN NIGERIA

Just as democracy was ill timed in Nigeria by collapsing oil prices, it was also cursed at its rebirth in 1979 by the Iranian revolution. This helped inspire similarly antidemocratic Nigerian ideologies. Critical to the explosion of fundamentalist violence which helped wreck Nigerian democracy was the impact of a remarkable Islamic prophet who denounced social injustice, Maitatsine. His movement was launched in Kano, one of the booming centres of the oil prosperity most deeply affected by soaring rents and deepening inequalities.

Maitatsine's Islamic movement, apart from its antidemocratic ideology, had something in common with reformist, spiritually based Gandhian and Catholic social-justice movements. As in these movements, Maitatsine's followers denounced police and military brutality. They also took practical steps to improve the welfare of the poor, such as encouraging gardening for food self-sufficiency. Unlike the Gandhians and disciples of Catholic base communities, Maitatsine was not interested in making democracy work more effectively. He was organizing, through violence, to create a separate Islamic state in northern Nigeria.

Gandhians and Catholic-base-community activists share much of Maitatsine's criticism of modern industrial technology, such as a condemnation of cars, and they too support interest in small-scale subsistence farming. Unlike Maitatsine, however, they would not condemn bicycles, seeing in them a practical way to improve the life of the poor. Maitatsine condemned bicycles because they are not mentioned in the Koran. Yet a lack of scriptural blessing did not apply to a condemnation of modern guns, which were to be the basis for the establishment of an Islamic state in northern Nigeria.

An armed insurrection was attempted in Kano, resulting in 5,000 deaths, and 15,000 injuries. Some 100,000 persons were made homeless. Maitatsine was killed and over 1,000 of his supporters arrested. Islamic fundamentalism, continued by his followers, still warred with democracy in Nigeria until it was overthrown by the military in 1983 [9].

Nigeria's restored dictatorship quickly became one of the world's worst despotisms. An authoritarian State Security edict of 1984, popularly known as "Decree Two" was proclaimed. This draconian measure allowed unchallenged detention by military authorities of anyone deemed harmful to state security [10]. Nigerian prison conditions soon resembled the death camps of Hitler and Stalin.

Maitatsine's idealistic followers were treated with special severity. By 1989, only 25 of his 100 incarcerated disciples were still alive after four years of imprisonment.

In the death camps of the Nigerian dictatorship prison wardens would routinely mark out for elimination anyone brave enough to protest abuses. Political dissidents, especially those from upper class backgrounds, were also targeted. Upon entering prison, guards would instruct prisoners to give such famous captives the "VIP treatment", characterized by beatings of exceptional severity.

Prisoners were frequently chained to cells. Whipping was another common punishment. Most prisoners were half naked or clothed in rags; they were seldom able to wash their ragged garments; cutlery was forbidden; and medical care was almost nonexistent [11].

ENVIRONMENTALISM BECOMES THE NEW FOCUS OF NIGERIA'S DEMOCRATIC MOVEMENT

Like most of the unfree world, Nigeria's seven-year-old petrotyranny was shaken by a green wave of democratic protest in 1990. The first spark of this flare-up took place in the October 1990 demonstrations directed against the Shell Petroleum Development Company (SPDC), which is the Nigerian subsidiary of Royal Dutch Shell.

The heroic anti-Shell protests were organized by the recently formed environmental group, the Movement for the Survival of the Ogoni

People (MOSOP), led by the former Nigerian government administrator and author Ken Saro-Wiwa. Although maligned and eventually executed by the Nigerian dictatorship on fraudulent murder charges, Saro-Wiwa bravely struggled to employ only non-violent methods in his challenge to petrotyranny. He persisted in his Gandhian path despite atrocious provocations by Nigerian military authorities. He often warned MOSOP colleagues of the dangers inherent in the use of violence. With considerable courage he exposed armed vigilante groups pretending to be affiliated with MOSOP but actually under the control of the Nigerian military dictatorship.

MOSOP's founding manifesto highlighted the environmental devastation caused by oil development in much of the Niger delta. It demanded an end to the flaring of natural gas, the clean up of oil spills and the burying of pipelines [12].

In its original declaration MOSOP accused Shell of "full responsibility for the genocide of the Ogoni." Two years later MOSOP sent its demands to Shell, Chevron, and the Nigerian National Petroleum Corporation, and their various joint ventures [13].

The demands of MOSOP emerged from the horrendous environmental impacts of oil extraction in repressive countries with widespread human-rights abuses. Unlined toxic waste pits cause contaminants to seep into drinking water, also driving fish away where there was open water. Acid rain has destroyed much of the delta's once fertile farmland. Nigeria's flaring of natural gas makes it one of the world's leaders in greenhouse gas emissions (carbon dioxide and methane). The flaring of gas is so bright that many children in the Niger delta have never experienced a dark evening. Noise from the flaring contributes to hearing loss. Flaring wastes a valuable resource, destroys plant life and causes soot to be deposited on homes.

Oil pollution is killing the Niger delta's mangrove wetlands. The natural mangroves are being replaced with exotic palm trees that are useless to the native wildlife on which subsistence communities in the delta depend for food [14].

MOSOP's first peaceful protests against pollution by SPDC were repressed with considerable violence and loss of life. Such a massacre took place on October 30 and 31, 1990, at Umuechem, an oil-producing community in the Niger delta.

On the second day of the Umuechem protests, brutal repression involving tear gas and gunfire was carried out by an elite unit of the Nigerian security services, the Mobile Police. This followed a request for assistance from the divisional manager of SPDC's eastern division for "security protection." The day following the protests saw indiscriminate shooting by the Mobile Police which resulted in 80 deaths and the torching of 495 homes [15].

The Umuechem bloodbath was an ominous precursor to the Nigerian petrotyranny's ruthless war against the nonviolent ecological activism of MOSOP. Despite the violent repression, the Ogoni's success in capturing the world's attention caused their ecological message to spread.

In October 1992, the Movement for the Survival of the Izon (Ijaw) Ethnic Nationality in the Niger Delta (MOSIEND) was formed. The next month, fifty-two traditional leaders from the Ogbia (an Ijaw subgroup) formed the Movement for the Reparation to Ogbia (MORETO). They demanded "protection against future effects of oil exploration." On October 4, 1993, 5,000 Ogbia disrupted activities at an Elf oil refinery [16].

On January 4, 1993, MOSOP staged the world's largest environmental rally. This involved 300,000 people — most of the Ogoni population [17].

MOSOP confronted Shell's efforts to extend exposed pipelines across farmlands. On April 28, 1993, an incident erupted with Willbros, a US pipeline contractor. It was commissioned by Shell. Willbros began bulldozing crops on farmland in the Ogoni village of Biara. Two days later its actions provoked a mass demonstration. The militant protests prompted Willbros to call in government troops. Eleven people were reportedly injured when security forces opened fire [18].

MOSOP's nonviolent protests were quite effective. Following the Biara confrontation, Shell closed all its facilities in Ogoniland. This terminated three percent of Nigeria's oil production. All Shell's flow stations in Ogoniland are closed to this day.

Despite their remarkable nonviolent victory in shutting down oil production, MOSOP continued its environmental agitation. Exposed pipelines still cross its homeland. Ogoniland remains contaminated by oil spills.

The largest spill in Ogoniland dates from a 1970 incident. Then the Biafran army set oil on fire to block federal troops. Oil continues to leach from this spill. It has a five-meter thick crust, and flow from the waste degrades downstream vegetation. Clean-up measures were stopped when Shell pulled all its personnel out of Ogoniland [19].

Repression against ecologists intensified in June 1993, when the Nigerian military dictatorship of General Babangida annulled the results of the presidential election victory by Moshood Abiola. The Babangida regime's plans to stage a transition to democracy became derailed after

Abiola's election victory was enhanced by his unexpected courage in distancing himself from Nigeria's military rulers.

Abiola was a respected liberal businessman and philanthropist who headed Nigeria's Social Democratic Party. A Muslim from the predominantly Christian southern Yoruba nation, Abiola was able to build significant national support from across Nigeria's diverse ethnic and religious groups in support of his program of social democratic reform. Later, in prison, he endured atrocious conditions.

SANI ABACHA

The annulment of Abiola's election unleashed a vicious cycle of state violence in Nigeria. One of the most ruthless figures in the repression of the protests against the nullification, which resulted in 400 deaths, was Babangida's Minister of National Defence, Sani Abacha [20].

With Abacha's encouragement, Babangida abruptly turned a transition to democracy into a return to petrotyranny. In the summer of 1993 hundreds of human-rights and pro-democracy activists, labour leaders, students and workers were arrested. Six media houses were proscribed. Many journalists who escaped arrest were declared wanted by security agents [21].

Abacha personally ordered soldiers to fire on unarmed demonstrators. Following this horrific carnage, he became President in November 1993. Shortly after becoming President he ordered the execution of 63 soldiers who resisted his dictatorship [22].

Abacha's rule was characterized by macabre brutality throughout Nigeria, but he was exceptionally ruthless over environmental protests against oil extraction in the Niger delta. Here he moved swiftly to stop growing green democratic contagion.

On November 19, 1993, the Mobile Police brutally attacked 3,000 demonstrators protesting peacefully outside an Agip terminal in the Niger delta community of Brass. After beating the environmentalists with clubs, they forced them to flee through an oil soaked drainage ditch, causing many to be bitten by snakes [23].

Shortly following Abacha's elevation to the Presidency, Ogoni police were withdrawn from their homeland. They were replaced with security personnel from other ethnic groups. Abacha also created a Rivers State Internal Security Task Force in January 1994 to intensify MOSOP's persecution [24].

Several Ogoni villages were burned down in April 1994. Abacha's terror climaxed in May 1994, following his arrest of Ken Saro-Wiwa. Over the next several months sixty towns and villages were raided in Ogoniland. Troops would enter towns and villages shooting at random with machine guns, causing villagers to flee into the surrounding bush. Before leaving they would loot money, food, livestock and other property. MOSOP activists who were not arrested were declared wanted by authorities.

Abacha's terror was unleashed against many Niger delta communities where environmentalists confronted the oil industry. On February 19, 1994, the Mobile Police destroyed and looted homes in Obagi, shooting indiscriminately and beating people who crossed their path. Villagers hid in the bush for more than six months following this attack.

On February 21, 1994 a similar attack was unleashed against several thousand environmental demonstrators. This incident took place in Rumuobiokani, a community located next to Shell's main compound at Port Harcourt. They were peacefully seeking to meet with Shell executives. Troops shot indiscriminately and beat environmental activists with their gun buts.

By the summer of 1994 Abacha's assault on the Ogoni had assumed a genocidal quality, expressing the full, terrifying logic of petrotyranny. Travel on bicycle in Ogoniland was outlawed. This gave troops a convenient pretext to shoot cyclists on sight. Anyone suspected of involvement with MOSOP risked summary execution in haphazard encounters with patrolling soldiers and Mobile Police. The Nigerian military destroyed 27 Ogoni villages, murdering 2,000 and leaving 30,000 homeless [25].

Shell has admitted that on one occasion it made direct payments to Nigerian security forces — in the form of "a very small fixed 'field allowance' in cases where members of the security forces have been deployed in connection with the protection of SPDC's facilities or SPDC personnel" [26].

The Nigerian military resented Shell's claims to have had nothing to do with their actions. Major Paul Okuntimo complained that Shell "had not been fair." Okuntimo had earlier ordered his troops to "shoot anyone you see" at a protest outside Shell's main headquarters. Protests over Shell's conduct resulted in a widespread international boycott of the company [27].

On June 26, 1994, Oronto Douglas and Uche Onyeagocha, both lawyers with the Nigeria Civil Liberties Organization, and Nicholas Ashton-Jones, a British environmentalist, were brutally beaten. They were kicked and slashed with electric cables and detained in prison [28].

Oronto Douglas was beaten at the time he was assisting in the legal defence of Ken Saro-Wiwa, who was finally executed along with eight other MOSOP leaders on November 10, 1995. During this period Abacha's terror met with growing protests from Nigeria's brave freedom movement, led by strong believers in democracy, including clergy, the country's trade union movement, the legal profession and teachers.

Prominent champions of democracy became singled out for terror and intimidation. On August 26, 1994, gasoline bombs were thrown at the home of Gani Fawehinimi, a respected human rights lawyer. Later, on September 2, 1994, the residence of a member of Nigeria's Constitutional Conference, Dr. Muyiwa Oladimeji, was firebombed. He had recently organized a demonstration against Abiola's imprisonment. Also firebombed were the headquarters of Nigeria's Campaign for Human Rights, and the home of Ayo Opadokun, the Secretary-General of the National Democratic Coalition. A month after his home was firebombed, on October 11, 1994, Opadokun was imprisoned for his opposition to Nigeria's dictatorship.

The firebombings of Nigeria's champions of freedom were part of a systematic campaign of terror against the country's democracy movement. Abiola's extensive publication network was shut-down and fake newspapers were circulated to discredit the democratic opposition.

Union headquarters and the office of journalists were sealed off. A march by members of the Nigerian Bar Association was stopped by 200 heavily armed riot police, resulting in the death of a 15 year old boy, Mufuau Preiva. On July 20, 1994, five protesters were killed in Abuja during a court appearance by Abiola [29].

After the execution of MOSOP's core leadership Abacha's tyranny worsened. During his detention Saro-Wiwa was severely beaten and kicked, manacled for prolonged periods, deprived of food, medical care and family visits. When Saro-Wiwa's mother attempted to visit her son at the Bori Military Camp she was flogged and briefly arrested [30]

The execution of the nine MOSOP leaders was particularly gruesome. To prevent their graves from becoming shrines to Nigeria's freedom movement, their bodies were buried in an unmarked common grave. The hangings were videotaped and viewed by Abacha and the military high command. MOSOP leaders who escaped execution were imprisoned. Until the death of Abacha, 20 MOSOP leaders were imprisoned on "holding charges."

The last three years of Abacha's tyranny, which ended with his unexpected and still mysterious death on June 8, 1998, were marked by increasing and more bizarre brutality. At one point soldiers invaded the Ibadan hospital and gunned down the wounded, other patients and staff [31].

Apart from terror, Abacha used a wide variety of cynical tricks to foster ethnic conflict, divide his opponents and manipulate a range of anti-democratic ideologies to cling to power. This was done with the compliance of oil corporations and allied petrotyrannies from around the world.

Abacha faced formidable opposition in the free world. Following Saro-Wiwa's execution, a coalition of American human-rights, environmental, black, and labour groups launched a campaign for sanctions against Abacha's dictatorship. This resulted in bipartisan proposals in the US Congress to cut off most investment by US firms and lay the basis for an international boycott of the purchase of Nigerian oil.

In response to human-rights crusaders, the Nigerian government purchased the services of nine American public relations and lobbying companies for $10 million. Opposition to sanctions was also supported by the 107-member Corporate Council on Africa, which urged dialogue rather than confrontation with the African dictatorships.

A strange American mix defended Abacha. Mobil, Chevron and Texaco all lobbied against US unilateral sanctions on Nigeria, as did USA Engage, a coalition of American corporations opposed to trade restrictions on dictatorships. Surprisingly, this corporate campaign was supported by the Nation of Islam, an American black Muslim organization [32].

Despite the Nigerian dictatorship's US oil-industry allies the Clinton administration did impose a ban on sales of military equipment, a reduction in humanitarian aid, the recall of the US ambassador, and a broadening of existing bans on visas for Nigerian officials and their families. In response to such measures, the Abacha dictatorship attempted to manipulate anti-Americanism.

State controlled Nigerian media highlighted "pro-government" rallies, where US flags were burned. These widely televised protests against American sympathies for Nigeria's freedom movement featured paid protesters, transported in government vehicles.

Nigerian government radio also stirred up hatred against America. It claimed that "so-called human rights and pro-democracy groups" assisted by the CIA were engaged in "devilish" plots to separate Nigeria into mini-states by civil war [33].

Abacha took particular care to restrict the growth of Nigeria's freedom movement in the country's largely Muslim North, especially among his own Hausa people, the country's most numerous nationality. The anti-American propaganda was used to scare northerners into acceptance of the Abacha dictatorship by depicting the democracy movement as a sinister foreign-controlled Christian separatist plot.

Government television and radio propaganda was particularly effective in the north where there was no independent press. The members of the northern pro-democracy Movement for Unity and Progress were targeted for arrest and harassment. State propaganda also attempted to depict riots between Igbo and Yoruba communities in Lagos as the work of democracy activists [34].

Despite Abacha's devious intrigues Nigeria's environmentally orientated democratic movement continued its struggle. It operated underground in Nigeria, while exiles built support for sanctions against the dictatorship around the world.

Unable to operate openly in Nigeria, the surviving leadership of MOSOP who escaped arrest moved to London. Despite extreme persecution, MOSOP was able to organize major protests on the January 4, Ogoni Day, and the November 10 anniversary of the executions. On the January 4, 1998 Ogoni Day, two environmental activists were killed in confrontations with soldiers [35].

New environmental organizations, such as the Niger Delta Human and Environmental Organization (ND-HERO), continued to oppose the Abacha dictatorship despite the risks. ND-HERO organized com-memorations of the executions of the Ogoni Nine.

Environmental activists continue to travel to democratic countries for training, despite frequent arrests for such actions. Anyakwee Nsirimovu was arrested and detained for several days for attending a human rights course in Canada. Nsirimovu's courage subsequently caused him to be imprisoned again, for protesting a January 1998, security crack-down on Ogoni Day.

Environmental and human-rights organizations in Nigeria persisted in their efforts despite their offices being regularly raided by the State Security Services (SSS). The offices of Environmental Rights Action (ERA) in Port Harcourt and Benin City were subject to constant SSS raids, as were those of ND-HERO. Since environmental and development organizations continued to receive aid from democratic countries they were treated as subversive, and so were subjected to constant SSS harassment.

Journalists were commonly arrested for reporting on blow-outs and oil spills. After armed men from the SSS came to arrest environmental activist Prince Ungo for launching a law suit against a petroleum development scheme, he fled to Togo [36].

Pirate radio stations were established by the democratic opposition off the Nigerian coast. These broadcast messages from MOSOP and reported on confrontations with the oil industry within Nigeria. In one incident in November 1997, the Nigerian opposition radio reported that 3,000 people from the Ekakpamre village near Ughelli in the Delta State forced the closure of the Ughelli West flow station. This protest over the destruction of farmland by oil was subsequently confirmed by Shell [37].

When Abacha died on June 8, 1998, the nation's military rulers faced a well organized and determined democratic opposition. Its underground power was combined with a growing movement for international sanctions.

By the spring of 1998 sanctions had begun to have some bite. Almost every country in the democratic world had by then imposed a tough arms embargo on Nigeria. It was also suspended from the Commonwealth; the first time such action had been taken. Several US and Canadian municipalities adopted sanctions resolutions to forbid municipal authorities from purchasing Nigerian and, in some instances, Shell products [38].

THE POST-ABACHA PERIOD

The considerable domestic and international pressure against dictatorship in Nigeria caused the new head of state, General Abdulsalami Abubakar, immediately to announce a transition to democracy. This resulted in the lifting of international sanctions. The stability of this transition was quickly threatened by the death of Moshood Abiola, shortly before his expected release from prison.

Until investigations by an international team of pathologists were completed there was concern over the possibility that Abiola had been secretly poisoned. However, the tragic deaths of many other Nigerian champions of freedom while in prison suggest that the abominable conditions in the jails may alone have been enough to end Abiola's life. Another victim was former Vice-President Musa Yar'Adu who died in prison in December 1997 of unknown causes. Some 10,000 persons died in detention from 1990 to 1995 largely because of unhealthy prison conditions. One leading dissident who became seriously ill in prison was journalist Chris Anyanwu. He had been convicted of treason in a 1995 show trial [39].

For several months progress in Nigeria's democratic transition was displayed in the less brutal treatment meted out to environmental protests of the Niger delta's Ijaw fishermen whose way of life is threatened by oil pollution. The transitional government of General Abubakar encouraged oil companies to negotiate with these injured parties [39].

Unfortunately, Nigeria's military rulers fell back to their old habits. On December 30, 1998, 240 people were killed in Yenagoa when soldiers fired on environmentalists protesting gas flaring. Soldiers have engaged in widespread arbitrary arrests and torture [40].

Part of the difficulty in uprooting oil dictatorship is that it is very profitable. The Nigerian section of Royal Dutch Shell is the most profitable of the company's worldwide corporate empire involving 110 nations. This exceptional profitability is not restrained as it would be in democratic states by environmental regulation. In the early 1990s the head of Shell's environmental division resigned in protest over such issues as the failure to bury oil pipelines [41].

Poor environmental regulation contributed to a disaster on October 17, 1998, when a thousand people died from an oil explosion. This inferno erupted on the third day of an oil spill. Some 44 days after the spill a former senior Shell executive reported that oil was still leaking at the site [42].

Nigerian youth question not only the environmental effects of oil production but also the consequences of its consumption. Nigeria's universities, which championed the country's freedom movement, have become harbingers of a renewal of bicycling. Cycling was common in Nigeria during its largely oilless first republic. With the country's oil boom, cycling became viewed as a "sin" and a sign of personal failure. Long line-ups for bus transit, involving up to two hours of waiting, became common after the oil boom faded. Despite such a powerful incentive to revive the bicycle, negative images of cycling still prevailed. The cult of oil-fired progress caused bicycles to be shunned, although for most urban workers, a third of their income would be spent in transit fares.

As Nigeria's students questioned dictatorship, skepticism grew about motorization. At the University of Ibadan, 72 percent of students surveyed supported cycling as a means of protecting the environment. Their demands for freedom were also combined with advocacy of bike lanes on campus [43].

NIGERIA'S ROCKY DEMOCRATIC TRANSITION

Nigeria's military rulers had given out their own golden handshakes. In one of their last acts before the scheduled transition to democratic rule in

May 1999, they pensioned themselves off by awarding lucrative areas of new potential oil fields to their cronies.

The recently elected President Olesegun Obasanjo has an honourable record as the architect of a previous democratic transition. He spent several years in Abacha's prisons. His biggest immediate challenges are ending state terror against environmentalists and recovering looted oil wealth from Abacha's cronies. When president-elect he was not consulted on the recent carve-up of future oil wealth among Nigeria's retiring military commanders.

Obasanjo has succeeded in collecting much of the money looted from Nigeria by its past petrodictators. A few weeks after his election the family of the late dictator Sani Abacha was forced to hand over $750 million. A court case in London is looking at corruption involving Nigeria's steel works, estimated to involve $2 billion in stolen funds. Early in October 1999 Switzerland froze the accounts of members of the Abacha family [44].

Today Nigeria illustrates the difficulties of democratic transitions when faced with the legacy of past authoritarianism financed by massive petroleum wealth. Even when blessed with the heroic legacy of brave freedom and ecological movements, new democracies face an arduous process in establishing the rule of law, instituting procedures for minority rights, fostering moderation and tolerance among competing political forces, and ensuring effective civilian control over security services. Oil wealth has created many toxic effects on Nigeria's ability to quickly become a stable, prosperous democracy.

One of the most severe challenges to Nigerian democracy is the imposition of the same regime of environmental controls on the petroleum industry that is the norm in free states. Despite a reduction in the persecution of environmental groups, this is still a source of violent conflict between the government of Nigeria and its citizens.

Although he has a distinguished record as a foe of Abacha's tyranny, Obasanjo is distrusted by Nigerian environmentalists because of his past Presidential record of attempting to reduce the land rights of communities in the Niger delta. The state's ability to take away communal land rights, previously recognized by the British colonial authorities, is one of the bitter points of controversy between Niger delta communities in authorities in both state and national governments [45].

Obasanjo's elected government has been plagued by violence in the Niger delta involving confrontations with oil corporations. Restive youths killed twelve policemen in the village of Odi, a small community in the oil-rich Bayelsa State. Subsequent military retaliation resulted in the destruction of the village. Obasanjo was subsequently ridiculed in a mock trial by human-rights and environmental activists in London. According to reliable media reports "dozens" of Odi residents were killed in this incident [46].

Repressive actions such as the assault on Odi will be difficult to repeat as Nigeria's democratic institutions mature. The Odi incident was quickly denounced by Nigerian Senate President Chuba Okadigbo, who led a Congressional investigating mission to the ruined village [47].

The green democratic champions of democracy in Nigeria were quickly empowered as the country's transition to freedom began following Abacha's death. Bans on the writings of Ken Saro-Wiwa were lifted. Twenty MOSOP activists held on "holding charges" were freed from prison on September 7, 1998.

On September 15, 1998 MOSOP was able to hold a demonstration of several thousand people without incident. By the end of October 1998, Ledum Mitee, acting President of MOSOP, was able to return safely to Ogoniland from exile in Britain. On November 10, tens of thousands of Ogonis were able to commemorate the third anniversary of Ken Saro-Wiwa's execution without the risk of death from police attack. In his memorial speech, Mitee called on Shell to "clean up the mess you have made by Ogoni Day 2,000 or clear out once and for all" [48].

MOSOP's considerable cohesion, discipline, commitment to nonviolence and ability to secure international publicity has encouraged better results for the Ogoni during Nigeria's transition to democracy than other Niger delta communities. While Shell's confrontation with the Ogoni was the stuff of headlines of the Abacha dictatorship, those between the Ijaw, the most numerous nationality of the Niger delta, and Chevron currently grab the attention of environmentalists around the world.

THE PLIGHT OF OTHER MINORITIES

In the last days of the Abacha regime, May 1998, 120 Ijaw youths occupied a tugboat, a construction barge and oil platform owned by the Chevron corporation, in Ondo State. They appealed for the company to help the plight of women who could no longer fish in the creeks because of siltation and sea water incursions caused by Chevron's operations. On May 28, 1998 three naval helicopters came to the platform with security forces, resulting in the deaths of two unarmed occupiers and other tragic consequences.

91

In an interview broadcast on Pacifica Radio in New York on October 1, 1998, Sola Omole, general manager of public affairs for Chevron in Nigeria, acknowledged that Chevron's management had authorized the Navy to intervene. It had also flown the Nigerian Navy and Mobile Police to its platform. Nigeria's acting head of security, James Neku, accompanied the troops to the platform. He confirmed that the Ijaw demonstrators had been unarmed [49]. Many of these villagers were tortured while under arrest [50].

On January 4, 1999, a violent confrontation took place between the Nigerian military and the Opia and Ikenyan Ijaw villages. This saw soldiers fire indiscriminately on the villagers with machine guns, killing and wounding dozens of people, including a traditional chief, Bright Pablogba. All houses were destroyed, and the villager's canoes were sunk. Three of the boats used in the attack were "sea trucks" obtained from a contractor used by Chevron. At the time of Human Rights Watch 1999 report, Chevron had not supplied any explanation for the use of its helicopters and boats in this assault. It had also not made any public statement critical of the Nigerian military's use of some of Chevron's equipment to destroy two communities [49].

In the United States Chevron's activities in Nigeria have been a focus of criticism by allied labour, human rights and environmental movements. This has resulted in calls for a congressional investigation into Chevron's role in abuses by the Nigerian security forces. Such an inquiry has won the support of liberal Democratic members of the US House of Representatives. Democratic Congressman Dennis J. Kucinich of Ohio has written a letter to the chair of the House International Relations Committee Ben Gilman that states, "we believe there is growing evidence that the US oil companies are accepting extra-judicial killings and other human-rights abuses as just another cost of doing business in Nigeria" [51].

Nigeria's human rights and ecological activists are at the forefront of global efforts to build a democratic and ecologically sustainable peace. Typical of this brave vanguard is Isaa Osuoka. He is an activist with ERA seconded to co-ordinate the African section of Oil Watch. This is an international coalition of organizations protesting the effects of oil company actions. Osuoka was arrested on May 26, 1998, in the last days of the Abacha regime, while attending a conference of the African Forest Network. A lawyer contracted by the ERA on Osuoka's behalf, Baidele Aturu, was subsequently himself arrested as he attempted to secure bail [52].

NIGERIA'S VISION OF PROGRESS

In many ways Nigeria's progress away from dictatorship can be seen in the way that it honours the memory of one of the critical martyrs of its new democracy, Ken Saro-Wiwa. While the ban on his writings was lifted immediately following Abacha's death, the transitional military government resisted calls for the exhumation of his body for a Christian funeral. This was not acceded to until the election of Obasanjo, who himself narrowly escaped execution in Abacha's prisons [53].

Since their bodies were once believed to be destroyed by acid, the suspected graves of the nine MOSOP leaders will be examined by a team of American pathologists to confirm their identity. Their courage is a fitting inspiration for many to achieve the growing vision of a democratic peace, in a world less reliant on oil.

The fishermen and peasants of the Niger delta and the urban democratic intelligentsia share a vision of a free Africa without oil. This is the greatest hope of Africa and will encourage co-operation between the new democracies of Nigeria and South Africa in creating a continental peace.

Nowhere in the world is there as full an appreciation of the connection between peace, freedom and environmental restoration as in Nigeria. This has been vividly captured by Ken Saro-Wiwa's Attorney, Oronto Douglas. Along with human rights and environmental groups he is leading the "No More Oil Campaign" to end the investment, projected at $150 billion, for oil exploration. A tenth of such finances, if put into renewables, would bring about lower costs and substantially reduce the need for oil.

Douglas has eloquently written, "It is simply immoral to carry on with an outmoded product such as oil. Petroleum is poisonous for the Earth's climate and has been the cause of so much suffering. The quest for more must end now" [54].

NOTES

1. Helen Chapin Merz ed., "Nigeria: A Country Study" (Washington: Library of Congress, 1991), p.46.

2. Michael Watts, "Black Gold, White Heat" in Steve Pile and Michael Keith eds. "Geography of Resistance" (London: Routledge, 1997) p.41.

3. Ken Saro-Wiwa, "Genocide in Nigeria" (London: Saros International, 1991) p.120.

4. Aaron Sachs, "Dying for Oil", *World Watch*, May/June, 1996, p.120.

5. Alan Gelb, "Oil Windfalls, Blessing or Curse?" (Oxford: Oxford University Press, 1994) p.245.

6. Jonathan Mantle, "Car Wars" (New York: Arcade Publishing, 1995) pp.92, 203.

7. Sarah Ahmad Khan, "Nigeria: The Political Economy of Oil" (Oxford: Oxford University Press, 1994) pp.190-200.

8. *Ibid*, pp.195-200.

9. Watts, *loc. cit.*, pp.41-43.

10. Freedom House Survey Team, "Freedom in the World: 1998-1999" (New York: Freedom House, 1999) p.347.

11. Human Rights Watch, "Nigeria Behind the Wall" (New York: Human Rights Watch, 1999) pp.1-19.

12. Bronwen Manby, "The Price of Oil" (New York: Human Rights Watch, 1999) pp.9-12.

13. *Ibid.*, p.124.

14. Ken Saro-Wiwa, *loc. cit.*, *passim.*

15. Manby, *loc. cit.*, p.15.

16. *Ibid.*, pp. 129-137.

17. Aaron Sashes, *loc. cit.*, pp. 119-121.

18. Human Rights Watch, "The Ogoni Crisis" (New York: Human Rights Watch, 1995) pp.10, 11.

19. Manby, *loc. cit.*, p.65.

20. Wole Soyinka, "A Year of Rapid Reverses", *Africa Today*, February 1999, pp.29-33.

21. Human Rights Watch, "The Dawn of a New Dark Age" (New York, Human Rights Watch, 1994), pp.1-16.

22. Soyinka, *loc. cit.*, pp.29-33.

23. Human Rights Watch, "The Ogoni Crisis", p.35.

24. Manby, *loc. cit.*, p.125.

25. Sachs, *loc. cit.*, pp.119-121.

26. Manby, *loc. cit.*, p.170.

27. Human Rights Watch, "The Ogoni Crisis", pp.39, 40.

28. *Ibid.*, pp.19-22.

29. Human Rights Watch, "The Dawn of a New Dark Age", *passim.*

30. Manby, *loc. cit.*, pp.124-128.

31. Soyinka, *loc. cit.*, pp.29-33; Norimitsu Onishi, "Not for a Nigerian Hero the Peace of the Grave", *New York Times*, March 22, 2000, p.3.

32. Raymond Tanter, "Rouge Regimes" (New York: St. Martin's Griffen, 1999) pp.23, 24.

33. Human Rights Watch, "The Dawn of a New Dark Age", pp.15, 16.

34. *Ibid.*, pp.14-16.

35. Manby, *loc. cit.*, p.126.

36. *Ibid.*, pp.128-144.

37. *Ibid.*, p. 135.

38. *Ibid.*, pp. 188-195.

39. Freedom House Survey Team, *loc. cit.*, p.396.

40. Sola Odunfa, "Drama in the Delta", *BBC Focus on Africa*, January-March, 1999, pp.22-25.

41. Danny Kennedy and Anne Rolfes, "Nigerian Protesters Killed" *Earth First*, February-March, 1999, p.4.

42. Monica Wilson, "Nigerian Youths Occupy Oil Wells", *Earth First*, January-February, p.7.

43. O.J. Okeadun Godwin, "Bicycle for Agriculture and Environment in Africa", in Robert Boivin and Jean Francois Pronovost eds., "The Bicycle: Global Perspectives" (Montreal: Velo Quebec, 1992), pp.85, 86; A.S. Gbadegsin, "Re-Introducing Bicycles Into Nigerian University Campuses" in Boivin and Pronovost, *loc. cit.*, pp.440, 441.

44. "Nigeria Probing the Past", *The Economist*, October 16, 1999, p.49.

45. Muyiwa Moyela, "Interview: Oronto Douglas", *Africa Today*, February 2000, pp.30-35.

46. Onishi, *loc. cit.*, p.3.

47. Muyiwa Akintunde, "Can the Center Hold", *Africa Today*, February 2000, p.21.

48. Freedom House Survey Team, "Freedom in the World, 1998-99", p.348; Manby, *loc. cit.*, p.128.

49. Human Rights Watch, "Crackdown in the Niger Delta" (New York: Human Rights Watch, 1999), pp.14-18.

50. Manby, *loc. cit.*, pp.148-152.

51. *Ibid.*, pp. 24, 25.

52. Manby, *loc. cit.*, p.132.

53. Onishi, *loc. cit.*, p. 3.

54. "No More Oil", *Earth Island Journal*, Fall 1998, p.23.

CHAPTER SIX
OIL VERSUS DEMOCRACY IN
SUB-SAHARAN AFRICA

The problems of sub-Saharan Africa are often equated with a chaotic dark age. What is missing in this equation, popularized by the famous American author, Robert Kaplan, is how such bleakness is induced by dictatorship, backed by substantial oil or mineral wealth [1].

While Nigeria was Africa's largest oil-rich dictatorship, there remain many smaller petrotyrants throughout the continent. In contrast to oil tyranny, each African country currently ranked as free by Freedom House — South Africa, Mali, Benin, Botswana, Namibia and Malawi — lacks proven oil reserves.

In southern Sahara and to the south, petrodictatorships include Angola, Chad, Equatorial Guinea, Cameroon, the Ivory Coast, Nigeria, the two Congos and Sudan. Human-rights abuses are also quite serious in the semidemocratic oil-rich Gabon. Its oppressive and corrupt rulers have been kept in power twice through French military intervention.

Kaplan's favourable portrait of French power in Africa ignores how it has been used to perpetuate tyranny, even in Rwanda at the crest of its 1994 wave of genocide. The oppressive dictatorship of Niger, although lacking in oil like Rwanda, has heavy financial support from France [2].

Much of the focus of French policy in Africa has been to secure control over oil. The African Affairs specialist for Freedom House, Thomas R. Lansner, has identified a critical barrier to freedom on the continent — what he has termed "Paris's blood-for-oil invoices" [3].

THE NEOCOLONIAL OIL DICTATORSHIP OF CONGO (BRAZZAVILLE)

Blood for oil on the part of France has been most striking in its former Congo colony. It is commonly called Congo (Brazzaville) after its capital city, to distinguish it from its larger neighbour, a former Belgian colony, whose capital city is Kinshasa. Congo (Brazzaville) is a country of 2.5

million people along the Congo River. It has oil reserves of 1.5 bbl thanks to six discoveries each year during the late 1990s. This new oil wealth gave Congo's ousted military rulers an opportunity to stage a comeback. In October 1997, the elected government of Pascal Lissouba was overthrown by military forces allied to the former dictator, Denis Sassou-Nguesso, assisted by an invasion from oil-rich Angola. The coup succeeded only after a brief civil war that resulted in 10,000 deaths [4].

Sassou-Nguesso had ruled the Congo as a one-party state since 1979 until international pressure and the local democracy movement forced multiparty elections in 1992. In this contest he received only 17 percent of the popular vote, coming third. After losing the elections, Sassou-Nguesso continued to plot his return to power through military means, building up a private army in northern Congo.

With the backing of the French government, Sassou-Nguesso declared himself President. The French decision had been supported by its former oil company, Elf. Since Sassou-Nguesso's return to power, the Congo had experienced an increase in illegal executions, police torture and violence by private militias. In exile Lissouba filed suit against Elf for its assistance to the antidemocratic forces. Unfortunately, the conflict was not mediated through the courts and the country is again wreaked by full-scale civil war which, after a few months of fighting, has created 250,000 refugees in a country of only 2.5 million people. The deserted southern suburbs of Brazzaville are now havens for looters who are mostly government soldiers [5].

French Neocolonial Oil Tyranny in the Ivory Coast and Gabon

The Ivory Coast's severe and rapid deforestation by commercial logging is tied up with the repression of a military dictatorship with small but increasing oil wealth, backed by a garrison of French troops. In pursuing criminals, police in the Ivory Coast have a policy of shoot to kill. Permits are required to have outdoor demonstrations and are commonly denied. Journalists are frequently beaten and jailed by police [6].

Since independence in 1960, oil-rich Gabon has been the former African colony maintaining the closest ties to France. Its current ruler, Omar Bongo, came to power in a military coup in 1967 with French support. This intervention actually undermined efforts by Gabon's military commanders to respect constitutional rule.

Upon coming to power Bongo officially outlawed all opposition, although his tyranny has weakened with the end of the Cold War. France maintains a garrison of 600 elite marine troops in Gabon. Bongo's personal wealth is estimated by Freedom House to be in the range of several billion dollars. Most of Gabon's oil reserves are controlled by French companies.

Gabon is one of many African countries that have felt pressure for democracy growing since the fall of the Berlin Wall. In 1990, widespread popular protests prompted Bongo to accept a transition process to democratic rule. While Gabon has improved its human rights status to that of a semi-democracy, rigged elections, the widespread use of torture, and a government monopoly over all broadcast media are employed by the Bongo regime to cling to power. Military attacks have recently been used to silence private radio stations. Although its $4,600 per capita income from oil wealth is one of Africa's highest, Gabon's continuing repression and corruption concentrate these riches in the country's small ruling elite [7].

Gabon's repression curtails environmental activism. In August 1999, the opposition newspaper, *La Griffe*, had its offices closed following a raid by soldiers who seized equipment. This followed an exposé of ivory smuggling by Gabon's national airline [8].

CHAD AND CAMEROON: TWINS OF OIL DICTATORSHIP

The jewel in the crown of France's oil-greased African neocolonial empire is the rapidly growing oil development of Cameroon and Chad, currently the focus of billions in international investment from both French and US oil corporations.

In 1995 Esso signed a framework agreement between the dictatorships of Chad and Cameroon. This was followed by a Treaty between the two states to move oil from landlocked Chad to the Atlantic coast for export, involving the construction of a 1,100-kilometre pipeline at an estimated $4 billion.

The Chad-Cameroon pipeline project has been condemned by the US Environmental Defense Fund as creating the basis for a future environmental disaster. If constructed, the pipeline would bisect the Atlantic Littoral Forest, a largely intact tropical rainforest that provides shelter for endangered gorillas, chimpanzees and elephants. This involves the homeland of the Pygmy minority of traditional hunters and gatherers who are the butt of persecution by various African oil dictatorships [9].

Cameroon's oil wealth has allowed the country to resist considerable international and domestic pressures for democratization. Massive cuts in aid by Canada, Germany, the International Monetary Fund (IMF) and the World Bank have failed to improve human rights because of Cameroon's oil boom. Transparency International identifies Cameroon as the world's most corrupt country.

Cameroon has many of the inherent weaknesses of oil dictatorships. One is the willingness to engage in armed conflict to control oil in border-disputed regions. In 1995, a dispute with Nigeria over the oil-rich Bakassi Island resulted in a violent clash with Nigerian soldiers, and 10 deaths. As in most of the world, border disputes in sub-Saharan Africa tend to get bloody when oil is involved [10]. Cameroon has one of Africa's most repressive censorship laws. Publications are regularly suspended, or released featuring blank spaces where cuts were ordered. Several journalists are currently jailed, and torture is common. The Pygmy population, whose homeland is scheduled for disruption by oil development, is subjected to widespread slavery.

Security forces have killed over 200 people in protests against the proposed Chad-Cameroon pipeline. The single parliamentarian, Ngarlégy Yorongar, who dared oppose the scheme was jailed for 10 months. His release was a result of pressure from the international environment movement [11].

The Republic of Chad, one of Africa's poorest dictatorships, is experiencing an oil-development boom. Over a thousand people have been killed since 1990 in political violence. Many of these victims were targeted by government security forces for their political opposition. The Chadian army has torched several villages. Here France maintains a garrison of 600 troops. In March 1998, 100 unarmed civilians were massacred by security forces [12].

Like neighbouring Sudan, Chad since independence has been involved in almost continuous dictatorship and civil war. Anti-crime policies involve summary executions and refugees continue to flee in the tens of thousands to escape such state-sanctioned violence [13].

EQUATORIAL GUINEA: MINI-SIZED OIL DICTATORSHIP

Equatorial Guinea, a small former Spanish colony, joined the ranks of commercial oil producers in 1996 when Mobil Corporation, and United Meridian of Houston started production from the Zafiro field. Then Equatorial Guinea conducted a crackdown, causing democratic activists to be arrested and tortured. No trade unions exist here to bother the oil companies.

Amnesty International has described Equatorial Guinea as governed by a "culture of terror." Illegal beatings, arrests and torture are routine. The country's leading exiled democratic opposition leader was recently sentenced *in absentia* to 101 years of imprisonment [14].

Oil development in Equatorial Guinea has resulted in major protests from environmentalists around the world who are opposing a new round of exploration by the world's largest corporation, Exxon-Mobil. Oil extraction on the island of Bioko threatens plants and animals found nowhere else in the world, including four distinct species of sea turtles and 10 species of primates [15].

The Bioko islanders have been subjected to intense repression. Eight Spanish journalists covering the trial of dissidents were expelled. One leader, Martin Puve, died after being jailed under conditions described by Amnesty International as tantamount to "slow execution."

Freedom House sees Equatorial Guinea as ruled by "political gangsterism." Any gathering of 10 or more people for political purposes is illegal. Citizens and residents must obtain permission for travel even within the country's borders. Membership in the ruling party is required for employment in government and the oil industry [16].

OIL-FINANCED ISLAMIC FUNDAMENTALISM AND BARRIERS TO DEMOCRATIZATION IN AFRICA

Oil power plays surprising roles in promoting wars and dictatorships even in African states that lack that resource. Islamic fundamentalism, backed by oil-rich powers such as Sudan and Iran, has been a major factor in diminishing civil liberties throughout sub-Saharan Africa. Even the most progressive and stable democracy in the region, South Africa, has recently endured a bout of terrorist bombings from Islamic fundamentalists. Such extremism fatally weakened Nigeria's second democratic republic from 1979 to 1983. Authoritarian elements in Chad, Uganda and Eritrea have been strengthened by fundamentalist Sudan's assistance to armed rebellions. These attempt to turn Sudan's neighbours into Islamic dictatorships on an Iranian model of clerical rule and exclusionary Shari'a law [17].

Southern Somalia is controlled by Islamic fundamentalists receiving aid from a variety of oil-rich nations such as Libya and Iran. Here executions and mutilations are imposed based on Shari'a law [16]. Libya has played a major role in the near disintegration of Sierra Leone by its aid to the insurgency of the Revolutionary United Force. Sierra Leone is also plagued by mercenary armies financed by mining companies and is rated the world's worst country in terms of the UN's Human Development Index (HDI). Libya is a backer of Gambia's dictatorship and is scheming to replace Exxon-Mobil as the developer of Chad's oil [18].

CHRONIC CIVIL WAR AND OIL IN CENTRAL AFRICA

In central Africa there is a low degree of democratic political culture. Before independence neither France nor Belgium sponsored local elections. France has not yet shown great concern for human rights in this region; it even altered the terms of reference of the War Crimes Tribunal to escape possible conviction for genocide in Rwanda.

Rwanda and Burundi have neither significant oil nor mineral wealth. These nations, suffering from widespread illiteracy but having some of Africa's best and most equitably distributed land for subsistence farming, are enmeshed in an ugly vortex of the politics of central Africa

Oil- and mineral-rich dictatorships in central Africa are dominant in the region's politics. Zaire's ruler, Mobutu Sesse Seko, had billions in foreign bank accounts acquired from his control over mineral wealth and oil. This was gained in a similar fashion to the plunder of Gabon's Bongo regime, which is still in power. The new government of the Congo (Kinshasa) — Zaire's new name under Laurent Kabila — is trying to recover $10 billion in looted funds from foreign banks in countries with secrecy laws, such as Switzerland.

During Angola's civil war Mobutu supported the diamond-enriched UNITA (National Union for the Total Independence of Angola) armed opposition which was allied to South Africa's apartheid government. This alliance and his tolerance of the use of Zairean territory as launching pads in the civil wars in Uganda, Rwanda and Burundi resulted in a coalition of these states with Angola against Mobutu.

The new Congo regime headed by Kabila, while attracting a flood of investment from foreign mineral and oil companies, did nothing to foster democratization and human rights. Congo also remained a base for Hutu armed extremists, causing Uganda and Rwanda to launch a new insurrection. Kabila was rescued by the intervention of oil-rich Angola [19].

ANGOLA: WAR-TORN PETROTYRANNY OF SOUTHERN AFRICA

After the twilight of the Soviet Union, Angola's civil war was kept to a low intensity through UN mediation. This has succeeded far less than in Mozambique which, while also a war-torn former Portuguese colony, is free of the curse of oil and diamonds. Angola's peace process has now degenerated into renewed civil war.

Another war for oil is the insurgency in the tiny, but petroleum-rich, northern Angolan enclave of Cabinda. It is surrounded, except for the coast, by the Congo. The rebel insurgency here is supported by the Belgium-based financial institutions that received $20 billion from Arab countries [20].

Apart from the Cabinda side show, armed conflict in Angola was protracted long after the peace accords, primarily by the refusal of the armed faction UNITA to accept its defeat in UN-supervised elections that took place in 1992. Peace-seeking efforts were focused on giving UNITA assured access to funding from diamond mines in its area of popular support. Instead of reconciling UNITA to the national government, this agreement provided the basis for more effectively financing its armed opposition. Diamond smuggling has undermined efforts by the United States, South Africa and the United Nations to impose sanctions on UNITA.

Most of Angola's wealth goes to an elite and to military spending. Its citizens are largely internal refugees. They swell the population of cities, creating havoc with sanitation. Some 70,000 people in Angola became amputees from land mines and 10 to 15 million land mines remain. Demining has not yet taken place in the areas under the control of UNITA. Angola is trapped in prolonged conflict between an oil-backed government, and a diamond-financed armed opposition.

DEMOCRATIZATION ADVANCES IN OILLESS EAST AFRICA

Throughout Africa democratization and peacekeeping efforts sponsored by the Organization of African Unity (OAU) and the UN have worked best when oil is not present, especially in the east African states of Mozambique, Tanzania, Zambia and Zimbabwe. These are all recognized as partially free by Freedom House. All but Zimbabwe have experienced a considerable improvement in human rights since the end of the Cold War. With the exception of Zambia's rich copper mines, these democratizing countries are relatively resource poor. Their progress towards democracy, which has been particularly impressive in Tanzania and Mozambique, illustrates how the advance of freedom has been helped by the power of international economic pressures on oilless states. Such pressure also caused oilless Malawi's democracy movement, led by Christian clergy, to triumph quickly after the end of apartheid.

During the Cold War, Tanzania was a one-party state ruled by a bureaucratic and dogmatically socialist elite. It was similar to much of post-colonial Africa where the concentration of power in the hands of the state made life as a civil servant the only alternative to subsistence agriculture. This group was responsible for some disastrous errors, such as the villagization program that introduced briefly the Soviet idea of collective farming to much of the countryside.

Part of Tanzania's surprising transition to democracy is that elite civil servants no longer have an aversion to getting their hands dirty. Many are now engaged in part-time farming, even in affluent suburban districts. Two-thirds of the faculty in one prestigious Tanzanian university devote much of their spare time to raising chickens in backyard coops. Tanzania has discovered recently that investments in donkeys and bicycles have impressive results in reducing rural poverty and making vaccines and other essential medical supplies available in isolated villages.

In Tanzania's capital city of Dar es Salaam, vegetables grow along the sides of roads wherever strips of land have been left vacant. Civil servants raise cows for milk production in backyard stables. Throughout the cities of democratizing, largely oilless sub-Saharan African states, urban agriculture, once suppressed by military authorities as a dirty nuisance to the elites, is now flourishing [21].

Tanzania is boldly developing appropriate technology for an oilless economy. In conjunction with the American aid organization, Tillers International, it is fostering improvements in traditional ox-powered machinery. This includes developing farmers' skills in cart and yoke making, small-scale drip irrigation, and home-made rope manufacture [22].

DEMOCRATIC SUCCESS IN OILLESS STATES IN WEST AFRICA

Most states lacking petroleum in former French West Africa have also made major strides towards democracy. The most successful has been oilless Benin, a largely animist state. Its democratic Prime Minister, Adrien Houngebedji, had been a long-time opposition leader and had been jailed and tortured under military rule. Although recently losing elections, Houngebedji accepted the results and made Benin a rare example of a democratic African state where power actually changes freely through multiparty elections. Benin has a powerful and independent labour movement.

Oilless Mali shows that democracy can succeed in an Islamic majority country, which is not cursed with oil wealth. Human rights abuses have largely ceased since a 1995 agreement that ended the country's previously brutal civil war. Mali's peace accords provided autonomy and linguistic recognition for its minority Tuareg people. While its authoritarian neighbours have state broadcasting monopolies, there are 60 independent radio stations in Mali. In this oilless, Islamic democratic state, solar pumps are increasingly used for irrigation, and photovoltaic power lights up the streets of isolated rural villages [23].

Most West African states without oil wealth have made considerable progress in the related areas of peace, human rights and economic development since the end of the Cold War. Senegal, Burkina Faso, Ghana, and Guinea-Bissau, are oilless states which have improved their human-rights situation since the fall of the Berlin Wall. These countries, along with most of resource-poor Africa, benefited from a combination of international pressure and the protests of domestic civil society. Ghana and Burkina Faso are experiencing an annual growth rate of five percent. Burkina Faso has a vibrant civil society, including strong agricultural, labour and environmental groups. Its independent media have flourished with little government interference. Human rights groups operate freely and effectively. Since the end of the Cold War democracy in Senegal has been strengthened by reducing media restrictions, lowering the voting age, and establishing an autonomous electoral commission. In March 2000, Senegal's President Abodou Diouf was defeated in free elections by veteran democratic opposition leader, Abdoulaye Wade.

By its support for Wade Senegal's Morides Sufi order played an important role in the country's democratization. Senegal's peaceful electoral change of government is a beacon of hope for both Africa and the Islamic world, demonstrating how freedom can advance where it is not blocked by the manipulation of great resource wealth [24].

THE SUCCESS OF OILLESS DEMOCRATIC SOUTH AFRICA

The most impressive strides towards freedom, social justice, and sustainable development have been achieved in the neighbouring southern oilless African democracies of Botswana, Namibia, Malawi and

South Africa. There has been in effect a Botswanization of this region, since this country was the first independent black African state to be recognized as a full democracy.

The success of democracy in oilless Botswana countered the propaganda of the apologists of apartheid, that independent black-majority nations in Africa could not be stable democratic states. Along with oilless Senegal, Botswana for many years has been the only state which, having achieved independence in the decade from 1957 to 1967, retained the freedoms and multiparty systems which were present at the end of colonial rule. Democratic freedoms in both Botswana and neighbouring oilless Zimbabwe helped these to be the sole African nations to escape famine as a result of drought in the 1970s and 1980s [25].

Oilless Botswana weakened apartheid by providing its subversive example showing that black-majority rule can work successfully. Eventually its success helped to bring democracy to another oil-free state, South Africa. Residents of Botswana's capital city, Gaborone, by 1994 had installed more than 3,000 solar water heaters, displacing nearly 15 percent of the country's electrical demand. South Africa's infant solar industry, whose growth was focused on providing water heaters to rural black areas, had been killed in 1961 by discriminatory rail freight charges [26].

The OPEC price hike of 1973, by ending dictatorship in Portugal [27], ended colonial rule in Angola and Mozambique. This loss of a repressive Portuguese colonial buffer made South Africa more isolated and vulnerable. It also generated an economic crisis that reversed decades of rapid economic growth. To obtain oil in the face of the embargo, South Africa had to pay premium prices. The price was $1 to $2 billion more than the impact of the OPEC cartel on any other country. Inflation sparked by higher oil prices triggered a wave of labour protests [28].

Autocratic South Africa's lack of oil helped give a positive legacy to the democratic postapartheid state. Under apartheid, South Africa made up for its lack of oil by heavy use of highly polluting coal for electric power. With freedom, coal mania has been replaced by greener strategies. The state-owned utility, Eskom, is now vigorously promoting energy conservation through such means as the free distribution of more energy efficient compact fluorescent lamps [29].

A favourable result of South Africa's democratic peace is cleaner air from the ending of coal subsidies. The reduced air pollution has saved the national treasury $614 million [30].

A critical goal of South Africa's ANC (African National Congress) leadership is to transform the country's energy system by providing the black majority with basic amenities such as electric lighting, while still reducing pollution through the increased application of clean alternative power sources. The country is well positioned to embark on such a path because of its solar and wind energy potential, and well capitalized industry. South Africa is an excellent location for solar power, since a square metre here typically receives an average power of 230 watts of sunlight daily. Only 150 watts per square metre on average are received in the USA.

The ANC has also incorporated passive solar designs into its ambitious housing program. Photovoltaic power is being installed on a priority basis in schools and rural clinics. By the year 2005, South Africa plans to have 14,000 schools and 2,000 rural clinics powered by the sun. This planned capacity of nine megawatts (MW) is one-tenth of the current world production of solar generated electricity. With the end of apartheid, South Africa has become a world leader in solar water heating. It has 160,000 units of this simple green technology that runs water through pipes heated by exposure to the sun.

The coming of peace and democracy to South Africa has nurtured sustainable development in many unreported ways. More democracy has meant stronger environmental assessment procedures to block mining projects that would blight ecologically sensitive areas. Former liberation fighters have found employment in the country's widely respected and growing national-parks service. Efforts at regional co-operation with neighbouring democracies have linked national parks across borders to expand effectively the large protected areas for threatened fauna. The South African army, in addition to being greatly reduced, has greener tasks such as addressing soil erosion, assisting wildlife counts, cleaning up oil spills, and removing invasive exotic vegetation [31].

South Africa's national parks are pioneering green technologies. In 1994, such efforts, combined with metering and public education, achieved a 74% decline in water use and 52% drop in electrical consumption in Kruger National Park [31]. Nelson Mandela's zeal for solar power made him the Sun President of a transition to a democratic peace in Africa. The growing strength of increasingly green and renewably powered states in Africa will hasten the decline of oil-based dictatorships that cling to power through brute force.

NOTES

1. Robert Kaplan, "The Ends of the Earth" (New York: Random House, 1997) pp.11-50.

2. Although Niger is a country without significant oil or any mineral resources, it is of considerable significance to France's neo-colonial strategy. French Gaullist strategy is obsessed with keeping Niger independent from the British Commonwealth state of Nigeria, a nation with which it has considerable geographic and cultural connections.

   Although not a "jewel in the crown" of the French-African Commonwealth, Niger is in the heart of its West-African core. In addition to concerns for oil wealth in other parts of her African Commonwealth, France has been captivated by nonmaterial reasons for its neo-colonial African policies, such as the status of the French language in the world. France continued the flow of money to Niger despite a January 1996 military coup that overthrew a democratically elected president and the National Assembly of Niger.

3. Thomas R. Lanser, "Africa: Democracy as Survival" in Freedom House Survey Team eds. "Freedom in the World, The Annual Survey of Political Rights and Civil Liberties, 1997-1998" (New York: Freedom House, 1999) pp.55-57.

4. Jim West, "International Petroleum Encyclopaedia, 1997" (Tulsa: Penn Well, 1997) pp.116, 117.

5. Freedom House Survey Team, *loc. cit.*, pp.81, 200-202.

6. *Ibid.*, pp.205, 206; 1995, pp.319-321.

7. *Ibid.*, 1998, pp.253355; 1998, pp.245, 246.

8. Freedom House Survey Team, "Freedom in the World, 1998-1999" (New York: Freedom House, 1999) pp. 90, 91.

9. Andrew Rowell, "Crude Operators", *The Ecologist*, May/June, 1991, p.105.

10. Freedom House Survey Team, "Freedom in the World" (New York: Freedom House, 1995) p.173.

11. Freedom House Survey Team, *loc. cit.*, pp.158-163; Al Graham, "The Seeds of Freedom" (Cornwallis: Canadian Peacekeeping Press, 1996) pp.158-163; "Stop the World Bank Funding of the Chad-Cameroon Oil Pipeline", *Earth First*, September/October, 1999, p.30.

12. "Same Oil Story", *Earth Island Journal*, Fall, 1998, p.18.

13. Freedom House Survey Team, *loc. cit.*, pp.183-184; 1998, 185-187.

14. *Ibid.*, pp.234-236; 1998, pp.231-233; "Bubi Harassed by Mobil", *Earth First*, September/October, 1999, p.14.

15. Freedom House Survey Team, *loc. cit.*, pp. 174-176.

16. The movement for Shari'a law and its imposition in several authoritarian states is one of the most formidable causes which retard the advancement of democracy in the world today. There are several versions of Shari'a law, which are themselves subject to numerous interpretations.

    The biggest problem regarding Shari'a law and democracy is that it is imposed on minority religious groups, making them second class citizens. During the Ottoman Empire many potential problems regarding Shari'a law were overcome by allowing religious minorities that did not believe in it to establish their own courts. This was called the millet system. Its main problem was that this tolerant pluralism existed without safeguards for civil liberties.

    In Lebanon, the cultural pluralism of the Ottoman millet system was adopted successfully into the country's liberal democratic order. This was accomplished by allowing various faith communities to have their own courts. India similarly has allowed its Muslim communities to have their own courts for family law.

    Unfortunately a liberal, pluralist adoption of Shari'a law has not been the norm in the world today. Most countries that have applied Shari'a law such as Iran, Sudan, the United Arab Emirates and Saudi Arabia, have not established separate courts for religious minorities.

    One of the reasons for the failure of the Nigerian second republic was a separatist movement that demanded Shari'a law. It wanted the predominately Muslim northern part of the country to separate so that the need for secular laws respecting the rights of Nigeria's many Christians living largely in the south could be avoided.

    A very harsh version of Shari'a law is used by the ruling dictatorship of Sudan. As in Saudi Arabia, it involves mutilations for minor crimes such as theft. This form of Shari'a law is also in use in southern Somalia, where it is imposed by armed factions backed by the oil dictatorships of Libya and Iran. Many peace talks have broken up over the issue of the application of Shari'a law to the whole of Sudan, even in the south of the country where most citizens are of the Christian faith.

17. Freedom House Survey Team, *loc. cit.*, pp. 15, 192, 193. Freedom House Survey Team, *loc. cit.*, 1998, pp.451, 465, 466.

18. *Ibid.*, pp.200-202.

19. *Angola Peace Bulletin*, October 1997.

20. United Nations Development Program, "Urban Agriculture" (New York: United Nations, 1997) *passim*.

21. "Tanzania Offers Lessons in Training", *Tiller News*, No. 14, Fall 1998, pp.14.

22. Freedom House Survey Team, 1998, *loc. cit.*, pp.352-354; Madanjeet Singh, "The Timeless Energy of the Sun" (San Francisco, Sierra Club, 1997) pp.164, 198.

23. Freedom House Survey Team, 1998, *loc. cit.*, pp.167-169, 254-56.

24. Paul Harrison, "The Greening of Africa" (New York: Harper Collins, 1989) pp.68-92, 250-255; "Victory For Democracy", *The Economist*, March 26, 2000, p. 48.

25. Ken Butil and John Perlin, "Golden Thread" (Palo Alto: Cheshire, 1979) p.241.

26. The causes of the fall of Portugal's dictatorship are briefly discussed in Chapter Thirteen under the subheading "The Long Road to Democratic Peace in Europe."

27. Robert Schaeffer, "Power to the People" (Boulder: Westview, 1997) pp.202-210.

28. "Oil Free Transport for South Africa", *Earth Island Journal*, Summer 1996, p.5.

29. Seth Dunn, "Can the North and South Get in Step?" *World Watch*, November/December, 1998, p.26.

30. Munyardzi Chenje and Phyliss Johnson ed. "State of the Environment in South Africa Report" (Johannesburg: ICUN, 1994) *passim*.

31. Paul Hawken, Amory Lovins and L. Hunter Lovins, "Natural Capitalism" (New York: Little, Brown, & Company, 1999) p. 224.

CHAPTER SEVEN
SUDAN'S NIGHTMARE VERSION OF OIL DICTATORSHIP

War, dictatorship, famine, starvation and slavery continue to plague Sudan, a rapidly expanding oil producer. Its oil industry is booming with the help of foreign enterprises; France, Iran, Italy, the Netherlands, Qatar, and the Canadian corporation Talisman with its partners from China and Malaysia are all involved. China has invested major resources with Sudan's dictatorship in order to get future access to oil. In May 1997 China's state-owned National Petroleum Corporation bought 40 percent of Sudan's Heglig oil field for $1 billion [1].

While Sudan is experiencing an oil boom its chronic civil war continues. It features the bombardment of towns, central markets, food warehouses, hospitals, and refugee camps. Christian religious processions have been disrupted by bombings [2].

DICTATORSHIP BACKED BY A COMBINATION OF ANTIDEMOCRATIC STATES

Authoritarian governments converge in their support for dictatorship in Sudan. Despite their numerous quarrels, Libya, Iraq and Iran are all firm allies of Sudan. Although a pariah state to every democracy, Sudan gets around such problems by obtaining arms from oil-rich dictatorships and Communist China.

Sudan has a food-for-oil program with Libya, which also receives slaves captured in Sudan's civil war. Libya has been a long-time supporter of Islamic extremism in Sudan, which it assisted through an attempted coup in 1976. The coup attempt, although defeated, helped propel the power of fundamentalists in the country.

Sudan was an ally of Iraq during its invasion of Kuwait and received extensive arms shipments for its expression of solidarity. The oil dictatorships of Libya, Iraq, Iran and Syria today are alone at the United

Nations in defending Sudan's human-rights abuses.

Iran has become Sudan's most important ally. Under a comprehensive trade agreement Iran supplies Sudan with one million tons of oil annually until its civil war is ended. It also provides a $300 million line of credit to allow Sudan to acquire more modern Chinese weapons, such as helicopter gunships [3].

SUDAN'S HOSTILITY TO DEMOCRATIZATION THROUGHOUT AFRICA

Sudan's rulers are hostile to a federal democratic peace, a concept whereby its authoritarian government could be removed through the United Nations. This is why, with its Iranian ally, Sudan did so much to prevent such a UN-assisted transition to democracy in Somalia. A successful intervention would have asserted the principle of the imposition of UN trusteeship on dictatorships until the restoration of conditions for democratic government.

In 1993, at the time of the Somalia debacle, Osama bin Laden, suspected mastermind of the bombing of US embassies in the summer of 1998, was based in Sudan. Here, with the support of the governments of Iran and Sudan, bin Laden defeated the UN forces, who mistakenly pursued the Aideed faction. Sudan supplied bin Laden with guns, mortars, and rocket-propelled grenades, delivered from Iran. Troops were also supplied from former Afghan Mujahideen forces [4]. Bin Laden's victory over the United Nations and the USA was followed by the application of Sudan's harsh version of Shari'a law.

Sudan's oil-financed muscle is used to export guerrilla war and terror to Chad, Egypt, Eritrea, Ethiopia, Algeria, Tunisia and Uganda. It is a haven and training centre for Hamas, and other extremist organizations that reject the PLO-Israeli peace accords. All movements towards democracy throughout Africa face the opposition of Sudan [5].

CIVIL WAR BASED ON AUTOCRACY, NOT CLASH OF CIVILIZATIONS

Contrary to the analysis of the US strategic studies expert, Samuel Huntington, Sudan's civil war is caused by the power of dictatorship, rather than civilizational conflict. While northern Sudan is heavily Muslim and Arabic-speaking it is also home to a sizeable Coptic Christian minority among the northern Nuba and Beja. Many of the Nuba are Muslims but this has not exempted them from ethnic cleansing orchestrated by the Sudanese government. Many Muslim Nuba have been killed and their mosques destroyed. Thousands have been deported from their villages and put in concentration camps.

Sudan's southern Christians are predominantly Anglicans and Catholics. Many have kinship ties to animists who resisted conversion efforts by British missionaries. Sudan has more than 50 ethnic groups, subdivided into nearly 600 tribes [6].

Sudan's authoritarian government, based on the returns of the last free elections held there in 1986 and subsequent results in student council elections, lacks the support of the majority of the country's Muslims, mostly Sufis — whose version of Islam is a liberal mystical one, introduced into Sudan between 1300 and 1500.

In Sudan, Sufism has strong support among the peasantry and working class. It is persecuted by the country's Sunni fundamentalist government. Sunni Islamic fundamentalism in Sudan is an elitist doctrine seeking to purify Islamic practice from what are disparagingly viewed as contaminated popular superstitions, such as older African traditions of nature worship.

While Shiite fundamentalism in Iran was a mass movement, Sudan's Iranian-backed Sunni extremism relies upon an affluent urban minority. In Sudan, as in the rest of Africa, the absence of a significant Shiite minority means that Iran's relations with extremist Sunni-dominated states are not complicated by the issue of minority Islamic rights. In Afghanistan, for instance, Iran is in serious conflict with the Sunni extremist Taliban (supported by Saudi Arabia) because of its persecution of the Shiite minority.

Sudan's Iranian-backed extremist Sunni political party is the National Islamic Front (NIF). In the 1986 elections the NIF received only 17 percent of the popular vote. Considering the elections were not held in southern areas controlled by rebel forces, its support nationwide would only be around 10 percent of the population. While the NIF's precoup support among the urban intelligentsia and middle class of Sudan was reflected in victories in student council elections prior to its seizure of power, these elections were banned after the NIF could no longer win them [7].

CURSED BY ITS OWN ADVANTAGES

Like many oil-rich states, Sudan has been cursed by several of its own advantages. It is the largest state in physical area on the African continent,

113

with 28 million people living along the longest stretch of the Nile's waters.

Sudan has lush wetlands in a continent having a dry interior. The wetlands remain a homeland for diverse tribal people and abundant wildlife.

The Nile's Sudd swamps are the largest wetlands in the world, providing habitat to millions of migrating birds, including storks, cranes, ibises, and herons. The population of the glossy ibis in these wetlands is estimated to reach 1.7 million during the early dry season. The swamps are also used for fishing and pastoral purposes by 450,000 tribal people [8].

The pristine wetlands of the Nile lie above what some have estimated to be the world's largest untapped oil reserves. Here the Calgary based Talisman Energy Corporation (formerly called Arakis Energy) has successfully spearheaded oil development involving the completion of a 1,600 kilometre pipeline from the Nile to the Red Sea at Port Sudan [9].

SUDAN: TARGET NATION FOR AUTHORITARIAN IDEOLOGISTS OF THE ISLAMIC AND ARABIC WORLD

Sudan's resources have made it the victim of intrigues by authoritarian ideologists around the Arab and Islamic world. Nasser's dam-building plans for Aswan, which caused disastrous soil erosion in Lower Egypt of the Nile delta, needed a supportive government in Sudan. In 1959, Nasser signed an agreement on the Nile River with Sudan, which committed the dual dictatorships to build the Jongeli canal to drain the Sudd swamps [10].

Dreams of food sufficiency for an Arab or Islamic block of nations in the Middle East and Africa invariably involve new massive water projects. Sudan is the only area in the predominantly Arabic-speaking and largely Islamic Middle East having the potential to become a large scale grain exporter and, as a result, schemes based on mechanized agriculture have been promoted by various dictatorships in the region. They are a focus for the lending activity of the country's Islamic banks, allied to the NIF. The banks' no-interest loans, originally made possible by heavy financial assistance from oil-rich states, have been used heavily by the NIF to build a political base. They have also helped to facilitate the acquisition of land for large-scale export-orientated agriculture, at the expense of subsistence farming. Sudan's Mechanized Farming Corporation rents vast tracts in 4,000-hectare units, some of the largest farms in the world. Such "agricultural strip mining", or "suitcase farming", has resulted in desertification after a few years of tractor cultivation. Among the backers of these schemes was Saudi businessman, Osama bin Laden, who would later do so much to delay democratization in Africa [11].

Agricultural development schemes also involve brutal ethnic cleansing of minority groups that stand in the way. This is one of the key reasons for Sudan's prolonged civil war as southern insurgents oppose the Jongeli canal's completion. The civil war's renewed outbreak in 1983 caused the project to halt abruptly before a diversion of the Nile could be made [12].

THE DEADLY MIX OF OIL, REPRESSION AND INDUSTRIAL AGRICULTURE

Since its independence in 1956, Sudan has enjoyed only one period of relatively democratic peace, which lasted from 1972 to 1983. While a turn to authoritarian Islamic government based on Shari'a law helped to reignite the civil war in 1983, democracy was restored in 1985. A return of the federal system was the goal of the predominantly Sufi elected government, but this possibility was destroyed by the NIF coup in 1989 and the return of dictatorship. Before and after Sudan's four-year restoration of democracy, authoritarian forces have used dictatorship to promote an oil-based version of industrial progress.

In 1983, Sudan's President Jarfar Numayari awarded the disputed petroleum-rich territory of Bentu to northern Sudan. This contentious move followed recent oil discoveries by the US Chevron Corporation. At the same time, Sudan's President used the NIF to terrorize communities opposed to his industrialization schemes. Some of the worst violence took place where ethnic minorities were cleared out of lands where Chevron had made major oil discoveries. The dictator also terminated conservation efforts that had been attempted by southern regional authorities. This caused the white rhino to become completely extirpated from Sudan [13].

Numayari's Arab nationalism encouraged the spread of tractor farming for cotton resulting in widespread evictions of subsistence farmers, and in deforestation. Well connected entrepreneurs would undertake illegal tractor schemes even in protected wildlife refuges. The spread of tractors resulted in erosion of 17 million hectares of land, almost half of Sudan's arable acreage. These are now a bleak dust bowl. Ninety-five percent of the forests of eastern Sudan have been cleared for mechanized farming schemes [14].

Dams, irrigation and tractorization in Sudan proceeded with a heavy ecological and human cost. Sudan's Gezira project encouraged massive cotton cash cropping. It produced the world's worst incidence of schistosomiasis, a parasitic worm that penetrates human skin that comes into contact with polluted water. The disease causes blood loss and disorders of the liver, bladder, lungs and nervous system. Only 10 percent of residents around Gezira were infected before the irrigation project began, but this soared to 80 percent afterwards [15].

Numayari used the NIF to punish communities opposed to his vision of oil-based industrial progress. The NIF achieved the approval of a version of Shari'a law with provisions for stoning and amputation. Two hundred former subsistence peasants who were displaced by tractor farming suffered amputation in Sudan during the first 19 months of Shari'a law. The use of Shari'a law to justify executions and mutilations was denounced by Sadiq al-Mahdi, a descendant of the famous 19th century Sufi foe of British imperialism, the Mahdi. A veteran democratic leader of the Sufi-connected Umma Party, Sadiq denied that the cruel and unusual punishment measures of the government were a proper interpretation of Islamic law [16].

Dictatorship and Shari'a law were combined to clear out subsistence farmers. The Nuer, who opposed schemes to drain the Sudd Swamps for tractors, had their villages destroyed by raiders who captured and enslaved hundreds of women and children [17]. The Nuba of northern Sudan have been similarly subjected to widespread ethnic cleansing. Displaced by military operations, their land has been sold to investors growing cotton using tractors [18].

EFFORTS TO RESTORE DEMOCRATIC PEACE IN SUDAN DESTROYED BY THE FUNDAMENTALIST NIF

Numayari's dictatorship came to an end in 1985, with a restoration of democracy, which lowered the war's intensity. The overthrow of dictatorship was a triumph of Sudan's civil society since, despite violent repression, strikes in favour of democracy were undertaken by judges, doctors, unionized railway workers and students. Unionists cut electricity, water and communications lines. Their protests closed Sudan's key airport and radio station, and eventually the army refused to join other security forces in repression [19].

Following Sadiq al-Mahdi's election as Prime Minister in 1986, Sudan's democratic civil society successfully pressured his government into a framework agreement to develop a compromise peace with the southern Sudan People's Liberation Army (SPLM/A). This was strongly opposed by the NIF, which used opposition to the peace process as a rallying cry for its authoritarian movement, supported by Iran. The NIF was able to win support among younger urban elites in Sudan, especially in the capital, Khartoum. It had won all student elections in Khartoum University from 1978 to 1984. The party won 40 percent of the vote in Khartoum, and also swept the polls in military barracks.

The NIF provided students with scholarships to study in Iran. It employed its supporters in NIF banks and companies and infiltrated the medical and engineering corps of the army. A separate NIF medical organization was formed, to oppose the prodemocracy Sudanese medical association. The NIF also gave a course on Islam for army officers.

The coup on June 30, 1989 initiated by middle-ranking officers brought to power Umar Hassan Ahamad Bashir. He has since ruled Sudan in alliance with the NIF. This coup took place on the day before Sudan's authoritarian laws favouring mutilations were to be suspended. Army officers connected with Sudan's peace movement were dismissed. It was announced that the civil war was to be conducted as a holy war, or jihad. The excuse of holy war was subsequently used to justify numerous crimes and atrocities. Its pretexts were even employed, during a court trial, to provide judicial immunity to a university student in Khartoum charged with murder as a result of the NIF's strong-arm tactics in student council elections [20].

COURAGEOUS MOVEMENTS FOR THE RESTORATION OF DEMOCRACY IN SUDAN

In 1990 military officers attempted a counter coup to restore democracy, which resulted in 28 executions. Protests by female relations of these officers have been conducted as valiant crusades for the right of free speech.

The NIF has attacked Sudan's labour movement because of its long support for democracy. Death sentences were imposed for organizing strikes. Trade unions and professional associations were closed and their estates confiscated. Over 3,000 railway workers were fired in 1990 after a failed strike for the restoration of democracy [21].

Strategic studies experts such as Huntington ignore Sudan's strong Sufi-connected movements for democracy, and its civil society. Another ignored brave theorist of the supportive relationship between Islam and democracy was Mahumoud Muhammad Taha, who founded Sudan's social democratic Republican Brothers Party. This democratic party has for over 40 years been in sharp conflict with the Muslim Brotherhood of Sudan, the basis for the NIF. The two parties have clashed bitterly over such issues as Shari'a law, holy war, and forced conversion to Islam.

Popularly revered as a saint because of his holy asceticism and devotion to the poor, Taha was a leader of Sudan's nonviolent anticolonial struggle against dictatorship. During the last days of dictatorship in 1985, he was executed for the crime of apostasy [22].

Sudan's champions of freedom are numerous. They use Sufi mosques as places of refuge, much in the fashion that churches provided safe havens during the last days of Communist rule in Europe. Even Sudan's most sacred holy places are not inviolable. After the Sufi spiritual leader, Sadiq al-Mahdi, gave a sermon for the return to multiparty democracy in 1995, a wave of repression followed. The Sufis' holiest shrine at Omdurman, containing the tomb of Mohammed Ahmed al-Mahdi, was nationalized.

Following the nationalization of the Mahdi's tomb, the Ansar Sufi order moved their communal prayers to the smaller Wad Noubawi mosque. It continues to be a holy citadel of non-violent resistance to Sudan's dictatorship, under the leadership of Sufi Imams, such as Mohammed al-Mahdi. One of the frequent topics of his sermons is religious tolerance and justice, which has resulted in his being arrested and held for several months at a time [23].

Following Iraq's invasion of Kuwait, demonstrations in solidarity with Kuwait took place in Sudan despite severe government repression. At the same time protesters called for an increased minimum wage. Sudan's rail system was paralysed by strikes. In the subsequent repression one union leader died in detention [24].

Symbolic violence by the democratic opposition in Khartoum has been directed against forms of property that display the oil-powered luxuries of Sudan's NIF elite, such as gas stations, cars, and motorcycles. Motorcycles are a favourite target for destruction since almost every one is owned by a member of Sudan's secret police. Mocking Sudan's authoritarian religious ties to Iranian dictatorship, student protesters in Khartoum have sarcastically called the tear gas used against them "Iranian gas for God" [25, 26].

International pressure has had some impact in modifying Sudan's use of starvation as a weapon in its civil war, which had fallen heavily on the Christian minority resulting in an estimated 500,000 deaths among the Nuba alone. A ceasefire between the Sudanese government and the largest armed opposition group was signed on May 4, 1998.

The ceasefire did bring some relief to the 2.6 million people facing starvation in zones of conflict. At the end of July 1998, UN observers were shocked by evidence of death from hunger — a mass grave in the southern town of Wau. One of the largest airdrops of food in history was made by the World Food Program (WFP) in the summer of 1998. After the ceasefire the UN relief workers were also given access to the Nuba mountains, although they are now banned from this war zone. Despite the ceasefire two employees of the WFP and one of the Sudanese Red Crescent were killed in an attack on a relief convoy on June 9, 1998. Fighting remains intense in the Upper Nile and Equatorial provinces where government-authorized militias continue to destroy Dinka villages in the "cease-fire zone" [27].

Continuing international pressure on Sudan resulted on January 1, 1999 in the slow beginnings of a democratization process. For the first time political parties were legalized in a formally democratic constitution which was proclaimed. Previously even the NIF had been technically banned in the military coup that brought it to power. It is now gambling that, like Mexico's long-ruling PRI, it can win elections in a semidemocracy through the control of vast oil wealth.

Initially the major Sufi parties, the Umma and the DUP, did not seek legalization under the new constitution, denouncing it from exile as a fraud. Sudan's former military dictator Numayari, however, returned from exile to embrace the government. Minority members in Sudan's major political parties also accepted the promise of elections [28].

HOW OIL PUMPED LIFE INTO SUDAN'S CRUMBLING DICTATORSHIP

Oil discoveries have literally pumped life into Sudan's previously crumbling dictatorship, although its rulers appear now to be attempting to stage a transition to a form of semidemocracy. Sudan's foes in neighbouring states are also preoccupied by their own internal divisions, such as the war over resource-rich Congo, and the bitter border dispute between Ethiopia and Eritrea. The US bombing of a Sudanese factory in the summer of 1998 proved to be a public relations disaster for efforts to undermine the dictatorship and seriously embarrassed the Sudanese democratic opposition.

US attacks on Sudan have not involved attempts to disrupt its oil installations, owned largely by its NATO allies. Critical were the pioneering efforts by two Canadian companies that commercialized discoveries abandoned by Chevron after the end of the Cold War when

US policy became more serious towards promoting human rights in Africa. The USA imposed sanctions on American firms that took part in Sudanese oil development.

Seldom has foreign investment in oil helped a more brutal regime than Sudan's. It proved critical after Canadian involvement began in 1992 when Sudan was on the brink of financial collapse. Then an accord between Chevron and Sudan caused US oil fields to be transferred to Canadians.

Canadian involvement in Sudan's oil began in 1993 when Arakis Energy Corporation (now Talisman Energy) of Vancouver acquired the State Petroleum Corporation. It acquired Chevron's former Muglad and Melut blocks. Arakis' drilling was delayed by monsoon rain until May 1994. Then it re-entered Sudan and began testing the last 29 of 34 Chevron wells in the Heglig and Unity fields. By late 1994 Arakis had begun drilling wells in the adjacent Kaikang field. Construction costs alone for the 250,000 barrels per day pipeline are expected to come to $1.2 billion.

Sudan began commercial oil production on a limited scale by trucking valuable low-sulphur crude to Port Sudan in connection with Gulf Petroleum of Qatar. By 1996, Sudan had nine producing wells, with a production of 2,000 barrels per day [29].

The Canadian-owned Arakis came close to cornering the market of all Sudan's commercially exploitable oil. Arakis, however, was rocked by scandal in 1995, weakening its ability to get the money together to build the pipeline and begin oil production. One of its principal investors, Terry Alexander, left Arakis under suspicion of share-price manipulation. Four years later Alexander was fined $1.2 million by the British Columbia Securities Commission, a record penalty for the province [30].

The financial manipulation behind Arakis' delays in getting production going were typical of many Canadian international oil companies. The delays by Arakis caused Sudan in 1996 to pressure it into a partnership with the state oil companies of China and Malaysia. This put close to $4 billion into the project.

In 1998 Arakis' 25 percent share in the Greater Nile Petroleum Company was purchased by Talisman Energy, Canada's largest independent, privately owned oil company. Talisman also has operations in Indonesia and is exploring for oil in Algeria. China put substantial manpower of its own into the construction of the Sudan pipeline. This speeded up its completion in June 1999, only a year after it began [30].

Oil corporation apologists for Sudan's oppression claimed their investments were working for moderation and peace in this war-torn dictatorship. Instead, the final completion of Sudan's oil pipeline in the summer of 1999 became a cause for intensified fighting.

Under a 1997 peace agreement, six former rebel groups were left in charge of security in oil areas. An attempt in May 1997 to put government militias in charge near oil-rich Bentu resulted in the resumption of warfare between parties that had been pacified by the 1997 truce. As a result of this incursion, one formerly pacified army of the United Democratic Salvation Front defected to the Sudan People's Liberation Army. This sparked an armed confrontation that has since escalated into one of the world's bloodiest current war zones following a September 20, 1999 bombing of the pipeline, which temporarily stopped the flow of crude oil to Red Sea tankers.

Sudan's response to the blowing up of its pipeline was quite brutal, escalating the civil war, despite recent efforts at international mediation. It repeated earlier efforts to use ethnic cleansing for petroleum development.

The Sudanese air force's Antonov bombers dropped bombs on starving civilians as they attempted to retrieve food dropped for them in airlifts by the UN's World Food Program. This was followed by attacks on the same people by helicopter gunships, tanks and machine guns.

In recent months numerous villages have been destroyed and their residents massacred near Sudan's oil fields. International observers from Christian Solidarity Worldwide have found huts reduced to ashes. Driven out of their homes, many former villagers seek refuge under trees to hide from bombardment. Some 6,000 homes have been burned along with 16 churches.

Talisman's Chief Executive Officer, Jim Buckee, who has denied the reality of global warming even to the point of calling other Canadian oil executives "spineless", has also disputed allegations of genocide in Sudan. His company has become the target of investor boycott. In October 1999 a New York City Council committee began hearings into whether it should pull out its 186,000 pension fund shares invested in Talisman [31].

Oil began to be exported from Sudan in major quantities in August 1999. As human-rights critics feared, oil revenues became a means for the Sudanese government to intensify the war by purchasing more expensive weapons. On the very day that the first 600,000 barrels of Sudanese crude left Port Sudan by tanker for refining in Singapore, 20 Russian-built T55 tanks, supposedly destined for Singapore, arrived to assist Sudan's dictatorship [32].

In October 1999, Canadian Foreign Minister Lloyd Axworthy appointed two special envoys to Sudan — John Harker, with a short-term mandate to investigate human-rights violations and the oil situation, and

Senator Lois Wilson, to diplomatic peace negotiations. The Harker Report is available from the Department of Foreign Affairs in Ottawa, while Senator Wilson's reports to Mr Axworthy were verbal. The peace negotiations are still ongoing [33].

Wilson's visit has stimulated more pressure for the democratization of Sudan. During her mission on November 26, 1999, a peace agreement was signed in the East African country of Djibouti. This achieved a peace accord between the Sudanese dictatorship and the democratic prime minister it deposed, the exiled Sadiq al-Mahdi [34].

Although al-Mahdi signed on behalf of his Umma Party, other party leaders of al-Mahdi's National Democratic Alliance still have not signed his peace accord. The former prime minister still has not indicated if he will return to Sudan. There is a risk his presence there would serve to legitimate repression rather than allow him to become a serious contender in promised free elections.

Refugees, fleeing bombardment by the Sudanese air force, continue to pour out of lands where Talisman extracts 150,000 barrels of oil a day. Allegations have been made that the company is assisting the Sudanese government, which employs soldiers from Iraq and Iran sent on a holy war. Talisman's oil pipelines are now attacked every few weeks according to reports by foreign aid agencies. Explosions from the shelling of villages can be heard in Talisman's oil fields 50 km away [34]. Foreign journalists interviewing refugees in Toureli found that at least one in four households had lost a child to slave raiders [36].

International pressure on Sudan's dictatorship has encouraged a rift within its ruling elite. In early December 1999, shortly following the peace accord with the Umma Party, the more pragmatic military officers who signed this agreement curbed the power of their fundamentalist allies by suspending their power base in Sudan's legislature. Such moves, although occasioned by the proclamation of martial law, appear to fulfill promises to al-Mahdi of a transition to democracy by curbing the power of hard-line extremists.

The turmoil within Sudan's ruling elite was intensified by sharp battles on Wall Street to deny both the China National Petroleum Company (CNCP) and Talisman a listing on the New York Stock Exchange. The United States Insurance and Annuity Association College Retirement Equities Fund, one of the world's largest pension funds, divested all of its shares in Talisman.

Foes of Sudan's outrages are hitting China via Wall Street over its strategic schemes to drill for oil. CNCP's hopes of becoming a multinational giant are based on plans for a global stock issue of $8 billion. In anticipation of punitive US actions it hived off its Sudanese investments into a front corporation. US human-rights activists however, saw through this shell game. They continued to denounce any listing of CNCP on the New York Stock Exchange and demanded that Talisman's coveted listing be revoked [37].

The human-rights activists that challenge Sudan's petrotyranny are building the foundations for global democratic peace. This assists efforts by democracy activists who build society in difficult circumstances by the nonviolent actions of underground organizations in Khartoum.

NOTES

1. Natasha Beschorner, "Water and Instability in the Middle East" (London: International Institute for Strategic Studies, 1992), p.59; Ahmed Rashid and Trish Saywell, "Beijing Gusher", *Far Eastern Economic Review*, February 26, 1998, p.47

2. John Bird, "When Food Aid is a Weapon", *United Church Observer*, July/August, 1998, p.46.

3. J. Millard Burr and Robert O. Collins, "Requiem for the Nile" (Boulder: Westview, 1995), pp.305, 306.

4. Bill Schiller, in *The Sunday Star*, February 6, 2000, pp.A1, A8. Previously it had been generally thought that the defeat of the UN forces in Somalia was primarily the work of the Aideed faction. The UN command had wrongly identified its prime foe.

5. Mark Muband, "Warriors of the Prophet" (Boulder: Westview Press, 1998) pp.4-40; Jessica Stern, "The Ultimate Terrorists" (Cambridge: Harvard University Press, 1999) pp.5, 6.

6. Ann Mosely Lesch, "The Destruction of Civil Society in the Middle East," in "Civil Society and the Middle East" (New York: E.J. Brill, 1996) 2, p.155; M. A. Mohammed Salih, "Land Alienation and Genocide in the Nuba Mountains, Sudan", *Cultural Survival Quarterly*, Winter 1999, pp.36-38.

7. Milton Viorst, "Shadow of the Prophet" (New York: Anchor, 1998) pp.108-140.

8. Sandra Postel, "Last Oasis: Facing Water Scarcity" (New York: W.W. Norton, 1992) p.85; Mohammed Suliman, "Civil War in the Sudan:

From Ethnic to Ecological Conflict", *The Ecologist*, Volume 23, no. 3, May/June, 1993, pp.104-109.

9. Bird, *loc. cit.*, p.48.

10. Postel, *loc. cit.*, p.85.

11. Lloyd Timberlake, "Africa in Crisis" (London: Earthscan, 1975), p.73.

12. *Ibid.*, pp.64, 65; Damazo Dut Majak, "Rape of Nature: The Environmental Destruction and Ethnic Cleansing of Sudan" in Joseph G. Jabbra and Nancy Jabbra ed. "Challenging Environmental Issues: The Middle Eastern Perspective" (New York: Brill, 1997) pp.135-149.

13. *Ibid.*, pp.135-149.

14. Suliman, *loc. cit.*, pp.104-109.

15. Postel, *loc. cit.*, p.57.

16. Burr and Collins, *loc. cit.*, p.16.

17. Sharon Hutchinson, "The Nuer of Sudan", *Cultural Survival Quarterly*, Fall 1993, p.45.

18. Peter Moxzynski, "Nuba of Sudan" in "State of the People", ed. Cultural Survival Staff (Cambridge, Cultural Survival, 1995) p.187.

19. Lesch, *loc. cit.*, p.151.

20. Human Rights Watch/Africa, "Behind the Red Line" (New York: Human Rights Watch, 1996) pp.79-81.

21. *Ibid.*, pp.160-172.

22. Francis Deng, "War of Visions: Conflict of Identities in Sudan" (Washington: The Brooking Institute, 1995), pp.169-171.

23. Human Rights Watch/Africa, *loc. cit.*, pp.217, 218.

24. Lesch, *loc. cit.*, pp.170-178.

25. Human Rights Watch/Africa, *loc. cit.*, p.251.

26. Bird, *loc. cit.*, p.46; Jeff Sallot, "Ottawa, Calgary oil firm pursues peace in Sudan", *The Globe and Mail*, March 18, 1998, p.3.

27. "Sudan", *UN Chronicle*, No. 3, 1998, pp.51, 52.

28. Andrea Useem, "Failure of Trust", *Africa Today*, February, 1999, pp.8, 9.

29. Jim West, "International Petroleum Encyclopedia, 1998" (Tulsa: Penn Well, 1999) p.315; Jim West, "International Petroleum Encyclopedia, 1995" (Tulsa: Penn Well, 1996) p.128.

30. Madeleine Drohan, "Into Africa", *The Globe and Mail Report on Business Magazine*, October, 1999, pp.82-90.

31. Susan Searead, "Calgary firm helps Sudan exploit its oil", *The Globe and Mail*, August 23, 1999, p.B6; Stephen Chase, "Explosion halts flow of Talisman's Sudan pipeline", *The Globe and Mail*, September 21, 1999, p.B7; Damien Lewis, "Fight for Sudan's oil is killing civilians", *The Globe and Mail*, October 4, 1999, p.A16; Stephen Chase, "Talisman plays with fire in Sudan", *The Globe and Mail*, October 5, 1999, pp.B1, B11.

32. Eric Reeves, "Sudan at War: Canada Responds", *The Globe and Mail*, October 27, 1999, p.A17.

33. Senator Lois Wilson, private communication to the editors, June 2000. Senator Wilson has also prepared a paper, "The Sudan" for the Canadian Institute of International Affairs, dated May 11, 2000, 8pp.

34. Associated Press, Cairo, "Sudan strikes peace deal with key group", *The Globe and Mail*, November 27, 1999, p. A15.

35. Barrie McKenna, "US protests of Sudan investment could hit Talisman", *The Globe and Mail*, December 14, 1999, p.B10.

36. Stephen Nolone, "Oil Drilling Makes Refugees of Sudanese Tribal People", *The Globe and Mail*, December 8, 1999, p.A13.

37. S. Nolen, "My week on the cusp of war", *The Globe and Mail*, December 17, 1999, pp.A20, A21.

CHAPTER EIGHT
OIL VERSUS DEMOCRACY IN THE INDIAN SUBCONTINENT

India has experienced a tragic decline in the quality of its democracy since the death of its great founder, J.P. Nehru. This degeneration has been greatly facilitated by oil discoveries.

Expensive schemes of industrialization in India have diverted attention from simple nutritional, health and education measures that could end its widespread poverty. Authoritarian ideologists have promoted militarism and drummed up unrealizable dreams of a universal motorized culture. Growing oil wealth has spurred India's increasing military ambitions, permitting its exchange reserves to fund growing arms expenditures rather than oil imports.

Indian democracy degenerated to the point that Freedom House gave India a rating of partly free from 1991-1998, but they then revised it to free in their 1998-1999 report. They explained the upgrading as due largely "to the continued growth of civil organizations that are actively working to strengthen human-rights protections." Much of the democratizing impact comes from India's Gandhian movements, concerned with peace, human rights, social justice, tolerance and environmental protection. Such organizations have been in conflict with the extremist National Volunteer Service (RSS) for over 70 years.

A low point for freedom in India was the national election triumph of the Bharatiya Janta Party (BJP). The BJP is dominated by upper-caste Hindus and is heir to the fundamentalist extremists responsible for the assassination of Mahatma Gandhi. India's recent oil boom has given more confidence to such intolerant megalomaniacs obsessed with military glory. The change in India from honouring Gandhi to electing a national government of the spiritually twisted heirs of his assassins is quite profound, but fortunately incomplete.

INDIAN DEMOCRACY WORKING BEST IN STATES WITHOUT OIL

In many regions of India, uncontaminated by the corrupting oil boom, the patterns of politics are healthier ones, such as characterized the 1951 general elections. Then the Hindu fundamentalists were banned and were in national disgrace following widespread shock over Gandhi's assassination. Wherever there is a strong, nonviolent Communist Party in India, committed to reformist, social democratic objectives, the BJP's fascistic fundamentalism has made little progress. All of these red reformist parts of India are free of oil.

The most successful oil-free zone in India is the state of Kerala. It is home to about 30 million people at the southeast tip of India, occupying an area about the size of Vancouver Island. Kerala has retained the older pattern of electoral alliances based on competition between a centrist Congress, and a left-wing Communist Party. The BJP, which nationally obtains close to 50 percent of the popular vote, wins only six percent of the electorate's support in Kerala. This has kept it from winning a single seat in the state legislature and from representing Kerala in the national parliament. Its weakness here has been a major factor in the absence of communal rioting in Kerala.

Congress and the Communists in Kerala have their own civic-minded organizations. The state's adult literacy movement has been helped by peaceful rivalry between a liberal Congress tied to an adult education organization and the Communist-influenced Science for People. While, in Kerala, a strong democratic political culture has encouraged all parties to co-operate against the BJP, the absence of such a civic spirit at the national level allowed the BJP to form a governing coalition government.

Despite its national resurgence the BJP is isolated in Kerala where there are no regional parties having separatist inclinations. Although Kerala is the only homeland for the Malayalam language, strategies to encourage its development avoid separatist agitation, and are focused instead on the state's remarkable achievement of universal literacy. Science for People has translated the great works of western science into the Malayalam language. It has encouraged an environmentally sustainable approach to development, without oil, nuclear power or massive hydro dams [1].

Kerala's position as a bastion of democratic peace and stability has been helped by an absence of oil. Its principal industries, processing coir (a fibre made from coconuts), and natural rubber, would boom if a carbon tax were applied to synthetic substitutes derived from oil. This would stimulate Kerala's relatively slow rate of economic growth.

Mumbai: Oil Tyrannopolis of India

Mumbai (formerly Bombay) is the service centre for India's booming offshore oil industry. In contrast to more equitable Kerala, it has been called a "tyrannopolis" by environmentalist Kisan Mehta. This term vividly captures the corruption and terror of the rule in Mumbai and the state of Maharashtra by the BJP. Only in Maharashtra has a significant Hindu fundamentalist political party emerged that is more extreme than the BJP. It is the Shiv Sena, named after a Hindu warrior king. For the past four years it has dominated the government of Maharashtra, with the BJP as a junior coalition partner. Some of its leading figures have been convicted in the courts of illegal use of public office for land speculation. The Shiv Sena attempted to prevent a cricket match between Pakistan and India. Having failed to prevent the games through demonstrations, its supporters dug up the wickets before the matches started. The Party has also vandalized cinemas [2].

The commissioning of the Bombay High Offshore Oilfields in 1980 reduced substantially India's oil-import bill. The rapid increase in oil production from 1980 to 1985 encouraged rising oil consumption. Although India's total oil bill rose, imports fell from 70 to 30 percent of the country's requirements. All of this extra production came from the Bombay High Offshore Fields.

With the Mumbai oil boom, India experienced its own version of the Asian car craze. Investments in railways and transit declined as car production soared. Middle class groups attempted to run expressways through already overcrowded slums. The oil boom encouraged the development of more chemical fertilizer factories [3].

Since 1991, a sharp expansion of India's car market has taken place largely from easier consumer credit. The annual output of car factories has doubled to 300,000 vehicles. With the entry of foreign automakers' production it was expected to reach one million by the year 2000 [4].

Mumbai is one of the most seriously polluted cities in India. Environmentalists have found that travel time was faster in horse drawn carriages during the 19th century. When fish in Mumbai harbour are not killed by oil slicks, chronic pollution makes them poisonous to eat. Since pollution penalties here are among the lightest in the world, Mumbai's harbour has become a cesspool for deliberate spillage [5].

More than any other Indian metropolis, Mumbai is characterized by extremes between rich and poor. With motorization such class distinctions have become more severe, as the luxuries of the affluent minority become the killers of the impoverished majority.

Mumbai's oil boom has given it a bigger elite with private automobiles than any other city in India. It has half the taxis in India, a fifth of all private motorized vehicles, and the worst air pollution. The high benzopyrene levels in Mumbai created by heavy automotive use have been linked to increased incidence of cancer.

Air pollution in Mumbai has become its leading cause of preventable early death. Tuberculosis and respiratory ailments are its largest cause of mortality while cardiovascular ailments have also increased.

Mumbai is defiled with the debris of an oil economy. Maharashtra's last remaining mangroves are littered with plastic bags and inorganic waste clogs the creeks and the lakes that supply Mumbai's drinking water [6].

Scientists are asking whether exposure to hazardous chemicals is linked to the breakdown of inhibitions to violence. If this hypothesis is correct, Mumbai may be a textbook example of a pollution-crazed city, as evidenced by clashes between Hindu and Islamic fundamentalists.

Mumbai is the focus of India's worst sectarian violence. The 1993 rioting in Mumbai and Ahmedabad resulted in 600 deaths and the wounding of 2,000 persons. Most victims were Muslims. Thousands of Muslim businesses and homes were looted and burned. Police tapes obtained by the *New York Times* proved that these riots had the character of a pogrom. The Mumbai police purposely avoided aiding Muslim victims and participated in violent acts.

Revenge for the anti-Muslim pogrom resulted in a bombing of the Mumbai Stock Exchange. Criminal charges may still result in the imprisonment of BJP officials who encouraged these riots. The BJP's control of the state government of Maharashtra has delayed justice by stalling the release of reports implicating its leaders [7].

Corruption is so widespread in Mumbai that collapsing buildings are a regular feature of life, taking place about every second day. This is a result of bribery and the adulteration of building materials. Rail lines are blocked for days from collapsing buildings.

Mumbai's oil and petrochemical boom has resulted in Asia's largest slum, Dharavi. It sprawls over 10 km^2 in central Mumbai. Only seven percent of children here attend school. Fights over limited supplies of water are daily affairs. Toilets are also scarce. Over half of greater Mumbai's population live in slums where 40 percent of the dwellings have more than two persons per room. In the worst one percent, more than 10 live in a room.

In oil-rich Mumbai, over 100,000 people live on sidewalks. Frequently the homeless are forced by police to move, or are arrested without warrants and held without bail. Corrupt local authorities demolish hut dwellers' homes and their few possessions are dumped into garbage trucks. Appeals to the respected Supreme Court of India are necessary to stop crazed demolition efforts by municipal authorities.

THE VIVID CONTRAST BETWEEN OILLESS KERALA
AND OIL-RICH MAHARASHTRA

Kerala's economic strategy is not based on the booming urbanization evidenced in Mumbai. Instead, it is focused on the development of rural cottage industries. Such innovations take advantage of Kerala's highly literate work force.

Community economic development in Kerala is being encouraged by a concept of land literacy. This involves preparing village-level plans for ecologically oriented goals such as reforestation, and using vacant land for subsistence crops [8].

The state of Kerala is also emerging as a daring champion of an innovative form of green energy, wave power. Kerala's capital Trivandrum in 1991 became the site of India's first wave power based electrical generating station, which harnesses the strength of crashing seas. The state government has identified 10 other sites and has proposed the construction of a two-megawatt plant, the world's largest [9].

OILLESS AND OIL-SOAKED PATHS FOR
INDIAN AGRICULTURE

Peaceful rural Kerala stands in vivid contrast to violence-torn Punjab, the region most affected by the oil-induced so-called *green* revolution. Violence in Punjab was increased as a result of the economic impact of high-input, chemically based agriculture.

Oil-powered agriculture has exacted a terrible human price in what Indian ecologists have termed the "Greed Revolution." In Punjab alone 10,000 people working on mechanized threshers have had their hands cut off through accidents. Cotton growing areas suffer from thousands of cases of pesticide poisoning. The ingestion of kerosene and agricultural chemicals by children is very common. The chemical industry is the most dangerous in the country, with around 100 workers being killed and 10,000 injured annually.

The Bhopal disaster of 1984 that killed 2,500 persons, is only the most extreme example of the violence of the oil industry. For instance, discharge of oil from refinery effluent in 1968 caused the sacred river Ganges to erupt in flames. Toxic discharges from oil refineries frequently result in massive fish and cattle deaths [10].

Mumbai is a centre of production of an especially deadly oil-based pesticide, ethylene dibromide. It is included in the UN's wish list for elimination of the most deadly pesticides. This pesticide has been described by the US National Cancer Institute as "the most potent cancer causing substance" found in its testing program [11].

India is a heavy user of pesticides banned in western countries, including DDT, and more toxic compounds such as methyl parathion, and Heptachlor. It is a major manufacturer of Agent Orange, which was used as a defoliant in Vietnam. DDT residues are now common in human milk in Punjab. Babies have been found to drink 21 times the acceptable amounts of DDT from their mothers' milk.

In India the heavy use of pesticides has actually contributed to secondary pest outbreaks from chemical impacts on the pests' natural enemies such as birds, spiders and worms. Earthworms critical to soil health have been targeted as pests in advertisements by Indian chemical companies [12].

KERALA: CORE OF AN EMERGING GREEN ASIAN CIVILIZATION

Kerala's oilless success is best expressed in comparative statistics regarding health, literacy and Gross National Product (GNP). The average life expectancy for a North American male is 72 years. Kerala's male life expectancy is 70. North America's GNP per capita is 59 times that of Kerala, although Kerala is not far behind in primary health care. Although the rest of India has a higher GNP per capita than Kerala, the national male life expectancy is much lower, only 58 years.

The United Nations recently certified Kerala as 100 percent literate. In India as a whole only about half the population is literate, a failure largely caused by 70 percent female illiteracy. Kerala's male-female ratios, and birth rates, which continue to fall, are both similar to the developed world. This is primarily caused by the empowering effect of female literacy [13].

Another green achievement of Kerala is the widespread use of smokeless stoves. They have replaced kerosene and inefficient wood stoves that encourage deforestation and pollute indoor air. One of the world's biggest pollution problems is the smoke inhaled by poor rural women while cooking. Smokeless stoves were first developed in the 1950s by Gandhians as part of their concern for appropriate technology. Only in Kerala however, is their use widespread, one of the most recent achievements of Science for People during the current term of Kerala's latest left front government. Science for People found that three hours spent cooking over a conventional stove in rural India is roughly equivalent to smoking 20 packets of cigarettes [14].

MISSIONARY STYLE EXTENSIONS OF GREEN OILLESS WAYS IN INDIA

Many of Kerala's achievements are shared with the rest of South India. Politics in southern India are more focused on combating poverty than the ethnic battles of the northern BJP dominated states. Southern India has also embarked on many green crusades. In Kerala's neighbouring state of Kanakara is India's largest organic farming movement, which has benefited a million farmers.

To the east of Kerala is the south Indian state of Tamil Nadu. It has become one of the world's major centres of wind power. Joint ventures between the state and foreign companies have produced 850 megawatts of power from over a thousand wind turbines [15].

An absence of oil is behind the profound achievements of numerous successful green rural communities. One is Auroville, a village founded largely by West European and North American pacifists, on the coast of Tamil Nadu. It uses organic farming and agroforestry. Similar success stories are symbolic of Gandhian triumphs. These range from the tree-hugging Chipko movement which has checked deforestation in the Himalayan mountains to the Gramdan villages based on communal land tenure.

One of the most spectacular success stories has been the Rishi Valley, in the state of Andhra Pradesh. This was achieved by the disciples of the liberal humanist reformer Khrishnamurti whose educational techniques are based on a missionary zeal for ecological restoration. The valley's many village schools are staffed by green and democratic reformists from Kerala. They focus on adult literacy, land reclamation, reforestation, hygiene, and bee keeping. As in Kerala, literacy rates in the Rishi Valley are substantially higher than the Indian average.

Once a barren desert, the Rishi Valley has become a shining example of the power of reforestation through the ecological principles of organic agriculture. Each school has a flower, fruit and vegetable nursery. A basic belief is that beautification is an antidote to violence.

Like Kerala and the various Gandhian and organic farming communities, the Rishi Valley has a creative mix of new and old green technologies that are free of oil. Its ancient Earth-friendly technologies include draft animals, neem cake for fertilizer, and thatch-roofed homes decorated with bougainvillea and hibiscus flowers. At the same time newer, environmentally focused technologies are applied. They include contour bunds and check dams to stop erosion. Percolation tanks assist ground water discharge. The presence of ancient ways, without flies and noxious smells, has caused American journalist Robert Kaplan to call the Rishi Valley a strange "airbrushed travel-magazine India" [16].

In India, there is a long tradition of oilless, organic agriculture. Sir Albert Howard, the great prophet of organic farming, developed his techniques based on the observation of what Indian peasants were doing.

Agricultural experts in contemporary India have discovered similar insights to Sir Albert Howard's. Narayan Reddy adapted the natural farming techniques of the Japanese agricultural scientist M. Fukuoka. Reddy found ploughing with oxen to be superior to tractors because the latter cause unnecessary soil erosion. He ridiculed farming experts who advocated chemical destruction of earthworms. Reddy combined the organic material on his farm with leaf litter collected from roadsides. After a transition process of seven years, Reddy demonstrated to much of the Indian agricultural-exten-sion community that organic methods could obtain equivalent yields at lower costs. Eventually he received a state award for high yields.

Reddy also pioneered techniques in agroforestry, using banana leaves successfully to feed a herd of 17 cattle. Soap water, the fruit of the neem tree, and ash dusting were successfully employed to replace oil-based pesticides. Agricultural wastes and leaf litter eliminated the need for herbicides to control weeds [17].

Southern Indian states also favour traditional sail-boat fishing over mechanized trawling. In response to widespread protests from fishers, southwestern states have all banned mechanized trawlers in their coastal fisheries during fish breeding. In Kerala, the state that introduced this measure first, fish harvests have rebounded since the ban was introduced in the late 1980s [18].

BUILDING ON DEMOCRATIC TRADITIONS

Contemporary Indian environmentalists are building on their country's democratic traditions. With a strong commitment to democratic principles, the governments of P.J. Nehru and Lal Bahadur Shastri had more Gandhian ideals concerning appropriate technology than is usually attributed to them. For instance, India's first five-year plan gave priority to railways and bicycles over roads and motorized transport.

At independence, there were only two factories with an installed capacity to make 1,200,000 bicycles annually. By 1956, this had increased to 63 factories with a capacity of 7,600,000. Bicycles became used for a variety of purposes. Indian dairymen and farmers cycled milk products to town. Hawkers used bikes to sell goods. University and secondary teaching in India expanded as more rural students could travel to urban schools by bicycle.

In rural India, the bullock cart remains critical in transporting bulk goods. About half the country's villages are completely inaccessible to trucks. Less isolated areas cannot be reached by heavy motor transport in the rainy season. Animal carts continue to handle about 70 percent of the goods in rural India. Motor travel, even by buses, is only a common mode for trips of more than 10 kilometres [19]. The first Congress Party governments developed strategies to improve bullock carts. This involved designing better wheels, which were put into use in 50 locations on an experimental basis. Bullock carts fitted with inflated rubber tires were also encouraged [20]. These and other technical improvements have been incorporated into slightly more expensive, but increasingly widely used bullock-cart designs. Public agencies in some of the more progressive Indian states provide credit to low-income families for the purchase of animal carts. Some programs provide subsidies that equal 25 to 50 percent of the cost of these carts, and also help purchase draft animals.

The above example of low-cost financing is being adopted to assist the broader diffusion of solar power. In Andhra Pradesh, the Syndicate Bank has developed credit for solar systems. The Solar Electric Company now markets and installs solar home systems through a network of five service centres in Karnatakata and Andhra Pradesh [21].

Indian democracy's greatest blessing is that, apart from areas such as the ugly and violent oil belt of Mumbai, it does not suffer from a time warp. Unlike the more repressive Russia and most of the former Soviet Union, India is able creatively to combine ancient and new green technologies.

One of the most stunning mixtures of the old and new green ways has taken place in the deserts of Rajasthan. Here photovoltaic panels are delivered to remote villages by camel. In a similar fashion, yak caravans deliver this space age technology to isolated Tibetan monasteries in northern Kashmir.

Solar power builds on ancient legacies of tradition in India while helping Gandhi's dream of creating an Indian democracy that does not mimic polluting, western ways. In Rajasthan, beautiful dancing girls are employed in markets to draw attention to unfamiliar solar water heaters. This technology in India's sunniest state has also liberated women for newer roles in the modern age. By lighting schools it is increasing female literacy. Women benefit the most from solar-powered pumps replacing hand-powered water pumps [22].

THE RECENT OIL-FIRED DEGENERATION OF INDIAN DEMOCRACY

As India's oil boom began in the 1970s the country's democracy took a turn for the worse. The dictatorial emergency, which saw the powerful son of Prime Minister Sanjay Gandhi engage in a futile effort to start a car industry independent of foreign control, was illustrative of the breakdown of a relatively equitable social democratic consensus. While India in the 1950s had been remarkably motorcycle- and scooter-free, these polluting machines began to emerge. In large cities the motor-vehicle explosion made the roads unsafe for pedestrians, cyclists, and drivers of bullock carts. The spread of private motorized transport, affordable only for a small elite, is widely viewed as a sign of class oppression. This perception is evident even in rural West Bengal, one of the strongholds of the Communist Party of India (Marxist), or CP(M).

The CP(M) government of West Bengal has a very mixed record. It has kept the state free of religious bigotry and violence and experienced some success in land reform, nutrition, agroforestry, and public works in rural areas. It has not achieved the impressive breakthroughs characteristic of Kerala. One of the reasons for this is that the Party has chosen not to antagonize its more affluent supporters by increasing taxes to pay for reforms. In the rural Communist hinterland of West Bengal, disgruntled comrades complain that the local Communist cadre, largely drawn from upper-caste backgrounds, drive scooters obtained corruptly [23].

HOW CULTURES CAN CO-OPERATE WHEN FREEDOM, NOT OIL, IS IN ABUNDANCE

Cultures can mutually enrich each other through co-operation instead of conflict. This is most evident in Kerala where freedom, not oil, flows in abundance.

Most of the world's dominant civilizations are found in Kerala. Although most people are Hindu, 20 percent are Muslim and a similar proportion are Christian. The cosmopolitan state has a small Jewish minority, which has lived peacefully with its neighbours for thousands of years.

There are many potential paths for cultural collision in Kerala. Marxism, often seen as a religious force, is very powerful here. Statues of Karl Marx and Friedrich Engels are found in many town squares. At the same time it is home to zealous followers of a great liberal critic of Communism, Khrishnamurti.

Despite great cultural diversity Kerala has established a pattern of successful, reformist and democratic politics. Its cultures work well together. Each has made a distinctive contribution to Kerala's success as a model for low-income societies.

Kerala has most of the world's great religious traditions, but in all of them fundamentalism is weak or absent. Its Christianity is Anglican, Catholic and Syrian. There is an absence of American-style Christian fundamentalism with its championing of right-wing politics favouring a weak state. Kerala's Christians have been in the vanguard of advocacy of important measures such as land reform. Their schools are important, and provide a healthy competition for the state run system.

Fundamentalism has not triumphed in the Hindu culture of Kerala. Tendencies in this direction have been challenged by the Communist parties, Science for People and a strong local Gandhian movement. Kerala's powerful Communist movement is generally led by Brahmins. Since Muslims in Kerala do not feel threatened this community is free of the extremism that in Mumbai resulted in bloody revenge bombings.

Communism, or socialism, is as much prone to fundamentalist extremism as any major religious faith of the 20th century. In Kerala, Communist fundamentalism also has been kept at bay. Unlike other parts of India, there have been no violent Naxalite insurgencies — Maoist armed struggles that have resulted in murders and mutilations. Naxalite guerrillas in Andhra Pradesh, Madhya Pradesh, Bihar and Orissa served as convenient pretexts to curb civil liberties, and reduce the protections of freedom provided by the rule of law. Communism in Kerala since 1950 has clung to a social democratic agenda. It has been favourably influenced through collaboration with important contemporary Gandhians such as Gandhi's heir Vinoba, who supported the first Kerala Communist state ministry of 1957.

All of Kerala's successes have been helped by an absence of oil. Advocacy of an oil-reliant economy would be clearly subversive to the state's economic interests that are based on coir, natural rubber, and cashew nuts. Efforts in the past to mechanize, such as the mechanization of fishing boats by the Norwegian government in the late 1950s, are now generally recognized as errors. Kerala's tree-lined coastline is still largely the preserve of sailboats and canoes, which benefit from solar-powered lanterns [24].

INDIA'S SECURITY

India's security depends on its ability to establish a *modus vivendi* with Pakistan [25] and in maintaining peaceful relations with China. Increasing India's defence spending will be seen as a threat by Pakistan and may also be interpreted as a threat by its one-time foe, China.

India's two great internal influences pull it in opposite directions. Hindu fundamentalism embodies greed and ambition that comprise a form of oil worship. A bizarre example can be seen in a current popular play, in Mumbai, in which Hindu fundamentalists praise Gandhi's assassination as removing a barrier to India's industrial progress.

India has within its borders all of the critical issues that affect the world. In contrast to the oil worship of fundamentalist Brahmins, and their enthusiasm for nuclear power and weapons, popular Hinduism is vividly identified with solar and wind power. These are celebrated in folk religious festivals. Solar collectors and wind generators obtain respect and reverence when they are identified with their natural deities: Surya, the Sun; Vayu, the wind; and the wind goddess, Indra. In a similarly humble, reverential way, prayers of thanks are made to the dried dung that widely serves as fuel [26]. Green advances are quite remarkable. For instance, India boasts two million clean biogas-cooking facilities and is installing 200,000 new units annually [27].

West Bengal is one of the states whose government has seen the importance of solar power. The region of West Bengal enjoying the best ethnic and religious peace in India is the Sundarbans, in the Ganges delta, where there is one of the world's boldest efforts at solarization. West

Bengal's Renewable Energy Development Agency, working with the Ramakrishna Mission, a respected humanitarian charity, has demonstrated the potential of photovoltaic power for home lighting, water pumping, vaccine refrigeration, communications and economic development. It has established a solar store, where subsidies can be arranged for the purchase of home lighting systems [28].

Given an ebb in the tide of oil fundamentalism, the subcontinent could evolve as a green version of Europe's common market. Such a democratic regional peace would be far more challenging to Chinese dictatorship than a nuclear arsenal. Rather than enter into a futile nuclear race with China, India's security needs to rely on people power and green energy, merging Kant's notion of perpetual peace with Gandhi's vision of one that is environmentally sustainable. China at one time antagonized India by allying itself with the then absolute monarchy of Nepal. This ended in 1990, part of the wave of democratization when the Berlin Wall came down. More dangerous to China than military fortifications are the temples of subverting ideas by which it is ringed, such as the solar-powered Buddhist shrines bordering imprisoned Tibet. Photovoltaic power illuminates the Tatopani Buddhist monastery in Nepal, overlooking the Chinese village of Khasa across the Bagamti River. Buddhist lamas have placed a stone statue of the Bodhisattva Vajrasattva to protect their PV panels. They also teach in their open-air schools what for Chinese Communists must be challenging doctrines of solar power [29].

While environmentalists are preparing for a sustainable Indian civilization based on solar power, the alternative oil- and nuclear-based future for India seems dismal in the long term. Strategic studies gurus and the hawkish Canadian journalist and broadcaster Eric Margolis point to battles over the control of oil as a potential spark for "a future major conflict in Asia." Margolis issues dark prophecies of a disastrous war for oil. These forebodings are based on former CIA director James Woolsey's estimates that India and China will in 30 years each consume 120 million barrels a day of oil, about double the current world usage. Margolis and his strategic studies associates are oblivious to the reality that petroleum guzzling on the predicted scale, through its contribution to global warming, poses an even more serious threat to the world that is environmental, not military.

BJP military thinkers, much like their Pentagon counterparts, point to the possibility of being cut off from oil supplies from the Persian Gulf and South East Asia [30]. Thus oil today and its possible shortage tomorrow are stimulating India's wasteful militarization by providing an excuse to build a high-technology navy having weaponry superior to that of much wealthier Japan [31]. India is also building its first nuclear submarine, which will be armed with a nuclear warhead — claimed to give India a survivable reserve nuclear force in response to a surprise nuclear attack.

The war-for-oil scenarios of India's bigoted extremists and opportunists now holding ministerial office are being challenged by the country's human-rights, ecology and peace movements, working in cooperation with their counterparts around the world. With reverence for life India's spiritual ecologists from diverse faith traditions are illustrating it is better to install a single solar panel than to curse the darkness. What holds back their influence is stubborn opposition from fundamentalist versions of diverse creeds.

NOTES

1. M. Zachariah and R. Sooyanmoorthy, "Science for People" (London: Zed Press, 1994) *passim.*

2. Kisan Mehta, "Mumbai by 2000 AD, A Tyrannopolis or Planned City?" in Rasmi Mayur and Rem Ratan Vohar eds. "Bombay by 2000 AD" (Bombay: Prem Ratan Vohra, 1997) p.218. Also, "Citizen Power in India", *The Economist*, March 20, 1999, p.45.

3. A.K.N. Reddy, "Energy for Development" in M.V. Nadkarni *et al.* eds, "India: The Emerging Challenges" (New Delhi: Sage Publications, 1991).

4. Odil Tunali, "A Billion Cars: The Road Ahead", *World Watch*, January/February, 1996.

5. Sheshagagri Rao, "Bombay Suffers From Many Ills" in Mayur and Vohra eds., *loc. cit.*, p.151.

6. Payal Sampat, "What Does India Want?", *World Watch*, July/August, 1998, p.36.

7. Freedom House Survey Team, "Freedom in the World, 1995" (New York: Freedom House, 1995) p.295.

8. Bill McKibben, "Hope, Human & Wild" (St. Paul: Hungry Mind Press, 1995) pp.157-169.

9. Madanjeet Singh, "The Timeless Energy of the Sun" (San Francisco, Sierra Club Books, 1998) p.98.

10. Centre for Science and the Environment, "State of India's Environment Report, 1984-85" (New Delhi: Centre for Science and the Environment, 1985) pp.198, 240-260.

11) *Ibid.*, pp.240-260.

12. McKibben *loc. cit.*, pp.120-130.

13. *Ibid.*, p.201.

14. Malcolm Adisehiah, "Natural Resource Environment in India" in "India: The Emerging Challenges", pp.208, 209.

15. Singh, *loc. cit.*, p.59.

16. Robert Kaplan, "The Ends of the Earth" (New York: Random House, 1997) pp.154-200.

17. M.V. Nadkarni, "The Crisis of Increasing Costs in Agriculture: Is There A Way Out?" in "India: The Emerging Challenges", pp.164-174.

18. Sampat, *loc. cit.*, p.37.

19. I.J. Barwell, et al., eds. "Rural Transport in Developing Countries" (Boulder: Westview, 1985), pp.21-33.

20. S.K. Srivastava, "Transport Development in India" (Delhi, S. Chand, 1964) pp.100-200.

21. Christopher Flavin and Molly O'Meara, "Shining Examples", *World Watch*, May/June, 1997, p.32.

22. Singh, *loc. cit.*, p.166.

23. Tony Beck, "The Experience of Poverty: Fighting for Respect and Resources in Village India" (London: International Technology Books, 1994) *passim*.

24. Singh, *loc. cit.*, p.197.

25. The biggest barrier to peace is the continuing semidemocracy in India and Pakistan, epitomized by the terrible civil rights situation on both sides of their disputed territory in Kashmir. Pakistan does not allow Kashmiri residents in its sector to vote. India's human rights abuses in Kashmir have become so pervasive that Freedom House now ranks the territory "not free."

26. Singh, *loc. cit.*, p.62.

27. *Ibid.*, p.40.

28. Eric Margolis, "War at the Top of the World" (Toronto: Key Porter, 1999) p.240.

29. Singh, *loc. cit.*, pp.6, 7.

30. Margolis, *loc. cit.*, pp.203-204, 215-216.

31. India has one aircraft carrier and a second on order. Japan has no aircraft carriers and fewer submarines than India, although its GNP is 11 times as large.

CHAPTER NINE
OIL-BASED ASIATIC DESPOTISM

The frontiers of freedom and peace in Eastern Asia are shaped by the distribution of petroleum wealth. The full democracies of Japan, Mongolia, the Philippines, South Korea, Taiwan and Thailand lack substantial oil reserves. Most Asiatic despotisms resistant to democratization — Malaysia, Myanmar (formerly Burma), Vietnam and China — are significant petroleum producers.

The exception to the pattern of Asiatic petrolized despotism is North Korea. However, it too is sustained by despotic oil wealth through its arms sales to Iran and other oil-rich Middle East states that are its critical source of foreign exchange.

Access to petroleum shapes the barriers to freedom more than do ancient cultural divisions. Taiwan and China have the same ancient religions and culture, yet China, with oil, is tyrannical while Taiwan, without oil, is democratic. Democratic Mongolia and tyrannical Myanmar are both predominantly Buddhist. Oilless democratic Mongolia is praised by environmentalists for its ambitious efforts at solar power and nature restoration. Tyrannical Myanmar is favoured by American energy corporations that exploit its substantial reserves of natural gas with the widespread use of slave labour.

HOW OIL, MILITARISM AND DICTATORSHIP
FOSTERED ASIA'S ECONOMIC COLLAPSE

China suffered from the blunders of massive investments in motorization, now unaffordable by more than a tiny elite. Producers of even the cheaper motorcycles had unsold inventories. China's state banks invested heavily in motorization and are now on the verge of collapse. Largely shunning cars, consumers preferred to put their savings into better shelter [1].

The over-investment in Asia's auto industry resulted in overproduction. In 1997, a drop in South Korea's car sales by seven percent forced its second largest automaker into bankruptcy. Car sales have now fallen by 49 percent. Although its car factories are operating at only 40 percent capacity, inventories are double their optimal level. The car owners' association of Korea itself predicts that 110,000 workers will lose their jobs. In Indonesia, the country's largest automaker, Astra International, axed 25,000 workers [2].

Calamity from car glut also hit Thailand. Here foreign automakers invested $1.7 billion. After its currency devaluation, output and sales fell by 73 percent. Toyota shut down two plants and closures also took place in the automotive industries of Indonesia and Malaysia.

Communist China's costly embrace of motorization through its massive debt now poses one of the greatest threats to the world capitalist economy. "Red chip" stocks of Communist Chinese companies were the source of most of Hong Kong's booming financial market. Now international bankers find that the more they discover about Chinese companies the more they want to run from them [3].

How Repression Intensified the Asian Crash

Throughout Asia the degree of crisis experienced by a national economy has become deeply exacerbated through curtailments of human rights. Democratic countries have all weathered the crisis with less dislocation than the region's dictatorships.

Thailand has adjusted to the crisis with the help of peaceful democratization. After its currency collapse in 1997 Thailand moved rapidly to improve its situation regarding fundamental human rights and freedoms, and is now rated as a full democracy.

Japan reformed its financial system after the Asian meltdown. This was accomplished through imposing institutional regulations by quiet parliamentary means. Not a single injury has taken place from violence associated with Japan's prolonged recession.

South Korea's austerity package was successfully implemented through its newly elected President, Kim Dae Jung. He has spent most of his life struggling for human rights. Kim has overseen the creation of a deeper democracy as part of South Korea's adjustment to economic change. One new component is a broader range of broadcasting through the creation of a new television network not controlled by the country's powerful conglomerates.

Where it is possible in response to the Asian crisis, popular discontent has been reasonably channelled into the informed protests of democratic civil society. By contrast in Indonesia, with its years of repression unbroken from the Dutch colonial empire, discontent tends to be expressed in destructive violence.

At the time of the Asian meltdown Indonesia had the worst human rights record of any of the impacted countries. Its economic collapse was accelerated by anti-Chinese riots that were encouraged by the Suharto dictatorship. An explosive cycle of violence erupted where destruction of churches and retaliatory action against mosques were taking place. This was fostered by the Indonesian army's inexperience at protecting civilians from violence. Soldiers frequently stood by passively as mob violence worsened. Nowhere else in Asia has economic decline produced widespread looting and massacres.

MYANMAR: A BUDDHIST VERSION OF PETRODICTATORSHIP

Myanmar's chronic civil war is the worst social catastrophe in Asia. It is financed through narcotics smuggling and petroleum development. Much of Myanmar's income comes from the export of natural gas. Myanmar's dictatorship has violated virtually every principle in the UN's Universal Declaration of Human Rights.

Dictatorship in Myanmar is based on a deadly mixture of Buddhist fundamentalism and petroleum. Oil-rich states and US energy corporations undermine trade sanctions imposed by most of the democratic world. While US trade sanctions have not hit older projects, legislation passed early in 1996 has stopped new investments in Myanmar by US oil companies.

Revenues from resource exploitation and exploration go directly into Myanmar's military, now a formidable force of 400,000 troops. In the last six years Myanmar has spent hundreds of millions of dollars on tanks, rockets, aircraft and helicopters from China, its main military supplier.

Oil companies doing business in Myanmar have been highly militarized in their style of operation. This is especially true of the French oil company Total that has transported Myanmar troops in its planes and helicopters in pursuit of its exploration objectives. Total's Myanmar headquarters resembles a fortress. It is surrounded by barbed wire fences, trenches and three on-site security battalions. Total's office is also garrisoned by truckloads of army escorts. Its involvement in Myanmar began when the

French government was a major shareholder. Its investments in the totalitarian regime are still subject to approval by the French government, which has retained some statutory authority over Total. Helicopter and weapons purchases have been paid for by Total for the benefit of Myanmar's military rulers. This was confirmed by former Polish President Lech Walesa who has acknowledged in several interviews that Poland was paid by Total for helicopters shipped to Myanmar [4].

In fighting its civil war Myanmar's military rulers are particularly concerned to secure territories for oil exploration. Some petroleum companies have abandoned the country, citing poor infrastructure as a stumbling block. Roads built by petroleum corporations become the basis for logging operations on previously isolated pristine tracts of tropical rainforests.

Myanmar's army in its war with the Chin National Front destroys churches and erects pagodas on their ruins. Such outrages have been a concern of human-rights organizations, labour unions, and ecology activists. An environmental group, the Rainforest Action Network, on September 19, 1998, filed a 127-page petition with the California state Attorney General's office to revoke the Charter of Union Oil (Unocal) for its collaboration with Myanmar's dictatorship. Denied by Unocal, these allegations contained in the petition were subsequently confirmed by a US Department of Labour report [5].

The oil-rich dictatorships of the Middle East have not applied sanctions to Myanmar despite its role as the world's most ruthless persecutor of Muslims. With government support in March 1997, Buddhist monks attacked Muslim mosques and properties in Mandalay. These shrines were subsequently levelled by tanks. Some 250,000 Muslims fled to Bangladesh to escape execution, religious persecution, forced labour, and portering; they also faced land confiscation. In defiance of the UN's Universal Declaration of Human Rights Muslims have been stripped of Myanmar citizenship and are denied basic social, health and educational services.

Myanmar's close alliance with China draws it into a cynical friendship with repressive oil-rich states such as Iran, Iraq, Sudan, and Libya which ignore the brutal persecution of Muslims in Myanmar and destruction of sacred Islamic shrines. To speak out in defence of Myanmar's persecuted Islamic minority would involve risking being cut off from Chinese weapons and profitable oil sales.

While Buddhism is normally characterized by its absence of bloodshed, Myanmar provides a unique petropowered fundamentalist version of this faith that justifies human-rights violations in the name of religion.

Myanmar's abundant natural gas supplies have resulted in powerful western energy corporations investing heavily in the Tenasserim region. Here a natural gas pipeline is being constructed. It will transport Myanmar's natural gas from offshore, across Myanmar's southern peninsula into Thailand.

Myanmar's army uses forced labour for roads and a railway line to assist in the Tenasserim project. Hundreds of villagers have been forcibly relocated. Porters frequently work without pay, and risk extrajudicial killings. Workers and their families are subjected to demands by soldiers for money and food. Unpaid workers are forced to pay for their own transportation, and have to rent bulldozers. Workers live in quite unsanitary conditions causing many to die or become ill from intestinal diseases. Many of the sick die along the way to their home villages.

Oil companies assist Myanmar's military rulers in complex and complementary ways. The roads they slash through the rainforest allow for more rapid deployment of troops. Since 1989, 10 foreign petroleum companies have bought exploration licences. They have invested around $500 million in Myanmar. Any oil or gas profits obtained by the state increase the military's efforts at repression. They are put into a fund administered for this purpose by Myanmar's ruling State Law and Order Council (SLORC).

Among the world's remaining dictatorships Myanmar has the world's strongest democracy movement. It is led nonviolently by Aung San Suu Kyi. She has been under house arrest since 1990, the year her party, the National League for Democracy (NLD), won Myanmar's last free elections. Myanmar's military rulers obtained only two percent of the popular vote. Suu Kyi's victory caused the military to nullify the results and arrest hundreds of NLD members.

Myanmar's tyranny has severely repressed liberal Buddhists who bravely champion democracy. Following the 1990 crackdown on the NLD, 300 Buddhist monks were placed in detention. Most are still in prison and 16 have died while incarcerated.

Myanmar's dictatorship is a critical barrier to the spread of a democratic peace. Its cynical mix of supporters illustrates vividly how war, dictatorship and petroleum are interconnected.

The nonviolent resistance to Myanmar's dictatorship is a vivid sign of the convergence of the ideals of freedom, environment and peace. This has brought the champions of social justice, the environment and freedom together from around the world. This nonviolent network contrasts greatly with the armed opponents of Myanmar's government, which are themselves frequently financed through the drug trade or co-opted into the repressive dictatorship.

In the United States over 100 university activist groups have launched campaigns against companies doing business in Myanmar. Twenty-one municipalities and one state have boycotted all firms doing business in Myanmar. When Indonesia became a democracy in December 1999 one of the first government actions was to give support to Myanmar's freedom movement.

Nonviolent people power although not yet successful in toppling the Myanmar dictatorship has weakened it, even its petroleum-rich base. The infamous Tenasserim pipeline has not produced any profits for its sponsors, a fact that should provide a vivid warning to foreign investors friendly to dictatorships. The Tenasserim pipeline is becoming a victim of the Asian economic collapse. The boycott against oil companies doing business in Myanmar has caused a number of corporations to pull out, including PetroCan and Texaco [6].

INDONESIA AND MALAYSIA: ASIAN ISLAMIC FUNDAMENTALISM, ECOCIDE AND OIL DICTATORSHIP

Malaysia and Indonesia share the oil fields of Borneo. Both countries during periods of dictatorships have manipulated Islamic fundamentalism. They have also directed repression against environmental groups.

Indonesia's recently deposed dictator, Suharto, attempted to divert protests against his rule into anti-Chinese riots. Apart from their prosperity, the Chinese were condemned because of their Christian religion, which makes them a small minority in predominantly Muslim Indonesia.

The repressive ruler of Malaysia, Mohammad Mahathir, is the leading theorist of "Asian Values". This was used to justify the alleged superiority of authoritarian capitalism over democracy. He has recently been named as among the top 10 of the world's "enemies of the press" by the New York City based Committee to Protect Journalists. His old use of Asian values now ringing hollow, Mahathir now employs fundamentalist homophobic interpretations of Islamic texts to justify the persecution of the country's leading champion of democracy, the former deputy-premier, Anwar Ibrahim. Typical of the way in which oil worship is linked to religious fundamentalism, Mahathir has organized a lengthy procession of Malaysian-built cars as a state-sponsored ritual.

What has not been reported in the mainstream western press is how

148

Mahathir's attacks on currency speculators have been combined with outbursts against environmentalists. Whenever the country experiences economic difficulties there are crackdowns in Malaysia against environmentalists who are denounced as "thorns in the flesh".

Allegations of green financial conspiracy were made when the crisis forced Mahathir to cancel the Bakun dam. It would have flooded an area the size of Singapore that provides critical habitat for dozens of endangered species. Despite Bakun dam's temporary cancellation, Malaysia is proceeding with the ethnic cleansing of animist indigenous people whose homes would be flooded by the dam's completion. Mahathir's crackdown on Malaysia's democracy movement was begun by raids on the offices of three environmental groups that opposed the Bakun dam [7].

Religious intolerance has contributed to repression in East Timor. After it was invaded and annexed by Indonesia in 1979, over 200,000 predominantly Catholic people were killed in the genocidal assault by the Indonesian army. Suharto's manipulation of hatreds was stimulated by a transmigration program. He moved 170,000 Javanese Muslims onto the lands of animist minority communities such as West Papua. During the Suharto dictatorship the worst repression was meted out to non-Muslim minorities. This was quite intense at the beginning of the regime with massacres of 500,000 people in the predominantly Hindu island of Bali.

The manipulation of hatred was a staple means for the Suharto dictatorship to cling to power. In 1994, a labour strike in the north-west city of Medan was manipulated by government intrigue into anti-Chinese riots. Ethnic violence in Borneo in early 1997 resulted in hundreds of deaths.

Some of the worst violence during the Suharto dictatorship was closely associated with resource extraction projects such as mining in West Papua. Here 800 villagers were killed by bombing. Repression was especially severe around the Grasberg copper and gold mine, where soldiers occupied villages, destroyed homes and enforced compulsory labour. In February 1997, Danny Kennedy, an activist of the US environmental group Project Underground was deported. His crime was to attempt to take water samples [8].

As in much of the world some of the worst violence in Indonesia comes in the form of persecuting the critics of petroleum development. This is the situation in the Aceh region of northern Sumatra where 2,000 people have been killed by Indonesia's military since 1989 [9].

Malaysia and Indonesia's cities' toxic fumes from unregulated motorization frequently blend noxiously with the acrid smoke of burning forests. In the summer of 1997, two million hectares of forests were set ablaze. Most of these fires were deliberately set on timber and palm oil plantations by a few politically well connected interests. Fees collected from logging companies were supposed to support reforestation and fire fighting projects. Investigations by the International Monetary Fund (IMF) later revealed that these revenues were diverted towards establishing a national car industry. This was undertaken by the Timor Putra Company, a firm controlled by the youngest son of now ex-President Suharto [10].

During Indonesia's economic collapse, owners of the automobiles produced by Timor Putra would keep them inside. To drive such symbols of theft by the powerful would cause the unfortunate owners to become targets for rioters enraged by the plundering of the country's oil wealth for its oligarchic elite.

Indonesia's national oil company, Pertamina, riddled with corruption and inefficiency, served the political goals of reinforcing the Suharto dictatorship. In the last years of the Suharto era, from 1996 to 1998, such fraud caused it to lose $6 billion. Malaysia's national oil company, Petronas, has been better managed, helping propel the continued success of the country's repressive rulers.

While collapsing oil prices destroyed the totalitarian Suharto dictatorship [Appendix I], Malaysia's Mahathir was able to ride out a storm of protest over the Asian crisis. Eventually he was bailed out by a 50 percent increase in oil prices engineered by the OPEC cartel. In contrast to the fumbling Suharto, Mahathir cagily used the wealth of Petronas to fuel his political and economic ambitions. Petronas is now purchasing control of Malaysia's troubled national car maker, Proton. Its 60 percent control of Malaysia's heavily polluting car market is enforced by exemptions from import duties that foreign competitors must pay.

Legally a nationalized oil corporation, Petronas functions more as a personal company controlled by Mahathir. He is one of the world's most powerful oil executives, having great political and economic power in the fashion of the Persian Gulf monarchies and the Sultan of Brunei.

Elected parliamentary representatives are unable to scrutinize Petronas' dealings fully. The company reports directly to the Prime Minister's office. Its accounts of $10 billion in annual spending are not put before parliament. Foreign oil companies that partner with Petronas are barred from talking to the media [10].

SOUTH EAST ASIA'S TRANSITION FROM COMMUNIST TO CAPITALIST OIL OLIGARCHY

The long war in South East Asia changed dictatorships. While in the past its military muscle was from an alliance with the oil-rich Soviet Union, Communist Vietnam is now experiencing its own petroleum boom in partnership with American multinational oil corporations such as Exxon-Mobil. Vietnam's continuing dictatorship is advantageous to the foreign oil corporations it is assiduously courting. Communist Vietnam has not tolerated any scope for private environmental groups in the country. Such groups operate out of Hanoi and have been given no autonomy. Vietnam also combines Communist dictatorship with a lack of health, safety and environmental-protection standards. A report by the American accounting firm Ernst & Young, found that levels of carcinogens in one of Nike's factories, exceeded safe levels by 177 times. A particularly infamous Hong Kong factory was shipped to Vietnam to continue its dirty business without being plagued by bothersome environmental regulations [11].

During the Asian economic boom, Communist Vietnam failed to emulate the success of its neighbours. As Samuel Huntington correctly points out, in every successful Asian Tiger economy — Thailand, Indonesia, the Philippines and Singapore — a critical role was played by Chinese immigrants. Vietnam, then comfortably subsidized by the oil-rich USSR, cut itself off from future prosperity through the expulsion of its Chinese ethnic minority.

After some 160,000 ethnic Chinese were expelled from Vietnam to China, China closed its border to refugees who then took to boats. Thailand refused naval protection, making the refugees vulnerable to piracy. Singapore's navy deliberately rammed refugee boats. This cast people adrift. Aid was refused to the drowning. Most of the surviving Chinese Vietnamese boat people obtained refuge in the democracies of the United States, Canada, Great Britain and France [12].

THE PHONEY WAR: DISPUTES OVER OIL IN THE SOUTH CHINA SEA

The most dangerous scaremongering over a war for oil in the South China Sea is Huntington's book *The Clash of Civilizations*. It climaxes with a portrait of World War III erupting over oil disputes between China and Vietnam. This fictional war for oil erupts after another

151

potential flashpoint, namely, the reunification of Korea and China, has been peacefully resolved.

Huntington's warnings of world war over South China Sea oil are a popularization of the hawkish views of Kent Calder. Like Huntington, he ominously warns of an "Islamic-Confucian entente that could decisively shift the balance of global power away from the west."

Calder has many reliable facts to justify his prognosis of war for oil in Asia. In 1974, China and Japan did come close to an armed clash over the petroleum-rich shoals of the Senkaku Islands. Both sides however, pulled back at the last moment, although the dispute remains unresolved. Conflicts between states over potential offshore oil reserves in the South China Sea have involved actual armed clashes. The most violent involved the claims of Vietnam and China to the Parcel Islands. Another contentious area is the too well named, Mischief Reef.

The shift from the Cold War to oil as the leading prop for military expenditure was evident in Indonesia's purchase of the entire navy of East Germany. This involved 35 ships although one sank before it arrived! Other big arms purchases were undertaken by Malaysia, Singapore and Thailand, and included mobile combat forces, long-range bomber attack squadrons and antiship missiles. Each state bordering the South China Sea upgraded its submarine fleet. China made massive purchases of long range bombers and military transports.

Heavy military expenditure over the phantom war for oil soon collapsed with the currencies of most of Asia. Thailand quickly cut its military spending by $1.5 billion. Its plans for armoured vehicles, light tanks, submarines and air defences were quickly discarded. Malaysia likewise quickly slashed 10 percent of its defence budget and announced that additional cuts of eight percent would soon follow. The Philippines shelved plans for purchases of two squadrons of fighter aircraft and a dozen patrol boats. Budget trimming is further eliminating in all previously booming Asian states military spending for fuel, ammunition and training exercises. [13].

SINGAPORE'S ALTERNATIVE TO ASIAN MOTOR MAYHEM

One of the little appreciated understandings of Singapore's economy is its successful restraints on private motor transport. This has been encouraged by its avoidance of the creation of a domestic motor industry, and heavy consumer taxation of all automotive imports.

Singapore's doubly green success has been fostered by the strength of its environmental movement. This began during the twilight of the British colonial era when the Nature Society of Singapore was founded in 1954. It has since consistently championed the cause of environmental protection.

The Nature Society of Singapore, with a membership of only 2,200 people, has won major victories. One was saving a bird sanctuary from a proposed agrotechnology park intended to boost the petrochemical industry. It has also crusaded for human rights in general and labour rights such as the protection of foreign maids from arbitrary abuses by employers.

In addition to its efficient public transport, Singapore has discouraged automotive use through area licensing, road user taxes, and parking restrictions and charges. Fees are adjusted on the basis of time and location. The heaviest penalties are imposed on drivers who use its downtown core in rush hours. A monthly fee is imposed on lone drivers for entering the downtown in rush hours enforced through electronic archways at entry points. These deduct fees from a "smart card" inserted into sensors inside every car. Annual road taxes are as high as $3,500 for vehicles with large engines [14].

DICTATORSHIP AND PETROTYRANNY IN ASIA

Although the World Bank encouraged policies to restrict motorized transportation on the Singapore model these were not adopted in Asia's oil-rich dictatorships. Malaysia ignored the car restraint policies of its more successful Tiger neighbour, Singapore. It spent over $200 million to develop a national automobile industry. At the same time billions were spent on new road and bridge construction as expenditures for rail and bus transport rapidly fell. From 1992 to 1996 car sales increased by 133 percent [15].

The combination of dictatorship and motorization was also evident in the Philippines during the Ferdinand Marcos era. Although the country's middle class eventually brought down the dictatorship it was bought off for a period by motorization. Marcos' last years in power saw an explosion of private cars in Manila, while bus numbers plummeted [16].

MALAYSIA'S ENDURING OIL DICTATORSHIP

By increasing repression, Malaysia's rulers have shown a degree of fierce consistency. Nowhere else has motorization and oil development been pursued with such single-minded determination. Malaysia embraces oil dictatorships around the world with a passionate fervour and stimulates motorization without regard for environmental consequences. Exhaust from oil burning is a holy incense here to the semidemocracy's attempts to achieve economic development without the restrictions commonly imposed by environmentalists in fully democratic states.

Like Marcos, Mahathir has kept the middle class onside with his repressive policies by aggressively pursuing motorization. Despite the financial meltdown his government has found more cash to pursue automotive dreams to keep the middle class away from his country's growing democracy movement. On January 27, 1999, motorists were blessed by lower fares on toll highways. Hunger and privation are less important priorities than the motorized pleasure of a powerful elite. Heavy subsidies for luxury middle class motorization are allocated by a country, which like the other Asian Tigers, lacks a comprehensive social safety net [17].

Malaysia's national capital, Kuala Lumpur, is one of the most polluted places in the world. Since 1993, Malaysia's Environment Ministry has suggested a simple regulation by which air pollution could be reduced, namely, banning the two-stroke engine commonly used to power small motorcycles. Even this minor measure was rejected.

Pollution is so severe in Kuala Lumpur that the Health Ministry has recommended that Malaysians wear gas masks. The city's hospitals are full of cases of severe bronchial problems among children that have been induced by air pollution [18].

THAILAND'S VERSION OF MOTORIZED REPRESSION

Some of the worst excesses of motorization have taken place in Bangkok. Before the Asian economic crash buying automobiles became a craze for the middle class. One such family would frequently own four automobiles. Commuting increased as the middle class fled the central core of Bangkok to escape air pollution.

Middle class family life in Bangkok became orientated to the car as it became a focal point for cooking, children's homework and feeding. Toilets were marketed for cars. Motorized air conditioning's chilly breezes provided protection from the city's terrible air pollution.

Motorization caused neighbourhood activism to decline in Bangkok because of the time demands of commuting. To avoid irritating air pollution, commuters would go to work at five or six a.m., arriving two or three hours early.

Motorcycles used by middle class youth contribute heavily to motor mayhem. In Thailand there are few age restrictions on motorization and eight-year old children commonly drive scooters. Pedestrians curse motorcyclists because of the deafening noise they create. Families will turn up the volume of television sets to drown out their racket.

The majority of Thailand's citizens are victimized by cars and motorcycles. Pedestrians, cyclists and transit users are exposed to heavily polluted air, made worse by the absence of restrictions on leaded gasoline. Air pollution results in headaches, eye irritation, and allergic reactions. Both school children and Thai traffic police have been found to suffer from significant brain and lung damage from automotive emissions.

One aspect of democratization in Thailand has been the recent improvement for traffic police. They are now provided with gas masks and regular health checks. Another recent labour victory was the provision of respite booths and oxygen tanks!

Thai drivers commonly ignore traffic rules. Until the 1990s, police seldom fined offenders. Low-income residents are frequently evicted for road improvements. Municipal buses are ageing, overloaded and poorly maintained. For the more affluent who can afford them, privately owned air-conditioned buses are available [19].

WAR ON BICYCLES IN COMMUNIST VIETNAM AND DICTATORIAL INDONESIA

Communist Vietnam and dictatorial Indonesia had a common love for motorized transport coupled with disdain for bicycles. Ho Chi Minh City and Jakarta had more municipal regulations to discourage cycling than any other cities in the world.

Indonesia never invested in rapid transit. Its military rulers looked upon the country's bicycle-powered cabs with disdain, as primitive modes of travel. Such bicycles were frequently gathered up by authorities and dumped into the sea. One incident in the 1980s saw 20,000 bicycles dumped into Jakarta Bay. Bikes were confined to nighttime operation on the edge of cities [20].

COMMUNIST CHINA: OIL-CURSED NO MATTER
WHAT COLOUR THE CAT

Deng Xiaoping, although abolishing ecocidal Maoism, lacked the environmental concern and democratic zeal of the otherwise similarly minded reform Communist leader, Mikhail Gorbachev. Both were sceptical of collective farms and did not care if a cat was socialist, as long as it caught mice. Gorbachev, however, had the additional concern that toxic oil-based substances be avoided in the capture of mice.

Both Maoist agricultural policies and Deng's reformed Communism favoured petrochemical inputs. The ping-pong diplomacy of Nixon and Mao was combined with deals with American oil companies. During the Cultural Revolution, China imported 13 ammonia-urea complexes, developed by the American Kellogg Company, at the cost of $2 billion. Targets were made to have the same level of agricultural petrochemical use as South Korea and Japan.

Deng followed Mao's oil-greased road. Cultivation of leguminous crops, which replenish the soil with nitrogen and are produced without petroleum products, steadily declined. Organic recycling fell. Pesticide damage devastated bee keeping. China's once formidable ability to recycle wastes shrank because of growing contamination of organic substances with petrochemicals [21].

Despite Huntington's worries about war for oil between China and Vietnam, the same western oil companies are heavily involved on both sides of the disputed offshore borders. Deng invited 48 foreign companies from 12 nations to undertake offshore exploration, with drilling getting underway in 1982. In contrast to impoverished donor democracies, China's oil wealth and potential mass market have turned it into a donor dictatorship [22].

The strong ties between Communist China and western oil, automotive and petrochemical companies helped prevent any effective economic sanctions being taken following the Tiananmen Square massacre. Recently revealed photographs, smuggled out of China by democracy activists, show that students were crushed by tanks on June 4, 1989. One tank mowed down 11 marchers from behind, killing seven student protesters instantly. Students that were able to escape from the tanks were forced to run a gauntlet of truncheons and fists [23].

The tanks in Tiananmen Square proved to be the shock that paved the way for the motorization of China. Three years following the 1989 Tiananmen slaughter the level of foreign investment tripled. It reached

$251 billion which amounts to a third of all foreign investment in developing countries. Vividly symbolic of the new direction of China, the square where the Goddess of Liberty briefly rose is now a parking lot [24].

The prospect of automotive development, as western executives dreamt of a market for 700 million cars, was critical to Communist China's ability to avoid sanctions. Japanese automakers were the first to breach the barriers to new investment in China. After Suzuki signed an agreement to produce a passenger car in Chongqing, other companies abandoned their earlier refusal to set up businesses there. The prospect of a Japanese dominated Chinese auto industry resulted in major investments by German, French, British and American automotive companies [25].

The biggest blunder in Deng's otherwise keen economic policies was a decision to foster the automobile as the basis for a future Chinese economy. It was propagated by a Communist Party think tank called the Strategic Development Research Team of China's Family Car.

Massive investments were made in motorization. Some 150,000 labourers in Beijing toiled to complete a ring road expressway around the city. Communist authorities in some cities launched an antibike campaign and cyclists were banned from downtown Shanghai and Guangzhou. This later was extended to streets in Beijing. Bicycles were blamed for the lack of road safety, and denounced for forcing cars to slow down. In Beijing a small army of police is employed to keep bicycles off of streets reserved for the Communist motorized elite. The Communist Party also sponsored an "international automotive car culture festival", featuring car parades.

Although still in its infancy, motorization is having a major impact on China. Farmland loss from transportation has jumped from 35,000 hectares to 400,000 annually. Already in Chapter Three we have seen a discussion of the disaster this would represent if continued for fifteen years.

The key to mass motoring in China is low car costs. To get around the difficulties of the limited group of Chinese consumers who can afford motorcars, General Motors plans to manufacture them in China without air cleansing catalytic converters. Fortunately Chinese consumers are rejecting this allure for more tangible pleasures such as better shelter. Massive investments in expressways financed by tolls appear to be headed for failure, given too few users of the costly bridge and highway infrastructure [26].

THE SECRET GREEN ANTI-OIL WEAPON OF DEMOCRATIC PEACE

Despite formidable repression in remaining dictatorships there is a powerful tendency towards a green peace in Asia. This convergence has been developing in Asia since democracy began in Japan during the Meji Restoration of the 1880s. Recent movements for a green peace were critical reasons for the triumph of democracy in Indonesia, the Philippines, South Korea, Taiwan and Thailand, and are important for freedom crusades in Malaysia and Myanmar.

From its birth Japan's environmental movement was identified with the struggle for democracy. It allied with the liberal elite of Meji Japan. These enlightened noblemen preferred real British constitutionalism to the fake, militaristic, German variety. Critical to the early unity of Japan's green and democratic movements was the remarkable prophet, Shozo Tanaka.

Shozo Tanaka's early battles for a liberal democratic constitution were combined with protest against the pollution of the Watarase River from copper mining. He was elected to the first Japanese Diet in 1890. Tanaka resigned a decade later in solidarity with farmers beaten in antipollution protests. His support came from both Japan's Christian and Buddhist communities [27].

Democracy in Japan after World War II was encouraged by its environmental movement. American tinkering with Japan's constitution was based on listening to the protests of the country's liberals who wanted an authentic British-style constitutional monarchy. Such veteran opponents of militarism subsequently prevailed after 1948, when these committed democrats prevented any amendments to Japan's democratic peace constitution.

Much of the free world in the early stages of the Cold War saw a new interest in solar power that was shared by Japan. The Japanese inventor, Sukeo Yamamoto, designed the country's first solar water heater. Mass production began in 1948 of simple units designed to facilitate hot baths on farms and more complex models were later developed for cities. By 1960, some 170,000 solar water heaters were sold in Japan. By the mid-1960s, the production of the five manufacturers had peaked. Low oil prices caused the solar water heating industry to decline in Japan after 1966. Japan's solar industry however, quickly revived after the shock of the 1973 OPEC price hike.

Japan's response to the OPEC price hike was awesome. Today its steel production is now 40 percent less energy intensive than the United States' and 10 percent below Germany's, part of a massive commitment to reduce its imported oil bill. In many industrial sectors conservation efforts caused oil consumption to fall by 20 to 30 percent within two or three years. Since 1980, following a second oil price shock caused by the Iranian revolution, Japanese industry has spent over $10 billion in improving its energy efficiency.

When it comes to confronting the oil and automotive industry, Japan's democracy has imposed higher environmental standards than western Europe or the United States. While US President Bill Clinton's plans for a million solar homes are still facing Republican opposition, Japan has ambitious government programs in operation for domestic solarization. It is already about half way to the target of a million homes, above the pace of the world's other democracies. Japan also mass produces 50 percent transparent glass windows as solar cells that achieve a peak output of 18 watts per square meter.

Japan's lack of oil has encouraged imaginative efforts for energy conservation and renewable power. Its leading insurance company is Sumitomo Marine and Fire Insurance which is one of the most active companies in drawing attention to the problems of global warming. Major housing companies have introduced a new type of dwelling with silicon roof tiles. This generates enough electricity to meet most of a family's needs. In 1997, Japan led the world in building 9,400 solar homes. By the year 2000 it is government policy to have 70,000 homes with solar cells.

Nowhere else have public subsidies for solar power been as impressive. Seven percent of photovoltaic system costs can be deducted from taxable income and low interest loans are provided for installation. For schools and other public facilities the Japanese government pays two-thirds of the costs for photovoltaic installation [28].

Japan is a world leader in the race to build zero emissions cars, and has recently dominated the World Solar Challenge held in the Australian desert since 1987. Honda also is in the lead in the automotive race to mass market a fuel-cell car by 2003. The world's first semi-automated fuel-cell assembly line was established by Fuji Electric [29].

Japan is way out in front in the commercial application of fuel-cell technology. Tokyo Electric Power has installed fuel cells that provide heat in hospitals, hotels, office buildings and other commercial facilities.

In the pursuit of oilless automotive technologies Japanese industry tends to lead. During the Kyoto Conference on global warming Toyota surprised the world with the delivery to its showrooms of the world's first hybrid electric car, the Prius. It has twice the fuel economy and half the CO_2 emissions of conventional cars. Its marketing as a green sedan helped

Prius sell so quickly in Japan that Toyota had to open a second assembly plant. Nissan is a world leader in electric cars, a move helped by an arrangement with Japanese municipal governments to provide a market for such clean vehicles.

Nowhere else in the high income, "developed" world do citizens tend to own fewer cars, and use them less than in Japan. Its 3.5 persons per car represents fewer cars per person than other industrialized countries with comparable incomes per capita.

Japan's car restraint is encouraged by a number of public policies. One element is gasoline taxes three times the level of those in the United States. Another is requiring car owners to pay $2,000 for registration every two years. Japan tends to avoid the construction of urban expressways, while heavily subsidizing rail transit [30].

In Japan, pedestrian travel is the dominant mode of transportation. Although only five percent of trips in the US are taken on foot some 50 percent of Japanese trips are taken the pedestrian way. Bicycling is also very popular. From 1975 to 1987, there was an increase from a half million to three million parked bikes in railway stations. This has subsequently grown to 3.5 million. Japan's cycling boom has caused it to develop the world's most elaborate bicycle parking storage facilities, featuring automated cranes [31].

Japan has the world's strongest organic agriculture movement. Some 16 percent of Japan's consumers, about double the norm elsewhere in industrialized nations, eat certified organic food. This has been assisted by a strong green matrix of health food stores, community-shared agriculture networks and co-operatives.

Japan's organic agriculture movement is consciously based on assisting the transition to an oilless society. This vision was articulated by Tsuchida Takashi in 1973. Takashi put forward the concept of an oilless world in founding the influential environmental group, the Society for Reflection on the Throwaway Age. It stresses that an oil-based civilization cannot endure [32].

THE SPREADING OF GREEN DEMOCRACY FROM ITS JAPANESE HAVEN

Environmentalism has been a critical factor in spreading democracy. The Environmental Diet of 1970 helped spark an exodus of polluting industries from Japan, especially to South Korea and Taiwan. However, the days of pollution zones surrounding Japan were numbered.

Japanese environmentalists were important in encouraging successful democracy movements in several Asian countries. Their actions in solidarity with persecuted environmental groups helped to expand the scope of civil society in South Korea, Taiwan, and the Philippines. Green-minded Japanese lawyers played an important role in the triumph of freedom by providing *pro-bono* work for persecuted environmentalists in other countries.

Environmentalists in Japan made strategic alliances with their counterparts, frequently from similar middle-to-lower-class backgrounds, in a number of Asian countries. This was helped greatly by the buying power of many green-minded Japanese consumers.

During the last years of the Marcos dictatorship, strong links were forged with farmers' organizations in the Philippines that were in conflict with major multinational corporations favoured by the regime in power. A Japanese food co-operative having a million members in 1986 contracted with farmers in Negros Island to purchase organic bananas free of oil-based chemical pesticides. By producing for environmentally concerned Japanese consumers the organic farmers were able to obtain three times the market price they would be paid by multinational corporations indifferent to the effects of synthetic pesticides.

Environmentalists throughout East Asia have been the vanguard of freedom. This tendency was seen recently after the election of South Korea's champion of democracy, President Kim Dae Jung. Following his inauguration, one of his first acts on March 9, 1998, was to lift court orders that had barred 52 Korean environmentalists from engaging in political activity. Among those freed were 17 activists who had opposed the ocean dumping of sewage [33].

Choi Yul is a leading Korean environmentalist, typical of the heroic visionaries around the world who are building a democratic peace. In the 1970s he spent four years in prison for daring to criticize the dictatorship of President Park Chung Hee. During his time in prison, Choi read about civil disobedience and environmental protection. Today in free Korea he is leader of the Federation of Environmental Protection, a national organization with 44,000 dues-paying members [34].

Taiwan's environmental movement used quite militant, although nonviolent, tactics to foster the island's democratization. Freedom was finally achieved at the same time that its environmental movement peaked in 1988-89 when the island averaged one antipollution demonstration per day. This caused the repeal in 1989 of repressive martial law legislation used to restrict independent organizations.

Originally sparked in the early 1980s to protect wilderness areas and scenic sites, Taiwan's environmental movement soon clashed with the polluting impacts of oil technologies. One early victory was the defeat of a proposed highway through a scenic wilderness. By 1986, Taiwan's greens were challenging petrochemical plants. Fishermen occupied 18 factories in the Linyuan Petrochemical zone because of their pollution, thus shutting them down until management agreed to demands for clean-up and compensation. Stronger environmental regulations from democratization caused some polluting factories to relocate in Communist China [35].

With only a decade of liberty to influence public policy Taiwan's environmental movement has already made on impact on national priorities. One is in curbing motorization. The lessons learned regarding the environmental cost of cars has meant that motorization is absent from Taiwan's future economic strategy. It has become the first nation to make the electronic highway the alternative to huge investments in road infrastructure.

Taiwan's economic strategy is quite appropriate to long-term planning to become a green banker of China's democratic reunification. Avoiding wasteful expenditures on motorization, Taiwan's foreign exchange surplus continues to increase despite the surrounding Asian crisis.

Taiwan is the only Asian state to have copied California's pioneering requirements about the development of zero emission vehicles. By the year 2000 two percent of its scooters must be emission free. Taiwan has targeted electric bikes as one of its six leading growth industries. The bicycles allow cyclists to achieve speeds of 15 miles per hour without pedalling. Much higher speeds are possible if pedalling and battery power are combined. This greener technology has the potential to eliminate gas-powered scooters and mopeds. It can make the sustainable democratic egalitarianism of a car-free world appear less archaic.

CHINA'S DEMOCRACY MOVEMENT: KEY TO A DEMOCRATIC PEACE

Sixty years ago Nationalist and Communist China had many similarities in their ideologies. While Communist China's democratization was arrested in 1989, liberty triumphed in Taiwan at the same time. China's democracy movement, although set back by the events of 1989, is still moving forward.

Before the 1989 crackdown China was moving in the direction of gradual democratization in the style of Eco-Glasnost in the Soviet Union. This green democratic ideology came quite close to winning over market Stalinism.

In many regards conditions for democratization were more favourable in China than in the Soviet Union in 1989. Unlike the USSR, China was no longer saddled with the collective farm system, having abolished it in 1979. Chinese decollectivization was made easier because the country did not have a highly subsidized petroleum-based agriculture, but one powered by draft animals. Its own version of Eco-Glasnost could have moved ahead without being disrupted by hunger and shortages.

After three years of severe repression in China a democratic opening was achieved in 1993 when authorities permitted the creation of the Friends of Nature. At the time it was the only legally registered environmental group. It has since assisted the growth of similar local organizations. One such recently formed ecological crusader is the Saunders' Gull Protection Committee, formed to protect the endangered Saunders' Gull, of which only 3,000 survive. One of its objectives is to protect this threatened species' coastal habitat from petroleum development [36].

With many now experiencing 10 years of a difficult struggle for freedom, China's democratic leadership has become more subtle and gradual in its tactics. The course it is adopting in many ways resembles the "self-limiting" objectives of the Polish Committee of Social Resistance that gave birth to the powerful Solidarity trade union movement. The Chinese democracy movement has become increasingly focused on environmental issues such as pollution and traffic chaos, concerns that are shared by more liberal leaning figures in the ruling party leadership [37].

Despite the aggressive pursuit of the creation of Chinese giant oil companies and auto manufacturing, there are powerful voices working towards making China another falling domino in the green march of freedom throughout Asia. Solar power has advanced especially in isolated rural areas outside electrical grids such as Inner Mongolia. The Chinese authorities who are permitting a new Eco-Glasnost are quite aware of how it became the basis for democratization in both the USSR and Mongolia. The latter's version of democratization is encouraging the example of freedom for the Chinese leadership. It was remarkably smooth, without violence or outbreaks of separatism. The country benefited from a situation wherein traditional agriculture was not uprooted through heavily subsidized collectivization [38].

One of the benefits of the democratization of China, if it occurs, could be the ensuing peaceful reunification with Taiwan. The united nation would provide a green basis for the investment of Taiwan's great surplus of foreign currency reserves. It would close another pollution zone. The end to the absurd race in military spending between China and Taiwan could finance solar roofs on every home in Asia [39].

One paradox in the handover of Hong Kong to China is that the power of its civil society and democratic movement has increased because it coincided with a growing environmental movement stimulated by massive and growing public protests against air pollution. Very much like Communism in Eastern Europe in the twilight of the Cold War, dictatorship in China is being undermined by green activism.

British colonial rule and pollution have long been linked in Hong Kong. During the British colonial era in 1996 the transport representative in the unelected Legislative Council was able to defeat a government proposal for banning highly polluting diesel fuels which belch out smoke.

However, Hong Kong's last minute transition to democracy did bring about the long delayed development of air pollution indexes, showing that Hong Kong has the most polluted air in the world. New records in global pollution have been reached frequently since the 1998 handover to Communist China.

Photochemical smog is now so severe in Hong Kong that visibility is often reduced to a few hundred yards. Surgical masks to filter out diesel particulates have become normal in highly polluted districts. Hong Kong's government now admits that air pollution accounts for at least 2,000 premature deaths annually.

Democratic civil society has exploded as a result of Hong Kong's growing air pollution crisis. Some estimates maintain that five percent of the city's population, a vigilant army of 250,000 people, have become members of local environmental groups such as Clean the Air, Friends of the Earth Hong Kong, and Green Power. Protests over air pollution have sparked the biggest public demonstrations in a decade. In November 1998, some 30,000 school children signed a petition demanding more action to curb pollution [40].

How Democratic Law Enforcement Can Solve Asian Environmental Threats

Growing democracy in Asia, based on the greening power of a government kept relatively honest by the informed pressures of civil society, is the only solution to its serious environmental problems. The powerful in repressive countries promote polluting machines such as scooters, motorcycles, and automobiles in an irresponsible way without any effective government regulation. This can only be challenged by the pressure of aware voters and a free press on both political leaders and civil servants.

The oligarchy of pollution is seen most vividly today in Communist China. Here cyclists are harassed by police to get out of the way of cars that would not meet the most primitive safety tests in the free world. Only people power can stop this kind of oppression, which is backed both by the Communist state and by the powerful international oil industries, as vividly witnessed by BP's bailout of the Petro-China Corporation.

There are countless examples of green people power in Asia's new democracies. Some of the most significant involve the imposition of rudimentary inspection and maintenance programs on car owners in Taiwan, Thailand and the Philippines.

In the Philippines democracy has been remarkably effective in protecting the pedestrian majority from the fumes of the powerful. In 1993 the country began an Auto Anti-Smoke-Belching Campaign. After six months of public education about the health hazards of air pollution and the need to reduce auto emissions, the program moved into the tougher mode of regulatory enforcement. Hundreds of vehicles were tested every day, with the result that 65 percent failed the tests. Owners of the failed vehicles were fined and had their licenses and registrations revoked until a second test determined that their cars were clean enough to be driven. This initial program was later strengthened by regular impromptu road inspections [41].

The magnitude of environmental challenges in Asia often seems formidable but so is the potential of a green and democratic peace. This is not understood by hawkish prophets who predict war over oil but ignore green and democratic trends that diminish oil's importance.

NOTES

1. Steven Kaye and Jack Egan, "China's new threat to the world economy", *US News and World Report*, August 17, 1998, p.24.

2. Charles S. Lee, "Collision Course", *Far Eastern Economic Review*, 9 April, 1998, pp.52, 53; Rodney Tasker, Murray Hiebert, John McBeth, Riogoberto Tiglao, "No One's Driving", *Far Eastern Economic Review*, October 30, 1997, pp.48-51.

3. Mark Landler, "Hong Kong Stocks Fall on China Debts", *New York Times*, January 12, 1999.

4. Jeasine Larsen, "Crude Investment: The Case of the Yadana Pipeline in Burma", Vol. *Bulletin of Concerned Asian Scholars*, **30**, No. 3. (1998) pp.3-13.

5. "US Study Reveals Unocal's Lies", *Earth Island Journal*, Winter/Spring, 1999, p.18.

6. Josef Silverstein, "East Asia: A Year of Uneven Progress", in "Freedom House Survey Team, Freedom in the World, 1997-98"(New York: Freedom House, 1998) pp.44-54, 168-172; Pamela Wellner, "Pipeline Killing Field", *The Ecologist*, September/October, 1994, pp.189-193; William Thomas, "Scorched Earth" (Gabriola Island: New Society, 1995) pp.11, 12; "Myanmar of Massachusetts", *Earth Island Journal*, Summer 1999, p.8.

7. S. Jayasankaran, Margot Cohen, Ben Dolyen, Shim Jane Hoon and Julian Baum, "Thorns in the Flesh", *Far Eastern Economic Review*, May 7, 1998, p.15.

8. Freedom House Survey Team, "Freedom in the World, 1997-1998" (New York: Freedom House, 1998) pp.282-284; "Unrest in Indonesia", 1998, *World Watch*, May/June, 1998, pp.17, 18.

9. "Unrest in Indonesia", *loc. cit.*, p.16.

10. "Tree-Fund Blazed", *Earth Island Journal*, Fall 1998, p.13; S. Jayasankaran, "Saviour Complex", *Far Eastern Economic Review*, August 12, 1999, pp.10-13.

11. Freedom House Survey Team, *loc. cit.*, pp.539-542; James Mittelman, "Globalization and Environmental Resistance", *Third World Quarterly*, **19**, No.5, pp.847-872.

12. Richard Rubinstein, "The Age of Triage" (New York: W.W. Norton, 1989) *passim*.

13. Kent Calder, "Pacific Defense", (New York: 1995) *passim*; Nate Thayer and Charles Bickers, "Market Misfire", *Far Eastern Economic Review*, February 5, 1998, pp.22, 23.

14. Wolfgang Zuckerman, "End of the Road" (Post Mills: Lutterworth Press, 1992) pp.203-205; Garry Rodan, "Singapore: state-society relations" in Garry Rodan ed. "Political Oppositions in Industrializing Asia" (London: Routledge, 1995) pp.106-110; Cerano, *loc. cit.*, pp.80-100.

15. Peter Freund and George Martin, "The Ecology of the Automobile" (Montreal: Black Rose Books, 1993) p.70.

16. V. Setty Pendakur, "Urban Transit in ASEAN" (Singapore: Institute of South East Asia Studies, 1984) p.13.

17. S. Jayasankaran, "Mahathir Bends", *Far Eastern Economic Review*, February 18, 1999, p.23.

18. S. Jayasankaran, "Smoke in Your Eyes", *Far Eastern Economic Review*, August 14, 1997, p.20.

19. Helen Ross and Anuchat Poungsomelee, "Environmental and Social Impact of Urbanization in Bangkok" in Jonathan Rigg, edited, "Counting the Costs: Economic Growth and Environmental Change in Thailand" (Singapore: Institute of Southeast Asia Studies, 1985) pp.131-154.

20. Pendakur, *loc. cit.*, pp.22-45.

21. Vaclav Smil, "China's Environmental Crisis" (London: M.E. Sharpe, 1993) pp.180-187.

22. Kim Woodward, "Development of China's Petroleum Industry" in Fereidun Fesharki and David Fridley ed. "China's Petroleum Industry in the International Context" (Boulder: Westview Press, 1986) pp.93-128.

23. Jan Wong, "Did tanks really roll over the students in Tiananmen Square" *The Globe and Mail*, June 2, 1999, pp.A1, A16.

24. Robert Schaeffer, "Power to the People" (New York: Westview Press, 1997) p.154.

25. Jonathan Mantle, "Car Wars" (New York: Arcade, 1995), p.210.

26. Gordon Laird, "China's Captive Market Falls in Love with the Car", *Transmission*, Winter, 1995-96, pp.24-26.

27. David Suzuki and Keib Oiwa, "The Japan We Never Knew" (Toronto: Stoddart, 1996) pp.200-220.

28. Curtis Moore and Alan Miller, "Green Gold" (Boston: Beacon Press, 1994) pp.39-58.

29. "Sol on Wheels", *Earth Island Quarterly*, Fall 1998, p.13; Madanjeet Singh, "The Timeless Energy of the Sun", (San Francisco, Sierra Club, 1998) p.182; Christopher Flavin and Nicholas Lenssen, "Power Surge" (New York: W.W. Norton. 1994) pp.102, 208.

30. Freund and Martin, *loc. cit.*, p.16.

31. Jane Holtz Katz, "Asphalt Nation" (New York: Crown Publishers, 1997) pp.128-130, 318, 319; Pryor Dodge, "The Bicycle" (New York: Flammarion, 1995) p.189.

32. Philip Conford, "A Future for the Land" (Bideford: Resurgence Books, 1992) pp.139-150.

33. "Ecological Amnesty", *Earth Island Journal*, Fall, 1998, p.13; Mittelman, *loc. cit.*, p.865.

34. Jayasankaran, Cohen, Dolven, Hoon and Baum, *loc. cit.*, p.15.

35. Walden Bello and Stephanie Rosenfeld, "Dragons in Distress" (San Francisco: Institute for Food and Development, 1990) pp.195-214.

36. Jayasankaran, Cohen, Dolven, Hoon and Baum, *loc. cit.*, p.12.

37. "Ten Years On", *The Economist*, June 5, 1999, pp.41, 42.

38. Trish Saywell, "Power to the People", *Far Eastern Economic Review*, January 29, 1998, p.36.

39. The arms race is estimated to cost China $34 billion annually and Taiwan $12.6 billion.

40. Maureen Pao and Alkman Granitsas, "Fragrant Harbour?", *Far Eastern Economic Review*, March 11, 1999, pp.38-40.

41. World Resources Institute, "World Resources" (New York: Oxford University Press, 1996) pp. 98, 129.

CHAPTER TEN
Mighty Mainland Oil Power versus Tiny Island Democracy

There is a basic conflict between small, largely democratic islands and big oil-rich dictatorships. Despite their numerous differences, the overwhelmingly democratic small-island nations are united in facing a common danger to their future survival. Failure to stop increased levels of oil consumption will compel their citizens to become stateless refugees.

Island democracies take issues of the environment more seriously than dictatorships do. They depend heavily on tourist dollars, which require sparkling waters and clean beaches. Apart from war and terrorism, nothing chases tourists away faster than an oil slick.

Environmental damage impacts rapidly on island environments, especially fragile coral reefs. Coral countries are only two metres above the sea level. Their drinking wells can easily become poisoned by infusions of salt water. Severe ecological degradation in the past has many times resulted in the human abandonment of coral built islands.

Ecodisaster Already Facing Coral Islands

Tales of islands being inundated by future melting of polar ice caps may sound to some readers like science fiction. Unfortunately this drama is real, even if poorly reported outside of Oceania.

Ecocidal disaster and the preparation of contingency plans for evacuation are increasingly the stuff of daily life in small islands states. In March 1996, during an international meeting on climate change, this reality was brought home by a newspaper clipping circulated to delegates. It reported a disaster in the Carteret archipelago, a chain of islands within the Solomon Islands state. All these islands, where 1,700 people live, had been recently inundated by a tidal wave. The disaster was not isolated, but was the worst incident caused by water rising steadily since 1991. The government of the Solomon Islands is preparing to evacuate the residents of the Carterets and hopes to move them to higher islands within five years [1].

The struggle of small island nations to survive in the face of climate change has a background with the epic character of the clash of freedom versus totalitarianism. With only one exception all the island states threatened by rising tides are to some degree democratic. The states that would benefit the most from the continued oil consumption are dictatorships.

THE MALDIVES: THE ONLY DICTATORSHIP ON CORAL REEFS

The Maldives, an 800-km string of 1,900 islands off the west coast of India, is the only coral island state that is currently ranked as not free by Freedom House. Despite religious ties that should bind it to oil-producing authoritarian Sunni Muslim states, the Maldives does not share their positions on global warming.

The threat of flooding causes the Maldives to challenge fellow Sunni Muslim dictatorships that have an interest in oil consumption. The main airport at Hulule would be flooded regularly at high tide if the sea rises by only half a metre. In contrast to most small island states without oil, the Maldives lacks a strong civil society and democratic culture. Little encouragement was given to democratization during the long period of British colonial rule, which ended in 1965. Since the end of its 815 years of absolute monarchy in 1968, the Maldives' republican era has been marked by numerous efforts at military coups [2].

With its weak civil society the Maldives lacks national parks and protected areas. There has been widespread destruction of coral reefs for new tourist resort islands, causing siltation and die-off. An increase in speed boating has also facilitated reef destruction [3].

DEMOCRACY AND ISLANDS GO WELL TOGETHER

The repressive Maldives is exceptional since resource-poor island states are largely democratic. The relative success of many free island states provides a contrast to the frequent failure of many oil-rich, mainland dictatorships to provide for basic health care, nutrition, clean water and education.

The island states of the Caribbean British Commonwealth escaped the authoritarianism of their mainland neighbours in Latin America during the 1960s and 1970s. The obsessive national security doctrines that twisted the minds of army officers in Central and South America, never had much impact in Jamaica. South of the US border, only the Commonwealth states and petroleum-free Costa Rica escaped from dictatorship continuously after 1950 [4].

In Africa freedom has also done much better on the surrounding island states than on the mainland. The free island republics lack the oil, diamonds and heavy metals associated with dictatorship and mercenaries who plague much of the continent. Stable African island democracies include Sao Tomé and Principe, Cabo Verde and Mauritius. While mainland successor states to Portugal's African empire have been plagued by war and dictatorship, its two island republics have done much better. They lack oil and mineral resources, and depend on fishing and agriculture. There is a growing environmental movement on Sao Tomé, led by the Society of the Friends of Nature.

MAURITIUS: SURPRISING GREEN DEMOCRATIC SUCCESS STORY IN THE INDIAN OCEAN

The former British colony of Mauritius in the Indian Ocean is a post-colonial African success story. It is a country of 1,100,000 people on an island of 1860 square kilometres (km²).

Mauritius is typical of how stable low-income democracies have been able to achieve high standards of human development. It has a low, three percent unemployment rate. Its 80 percent literacy rate is the best in Africa. Its annual rate of population increase is 1.8 percent, half of the overall African rate.

Six percent of Mauritius' land base is designated as protected nature reserves and these are expanding. Smaller adjacent islands that are part of the state of Mauritius, are the scene of intensive efforts at ecological restoration. This involves the removal of exotic plants and animals not native to the area. Mangrove forests are also being restored [5].

Clean water is one of the magnets of Mauritius for tourists. The island's business community, aware of the economic importance of its ecological wonders, plays a major role in restoration efforts. Mauritius has numerous environmental groups and environmental education is stressed in schools. A free press and television also send out a strong environmental message [6].

SEYCHELLES: BEAUTY PAGEANTS AND ECOLOGICAL RESTORATION

The Seychelles is another Indian ocean success story that has become a pioneer in ecological restoration. Although more famous for its Miss World Beauty pageants, which have revived its formerly stagnant economy, the Seychelles is also focused on restoring the splendours of the natural world. It has the world's most draconian car restrictions with only 12 vehicles being currently permitted for a population of 75,000.

The Seychelles has the world's largest coral atoll, which is protected as a national park. Its extensive protected areas have management plans, and a well trained staff of park rangers. Also, three nongovernmental organizations are quite active in environmental protection. The Royal Society for Nature Conservation and the International Council for Bird Preservation protect and restore the fragile ecosystems of entire islands. The Seychelles Island Foundation has undertaken research on how to reverse the ecological degradation of coral reefs. It has succeeded in attracting wildlife to formerly abandoned islands [7].

COMBINING PEACE, FREEDOM AND ENVIRONMENTAL PROTECTION

The ranks of resource-poor, low-income but democratic, island ministates include Cabo Verde, Kiribati, Vanuatu, Tuvalu, Mauritius, the Solomon Islands, Western Samoa, the Marshall Islands, Micronesia, and Palau. All have been able to protect a broad range of civil liberties and political rights for their citizens. Their success in safeguarding fundamental freedoms illustrates that although poverty and other economic factors can contribute to war and dictatorship, wealth is not a prerequisite for freedom [8].

The mini-island democracies benefit from their very lack of oil and other mineral wealth. None of the free island democracies, with the exception of Trinidad & Tobago, have any commercially significant oil reserves. Nor is Trinidad & Tobago a producer on a scale comparable to any oil dictatorship. Its parliamentary democracy has contributed to the wise use of Trinidad's modest oil income. Decision making in this transparent, accountable democracy has encouraged placing much of the profit from oil wealth in stable, well managed, foreign securities. Almost all island democracies have been blessed with freedom from oil. In many such states the horse and cart is the main mode of travel.

How Democracy is Delayed by Oil and Resource Riches

Some potential island states with oil or mineral wealth remain in colonial relationships because of it. The Netherlands Antilles is an oil-soaked relic of empire, with its origins in piracy and the slave trade. Here fragile coral reefs have been devastated by oil spills and pollution from the giant Aruba petroleum refinery. Such pollution can cause massive coral deaths near oil refineries [9].

Nickel-rich French-controlled New Caledonia is another mineral-rich relic of European imperialism. It suffered from serious outbreaks of violence in the 1980s during an anticolonial struggle. New Caledonia has 40 percent of the world's nickel deposits and one of the highest rates of lung cancer, asthma and childhood leukemia [9].

Conflict over mineral wealth is the main reason an otherwise successful island semidemocracy, Papua New Guinea, is rated as only partially free. Disastrous violence erupted in Bougainville, from protests against the environmental impacts of mining, such as the sea dumping of 80,000 tons of rock and tailings. Over 100 deaths have been linked to toxic emissions of lead and zinc from mining [10].

The Fragility of Coral in the Face of Oil

Coral reefs are the rainforests of the oceans, being the source of the greatest diversity of life in the seas. Although living corals cover only 900,000 km^2, they host one out of four species to be found in the oceans. The rich biota produced at these ocean oases provide food for 40 million people. This abundance is the foundation for human cultures that have lived sustainably with their environment for thousands of years.

Close to 1,000 reef-building corals exist in diverse forms ranging from mushrooms to wrinkled brains constructed through secretions of the living coral polyps. Their reefs grow slowly in shallow seas at no more than half an inch annually.

The ecological requirements that nurture coral reefs are quite stringent. They involve numerous relationships of co-operation between species. These begin with plankton-feeding polyps, which sustain a great biodiversity in a nutrient poor environment. This delicate balance can easily be upset by radiation, sedimentation and pollution. Even dropping anchors can bring devastation.

The skeletons of the dead corals support the reefs that are built up annually by the living polyps. The mining of reefs in such fragile environments can bury living corals in muddy sediments. Mined reefs are also more vulnerable to inundation by storms. A tenth of the world's corals have been destroyed by pollution, overfishing, the development of coastlines, and direct mining of the coral itself. Another third of the surviving living reefs are seriously degraded.

One of the worst devastations of coral took place in the oil-rich dictatorship of Indonesia. Here only 10 percent of its coral reefs remain in pristine condition.

In Indonesia's dictatorship there were acts of environmental vandalism commonly prohibited elsewhere. Indonesia's corals suffer from the widespread use of explosives and poisons in fishing. This involves pouring cyanide and bleach directly onto coral reefs.

One happy consequence of democratization in the Philippines is that fishermen who once used poison are being retrained by the International Marinelife Alliance in the use of hand-carried nets.

The presence of ecologically fragile coral reefs has served as a successful deterrent to oil exploration in many parts of the free world. Oil exploration kills coral reefs, flushing toxic muds into the sea from bore holes. In the Philippines, during the Marcos dictatorship, such muds killed 90 percent of corals within 100 metres of an exploratory well. Democratic Australia and the United States have both banned oil exploration on their coral reefs [11].

ISLAND NATIONS' ROLE AS GREEN CRUSADERS

Island democracies in the South Pacific have a long history of combating pollution, which was tied in many instances to their quest for freedom from colonial rule. The South Pacific ministates, in alliance with the world environmental movement, notably Greenpeace, were successful in making the region a nuclear-free zone. French and US colonialism exploited the South Pacific as a nuclear testing ground. The end of nuclear testing in Oceania finally came in 1993, the result of the campaigns of democratic island states in the region, notably Vanuatu.

Vanuatu is a predominantly Melanesian archipelago in the South Pacific, home to 170,000 people. Its Earth-revering ancient spiritual traditions have been harnessed to the objectives of environmental preservation. Wildlife such as dugong, fish and turtles continue to be protected by customary taboos. Vanuatu also has a low population density of about four persons per km² in rural areas, which has helped keep its environment relatively undisturbed [12].

In its campaign against global warming, Vanuatu is now without its former antinuclear ally, New Zealand. New Zealand's fossil-fuel industries, notably coal, keep it aligned with its big oil-producing neighbour, Australia. They have the worst positions on global warming issues of any democratic states.

The South Pacific ministates have attempted to influence the largely indifferent public opinion in New Zealand. In November 1997 Tuvalu's Prime Minister, Bikenibeu Paeniu, told Radio New Zealand that without cuts in greenhouse gas emissions, sea levels would rise so high as to put the survival of his country at risk. Paeniu has traveled the world to confront the voters in democracies about the predictions of coastal destruction by global warming. During the first months of the Clinton administration, he toured the United States in support of its embattled efforts to increase fossil-fuel taxes. On this mission he developed a sister-city arrangement with Florida City [13].

THE SOUTH PACIFIC: AN OILLESS SEA OF DEMOCRATIC PEACE

The independent island states of the South Pacific are all full or partial democracies. This region, unlike the ecologically similar tropical Indian Ocean, is not blighted by exclusionary, fundamentalist religious creeds. Spiritual passion instead goes into reverential care for the environment. In the New Zealand Overseas Territory of Tokelau sacred tree planting overseen by a traditional council of elders is one of the principal aims of an annual conservation week [14].

The only armed conflicts arising from dictatorship in Oceania are stoked by mineral resources in Papua New Guinea and French New Caledonia. While these mineral-rich mountainous outcrops have war and repression, the more fragile coral reefs are outposts of freedom and peace.

Since independence, Fiji has experienced the most difficulty of all Pacific islands in making democracy work. Tonga is taking strong environmental initiatives in the preservation of wildlife, and in the establishment of protected areas. Pushed forward by a variety of citizen environmental activism and the reforms of democratic governments, the South Pacific is increasingly becoming a nuclear- and oil-free zone of democratic peace.

Oceania's Free States Threatened by Global Warming

Unfortunately, the Earth-revering and environment-protecting nations based on coral reefs in Oceania face fundamental threats to their survival. Scientists believe Tuvalu, a state of nine coral islands, is already being eroded by storms and is sinking into the Pacific. An atmospheric warming of between one and two degrees centigrade will cause polar ice caps to melt and water levels to rise. Today global warming is causing sea levels to rise faster than corals can keep pace through new growth. Oceans may rise as much as 1.5 metres in 70 years. Many coral atolls stand only about one metre above the highest tides and none stand higher than two metres.

Flooding by storms can result in long term damage to coral reefs. Fresh water pits become brackish with salt, and storm waves can sweep palms from the land.

Scientists predict that the states of Kiribati and Tuvalu and New Zealand's dependency of Tokelau will vanish below the sea in less than a century due to global warming. Threats to freshwater supplies, land loss and increased destruction by hurricanes threaten to soon make such islands uninhabitable [15].

Another ominous sign of global warming is a newly discovered phenomenon called coral bleaching. Branching corals, usually coloured in a variety of vibrant hues, turn white when sea temperatures rise. This phenomenon which, if not reversed by more stable temperatures, can eventually kill corals, has increased rapidly since the early 1980s. In the winter of 1982-3 vast areas of coral bleached in the eastern Pacific. Massive coral-reef death took place following bleaching in the Pacific coasts of Costa Rica, Panama and the Galapagos Islands. Major bleachings later were subsequently reported in Florida, Puerto Rico, Jamaica, the Gulf of California and the South Pacific. All followed increases in ocean temperatures, caused by changes of the El Niño current [16].

Coral bleaching was followed by more deadly diseases, such as "black band", and "white plague". Then, between January and August of 1997 came the mysterious "rapid wasting disease". It wiped out huge patches of coral in a 3,200-km swath from Mexico to the Caribbean. All over the world in 1997 reefs were struck by new diseases not recorded earlier. One new epidemic named "white pox" broke out off Key West, Florida [17].

While coral bleaching has been associated with warmer water because of its tendency to take place in even pristine nature reserves, the other plagues facing corals may have more complex, but sinister causes.

The greatest worry of scientists working on threats to corals is that global warming, pollution, and the use of toxic chemicals and explosives may be complementary. Their harm could involve synergistic effects that are not yet understood. This assumption would illustrate that a potent chemical cocktail of oil technology is proving to be a devil's brew. This vile concoction may be transforming one of the richest zones of life into a biologically impoverished sphere of death [18].

Western Samoa's Democratic Challenge to Oil Dictatorship

One of the leading islands to challenge the power of oil oligarchies is Western Samoa, which has a population of only 212,000. Its governing political movement, which is focused on global environmental threats to the island's future, is the Human Rights Protection Party.

Western Samoa's concerns about global warming were increased by devastating hurricanes in 1991 and 1992. These wiped out the country's copra and oil exports, which quickly depleted its foreign exchange reserves. The disaster made thousands homeless and entire villages were destroyed by four days of winds up to 300 km per hour and gigantic waves pounding the coast. Seven deaths were caused by the record-setting disaster, which resulted in $170 million in property damage [19].

Earth-revering Western Samoa has taken a number of environmental initiatives. It is a leader among Oceania's states in establishing natural parks and wildlife refuges. A lowland rainforest has been protected by a village through an agreement with an American conservation group. Its largest national park, O Le Pupu Pu'e, protects a great diversity of rare forest species [20].

The rainforests of Western Samoa are being recognized as a potential medicinal treasure house. Native shamans have identified 74 plants as having medicinal properties. The most dramatic potential comes from a tree that Samoans have traditionally used to combat hepatitis. It is now being studied by the US National Cancer Institute as a part of a combination therapy for AIDS. This promising research began after prostratin, a compound of its bark was isolated [21].

Western Samoa is used to making environmentally innovative responses to challenges posed by the petroleum industry. When it was hit by the OPEC price increase of 1973, the country promoted horse-drawn carts. It was found that for a year the cost of these carts came to only $65, about two days' truck rental. Horses and carts were found to have a lower investment cost, $570, versus $9,000. This green technology was a great blessing to the low income families of Western Samoa, since horses and carts made it easier to collect coconuts and process coir fibre [22].

Western Samoa's governing Human Rights Protection Party helped unify the South Pacific states around the curbing of greenhouse gas emissions. It spearheaded the Alliance of Small Island States (AOSIS) to encourage a dramatic reduction in fossil-fuel use. AOSIS calls for a 20 percent reduction in CO_2 emissions by industrialized nations from 1990 levels by the year 2005. This is much bolder than the targets set for industrialized states, even the oil-poor European Union.

AOSIS: A PACT FOR ENVIRONMENTAL SECURITY

In contrast to other international alliances, AOSIS was formed to counter an environmental threat. It was created because of the failure to follow through on the commitments to curb greenhouse gas emissions made at the June 1988 Toronto Conference on Global Warming representing 48 nations. The Toronto Conference advocated a 20 percent reduction by the year 2005. After this recommendation fell on deaf ears it became the basis for the formation of AOSIS. The primary tool advocated was a carbon tax. It would have been a powerful stimulus to energy conservation, while also making renewable technologies, such as wind and solar power, more cost competitive with fossil fuels [23].

With the failure of carbon taxes to be imposed by the deadlines anticipated in the Toronto Conference, the threatened democracies of the South Pacific began to act in concert. A crucial event was the 1988 South Pacific Forum, organized by coral atoll states most at risk from global warming. AOSIS was organized following this conference, and now represents 36 countries [24].

AOSIS has put forward simple, but effective and relatively painless solutions for reducing greenhouse gas emissions. In March 1996 it suggested that world automobile manufacturers should co-operate in developing more fuel-efficient vehicles. This suggestion, put forward at a meeting of the International Panel on Climate Change (IPCC), met with loud, dismissive and cynical laughter. Oil interests suggested that coral islands' survival problems could be solved by building concrete sea walls.

The experience of the dictatorial Maldives illustrates the folly of relying on sea walls for protection. A protective belt of living and expanding coral reefs, not dead concrete walls vulnerable to erosion, provide the best protection from the turbulence of the sea. They dissipate between 70 and 90 percent of a wave's energy upon impact. Corals also serve, like forests, as carbon sinks. Also, diverse reef organisms remove excess carbon dioxide from the atmosphere.

The dictatorial Maldives discovered the protective qualities of coral reefs in an unfortunate after-the-fact fashion. Land reclaimed for the expansion of its capital city used 905,000 cubic metres of dead coral stone taken from an adjacent reef. High waves during a tropical storm destroyed this breakwater [25].

Support for sea walls illustrates the cynical nature of oil-industry positions on global warming. Ignoring scientific reasoning, they are akin to ordering the waters of the sea to recede in response to royal commands of concrete barriers. The concrete blocks would be much more fragile than the volcano cones that the seas long ago washed away from the enduring coral atolls.

In contrast to the oil industry's cynicism, AOSIS' positions have been moderate and reasonable. It supports, for instance, tougher building codes and improved energy efficiency standards for home appliances. Unfortunately, the oil industry was able to have these modest proposals defeated at the IPCC. It claimed these restrictions were nonregulatory barriers to trade prohibited by the General Agreement on Tariffs and Trade (GATT) [26].

The simple measures advocated by AOSIS such as improving fuel and energy efficiencies are easy to implement. The main reason they have not been acted upon is the self-interest of the oil industry, and the largely dictatorial governments that benefit. Only an arrogance of power from the control of vast oil wealth allows for callous indifference to the threat of evacuation of 500,000 people who live on vulnerable coral islands. This danger includes loss of the treasury of the biological wealth of the past, which discards medicinal cures from thousands of unstudied plants.

While AOSIS' reasonable suggestions generated laughter in the past, they are now being taken more seriously. In the 1997 December Kyoto Conference, an impassioned speech by the President of Nauru, Kinza Clodumar, was critical to preventing deadlock. Dressed in a colourful robe in a sea of dark suits, Clodumar warned of "a terrifying, rising flood of biblical proportions", and called the destruction of small islands a crime against humanity. His moving appeal weakened opposition from the American delegation to reducing US greenhouse gas emissions [27].

Strange climatic events have underscored the warnings of Clodumar's prophetic message. In addition to increased frequency of hurricanes, new phenomena are emerging to threaten the world's threatened island democracies.

In the South Pacific state of Kiribati, two tidal surges rolled across the Tarawa Atoll in early 1997, although they came without rain or storm. Homes were swallowed up in unrelenting but unexplained tides in the stillness of the day, in a manner not recorded in the living memory of any of the threatened atoll's residents [28].

Informed residents of the world's free island states understand that the ratification of the Kyoto Treaty has essentially given them a race against time for the deep cuts needed in carbon emissions to prevent their destruction by global warming. This is why their freely elected leaders have been the first to ratify the Kyoto Protocol, which requires ratification by 55 countries to become legally binding. A year after the December 10, 1997 signing of the Protocol only three countries had ratified it. These are the threatened island democracies of Antigua & Barbuda, Fiji and Tuvalu [29].

NOTES

1. Paul Brown, "Global Warming, Can Civilization Survive?" (London: Blandford, 1996) p.214.

2. Sue Wells and Nick Hanna, "The Greenpeace Book of Coral Reefs" (New York: Sterling, 1992) p.57.

3. International Union for the Conservation of Nature (ICUN), "Protected Areas of the World" (Cambridge: ICUN, 1992) p.85.

4. E.H. Stephen and J.D. Stephens, "Jamaica", in J. Donnelly and R.E. Howard, eds. "International Handbook on Human Rights" (New York: 1988) *passim*.

5. ICUN, *loc. cit.*, pp.179-183.

6. F. Falloux and L.M. Talbot, "Crisis and Opportunity" (London: Clarendon Press, 1989) pp.70-75.

7. ICUN, *loc. cit.*, pp.241-248.

8. Freedom House Survey Team, "Freedom in the World, 1997-8" (New York: Freedom House, 1998) p.7.

9. Wells and Hanna, *loc. cit.*, p.85.

10. Marc Miller, "State of the Peoples: A Global Human Rights Report on Societies in Danger" (Boston: Beacon Press, 1993) p.7.

11. Anouk Ride, "The Dark Side of the Moon", *New Internationalist*, March 1988, p.8.

12. ICUN, *loc. cit.*, p.273.

13. Freedom House Survey Team, *loc. cit.*, pp.512, 513; Jeremy Leggett, "The Carbon Club" (London: Penguin, 1999) pp.130-133.

14. ICUN, *loc. cit.*, Volume One, p.238.

15. Wells and Hanna, *loc. cit.*, p.85; David Boubilet, "Coral Eden," *National Geographic*, Jan., 1999, pp.32-34.

16. Wells and Hanna, *loc. cit.*, pp.54-56.

17. Dick Russel, "Where the Land Meets the Sea", *E Magazine*, March/April, 1998, p.37.

18. Boubilet, *loc. cit.*, p.34.

19. Freedom House Survey Team, "Freedom in the World, 1994-5" (New York: Freedom House, 1995) pp.60-68; Leggett, *loc. cit.*, p. 72.

20. ICUN, Volume 1, *loc. cit.*, p.279.

21. Christopher Hallowell, "Rainforest Pharmacist", *Audubon*, January-February, 1999, pp.28, 29.

22. J.J. Barwell *et al.*, "Rural Transport in Developing Countries" (Boulder: Westview, 1985) pp.61-70.

23. Brown, *loc. cit.*, p.19.

24. *Ibid.*, pp.19, 20, 94.

25. Wells and Hanna, *loc. cit.*, p.20.

26. Ross Gelbspan, "The Heat is On" (New York: Addison-Wesley, 1997) pp.109-125.

27. Seth Dunn, "Can the North and South Get in Step?", *World Watch*, November/December, 1998, p.19.

28. Leggett, *loc. cit.*, p. 266.

29. "Green is Good", *Scientific American*, March, 1999, p. 39.

CHAPTER ELEVEN
THE RED VERSION OF THE
OIL TIME WARP AND ITS SUCCESSORS

The USSR became a superpower by living off its oil resources, a Red version of the luxurious petroauthoritarianism usually associated with Arab sheikdoms. Declining oil wealth tragically became the biggest obstacle to Mikhail Gorbachev's efforts to create a unified and democratic USSR.

Today's semidemocratic Russian and neighbouring Asian oil despotisms are still mired in low oil revenues. The successor states of the USSR are caught in an oil time warp. Here old green ways were destroyed while powerful interests in the coal, oil and nuclear-energy sectors forestalled the emergence of a renewable resource economy.

THE USSR'S ROLE AS AN OIL-SOAKED LENINIST IDEOLOGY

Lenin failed to grasp the essence of the state he inherited from the Russian czars, truncated as it was by the Treaty of Brest-Litovsk. The German militarists who imposed this Treaty failed likewise. While the Treaty shrank Russian territory dramatically, it allowed the new revolutionary state to keep its most crucial commodity — oil.

Lenin was familiar with war for the control of gold and diamonds from the writings of British anti-imperialists denouncing the Boer War. Russia's vast storehouse of such precious minerals, however, would be far less significant than its situation as the leading oil producer outside of the United States at the onset of the age of motorization. This would allow oil wealth to subsidize the economic follies of Leninist ideology, although at a terrible environmental price.

The hammer and sickle, a sign of solidarity between workers and peasants, also failed to show the source of Communist strength. A more appropriate symbol would have been a gushing oil well pouring crude into the Caspian Sea.

Soviet Communism was to turn the Caspian Sea into one of the most polluted areas in the world. Seepage from the oil wells at Baku contain mercury and other heavy metals including deadly radioactive material such as radium 226. In Baku Bay the hundreds of derricks that are still in use are severely corroded. The Bay is depleted of oxygen and is recognized as a dead zone [1].

THE USSR's ECOCIDAL FOLLY IN COMBINING NUCLEAR EXPLOSIONS AND OIL EXTRACTION

The lack of democracy in the USSR was critical to its disastrous ecocidal evolution. In the United States, hawkish scientists such as Edward Teller dreamed of using nuclear bombs for civil purposes, but were stopped by environmental protests. In the USSR there was no opportunity for critics of the powerful industrial establishments to express open dissent.

Underground nuclear explosions in the Soviet Union were applied as a recovery method in the Soviet petroleum industry. Such blasts were used to force oil to the surface in a wasteful manner, boosting immediate production at the expense of longer term total yields [2].

THE USSR's APPROACH TO OIL EXTRACTION

Another environmentally destructive method of increasing petroleum output, widely used in the USSR and its successor states, is to force oil rapidly to the surface by pumping in large amounts of water. One of the consequences of the use of this outdated technology is widespread groundwater contamination.

Often a two percent solution of hydrochloric acid is injected into the water. The resulting blend of oil, water, and hydrochloric acid corrodes oil pipelines. This shortens their life spans and contributes to disastrous leaks.

In 1995 a Russian parliamentary commission found that some five million tons of oil and gas, worth 72 billion rubles, escape into the environment every year through leaky, antiquated pipelines, and negligence. This wastage has been estimated as sufficient to cover Russia's current budget deficit [2].

Water and bombs were used in the USSR to lift oil to the surface as an alternative to manufacturing, or importing, modern state-of-the-art compressing equipment. In 1982, the water in the liquid mixture pumped upwards was only 38 percent. In 1989, two-thirds of the liquid brought to the surface was water [3].

The Soviet Bastion of War and Dictatorship Empowered by Oil

Oil wealth made it possible for the Soviets to prop up dictatorships through much of the 20th century. Critical was the alliance between oilless Germany and the USSR, which endured from Germany's defeat in World War I until its invasion of the Soviet Union in 1941.

Outside the Soviet Union, most of the world's oil supplies were controlled by the democratic Allied Powers which drafted the Versailles Treaty. Hitler's infamous pact with Stalin was occasioned by his need for access to Romanian oil supplies — which were largely exhausted in WWII. Without this agreement his efforts to use Romanian oil, essential for his war plans, would have failed.

After the Hitler-Stalin pact, Russian oil supplies became critical to the initial German war successes. Great Britain and France only avoided bombing Soviet oil facilities because it would have risked extending the war into neutral Turkey [4].

The Soviet role in the nuclear nightmare of the later Cold War was sustained by the USSR's great oil wealth. At its peak in 1985, the value of Soviet petroleum exports came to $30.2 billion. This amounted to 57.5 percent of its foreign exchange earnings [5]. Today the downsized nuclear-equipped Russian military and its ongoing research into weapons of mass destruction, including germ warfare, remains possible only because of exports of oil and natural gas.

Oil-Financed Collective Farming: Disastrous Ideological Consumption

The Soviet Union's collective farm system was ideological and was a grandiose effort at conspicuous consumption. Its waste and inefficiency gobbled up most of the USSR's oil-financed foreign currency reserves to pay for grain imports, production levels having remained below the figures achieved before the revolution. Efforts at collectivization under Stalin in the early 1930s resulted in the deaths of over five million people from starvation. After Stalin's death in 1953 the USSR experienced an economic boom from the new encouragement given to private plots. Tragically, however, this prosperity of peasant agriculture alarmed ideological extremists in the Kremlin and, in 1958, Nikita Kruschev launched a new campaign against family plots. This attempted to demonstrate the superiority of socialist agriculture through the heavy use of petrochemical inputs.

After 1958 a pattern emerged whereby Soviet oil profits and production held the Communist bloc together in spite of it being pulled apart by the waste of its collective farm system. In the USSR and every other Communist country but Poland, the size of family plots was substantially reduced. More state farms were created. On these superfarms private plots had smaller acreage. Large agrotowns were created on the biggest state farms. These housed agricultural workers in large apartment buildings and made no provisions for private farming. Farm workers frequently were bused to the fields. Farm families, even on collective farms that still permitted small plots, relied less on them for income. Private plots were less important since government subsidies increased wages and pensions.

Various forms of environmental damage were added to the economic problems of socialist farming. Hay production was slashed as corn soared in price. Massive erosion on fragile lands formerly used for pasture remained a chronic problem. At the time of the break-up of the USSR, it was losing a million hectares of arable land annually from erosion [6].

The application of synthetic agricultural chemicals was most catastrophic in the oil-rich Asian republics of the USSR. In the 1970s, these areas began intensive applications of petrochemical inputs for extensive cotton monoculture. Pesticide use here was so heavy in the 1980s that experts considered 90 percent of the applications to be wasted. The Asian republics experienced the most extreme prohibitions of private plots. Massive deforestation and tree cutting created the giant fields necessary for cotton monoculture.

Irrigation for cotton resulted in the draining of 44 percent of the surface of the Aral Sea. The former waters have become a toxic desert that now generates poisonous dust storms. A biological disaster threatens as a former island top secret research station in the Aral Sea may become linked to the mainland by the receding waters [7].

COLOSSAL WASTE INDUCED BY LACK OF METERING

Among the tragic consequences of the USSR's approach to energy was colossal waste induced by too low pricing and a lack of any metering or controls. When Gorbachev's reforms began to prod industries for energy accounting many managers refused. A legacy of Stalinism was an emphasis on production to the neglect of cost accounting.

Energy consumption in space heating and domestic hot water in the USSR was 50 percent higher than in OECD countries. This was caused by heat losses due to poor insulation, and the aforesaid absence of meters and heat controls. Half the apartments were constructed without any individual ability to regulate heating. No minimum performance standards were developed for the energy efficiency of consumer products.

Opportunities for the co-generation of electricity were missed despite the USSR's abundant natural gas and tracts of housing using district heating. Overheating frequently resulted from the use of open windows as heat ventors. This common open air venting makes insulation impractical. The situation persists in part because residential energy prices are too low to make metering economical [8].

FORMIDABLE BARRIERS TO GORBACHEV'S PLANS FOR DEMOCRATIC REFORM

Apart from authoritarian manipulations of ethnic nationalism, Mikhail Gorbachev's difficult path to democratic reform was strained by two intertwined economic factors — formidable oil power and the massive agricultural subsidies its wealth permitted.

Gorbachev did not have the easy solution to achieve an economic boom that was possible for other liberal Communist reformers. This escape mechanism stretched back all the way to the New Economic Program. It was applied in 1921, just three years after the Russian revolution. What China in 1979, and the USSR many times in its history, could do to get more food on the table was to decollectivize and raise prices paid to farmers.

In the USSR during Gorbachev's courageous period of remarkable green leadership the old way to prosperity was no longer possible. Massive subsidies to agriculture, permitted by the USSR's petroleum wealth, made the majority of farmers in collectives the biggest obstacles to decollectivization.

A long litany of reforms, which had worked well in the past before the distortions of subsidies, was tried. One was family work teams made responsible for the management of sections of collective farms on a leasehold basis. Opportunities to leave collective farms for private farms were provided. All these imaginative measures, and others that in the past resulted in massive expansions in yields, brought only marginal results. Many who tried to operate private farms with expensive machinery, such as tractors, went broke. For a time in the early 1990s, such failures exceeded new family farms.

Expanded family plots and miniprivate farms now only cover 20 percent of Russia's arable land. Most land in both Russia and the Ukraine is still under the control of state and collective farms. Elections in Russia in rural areas are dominated by the Communist-allied Agrarian Party. Its power reflects the economic self-interest of collective farm workers in perpetuating the oil-subsidized state system.

Gorbachev tried every skilful tool of past liberal-minded Communist reformers. Outdoing any of his predecessors, he turned for advice to the agricultural extension services of the western ecological movement. Close co-operation was developed with the Rodale Institute of the United States, which continues to publish a Russian language magazine on organic agriculture. The mechanized collective farms however, simply offered higher incomes, for shorter hours.

While oil wealth put agriculture into a subsidized, low productivity straitjacket, the USSR's oil revenues declined. Apart from production problems, a legacy of past Communist mismanagement, the fall in revenues was caused by the worldwide collapse in oil prices following the end of the OPEC oil boom.

Gorbachev's leadership had to endure a dramatic economic shock to the USSR's economy from falling oil wealth [Appendix I]. Lower prices led to a reduction in revenue from $30.2 billion in 1985 to $28.7 billion in 1989. An inability to boost output in response to lower prices was a legacy of past strategies which involved moving from one easily exploitable oil field to the next. Crude oil production in 1989 fell by nine percent from the peak experienced in 1987-88. These circumstances caused Gorbachev's last days as President of a disintegrating federation to be a time of one-third less petroleum revenue than he could command when he had been General-Secretary of the Communist Party [9].

Declining oil revenues continued to plague Russia after Gorbachev's fall. The USSR experienced a decline in oil production of 13 percent in 1993, and 11 percent in 1994 when for the first time since the break-up of the USSR the rate of decline had diminished. This was helped by western assistance in bringing idle wells back into production.

Today oil production has crashed to 46 percent below its 1994 level, and has caused Yeltsin's reformers to be blamed for declines in living conditions. Most of these problems were caused by past suboptimal technologies, failure to carry out proper well maintenance, poor oil reservoir management and declining crude prices [10].

Gorbachev could not use oil wealth to buy more imported goods and social peace. At the same time, agricultural subsidies funded by continued petroleum exports reduced decollectivization to a small-scale effort by essentially part-time private farmers.

THE CHALLENGE OF CURBING SUBSIDIES TO WASTE

Gorbachev bravely slashed energy subsidies amounting to $130 billion per annum, roughly 10 percent of the Soviet bloc's GNP. These subsidies had been used to hold down fuel prices below the levels of North America and Western Europe. Subsidies were also slashed for petrochemical fertilizers, resulting in consumption declines from 25 million tons in 1989 to 5 million by 1995 [11].

So great were the distortions produced by Communist era subsidies that the post-Soviet era in the former USSR and Eastern Europe has been one of the few bright spots in efforts to lower greenhouse gas emissions. Since reductions here have been deep and opportunities for further decreases in emissions so inexpensive, the former Soviet bloc is the favourite example of the advocates of emissions trading [12].

Unrestricted emissions trading would avoid the need for measures to curb emissions in industrialized countries. The greatest beneficiary would be the United States. It produces 36 percent of greenhouse gas emissions. Unrestricted trading would also encourage the perpetuation of luxury emissions of the developed world, ultimately based on the heavy use of private motorized transport.

The closing of factories in the former Communist bloc since 1990 resulted in a reduction of 830 megatonnes of greenhouse gas emissions annually. Largely by improving fuel efficiency in former Soviet-bloc vehicles an annual reduction of a further 169.5 megatonnes could be achieved.

The potential of cheap pollution control in the former Communist world has resulted in the formation of the JUSCANZ bloc. This is a consortium of Japan, the United States, Canada, Australia, Ukraine, Norway, Russia, and New Zealand. Many of these nations, notably Norway, Canada, Australia, New Zealand and the United States, have powerful fossil fuel industries. Although Japan's fossil-fuel industries are marginal it has already made relatively inexpensive investments needed to reduce greenhouse gas emissions. The Ukraine and Russia would benefit from massive investments of emissions trading to reduce their impacts on global warming. These are expected to be in the range of $10 to $20 billion dollars, indicative of the mammoth scale of action required.

JUSCANZ favours a situation whereby greenhouse gas emissions in advanced capitalist industrialized nations are allowed to continue with little change. They would be pleased to pay for relatively inexpensive methods to reduce pollution in the former Communist world. This strange paradox of achieving a painless way of stabilizing emissions while avoiding serious cuts illustrates the ecocidal legacy of Soviet Communism as well as the failure of North-American leaders to appreciate the full impact of climate change and the responses that will be needed [13].

A NEW BELT OF OIL DICTATORSHIPS

One of the most unfortunate consequences of the break-up of the USSR was the creation of a new belt of petrodictatorships in Asia, a region heavily dominated by oil technology. The break-up took place when it appeared that Russia through its Siberian fields had control over most of the USSR's petroleum resources. This situation soon changed after major discoveries were made in 1997 in the Caspian Sea region. Cheap oil here is now estimated to be sufficient to extend the world's current gas guzzling patterns for at least another decade.

Russian democrats did not favour a united USSR without the Ukraine since they feared the undemocratic influence of the Communist bosses of the petroleum rich, southern republics. While they did not initiate the break-up of the USSR, the Communist *nomenclatura* (self-appointing elite) of the oil-rich Asian republics benefited greatly by it. Gorbachev, whose position as chief of state of the Soviet Union ended with its destruction, had begun to undercut their power. He cancelled plans for a massive southward diversion of water from Siberian rivers flowing naturally to the Arctic Ocean. *Glasnost* also exposed the various ecocidal actions of Asian republics, such as the draining of the Aral Sea.

Gorbachev's encouragement for a green civil society clashed with the cotton, chemicals and oil priorities of the leaders of the southern Asian republics. His reforms to foster civil society had slight impact south of the mouth of the Volga. They failed to stimulate private agriculture and organic farming outside of Europe. Oil power in the former southern Asian republics of the USSR traded authoritarian versions of Marx for state approved versions of Islam, backed by pacts between Teheran and Moscow.

THE DEEPENING OF THE ECOCIDAL FOLLY
OF THE NEW PETRODICTATORSHIPS

Independence has served to intensify the oil-worshipping oligarchic petrophilia of the Asian republics. Most of its press has returned to the Stalinist-style propaganda, which features the lauding of government achievements. Unlike European Russia, there has been no growth of small scale, private organic agriculture. Agricultural production here crashed more severely than in the European successor states of the former USSR. Kazakhstan, the largest oil-rich Asian republic, has experienced a 68 percent decline in agricultural production [14].

The tendency to devote more acreage to vast petrochemical consuming cotton monocultures has increased in the new petrorepublics. Dried up streambeds have become a new source of cotton growing lands. Pastures continue to be rapidly converted to cotton at the expense of forests and livestock. Food supplies have fallen, causing meat shortages in major cities such as Tashkent.

The people of the despotic states of former Soviet Asia continue to experience some of the world's worst pollution-related illness. The Karkalpaks of Uzbekistan suffer from one of the world's highest infant mortality rates of 92 per 1,000 children. This disaster was created by the heavy use of pesticides [15].

Tragically, the drying of the Aral Sea has accelerated. Plans by environmentalists to save it by lining irrigation canals, thereby making more efficient use of irrigation water, have been rejected. It is obvious that the government of Uzbekistan is more interested in exploiting potential oil and gas than restoring the Aral's waters [16].

RUSSIAN-IRANIAN CO-OPERATION ENSURES AUTHORITARIAN STABILITY

A tyrannical but frequently disrupted stability has been achieved in the oil-rich southern republics by authoritarian power sharing between Russia and Iran. Violent armed Muslim extremists in this region are discouraged by Iran. It is concerned with the protection of the region's small Shiite minority against militant Sunni movements such as the Taliban. Iran shares Russia's and the ex-Communist elite's desire for rapid petroleum development. Russian-Iranian co-operation terminated the worst civil war of the post-USSR period in Tajikistan's Fergamma valley. The five years of turmoil resulted in 20,000 deaths. A peace accord was signed in Moscow on June 27, 1997. Fighting however, still continues although at a much reduced level of intensity, now largely restricted to political kidnappings and hostage taking [17].

THE ECONOMIC MESS OF
AUTHORITARIAN PETROLEUM-RICH TURKMENISTAN

The ex-Communist elite and Iran have co-operated in an authoritarian fashion in Turkmenistan. It has the worst human rights record of any successor state of the former USSR. Here all opposition parties are banned and most dissidents have fled. In keeping with Soviet-era methods, political prisoners are detained in psychiatric hospitals. In 1997, a correspondent from Radio Free Europe/Radio Liberty was detained for two weeks in retaliation for interviews broadcast with Turkmen opposition leaders living in exile in Moscow.

There have been no reforms of collective farming in Turkmenistan. Here small plots are not encouraged despite a shortage of basic foodstuffs. As in most dictatorships hunger has little impact on government priorities. The regime is constructing expensive Presidential palaces, a move typical of the Stalinist style of its President, Saparmurad Niyazov, former First Secretary of the Turkmen Communist party.

Despite its considerable petroleum wealth, Turkmenistan's education system is in complete collapse, with all secondary technical education institutions shut down.

Human rights abuses and deepening poverty in Turkmenistan have not generated international concern. Rather than being disciplined by IMF-style restructuring or conditional aid, Turkmenistan has experienced a flood of foreign investment. Iran has completed a rail link and is developing a gas pipeline. The European Union has constructed a container port on the Caspian Sea. Malaysia's national oil corporation, Petronas is seeking to move into the ranks of the Fortune 500 by its petroleum development here. It is developing a $10 billion scheme to export natural gas from Turkmenistan to Japan, a scheme involving close co-operation between Petronas, Exxon, the Mitsubishi Corporation of Japan, and China's state oil corporation [18].

The Speculative Oil Boom of the Southern Republics

The 1997 Caspian Sea oil boom, which might have been expected to sustain prosperity, was narrowly preceded by an economic collapse of several of the former Soviet states, and a similar economic downturn occurred in Russia only one year later. Discoveries in 1997, found that the Caspian Sea and Central Asia have commercial oil reserves of more than one hundred billion barrels. Powerful companies from Europe, Russia, the United States and China are planning $60 billion in investments. They compete for pipeline routes across the Taliban-dominated zones of Afghanistan [19].

The strange paradox of oil boom and economic collapse was most evident in the strongest new petrodictatorship of Central Asia, Kazakhstan, a republic of 16.4 million people. It is the size of India and stretches from the Caspian Sea to China. It is simultaneously experiencing a boom in petroleum development and deepening poverty.

Despite severe human rights violations, the World Bank in 1997 made Kazakhstan a $200 million loan. Police have broken up peaceful protests against growing hunger and privation [20].

Democracy Versus Oil Oligarchy in Russia

Russia's relative civil liberties, growing organic farming movement and small-business sector insulated it from some of the follies of the southern Asian republics. Still, the overall tendency was the same. Both experienced the paradox of an oil boom coupled with overall economic collapse. A fall in oil prices through its impact on the Russian ruble created the conditions for a sudden and catastrophic financial meltdown in the summer of 1998.

What has proved to be Russia's stabilizing safety net was encouraged by the reforms of Mikhail Gorbachev, based on the development of co-operatives, small business and an explosion of activity in private farming. Democratic stability has not been helped by the rigid privatization mantras of his successors. Privatization has proven especially disastrous in Russia's resource sector, its major source of foreign exchange.

Now former state managers of energy enterprises have greater power than during the reforming crusades of Gorbachev when their power was more accountable to political control and supervision. In the privatization process managers received a substantial share of the stock, making them more powerful than ever. They became much less accountable than is normal in any democratic capitalist economy [21].

EFFORTS BY OIL COMPANIES TO DOMINATE THE RUSSIAN MEDIA

While Gorbachev's *glasnost* encouraged exposés of environmental follies of the Soviet oil industry the mass media in Russia are now more tightly controlled by their managers. The media, and the now collapsed banking system, quickly became dominated by managers of energy corporations. A World Bank study of the Russian oil sector found that privatization of petroleum did not result in the hoped for creation of healthy competition but increased the power of the managerial group running the companies [22].

The oligarchic corruption and waste of oil revenues in Russia are epitomized by the lengths the managers of Russian petroleum corporations went to in order to increase their media domination. This is especially evident with the most powerful Russian corporation, Gazprom.

Gazprom is the semiprivatized successor to the former Soviet Natural Gas Ministry. It has been the most successful enterprise in Russia's democratic transition. Its supplies have continued through the country's considerable turmoil, increasing its credibility with western bankers. Gazprom is the only petroleum corporation in Russia to have retained a substantial capacity in research and development.

Gazprom controls Russia's major media outlets, including Russian State Television (ORT) and NVT, a Moscow TV station which broadcasts nationally. The largest privatized oil corporation is Luk-Oil which also has major media investments.

Russian banks helped facilitate the petroleum companies' control over the mass media. These were so ideologically driven that they were not good commercial investments. The old quip of Communist party bosses that when it comes to ideology no expense should be spared was carried over into the new market era by Russia's fossil-fuel tycoons. Costly efforts to obtain media monopolies consequently became a significant factor in the collapse of the Russian banking industry.

The zeal by which managers of petroleum companies pursued a strategy of media control was epitomized by their response to an article exposing the most revealing aspects of their political power. In April 1997 *Izvestia*, Russia's largest circulation national newspaper, claimed that then Prime Minister, Victor Chernomyrdin, had accumulated a fortune of $5 billion through his links with Gazprom. No libel action was taken to dispute the allegations; instead Luk Oil moved swiftly to obtain total ownership of *Izvestia*. With the help of Russia's soon-to-collapse banks it paid several times more for *Izvestia* than its commercial worth. This hostile takeover sparked a split in the newspaper. Outraged journalists who supported the crusading investigative reporters launched a new paper, *Noviye Izvestia* [23]. Eventually *Noviye Izvestia* was itself taken over by the oil baron Boris Berezovsky, Secretary of the Commonwealth of Independent States!

CORRUPT INFLUENCE OF OLIGARCHIC JOINT VENTURES

The power of Russia's petroleum magnates has been aided by the privatized companies' joint ventures with western business, creating great opportunities for corruption. Billions have found their way into Swiss bank accounts [24].

The amount of foreign money invested in Russia's private oil companies is quite large. One such joint venture is Polar Lights, which received $430 million from various US and European development banks. The European Bank of Reconstruction gave $80 million to help facilitate the purchase of shares in Komi Arctic Oil by Gulf Canada. In total about $800 million was invested in the Russian oil industry in the first years of Russia's independence. This was all in relatively small projects with rapid payout [25].

Privatization of the revenue-generating resource sector and requirements for western investment for joint ventures has contributed to Russia's crisis in public revenues. This has resulted in millions of civil servants being unpaid. While foreign exchange revenues in the past largely paid for the expenses of the Russian state these are now in the hands of the managers of the resource industry and their foreign partners.

One of the problems of the privatization of the Russian resource sector has been an increase in crime, resulting in the evasion of taxes and other revenues that would have otherwise brought greater oil revenues to the state. In 1992, the Department for Economic Crimes in the Russian Internal Affairs Ministry announced that the flow of unlicensed oil to Europe resulted annually in a $950 million loss to government revenues. Such private Russian crude sells for three to four dollars a ton below the official government price [26].

In 1993 privatization was accompanied by new tax advantages given to oil companies. These changes were heavily lobbied for by Mobil, Exxon, Shell, Elf and Phribro Energy. To obtain lower taxes they formed the umbrella of the Petroleum Advisory Committee. Following this pressure in October 1994, six major joint ventures were granted 100 percent relief on any export duties from oil exports for three years. This decree was signed by Chernomyrdin on October 11, 1994, but was not made public until it appeared in the western trade press [27].

Foreign companies have arranged for protection from decaying Russian oil pipelines through oil swap deals and allowing companies to be paid on the basis of oil production from wells, not actual deliveries. This removes incentives to worry about leaking pipelines. Highly profitable production was given to foreign companies while the Russian State maintained ownership of poorly maintained pipelines that need costly upgrading [28].

The disastrous combination of concessions to foreign oil companies and traditional secrecy was seen in the Komi Arctic Oil spill of 1994, the world's third largest. Russian authorities did not admit the pipelines were leaking until three months after the disaster began. Foreign corporations who were pumping the oil continued to be paid although most of the petroleum leaked out. The oil breached dams and flooded waste storage pits. Clean-up workers did not have access to modern equipment, but had to scrape waste oil into buckets [29].

After the Komi spill international pressure resulted in the disclosure of smaller scale disasters. One was a 450,000 ton spill in the Tyumen region of Siberia. It was also announced that spills under 10,000 tons were deemed too small to report [30].

CORROSION OF RUSSIAN DEMOCRACY BY OIL POWER

Russian environmentalists encounter great personal risk in their challenges to the oligarchy of oil. Some companies have hired assassins to reduce opposition to their projects. The Russian Green Party has reported the murder of 18 environmentalists [31].

The use of gangsters against environmentalists by petroleum companies illustrates why the powerful Russian mafias are tolerated by the country's powerful energy barons. A more adequately financed justice system that could afford, for instance, the postage to mail subpoenas, would place more demands on the resource sector to share its profits with the state. In contrast, the use of mafias to solve disputes between businesses empowers the wealthiest companies that can afford to pay them [32].

Large-scale new oil-exploration activities in Russia are sometimes carried on in a bizarre fashion, where the worlds of crime, high finance and international intrigue meet. Such antics would be impossible in a fully democratic state. One of the most recent examples of such intrigue, verging on the criminal, took place when Greenpeace on October 24, 1998, discovered a previously secret oil-drilling rig in the Pacific Ocean off the coast of the Sakhalin Peninsula. It had been exploring for oil for an entire year before being discovered by Greenpeace.

The mysterious oil-drilling platform uses a flag of convenience, that of Panama. Greenpeace believes the flag of Panama is used to disguise potential liability for a future oil spill. Greenpeace's exposé found that considerable environmental damage had already been done by the construction of the drilling platform. Dumping for its construction has impacted negatively on fish habitat. Some 40 km^2 of soil were removed from nearby land in the processes of its construction. The dumping of stone around the platform threatens the endangered grey whale [33].

Gazprom: Green Hope but Marred by the Style of Petro-Oligarchy

Gazprom's exports continue to increase in revenue. It now earns annually $7 billion in hard currency from gas exports to Europe [34]. Such exports provide Europe with a cheap way to reduce greenhouse gas emissions and close down nuclear power plants simultaneously.

Despite increased use of gas peculiar barriers still restrict Russian exports. One factor is the remaining heavy coal subsidies that delay the use of natural gas for electrical power generation. In 1990, these subsidies were close to $10 billion. They have fallen by about 10 percent but these small cuts sparked major demonstrations by coal miners [35]. Demarcation zones favour European gas producers. The volume of gas imports is also held down by a buying monopoly — a consortium led by Ruhrgas that purchases most of the presently imported Russian gas [36].

Russia's gas production, as environmentalists have shown, can be expanded by better pipeline maintenance and the ending of natural gas flaring. These methods would bring major environmental benefits while preventing the need for embarking on disruptive projects in the fragile wilderness. In West Siberia alone 10 million tons of soot are produced annually by gas flaring [37].

The most controversial new natural gas project involves a partnership between Gazprom and the American Amoco Corporation on the Yamal Peninsula. This is the homeland of the Nenets, a nomadic reindeer-herding people. The Nenets continue to use reindeer as draft animals for their sleighs and they depend on reindeer for clothes, tents, food and tools. Although similar struggles in Canada, Scandinavia and Alaska of subsistence caribou cultures in conflict with energy development have garnered widespread public sympathy, the Nenets' struggle is largely unknown. Their leader Hoodi Nudelit committed suicide in 1995, in despair at his difficulty in challenging Gazprom and Amoco.

Despite formidable challenges the Nenets have found democratic space in Russia to build alliances with environmentalists to challenge petroleum power. Shortly following Nudelit's suicide, publicized by environmentalists sympathetic to the Nenet's caribou culture, Gazprom and Amoco announced a five-to-ten year moratorium on further construction of the Yamal development. This will make the most environmentally damaging aspects of the project vulnerable to demands for its cancellation by a concerned global environmental movement [38].

Aware of the devastation to the fragile tundra and taiga of new oil development Russian and western environmentalists have opposed frontier projects. They note that close to half of Russia's caribou habitat has been rendered useless to herds by the combined effects of logging and oil development. Environmentalists have pointed to the potential riches below Russia's already producing oil fields if drilling operations were repaired and modernized. This has resulted in some western development loans. Russian oil managers give such conservation-orientated projects a lower priority than developing new fields [39].

RUSSIA'S FINANCIAL COLLAPSE DUE TO A CORRUPT OIL EMPIRE

The inability of the newly privatized energy corporations to pay dividends is illustrative of the pseudo-capitalism that was introduced into Russia. Here shareholder power pales in comparison to the strength of omnipotent managers.

Oil industry managers were more concerned with dominating the Russian media than rehabilitating oil fields and stopping the flaring of natural gas. Russia's stock market was dominated by shares in oil companies, amounting to 55 percent of the share value of all the firms traded on the exchange [40].

Oil provided the basis of the speculative stack of cards that came falling down as reduced prices resulted in a currency devaluation in the summer of 1998. This collapse was predicted in a scenario described by the American environmentalist and oil industry's analyst, Daniel Yergin, published in 1993. He wrote of the possibility of a Russian business panic in 2006. It would be based on a trough in export revenues caused by reduced oil prices that would expose the weakness and corruption of Russian capitalism. Although Yergin's timing was off, his prophecy of collapse throughout the entire financial services sector was otherwise quite accurate.

Yergin's predictions of Russian financial panic in 2006 were based on growing environmental concerns and technological changes such as the mass production of electric cars. While falling oil prices from the Asian collapse, rather than massive shifts toward green technology, caused the Russian meltdown, Yergin was prophetic in predicting a crash after the oil-induced speculative bubble broke [41].

Russia's Green and Democratic Hope

Russia's economic collapse was based on unrealizable revenue projections from oil development. Fortunately this disaster was offset by more favourable developments in other areas of the Russian economy.

In contrast to the dictatorship and semidemocracy that envelops most of the former USSR, the oilless Baltic states have more happily evolved as full democracies. Their relative success points to the sustainable direction that Gorbachev attempted to launch for the Soviet Union.

The unfortunate paradox of the Baltic states is that while they rejected Gorbachev's efforts to hold the Soviet Union together, their liberal political and economic ideals were similar to his own. It is this part of the Soviet Union where the ecologically orientated civil society he was encouraging received the greatest popular support. Eco-Glasnost became a powerful movement here. It saw massive protests against paper mills that pollute before it became overwhelmed by separatist agitation.

The Baltic states had several advantages in their democratic transitions. Collective farms were not established here until 1950. They were run, moreover, in a more ecologically sustainable fashion, using less petrochemical input than anywhere else in the USSR. Typical of the stubborn Baltic resistance to mechanization was the survival of draft horses. Here the Lithuanian heavy horse breed did not die out but was assisted by breeding efforts in state farms.

The Baltic states were pioneers in setting aside protected nature reserves and parks. Only here in the USSR were moves begun to embrace cycling as a transportation strategy. Pedestrian zones are common in the historic cores of cities. The Lithuanian city of Siauliai, a cultural centre and university town, launched the USSR's first comprehensive cycling program in 1979. It built bicycle paths and developed extensive parking facilities for them and successfully increased cycling. Western cyclists view the city as an eastern green haven where their environmental values are broadly shared [42].

Gorbachev's desire to keep the Baltic states in the USSR was motivated by a fear that independence would result in a domino effect that would shatter the Soviet Union. The representation of the Baltic states in a democratic USSR would also encourage support for his own ecological and democratic ideas. These were less welcomed especially by the politically active elements in the rest of the country.

While the Baltic states rejected Gorbachev's federalism they embraced his support for oilless farming. In Lithuania there is an organic Gaia agricultural movement, named to honour the Greek goddess of the Earth, Gaia. Estonia's biodynamic farming movement is organized around mystic Earth-reverencing principles quite alien to Marxist atheism. All the Baltic states give state support to oilless agriculture and have passed legislation for organic certification [43].

THE GROWING SUCCESS OF OILLESS ECOLOGICAL FARMING IN RUSSIA

Despite its limited impact, partial decollectivization has improved the efficiency of Russia's remaining collective farms. They tended to do better in the mass production of grain than in more labour-intensive farm tasks such the production of vegetables and caring for livestock. Intensive horticulture and animal husbandry are now largely performed on private plots and minifarms.

The 10 percent of Russia's land base that has been decollectivized is now mainly farmed by organic methods without the use of expensive machines. Fossil-fuelled machines such as tractors remain under the ownership of collective farms. Private farmers who buy tractors increase their risk of bankruptcy.

There is an ecologically favourable movement in Russia to bring back horse power, carried out in co-operation with western organic farmers. Russian ecologists have found that the traditional wooden horse plough leaves the soil in better condition than the erosion-inducing deep furrows created by Soviet style ploughs drawn by gigantic tractors.

The transition from tractors to horses has appeared in a 30-hectare factory complex that once made parts for nuclear submarines, a case of turning swords into modernized draft-horse equipment. The Draft Horse and Mule Association of the United States came to the aid of Russian farmers through its Russian Draft Horse Revitalization Project. It made draft horses more widely available on Russian farms by donating equipment of types that had vanished during the Communist mechanization craze [44].

Another surprising green revival is antique traditional Dutch-style windmills. Small-scale farmers favour these since larger state owned mills are too far away and are not suited to mill small amounts of grain [45].

Before becoming First Secretary of the Soviet Communist Party, Gorbachev as Minister of Agriculture attempted to boost private plots. These were constrained by bewildering regulations, making it difficult to wholesale a product. Also individual collective farm managers would sometimes take a hostile attitude towards small plots.

One novel Gorbachev reform was to require factories to make land available for workers who wanted to grow vegetables on subsistence plots. He also encouraged private plots by allowing small cottages next to them. Yeltsin's Russian reformers later recognized these plots as private property.

Private plots near collective farms now provide 40 percent of Russia's food, including most of the meat and a high proportion of its milk and eggs. Russia's greatest farming boom comes from subsistence farming by urban workers, now carried out on 30 million plots, covering two million hectares of land. Almost every town family in Russia has a vegetable plot. This pattern is found even in far northern towns on the Arctic Ocean, such as Murmansk and Archangel. Such plots on average produced 540 kilograms of vegetables and 250 kilograms of fruit yearly. At 1997 market prices, this yield is twice the size of an average pension. Production on subsistence plots accounts for 20 percent of family income. The figure is lower in the large, more affluent cities of Moscow and St. Petersburg and higher in provincial towns. Almost half the calories that urban dwellers receive outside big cities come from their own plots, which now account for 13 percent of Russia's food [46].

The diffusion of farming skills is a decade-long achievement that was encouraged by Gorbachev. One important measure was the development of a television program on how to carry out organic gardening on small plots. In 1970, only 20 percent of households in Moscow were engaged in urban agriculture; by 1995, this figure had leapt to 65 percent [47].

RUSSIA'S EMERGING GREEN ECONOMY

The strength of Russia's emerging green economy has prevented its financial collapse so far from becoming a time of starvation. The recent multiparty compromises following the Russian financial meltdown offer hope that Russia's maturing democracy is displaying more compromise and civility.

As in the rest of the world, the environmental movement in Russia is at the forefront of the country's democratization, frequently involving conflict with oil companies. In Russia's far east Sakhalin Island, environmentalists are being assisted by neighbouring green critics of the oil industry in Japan's Hokkaido Island only 65 km away. Benefiting from these contacts, fishermen in this region have called for a moratorium on offshore oil drilling, similar to what already exists in the United States.

Russian environmentalists were able to stop oil industry efforts to dismantle the Federal Agency for Sea Inspection, which monitors critical oil developments in the Russian Pacific. This was assisted by legal suits brought by public-interest law firms in Moscow [48].

RECENTLY INTENSIFIED PETROTYRANNY

One of the biggest setbacks for the momentum of the combined ecological, peace and democracy movements around the world was replacing Mikhail Gorbachev with Russian petrotyrants. This unfortunate rebirth of petrotryanny from Communism to capitalism was recently reinforced by the change in the Russian presidency from Boris Yeltsin to Vladimir Putin — who had been prime minister. This authoritarian former KGB agent reaped popular support by using a Russian budget surplus, brought about by a sudden windfall from higher oil prices, to launch a second war in Chechnya [Appendix I].

The renewed war adds to the number and already large proportion of armed conflicts that are disputes between petrotyrants. Following the late 1996 peace agreement a moderate government headed by President Aslan Maskhadov was elected in Chechnya with a strong majority. It defeated Islamic fundamentalists who sought further confrontation with Russia in their quest to create an empire in Central Asia in co-operation with Osama bin Laden and the Taliban.

Maskhadov's democratic government was undermined by Russia's oil oligarchy collaborating with Chechen Islamic extremists. An agreement between them and Russian oil czar Boris Berezovsky, an influential Yeltsin presidential adviser, permitted fundamentalists to make armed incursions into Dagestan villages, without opposition from Russian troops. Following the eruption of frontier violence Berezovsky's media later inflamed anti-Chechen hatred with nationalistic propaganda as the war began [49].

Putin's nationalist government has also severely persecuted environmental and human-rights groups. During his tenure as prime minister half of the Russian public organizations were denied requests for reregistration. This banning fell heavily on human rights and ecology groups. In the oil-industry dominated Russian mass media, this persecution is justified by depicting them as western paid intelligence agents.

Environmental groups concerned with global warming are singled out for especially severe persecution by Russian authorities. Foreign scientists working in co-operation with Russian environmentalists have frequently had their Global Positioning instruments seized for alleged espionage. Today Russian environmentalists' courage is similar to that shown by the dissidents in the Communist era who hammered out samizdat newsletters at the risk of being found by the hostile eye of the KGB.

Despite formidable challenges, Russia's human rights, peace and ecological movements continue their brave crusade to green, democratize and pacify their country. In many cases these actions are carried out by the same people who suffered imprisonment as Soviet dissidents, championed Gorbachev's *Glasnost* and resisted the failed Communist coup. In the Russian Duma their views are expressed by the Yabloko Party. It alone in parliament has opposed the recent war in Chechnya. Unfortunately Russia's three green parties receive support below the minimum five percent needed for Duma representation, but they continue important campaigns despite heavy persecution.

Russia's civil society bravely nurtures civility and struggles to protect the Earth as it grasps for more liberty in a semidemocratic state. Its gradual but real progress is highlighted by the work of the Gorbachev Foundation, which champions many environmental groups in conflict with the oil industry. It assisted the Sami in the Kola Peninsula, who are keeping petroleum development out of their newly mapped and protected reindeer-herding range [50].

The struggle for freedom in Russia is similar to that the world over. Democrats use civil liberties and people power to protect nature, while authoritarian elites with great oil wealth employ repression and militarism to enhance their well financed oil empires.

Although the silence of NATO countries towards the war in Chechnya, is usually explained in terms of Russia's military strength, this ignores how powerful oil companies in these democratic nations have close ties to petrotyrants. Economic interests with a stake in fossil-fuel development place a blanket of silence over Russian repression. Foreign plans for fossil-fuel investment in Russia are truly massive. They include loans for coal mining recently approved by the World Bank despite the need for a rapid shutdown of this industry to avert catastrophe from global warming. In total $120 billion in investment by foreign energy corporations is projected for Russia during the next two decades [51].

Despite their arrogance and power, Russia's *oilygarchs* are doomed by creative destruction within the capitalism that Marx mocked. The fantastic superfluity of investment in fossil fuels will never materialize because renewable energy technology is bound to get cheaper, being advanced by determined defenders of the Earth around the world. Russia's democratic champions of a green peace are pushing this visionary agenda forward in one of the world's most ideologically hostile and polluted environments.

NOTES

1. Mark Jacobson, "Big Oil Comes Back to Baku", *Natural History*, 3/99, pp.20-30.

2. Ellen Schmidt, "The World Bank and Russian Oil", *The Ecologist*, January/February, 1995, pp.23-31.

3. Murray Feshback and Alfred Friendly, "Ecocide in the USSR" (New York: Basic Books, 1992) p.137.

4. Geoffrey Kemp and Robert Harkavy, "Strategic Geography of the Middle East" (Washington: Carnegie Endowment for International Peace, 1997) pp.41-63.

5. Feshback and Friendly, *loc. cit.*, 4, p.136.

6. *Ibid.*, pp.57, 58.

7. *Ibid.*, pp.86-96.

8. International Energy Association, "Energy Policies of the Russian Federation" (Paris: OECD/IEA, 1995), pp.55-69, 249-256.

9. Feshback and Friendly, *loc. cit.*, p.136.

10. Dale Gray, "Reforming the Energy Sector in Transition Economies" (Washington: The World Bank, 1995) p.9.

11. Lester Brown, Michael Renner, Christopher Flavin, "Vital Signs, 1998" (New York: W.W. Norton, 1998) pp.44, 142.

12. Emissions' trading allows polluters to offset emissions by paying others to reduce theirs. The trading seeks to produce the most benefit to the environment for the least cost.

13. "Buenos Aires/COP4 report" *Environment News*, Fall, 1998, pp.17-19; Christopher Flavin, "Last Tango in Buenos Aires", November/December, 1998, p.15.

14. Zhores A. Medvedev, "The Agricultural Crisis and Land Reform in Russia", *Small Farmers Journal*, Fall, 1998, p.43.

15. David Smith, "Culture and Water", *Cultural Survival Quarterly*, Winter, 1992, pp.49-52.

16. Freedom House Survey Team, "Freedom in the World, 1997-98" (New York: Freedom House, 1998) p.53.

17. *Ibid.*, p.305.

18. *Ibid.*, pp.517, 518; Kemp and Harkavy, *loc. cit.*, p.151.

19. Christopher Flavin, "Oil and Gas Reach New Heights" in Renner and Flavin, *loc. cit.*, p.50.

20. Freedom House Survey Team, *loc. cit.*, pp.105-109.

21. Gray, *loc. cit.*, pp.36-46.

22. Schmidt, *loc. cit.*, p.24.

23. Otto Lastis, "Russia: Man on His Own" in Freedom House Survey Team, *loc. cit.*, pp.426-433.

24. Schmidt, *loc. cit.*, p.26.

25. Greenpeace International, "Black Ice: The Behaviour of Multinational Oil Companies in Russia", November, 1994, pp.4-7; Gray, *loc. cit.*, p.9.

26. Stephen Handelman, "Comrade Criminel: The Theft of the Second Russian Revolution" (London: Michael Joseph, 1994) pp.113, 114, 226.

27. Greenpeace International, *loc. cit.*, pp.8, 9.

28. *Ibid.*, p.9.

29. Greenpeace International, "Spring Thaw Reveals Full Extent of Russian Oil Disaster", 1995.

30. Greenpeace International, "Black Ice", *loc. cit.*, pp.2-3.

31. Schmidt, *loc., cit.*, p.26.

32. Otto Lastis, *loc. cit.*, pp.19-23.

33. "Greenpeace Exposes Sakhalin Drillers", *Earth Island Journal*, Winter/Spring, 1999, p.25.

34. Gray, *loc. cit.*, p.45.

35. Brown, Renner, Flavin, *loc. cit.*, pp.52, 142.

36. Gray, *loc. cit.*, p.83.

37. Feshback and Friendly, *loc. cit.*, p.138.

38. Bruce Forbes, "The End of the Earth", *Wild Earth*, Fall, 1999, pp.46-50.

39. Schmidt, *loc. cit.*, p.25.

40. Gray, *loc. cit.*, p.45.

41. Daniel Yergin and Thane Gustafson, "Russia 2010" (New York: Random House, 1997) pp.194, 195.

42. Marcie Lowe, "The Bicycle: Vehicle for a Small Planet" (Washington: World Watch, 1989) p.8.

43. Walter Goldstein, "Ecological Agricultural Survey", *Surviving Together*, Spring, 1993, pp.22, 23.

44. "The Teamster 2,000 Goes International", *Draft Horse Journal*, Summer, 1998, pp.132-135.

45. Medvedev, *loc. cit.*, p.41.

46. *Ibid.*, pp.42, 43.

47. United Nations Human Development Program, "Urban Agriculture", (New York: United Nations, 1997), p.55.

48. Gary Cook, "Oil in the Russian Pacific", *Earth Island Journal*, Fall 1999, pp. 25, 28.

49. Krimsky Val, "The War in Chechnya and the Situation in Russia" (Moscow: The Glasnost Foundation, December 1999) pp.1-7; "Russia's Election", *The Economist*, December 18, 1999, pp.19-21.

50. Daniel Gawthrop, "Vanishing Halo" (Toronto: Greystone Books, 1999) pp.170-172.

51. *Ibid.*, pp.71-75.

CHAPTER TWELVE
OIL, MILITARISM AND REPRESSION IN LATIN AMERICA

Latin America's most striking contrast is between countries with tendencies towards oil, militarism and dictatorship and those that foster peace, human rights and the protection of the environment. The key to achieving peace and democracy in Latin America is the avoidance of oil and narcotics. Most states attempt to co-operate to suppress the illegal drug trade but conflicts over oil are the most likely cause of interstate war.

Oil wealth increases the corruption and repression that allows violent organized crime to flourish. Luxury oil consumption is the starkest expression of inequality. Here the majority of families now alive will never be able to afford an automobile, motorcycle, or scooter. Nations in the region with the most effective democratic systems tend to import most of their oil.

LATIN AMERICA'S CLASHES BETWEEN STATES OVER OIL

The last full scale war between Latin American states was a conflict between dictatorships over oil. It took place in 1941 between Peru and Ecuador over the oil-rich region of the Oriente in western Amazonia. Fighting here flared up again in 1983 and 1993. The conflict was not resolved to the mutual satisfaction of both nations until a peace accord was signed on October 25, 1997.

For more than a half century the oil-rich Oriente was under martial law. This facilitated army harassment of native residents and their environmental allies.

After its defeat in the 1941 oil war, Ecuador refused to recognize the resulting boundaries. Successive governments, their views repeated in the school system, claimed Ecuador had been stripped of 200,000 km² of national territory. It engaged in military infiltrations over the border in an attempt to reopen the issue. In 1995, Ecuador's advances were defended with land mines and sophisticated military technologies.

The 1997 treaty was an important step in the spread of a democratic peace throughout Latin America. In exchange for abandoning its claim to most of the disputed oil-rich territory Ecuador was given some face-saving compensation. This included the one km^2 of the former Tiwinza battleground, the right to build port facilities on the Amazon and an additional 26 km^2 along the unmapped border. For the first time school texts in Ecuador reflect the border on the rest of the world's maps. The peace accord has contributed to major military defence reductions in Peru and Ecuador and has accelerated such trends throughout the region [1].

ANTIDEMOCRATIC OIL POWER AND
PROTESTANT FUNDAMENTALISM IN LATIN AMERICA

One of the reasons that Latin America has seen relatively few interstate wars is the region's dominant Catholic faith. This pacifying trend stretches back to the colonial era where conflicts between Portugal and Spain were avoided through papal mediation. A more militant creed however is Protestant fundamentalism. This trend was strong in many extremist political parties linked during the Cold War to death squads.

In the past Catholicism was blamed for the slowness in the spread of democracy in Latin America. Whatever validity these arguments had in the past, when Catholics were identified with corporatist authoritarian movements, they are rapidly fading.

Catholic-based Christian Democratic parties are one of the great bulwarks of democratic currents in Latin America. Apart from recent political changes toward despotism, Venezuela has since 1958 been a relative haven of democracy and civil peace despite its considerable oil wealth. One of the reasons for Venezuela's relative success was a strong Christian Democratic Party. Similar parties have also been important for the success of democracy in Chile and Costa Rica.

Catholic liberation theologies to the left of Christian Democracy were also critical to the eventual triumph of most democratic movements in Latin America. These have encouraged nonviolent base communities, who have fostered training in organic farming methods.

In contrast to the deepening identification of Catholicism with democracy in Latin America is the recurring authoritarianism associated with fundamentalist Protestantism. Unlike Catholicism which evolved in the region over four centuries, it has been newly imported from the United States, sometimes accomplished with the help of missionaries paid by oil companies.

US Protestant fundamentalism emerged between 1910 and 1920. Its advocates consciously called for a return to the "fundamentals", based on a literal reading of the Bible which involved attacks upon the evolutionary theories of Charles Darwin. Their crusades were heavily financed by several oil companies based in California and Texas, including Sun Oil (Sunoco), Placid Oil, Union Oil and Ayetec Oil. Their grants to American Christian churches and their overseas missions, pushed aggressively by Milton Stewart of Union Oil, favoured those espousing fundamentalist doctrine. Stewart also made major donations to Protestant churches, one in the amount of $1,750,000 in return for acceptance of the fundamentalist creed. The Stewart brothers, Milton and Lyman, unleashed the fundamentalist revolution between 1910 and 1915, by commissioning the publication of a 12-volume paperback series, *The Fundamentals*. These books were distributed by the Stewarts free of charge at a cost to themselves of one million dollars [2].

Protestant fundamentalism's introduction into militarized, repressive and oil-rich areas of Latin America had harmful consequences which were not experienced in oilless democratic countries. In Costa Rica, Protestant fundamentalism advanced on the basis of its ability to encourage the faithful to embrace a life of sobriety. In less democratic countries a wide variety of Protestant faiths became associated with state terror. Conversion often became a move by native communities, suspected by the authorities of being guerrillas, to escape death squad violence [3].

The American-sponsored fundamentalists' Latin-American beachhead was established deep in the Mexican rainforest of Chiapas in the 1930s. Then the Sumner Institute of Linguistics (SIL) was permitted to establish a training school for missionaries funded by Lyman Stewart's Church of the Open Door and several American petroleum corporations [4].

There was a close collaboration between oil companies, military dictatorships and Protestant fundamentalists in the ecocidal assault on the Amazonian rainforest. Oil spearheaded the assault on Amazonia since its potential riches justified costly road construction. Oil roads subsequently became the basis for less lucrative logging and cattle ranching. Missionary airstrips were used by oil companies, who employed loudspeakers from planes to scare natives away from the territories they wished to explore.

Initial contacts between American fundamentalists and the Huorani, an Amazonian nation in Ecuador's oil-rich Oriente, were financed by oil companies in the early 1950s. These conversion efforts were celebrated by mass Christian fundamentalist rallies in the United States. Texaco gave SIL an open chequebook to relocate the Huorani. After moving to an SIL mission almost all of the converts became infected with polio and sixteen subsequently died, while many were permanently injured.

Protestant fundamentalists and Catholic missionaries have very different visions for Ecuador's Oriente. American fundamentalist organizations backed by the allied oil and Bible belt of Oklahoma support continued oil development. This is opposed by Catholic missionaries of the Capuchin order who are struggling to keep oil companies out of the homeland of the remaining Tageri-Taromenga. These natives have resisted Christian conversion and European contact. They occupy 50,000 acres of pristine rainforest which the Capuchins and environmentalists are struggling to protect as an ethnic reserve. The Capuchins are also encouraging oilless organic agriculture among natives in the region [5].

Coming out of its Chiapas rainforest training centre the American fundamentalist religion spread across the border in Guatemala. After the CIA's imposition of a military coup in 1954, Guatemala was opened up to Protestant fundamentalists and US oil companies. The US-installed regime of General Castiolo Armas gave 20 oil companies, largely American, 40-year concessions involving subsoil rights to half of the country.

The displacement of one million people and the deaths of 100,000 from military terror between 1975 to 1990 were in large part ethnic cleansing for the oil industry. It was assisted by US Protestant missionaries. Their conversion efforts benefited from fortified strategic hamlets to which many exiled natives were relocated. Here their chapels became the focal point of the new communities replacing traditional Catholic shrines. Missionary efforts were encouraged by the US petroleum industry-funded Wycliffe Bible Translators.

The height of the Guatemala terror, in which approximately 10,000 people were killed, took place during the Presidency of Rios Montt, 1982-83. Montt was a Protestant fundamentalist trained in the United States. His "born again" conversion took place at Gospel Outreach Church, in Eureka, California. This church provided substantial funds and missionaries during the height of Montt's scorched-earth policies. Many of his key advisers were US fundamentalists who discouraged the counsel of the country's more moderate Catholic hierarchy.

Guatemala's strategic hamlets eliminated traditional organic farming methods based on ancient Mayan techniques of the symbiotic relations between corn, beans and squash. Instead methods dependent on the heavy use of synthetic inputs of petrochemicals were adopted.

Settlement in model villages took place after a few years in relocation camps where traditional agricultural skills were frequently forgotten. Native religious festivals that celebrated the three sisters were forbidden. A program called "Bullets and Beans" caused Mayan communities to become dependent on food provided by fundamentalist relief agencies.

Montt's regime massacred entire native villages. Crops were burned and domestic animals killed. Parts of the Guatemala Highlands considered to be strategic areas, such as along the route of the Pan-American Highway, had all their native communities "erased." Another strip was bulldozed five to 10 kilometres wide along the border with Mexico. In this "no man's land" everything was burned, with the help of phosphorous and napalm bombs. After villages were destroyed only soldiers were permitted to live in border areas. Massacres took place where native communities had opposed the seizure of their land for oil exploration and development. Many victimized nations, notably the Xil, had their lands granted to Guatemala's National Oil Company [6].

Although terror had existed before Montt's presidency his actions brought the worst terror in Guatemala's history. Over a hundred people were burned alive by army troops in a church. The first strategic hamlets were organized. For the first time identification with Protestants became a tool of survival for many native people. Montt imposed a state of siege and press censorship. He created "special tribunals" which were clandestine military courts where suspected subversives could be tried without lawyers and shot if found guilty.

While most of Guatemala's Protestant fundamentalists dismissed the criticism from human rights organizations, the country's Catholic Bishops accused the regime of genocide against Indians. An army coup against Montt on August 6, 1983, began Guatemala's painful and still uncompleted transition from civil war to democratic peace. It ended the previous regime's clash with the Catholic Church and began to allow more space for civil society. Democratic opposition grew in 1984 with the resurgence of labour unions and the formation of the Mutual Support Group, GAM, an organization of relatives of the disappeared.

One of the signs of growing strength of freedom in Guatemala was the ability of its civil society finally to defeat development schemes of the oil industry. This took place in 1989 at the same time as democracy and environmental movements triumphed in much of the world. Then Exxon was defeated in attempts to secure exploratory drilling in the rainforests surrounding Ceibal, one of the country's most prestigious archaeological sites.

The restoration of democracy received a further boost in 1993 when Guatemala's Congress removed Montt's stand-in president, Jorge Serrano, and replaced him with human-rights ombudsman, Leon Caripo, who launched successful UN-mediated peace talks [7].

OIL POWER AND THE CONTINUING PROBLEM OF SEMIDEMOCRACY

Oil wealth remains critical to the problem of semidemocracy in Guatemala and in a number of Latin American states. Only one full democratic state — Venezuela is an oil exporter. The other full democracies — Costa Rica, El Salvador, Honduras, Argentina, Chile, Uruguay and Panama — are all oil importers. The most durable democracy in the region is oilless Costa Rica. Here environmentalists recently routed an oil pipeline away from a threatened rainforest.

Most mainland Latin American states that are now rated as only partially free — Brazil, Ecuador, Guatemala, Ecuador, Colombia, Peru and Mexico — have significant oil reserves. All these countries have violent struggles between native communities and interests favouring oil development, involving horrendous human rights violations by private armies and death squads.

Throughout Latin America nations that have experienced the greatest success in eliminating poverty, protecting the environment and establishing democracy lack significant oil wealth. They achieve higher levels of human development and notably better results in public health and education. The power of the military, where it has not been abolished altogether as in Panama and Costa Rica, is gradually being reduced.

Increases in taxes have combined with higher family allowances, pensions and improved health and nutrition programs following democratization in oil-importing democracies. Three years after the restoration of democracy in Chile the purchasing power of families increased by 70 percent. Four years of freedom saw the percentage of people living in poverty fall from 46 percent to 28 percent. Chile's restored democracy recently abolished compulsory military service. It was the first Latin-American country to elect Green Party representatives to the national legislature and cabinet [8].

Oilless Costa Rica, Uruguay and Chile were Latin America's only relatively durable democracies for most of the 20th century. Their success in pioneering social welfare was based on taxation — not the less predictable revenues generated by oil wealth. Today fully democratic Chile, Costa Rica, Uruguay, Argentina and Panama have better Human Development Index (HDI) rankings than oil-rich Venezuela.

GREENING STRATEGIES IN DEMOCRATIC OILLESS FREE STATES

The oilless democracies of Latin America are developing impressive greening strategies to halt global warming. Costa Rica, Honduras, Nicaragua, Belize and Panama have become recognized as "emissions entrepreneurs". They are home to 17 projects that are already part of emissions trading schemes. One such venture by Panama is the reforestation of the Panama Canal's headwaters. In Honduras photovoltaic water purification was launched as part of a larger health clinic electrification project. By replacing kerosene lamps with photovoltaic lights a surprising reduction in carbon emissions has been achieved. Honduras is making increasing use of photovoltaics also for water pumping and communications for environmental conservation efforts.

Costa Rica has developed one of the world's most ambitious strategies of greenhouse gas reduction. By 2010, it plans to have all of its electricity produced by renewable power. Costa Rica has already imposed a 15 percent carbon tax on fossil fuels. A third of its revenues support tree planting by farmers. An emissions trading program has been developed to sell credits on the Chicago Board of Trade. Some 16 million tons of carbon credits have been certified by Costa Rica through nine projects for clean energy and forest protection. It will generate $300 million in government revenues by emissions trading to protect 1.25 million acres of tropical rainforest.

Argentina is another fully democratic Latin American country and a major oil importer advocating emissions trading. It is planning to spend $700 million for reforestation projects. Argentina's announcement that it would not delay action on global warming until industrial countries made reductions was widely hailed by environmental groups. It marked a clear break with past claims of developing countries that increased carbon emissions were needed for economic growth [9].

THE PARADOX OF OILLESS COSTA RICA AND OIL-RICH VENEZUELA

Costa Rica has done far better in terms of education, health care, social justice and a reduction in poverty than Venezuela. Democracy in oil-rich

Venezuela was only achieved after the country's future ruling social democratic political elite had spent a decade of exile in Costa Rica after being ousted from power in 1949 by a military coup. Here from 1949 to 1958, they analyzed how Venezuela's military dictatorship was supported by US oil companies. After their return to power following the restoration of democracy in 1958 this study fostered the creation of OPEC in 1960. As intended, OPEC did increase Venezuela's oil income. Still, despite huge oil windfalls, the restored social democrats would not be as successful as their former Costa Rican hosts.

Venezuela's President after the restoration of democracy in 1958, Romulo Belancourt, and his Oil Minister, Juan Pablo Perez Alfonso, were ultimately frustrated in their dreams by the forces of oil wealth they were seeking to tame for national development.

Belancourt had a stronger sense of the relationship between democracy and peace than any statesman of the 20th century. He undertook a courageous foreign policy to deny diplomatic recognition to any dictatorship in Latin America, at the considerable risk of assassination. Perez Alfonso had similar ideals nurtured by their long exile in the US and Costa Rica.

Greatly concerned with the environmental damage and waste caused by profligate use of petroleum resources, Perez Alfonso set about establishing OPEC, primarily for conservation purposes. He sought not only to increase oil prices, but to reduce the harmful environmental impacts from the waste and premature development of petroleum resources. He conceived OPEC as a globalized version of the Texas Railways Commission, a regulatory agency in the United States that stabilizes oil prices and cuts down the waste. Perez Alfonso lived long enough to regret his creation of OPEC, which can now be seen as empowering dictatorship.

Costa Rica and Venezuela are currently the only fully democratic Latin American states which did not descend into dictatorship during the US Republican administrations of Richard Nixon and Gerald Ford. Although both democracies are similarly durable, the Costa Rican is far more effective. In 1994, Venezuela's per capita income was $8,120. Costa Rica's was only $5, 919. Despite having lower per capita GNP Costa Rica outperformed Venezuela in terms of literacy, life expectancy, low infant mortality and the fraction of underweight children under the age of five. The difference in life expectancy is significant: Costa Rica's 76.6 years as against Venezuela's 72.1 [10].

Venezuela's huge oil wealth has been its military's means of justifying its existence. Costa Rica's military has been abolished. Venezuela's has attempted numerous coups. Much of Venezuela's oil wealth has been wasted in expensive schemes for tractorization, agricultural subsidies, steel mills, automotive manufacturing and petrochemicals. In contrast, Costa Rica has put a major investment into developing ecotourism and pharmaceuticals from rainforest plants [11].

OIL, POLLUTION AND REPRESSION IN MEXICO

Mexico's great oil wealth accounts for a third of its public revenues. Oil's abundance is one of the principal reasons for Mexico's inability to evolve into a full democracy that respects human rights.

Mexico City's air is actually dangerous to breathe. In 1987, it was discovered that nitrogen oxide and hydrocarbon levels in Mexico City are comparable to those found in New York City's Lincoln Tunnel. Infants are born with high levels of lead in their blood. The elderly and young are routinely hospitalized for laboured breathing. Lung cancer rates are growing and rising pollution levels have increased incidences of skin disease, heart attacks and mental retardation.

The power of Mexico's nationalized petroleum corporation, PEMEX, is behind a surprising variety of the country's air pollution ills. PEMEX provides high sulphur bus-oil fuel to the state electrical commission for use in power plants. Little electricity in Mexico is generated from the cleaner natural gas. Most natural gas is flared off causing considerable pollution. Low oil prices and government subsidies lead to overconsumption. Poorly formulated cooking gas supplied by PEMEX is a major source of smog [12].

Mexico's long-ruling Party of Revolutionary Institutions (PRI) sustained its rule primarily by fostering dependence on synthetic fertilizers in southern rural areas. Bag loads of such fertilizers were given away to PRI supporters prior to elections. Voters were warned that such inputs would be cut off should PRI lose at the polls. In many parts of rural Mexico farm families have forgotten how to grow subsistence crops such as corn without the aid of petrochemicals. The environmental harm of such products is increased by the use of many pesticides that are banned in the United States. Annually pesticide poisoning kills 5,000 people in Mexico. Heavy pesticide applications have been linked to rising cancer rates and contaminated human breast milk.

Oil development was a major factor in the outbreak of the Zapatista insurrection in Chiapas. Roads constructed by PEMEX were the major reason for the invasion of tropical rainforest by settlers. This sparked the land-use conflict which was at the heart of the insurgency [13].

AUTOTYRANNY IN BRAZIL

Brazil's increasingly automobile-based economy is an inherently fragile one. It is based on luxury goods that are not affordable by most Latin American families.

Brazil has now become the world's fourth largest automobile manufacturer but has not been able to rely on a stable market of domestic consumers who can afford to pay for motorized transport. An investment of $17 billion in Brazil was planned by Asian, European and North American automakers before the year 2000. This was rescued from meltdown by the IMF's last-minute bailout [14].

Despite the initial IMF bailout, Brazil's economy lurches from crisis to crisis. Its January 1999 devaluation caused a 10 percent drop in car company earnings. Ford was required to lay off 2,500 workers at its Sao Bernado Assembly plant [15].

Although the limited democracy in Brazil has brought major gains for native people, such as the creation of extractive reserves for rubber tappers, frontier violence endures. This has been encouraged by cuts in funding to protect the rights of native people, such as the demarcation of native reserves. Attempts to introduce motorization as the economic basis of an economy in a low-income nation is strategically doomed to failure, especially if any serious effort is made to reduce pollution.

OIL AND CIVIL WAR IN COLOMBIA

Oil has been an important reason behind the complex civil war in Colombia involving numerous parties. Its petroleum revenues finance Latin America's most repressive military regime. Cases involving police and military personnel are not tried in civilian courts.

Oil pipelines have been made a major target of armed guerrilla groups. During the first three months of 1997, 21 attempts were made to blow up the pipelines of Occidental Petroleum. The yearly average during the 1990s has been 45 attacks. Five Occidental employees were killed in 1997. Ten percent of its costs in the Cano field are for security.

Colombia's Cusina oil field has been the scene of some of the worst violence in Latin America in the 1990s. Here in 1991, a special unit of the Colombian army was established through oil company money. Known as the XVI brigade, it has murdered and tortured unarmed oil critics.

All 5,000 U'was in Colombia have threatened mass suicide because of oil activity in their homeland. Oil development threatens to pollute their sacred lakes. They have engaged in lengthy fasts as part of their campaign to be left alone.

Critical to the success of the U'wa in blocking oil development was a 1997 appeal to the Organization of American States, (OAS) in Washington. Following the appeal, the OAS' Inter-American Commission on Human Rights persuaded the Colombian government to lift Occidental's licence for oil exploration. The OAS produced a document stating that any oil development could only be permitted with the U'was' consent.

The U'wa campaign has strengthened Colombia's democratic civil society. It has a number of effective champions within the country, most notably the Colombian Committee for the U'was [16]. The U'wa have for eight years blocked oil development in their homeland, which spans the cloud forests and plains of northeast Colombia. They believe that drilling for oil is tantamount to sucking the lifeblood of Mother Earth. In August 1999, the U'wa won another victory by achieving the expansion of their reservation from 7,300 to 220,000 hectares.

The U'wa, however, have not yet succeeded in stopping oil development on another 200,000-hectare block just outside of their expanded reserve. On September 21, 1999, the Colombian government gave Occidental Petroleum, an American corporation associated with the environmental disaster of the Love Canal, drilling rights at a proposed test well a few miles outside the U'wa's reservation. Early in February 2000, armed only with clubs and bows and arrows, hundreds of U'wa blockaded a road where construction trucks were travelling to Occidental's drilling sites and were assaulted by 150 riot police who flew into the forest by helicopter. After the attack three children were reported dead from drowning in a fast flowing river [17]. The deaths of the three children created widespread popular outrage in Colombia against the oil industry. This facilitated the building of a stronger nonviolent blockade, which has so far successfully prevented the oil exploration. Thousands of *campesinos*, students, union members and native people from across Colombia have joined the U'wa in the successful defence of their lands from the petroleum industry. They have prevailed despite government attempts to stop shipments of food and medical supplies for the U'wa [18].

Despite considerable turmoil and violence, democracy in Colombia is being strengthened by a combination of international and domestic pressures. Only a few years ago, leaders of similar native anti-oil crusades would have been killed. In 1992, a leader of the Ingano nation of

Colombia was murdered while preparing for negotiations with government authorities over the environmental impact of petroleum development. At the time of his assassination, he was seeking compensation for his people's loss of their traditional lands [19].

The most recent profiles in outstanding courage for an oilless, democratic peace are those of three native Americans from the United States. They journeyed to Colombia to help the U'wa nation defend their homeland from petroleum development, and were recently executed on the orders of Leninist guerrillas. These terrorists not only attack democratic environmentalists, but frequently blow up oil pipelines, creating environmental havoc from massive spills. Terrence Frietas, of Oakland, California, Ingrid Washinawatok of the Menominee nation and Lahen'ena'e Gay of Hawaii died as part of the vanguard of freedom that seeks to heal the oil madness so threatening to the very atmosphere of the planet [20].

OIL AND FUJIMORI AUTHORITARIANISM IN PERU

One of the principal reasons for the international tolerance of the antidemocratic antics of Peru's President Alberto Fujimori is his government's subservience to multinational oil corporations. International protests over Peru's involvement with drug smuggling, its sabre rattling with Ecuador and the jailing of 200 prisoners of conscience, have been muted because of the alliance with oil power.

In 1996, some 169 kg of cocaine were found in the Peruvian presidential plane, while major deals were made with foreign corporations to gain access to seven million hectares of native lands in Peruvian Amazonia. No consent was obtained from the native residents [21].

During Fujimori's Presidency a massive wave of oil industry investment has entered Peru. His repression was praised by US strategic studies expert Samuel Huntington, who claimed, apparently without intending irony, that the President saved democracy by destroying it [22].

Fujimori's government has used the military with considerable ruthlessness against the Aguaruna and Huambisa nations. They oppose the invasion of their ancestral lands by the Edward Callan Interests and Halliburton Geophysical Services. These oil companies are both based in Houston, Texas.

In 1996, Peru signed an agreement with Shell to drill an oil well on the reservations of the Kugapakori and Nahua nations. Half the Nahua were killed as a result of Shell's explorations for oil in the 1980s through the accidental spread of germs. Peru's concession to Shell resulted in a $2.7 billion investment in Peru. It is the focus of Peru's industrialization and mining strategies [23].

The Fujimori presidency has eroded Peru's policies to protect nature, in favour of facilitating oil development. The most toxic impacts of what has been termed "Fuji shock" have been on the environment — worsening air pollution by lifting import controls on cars, while banning the creation of new national parks.

Peru's most significant ecological treasure is its Amazonian rainforest preserve of Manu National Park. It contains more biodiversity than any national park in the world. Its bird list contains almost 1,000 species. Two hundred mammals roam here, including jaguars, pumas, ocelots, giant anteaters and spectacled bears. One section of the park alone contains 90 species of frogs and toads.

Manu National Park is also a refuge to significant groups of uncontacted native people. The park is one of the closest areas on Earth to being a massive oil-free zone. Electricity in the office of its park ranger administration is supplied from solar power. Even its long contacted native communities continue to paddle canoes and hunt with bows and arrows.

While oil exploration is prohibited inside Manu National Park, its future as a treasure house of human and biological diversity is threatened by oil development just outside of its borders. Exxon-Mobil has been granted an oil concession to the north of the park, while Shell is drilling to the west. Shell has discovered natural gas and is in the process of constructing a pipeline to the Pacific coast. Manu National Park is threatened by a potential massive influx of native people displaced by oil development. If, as expected, close to a thousand ecological refugees flood the park because of the destruction caused by oil development, hunting and fishing pressures could bring about the loss of many of the reserve's rare species [24].

THE DISASTER OF OIL WEALTH IN ECUADOR

In Ecuador oil has been used to corrupt democracy and block social reforms. Although the country has strong native organizations increasingly allied with environmentalists, their efforts are blunted by the power of oil wealth. Since 1970, Ecuador has been heavily dependent on oil for its public revenues. It has now fallen behind both Cuba and the oilless democracies of Latin America in achieving basic literacy and public health targets.

The discovery of oil was used to block plans for a Costa Rican-style program of land reform advocated by Ecuador's native majority. Land instead would be provided in the tropical rainforest in the Amazon. At the end of 1993, Ecuador suffered from a foreign exchange crisis brought about by an oil-induced debt. It is still in a situation where oil revenues are eaten up by the costs of oil development, military spending and debt service. This debt is $12 billion, more than Ecuador's entire GNP [25].

The use of oil development as an alternative to land reform has been a disaster. In the colonized Napo province malnutrition problems are among the worst in Ecuador and are predicted to result in widespread mental retardation caused by deficiencies in protein, Vitamin A and riboflavin. Infant mortality here exceeds the national average. New towns such as Coca lack basic water and sanitation facilities. The region's population jumped from 40,000 to 400,000 owing to oil development. Despite the oil boom most people are worse off than when they were living in the Andean highlands [26].

Texaco's first well was drilled at Lago Agrio. This was the site of a village of the Tetete, now an extinct nation. Texaco's main Amazon refinery was constructed at Shushufindi in Cofan territory. This nation's population crashed in three decades from 30,000 to 300 because of hunger and disease.

Oil has had a devastating environmental impact in Ecuador. Here genocide and ecocide are inextricably linked. Acid rain has been caused by the flaring of natural gas. Much of the damage comes from the absence of periodic cut-off valves common in more expensively maintained pipelines in North America. Since Ecuador lacks any oil-spill response equipment crude will gush for days before the damaged line is abandoned. Some 16.8 million gallons of oil have been spilled. There have also been massive spills from smaller connecting pipelines, wells and tanks, and from breached waste pits. Texaco abandoned 1,000 waste pits, where over 20 billion gallons of contaminated wastes have been left. Sixty percent of the pits are now uncovered, with wastes washing into streams [27].

THE CURBING OF OIL POWER IN THE TROPICAL RAINFOREST

Efforts to stop oil development in Amazonia are consciously being linked to a vision of a world without oil. The images of devastation in an otherwise green paradise have given the most eloquent evidence of the costs of oil. Green ecotourism is encouraged as an alternative to oil for the rainforest.

One rainforest visionary is the nonconformist son of an SIL missionary, Randy Borman. This wilderness prophet of an oilless economy has married into a native nation and is now the leading Cofan chief.

The Cofan have secured a land base of 80,000 acres within the Cuyabeneo wildlife reserve for their subsistence economy. It has increasingly become an oil-free zone in Ecuador's Oriente. Under Borman's leadership the Cofan have destroyed oil equipment and taken videos of illegal exploration efforts. They have also employed solar power for electricity, giving their thatched homes a post-modern blue-white fluorescent glow.

The Cofan have embraced an environmental agenda with considerable passion. They are breeding endangered turtles. This restoration activity assists their ecotourism business, Transturi Tourism. It is a missionary endeavour to broaden public awareness of the harm of an oil economy [28].

The Cofan's struggles are part of an ongoing campaign to keep oil development out of new regions of the Oriente. Critical has been Yasuni National Park, a last refuge for a number of spectacular species, such as the Giant Otter. The Park's streams are used by fresh water dolphins. A refugia during the Pleistocene ice sheets, it is believed to have the greatest biodiversity on Earth. Native Huorani, foes of oil in Yasuni, were paid off by the government to become wardens in a national park where oil drilling is permitted. In 1995 they unexpectedly used this authority to destroy drilling rigs [29].

THE REVIVAL OF THE THREE SISTERS AND DEMOCRACY

The peace accords in Guatemala, El Salvador and Nicaragua all had provisions for the redistribution of land. Organic farming is being used to keep native farmers in control of their lands. This brings a higher price for their product while lowering input costs.

Low-cost farming with draft animals increasingly interests peasant political leadership. The Faribundo Marti Liberation Front, a former guerrilla group, has now become El Salvador's largest political party. It is encouraging organic agriculture as an alternative to life in a Macquiladora factory. Green transitions have helped many Mexican communities retain common land despite a Constitutional amendment which facilitated privatization of ejido, or communal lands. In Guatemala many natives remained true to their traditions by fleeing into the highland forest or into exile in Mexico. They survived bombing and deliberate forest fires and have returned with the coming of peace.

Many native communities throughout Latin America have been able to secure self-sufficiency in food while generating additional crops for markets. This was recently demonstrated in a study of an Indian community near Papantala, Veracruz. It rejected petrochemical fertilizers and the credits for their use. Subsistence vegetable farming is combined with the production of vanilla and livestock on small areas of pasture. Families are able to grow their own food. They earn cash by selling surplus corn, milk, meat, vanilla and some forest products on the market. These traditional native communities appear as diversified green islands in a sea of oil-soaked, chemical monoculture [30].

ORGANIC FARMING IN THE CITY

Another aspect of Latin America's democratization is an increase in oilless, organic farming in urban environments. In many countries this emerged out of earlier opposition by women's groups to the military dictatorships. It has provided a highly practical way to realize their dreams of democracy and provide a better life for their families.

As Latin America's longest established democracy Costa Rica remains a leader in urban agriculture. Some 60 percent of the land in the metropolitan area of its capital city, San José, is in urban agriculture. In Costa Rica the Women's Solar Collective Group also promotes the distribution of hundreds of highly efficient fuel-free cookers obtained at the cost of only five dollars each [31].

One of the blessings of the coming of democracy to Argentina has been the growth of urban agriculture. In Buenos Aires backyard gardeners can supply 10 to 30 percent of a nutritious diet. Such farmers supply 20 percent of the city's food. Here residents who take up backyard gardening eat 70 kg of vegetables for every 30 kg consumed by their nonfarming neighbours.

The coming of freedom to Argentina saw the creation in 1990 of Pro Huerta. It is a national agency that supports 500,000 part-time farming operations. Teaching organic techniques is part of its basic mission [32].

THE DEMOCRATIC LEFT BREAKS WITH MOTORIZATION

A growing tendency of the democratic left in Latin America has been to break with the past attitude that identifies increasing motorization with progress. Bicycles are growing in popularity in democratic Costa Rica and Argentina. Bicycles, affordable even in poor countries, provide an alternative to head loading (a practice that causes spinal damage to many who carry heavy loads in this way). Also there are alternatives to the luxury motor travel of a tiny elite in such countries. Providing for safe bicycling conditions has become a new source of class struggle in recently democratic Latin America.

One of Latin America's most distinguished social democratic political theorists is the novelist and historian Edwardo Galaneo. He has developed one of the most compelling critiques of motorization as a cruel form of luxury consumption.

Galaneo has demonstrated that automotive transport is now the primary cause of death among young people in Latin America. An advocate of bike lanes, he believes that the "great majority" of families in the western hemisphere south of the Rio Grande will never be able to afford to drive a car, although unsafe cycling conditions pressure many low income persons to pay a considerable part of their wages for bus fares.

The democratic left in Latin America is increasingly aware of how policies that promote cars and motorcycles favour an affluent minority. Raising transit subsidies was one of the first acts of the new municipal council of Uruguay's capital, Montevideo following the restoration of democracy [33].

Encouraging cycling has long been a feature of the Sandinistas of Nicaragua. Importing affordable bicycles remains a target of Sandinista development projects, in collaboration with aid organizations such as Tools for Peace.

One of the most remarkable signs of the restoration of democracy in Argentina was the promotion of cycling by Argentina's past president Carlos Menem. He had urged citizens to deal with rising gasoline prices by following his example and riding a bike. No more vivid contrast to the motorcade of a despot can be imagined than a cycling chief of state [34].

Environmentally motivated cyclists in Latin America have much in common with the brave Catholics in base communities who work peacefully for social change. Cycling clubs with a missionary environmental message have taken root even in automobile-dominated Mexico City. Here the *Movimento Bicicleto* campaigns for bike trails, pedestrian zones and combats the negative association of cycling with rural backwardness.

Despite Mexico City's association with the corrupting wealth of oil, social democratic and environmental breakthroughs are happening. The city became the first in Mexico to elect a social democratic government. This has brought an explosion of reforestation efforts and support for Catholic base communities and environmental groups [35].

CURITIBA'S EMERGENCE AS A CORE GREEN ALTERNATIVE

The Brazilian city of Curitiba, a metropolis of 1.5 million people, has widespread programs of urban agriculture, reforestation, extensive parks and ambitious recycling programs. Like most northern European cities its downtown district is an autofree pedestrian mall. A network of group homes are combined with recreation and youth employment activities. This has prevented the common blight of street children.

Like European social democratic cities Curitiba has benefited from the extensive municipal ownership of urban land. This has facilitated its impressive transit system, based on reserved bus lanes on roads. Its transit features subway style loading platforms that provide easy level access for the elderly and disabled. Such reforms have considerably curbed automotive use. Curitiba's creative promotion of transit has made it a centre of Brazil's bus manufacturing industry by attracting international investment.

Curitiba is one of the safest large Latin America cities in which to cycle. Before the 1980s prevailing perceptions of danger made cycling rare. To change attitudes the city created a 150-kilometre network of bicycle trails, many of them tree-lined through parks [36].

PROGRESS TOWARDS A GREEN AND DEMOCRATIC PEACE

Although the combined forces of oil power, religious fundamentalism, organized crime and militarism remain formidable in Latin America they are on the decline. The OAS is increasingly emerging as a champion of human rights and democracy. Strategic policies are largely unified through a hemispheric joint board of defence, modeled on the example of democratic cooperation between Canada and the United States. Latin America is now free of tyrants seeking global domination through the acquisition of weapons of mass destruction. The southern half of the western hemisphere is emerging as the world's largest nuclear free zone.

Outside of the oil-rich semidictatorships of Mexico and Colombia civil war in Latin America has been replaced by electoral competition at the ballot box. Although Cuba remains a dictatorship, it is showing increased signs of pluralism such as the growth of private and increasingly organic agriculture and the increased strength of the Catholic Church.

In spite of petrotyranny in Latin America the region is emerging as a champion of a democratic peace. The spread of pedestrian zones, organic farming and bicycle trails has been encouraged by an increasingly vibrant civil society. This movement towards an ethical, green politics provides encouraging signs that the future of the region will be on the lines of sustainable, voluntary simplicity.

The greening of Latin America will accelerate as the oil industry continues to decline and the limits of mass motorization become evident. Both the ethical politics of Christianity and the class-conscious analysis of the left are converging against the sin and oppression of motorization. Salvador Allende is being recognized as a regional martyr of a prophetic green and democratic peace who, in his time acted in the same heroic fashion of courageous statecraft as Petra Kelly, Yitzhak Rabin and Mahatma Gandhi in other corners of the planet.

NOTES

1. Nelson Manrique, "Perils of Nationalism: The Peru-Ecuador Conflict", *NACLA Report on the Americas*, January/February, 1999, pp.6-10.

2. Gerald Colby and Charlotte Dennett, "Thy Will be Done" (New York: Harper Collins, 1995), p.24; George Marsden, "Understanding Fundamentalism and Evangelism" (Grand Rapids: Will Erdmanns, 1991) pp.41-55.

3. Phillip Berryman "Stubborn Hope" (New York: Orbis Books, 1993) pp.145-169.

4. Colby and Dennett, *loc. cit.*, pp.63, 64.

5. Judith Kimmerling, "Petroleum Development in Amazonian Ecuador: Environmental and SocioCultural Impact" (Quito: National Resources Defense Council, 1989) *passim.*

6. Colby and Dennett, *loc. cit.*, pp.200-260, 815-821; Frank Lucia and Philip Wheaton, "Indian Guatemala: Path to Liberation" (Washington: EPICA Task Force, 1984) pp.70-85.

7. Freedom House Survey Team, "Freedom in the World, 1997-98" (New York: Freedom House, 1998) pp.260-263.

8. Phillip Vergara, "In Pursuit of Growth With Equity", *NACLA Report on the Americas*, May/June, 1996, pp.37-42.

9. Seth Dunn, "Can the North and South Get in Step?" *World Watch*, November/December, 1998, pp.21, 22; "Argentina Takes a Lead in Setting Goals on Greenhouse Gases", *New York Times*, November 12, 1999, p.A7; André Verano. Chad Nielsen and Phillip Covi, "PV Powers Rural Communities" *Solar Today*, May/ June, 1999, pp.30-33.

10. "From Deconsolidation to Re-equilibration Prospects for the Renewal of Democracy in Venezuela" in Jennifer McCoy, *et al.* eds., "Venezuelan Democracy Under Stress" (Miami: North South Center Press, 1995) p.265; Jahangir Amuzegar, "Oil Wealth: A Very Mixed Blessing", *Foreign Affairs*, 1983, pp.814-835; Alan Gelb and Associates, "Oil Windfalls: Blessing or Curse?" (Washington: Oxford University Press, 1988) pp.3-12.

11. Joel Simon, "Endangered Mexico" (San Francisco: Sierra Club Books, 1997) pp.80-90.

12. James Nation, "The Ecology of the Zapatista Revolt", *Cultural Survival Quarterly*, Spring, 1994, pp.31-33.

13. Seth Dunn, "Automobile Production Sets Record" in Lester Brown, Michael Renner and Christopher Flavin eds. "Vital Signs" (New York: W.W. Norton, 1998), p.85.

14. "Brazil's Woes Chill Some Profit Forecasts", *Wall Street Journal*, January 14, 1999.

15. Monica del Pilar Urbie Marin, translated by Peter Bunyard, "Occidental in U'wa Territory in Colombia", *The Ecologist*, Volume, 27, No.3, May/June, 1997; "Where Development will lead to Mass Suicide", *The Ecologist*, January/February, 1999, pp.42-46.

16. Adolfo Triana, "Ingano of Colombia" in Julian Berger et al. eds. "State of the Peoples" (Boston: Beacon Press, 1993) pp.245, 246.

17. "OXY Granted Drilling Rights", *Earth First*, November-December 1999, p.14; "Colombian Indians and Police Clash over Oil Company Site", *New York Times*, February 14, 2000, p.A13.

18. Patrick Reinsborough, "U'was Brutally Crushed at Gibraltar One then Re-occupy Drill Site", *Earth First*, March-April, 2000, pp.1, 24.

19. Derrick Jesen, "Lessons From Peru", *Earth Island Journal*, Summer, 1997, pp.40, 41.

20. "Activists murdered", *Earth Island Journal*, Summer, 1998, p.39.

21. Senator Al Graham, "Seeds of Freedom" (Cornwallis Park: Canadian Peacekeeping Press, 1996) pp.36, 37.

22. Jason Clay, "Looking Back To Go Forward: Predicting Human Rights Violations" in Julian Berger, ed. *loc. cit.*, p.79.

23. Chamine Oakley, "The Media Missed the Mark on Peru", *Earth Island Journal*, Summer, 1997, p.42.

24. John Terborgh, "Requiem For Nature" (Washington: Island Press, 1999) pp. 40-58.

25. Joe Kane, "Savages" (New York: Alfred A. Knopf, 1996), pp.111, 112; Gelb, *loc. cit.*, pp.170-195.

26. Judith Kimmerling, *loc. cit., passim.*

27. Glen Sitkes, "The People Versus Texaco", *NACLA Report on the Americas*, Sept./Oct. 1994, pp.7, 8.

28. Mike Tidewell, "Amazon Stranger", (New York: Lyons & Burford, 1996) *passim.*

29. Kane, *loc. cit.*, p.255. A refugia is an area that was spared from glaciation throughout the ice age.

30. Victor, M. Toledo, "The Ecology of Indian Campesinos", *Akwekon Journal*, Summer, 1994, pp.44-46.

31. Tracy C. Rembert, "Electric Currents", *E Magazine*, November/ December, 1997.

32. United Nations Development Program, "Urban Agriculture" (New York: United Nations, 1997) passim.

33. Peter Winn, "Frente Amplilo Montevideo", *NACLA Report on the Americas*, July/August, 1995, p.22.

34. Marcia Lowe, "The Bicycle: Vehicle for a Small Planet" (New York: World Watch, 1989) p.45.

35. Armando Roa Bejar, "Bike Activism in the World's Worst City for Cycling" in Robert Boivin and Jean-Francois Pronovost eds. "The Bicycle: Global Perspectives" (Montreal: Velo Quebec, 1992) pp.91, 92.

36. Bill McKibben, "Hope, Human and Wild" (St. Paul: Hungry Mind Press) 1995, pp.59-115.

CHAPTER THIRTEEN
Oil-free Europe as an Emerging Green Bastion of Liberty

The success of Europe's strong democratic political culture in making it a region of free states has been helped by its absence of oil wealth, which could have entrenched authoritarian rentier elites. The European Union is the most democratic multinational federation in the world. Its operations, monitored by a freely elected parliament, stand in sharp contrast to trade pacts such as the North American Free Trade Agreement (NAFTA) which lack accountability to an electorate protected by extensive civil liberties.

The OPEC oil hike of 1973 was paradoxically Europe's greatest blessing. It quickly destroyed the last vestiges of dictatorship west of the Iron Curtain and gave new life to green technologies such as cycling and windmills.

The production of North-Sea oil by Great Britain and Norway, which started only in the 1970s, is already declining. Future European oil prospects rely on more expensive deep-sea exploration, requiring huge and expensive drilling ships that can reach the sea bottom at the edge of the continental shelf. The techniques for doing this are untried and would likely be made possible only through massive government subsidy.

Europe's oil volume is small on a global scale. Norway, the continent's largest oil exporter, is increasingly politically isolated from its continental neighbours as its national oil company contributes to petroleum industry efforts to disprove human induced global warming.

Oil-Rich Norway — Odd Man Out of Europe

Norway's earlier hesitant rejection of membership in the European Union (EU) is further compounded by its preference for weak policies to curb global warming. Out of pure self-interest to sell more oil, it is part of the JUSCANZ group — Japan, United States, Canada, Australia,

Norway, New Zealand, Russia, Ukraine — and thereby opposes the EU's preference for substantial emissions cuts by 2010. Norway has also slashed public subsidies for solar power.

During the Gulf War its government received a sudden $3 billion infusion in revenues from a short-lived price hike. Early in 1999 it assisted OPEC in its renewed attempts to boost oil prices by lowering production. The previous, lower oil price was making Europe's rapidly declining reserves unprofitable to extract.

While Norway's oil has caused it to adopt opportunistic — unsound — policies on global warming, by being a full democracy it has managed to invest its petroleum wealth prudently. Norway has put its periodic oil windfalls into a fund to supplement future pensions [1].

THE NORTH SEA: OILY HEADACHE

Public policy in Europe is uniquely shaped to discourage oil consumption, which is taxed at a punitive rate as a form of environmental sin. Taxes now account for 80 percent of the retail price in Europe — compare one dollar or more per litre in Europe to 40 cents a litre in the United States.

As new discoveries are made in Europe a cleanup headache is being created by toxic chemicals leached from drilling debris and accumulating around oil derricks. The pollution from Norway's North Sea wells annually has been equated to all the emissions from its motor vehicles [2].

Europe is getting all of oil's headaches and few of its profits. It suffers from oil slicks on its shores and increasing damage from climate instability associated with global warming.

The major controversy over the planned deep-water disposal of the Brent Spar North Sea oil platform in 1995 made some of the costs of oil clearer to the European public. It resulted in a widespread boycott of Shell Oil in northern Europe that cost the company $10 million per day in Germany alone. Plans to dispose of the Brent Spar rig would have resulted in dumping 1,000 tonnes of toxic waste, including arsenic, cadmium, lead and PCBs into the sea. Now that environmental protests have forced oil rigs to be towed to land and dismantled, the North Sea disposal will cost Europeans $7.5 billion [3].

EUROPE'S WINDS OF FREEDOM

Blessed with strong winds, the seas and coasts of Europe are becoming sources of wind power, as well as wave and tidal power. Europe has become a pioneer in modern wind technology. The striking growth of this industry can be traced to the oil-price hike of 1973, and viewed as a free society's response to petrotyranny [4].

Wind power is now being planned on a massive scale, the largest project being situated 38 km east of the Baltic island of Rugen. It involves 200 turbines having a total capacity of 1,000 megawatts of electricity, similar to that generated by a large nuclear reactor [5].

Through joint ventures with Danish firms that supplied the technology, Spain has emerged as a major wind-power producer. In 1998 its wind power increased by 350 megawatts. The Spanish state of Navarra now leads the world with 23 percent of its electricity from wind. On the Greek Aegean island of Andros seven windmills provide 12 percent of its electrical requirements. Electrical-generating windmills line drainage dikes in the Netherlands. Rooftop units have even begun to appear above restaurants. Near the German port of Kiel there is one on a McDonald's, humorously called McVentis because of the company that provided the blades.

One of the favourable consequences of German reunification was the rapid expansion of wind power into the former East Germany, which had been heavily polluted by fossil fuels. Subsequently the coastline of Mecklenburg-Vorpomern became a booming area for wind power [6].

During the 1990s Europe's electrical supply from wind has grown by more than 250 megawatts annually. The European Wind Atlas reports that the continent has more than enough wind power to meet all the EU's electricity needs [7].

THE VISION OF AN OILLESS WORLD

The recent red-green coalition election victory in Germany was a tribute to one of its former leaders, the late parliamentarian Petra Kelly. She had sufficient vision during the Cold War to dream of an oilless democratic peace in Europe. The self-styled realists of left and right did not believe in her dream.

So-called red-green governments of France, Italy and Germany are now embarked on bold measures to increase democracy at home and abroad. These policies are shared by most of the smaller northern democracies in the European Union, all curbing the power of the oil interests. Critical early moves were to lower employment taxes, an infamous job killer, and to boost gasoline taxes.

The protests that brought the current wave of red-green governments are typified by the global street party, a social phenomenon that halts traffic while anticar activists fill the streets with sofas, carpets, toys, food stalls, and cups of hot tea. In Utrecht, Netherlands, rebellious pedestrians occupied a six-lane highway in a 1998 street party [8]. A response of red-green governments was to declare a "Downtown without-my-car day." In France, Italy and Switzerland on September 22, 1999, 150 cities banned automobiles downtown. As a result of estimates that air pollution had dropped as much as 30 percent, French Environment Minister Dominique Voynet urged all European cities to adopt such actions next year [9].

France's socialist Premier Lionel Jospin is attempting to bring home the French neocolonial troops that prop up Africa's petrodictators, reversing years of French policy. At the same time Germany's red-green government has removed a barrier to stronger democracy in Europe — the exclusion of millions of immigrants from full citizenship because of restrictive naturalization laws. Both France and Germany now seek to expand the EU so that it embraces and democratizes its authoritarian fringes. France's socialists are avoiding the aggressive nationalist scheming by conservative Gaullists who are backed by oil companies with heavy investments in dictatorships in the Middle East and Africa.

The first red-green government of Germany came to power in the wake of major demonstrations against the Christian Democratic Union (CDU) administration's cuts to subsidies for the development of wind power. That this previously marginalized political issue should evoke major protests shows how vividly the winds of change are shaking the continent. Germany has embarked on an ambitious new deal featuring a 100,000 solar-roof project, Europe's largest solar initiative. It has moved to shift taxes towards carbon emissions and away from wages. Higher taxes on gasoline, natural gas and electricity marked the first phase of a $22 billion tax shift [10].

THE LONG ROAD TO A DEMOCRATIC PEACE IN EUROPE

Immanuel Kant's late 18th century dream of a democratic peace was retarded by the cunning of another Prussian, the authoritarian militarist Otto von Bismarck. Bismarck's Germany and its successors were Europe's biggest barrier to peace for 75 years. However, German reunification in 1992 gave new impetus to the creation of a united and democratic continent. The shutting down of East Germany's superpolluting industries allowed the EU to meet guidelines for fossil-fuel reductions set by the Rio Summit. The awesome $128 billion cost of having former East Germany's environmental standards meet those of the West were paid for by a 10 cents per litre hike in gasoline taxes and new charges on toxic waste and carbon dioxide.

Western Europe was fortunate in being fully democratic when the Berlin Wall came down. The last strongholds of dictatorship, Portugal, Spain and Greece, had fallen like dominoes following the oil price shock in 1973 as their economies contracted. By 1975 all three were democratic. The economic vulnerability of Western Europe's last dictatorships had been hidden by a boom arising from the export of workers and influx of tourists. With higher oil prices and transportation costs tourism declined. Workers returned home where their presence increased unemployment. The combination of rapid inflation and growing unemployment meant that the last dictatorships could no longer buy off social protest with prosperity. Declining living standards gave rise to strikes led by socialist and Euro-Communist parties that demanded democracy [11].

GREENS SAVED BY EXPOSÉS OF OIL CORRUPTION

Germany's new red-green government for a few months alienated core voters more familiar with the language of class struggle than green economics. It was saved by public outrage over the disclosure of illegal campaign contributions to Helmut Kohl for the Christian Democratic Union (CDU) under the previous government. Kohl had for many years resisted radical green demands. The scandals, however, gave a more sinister explanation of that resistance than had been believed by voters: reports by German and French television stations revealed that Elf, then a French state-owned oil company, was engaged in illegal financing of the CDU. Documents allegedly supporting these charges, compiled by a "high ranking aide" of Former French President François Mitterand, "have gone conveniently missing" [12].

EUROPEAN DEMOCRATIC IDEOLOGY AND THE
CURBING OF AUTOMOTIVE POWER

One of the main differences between North America and Europe is that there has never been the same political acceptance of automotive culture. It was ridiculed as "Fordism" by the Italian humanist Antoni Gramsci, distinguished for his theory of socialism. Democrats in Europe tended to be sceptical of the car, oil power and all its consequences. One Swiss canton, Graubunden, banned automobiles until 1922. The ban was upheld by numerous referendums until automotive passage through its roads was ordered by the federal government of Switzerland. That canton remains opposed to motorization. In 1994, a Swiss referendum proved to be a blessing for the rail freight industry throughout Europe when voters decided to ban all trans-alpine truck traffic by 2004 [13].

One sceptic of mechanization, George Orwell, was the articulate foe of totalitarian ideology of the left and right. Like his working class friends in the Glasgow dockyards Orwell preferred horses to automobiles. The widely respected British postwar Labour Party government of 1945-51 was heavily influenced by his thinking. So it encouraged rail transit and built no expressways.

One of the interesting tendencies of the "New Labour" government of Prime Minister Tony Blair is to bring back some very old Labour thinking. Less than a year after Blair assumed office every new expressway project in Great Britain had been cancelled. The Labour government's Minister of Transport is actress, Glenda Jackson, an outspoken automotive critic. One of her actions was to secure through parliament the passage of the Road Traffic Reduction Act requiring municipalities to produce motorization reduction strategies [14].

The environmental toughness of Blair's government has frequently gone unnoticed. It supports both carbon dioxide reductions of 20 percent by 2010 and the phasing out of nuclear power. These ambitious targets have been combined with a program for the creation of 50,000 new jobs through energy conservation [15].

Before World War II European democrats offered gentler pleasures than those promised by authoritarians. The French Popular Front, having won two weeks of paid vacations, suggested workers explore the countryside by bicycle. Democratic reformists also promoted vegetable plots and better housing that made conscious use of passive solar designs; whereas authoritarians promised every male-headed household a car.

Antidemocrats were able to gain popular support by exploiting the imagery of petroleum power. Nazi propaganda films in Germany in the 1930s boasted that car owners were able to win prettier women! Among the dictator's closest friends were Germany's automotive manufacturers [16].

The great enthusiasts for the automobile and petroleum power in Europe were the antidemocratic extremes of left and right. Lenin thought the tractor would reconcile the Russian peasant to the loss of his horse and land. Hitler's popularizing the car and constructing autobahns were integral to German militarists' plans for an oil-powered, lightning-quick war. The Nazi strategy of having every German male become a motorized warrior was crucial to their scheme for global domination.

Democratic European political culture has been in its essence ethical. This is what distinguished the social democratic ideals of Edward Bernstein from his materialist Marxist opponents. Christian democracy became Western Europe's other mainstream ideology. Tendencies toward ethical politics were reinforced in the 1970s by the emergence of green parties. The only anti-environmentalist movements are fringe separatist groupings and far right extremists such as the French National Front.

In Eastern Europe the connection between enthusiasts for motorization and the antidemocratic right still endures. Ecologists in the Czech Republic are determined to keep their country a relatively car-free haven. This has enraged the country's far right. One anti-car street occupation in the summer of 1998 was attacked by 30 Nazi skinheads [17].

The opposite of the European fascists' fascination with machines that pollute is voluntary (Gandhian) simplicity. It stresses the need for conscious personal decisions to refrain from harmful patterns of consumption and to protect the Earth. It encourages recycling, waste reduction, the use of energy efficient products, and organic growing.

One version of voluntary simplicity encourages cutting one's personal share of carbon emissions. A more radical version involves refusing to use private motorized transport. There are many less severe applications of this philosophy, such as having only one automobile per household, or encouraging co-operative car-sharing arrangements. This is frequently combined with efforts to encourage smaller, lighter and more fuel efficient cars, in contrast to the current craze for sport utility vehicles.

Northern European acceptance of car restraint was helped by timing. At the time of the OPEC oil shock in 1973, most European families still had a car-free simplicity imposed on them by income. Although such income restraints were easing, the sudden gas hike made the still unattained American dream of most families owning an automobile appear less attractive.

European greens had several advantages over their North American counterparts in anti-car campaigns. These included higher national population densities, milder winters and shorter distances to travel within common linguistic borders. On top of such factors, Europe's majority of carless voters made it much easier for environmentalists to encourage their citizens and politicians to embrace car restraint policies.

In advocating voluntary simplicity, environmentalists have striven to make car-free living appear to be a pleasurable experience, citing many advantages. One is savings made by replacing the family car with a fleet of bicycles. Other versions stress the potential for retirement savings and enhanced ability for leisure pursuits. Such advice, combined with public policies, has had the greatest impact on the Dutch city of Groningen, where 57 percent of the people use bicycles for most of their daily travel. This city has taken the most extreme measures against cars. It has dug up motorways, narrowed roads and banned cars from many streets, while building cycleways. Grenit van Werin, one of the architects of this triumph, has stressed, "We don't ride bicycles because we are poor. We ride them because it is fun, it is faster, it's convenient [18]."

Denmark, Austria, Belgium, Switzerland and the Netherlands all have levels of per capita family income comparable to the United States. Despite this affluence these countries all average lower distances driven per person than the US. Although more affluent than most European states, Austria has Europe's lowest distance driven per person annually of 3,400 km. The average in the US is 7,200 km [19].

The Netherlands and Denmark are the only two countries that have acted rationally and in an informed, democratic way to curb greenhouse gas emissions. Part of this has been a concerted effort to reduce the use of private motor vehicles. These two countries tax cars the most heavily and channel the largest shares of their transportation budgets into public transit and cycling [20].

Vienna: The Reformist Valhalla of European Social Democracy

For most of the 20th century, the city of Vienna has been a showcase of the achievements of social democracy. The "Vienna Model" is a widespread planning term used to describe efficient land use patterns without sprawl. In the 1920s this term expressed admiration for Vienna's social democratic municipal administration, which developed an extensive network of allotment gardens, beautiful low-income housing and efficient public transit. Vienna also boasted major cultural achievements such as libraries and extensive recreational services, including hiking and discussion clubs. Social democratic theorists took pride in how these working-class victories had been won without curbing civil liberties as in the Soviet Union.

Vienna's model before World War II reflected the fact that motorized travel could not be afforded by the social democrats' working-class political base. After motorization became affordable to most citizens more deliberate strategies were adopted. Vienna is the largest European city without expressways. Automobiles are prevented from driving through its historic core. Its streetcars remain the basis for one of the most efficient systems of public transit in Europe [21].

THE REMARKABLE ACHIEVEMENTS OF ITALY'S SOCIAL HUMANISTS

Similar to the remarkable Austro-socialism in promoting oilless voluntary simplicity have been the achievements of Italy's Euro-Communists. These began in 1964 when the Italian Communist Party (PCI) made its first major breakthrough at the municipal level in Bologna.

Following the end of the Cold War the Euro-Communist mayors who directed the remarkable car-curbing strategy rejected the appeals of the authoritarian Refoundation splinter group. These visionary mayors stayed with the PCI's successor, the Democratic Party of the Left. Before the PCI split during the Cold War, the extremist Refoundation leaders had sided with Russian Stalinists. Such authoritarian leaders had close ties to the Italian capitalist strategy of Fiat whose joint ventures in the Soviet Union have been the basis for much of the USSR's automotive production.

The PCI's remarkable policies followed the Party's humanist traditions, placing more importance on people than machines. Italian humanism helped shape the idealistic environmental crusades of Mikhail Gorbachev. He was a long-time supporter of the liberal-minded PCI during a period of remarkable environmental policies. Gorbachev headed the Soviet delegation to the funeral of the PCI's leader, Enrico Berlinguer, a widely respected international statesman of the Communist movement who pioneered Gorbachev's own diplomatic efforts to wind down the Cold War. Like Petra Kelly and her supporters in the green parties of Europe, Italy's Communists rallied to the support of human-rights movements in Eastern Europe, such as the Polish Solidarity union.

Over the past 34 years Bologna, through its traffic restraint program, had the greatest success in curbing automotive use of any metropolitan region in the developed world. Many streets have been converted into pedestrian malls. Parking rates have steeply increased. Transit subsidies have facilitated the extension of trolley lines and rapid transit. In 1964, one million cars entered the city; in 1990 this had dropped to 160,000 [22].

The PCI's success in taming the car contributed to its growing popularity. By the late 1990s this caused the Democratic Party of the Left to become Italy's dominant governing party. Similar policies have been introduced by the Party in a number of northern Italian cities, notably Milan. It has closed its downtown business district to cars on some weekends when pedestrians share the streets with cyclists and horses. The Red Belt of northern Italy, named for the areas where the Communist Party tends to dominate local and state elections, is increasingly emerging as a distinctive, affluent land without shopping centres and their massive parking lots. Nestled in the Red Belt is Ferrara, a community of 140,000 people, a cyclist's paradise. Most of its medieval core is off limits to private cars. The top of its ancient walls serve as an elevated bicycle path. Hotels provide free bikes for guests. Ferrara is a champion of Europe's "Cities for Cyclists" [23].

The PCI's success in northern Italian cities was due to the strong civic spirit in these communities dating back to their history as city states in the Middle Ages. In these towns we find civic-minded groups such as bird-watching societies, trade unions and co-operatives. Bologna's carless central piazza is famous for nightly debates among community activists.

The municipal governments of northern Italy are at the forefront of a number of environmental controls, such as wildlife and forest protection. The strong participation by citizens in local government helps facilitate the observation of traffic laws. These are more widely ignored in southern Italy where the Democratic Party of the Left has weak roots in a political system dominated by Mafias [24].

CURBING AUTOMOBILES IN NORTHERN EUROPE

Low income is still the biggest factor curbing cars and scooters in the infant democracies of southern Europe, such as Greece, Spain and Portugal. Here the environmental movement still has not even achieved a ban on leaded gasoline. There are few pedestrian zones and bicycle paths. The complex constraining web of civil society, government regulation and individual moral choice has been stronger in the more affluent north of Europe. This is a political pattern which replicates to a surprising degree Italy's own contrast in democratic effectiveness between north and south.

Northern European cities are rejecting the motorized American dream. Pedestrian zones are increasing and "traffic calming" measures are being adopted [25].

The various ways that Europeans have curbed greenhouse gas emissions are quite surprising. Oil-based asphalt paving, which adds toxins to the air and contributes to global warming, has been stripped away in favour of bricks or cobblestones. The old paving stones slow down vehicles in the heart of cities and even discourage such trips. In Germany alone 500 urban areas have banned cars and converted portions of streets into *Fussgänger* for the exclusive use of pedestrians and cyclists. Many have closed their main streets to traffic and have restricted truck deliveries to morning and evening hours. Handcart deliveries are often required during the day. Such restrictions on cars have brought impressive results. Before its downtown pedestrian zone was created in 1972, the German city of Karlsruhe frequently violated national air-quality standards for ozone and carbon monoxide. Today its air is much cleaner and trees and other vegetation thrive.

The growing movement toward banning cars in Europe has produced impressive results in diverse areas. One is the medieval village of Bretten. It is the smallest community in Europe to have a multistreet pedestrian zone that spans more than a kilometre. With ecological zeal the mayor and town council removed car traffic from the village centre and built an internal bike path system [26].

Transit authorities in Europe have been much more effective than those of North America in discouraging automotive use. They have successfully lobbied to have transit passes replace free parking for employee benefits. Payroll deductions, price discounts and university semester passes help fund municipal transit. Tickets are marketed as part of the price to sport events, concerts, conventions, and amusement parks [27].

European transit authorities have taken a number of creative steps to encourage cycling. Buses and trams were redesigned to accommodate bikes. The Dutch railways have 200,000 guarded bicycle parking spaces and bicycle access has been provided on the Eurostar trains of the Eurotunnel between Great Britain and Europe.

In contrast to the stagnant or declining passenger rail service in North America, European railways have been experiencing a remarkable revival. Every nation is co-operating with plans for 300-km-per-hour rail travel. The strategy is designed to reduce both automotive and air travel. Fast corridors are planned from London to Lisbon and between Helsinki and Ankara [28].

BICYCLE CULTURE VERSUS CAR CULTURE IN NORTHERN EUROPE

In North America cycling accounts for only one percent of trips whereas 30 percent of trips in the Netherlands are made by bicycle. In Denmark bikes account for 20 percent of trips and 75 percent of the main roads have bicycle paths alongside. Germany has experienced a 50 percent increase in cycling over the past 20 years [29].

Cycling levels in Europe never declined to an occasional recreational activity as they did in North America. In 1973, European cycling was given a fortunate boost by the OPEC oil embargo.

The European and American responses to gas shortages caused by the embargo were quite different. Because of its strong support of Israel, and in response to a singular Arab oil embargo, the Netherlands pursued a conscious strategy to promote bicycle use. Cycling had not declined significantly in rural areas. However, in Dutch cities many potential cyclists were intimidated by motor traffic. Public policy sought to build the necessary infrastructure to have safer roads for cyclists and thereby encourage biker confidence.

Between 1975 and 1985, the Dutch government spent $230 million to construct cycleways and bicycle parking facilities while cutting out funds for new highways. In the early 1980s, government capital expenditures for bicycle infrastructure had begun to exceed the capital costs on automotive road maintenance. By 1986, bicycle trails covered 13,500 kilometres. Pavement lines at intersections allowing cyclists to step ahead of traffic and move first were introduced and bicycle-sensitive traffic signals were developed. Cycling underpasses and overpasses were built at dangerous intersections [30].

Cycling in the Netherlands was promoted by a surprising coalition of the environmentally minded. One of the early champions of pedestrian zones and bicycles was the anarchist and Amsterdam municipal councillor, Luud Schimmelpenninck. His green movement gained in popularity after Queen Beatrix began to lead bicycle rides [31]. The Dutch democratic "bicycle monarchy" makes a vivid contrast with the absolutist oil-loving emirs and sheikhs of the Persian Gulf.

Street closings banning motor vehicles spread through Delft,

Groningen, and Amsterdam. This led many European cities to ban motor traffic in their central areas built before the appearance of the car.

Oilless Europe's Strategy for Global Warming

The EU has taken a much tougher approach on oil use and other greenhouse gas emissions than the rest of the affluent world. It advocates a 20 percent reduction in emissions by 2010, close to the 25 percent reductions advocated by the Alliance of Small Island States (AOSIS). The EU's desire for tough reductions is quite different from the positions of the JUSCANZ countries, which are evading the reality that oil burning must cease in the medium term.

In Sweden and Switzerland dozens of office buildings are now equipped with solar cells. The Finnish village of Kerava is now largely solar powered. Across the plains of northern Germany wind power provides a new source of farm income. The Netherlands plans to have 250 megawatts of photovoltaic systems by 2010. Bankers there are advising Dutch farmers to solve their financial woes by combining agriculture with wind-powered electrical generation. Dutch bankers displayed their green zeal in the design of a bank with 12 times the energy efficiency of its predecessor. Homes nestled in Germany's Black Forest generate their own heat and electric power from solar energy [32].

Solar power in Europe has the greatest variety of existing and planned uses in the world. Sweden leads in the number of solar powered district heating projects, with a dozen large schemes built or nearing completion. Thousands of PV-powered pumps put water in drinking troughs for cattle across Europe. Deutsche Airbus is working on applications of solar power for its aircraft. Since 1990 the German electronics company Siemens has been the largest producer of photovoltaic cells [33].

Switzerland is one of Europe's oldest democracies and has one of Europe's highest carbon taxes. It is also the staunchest advocate of solar power, an appropriate energy strategy for its interior position in Europe. No other country has come close to the three dollars per capita Switzerland has spent promoting solar energy research. One promising line of research being pursued by the Swiss Federal Institute of Technology features solar cells that mimic photosynthesis. Two large Swiss corporations, Brown Boveri and Sandoz, are developing such "nanocrystalline" cells, whose cost, it is estimated, will go down to one fifth the cost of current photovoltaics.

Switzerland's picturesque Alpine farms commonly use solar heaters for hay drying. Some 1,500 solar space heaters are installed annually. A 100-kilowatt PV system now lines a highway near Chur. However, to avoid the waste of land for power generation the country has become a pioneer in the development of building-integrated PV systems, such as a PV roof-tile system with quick-connect, plug-in electrical connectors. Switzerland has a national goal of having at least one PV system in each of the country's 3,029 villages by the year 2000 [34].

THE GREEN GNOMES OF ZURICH

The Swiss financial city of Zurich is often portrayed as the archetypal capitalist centre, with its financial czars secretively orchestrating major events around the world. If such scenarios are true, these "Gnomes of Zurich" could prove central to solving the climate change dilemma.

Zurich in many ways is the very model of a well planned northern European city. Its affluent bankers reside in a largely car-free core, lured by an artistic mix of niceties such as courtyards, parks, refurbished shopping arcades, museums and outdoor cafés. Surrounded by the quaint landscape of the horse-and-buggy era, its visionary financiers have entered indirectly into conflict with the oil barons.

Nowhere else in the world are the financial tycoons as determined to foster the transition from fossil fuels to renewables as in Zurich. The role of Swiss Reinsurance (Swiss Re), the world's second-largest reinsurance company, is critical. Its elegant headquarters beside a lake is home to a remarkable group of visionary green prophets. These are the company's special service for study of the risk of natural catastrophes, a group of 12 experts in fields that include mathematics, engineering, physics, meteorology and geology.

In April 1992 Swiss Re's special risk service issued an alarm to the Gnomes of Zurich. It predicted an increase in the risk of flooding from torrential rains, worse storms and droughts, and more thunderstorms, forest fires, hailstorms and tornadoes. It warned that major coastal cities such as Tokyo and New York were likely to have increased hurricanes. The next year Swiss Re began to tell the press that its recent pattern of losses were due to the greenhouse effect.

In November 1993 at their Zurich headquarters Swiss Re convened a two-day seminar to discuss predictions by Greenpeace of the dangers of global warming. Here its special service for natural disasters, headed by

Andreas Schraft, warned that it would be pointless to extract short-term profits while the world disappeared. Schraft urged that Swiss Re take actions such as investing preferentially in cleaner technologies, even if this meant taking short-term losses. Moved by Schraft's appeal, Walther Kielholz, a senior executive, told Swiss television that the insurance industry should take a major role in preventing climate change.

Kielholz's concerns have prodded Swiss bankers to investigate setting up the world's first investment fund dedicated to promoting solar power. This is intended to provide a means for big insurance companies to invest in solar energy by spreading their risk among a portfolio of companies [35].

GREEN VISION BECOMES MAINSTREAM

Already in much of northern Europe green vision is entering the mainstream. In Austria a new town is being constructed on green principles. This Solar City of Pichling will be completed in 2001 and will feature 1,500 homes with passive solar designs, natural lighting and solar water heaters. No cars will be permitted on its streets [36].

In Europe no new coal or nuclear electrical generating stations are being built. France is planning a fairly rapid phaseout of its entire coal-mining industry. One of the first acts of France's red-green government was to close down the *Superphénix* fast breeder reactor, ending the expansion of the only growing nuclear program anywhere in Western Europe. At the same time the Netherlands closed a major reactor. Immediately upon its formation, Germany's red-green government announced plans for a nuclear phase-out which is expected to boost further wind generation.

Renewable power and efficient combined-cycle gas generation are the only sources of new electrical generation in Western Europe. Coal subsidies are declining and mine closures accelerating. This change is taking place on both sides of the former Iron Curtain. In 1997, coal subsidies in Germany were slashed despite major demonstrations by miners. Overall coal consumption in Europe has declined 27 percent since 1990 [37].

Democratic Europe exceeds the rest of the world in the development of nonpolluting, renewable forms of energy. Wind power in Denmark is an industry employing 20,000 people. Danish turbines are a major export, a billion-dollar industry. Danish branch plants and partnerships with its global green corporate champion, Vestas, are adapting wind energy technology to particular local conditions in the free world. While promoting Vestas, the Danish government does not export nuclear or fossil-fuel technologies. It banned a proposed coal power plant sale to India, on the grounds that new facilities of this nature cannot be established in Denmark [38].

Germany and Denmark have contributed most to the growth of wind-generated electricity. Critical to their success has been a high buyback price for the power produced by independent operators. The utilities pay such operators close to 90 percent of their normal retail price. This encourages farm cooperatives to build efficient windmills to generate power surplus to their needs.

Revenues earned from the generation of renewable power are tax-free, while fossil-fuel profits are heavily taxed. Danish financial institutions linked to the country's strong co-operative movement have been very supportive of renewables. Unlike many other countries they have supplied 10- to 12-year loans for 80 percent of capital costs.

Denmark's growing dominance in the world of renewables is a tribute to its democratic elements. Just as oil and oligarchy are intertwined so are wind power and Denmark's remarkable co-operative culture. Denmark's support for green power has deep roots in its liberal 19th century Lutheran zeal for the principles of democratic co-operation, vividly expressed by the folk school movement, which has helped generate public acceptance of green power.

In many nations wind power development has proceeded through expensive experimentation by aerospace engineers, resulting in some costly failures. By contrast wind power in Denmark has proceeded incrementally. It took advantage of some significant electrical power-generating windmills developed in the mid-1950s and still in use. Danish wind power also benefited from the experience of back-yard inventors, agricultural equipment manufacturers and the active participation of its co-operative movement.

Official Danish interest in wind power expansion emerged after the 1973 OPEC price hike, when imported oil met 95 percent of the country's energy needs. Since the price hike, and despite the later discovery of North Sea oil and natural gas, Denmark has become a leader in wind power now achieving a remarkable seven percent of its electrical supply through wind energy. The nation's government has an ambitious goal of providing 50 percent of its electrical consumption through wind power by the year 2030, part of a strategy for making renewable energy the country's dominant energy source.

Through a gradual process of innovation over 30 years the costs of wind power have fallen by 40 percent. Wind-generated electricity on the mountains of California now costs only four cents (US) per kW-hour, and Danish windmills installed on the west coast of Ireland are guaranteed to supply power at about the same cost, far below that of electricity from coal burning. Only natural gas today is competitive with wind in the better wind fields.

Critical to the early success of Danish wind power was the development of minimum design standards, especially fail-safe braking systems. The Danish Windmill Owners Society helped keep manufacturers on their toes through owners surveys and reliability reports.

Today about 100,000 Danish households, or five percent of the country's population, own a stake in a windmill guild or co-operative. While originally these were dominated by farmers and rural people, windmill co-operatives have now been formed in urban areas. The Avedore Vinkraft co-operative recently constructed Copenhagen's first wind power plant. It was founded by the Danish Green Party and the municipal utility [39].

Denmark is also Europe's leader in energy conservation. Through clever appliance design and minimum standards' setting Denmark has cut electricity use by 74 percent compared with 1988 levels. With subsidies the Danish state is encouraging the widespread installation of solar water heating systems. Costs are falling so rapidly that this assistance is expected to be removed by the year 2000. A solar heating plant on the Danish offshore islands provides the district-heating grid for 5,000 persons. Denmark now gets two fifths of its electricity from co-generation, and is seeking to obtain three fifths of its power by this method in 2005 [40].

Few places in the world have shown as much determination to curb polluting means of transport as Denmark. Since the mid-1980s Copenhagen has been expropriating car lanes and curbside parking spaces for the sole use of cyclists. Over the past decade parking in the city has been cut by two-to-three percent per year. Curbside parking in the downtown costs the equivalent of $4 per hour. To discourage gas guzzlers road taxes are scaled to vehicle weight and engine size.

Even in sleet, snow and frost, 30 percent of Copenhagen's cyclists will bicycle to work. In the entire affluent world that can afford automobiles, Danes tend to own and use them least. Its average of 330 cars per 1,000 inhabitants is below that of 10 European countries, including poorer nations such as Spain.

Denmark's minority of car owners tends to be concentrated in rural areas, the most difficult to service by cycling, walking and transit. Copenhagen has fewer cars than the national average, only 185 per

1,000 residents. This is fewer than Bangkok, which has a far lower per capita income [41].

Finland's national oil company Neste, in the less profitable business of importing rather than exporting petroleum, is selling photovoltaic units for Finnish cottages and applying photovoltaic power to the building sector.

Germany has become the only country in the world to reach an installed wind power capacity of 2,000 megawatts, providing five percent of its electrical needs. One hundred large centralized solar-assisted heating systems are being installed in public buildings. Germany became Europe's biggest producer of wind power primarily because of changes in public policy following the Chernobyl nuclear disaster that gave rise to a surge in Green Party support. Germany's Danish border state of Schleswig-Holstein produces 17 percent of its electricity by wind.

Europe is pioneering energy conservation. The German Siemens corporation leads the world in the production of energy-efficient turbines and compact fluorescent light bulbs. New German washing machines have computer microchips that sense the weight of a load and meter water and soap accordingly. In the US such energy efficient appliances are dismissed as a "distant vision." Corex, a German company, has pioneered the development of the world's first cokeless steel mill [42].

MUCH OF BIG BUSINESS IN EUROPE GOES GREEN

Europe's greening has widespread participation by big business, in contrast to the United States, where powerful energy corporations gradually abandoned the development of renewable energy after a surge of interest during the Carter administration

The second- and third-largest oil companies in the world are respectively Royal Dutch Shell and British Petroleum (BP). They recently made investments in renewable energy amounting to $1.5 billion, some of which has gone into photovoltaics (PVs). Shell is constructing a 25-megawatt PV plant in Germany. It is taking part in a three-party consortium that is testing various applications using hydrogen, or hydrogen carriers with fuel cells that will make Iceland the world's first "hydrogen economy."

In March 1999, Shell opened its first solar service stations in Germany and the Netherlands. These four stations allow drivers of electric vehicles to recharge with solar electricity in return for a contribution to the costs. The Dutch stations are themselves powered by the Sun [43].

BP has broken ranks with oil companies on the issue of global warming. Its president, Sir John Browne, has announced BP will go beyond the cuts in CO_2 emissions set at the 1997 Kyoto Climate Conference. In its strategy of curbing emissions by 10 percent below the company's 1990 levels, BP committed to cutting the flaring of waste gas, and installing devices to capture vapours when tankers load oil.

In April 1999, BP began a program of having 200 of its retail petrol stations powered by solar panels. This was a clever business move since gas sales increased at these greened service stations. With the help of the Environmental Defence Fund, BP has launched an internal market for emissions trading among its divisions around the world. It is sponsoring a program called Global Solar Partners in 50 Scottish secondary schools [44].

The American Petroleum Institute issued an edict against Shell's and BP's heretical deviations of "leaving the church." This anathema was issued following Shell's and BP's decision to withdraw from the US oil- and auto-dominated Global Climate Coalition [45].

Several European big business interests were already ahead of Shell and BP. The Swiss Reinsurance Company, the Union Bank of Switzerland and the British Bankers Association have made common cause with Greenpeace in pointing out the dangers caused by global warming. In 1995, an environmental report published by the British Bankers Association pointed out that there are already parts of the world which are uninsurable due to climate change phenomena such as increased hurricanes, rising temperatures and sea levels. Munich Re has indicated that the first 11 months of 1998 set a world record for damage from violent weather. The $89 billion lost was greater than all such damage during the 1980s. Swiss Re has led the way in putting its money into strategies curbing global warming, including $2.75 million in Sunlight Power International [46].

Falling oil prices early in 1999 encouraged a spate of corporate mergers among petroleum giants. BP's acquisitions (still in progress) of Amoco, ARCO and Atlantic Richfield were based on the latter companies' major reserves of natural gas. Amoco had withdrawn from the Global Climate Coalition previous to its acquisition by BP, giving the takeover the character of a marriage of ideological compatibility. The creation of BP-ARCO-Amoco shows an acceptance of the Kyoto process by all these companies, as well as their recognition of the need to reduce gas flaring and adopt other measures to reduce greenhouse gas emissions.

On April 6, 1999, BP became the leading producer of photovoltaics with the purchase for $45 million of Solarex. Now part of BP's expanded solar division, Solarex was a pioneer in the development of thin-film solar cells which are cheaper than single-crystal silicon cells and offer considerable promise in reducing the costs of solar technology.

Despite the importance of the solar divisions of BP and Shell, the senior management of these corporations has failed to give these junior branches the resources needed to make the cost-cutting breakthroughs to have renewable power capture more of the market now served by fossil fuels. The top decision makers prefer solar to stay in niche markets such as off-grid power, communication technologies and navigational equipment.

Although Shell has won brownie points by its solar support of Nelson Mandela, it seeks to take the oil-soaked path with powerful Chinese Communist dictators. Shell Renewables has been kept away from deal making in Beijing. Instead, Shell's South-East Asia division has made big investments in Communist China.

BP's solar division published a paper indicating that solar electricity could be competitive with coal and oil if a big enough factory was built to bring production costs down. The cost of such investment would be close to $250 million, equivalent to just nine weeks of BP's exploration for oil in 1998. Rather than abandoning its quest for more oil reserves in the deep seas, high arctic tundra and tropical rainforests, BP's head office rejected plans to make the investments required for a solar breakthrough.

However, a British merchant bank is funding Oxford University's Environmental Change Unit. One of its key strategies, put forward by Oxford's Charterhouse Fellow in Solar Energy, Jeremy Leggett, is to achieve a "pricebusting" solar energy plant. This it believes can be achieved at half the cost estimated by BP's solar division. Using the same recent thin-film technology, a plant of solar panels producing 100 megawatts (MW) would bring down solar electricity prices to a level competitive with coal. The estimated $100 million cost of such a plant is no more than that of a single oil rig. Currently the biggest thin-film PV power plant produces less than 10 MW. A number of partners including potential customers are being networked for mass PV production. In 1999, a hundred homes with photovoltaic roofs were to be installed in Great Britain and sold with favourable financing. Simultaneously the green Charterhouse at Oxford was making plans with financial institutions concerned with global warming to be part of the market for a 100 MW photovoltaic plant [47].

Price busting is moving faster in fuel cell development than solar. One of Europe's auto giants, Daimler-Benz, took a critical role in commercializing fuel cells through its partnership with Ballard Power, launched in April 1997, with a $350 million investment. In March 2000, it announced plans for commercial production of fuel-cell buses with Ballard. It pledged to produce 100,000 such vehicles annually by 2005. Mass production is expected to make the technology competitive with the established forms of internal combustion engine [48].

GREEN AND BROWN TRANSITIONS OF EASTERN EUROPE

The democratic transitions in Eastern Europe have been quite chequered. While this problem is most evident in the former Yugoslavia, the last undemocratic corner of Europe, examples of democratic deficit are common. Yugoslavia followed the tragic pattern of the Soviet Union, with only Slovenia emerging as a full democracy. Similarly, the Baltic states are the only full democracies among the successor states of the USSR.

Another similarity between Slovenia and the Baltic states is that they were the parts of their federation with the strongest commitment to democracy, human rights and environmental protection. They had strong civil societies, with brave dissidents willing to challenge polluters, arms exporters and the military establishment. Unfortunately this green, democratic fervour took a separatist direction.

Slovenia's clash with Yugoslavia was sparked by the denial of autonomy to Serbia's Albanian minority in Kosovo. The exit of liberal Slovenia made the Albanians and other national minorities more vulnerable to the domination of Serbian nationalism than ever. This led to war in Croatia, Bosnia and eventually in Kosovo.

Slovenia during the last years of Communist power in Europe was a critical link in the passage of green, democratic dissidents between East and West. The country's Communism shared much of the liberal, environmentally friendly spirit of their neighbouring Italian comrades in the PCI.

Slovenia escaped the oppressive collective farm system that is dependent on fossil fuel. Its private farmers were part of a vigorous small business community before the end of Communism. Slovenia's constitution had special provisions for the protection of the rights of its Italian and Hungarian minorities, including special parliamentary representation.

Slovenia has prospered without oil or mineral wealth and is integrating well into oil-free Europe. It has the highest per capita income of any ex-Communist state in Europe, around $9,300. Its success is a good indicator of the connections between peace, economic prosperity and democracy [49].

The conflict between NATO and Yugoslavia in Kosovo took place in an oilless dictatorship that has powerful oil-rich friends in the repressive ex-Communist bloc. The Danube Convention of 1948, which allowed Russian oil passage into Yugoslavia, is itself a relic of Stalinism as the Treaty was never signed by democratic Germany [50].

Despite Gorbachev's encouragement, expressing dissent during the last years of Communism required considerable courage. Protecting nature was a sufficiently heroic goal. The secret police in Germany saw signs of trouble in the Lutheran churches that had become conveyors of the message of a green peace. A favourite message was "Ride a bike, don't ride a car" [51]. Today environmentally minded Western cyclists touring Eastern Europe are pleased with the relative absence of motor traffic, but are surprised to be asked why bikes are used when they can afford cars.

Like the new democracies of southern Europe, which give a relatively low priority to the environment, Eastern Europe's new free states have not yet banned lead in gasoline. Despite such failures environmental activists have achieved notable victories in the post-Communist era. Hungary, Bulgaria and Poland all stopped plans for the construction of new nuclear generating plant within a few months of gaining their freedom [52].

POLAND'S POSSIBLE MODEL FOR A GREEN AND DEMOCRATIC EUROPE

Some of Karl Marx's optimism about the impact of a democratic Poland appears to be justified by the remarkable potential it has shown to become a core nation for Europe's emerging democratic peace. It is the last bastion of the European peasantry, which still makes up 37 percent of Poland's population. They have benefited in Poland's democratic transition because the petroleum-based farming of Western Europe cannot be afforded owing to the relative lack of agricultural subsidies and high interest rates. Poland remains the only European country with a substantial manufacturing industry in horse-drawn farm equipment. Despite its awesome economic challenges, Poland, since the end of Communism, has consistently spent a higher fraction of its GNP than the OECD average on protecting the environment.

The transition in rural Poland has been a mixed blessing for the environment. Under Communism following the death of Stalin, the combined power of Church and State protected the unique rural economy from both capitalist pesticides and extreme Communist ideology. Now western multinational chemical companies are free to market their products. This has resulted in peculiar compromises. Some farmers will avoid chemical inputs for subsistence food, while marketing sprayed crops to the public. Such opportunism fortunately is quite limited, as it threatens consumer confidence. Poland's environmental movement is educating consumers on organic standards. There is also a movement for organic certification among Polish farmers. Environmental organizations such as the Polish Ecology Club are encouraging farmers whose produce is contaminated by neighbouring industries, to switch to nonfood crops such as flax, used for textiles [53].

Poland is undergoing environmental debates as General Motors plans major investments there. Despite such trends towards motorization the historic cores of Polish cities have widespread pedestrian zones where motor travel is prohibited. Its strong civil society is pioneering advances in environmental standards. It has also facilitated acceptance of the phase-out of the country's heavily polluting coal and steel industries. Environmental NGOs helped secure a "debt swap" whereby an environmental protection program was established administered by a independent nonprofit foundation, Ecofund, with a clear set of government rules to ensure transparency and nonpartisanship. Ecofund has given grants for curbing greenhouse gas emissions, phasing out ozone depleting substances, reducing sulphur and nitrogen oxides, conserving biodiversity and reducing water pollution [54].

GEORGE ORWELL'S EMERGENCE AS A PROPHET OF EUROPEAN DEMOCRATIC PEACE

The British working-class affection for horses, admired by George Orwell, has come to renewed prominence through the actions of Labour Party municipal councils across Great Britain. Glasgow now uses horses for transport in its largest city park. They are also employed in recycling programs in Manchester. The city of Aberdeen maintains a stable of 14 horses to pull vans and lorries and provide a park stagecoach service. Dartford has replaced tractors with horses for grass cutting and Birmingham uses horses to clean canals.

The radical demotorizing action by Labour Councils was praised by the conservative *Sunday Times* for its "extraordinary courage and immunity to ridicule in pursuing and proving a seemingly unlikely practical point: that heavy horses are not only more attractive than tractors but no less efficient and — closest to the heart of municipal treasurers — actually cheaper to run" [55].

EUROPE'S GROWING GREEN CONSENSUS

In the past European companies were able to exploit oil reserves based on colonial domination. Almost all of the oil of the Middle East fell under the control of nationalized corporations a few years after the OPEC price hike. One relic of empire going back to the turn of the century was the Anglo-Iranian Corporation. It vanished along with the bulk of the British Empire in the 1950s becoming transformed into British Petroleum and no longer owning its former Iranian wells. The last colonial outposts in the Middle East became independent by 1971. The OPEC price hike two years later was the final blow. Stripped of its colonial wells, BP is now, albeit at a slow pace, moving away from oil as the Sun finally set on its parent country's empire. Likewise Royal Dutch Shell, another green pioneer among the oil giants, was stripped of the wells now owned by Indonesia's national oil company.

Oil companies' ties to dictatorships have on occasion resulted in consumer boycotts in democracies. Such negative publicity played a role in the greening of Shell and BP.

Europe's democratic, nonviolent, environmental activists are able to keep the heat on to encourage democratic transitions in countries plagued with oil oligarchy around the world. On January 4, 1999, Ogoni Day in Nigeria, 12 well-dressed British environmentalists occupied Shellmex House, the headquarters of Shell UK. Here they unloaded a spoof website, mimicking Shell's own. It detailed the truth about continuing human rights violations in Nigeria. News of the actions soon reached the Niger delta, giving encouragement to many democratic environmental activists confronting the problems of oil pollution [56].

Anglo-Iranian's evolution from petrotyranny toward green liberty under the bold knight, John Browne, is a fortunate result of the end of empire. Anglo-Iranian was for the first half of the 20th century the only really profitable part of the British Empire. It brought huge revenues to the British navy and the state that, for most of the Corporation's history, was a substantial shareholder. This colonial relic, quite an embarrassment to the postwar Labour government that benefited by it, has now vanished.

The greening of Shell and BP were not inevitable results of decolonialization. They required, despite Margaret Thatcher's ideology of laissez-faire, the intervention of the state. OPEC members were able, through increased oil revenues in the 1970s, to nationalize the previously owned wells in their countries. The flood of oil revenues proved to be so profitable that many countries previously dominated in a colonial fashion by these energy giants came close to buying out their entire operations.

In the United States a close relationship between Persian Gulf states and oil companies spawned the Global Climate Coalition. Texaco in particular developed ties with Saudi Arabia, which saved the company from a potential hostile takeover. Kuwait came close to acquiring the dominant ownership of BP after British Prime Minister Margaret Thatcher put the UK government's shares on the market [57].

In the recent merger mania of oil giants, sparked in 1998 by low oil prices, there were differing attitudes in North America and Europe. The recently merged Exxon and Mobil, and Texaco and Chevron, which are engaged in merger talks, all opposed ratification of the Kyoto Agreement at that time. They have a number of other features which complement their die-hard defence of oil. Unlike Shell and the expanded BP, their corporate headquarters are in the US. In contrast to Shell and BP, they have retained extensive coal operations, especially in Australia, which is the biggest coal exporter and most determined foe of greenhouse gas reductions among democratic states. Australia is even pressuring small island states with tied foreign aid to be less provocative over global-warming issues.

In addition to their European ecologically influenced sensibilities and lack of coal mining subsidiaries, the greener energy giants, shunning rather than embracing investors from Persian Gulf dictatorships, began a process of transition in 1989. This time of democratic ferment, which saw the fall of the Berlin Wall and the birth of freedom in many other countries, was a low point for the image of the international oil industry, further damaged by the sinking of the Exxon Valdez.

Exxon did not learn much from the Exxon Valdez disaster. Nor did Occidental learn enough from the equally great catastrophe of the Love Canal to do any serious rethinking of its corporate mandate. These firms are still rated among the worst US corporations in terms of their environmental responsibility.

Nevertheless, other petroleum companies did take lessons from the Exxon Valdez disaster and from a spate of other oil mishaps. This is particularly true for BP and its later acquisitions, ARCO and Amoco.

In 1989, BP formed an environmental audit committee on its Board of Directors. Only board members having an arm's-length involvement with BP were allowed to serve while all its health, safety and environmental policies were reviewed. Staff was increased in these areas. A new position of crisis management was created and given an important part in BP's corporate hierarchy. The company's winter annual meeting focused on environmental issues, which contributed to the development of a waste minimization program. A critical step was an environmental research and development facility in Cleveland staffed by 30 scientists. One of its early achievements was to develop an improved technology to clean up oil wastes. ARCO similarly moved boldly in response to the Exxon Valdez disaster. It openly stated that the US petroleum industry could not respond adequately to spills and advocated a national spill response and cleanup capability program to be enforced by the US Coast Guard.

As a precautionary step to avoid an oil-spill disaster BP inspected 3,000 tankers. This resulted in a third of them being blacklisted. Many were now over 15 years old and were not maintained to the standards of BP's own ships [58].

ARCO has become one of the boldest advocates of the end of oil. Mike Bowlin, its Chair and Chief Executive Officer, has openly stated that the world has entered "the last days of the Age of Oil." He has predicted that global demand for clean energy and natural gas, will grow faster than the overall power demand. Having an abundance of natural gas and absence of coal, BP-Amoco-ARCO is in a better position to profit from some such transition than are such unyielding competitors as Exxon-Mobil, Occidental, Texaco, Chevron and the European dinosaurs. Shell is displaying a similar emphasis on natural gas and is beginning to retail it [59], while selling off its coal assets.

France has been the most wayward European country in its nonaligned pursuit of oil power. It broke with the common military command of NATO while wooing Soviet-allied oil dictatorships in Algeria, Libya and Iraq. Its oil companies, now merged, are aligned with some of the most repressive dictatorships in the world. France has the worst record in the democratic world for failing to tie aid and investment to human rights. It has scooped up, for instance, oil exploration contracts in Iran prohibited by US sanctions. France and Italy together assisted Iraq in its attempt to develop nuclear weapons through joint agreements from 1974 to 1978. France supplied two nuclear reactors while Italy sold a set of reprocessing laboratories. Its diplomacy failing, Israel had in 1981 to resort to bombing the French reactor in Iraq to destroy it a few months before it became operational. European and Russian assistance to Iraq in its nuclear program continued even after the Gulf War. Iraq continued to attempt to construct a nuclear device with French and Russian fuel, which was delivered notwithstanding International Atomic Energy Agency safeguards forbidding such deliveries [60].

Despite the influence of petrotyrannies, European governments and companies are increasingly adopting the viewpoint of Petra Kelly that the issues of peace, human rights and ecology are inextricably connected. What once seemed like radical heresy is eventually becoming conventional wisdom, even in cabinets and boardrooms.

NOTES

1. Harald Rostick, "The Sunshine Revolution", (Oslo: Peter Opsvik, 1992), p.2; "Cheap Oil", *The Economist*, March 6, 1999, p.25.

2. Rostick, *loc. cit.,* p.13; *The Economist*, pp.22-25; Christopher Flavin, "Oil's Shaken Foundation", *World Watch*, January/February, 1992; 5, No.1, p.8.

3. Jeremy Leggett, "The Carbon War" (London: Penguin, 1999) pp.210-213.

4. By contrast, the Communist bloc, isolated from rising fuel prices, became a rusting museum of polluting technology. Its democratic opposition was spearheaded by courageous environmentalists well aware of the contrasting ecological protection standards on either side of the Iron Curtain.

5. Christopher Bourillon, "Winds of Europe", *Solar Today*, January/February, 1999, p.23.

6. Paul Gipe, "Wind Energy Comes of Age" (New York: John Wiley, 1995) p.37; Christopher Flavin, "Bull Market in Wind Energy", *World Watch*, March/April, pp.24-27.

7. Derek Denniston, "Second Wind", *World Watch*, March/April, 1993, p.34.

8. "Seize the Streets", *Earth Island Journal*, Fall, 1998, p.15.

9. "France urges Europe to join car free day in 2000", *Auto-free Times*, Spring 2000, p.16.

10. "Germany's New Green Agenda", *World Watch*, March/April, 1999, p.8.

11. Elizabeth Gleick, "Do as We Say", *Time Magazine*, November 1997; Robert Schaeffer, "Power to the People" (New York:

Westview Press, 1997), pp.57-63; Curtis More and Alan Miller, "Green Gold" (Boston: Beacon Press, 1994) p.26,

12. "France's secret loves, *The Economist*, January 29, 2000, p.58.

13. Wolfgang Sachs, "If Wishes Were Horses", *The Ecologist*, Volume 24, No. 3, May/June, 1994, p.95; Christopher Flavin and Nicholas Lenssen, "Power Surge" (New York: W.W. Norton, 1994) pp.220, 221.

14. *Earth Island Journal*, Fall, 1998, p.20.

15. Paul Brown, "Global Warming" (London: Blandford Books, 1996), p.224.

16. Wolfgang Zuckerman, "The End of the Road" (Cambridge: Lutterworth, 1991) pp.16, 17.

17. Hubert, "Street Party Lands in Prague", *AutoFree Times*, Early Spring, 1999, p.29.

18. Jennifer McCullough, "Taking Stock", *Yes Magazine!*, Winter 1999-2000, pp.24, 25.

19. Marcie Lowe, "The Bicycle: Vehicle for a Small Planet" (Washington: World Watch, 1989), pp.40, 41.

20. Robert Cervero, "The Transit Metropolis" (Washington: Island Press, 1995) pp.1-50.

21. Zuckerman, *loc. cit.*, pp.65-80.

22. *Ibid.*, p.100.

23. *Ibid.*, pp.80-120; Tooker Gomberg, "When in Italy", *Auto-Free Times*, Spring 2000, pp.28, 29.

24. Robert Putman, "Making Democracy Work: Civic Traditions in Modern Italy" (Princeton: Princeton University Press, 1993) *passim*.

25. Zuckerman, *loc. cit.*, pp.100-120.

26. Cervero, *loc. cit.*, pp.180-200; Richard Untermann, "Accommodating the Pedestrian" (New York: Van Nostrand Reinhold, 1984) p.185.

27. John Puchee, "Back on Track", *Alternatives Journal*, Winter, 1998, p.31.

28. Jurgen Bunsing, "Public Transport and Cycling: Experience of Modal Integration in Germany" in Rodney Tolley ed., "Greening Urban Transit" (London: Belhaven Press, 1990) pp.60-80; Pryor Dodge, "The Bicycle" (New York: Flammarion) p.189; More and Miller, *loc. cit.*, pp.30, 31.

29. Lester Brown, "Overview", in Lester Brown, Michael Renner, Christopher Flavin, "Vital Signs, 1998" (New York: WW Norton, 1998) pp.18, 19.

30. Lowe, *loc. cit.*, p.35.

31. Dodge, *loc. cit.*, p.190.

32. Christopher Flavin, "Clean As A Breeze", *Time Magazine*, December, 1997.

33. Rostick, *loc. cit.*, pp.81-99.

34. *Ibid.*, p.142; Flavin and Lenssen, *loc. cit.*, pp.163, 164.

35. Cervero, *loc. cit.*, pp.20-40; Jeremy Leggett, "The Carbon War" (London: Penguin, 1999) pp.108-109, 123, 145, 188, 233, 322.

36. "Solar City Up Above", *Earth Island Journal*, Winter, 1999, p.16.

37. Seth Dunn, "Coal Use Rebounds", in Brown, Renner, Flavin, *loc. cit.*, p.52.

38. Paul Hawken, Amory Lovins. L. Hunter Lovins, "Natural Capitalism", (New York: Little, Brown & Company, 1999), p. 25.

39. Gipe, *passim*; Danish Trade Commission, 1999, personal communication.

40. Hawken, Lovins and Lovins, *loc. cit.*, p.247.

41. Cervero, *loc.cit.*, pp.100-120.

42. Pamela Murphy Kunz, "Solar Energy in Europe", *Solar Today*, January/February, 1999, p.31; More and Miller, *loc. cit.*, p.23.

43. Christopher Flavin, "Wind Power Sets Record", Molly O'Meara, "Solar Cell Shipments Hit New High", in Brown, Renner, Flavin, *loc. cit.*, pp.58-61; "Shell and Renewable Energy", *Solar Today*, May/June, 1999, p.55.

44. "BP Fights Global Warming as Car Crisis Grows", *Earth Island Journal*, Fall, 1998, p.20; Lester Brown," Threshold: Early Signs of An Environmental Awakening", *World Watch*, March/April, p.18; "How Green is Browne?" *The Economist*, April 17, 1999, p.74; "Scottish Solar Schools", *Solar Today*, May/June, 1999, p.22.

45. Christopher Flavin, "Last Tango in Buenos Aires", *World Watch*, November/December, 1998, p.16; Brown, *loc. cit.*, p.18.

46. Jeff Johnson, "The New World Of Solar Energy", *Chemistry and Engineering News*, March 30, 1998, pp.24-28; Paul Brown, "Global

Warming" (London: Blandford, 1996), p.194.

47. Jeff Johnson, *ibid.*; Stewart Boyle, "Making Progress Towards A Fossil Fuel Energy Future", Mathew Spencer, "Fossil Crunch: The Arithmetic of Climate Protection", Stewart Boyle, "Making Progress Towards a Fossil Free Energy Future", Jeremy Leggett, "Solar PV: Talisman for Hope in the Greenhouse", *The Ecologist*, March/April 1999, pp.126-134; Jeremy Leggett, "The Carbon War " (London: Penguin, 1999) pp.322-328.

48. "Solarize Now", *Earth Island Journal*, Spring 2000 p. 18; Hawken, Lovins and Lovins, pp. 34, 94-104.

49. Freedom House Survey Team, "Freedom in the World, 1997-98 (New York: Freedom House, 1998) pp.446-463.

50. "Oil Flowing to Yugoslavia Despite NATO's Exertions", *New York Times*, May 25, 1999, p.7.

51. Mark Mazower, "Dark Continent" (New York: Alfred A. Knopf, 1999) p.375.

52. Robert Manser, "Failed Transitions" (New York: New Press, 1993) pp.126-145.

53. Anne Bellown, "Where Kitchen and Laboratory Meet" in Diane Roheleau, Barbara Thomas-Slayter and Esther Wargari eds., "Feminist Political Ecology" (London: Routledge, 1993), pp.251-270.

54. Ruth Greenspan Bell, "Building Trust: Laying a Foundation for Environmental Regulation in the Former Soviet Bloc", *Environment*, March 2,000, pp. 20-30.

55. Keith Chives, "History With A Future" (Peterborough: Shire Horse Society", 1988) pp.50-59.

56. "Shell Complicity", *Earth First*, February/March, p.4.

57. Leo Drollas & Jon Greenman, "Oil: The Devil's Gold" (London: Duckworth, 1989) pp.285-289.

58. Leggett, *loc. cit.*, p.17.

59. "Oil Be Seeing You", *Earth Island Journal*, Summer, 1999, p.8; Jim West, "1990s: Decade of the Environment" (International Petroleum Encyclopedia, 1990) pp.30-40; "Energy: the New Convergence", *The Economist*, May 29, 1999, pp.59, 60.

60. Jessica Stern, "The Ultimate Terrorists" (London: Harvard University Press, 1999) pp.115, 116.

CHAPTER FOURTEEN
OIL MOCKS DEMOCRATIC POWER

THE FREE WORLD'S WEAKNESS IN THE FACE OF OIL

The democracies control most of the world's wealth and weapons, but they are relatively oil-poor, a fact that hobbles US leadership of the free world whose prosperity can be easily disrupted by a handful of oil dictatorships. From these countries must come the oil needed, as things are today, to drive most people to work.

The United States and its allies may boast of superiority in hightech weapons, recently used in Yugoslavia, but their economies are vulnerable to repressive rulers who control oil. The most hopeful economic forecasts are hedged with caution in case of a sudden increase in oil prices.

The paralyzing grip that getting access to cheap oil has on democratic politics is understandable. Voters tend to reward politicians for low inflation, high employment and booming economic growth. The easiest way to do this is to have cheap oil, with prices close to the production cost in the Persian Gulf. This causes bowing and scraping to dictatorships by the American superpower.

Low oil prices, such as were experienced between 1992 and 1999, amount to the best prescription for an inflation-free economic boom. Since 1973, business cycles have echoed the patterns of oil prices. Between 1973 and 1998 oil played a stronger and statistically more significant role in American unemployment levels than interest rates.

Profit margins widen dramatically as the price of energy falls. Inflation subsides even as demand gains strength under the influence of rising stockmarkets and higher wages. Unemployment under stable inflation appears to fall. The boom from 1993 to 1999, originally thought to be the product of technological revolutions such as the Internet, is now understood as the product of an oil glut and breakdown of OPEC discipline.

With oil pegged above $20 per barrel, low inflation can be maintained at the cost only of higher unemployment. After oil prices rose rapidly in 1973, American unemployment more than doubled to 9 percent by 1975. The business cycle returned to prosperity through the breaking of OPEC's might, but it was disrupted by the boost in prices caused by the contraction of supplies during the Gulf War.

OPEC's recent success in disciplining its members offers the first instance of oil shock caused purely by OPEC discipline. OPEC's new muscle is operating on the basis of the insights of its Venezuelan founders, notably Perez Alfonso, whose strategy was to stabilize both production and higher than average rates of return. OPEC functions according to the long-time goals of the government of Venezuela.

Venezuela's current oil Minister, Ali Rodriguez, now President of OPEC, is the architect of a grand scheme to keep prices in the range of $22 to $28 a barrel. If the price of a basket of seven OPEC crudes stays below $22 for 20 trading days, the cartel cuts production by 500,000 barrels a day. A similar rise in production is ordered if prices rise above $28.

The moderate strategies of democratic Venezuela, an American ally, frequently have been negated by hostile dictatorships. The latter are determined to use higher windfall profits to pursue militaristic ambitions and finance repression; and they have frequently succeeded in overruling the OPEC doves. Such petrotyrannical OPEC hawks as Libya are attempting to bring prices up to $30 per barrel or more. This was achieved briefly in the winter of 2000 before the American government pressured the cartel to accept Venezuela's strategy [1].

The dependence on imported oil is serious for European countries. The Americas are relatively self-sufficient in oil, with semidemocratic Mexico and Venezuela being the largest oil producers. Combined, the Americas' reserves are 153 billion barrels (bbl). Europe's total only 18 bbl. The United States itself, with reserves of 22 bbl, has more oil than all of Europe west of the former Iron Curtain [2].

Although much of the Western Hemisphere's oil is controlled by semidemocracies, Latin America's producers have never attempted to use oil as a political weapon to challenge US foreign policy. Mexico has long curried US favour by staying out of OPEC.

Despite its gas-guzzling ways the US only imports 16 percent of the energy of all types that it consumes. If we look at oil imports only, however, in the past decade they have risen and now account for 44 percent of US oil consumption. Most of the USA's imported oil comes from Canada and Latin America; less than a quarter comes from the Persian Gulf.

American dependency on Persian Gulf oil could easily be eliminated by a selection of prudent measures — an example would be land-use planning that discourages automotive use. Two-thirds of US oil is used for motor vehicles. Most of this gas is guzzled by trips of less than eight km. Some 87 percent of all personal trips in the US are made by private motor vehicles. Portland, Oregon in the 1970s discovered it could cut gasoline consumption five percent just by restoring the idea of the neighbourhood store.

Since Canada and the US are relatively self-sufficient in oil, a sudden cessation of Middle Eastern supplies would have a much smaller effect on them than on their chief trading partners in Europe and Japan. Fuel imports of Japan and southern Europe amount to between 80 and 90 percent of their total consumption. This has discouraged these countries from taking part in US sanctions directed against the oil dictatorships of Libya and Iran [3].

While Italy is frequently compromised by its close ties with its neighbouring petrotyrant, Libya, the US efforts to encourage greater democracy in Latin America are also impeded by sheer greed for oil. As part of its efforts to encourage the principle of a democratic peace, the United States in 1991 helped persuade the Organization of American States (OAS) to adopt a commitment to defend representative government against all threats. This policy would soon be tested when in April 1992 Peru's President Alberto Fujimori, backed by his military, dissolved his country's legislature and suspended the constitution. The OAS did impose sanctions; however, these were lifted after Peru accepted face-saving state-engineered elections for a new Congress. Acceptance of this deal was encouraged by Fujimori's currying favour with US oil companies. Most notable was the widespread privatization of Peru's previously state-controlled energy industry [4].

OIL POWER CREATED US WEAKNESS IN THE BALKANS

The central importance of human rights as a guide to foreign policy priorities is illustrated by the post-Communist transitions in Eastern Europe. Where these countries were able to evolve into fully democratic countries in the past decade, peace has prevailed.

Despite serious challenges, the United States and its democratic allies did eventually succeed in integrating most of former Communist Eastern Europe into a peaceful community of democratic states in the decade following the collapse of the Berlin Wall. The process was facilitated by the rational discussion of controversial issues, such as the rights of linguistic minorities, via Radio Free Europe. Despite potential flash points favouring exploitation by authoritarians, such as the rights of the Hungarian minority in Romania, all ex-Communist states of the Soviet bloc are now recognized as full democracies by Freedom House. These states are also free of violent political conflict and have either joined NATO or become prospective members.

Despite the real success of US policy in former Warsaw-Pact states, it failed in Yugoslavia. While US policy supported the same moderate Communist leaders favoured by Gorbachev, both superpowers ultimately had as little influence during Peristroika on events in Yugoslavia as they did in attempting to foster a similar course of democratization for Afghanistan. Even the close co-operation between Russia and the USA in the first two years of the Yeltsin government was unable to influence events in Yugoslavia.

US power had little effect on Yugoslavia even after all the arm-twisting that produced the Dayton Agreement that finally ended the Bosnian civil war. This failed because Yugoslavia's economy could be subsidized by low fuel prices from semidemocratic Russia, which supported a nationalist course in the Balkans after 1992.

Russia, by subsidizing Yugoslavia from its oil profits, negated American and European Union sanctions intended to encourage democratization in Yugoslavia. Such incentives did eventually triumph in the Yugoslavian province of Montenegro, but success here underscores the catastrophic US failure in Serbia.

Russia's oil subsidy exacerbated tensions caused by the monopoly of media power within Yugoslavia by extreme nationalists. They inflamed ethnic tensions using distorted propaganda against minorities such as the Kosovo Albanians. Unlike the former situation in Eastern Europe, this was not effectively challenged by broadcasting from democratic countries. It was largely a legacy of the failure of Radio Free Europe to undertake Serbian broadcasts during the Cold War — Yugoslavia was considered a US ally.

Russia was able to fuel the armies engaging in ethnic cleansing and widespread atrocities, without provoking domestic protests. No outrage over Yugoslavian war crimes appeared in Russian media, which are dominated by the very oil companies that profited from their client state's brutal action.

The US was not prepared to confront Russian oil media power. The oil-controlled press was important for the US government's limited influence there, helping, for instance, to secure the re-election of President Boris Yeltsin. His re-election was achieved in the face of a stridently anti-American "red-black" alliance by Communists and extreme nationalists.

They were more threatening, with their outspoken anti-Semitism and sabre rattling, than the oil barons [5].

Nor could America devise effective ways to let the majority of Yugoslavs who lived outside Belgrade understand what was happening in Kosovo. Yugoslavia's prolonged defiance of NATO in its war in Bosnia and its brutal persecution of ethnic Albanians is only understandable in the context of the politics of oil. It took place with the help of Russian oil wealth.

Continued albeit diminished Russian economic strength from the export of petroleum is what fuels the fantasies of authoritarian nationalists of a Slavic Federation of Russia, Yugoslavia and Belarus. This dream of protecting the dictatorships of Yugoslavia and Belarus under the Russian nuclear umbrella is possible because expensive armaments can be afforded through petroleum exports. The sailing of Russia's rusting Black Sea fleet to Yugoslavia during the Kosovo war is evidence of this.

Repression in Belarus is encouraged by ties to oil-rich Russia. Reunion with Russia is vigorously pursued by Belarus' dictator, President Aleksandr Lukashenka who secured a ratification of a union treaty of Belarus and Russia on June 10, 1997.

American weakness in the face of increasing repression in Belarus was vividly illustrated in the arrest and expulsion of the US Embassy's first secretary, Serzh Alexandrov. This took place in the spring of 1997 as human-rights supporters were subjected to increased beatings and repression. Pro-American organizations, such as the country's independent trade unions and the George Soros Foundation, were closed down [6].

A litmus test of democratization in the post-Communist world comes from the varying degree of success enjoyed by organizations assisted by the George Soros Foundation. Soros, a wealthy Hungarian-American financier and philanthropist, funds the Foundation himself. It helped foster successful democratic transitions in much of Eastern Europe, by providing small groups with enlightened ideas for promoting peace, ecology, human rights and social justice. However, it has not had much success in Yugoslavia or Belarus.

In Yugoslavia the Soros Foundation supported the work of Sonja Licht, a dedicated peace activist and human-rights champion. Her organization (the Serbian Soros foundation) was one of the few Serbian organizations to advocate a compromise peace in Kosovo based on respect for Albanian human rights. To this end she organized a joint statement by respected Serbian and Albanian intellectuals [7].

American-funded efforts to promote peace in Serbia went nowhere. Newspapers that supported democracy were purchased by the government or had their newspaper and printing supplies cut off. The reformist directors of an independent TV station were fired as a result of pressure from the Yugoslav government [8].

Only after the end of the war in Kosovo, with the belated help of the Serbian Orthodox Church, has the truth about Yugoslavian atrocities been told to the majority of the country outside of Belgrade. These revelations have helped fuel a growing democracy movement whose success, however, is still uncertain.

The greatest barrier to the champions of integration into democratic Europe is the authoritarian nationalist dream of a Slavic Federation. This despotic fantasy is rendered possible by Russia's petroleum wealth, which is enough to finance neo-Stalinism in a new Cold War.

OIL WEALTH SETS BACK US EFFORTS FOR ARAB-ISRAELI PEACE

US weakness has also been revealed by the painfully slow progress of the Oslo peace process, agreed to in 1993 by the government of Prime Minister Yitzhak Rabin and PLO Chairman Yasser Arafat. Since that time the US has consistently supported groups in Israel and throughout the Arab and Islamic world that want peace on the basis of the eventual two-state formulae enshrined in the Oslo Declaration of Principles. However, it has experienced considerable frustration in realising its goals, especially after the election of a Likud government headed by Benjamin Netanyahu in 1996.

What is not generally appreciated is how the American government's considerable efforts to facilitate the re-election of the Labour party government that signed the Oslo Accords were defeated by the determined use of terrorism financed by the oil-rich dictatorships of Iran, Syria, Iraq and Libya. Profits from oil flowing to these dictatorships financed the terror which secured the defeat of a Labour Party government that courageously sought peace.

Following the assassination of Israeli Prime Minister Yitzhak Rabin, the Labour Party headed by the dovish architect of the Oslo Accords, Shimon Peres, enjoyed a commanding lead in the polls. This soon vanished after the Hezbollah and Hamas suicide bombings in late February and March of 1995. The bombings killed over 80 civilians and turned the Israeli election campaign upside down. A poll conducted within hours of the first blast saw Peres' lead slashed from nine to two percent. Continued bombings completed the process, in part by driving more dovish Likud supporters such as former Foreign Minister David Levy, to rally behind the hawkish Netanyahu [9].

The terror bombings of the spring of 1995 were financed by various petrotryannies that supported extremist groups having their own brands of authoritarianism. Hezbollah is a Lebanese franchise for the Iranian revolution, with support drawn from the country's Shiite Muslims. It essentially seeks to export the Iranian model of state rule through theocratic dictatorship.

In the assault on the Oslo Accords, Iran displayed close co-operation with Syria. Syria controls areas of the Bekaa valley in Lebanon where Hamas and a variety of other terrorist groups that oppose the peace process are based. Both Iran and Syria back the terrorist Popular Front for the Liberation of Palestine, headed by Ahmad Jibril, a former captain in the Syrian army. Two Syrian-backed terrorist organizations in the Bekaa valley are the Popular Front for the Liberation of Palestine and the Japanese Red Army. Syria also supports Hamas, a Sunni Muslim extremist group that receives funds from wealthy families in Saudi Arabia.

There are several different terrorist organizations supported by the wealthy petrotyrannies of Libya and Iraq. They will likely continue to oppose the peace process if, as expected, Syria makes peace with the newly elected Israeli Labour government headed by Prime Minister Ehuad Barak. One is the Libyan-based Abu Nidal organization. It long delayed the Oslo Accords by assassinating many PLO diplomats and a Jordanian official. Libya and Iraq back two other extremist groups. One is the Palestinian Liberation Front, headed by Abu Abbas. Syria and Libya both support the Democratic Front for the Liberation of Palestine whose 500 fighters are focused on destroying the Palestinian-Israeli peace process [10].

When faced with the hostility of so many petrotyrannies, the United States did all it could to encourage the re-election of Peres' government. One step was to encourage moderation and respect for human rights in the new Palestinian National Authority (PNA). To this end it gave $1.5 billion in funding to the PNA for its first elections and interim administration.

While the PNA has engaged in its own human-rights violations, it is generally American Palestinians, frequently backed by the US government, that have been the most vigilant in pressing for respect for human rights. Daoud Kuttab, a Palestinian-American journalist was arrested and detained for a week for such efforts. His crime was broadcasting the live legislative sessions of the PNA [11].

US encouragement for democracy and moderation among Palestinians was combined with creative measures to bolster Israel's confidence in its own security. Pan-Arabism, the idea of a single Arab state, is a notion that usually is quite intimidating to the Israeli electorate. The US gave this idea a different twist by organizing a pan-Arab conference against terrorism, which excluded Farsi-speaking Iran. With the exception of Sudan, Libya, Syria and Iraq, every Arabic-speaking nation in the Middle East condemned terrorism at the conference. Despite this impressive display of Arab unity for peace, the US could not undo the effects of the bombings. Its intelligent interventions helped Labour secure a respectful share of the vote, but it still could not reverse its slide towards defeat [12].

Failing to secure Labour's re-election the US government had to endure three years of provocative antics under Netanyahu. The worst took place when a tunnel that had been sealed since 1947 was opened under Islamic holy places in East Jerusalem. This resulted in riots leading to 50 deaths. It was climaxed by a gunfight between police of the PNA and Israeli soldiers. Other outrageous antics included the destruction of Palestinian homes and the construction of a Jewish settlement at Har Homa in East Jerusalem. Undermined by Netanyahu's mischief, US efforts at keeping the peace process alive were further strained by the deaths of 20 people through renewed suicide bombings. Every delay in the schedule of the Oslo process' land-for-peace formula was used by Saddam Hussein to justify confrontations with UN weapons inspectors [13].

US power is now focused on assisting the peace negotiations between the Barak government and Syria. Even if this is successful, the process invites the continuation of war by the terrorist agents of Libya, Iran and Iraq. Save for the end of US economic sanctions, there is not a carrot comparable to the return of the Golan Heights that would make these countries amenable to the peace process. Unlike Syria, moreover, these states have never participated in negotiations with Israel to end their state of war by terrorist proxy. Continued manipulation of Palestinian grievances, even if peace is achieved between Syria and Israel, will still provide several dictatorships in the Middle East with new pretexts to justify their repressive rule and quest for weapons of mass destruction.

US CONFLICT WITH SAUDI ARABIA

Although Saudi Arabia has generally been supportive of the peace process between Israel and the PNA, its policies are based on the export of its own brand of authoritarian, Sunni Islamic ideology, have undermined US policies in many parts of the Middle East. Despite close economic and military ties, Saudi Arabia's absolute monarchy clashes with the interests of the democratic United States in many parts of the world.

Even though financially supportive of the PNA, the House of Saud has not chosen to follow the example of its old Jordanian Hashemite rivals to extend diplomatic recognition to Israel. Even its funding of the PNA is a mixed blessing. Saudi largesse tends to duplicate a common problem in the Middle East — funding from oil-rich repressive governments having the effect of sustaining human-rights abuses. Unlike funding from US and European sources, Saudi assistance, tied to prestige projects such as the Gaza airport, has not been linked to improvements in the PNA's human-rights performance.

The largely symbolic disagreement over Saudi Arabia's continuing nonrecognition of Israel is the least significant of very real conflicts between the US and Saudi Arabia. One of the most serious is the attempt to spread Sunni extremism to one of America's most important allies in the Middle East, Egypt.

A common Arabic language and opportunities for employment in its oil facilities gives Saudi Arabia considerable influence in Egypt. After Egyptian peasants work in Saudi oil fields, they frequently bring back more authoritarian formulations of Islam than those taught at home. Saudi oil wealth also has strong attractions for Egyptian intellectuals. Higher pay has attracted Egyptian journalists to write for Saudi newspapers and similar tendencies have influenced Egypt's judiciary, educational and legal professions. Only semidemocratic Kuwait has denounced the Islamic extremist groups operating in Egypt. These were originally encouraged by US policy in the Cold War to undermine Nasser's secular Arab nationalism [14].

One unfortunate feature of the entire post-Cold-War period has been the alienation between many Saudis and the United States. This was almost an inevitable outcome of Gorbachev's efforts to wind down the Cold War which sought a compromise peace in Afghanistan, backed by Iran, the United States and the USSR.

Iran shared superpower efforts at compromise since such a peace would protect its Shiite minority in Afghanistan from quite extreme Sunni intolerance. An example of a Sunni extremist organization is the Saudi-financed Sipahe-Sahaba Pakistan (SSP), which has called for the "termination" of Shiites [15].

Since the Taliban captured Afghanistan's capital, Kabul, in 1996, particularly harsh treatment has been accorded the country's Hazara Shiite minority. On September 14, 1997, 70 Hazara Shiite civilians were massacred by retreating Taliban soldiers. In the past three years Afghanistan's civil war has resulted in the displacement of 250,000 persons. In 1999 Taliban blockades left a million civilians in danger of starvation. The Taliban has applied Saudi Arabia's harsh version of Shari'a law, which features public executions, amputations, and stoning to death for adultery [16].

Factions of the Saudi elite frequently use terrorist groups as proxies in power struggles. Exiled Saudi extremists, waging wars in Afghanistan and Algeria, are viewed by the nation's security services as being beneficially out of the country. They are essentially paid to stay away, spreading their violence to other lands.

The Saudi export of armed trouble makers began as aid to Afghans resisting the Soviet invasion, but has been extended to other nations that are predominantly Islamic, so as to spread mayhem and retard democracy. It also frustrated efforts to speed the Arab-Israeli peace process, through the terrorists' collaboration with Syrian and Iranian intelligence.

Saudi Arabia has helped the Taliban in their triumph over much of Afghanistan. Such help has been strongly advocated by Sheik Mohammad bin Jubier, the current chair of the Saudi Consultative Council. He has served as the leading "exporter" of the Wahhabi version of Islam to other areas of the Islamic world, creating new barriers to democratic transitions by fostering religious intolerance and persecution of minorities.

The Wahhabi export to Afghanistan has been particularly tragic since it has been at the expense of the country's native Sufi traditions. The country was actually the birthplace of the Sufi mystic Melylana Selalenttin Rumi who founded the dervish order in the 11th century and preached love and tolerance.

Sufism was tolerant towards Afghanistan's minority faiths such as Sikhs, who have now fled the country. The strength of the Wahhabi creed among the Taliban has also encouraged conflict with Shiite Iran, which has frequently been on the verge of war with the Taliban over its persecution of Shiites. War between the Taliban and Iran has been averted largely by the mediation efforts of Osama bin Laden. He has played a remarkable role in uniting diverse anti-American groups hostile to the emergence of democracy in much of the Islamic world.

OSAMA BIN LADEN: KING OF PETROTYRANNY?

Osama bin Laden's skill as a mediator enhances his status among authoritarian extremists. It makes him the virtual ruler of petrotyrannies united by their hostility to the emergence of democracy. Despite their profound differences, petrotyrannies from Beirut to the Khyber Pass are able to demonstrate a unity of purpose, hostile to the spread of human rights.

While many devout Muslims would be shocked at bin Laden's defence of the aggressively secular dictatorship of Iraq, which has desecrated so many Islamic shrines, books, and holy places, his supporters understand that, if the Hussein regime were replaced by a democratic state, it would undermine petrotyrannies throughout the Middle East that provide them financial support. This allows him to mobilize protests against Middle Eastern governments that co-operate with the United Nations against the Iraqi dictatorship.

The brutality of Taliban rule has much in common with the severity of Iraq's dictatorship. This was vividly illustrated on August 8, 1998 when its forces captured the city of Mazari-i Sharif in northwestern Afghanistan. It was the last major city in the country under the control of the opposition United Front. Its capture became a massacre when, a few hours later, Taliban troops killed scores of civilians in indiscriminate attacks. Witnesses described a "killing frenzy" where advancing forces shot at "anything that moved" [17].

The Taliban's brutal triumph in Mazari-i Sharif was assisted by Saudi Arabia's oil wealth in an arrangement hammered out in July 1998, at a meeting of Prince Turki, head of Saudi intelligence, Taliban officials, senior officers in the Pakistan Intelligence Service (ISI) and representatives of Osama bin Laden. The Taliban agreed not to use their lands to launch subversion against Saudi Arabia. In exchange Prince Turki agreed to provide abundant oil and financial assistance to both Pakistan and the Taliban.

Soon after, large sums of money were transferred from Saudi Arabia and the United Arab Emirates to the Ukraine, to pay for the purchase and quick delivery of weapons to both Pakistan and the Taliban. The weapons proved crucial in the capture of Mazari-i Sharif a few weeks later [18].

The bombing of the US embassies in Dar es Salaam and Nairobi, the day before Taliban's triumph in Mazari-i Sharif, resulted in 250 deaths and 5,500 injuries. Following this spectacular terrorist success, Osama bin Laden conveniently vanished from his former Afghan base. Apart from frustrating American revenge, he sought to reduce the Taliban's difficulties as they were negotiating with American investors to build an oil pipeline across Afghanistan from Central Asia to Pakistan.

By February 1999, Osama bin Laden had established a new base in the mountains of the Helmand Valley, the centre of Afghanistan's drug production. Here his organization received extensive military protection from the Taliban, which they explained to potential foreign investors as an antidrug operation.

Osama bin Laden subsequently traveled to Islam Dara, an abandoned underground base in the Sheikh Hazrat Mountain, surrounded by minefields and other entrapments.

Eventually all of Osama bin Laden's moves in Afghanistan to help the Taliban in its negotiations with the American oil company, Unocal, were in vain. Catching on to his game, the US State Department refused to accept the Taliban's claim that bin Laden was not in their occupied territory, but in lands controlled by their allies, the Hibi-i Islami [19].

The unexpected slamming of the door to a major American oil company was part of a growing concern in US foreign policy under the Clinton administration that international terrorism, human-rights violations and the drug trade should take priority over outdated obsessions about access to petroleum. The American Petroleum Institute in a 1998 study denounced this evolving human security orientation of American foreign policy. It found there were 35 countries in which American government policy banned US companies from investing in strategic petroleum industries. This was estimated to account for 10 percent of world oil production and 16 percent of reserves [20].

Although cut off by the US government from co-operation with its own companies, the Taliban regime has control over enormous revenues from the drug trade stimulated by massive opium cultivation, estimated at $6 billion per annum. These funds are laundered through the Russian Mafia, in return for a commission of about 15 percent, and provide bin Laden with an estimated annual income of about one billion. Osama bin Laden also launders operational funds the Taliban receive from Pakistan and Saudi Arabia, and gets an estimated $400 million a year from Wahhabi organizations in the Persian Gulf [21].

TERRORISM, DICTATORSHIP AND OSAMA BIN LADEN

Osama bin Laden's success as the man who defies America is understandable only in the light of support he gets from autocracies having great oil wealth. He has disrupted the path of freedom in many parts of the world. The bold acts of anti-American terrorism associated with his name have served to create a sensationalist unity that covers up the profound differences between the various groups and states allied with his cause of armed struggle.

Throughout the world, oil wealth gives muscle to various tyrannies.

For instance, Angola props up the tyranny of the misnamed Democratic Republic of the Congo. Libya has assisted with mayhem in West Africa, aiding dictatorship in Gambia and armed insurgencies in Sierra Leone and Senegal. China seeks comfort in friendly dictatorships in neighbouring Myanmar and North Korea. All these repressive countries tend to co-operate with each other and the dictatorships of Iraq, Libya and Iran.

What is remarkable about Osama bin Laden is the globalized nature of his role in sustaining and spreading petrotyranny. His actions are critical in retarding democracy in the Horn of Africa and Central Asia. They cause turmoil in the depths of India's forests in Assam and the mountains of Kashmir. His followers have attempted to sabotage the Olympic games in Sydney, Australia [22].

Bin Laden and the Sudanese government have supported Christian fundamentalists (the Lord's Resistance Army) in Uganda. This group has murdered or abducted thousands of civilians in northern Uganda in its quest for a separate Christian fundamentalist state based on a literal reading of the Ten Commandments [23].

Sudan gave Osama bin Laden the base to defeat United Nations forces in Somalia. [See Chapter Seven]. In southern Somalia, still wreaked by civil war between clans, he has a base in the Gedo region. Here in the coastal town of Ras Kamboni, a secure communications system is being set up by experts in the service of petrodictatorships. This region is under the control of the Al-Ittihad movement, an offshoot of the Somali Islamic Union Party, linked to bin Laden since 1993. His control of the region was discovered after a US aid worker was gunned down in a tea shop in Ras Kamboni [24].

Osama bin Laden's supporters wreak havoc in Eritrea and Ethiopia, fostering civil wars in two desperately poor nations. His supporters in the Eritrean Islamic Jihad, backed by Sudan, carry out guerrilla actions in the country's western lowlands. In Ethiopia, bin Laden's Al-Ittahad Al-Islam movement, co-operates with the Oromo Liberation Front, and the Islamic Front for the Liberation of Oromo. Their armed militias now work in co-operation with their former opponents, the Dergue, with whom they clashed when the Dergue ruled Ethiopia as a Communist dictatorship. This extremist alliance of Communist atheists and Islamic fundamentalists was galvanized by Sudan's effective anti-American propaganda following the 1998 US embassy bombings. The alliance now has established military bases on the border region between Somalia, Ethiopia and Kenya [25].

The same pattern of fostering an alliance of diverse organizations committed to armed struggle and supportive of dictatorship has been successfully manipulated by bin Laden to undermine democracy in India.

Here he has worked closely with Pakistan's ISI, which has mastered such devious tricks as aiding Sikhs committed to armed struggle seeking separation from India, while driving their religious brethren out of Afghanistan and Kashmir!

In mid-January 1999, Indian security authorities averted a complex plan to blow up simultaneously the US Embassy in New Delhi and the American consulates in Chennai and Calcutta. The plan failed after the arrest of one of its key operatives Syed Abu Nasir, carrying four pounds of explosives received from an ISI agent in India. Nasir had previously taken military-terrorism training in Afghanistan [26].

To his credit Pakistan's elected President Nawaz Sharif, courageously resisted demands by the ISI and bin Laden's allies to intensify confrontation with India across their line of control in Kashmir. Soon afterwards the government of Pakistan was overthrown in a military coup.

The new Pakistan dictatorship's ties to terrorist groups (later suspected in an airline hijacking, an attempted embassy bombing and the brutal massacre of 35 Kashmiri Sikhs) eventually resulted in the United States favouring democratic India. Following the coup by Pakistani General Perves Musharraf, it appeared to the US security establishment that America's interests were the same as India's since they faced identical foes. Osama bin Laden essentially pushed the US and India together, since he is their public enemy number one.

In an address to the Indian parliament during his March 2000 visit to South Asia, US President Clinton signaled a new alliance. He expressed solidarity with democratic India because of its encirclement by dictatorships. He also announced annual meetings of foreign ministers between the two countries on issues of common concern, most notably, terrorism [27].

OIL OVERWHELMS US POWER

Time and time again dictatorships with oil money frustrate American power. This contrasts with the growing list of "donor democracies" such as Mali and Malawi where democratization has advanced as a result of pressures from aid agencies.

For a decade, Libya refused to release its agents charged with blowing up a commercial airliner. Iran adds Chinese front line ballistic missiles to its considerable arsenal of Soviet-made Scuds. Russia helps Iran build a nuclear reactor. Despite widespread starvation Iraq rebuilds production facilities to turn out an upgraded Scud missile called El-Hussein. Similarly starving North Korea, assisted by Iran, toils away at its long-range Taepo Dong missiles which soon should be able to hit the United States. China seeks to make its intercontinental ballistic missiles capable of carrying multiple warheads. Even Peru under the lawless Fujimori regime, after its setback in a border skirmish for oil with Ecuador, attempted to negotiate with North Korea to obtain ballistic missiles [28].

In their cramped focus on access to oil as the badge of US power, strategic studies experts ignore how this has blinded the United States to more critical goals of a democratic peace that would eliminate the need for continued massive military expenditure and facilitate more secure business investments. Such an agenda involves the spread of the rule of law, safeguarding human rights and discouraging the proliferation of nuclear weapons.

These more important foreign policy objectives are blunted by goals such as selling cars to China, stretching oil lines across Afghanistan, petroleum development in Chad and Cameroon and the search for oil in the Amazon rainforest. All of these narrow, commercial goals that benefit the oil industry also clash with efforts to halt global warming.

Democratic power is best enhanced by cutting off the biggest form of tribute from democracies to dictatorships — payment for oil. The fortunes of Osama bin Laden, funds for infiltrators into Kashmir, the scheming for an authoritarian Slavic Federation, nuclear proliferation and the plotting by terrorists to blow up the Arab-Israeli peace process are all paid for eventually by democracies through their purchase of oil.

NOTES

1. "Oil and the new economy", The Economist, April 1, 2000, p. 72; "Oil The end of opaque", The Economist, April 22, 2000, pp. 61, 62.

2. Jim West, "International Petroleum Encyclopaedia, 1998" (Tulsa: Penn Well, 1998) pp.290-300.

3. Kent Calder, "Pacific Defense" (New York: William Morrow, 1998) pp.4381; Daniel Sitaz ed., "Sustainable America" (Carbondale: Earth Press, 1998) pp.191-197.

4. Freedom House Survey Team, "Freedom in the World, 1997-98" (New York: Freedom House, 1998) pp.412-415.

5. *Ibid.*, pp.423-428; George Urban, "Radio Free Europe and the Pursuit of Democracy" (New Haven: Yale University Press, 1997) *passim.*

6. House Survey Team, *loc. cit.*, pp.141-143.

7. Personal Interview with Sonja Licht, 1998.

8. Freedom House Survey Team, *loc. cit.*, pp.546-549.

9. James Ciment, "Palestine/Israel" (New York: 1997, Facts on File) p.215.

10. Raymond Tanter, "Rogue Regimes" (New York: St. Martin's Griffen) pp.269-274.

11. Freedom House Survey Team, *loc. cit.*, pp.575-578.

12 Ciment, *loc. cit.*, p.215.

13. Tanter, *loc. cit.*, pp.83-128.

14. Mary Anne Weaver, "A Portrait of Egypt" (New York: Farrar, Straus and Giroux, 1999) p.190.

15. *Ibid.*, p.209.

16. Freedom House Survey Team, *loc. cit.*, pp.106-108.

17. Human Rights Watch, "Publication Catalogue", (New York: Winter 1999) p. 12

18. Yossef Bodansky, "Bin Laden: The Man Who Declared War on America", (Rockland: Prima, 1999) pp., 282, 283.

19. *Ibid.*, p. 383.

20. "Talisman case spotlights Canadian edge as global business base", *Oil Week*, February 7, 2000, p.3.

21. Bodansky, *loc. cit.*, p. 315.

22. *Ibid.*, p.402.

23. *Ibid.*, p. 272; Freedom House Survey Team, "Freedom in the World, 1998-99" (New York: Freedom House, 1999) p.471.

24. Bodansky, *loc. cit.*, p. 392.

25. *Ibid.*, p. 272.

26. *Ibid.*

27. "Clinton warms to India", *The Economist*, March 25, 2000, pp. 41, 42.

28. Ralph Kinney, "Defenseless against Missile Terror", in Bernard Schechterman and Martin Slann eds., "Violence and Terrorism, 1999/2000" (Guilford, McGraw-Hill, 1999) pp.158-161.

CHAPTER FIFTEEN
OIL AND DEMOCRACY IN NORTH AMERICA: THE HEART OF POLITICAL CONFLICT

The struggle between oil companies and their environmental critics in North America is a battle between giants. Massive oil corporations with considerable wealth and power clash with vigilant environmental groups having millions of dedicated members.

Environmentalists have won many battles in their nonviolent war with the oil industry, holding on through titanic disputes for small, albeit significant gains. This is best illustrated by the Exxon Valdez disaster of 1989.

The Exxon Valdez spilled 11 million gallons of oil, killing millions of fish, an estimated 300,000 birds and 2,650 sea otters. Some 2,060 km of coastline were contaminated. Oil in rocky crevices continues to wreak havoc among salmon that spawn near shore.

Before the Exxon Valdez calamity took place environmentalists had pushed for comprehensive oil-spill regulations for 14 years. One aspect of their agenda was legislated requirements for spill-resistant double hulls. A year-and-a-half after the Exxon Valdez wreck an oil-spill bill was passed by the US Congress. Oil spills of more than 100,000 gallons declined by 66 percent following the bill's passage. Tankers are now escorted by tugboats while navigating the Gulf of Alaska. However, the bill's requirements for double hulls, which should have prevented the Exxon Valdez spill, will not come into effect until 2015.

Oil companies and environmentalists keep watch on each other very carefully in North America. Greens pioneered web pages; oil corporations followed suit. There are now web pages for and against oil drilling in the Arctic National Wildlife Refuge. Both urge internet readers to write to the Secretary of the Interior, Bruce Babbitt [1].

Many US oil executives see themselves as under siege by green crusaders. Chairman Frank Pitts of the Pitts Energy Group of Dallas is one such alarmist. In a March 1992, speech to the Natural Gas Society of North Texas he calculated that the budgets of US environmental groups are greater than the annual combined spending of US Republican and Democratic parties. He complains that environmentalists "are calling the shots in Washington today." Pitts fears they are now able to "make or break elections in many Congressional districts [2]."

The "International Petroleum Encyclopaedia" editor is Jim West, a self-styled expert in "confronting greens." West believes that environmental regulations have sparked an oil industry exodus. Indeed, Texas wildcatters are now on the prowl in a variety of repressive oil sanctuaries: Colombia's Cusina field, Yemen's Jannah block, Myanmar, Tunisia and Indonesia.

Ken Deer, Chairman of the Chevron Corporation, has called US environmental regulation a "national scandal." In 1992, Deer boasted that Chevron moved 600 employees out of democratic USA. Most moved to repressive lands such as the booming oil dictatorships of the Caspian Sea. Deer has painted the US oil industry as a victim of "capital expulsion." Mobil Oil Chairman Allen Murray has similarly complained, "We're not leaving, we're being kicked out [3]."

Typical of the insider oil company versus environmentalist nature of US politics was the attitude toward Vice-President Al Gore's role in the selection of Carol Browner as head of the US Environmental Protection Agency (EPA). While mainstream media were largely silent on who held up this post, the US oil industries and its environmental foes watched closely. Bob Williams is editor of the petroleum industry trade publication, the *Oil and Gas Journal*. He warned that Gore's coup "raised a chorus of cheers among the green lobby and shudders among a US petroleum industry already grappling with the world's most onerous environmental regime [4]."

Europe and North America differ considerably in the size of their oil reserves and in attitudes towards oil. All of Europe's oil is less than half of North America's reserves. A new oil rush is underway in Alaska's huge Naval Petroleum Reserve. Most of America's financial giants keep quiet about global warming because they have quiet connections with the energy corporations, apart from a few mavericks, such as Frank Nutter, president of the Reinsurance Corporation of America.

Oil in North America conveys great political power unequalled among the nation states of the free world. Oil companies have a massive work force that is at critical moments effectively mobilized to lobby politicians. Ranked by sales, oil companies account for the top nine of the leading 25 American corporations, and for almost a third of the next highest earning. Exxon-Mobil, despite billion-dollar penalties arising from the Exxon-Valdez spill, was able to become the world's largest oil corporation through its recent merger. The enlarged corporation has a capital market value of $253 billion [5].

ANTI-OIL POLITICS IN NORTH AMERICA

Before the 1960s the United States lacked a debate over the negative consequences of oil-powered motorization, outside of the communities of old-order Mennonites and wilderness back packers. Streetcars, still common in Europe, faded as a significant part of the urban transportation scene on the American continent. Only Toronto, the largest city of Canada, broke this trend. Motorists wanted streetcars off the road because — like the horse drawn milk delivery wagons that also perished in the 1950s — they slowed down automotive traffic.

Canada has a slightly lower rate of car ownership and use than the United States. This is a product of its antifreeway activists, transit supporters and neighbourhood lobbyists. Canada has also been more vigilant in its formation of metropolitan governments and application of land-use-planning controls. However, the best records of Canadian cities in controlling cars are poor in comparison with Europe and Japan. None of the megacities of the affluent democratic world that depend least on cars are in North America [6].

It was easy for the automotive companies to dismantle streetcar lines in the United States. General Motors, Firestone Tire and Standard Oil of California achieved transit deconstruction without it becoming a major political issue [7].

Near the end of his life, the visionary environmental writer, Lewis Mumford, regretted how he attempted to modify America's landscape to accommodate the automobile. His deathbed confession was part of a general trend among urbanists. Before the 1960s, the American environmental movement would clash with important business interests but not automobile companies. Regulations prohibiting automobiles from national parks did not survive World War I. By the 1920s, environmental groups with close ties to the national-parks services of both Canada and the United States tended to positively promote automotive tourism. It was widely believed, for instance, that cars were the best way to tour the scenic redwoods.

Early North American environmentalists did not have an important clash with the oil and auto lobbies until the 1960s. The extensive US network of protected areas did not come into conflict with petroleum interests until late in its development. Much of the current agenda of environmentalists — organic agriculture, the elimination of oil-based plastics, the substitution of cars — is of relatively recent origin. In the US, the more subsistence-oriented family farms vanished without substantial debate because of the higher costs of motorized agriculture, largely in the 1920s. Farm programs introduced by the New Deal simply accelerated this trend by encouraging more capital-intensive farming vulnerable to debt.

Oil-financed authoritarians were able in the booming twenties to divert attention from the effects of displacement by high cost motorization on small farms and businesses. This was evident in fiery diatribes over alleged assaults on the threatened "fundamentals" of Christian religious doctrine, a concept propagated by the Union Oil tycoons, the Stewart brothers. Prodded by aggressive lobbying by fundamentalists most state legislatures banned the teaching of evolution in schools. However, the more fundamentally disrupting inventions of automobiles and tractors received little censure. Widespread farm foreclosures and the great depression were interpreted in fundamentalist pulpits as the sign of the second coming of Christ. Few thought through the cruel realities of tractor economics.

A different attitude towards motorization was shown by the pacifist Amish and Mennonite faiths. Their old orders emerged in the 1920s through their stubborn use of horse and wind power, causing their communities to become tourist attractions in the 1930s. By this time both modernist and fundamentalist Christians had abandoned the windmill and horse.

THE SURPRISING OILLESS EXAMPLE OF THE OLD-ORDER AMISH

Inspired by the old-order communities, North American environmentalists are embarking on daring visions of an oilless economy, even exporting horse farming to Europe. Here the pacifist Anabaptist faith began in the 17th century in protest against militarism and dictatorship. Anabaptist ecopacifism died out in 19th century Europe, but flourished in then more democratic North America, allowing the old orders to become the guardians of secrets of oilless technologies that would have otherwise vanished.

Much of the Amish rejection of oil technology is favourably viewed by American environmentalists. They note that the Amish preferred horses to tractors since the machines don't produce manure. Horse power also favours crop rotations instead of the use of chemical nitrogen fertilizer.

The Amish and environmentalists have come together in a number of common causes. One is to oppose increased strip coal mining. Another is opposition to toxic waste treatment facilities that incinerate petrochemical byproducts, not used on Amish farms [8].

Many environmentalists in North America, while not becoming Amish or Mennonites, have adapted certain aspects of their way of life to their own earth-respecting creeds. They have encouraged farming and logging with horses and, after the Gulf War, some began to use the distinctive style Amish horse and buggy for personal transportation.

Many old-order communities have been influenced by the environmental movement. Some have their farms organically certified and share ecologists' Earth-respecting rituals such as birdwatching. One green Amish prophet, David Kline, notes that care is taken in his community's religious meetings not to disturb the peace of endangered barn owls. This complex exchange illustrates the development of a counter culture more profound in its clash with corporate power than the youth protests of the 1960s. Nevertheless the media made a sensation out of the protests of the 1960s whereas today they are ignoring the more radical movement that is trying to build organic agriculture [9].

THE ORIGINS OF CONFLICT BETWEEN OIL AND ENVIRONMENTALISM

The one area where the conflict between US greens and the oil industry stretches close to a century is the roadless nature of wilderness sanctuaries. The creation of these protected areas involves millions of acres of US public lands. They were encouraged by the active lobbying of outfitting groups catering to back packers and wilderness tourism that used pack animals; such interests were hostile to motor travel, beginning back in the 1920s. Wilderness protection can be seen as the one significant political victory for the American Horse Association, which opposed the introduction of motor transport into agriculture.

The concept of wilderness protection was generated by the advent of motor transport in the woods. It was first advocated by Aldo Leopold, who wanted to get rid of "Ford dust" from the wilds. Wilderness areas were created first through administrative regulations in the US National Forest system. However, by 1964, Congressional legislation entrenched this protection and extended such roadless zones to national parks and other federal lands. Native American communities have also created their own wilderness areas to protect sacred sites.

WILDERNESS PROTECTION:
A MAJOR CONFLICT BETWEEN GREENS AND THE OIL INDUSTRY

As the extent of designated wilderness increases so does conflict with the motorized recreational vehicle industry. Use of such vehicles is scorned by environmentalists as "pollution for pleasure." An important recent victory for US environmentalists was the California Desert Land Act. It extended wilderness areas on federal lands in California and banned motor vehicles such as dirt bikes, jeeps, and all-terrain vehicles on large tracts of California's wilds. Federal legislation to protect the California desert from motor vehicles was approved despite strong opposition of an anti-environmental group, the motorcyclist Sahara Club.

Environmentalists seek to ban airplanes and helicopters over the Grand Canyon, airboats on the Everglades, outboard motors on mountain lakes, skidoos in Yellowstone National Park and dirt bikes where they threaten the endangered desert tortoise. These are major and growing conflicts. Current battles before the US Congress include flight-free zones in national parks and the closing of 65 km of roads in the Grand Canyon. Another battle is over banning snowmobiles and stopping a proposed road in Alaska's Denali park [10].

Manufacturers of motor equipment are opposed to efforts to restrict the use of this technology on public lands and they clash with vacationers who travel on foot or by horse, mule and other more exotic animals such as llamas and alpacas. Producers of wilderness equipment such as tents and cross country skis frequently make heavy donations to environmental groups. Many of their products are imitative of a traditional native lifestyle, such as tepees and Mongolian yurts [10].

The battles with dirt bikers, motor-boat owners and skidooers are quite serious. Snowmobilers have killed endangered gray wolves and bison. Snowmobiles have no air pollution emissions controls.

The air quality of certain corners of Yellowstone National Park in winter is so bad that park rangers will in certain situations feel compelled to use gas masks. In winter it now has the worst carbon monoxide readings of any region of America. Each winter pollution from skidoos equals 55 years of the park's automotive traffic. Park ranger booths now are enclosed and have fresh air piped inside to cure dizziness and nausea. Banning snowmobiles from US public lands is an intense battle between the automotive industry-funded Blue Ribbon Coalition and the green Bluewater Network [11].

GREENS AND THE OIL INDUSTRY
ON A COLLISION COURSE IN THE LATE 1950S

Despite their former lack of attention to energy issues environmentalists almost lucked into the elimination of oil through the strategic grounds of the Cold War. This near victory came in the early stages of the Cold War under the presidential leadership of the Missouri mule enthusiast Harry Truman. Questioning the need to move away from oil began in 1948, the start of the USA's chronic condition of being a net oil importer.

During Truman's formidable leadership of the US crusade for freedom it appeared that green power would be allied to US struggles against the oil-financed Communist block. During his presidency southern public housing projects commonly began to use solar power. The federal government also used solar water heating installations in Florida defence facilities.

At the start of the Cold War all the centres of the world's growing solar industry were focused exclusively in the democratic free world states. The United States, Japan, Australia and Israel spearheaded the development of solar power. Miami was one of the leading centres for solar water heaters. They outsold electric and gas competitors by two to one. Major innovations were also being made in solar space heating. The Rose Elementary School, built in Tucson, Arizona, in 1948, became the world's first solarheated public building.

Truman commissioned a strategic materials commission whose report, appropriately titled "Resources For Freedom", advocated 13 million solar-heated homes for America by 1975.

Truman's interest in alternative energy was not shared by his successor Dwight Eisenhower. His Republican administration was closely linked to business groups in the allied oil and automotive industries. The confirmation hearings of his Secretary of Defence, former automotive executive "Engine Charlie" Wilson, unintentionally created that expressive slogan "what's good for General Motors is good for the USA."

Eisenhower's Republican administration turned the thrust of the Cold War away from Truman's social democratic crusade for freedom, into an oil industry-dominated strategy for corporate control. This new thrust emerged in CIA-sponsored coups in Guatemala and Iran during the first two years of Eisenhower's administration. At the same time the United States strongly supported an oil dictatorship in Venezuela until it was overthrown nonviolently in a coup supported by massive popular demonstrations in 1958.

The collusion between the US government and repression abroad was advantageous for US oil corporations but disastrous for stable international security. The might of the US oil companies inspired a revolt among American NATO allies in Europe, which were heavy oil importers. They were shocked at the ability of the hated oil multinationals, the "seven sisters", to boycott Iran's nationalized oil until a CIA-inspired coup succeeded. France eventually pulled out of the military command of NATO. The CIA coup in Iran set back democratic movements in the Middle East, encouraging the later rise of Islamic fundamentalism. The left in Latin America, in response to the US-plotted Guatemala coup, became stridently anti-American, resulting in the move of Cuba to the Communist bloc. Blinded by the power of oil wealth, the Eisenhower-Nixon administration disregarded human rights in foreign policy, a strategic blunder that would be repeated later in the Nixon-Ford administrations guided by Henry Kissinger.

Supportive of nuclear and fossil fuels, the Republicans in the 1950s had no interest in solar power. Despite the revolutionary discoveries by Bell Telephone Laboratories in 1956, which set the basis for current models of silicon based photovoltaic cells, no government efforts were made to commercialize this technology. It was applied only to the limited Cold-War aims of the race in space with the Soviet Union [12].

The marginalizing of solar power was facilitated by the lack of awareness in the 1950s of the environmental costs of oil. One move which slowly contributed to this understanding was the designation, in the last days of the Eisenhower administration, of the Arctic National Wildlife Refuge (ANWR) in 1960. This was the culmination of efforts begun by a few visionaries in the 1930s, most notably George Marshall, founder of the Wilderness Society.

The creation of ANWR took place during the controversy over Rachel Carson's warning in her book *Silent Spring* about petrochemical pesticides. Leading members of the Audubon Society who were chemical corporation executives, resigned from the Society after it backed her ultimately successful campaign to outlaw DDT.

The Audubon Society is now one of biggest environmental groups in the US. The Canadian Nature Federation is in a similar position north of the border. Both groups bring together organizations devoted to various facets of nature appreciation.

Today the emerging anti-oil basis of the US Audubon is shown in its offices and wildlife interpretation centres. These buildings are models for energy efficiency and the use of oil-substituting technologies such as solar power. In Manhattan, the Audubon Society reduced energy use in a turn-of-the-century office tower by 60 percent. Recycled and natural materials were used wherever possible. A similar concern was shown in the office design for the Union of Concerned Scientists whose Cambridge headquarters avoids fossil fuels by employing daylight and rooftop photovoltaic (PV) solar panels [13].

The Sierra Club is a vigorous advocate of bicycle commuting. It encourages the use of folding bicycles that can be put in briefcases [14].

Another green crusade to reduce automotive emissions resulted in the passage of the Motor Vehicle Air Pollution Act of 1965. This began the pattern for serious standards still not met by most oil dictatorships. Environmentalists are attempting to restrict emissions on light trucks, minivans, motorcycles, skidoos and lawnmowers, all unregulated outside of smog bound California. Such moves are strongly opposed by the Republican majority in the US Congress. They have kept pollution standards below those currently prevailing in oilless Europe and Japan.

THE EMERGENCE OF AN INTERNATIONAL PACIFIC WEST COAST ANTI-OIL ALLIANCE

Both sides of the border of the North American Pacific coast have become opposed to the power of the oil industry. This has helped commercialize one of democracy's most critical weapons for independence from oil dictatorships, the fuel cell.

Fuel cells produce electricity directly from chemical reactions rather than by combustion. When the fuels are hydrogen and oxygen the exhaust from this process is water. It simply reverses the splitting of water into hydrogen and oxygen by electrolysis. There is no interest in fuel-cell technology in the more autarchic oil-rich dictatorships and semidemocracies. The fuel cell has, however, obtained major investment from automakers in Japan, Europe and the United States.

With fuel cells there are no noxious pollutants created or carbon dioxide emissions that contribute to global warming. The first fuel cell was invented by British physicist William Grove in 1839. His breakthrough took place 40 years before the invention of the petrol engine [15].

Fuel cells have been a common source of power in US spacecraft since the early 1960s when the Gemini rocket series was developed. They now power both the US Space Shuttle and small research submarines. Price had been the biggest barrier to their commercial use. This situation began to change in the 1990s. The great transformation came because of

California's anti-smog regulations and taxes that encouraged the Southern California Gas Company (SoCal) to order fuel cells for installation in hospitals and office complexes. Exemptions from pollution taxes helped to make the cells a profitable investment for SoCal. Since 1996, General Public Utilities in the United States has developed a partnership with the Canadian company, Ballard Power, which develops fuel cells for power generation. Within five years the price for a combined furnace-generator for a home is predicted to be $3,000.

Canada's success in the commercialization of fuel-cell technology is its biggest technical triumph since the development of the supersonic Avro Arrow aircraft in the 1950s. Daimler-Chrysler already has a compact prototype car, powered by Ballard fuel cells, on the road in Germany. It has announced its intention to put fuel cells on the market by 2004. Nearly every other car company having major sales in British Columbia (BC) and California expects to do the same by 2010. Even some oil companies, notably Shell, Texaco and BP-Amoco-ARCO have announced their intention to supply the necessary infrastructure for fuel cells.

Considering the likely role Ballard Power's developments will have in ultimately weakening the power of oil, it is interesting that Canada's Department of National Defence (DND) invested heavily in the development of the fuel cell. They did so when earlier funding of Ballard Power from the National Energy program dried up. Their motive at that time was to provide an energy source for submerged submarines, so that the Canadian navy wouldn't have to adopt nuclear propulsion.

California's zero-emissions legislation was quite creative in stimulating new technology. Most automakers want to sell cars in California. All such companies are effectively required to help pay for the development of zero-emission vehicles. In California zero-emission vehicle credits are tradable. This allows major automobile manufacturers to purchase credits from innovative smaller companies that pioneer clean technologies. These cash payments have caused hundreds of companies to spring up and invest in aspects of zero-pollution car development. Innovations are being developed in flywheels, batteries, ultracapacitors, and super-efficient tires and heaters [16].

California and BC have developed an alliance to encourage zero-emission vehicles. The alliance now also includes New York and Massachussetts. Both California and BC law requires that in the future a certain percentage of vehicles sold in their jurisdictions must be zero-emission cars. California's deadline for the fraction to reach 10 percent is 2003.

The BC government has sponsored Ballard Power's prototype fuel-cell buses. These are already used on a test basis in Vancouver and Chicago. The rapidly growing company has made a major alliance with several automakers, notably Ford and Mercedes-Benz.

Ballard Power's research team involves 450 employees in a laboratory the size of two football fields. Since Ballard's fuel-cell research involves several competing automotive companies, it has been compared to a "black program in the military" for its high degree of secrecy involved. Rapid co-operative development of the technology would be more likely than secret compartmentalized development to lead to early success; such a result would contribute to destroying the lifeblood of dictatorship [17].

THE POLARIZED POLITICS OF FUEL EFFICIENCY

The strength of the US oil lobby is best revealed by the fact that automotive efficiency standards are still weaker than those of Japan and Europe. With proposals for tighter regulations in Europe being advocated by car producers themselves, this gap will increase rapidly [18].

North American automakers have gone to extreme lengths in fighting federally mandated fuel efficiency standards. The Coalition for Vehicle Choice is a US lobbying organization created by the oil and automotive industries to fight tougher fuel-efficiency rules. This lobby has received over $10 million in funding from the automotive industry. Between 1981 and 1988, General Motors spent $1.8 million to combat clean air legislation and corporate political action committees spent $23 million in total to combat clean-air laws. The Global Climate Coalition also ran advertisements against the theory of human-induced global warming prior to the Kyoto Conference [19].

THE EPIC BATTLE TO SAVE THE PORCUPINE CARIBOU HERD

The most contentious anti-oil battle conducted by environmentalists in North America has been their successful effort to block oil exploration in the Arctic National Wildlife Refuge (ANWR) and adjacent lands in Canada. This refuge protects one of the most intact ecosystems of the Arctic wilderness. It provides habitat for the 180,000-strong Porcupine Caribou herd. The herd is the staple of the subsistence economy of the native Gwich'in, whose homeland is about the size of New England.

Wealthy environmentalists such as the Marshall brothers were influenced in their selection of Alaska's northeast corner for a wilderness refuge by reliable US government geologists' reports. They concluded that a refuge on the eastern edge of the north slope would only eliminate insignificant areas from oil production. This advice proved correct.

Oil companies anticipated that Canada would be a weak link in the American environmentalists' defence of ANWR. For two decades, successful oil-industry lobbying caused Canada to reject attempts to complement this US refuge through a cross border national park. A consortium of major oil corporations in Canada attempted to persuade the Canadian government to approve the construction of a pipeline that would allow Alaskan oil to be transported through the Mackenzie Valley. Such a route would have passed through ANWR's most environmentally sensitive caribou calving grounds. Here young caribou are born in conditions which can be easily disrupted.

Fortunately, Canada's democratic political culture would not be swayed by US oil power. Critical to Canada's rejection of oil lobbies were the recommendations of a royal commission chaired by Justice Thomas Berger. He was appointed to the commission during a period of a Liberal minority government, headed by the wilderness-loving Canadian Prime Minister Pierre Trudeau. Berger had risen to national prominence as former provincial leader of British Columbia's New Democratic Party (NDP). Berger supported ANWR's twinning by a crossborder Canadian Arctic Wilderness Park. Despite considerable opposition from oil companies, Berger's report was eventually accepted. Through a federal cabinet order-in-council, mineral and oil prospecting were prohibited. Following the resolution of native land claims, two national parks were established immediately adjacent to ANWR.

After Canada had undertaken to protect its half of the Porcupine Caribou herd's range the federal government became a strong defender of conservation on the US side of the border. It would not sacrifice oil revenues only to see benefits flow to Alaska. Despite the Conservative Party government efforts under Prime Minister Brian Mulroney to cultivate a close relationship with pro-oil Republican administrations Canada never wavered from a defence of the Porcupine caribou herd. Through the resolution of the Gwich'in land claim, the protection of the Porcupine herd's range has achieved an entrenched status in the Canadian constitution. Only the extreme right elements in Canadian politics challenge this protection.

Further protection was created by an international treaty that established joint management agreements for the Porcupine caribou herd.

Combining scientific biology studies with traditional knowledge based on native occupancy, these arrangements have ensured a sustainable level of subsistence hunting. Canada has invoked this treaty on numerous occasions to stop oil drilling in ANWR [20].

In January 1988, a traditional assembly of Gwich'in chiefs was held at Fort Yukon, Alaska. The international council sought to combat oil company exploration plans. Major environmental groups were invited to attend as observers so that the message could spread beyond Alaska.

At a subsequent seven-day tribal meeting in Arctic Village, many relatives from both sides of the border met for the first time. An international Gwich'in Steering Committee was created to oppose oil exploration. The Gwich'in were supported by the Episcopal Church and environmental groups. This defeated a $3 million campaign in support of oil exploration by the Alaskan State legislature.

The battle to defend the Porcupine caribou herd still continues. Republicans in the US Congress have lined up to support the Arctic Coastal Plain Domestic Security Act, introduced in May 1999, their latest attempt to permit oil drilling within ANWR. To counter such efforts, a multimedia "caribou" concert went on a cross-country tour in 1999, culminating in an engagement at the Canadian Embassy in Washington. The Yukon Old Crow Gwich'in community is networking with environmental organizations around the world via satellite, FAX and the internet to advance its defence of the Porcupine herd.

Despite strong Canadian government support for the protection of the calving grounds on the coastal plain, oil development threatens the southerly Yukon wintering range of the Porcupine herd. In January 1999 the Supreme Court of Canada dismissed an appeal by the Vutut Gwich'in First Nation to stop oil exploration here [21].

After failed attempts from Democratic congressional opposition during the energy bills of the Republican Bush administration, oil lobbyists made another charge on ANWR. This took place after the Republicans gained control of the US Congress following the triumph of the Contract With America. Opposition by the Democratic Clinton administration, pushed by both environmental lobbyists, the Gwich'in and the Canadian government, resulted in another oil industry defeat. In defence of oil interests, however, the Republican majority in Congress had temporarily shut down much of the US government through budgetary blockage.

The Politics of Oil Consumption versus Conservation and Renewables

Quite dramatic, political battles over oil in North America have seldom captured the headlines. This was quite evident in the treatment of the environmental and energy politics of the Carter administration. Carter protected Alaskan lands from oil development and encouraged solar power. These achievements built on those made by the Democratic Congressional majority in co-operation with Republican President Richard Nixon during the first Arab oil embargo. One was a national speed limit of 55 miles per hour on rural roads and expressways, imposed in 1974. In one decade, the measure saved 730 million barrels of oil. Foreign oil imports were reduced by three percent. In the first year, it also saved between 3,000 and 5,000 lives — a drop close to 10 percent in road fatalities; there were 2,500 to 4,500 fewer accidents resulting in serious human injuries; and a reduction was achieved of between 34,000 to 61,000 accidents involving minor and moderate injuries. The 55-mile per hour speed limit was lifted when the Republican Party was elected, having made its abolition a major plank of its national platform [22].

Carter's green direction was a triumph for the elements of democratic society pushing for energy conservation, wilderness protection and renewable energy. This course was favoured by a liberal Congressional group, "the Solar Coalition", based in states such as Wisconsin, New York and Hawaii that lacked significant fossil-fuel lobbies. It was advocated by the Democratic administrations of Colorado and California, then headed by liberal Democratic politicians Gary Hart and Jerry Brown. Green power was also the political platform of Carter's left opposition, the short-lived Citizens Party, headed by environmentalist, Dr. Barry Commoner.

During the Carter administration the connection between a durable peace and green power was stressed by the iconoclastic environmentalist Amory Lovins, who wrote *Soft Energy Paths* in 1977. A "solar day" in May 1978 was organized by renewable power supporters and this succeeded in prodding an additional $100 million for solar power research out of the US government. At this time, as solar advocate Ray Reece pointed out in his 1979 book, *The Sun Betrayed*, public interest in solar development was producing a "heavier volume of letters and phone calls to members of Congress than almost any other single issue [23]."

Reece noted how during the Carter administration the popular movement for conservation and renewable energy had become a crusade against corporate power. "Federal solar energy funds" became directed to "building a mass movement toward community independence and self-determination." One example of such people power was the Bronx Frontier. It used windpower to aerate compost for a community gardening project. Similarly a 12-week "energy auditor" training program in Harlem equipped the unemployed with the skills required to analyze and improve the energy efficiency of tenant owned buildings. Lower East Side New York youth built a solar wall producing heat for a community gymnasium. Tenant owned co-operative apartment buildings kept solvent by cutting their energy bills through wind generation. Similar grass roots green power was encouraged by California Governor Jerry Brown's maverick environmentalism, which had a complementary program of solar tax credits. Brown's policies fostered the San Francisco Solar Center, a worker co-operative that installed hundreds of solar hot water heating systems [24].

Apart from the greening pressure of American civil society, it is understandable that, as a democratic politician facing the might of oil dictatorships, Carter wished to encourage the transition to other forms of energy. Carter dared to advocate nonviolence toward the Earth by appearing on television in a cardigan sweater and installing solar water heaters in the White House. He secured tax credits for the purchasers of solar energy equipment and created a Solar Energy and Conservation Bank that provided subsidized loans for solar equipment and energy conservation. Some six million Americans took advantage of government conservation tax credits. US research and development programs assisted in the rapid commercialization of heat pumps and energy-efficient refrigerators. Government policies helped create a boom in private energy-service companies promoting conservation, which leapt from only 10 to 75 in a decade. Federal projects demonstrated the considerable potential for energy savings in the industrial sector through cogeneration, which led to subsequent imitation without federal involvement [25].

The Reagan Revolution marked a profound change in direction of US energy policy. For a political mandate for these changes, it lucked into the widespread hostility to the Carter administration unleashed by the protracted nature of the Iranian hostage crisis. Rather than expressing a clear attack on renewable energy and conservation, Carter's critics in their media advertisements focused on the alleged abandonment of US "friends and allies", such as the Shah of Iran. This simplistic criticism ignored the Carter administration's efforts to promote a stable democratic transition in Iran towards a constitutional monarchy rather than the Islamic fundamentalism which eventually triumphed. The authoritarian clerical victory in Iran was the product of policies that discouraged democracy, going back to the CIA-inspired coup of 1953 and more recent efforts by Republican administrations [26].

Ignoring the authoritarian politics of oil which gave the Iranian revolution such brutal power, the Reagan administration abruptly reversed course on energy policy. Even if conspiracy theories suggesting its supporters engineered the hostage taking are untrue, it blindly chose to become more dependent on unstable petrotyrants that had created the past outrage of the Iranian embassy seizure. This dangerous pattern was the reverse of what the Carter Administration had been trying to do, following the advice of environmentally concerned scientists such as Amory Lovins.

The Reagan administration ended Carter's tax credits for solar power and subsidies for conservation. These changes were intensified by Republican victories at the state level, most notably in California in 1985 with the election of Governor George Dukmejian, who promptly terminated state renewable power and energy conservation tax credits, resulting in the sudden shrinkage in the state's previously booming wind and solar industries. The Solar Bank was weakened by the Reagan administration's refusal to staff it or request funds for it. Only funds pushed through by the Democratic-controlled Congress and a successful court action kept the Solar Bank from disappearing completely. Programs to increase energy efficiency in refrigerators, air conditioners and other large appliances ended. White House solar panels and heaters were placed in government storage. Fuel efficiency standards for vehicles were eased. Between 1980, the last year of the Carter administration, and 1990, US funds for research and development in renewable power sank by 90 percent [27].

The cost of solar power was targeted by the Carter administration to reach $2 per peak watt-day by 1995. This would have made the up-front expense comparable to electricity produced by coal or nuclear power. The Reagan Revolution thus ended the Carter administration's plans for a quick breakthrough to the solar age [28].

In addition to slowing the growth of renewables, the Reagan administration played havoc with government efforts to encourage energy conservation. A symbolic action in this regard was the firing of the supervisor of conservation and renewable energy programs in the Department of Energy, Maxine Savitz [29]. This showed the new ideological fervour against environmentalism by the Republican Party, similar in temperament to the McCarthyite hysteria of the far right during the Cold War.

Although keeping many of Carter's prohuman-rights policies, especially outside the oil-rich Middle East, the Reagan Revolution destroyed the holistic effort to encourage democracy, peace and renewable power. David Stockman, Reagan's Director of Office Management and Budget, ridiculed Carter's policies as being based on "Chicken Little" warnings. He believed that any threats to American access to low-priced Persian Gulf oil could be met with "strategic forces" [30].

Stockman, in co-operation with Persian Gulf states such as Saudi Arabia and Kuwait, who benefited from the higher volume of sales at lower prices, did bring about a 45 percent decline in gasoline prices at the pump. Meanwhile Japan and the European Union kept up oil prices through taxation. The low price in the USA increased the havoc in the American renewable energy industry, already reeling from the Republicans' unfavourable tax and subsidy changes [31].

Although the Gulf War would expose the inherent danger of Stockman's doctrines, their folly was apparent earlier in the brutal Iran/Iraq war. It ultimately tainted the Reagan administration in the scandal of the Iran-Contra affair. Again and again the folly of what Amory Lovins called the "hard" energy path has produced disaster. This is apparent in the Iran-Iraq war, the Gulf War, scheming by oil-rich states to sabotage the Arab-Israeli peace process and endless efforts by Iran and Iraq to produce weapons of mass destruction.

What is astonishing is how the tragedy of trading guns for oil could be claimed to be a national asset by Republican defenders of American reliance on Persian Gulf oil. A Republican Secretary of State, James Baker, defended the guns-for-oil exchange in terms of "jobs, jobs, jobs". A lobby group, US Jobs Now, took up this cause. It was composed of six defence contractors and six labour unions in the arms industry and promised new job opportunities to Americans through arms sales to the states of the Persian Gulf [32].

After 12 years of Republican administrations, Democratic President Bill Clinton returned to the solar policies of Carter. In his first two years in office there was a 35 percent increase in funding for research and development of photovoltaics. Clinton boldly attempted an energy tax increase that was watered down to a four-cent-a-gallon increase in the gasoline tax. It was only narrowly approved because of strong Republican opposition. Congressional Republicans also succeeded in weakening fuel efficiency standards by exempting sport utility vehicles which now account for half the new cars being purchased and only get 14 miles to the US gallon.

The initial energy tax proposal of the Clinton administration sparked the creation of corporate-funded lobbies against it. One was Citizens for a Sound Economy; another was the Affordable Energy Alliance. They organized massive rallies against the tax in oil producing states such as Oklahoma and Louisiana by direct mail to oil company employees [33].

Clinton's 1999 budget package included $6.3 billion for American-made clean-energy technologies and a five year extension of the wind energy tax credit. Like the leaders of America's allied democracies, Japan and the EU, Clinton has a goal of one million solar roofs for America by 2010. His proposal is now approved [34].

The Clinton administration has viewed the development of renewable energy as a critical battleground in its quest for a democratic peace. It is turning vast military laboratories of the Cold War toward researching renewable technologies so as to end dependence on foreign oil. It is also pursuing the same objective through the Clean-Car Initiative. This seeks to create a government-business partnership to replace conventional cars with zero-emission vehicles. It will accelerate electric propulsion, lightweight technologies and advanced manufacturing processes. The program has been given a significance equivalent to the mission to put a man on the Moon. At the time of the launch of the Clean-Car Initiative, about $3 billion annually was being spent on weapons development at government laboratories such as Los Alamos. The initiative's purpose is to redirect the funds into creating automotive vehicles that do not require oil [35].

The conversion of US military laboratories has already brought some promising results. The Los Alamos National Laboratory, which formerly funded research on nuclear bombs, developed a mobile education trailer on renewable technologies. It demonstrates operational solar technologies such as water heaters. The trailer was unveiled at a September 1998 Ghost Ranch Conference held in New Mexico. This sacred gathering to heal the scars of militarism was opened by the blessings of Running Deer, a native American shaman from the Taos Pueblo [36].

Sitting strategically in a line between the Pentagon and the Oval Office there are now four concentric arcs of iridescent silicon making up a 30 kW photovoltaic (PV) array to supply electricity to the Pentagon. This high profile PV project was intended to provide the Pentagon with a low-risk introduction to green power along with direct hands-on experience. The Pentagon's energy management team is rapidly becoming a resource for others in the federal government strategy to shift to solar power [37].

Renewable Power as the Basis for Community Activism

The surprising sunrise blessings of a Taos shaman illustrate how native American communities are playing a pioneering role in the development of renewable power. The Papago Indians of Arizona are renowned for remarkable achievements in protecting biodiversity. They are also leaders in solar energy. In 1978, the Papago village of Shuchuil became the world's first completely solar powered community [38].

Native communities have used solar power as an instrument of community economic development. The Hopi of the traditional communities of Hotevilla, Walpi, Lower Monenkopi and Old Oraibi have long refused to have their communities connected to electric power grids. Today many Hopi offer prayer feathers to their PV panels as they would to their crops, to the Sun and the Earth [39].

Likewise, Yukon native communities have been heartened by their territory's role in windpower development. The 150 kW Haeckel Hill turbine, west of Whitehorse, now feeds enough energy for 25 homes into the local power grid. This success recently caused Yukon's NDP territorial government to earmark $2 million for additional wind-power development.

The green civil society that blossomed during the Carter administration survived the assaults of the hostile Reagan administration, although its growth was slowed. Stripped of the support of the state, civil society tenaciously clung to its ideals. Although many alternative-energy businesses were destroyed, a core remained. Some of the state roles were assumed by civil society. For instance, after the Reagan administration stopped publishing statistics indicating the growth of renewable power, this task was taken up by Public Citizen, an environmental group founded by Ralph Nader. The co-operative San Francisco Solar Center still produces heating units for apartments, an effort spearheaded by trade unions [40].

Even in the state of Texas, its capital city, Austin, has become a liberal island of renewable power pushed forward by local solar champion Ray Reece. Here decomposing sewage generates 800 kilowatts of electricity, while reducing greenhouse gas emissions from methane. PV panels power both homes and traffic lights. Sacramento, the state capital of California, also went green. Its municipal utility has installed solar water heaters in 14,000 homes and promotes tree planting [41]. Sacramento has the world's biggest solar power plant, generating two megawatts of electricity. Funding was opposed by the US Department of Energy whose objections were overcome through appropriations in the mid-1980s by the then Democratic Party-controlled US Congress.

293

Many American communities have become remarkably oil free. Soldiers Grove, Wisconsin, a village of six hundred people, has become America's first community outside of an Indian reservation to obtain all its electricity from solar conversion. The Northwest Missouri State University became the premier university to be free of fossil fuels. University towns also have become the centres of cycling advocacy and use. Such battles are easier there than in other American cities since most students do not own cars [42].

CORPORATE OIL POWER AND THE AMERICAN DREAM

There are many green islands of civil society, such as Indian reservations, Amish communities and university towns, which are surrounded by a sea of oil money and power. Outside such green ghettos renewable technologies are simply unheard of. Views are shaped by mass media heavily influenced by the energy industry. The most disturbing aspect of "manufacturing consent," to use the phrase of critic Noam Chomsky, is the consent it gives to global warming. Nowhere else is this more apparent than in the huge audience of global warming sceptic Rush Limbaugh, whose broadcasts are an influential political commentary on the airwaves of much of the United States.

The strength of the oil industry in mainstream United States is vividly shown by the fact that only three Senators would vote to ratify the Kyoto Treaty. The defeat of Kyoto was helped by the massive political contributions of energy corporations who invested $64.4 million into US political parties between 1992 and 1998.

The US oil giants that have used considerable political influence to fight the Kyoto Treaty have been termed the "dinosaurs" of the global energy industry. Unlike transitional European giants such as BP and Shell, major American-owned oil companies such as Exxon-Mobil, Chevron and Texaco, continue to deny global warming and remain in the Global Climate Coalition. Their fundamentalist oil-worshipping faith has survived a November 1998 corporate exodus from this doomed cult by Ford, General Motors, Boeing, Enron, Lockheed Martin, Minnesota Mining & Manufacturing, and United Technologies — this last coupling its pull-out with a pledge to reduce its own greenhouse gas emissions.

In their assault on the Kyoto convention, American oil companies have been particularly energetic. Lee Raymond, president of Exxon-Mobil, gave an important address in China in which he said that if they want to continue to attract corporate investment from multinational giants, such as Exxon-Mobil, they should not participate in the international treaty process on climate change [43].

With the help of OPEC, American oil companies lobbied hard for exemptions from greenhouse gas reductions for developing countries in the Kyoto Treaty. They have then used these "catch up" provisions, intended to encourage economic growth, in the United States to lobby against the Treaty. Through extensive television advertisements they have claimed the Treaty will not work because of the increased emissions permitted to Third-World countries, ignoring, of course, how these advertisements' sponsors encouraged these very provisions [43, 44].

Refusal to believe in global warming, and a willingness to deny the truth of scientific findings are implicit prerequisites for corporations to be members in the Global Climate Coalition. The fixation on oil, which goes beyond profit rationality, is sowing the seeds of destruction of these same companies. Many years ago Amory Lovins noted that consumers want to keep warm, have cold drinks and hot showers, but not consume energy just for the sake of doing so. Energy corporations have largely ignored Lovins, though it is noteworthy that some are now moving in the direction of renewables.

Encouraged by the current federal research and development efforts, new energy-service companies are giving consumers what they want. Enron is such a growing US energy company without any oil wells. It began as a gas pipeline company, but has diversified into solar, wind and energy efficiency services. This has helped it devise products that consumers, increasingly aware of the potential for reducing their energy bills, want. Enron's strategy has proven especially effective in California. Here customers from the state university system to the San Francisco Giants baseball team have signed longterm outsourcing contracts with Enron to take care of their varied energy needs, including risk management.

Enron is the only major natural-gas based and US-owned energy company to break with the Global Climate Coalition and support the Kyoto Treaty. One of the most important benefits of the Treaty has been to generate debate over the future of oil within the American business elite. Major electrical utilities, which can switch from coal to natural gas, have also pulled out of the Global Climate Coalition [45].

The most conservative environmental groups have been outraged at TV ads featuring sport vehicles ploughing through streams. Another objectionable advertising feature is to promote desert crossings without roads.

Automotive culture is strong in North America, but has its limits. Safety standards are stricter than in most of Europe. Outrage over the amphibious Jeeps caused the National Wildlife Federation, an organization of environmentally concerned hunters and fishermen, to have the ads pulled. Although driving is considered to be a right, stronger than access to clean air and water, its power rests essentially on a consent perpetually being manufactured. Its unspoken restrictions on freedom are so strong that several television networks have not permitted paid anti-car advertisements from environmental organizations.

More than anywhere else in the world automotive culture tends to bond citizens in North America. Access to motorized luxuries remains an allure for immigration and driving has become a teenage rite of passage. This trend is encouraged by corporate strategists, aware of what must be encouraged to have consumers buy a product. However, the scale of employment in the automotive industry has in itself become one of the biggest barriers to shifts in public policy to encourage greener transport.

Nowhere has the tendency to promote trucking at the expense of rail freight been more severe than in North America. The increase in truck transport has prompted an expansion of the continent's expressway system — a hidden subsidy for truck haulage. More efficient haulage is not subject to much debate. As an illustration, the roads of southeast Michigan are barely passable, with every major highway in metropolitan Detroit being under construction at the time of writing [46].

In manufacturing consent a critical element has been to have widespread employment tied up in the automotive industry and its allies. This has encouraged the environmental movement to develop an anti-oil counterculture, analogous to that used by the prohibition movement. The "demon" *oil* is every bit as real as *rum*. It has caused many around the continent to take the pledge to avoid its use, through counterculture groups in such diverse areas as organic agriculture and cycling. Although still a small minority many North Americans are now trying to break their dependence on oil, much as alcoholics seek salvation from the bottle.

Part of the older American dream of small family farms and independent mechanics was ruined by the very oil interests now promoting speed and mobility. An oilless American counterdream could, however, arise to bring back family independence on the small farm.

OIL POWER VERSUS DEMOCRACY IN NORTH AMERICA

The so far successful battle to keep oil drilling out of the Arctic National Wildlife Refuge (ANWR) and its two complementary Canadian National Parks shows oil power in a fully democratic society ultimately loses when confronted by a strong environmental movement that sticks to peaceful means of protest. In over four decades of uncompromising political disputes over ANWR neither side has ever engaged in violence.

In all the bitter disputes between environmentalists and the petroleum industry, there is only one episode that has involved state violence remotely comparable to the atrocities of Third-World tyrants. The conflict was in northern Alberta, Canada, and was caused by the flaring of natural gas, a process that saves companies from having to collect the gas or re-inject it back into the ground.

Efforts at prosecuting a determined critic of the Alberta gas flaring, farmer Wiebo Ludwig, have involved a confessed false bombing of an oil facility. Blamed on environmental zealots, the crime was actually committed by Royal Canadian Mounted Police and involved extensive media manipulation. In addition, Ludwig's van was destroyed in an explosion which did not result in any charges being laid against those who carried out the crime. Despite such outrages, the incident serves to illustrate the importance of independent jurisprudence, since it was through the integrity of the judicial process, one of the cornerstones of democracy, that the police mischief was brought to light [47].

The continuing problems of Canadian farmers with gas flaring tend to overshadow the numerous victories that they have won through the democratic process to regulate the oil industry, especially outside Alberta (a province long dominated by a Conservative government having unusually close ties with the petroleum industry). Ontario farmer Peter Lewington has taken pride in his life's crusades for "democracy come to the oil patch." On one occasion Lewington persuaded Canadian Prime Minister Lester Pearson to reopen a National Energy Board (NEB) hearing into the environmental impacts of the oil industry on agriculture. The NEB eventually developed into what Lewington considered an excellent environmental department and made the protection of farmland a top priority.

By determined lobbying and court actions, Lewington and other Canadian farmers forced oil companies to protect their tile drains and achieved "sweeping reforms" to such federal legislation as the National Energy Board Act, the Railway Act and the Expropriation Act. Lewington's photographs showing how an oil fire destroyed his neighbour's white-ash grove convinced the NEB to develop "vastly better oil policies."

The worst horrors that Lewington faced include the elevated welded oil pipeline that became an impenetrable barrier through his farm for several weeks. Such assaults on the environment, now illegal in Canada, are the norm in dictatorships where exposed pipelines commonly devastate farmlands through leaks.

The flaring of natural gas is one of the many ways in which the true costs of fossil fuel are disguised in the marketplace, since injecting it back into the ground is more directly expensive, whereas the environmental costs of flaring are unknown, but likely huge, being spread over centuries.

Increasing the rate of descent in the cost of solar power is critical to phasing out fossil fuels at a suitably early date. Republicans in Congress who are allied to oil interests understand this quite well in a negative sense. They recently attempted to use the Monica Lewinsky scandal to gut $110 million from the US budget for renewable energy and efficiency programs. Their efforts failed because Clinton used a loophole in existing appropriation rules to ensure the measure's passage [48].

The world's most powerful oil companies have used violent tactics based on the power of the gun in repressive dictatorships and semidemocracies, but this has not been their method of operation in democracies, even in the Arctic wilds. While more conservative American environmental groups, notably the National Resources Defense Council (NRDC), have compromised in suggesting oil extraction in protected areas in Latin America, they have never taken such positions toward US national parks.

With their experience in the dramatic ecopolitics of North America, oil interests cannot be expected to promote the expansion of human rights in dictatorships. Friends of the Rainforest, an environmental group in Ecuador, seeks justice in US courts. US courts have greater powers, resources and independence to prosecute oil companies than the courts of Ecuador. The lawsuit against Texaco is based on its spillage of 16.8 million gallons of oil into Ecuador's rainforest. Since 1993, the Texaco suit has been in US courts. In 1995 environmentalists won a major victory when Federal District Judge Vincent Broderick cited international conventions for accepting jurisdiction. However, one year later Judge Broderick died and the case was assumed by Judge Jed Rakoff, who claimed the case could be pursued through the Ecuadorian judicial system. Rakoff's ruling was itself reversed in a unanimous decision of the US Court of Appeals for the Second Circuit Court [49].

Court battles in Manhattan against the oil industry illustrate repercussions of unrestricted exploitation — as permitted by dictatorships — in a democracy where most of the product is consumed. Although the slick commercials of automotive ads may equate personalized motor transport with the Statue of Liberty, reality puts freedom in democratic society into conflict with the power of oil.

NOTES

1. Jim West, "Tapping the Internet for Petroleum Data" in "International Petroleum Encyclopaedia, 1996" (Tulsa: Penn Well, 1996) pp.210; Jon R. Ludma, "The Price of Oil" *Audubon*, March/April, 1999, pp.53, 54.

2. Jim West, "Industry Broadening Scope of Environmental Initiatives" in "International Petroleum Encyclopaedia, 1993" (Tulsa: Penn Well, 1993) pp.193, 194.

3. *Ibid.*, pp.192-201.

4. Bob Williams, "Forward", *Oil and Gas Journal*, 1993 Edition (Tulsa: Penn Well, 1993) p.vii.

5. Ross Gelbspan, "The Heat is On" (New York: Random House, 1997) pp.87-100; Curtis Moore and Alan Miller, "Green Gold" (Boston, Beacon Press, 1993) p.83; "Why big is still beautiful", *The Economist*, April 3, 1999, pp.53, 54.

6. Wolfgang Zuckerman, "End of the Road" (Cambridge: Lutterworth, 1991) pp.42, 43.

7. Peter Freund and George Martin, "The Ecology of the Automobile" (Montreal: Black Rose Books, 1993) p.135.

8. David Kline, "Great Possessions" (San Francisco: North Point Press, 1990) *passim*.

9. Personal Communication from Quaker organic farmer Ken Laing (1995)

10. US National Parks and Conservation Association, *National Parks,* November/December, 1998, *passim*.

11. Brooke Coleman, "Bluewater Battles Snowmobiles", *Earth Island Journal*, Winter/Spring, 1999, p.8.

12. Ken Butti and John Perlin, "A Golden Thread" (New York: Cheshire Books, 1980), pp.221-231; Manucher Farmanfarmaian and Roxane Farmanfarmaian, "Blood and Oil" (New York: Modern Library, 1997) p.287; M. A. Adelman, "The Genie out of the Bottle" (Cambridge: MIT Press, 1995) p.47.

13. Nancy Cole and P.J. Skerrett, "Renewables Are Ready" (White River: Chelsea Green, 1995) pp.159, 160.

14. Bob Schilden, "Carless Behaviour", *Sierra*, March/April, **83**, No.2, p.28.

15. "At Last the Fuel Cell", *The Economist*, October 25, 1997, pp.89-92.

16. David Sperling, "Future Drive" (Washington: Island Press, 1995), pp.99-120.

17. Ron Stodhill, "Heaven on Wheels" *Time Magazine*, November, 1997, pp.30-40; Jeffery Ball, "Auto Makers Are Racing to Market 'Green Cars' Powered By Fuel Cells", *Wall Street Journal*, March 15, 1999, pp.A1, A8.

18. Freund and Martin, *loc. cit.*, p.90.

19. *Ibid.*, p.136; Tom Koppel, "The Power to Change the World", *The Globe and Mail Report on Business Magazine*, October, 1999, pp.81-87.

20. Debbie Miller, "Midnight Wilderness: Journeys in Alaska's National Wildlife Refuge" (San Francisco: Sierra Club Books, 1989) *passim.*

21. Michael Bedford, "Saving a Refuge", *Cultural Survival Quarterly*, Spring, 1992, pp.38-42; Raymond J. Parker, "A Natural Resource", *Nature Canada*, Autumn, 1999, pp.33-37.

22. Franklin Tugwell, "The Energy Crisis and the American Political Economy" (Stanford: Stanford University Press, 1996), pp.105, 140-149, 258, 259.

23. Ray Reece, "The Sun Betrayed", (Montreal: Black Rose Books, 1979) pp.191-222; Amory Lovins, "Soft Energy Paths: Toward a Durable Peace (New York: Friends of the Earth, 1977) *passim.*

24. *Ibid.*, Daniel Berman & John T. O'Conner, "Who Owns The Sun" (White River: Chelsea Green Publishing, 1996) pp.29-31.

25. Maxine Savitz, "The Federal Role in Conservation Research and Development" in John Byrne and Daniel Rich eds., "The Politics of Energy Research and Development" (New Brunswick: Transaction Books, 1986) pp.89-118.

26. Manucher Farmanfarmaian and Roxane Farmanfarmaian, *loc. cit.*, pp.166, 187-189, 292-295, 300, 452, 457.

27. Berman and O'Conner, *loc. cit.*, pp.32-35, 54-56, 194; Eugene Frankel "Technology, Politics and Ideology: The Vicissitudes of Federal Solar Energy Policy, 1974-83" in John Byrne and Daniel Rich, *loc. cit.*, pp.61-88.

28. Tugwell, *loc. cit.*, pp.112-140.

29. Richard Ottinger, "Introduction: The Tragedy of US. Energy R&D Policy", in Byrne and Rich, *loc. cit.*, p.5.

30. Paul Maycock and Edward Stirewell, "A Guide to the Photovoltaic Revolution" (Emmaaus: Roedale Press, 1995), pp.189-203.

31. Moore and Miller, *loc. cit.*, pp.99, 101; Berman and O'Conner, *loc. cit.*, p.55.

32. William Keller and Jane E. Nolan, "The Arms Trade: Business As Usual?" *Foreign Affairs*, Winter, 1997-98, pp.113-118.

33. Moore and Miller, *loc. cit.*, pp.84, 85.

34. "Clinton preparing to help renewables" *IPSO FACTO*, **12**, No. 1, February, 1998, p.5.

35. Sperling, *loc. cit.*, pp.110-130.

36. "Ghost Ranch Conference" *Solar Today*, Winter, 1999, p.12.

37. James Bing, "PV At the Pentagon", *Solar Today*, January/February, 2000, pp.32-35.

38. Paul Maycock and Edward Stirewell, "Photovoltaics: Sunlight to Electricity in One Step" (Andover: Brick House, 1981) pp.72, 73.

39. Cole and Skerrett, *loc. cit.*, pp.49-51, 124-126.

40. Berman and O'Conner, *loc. cit.*, p.31.

41. *Ibid.*, pp.29-31, 94-111.

42. Maycock and Stirewell, "Guide to the Photovoltaic Revolution", *loc. cit.*, p.198.

43. Shrong Beder, "Corporate Hijacking of the Greenhouse Debate", pp.119-122, Simon Retallack, "How US Politics is Letting the World Down", pp.111-118; Simon Retallack, "Primary Target: Derailing the International Negotiations", *The Ecologist*, March/April, 1999, p.119.

44. "Energy, the new convergence", *The Economist*, May 29, 1999, pp.59, 60.

45. Tom Murphy, "When ASAP Isn't Good Enough", *Ward's Auto World*, May, 1999, pp.67, 68.

46. *Ibid.*, pp.111-113, 155.

47. "Shooting remains a mystery", *The Globe and Mail*, June 22, 1999, p.A3.

48. "Editorial", *Solar Today*, Winter 1999, p.5; Peter Lewington, "No Right of Way: How Democracy Came to the Oil Patch" (Ames: Iowa University Press, 1991) *passim*.

49. Eyal Press, "Texaco on Trial", *The Nation*, May 30, 1999, pp.11-15.

CHAPTER SIXTEEN
THE EMERGENCE OF A
GREEN AND DEMOCRATIC PEACE

Europe, a continent lacking substantial petroleum wealth, has moved steadily in the direction of a democratic peace since the end of the Cold War, despite the temporary set-back of conflicts in the former Yugoslavia. The open conflicts in Bosnia and Kosovo were eventually ended with the establishment of police forces involving troops from Russia, the United States and its allies. The rest of Europe's evolving democratic peace is quite different from what one finds in less fortunate parts of the world that are still plagued by dictatorship, famine and civil wars

DEMOCRACY AS THE KEY TO EFFECTIVE REGIONAL SECURITY

NATO became the police instrument for the Dayton Accords that ended the war in Bosnia through the creation of the International Stabilization Force (IFOR). IFOR's 35,000 troops have served to keep the warring parties in Bosnia apart under its supervision and has assisted in the prosecution of war crimes. NATO and the European Union have poured $6 billion a year into Bosnia since the signing of the Dayton Accords in 1995. A critical achievement toward peace has been the creation of a television network, the Open Broadcast News, which has promoted a message of ethnic tolerance. IFOR's model was subsequently followed by SFOR which ended the civil war in the Serbian province of Kosovo.

Various dictatorships in the world are hostile to efforts to establish a democratic peace to defuse the Balkan powderkeg. China vetoed the UN's extension of an observer force patrolling the border between Macedonia and Yugoslavia; it was also critical of the creation of SFOR.

NATO's evolution since the end of the Cold War gives the clearest indication of it becoming an explicit instrument of a regional democratic peace. Its strategy to become a democratic alliance was critical in its mid-1997 decision to accept only Poland, Hungary and the Czech Republic as new members. Undemocratic Slovakia, which at the time had a Freedom House rating of "partially free", was left out, despite earlier plans to include it. This sent out a political message that only countries whose democratic credentials are beyond dispute will be invited to join NATO. It reinforced an earlier decision in the 1960s not to admit Spain into the alliance because of the lingering dictatorship of Franco [1].

Strategic studies experts and their conservative political allies have stressed national interests, such as oil, over human rights as a foreign policy objective. The error in such thinking is clear in Europe's post-war evolution. Security in Europe has increased with the protection of human rights, or decreased without it. The civil wars in former Yugoslavia have been primarily caused by the fact that the successor states which have sparked them, including both Croatia and Serbia, have been repressive regimes and serious abusers of human rights. A vivid contrast to the disintegration of Yugoslavia has been the democratization and respect for cultural pluralism shown in democratic Romania.

Hungary and Romania before the fall of the Berlin Wall were on the brink of war over Romania's brutal repression of its Hungarian minority. In their democratization, they moved to prevent conflict over abuses of human rights of national minorities. A private team from Princeton [2] was able to persuade the Romanian government to allow its Hungarian minority to use its own language in return for a promise not to promote separatism. One of the recent democratization moves by Romania's government, attacked by nationalist extremists, permits Hungarians to study history and geography in their own language.

The Organization for Security and Co-operation in Europe, with its stress on seeking peace through pluralist federalism and accommodation, is a good example of a democratic, regional peacemaker. Its approach is not taken in regions dominated by dictators. Repressive states tend to co-operate only to cause difficulty for the emergence of democracy. This has encouraged some bizarre combinations of extremists. Both Jewish and Islamic fundamentalists have shouted down advocates of peace who bravely appeared on the same platform.

FUNDAMENTALISM AND THE DEADLY MIX OF OIL, MILITARISM AND DICTATORSHIP

Religious fundamentalism has been a critical component in the deadly mix of oil, militarism and dictatorship. Fundamentalists of various stripes ignore how the great Hindu, Christian, Islamic, Confucian and Buddhist faiths have borrowed concepts from each other and integrated each others' creeds.

Ecumenism is a liberal approach to religious teachings that stresses mutual respect for the validity and common truths in various faith traditions. It is alien to fundamentalism, which stresses the exclusive truth of one revelation. Early American Protestant fundamentalists were hostile to ecumenism, opposing the incorporation of Roman Catholic ritual into Protestant worship. The ecumenical reality is recognized by the World Conference on Religion and Peace, composed of 15 faiths and 100 denominations. It stresses the need for interfaith actions on the issues of human rights, environmental protection and peace. The Conference emerged as the strongest expression of civil society in Sierra Leone. Under its ecumenical banner, brave actions for peace were undertaken successfully by lay Muslim and Christian women to end its terrible civil war.

The term fundamentalist was fashioned by the disciples of American oil tycoon Milton Stewart. It has subsequently become widely used to describe religious intolerance and authoritarianism across faith traditions. Such bigoted creeds are upheld by religious communities having the ability to employ state power over minorities. Fundamentalism is absent, for instance, among the Hindu community in predominantly Islamic Bangladesh. Fundamentalism hardens faith communities into polarized camps frequently through distorted interpretations of history. This was evident in India when in 1992 150,000 rioting fundamentalists destroyed the 16th century Ayodhya mosque. Like many holy places in India it was a delicate fusion of the architectural styles of the Islamic and Hindu faiths [3].

Fundamentalist interpretations tend to favour uniformity, military solutions and dictatorship. These faith interpretations are frequently encouraged by those in command of great oil wealth. Both Christian and Islamic fundamentalisms use confrontational style while *de facto* praising oil consumption and ignoring environmental concerns.

DECLINE IN OIL-BASED FUNDAMENTALISM

In December 1999, the Third Parliament of the World's Religions was held in Cape Town, South Africa, conducting among other events, a peace pilgrimage to the former apartheid prison of Robben Island. A tiny band of oil-financed Islamic fundamentalists denounced this conference, branding it as a "satanic, Zionist conspiracy." [4]

However, oil worshipping fundamentalism is on the decline even in some of its strongholds, such as the middle class of Sudan and Guatemala. Here fundamentalists unleashed horrific scorched-earth policies against traditional peasant cultures living in harmony with the Earth.

The foreign sponsors of the genocidal devastation in Sudan and Guatemala are also receding. Iran has a blossoming democracy movement. In the United States environmentalists are separating the toxic combination of oil and fundamentalism, as Christian environmentalists crusade to save endangered species in the spirit of Noah.

It is difficult to equate squeezing of precious oil from the sacred body of Mother Earth with a profound spiritual purpose, no matter what distortions are employed. Union Oil of California, whose riches financed the first fundamentalist manifesto and later became tainted by the Santa Barbara spill, is now the target of an effort by environmental and human-rights advocates for the repeal of its corporate charter. One of the reasons cited is its close ties with Myanmar's dictatorship, one of the world's worst oppressors of Christians [5].

The Acceptance of a Green Democratic Peace in Mainstream US Politics

The policy of promoting a green democratic peace has been a consistent thread for two decades in the policies of the US Democratic Party. First apparent in strategic concepts of the Truman administration, it was resurrected by President Jimmy Carter's promotion of alternative power and championing of human rights. For instance, he succeeded in toppling most of the repressive regimes that had been imposed on Latin America during the Republican administrations of Nixon and Ford. Quickly after Carter's inauguration, hundreds of Chilean prisoners of conscience were released from conditions in which they had been subjected to horrific torture. An element of bipartisanship towards human rights appeared in the subsequent Republican administrations of Reagan and Bush. Although oil - loving they tended to accept the human-rights elements of Carter's foreign policy. This encouraged democratization in a number of nations, especially those with little oil such as Chile and the Philippines.

The Clinton administration has also favoured the ideal of a democratic peace, encouraging it by measures such as increased funding for the National Endowment for Democracy and Radio Free Asia. A new initiative is the creation of a Radio Free Africa.

Much of the force behind the notion of green and democratic peace was supplied by the dynamic duo of birdwatching environmentalists, Jimmy Carter and his energy adviser, James Schlesinger. While CIA Director, Schlesinger would pursue his birdwatching hobby in off hours. His maverick environmentalism was combined with hostility to the negation of US power by oil-rich dictatorships. Carter saw the challenge as a contemporary version of William James' notion of a moral substitute for war [6].

The democratic "Sun" presidents, Carter and Clinton, have adopted a solar strategy for a green and democratic peace. Such a Sun-powered course is favoured by most democratic governments, including oilless South Africa, Japan, and the European Union [7].

CAPITALIST CREATIVE DESTRUCTION — THE ULTIMATE TOOL FOR A GREEN AND DEMOCRATIC PEACE

One of the greatest economists in the 20th century was the Austrian social democratic statesman and scholar Joseph Schumpater. He was the prophetic author of the phrase "creative destruction" which means eliminating the problems posed by fossil fuels and nuclear power as the cost of alternatives fall. This process will be hastened by reduced fossil-fuel subsidies, eventually turning the oil patch of the Persian Gulf into an archaic relic.

All automotive manufacturers in the developed democratic capitalist economies are spending considerable research and development money on some form of zero-emissions technology. This technological offensive is isolating the pariah states of oil dictatorships, such as Iran, Russia and its former allied oil dictatorships, Syria, Iraq and Libya. Their motor vehicles, already superpolluting, will ultimately become much more expensive to operate in comparison with fuel-cell cars.

Sharing new green technologies with less developed nations offers incentives for co-operation on other fronts. Democratization and demilitarization can be made conditions for technology transfers.

In the late 1990s the oil dictatorships were hit by a double whammy. Oil prices declined while their own manufacturing industries failed to keep up with efficiency innovations of the free world. This fostered democratic transitions in Indonesia and Nigeria [Appendix I]. Such pressures on dictatorships will be further increased with the declining costs of renewable technologies such as fuel cells and solar power.

Any rise in petroleum prices from trends such as an Asian economic revival, OPEC's recent production cutbacks or declining petroleum reserves, will make renewable energy technologies more cost-competitive with fossil fuels. The benefits to petrodictatorships of such price increases will thus only be temporary.

Creative destruction is the weapon of liberty in the struggle against petrotyranny. Its emergence highlights the tyrannies' essential weakness and state of underdevelopment.

Future Political Conflict in the Era of Green and Democratic Peace

Optimism over the green and democratic peace is tempered by its late arrival. Since the Pleistocene extinctions humans have harmed the stability and diversity of the natural world. There are of course exceptions to this trend; among the most impressive are unusual ecopacifist communities such as the Bishnoi of India and the old-order Amish. These unmotorized and peace-oriented exceptions serve to highlight the tragic impact of the general rule.

With a democratic world federation guns will stop blazing. However, there will be intense and fierce debates galore.

Optimistic and Pessimistic Scenarios for the Post-Cold-War World

Among predictions for the directions of the post-Cold-War world there are two which have served as a focus for debate. One is Francis Fukuyama's *End of History*, the other is Samuel Huntington's *Clash of Civilizations*.

The End of History thesis is based on universal peace through the spread of democracy and the free-market system. Samuel Huntington denies that democracy will be triumphant. He sees freedom as a product of Western culture forged by the medieval Catholic church and warns of wars sparked by disputes over oil.

Both Huntington's and Fukuyama's predictions suffer from a lack of attention to environmental issues. The problems of climate change, global warming, the hole in the ozone layer, species extinctions, deforestation, desertification, pollution and soil erosion are ignored in their sweeping prophecies. However, Fukuyama's optimism shows a kernel of green wisdom. He predicted liberal democracy would be combined with easy access to stereos and VCRs but not to universal scooters or automobiles [8].

The problem of the unsustainability of motor transport points to the remarkable convergence in the thinking of three leading peace prophets — Gandhi, Kant, and the Canadian statesman, J.S. Woodsworth. All of these practical-minded visionaries had a notion that consumption patterns should be restricted to what could be afforded by the whole human community. Kant's famous "categorical imperative" was to "so act that you would be willing to have everyone act that way." Likewise, J.S. Woodsworth remarked that "What we want for ourselves, we want for all." Gandhi rejected the British style of living for India since he did not believe it was physically possible to achieve it within the constraints of the world's resources [9].

The prophetic words of Kant, Woodsworth and Gandhi are a visionary condemnation of oil-based motorization. Oil-burning cars, scooters and motorcycles cannot be universally afforded by the world's families either in terms of price or environmental impacts. To paraphrase Woodsworth's famous prayer, such deadly toys should not be wished for all. What could be wished in a universal sense is greener private transportation technology, such as a nonemitting electric bike.

Fortunately the threats of oil, dictatorship and militarism do get considerable attention from democratic leaders. The world's most powerful democracies — the United States, Japan and the European Union — all have ambitious plans for a million solar roofs by 2010, although America's program is opposed by the Republican-dominated Congress.

When environmental threats and the problems of oil and dictatorship are considered, it is possible to modify Fukuyama's utopianism and Huntington's pessimism. Continued problems caused by ecological degradation will be the source of intense disputes. Debate over these hotly contested environmental issues will mean that there will be a continuation of history, despite democracy and the market economy and the abundance of stereos and VCRs. These disputes can in principle be resolved in a nonviolent fashion between democracies in a world federation.

A VISION OF HOPE FOR 2015

Samuel Huntington's provocative challenge of a world war over oil by 2010 cries out for a more positive alternative for the first decades of the new millennium. While there will still be plenty of conflict such disputes will be

309

resolved nonviolently within a politically united humanity. To parody Huntington, there could in the near future be a conflict of environmental agendas reflecting clashes of comforts rather than civilizations. Not all aspects of such a vision will ever be realised, but it lights a candle of hope to brighten the bleak prophesies of war for oil churned out by Huntington and similarly minded writers of the strategic-studies genre.

THE CLASH OF ENVIRONMENTAL AGENDAS FROM 2010-2015

By 2010, an international democratic federation is achieved. This took place after the member states of the United Nations became full democracies. The reduced value of oil was provoked by the lower costs of alternative energy. This crash caused even relatively clean natural gas to be widely replaced with hydrogen and methane from animal manure and biomass. Communist China, after making huge investments around the world in the oil economy, quickly became insolvent after these assets devalued. Remaining oil production is increasingly restricted to serving the needs of industrial raw material.

Rapid devaluation of petroleum made the remaining dictatorships fall like collapsing dominoes. The final transition took place in only seven days.

Armies are abolished except for a UN police force. All weapons of mass destruction are outlawed and abolished. The nuclear fuel cycle is being phased out prior to its prohibition. Unemployed uranium and coal miners find jobs in the booming solar and wind-power industries.

UN auditors inspect the world's financial institutions. This contributes to economic security by effectively prohibiting speculative practices that resulted in the 1998 Asian meltdown.

There is an international prohibition on banking secrecy. The assets of former dictators are seized by an order of the International Criminal Court. The $200 billion in confiscated dictators' plunder improves basic public health and literacy in low-income nations.

The UN police force stands ready to intervene and put a nation under trusteeship if it violates basic human rights. For three years Somalia had such a trusteeship imposed upon it by the Security Council. This lasted until Somalia was able to function as a full democracy. After the transition was completed it was readmitted to the UN.

A new, decisive action by the UN in Somalia served to forewarn a variety of would-be dictators, most notably leaders of Hutu and Tutsi extremist factions in Central Africa. What resolve they had was shattered after their radio stations attempting to broadcast hate messages of genocide were sabotaged. The mission was carried out by a special detachment of the UN police force.

Peace, environmental restoration and democracy are encouraged by US President Ralph Nader and his national security adviser, former Vice-President, Al Gore. They have redirected the covert operations capacity of the CIA which now stimulates the growth of grass-roots environmental groups in new democracies. This encourages tree planting, energy conservation, and creating bicycle paths. An international space agency directs previous military hostilities towards developing protection from comets and asteroids. It sends a solar ship to explore such heavenly threats.

In keeping with the new focus on environmental security most of the former US Army is redirected to the task of restoring the great plains, which become a vast wild buffalo commons and a Mecca to millions of ecotourists. Other countries try to initiate the audacious green example of the world's leading superpower. This creates a surprising environmental restoration race. Russia declares it will outdo the United States by bringing back the Woolly Mammoth from extinction through genetic engineering based on surviving DNA obtained from animals frozen in ice. Land formerly set aside for oil exploration in Russia is designated as a gigantic "Pleistocene Park", believed to be of a sufficient size to have great herds of the restored Mammoths together with millions of free-roaming caribou.

Unusual ideas for environmental restoration spring up around the world. One is a joint Palestinian-Israeli initiative to instal waterless composting toilets throughout Palestine and Israel. This is a green feather in the cap of the new Israeli Prime Minister, Mordechai Vanunu. He is revered throughout the Middle East because of his long imprisonment for opposing nuclear weapons. Vanunu's election brought a fresh trust towards Israel by the new Arab democracies.

Encouraged by grass-roots mobilizations and demonstrations the Arab League has former soldiers (those not absorbed into the UN force) assigned to reclaiming desert. Thus, plants now grow in the oil-tarred sand dunes of Kuwait.

Islamic scholars have become passionate environmentalists. Their green vision was encouraged by participation in one of the UN's educational space missions which showed the dramatic advances of the desert in the Middle East.

A world federation has been developed through reforms to the United Nations. A system of weighted voting is instituted for its parliament, based largely on population [10].

The UN is now dominated by ecologists who do not share the US love of the car. In 2012, two years into the mandate of the UN's directly elected People's Assembly, the Prime Minister of China, Mah Tin Lee, demands a draconian auto ban, so that greenhouse gas emissions will fall to the level of 1880. Using land-use and population figures Lee illustrates how if Asia copied US motor methods starvation would ensue.

Lee's UN plea came after the Chinese auto debate resulted in a demand for a world auto ban. Lee announced the application of the ban to China after popular agitation against cars exploded when a treasured refuge for endangered species became threatened by an expressway interchange.

The Chinese government acted on the advice of their agronomists who demonstrated that the best way to expand food production was to dig up the expressways constructed during the last years of Communist rule in southern China. These were on the nation's most productive lands, which had yielded three crops a year.

The Chinese parliament's car ban resulted in widespread turmoil. Publishers were angered at the sudden loss of automotive ads. They complained that China did not struggle for democracy to go back to the ox and cart.

Chinese ecologists were supportive of the auto ban but wished to inflict further economic damage on the global automakers that had collaborated with Communist rule in the last years of dictatorship. Many ecologists had been tortured. They mounted massive demonstrations demanding a universal car ban. The US flag was burned among shouts of "Death to the Car".

Chinese citizens are incensed at TV images of foreigners enjoying motor luxury. Scenes of US families travelling gleefully through the vast buffalo commons in jeeps and minivans do not go down well among toiling Chinese peasants.

The democrats are having to explain to the nation that the dream promised by the Communists of a car for every Chinese family is not obtainable. To placate the outraged demonstrators Lee seizes the automobiles of western residents in China. They are destroyed in rallies across the nation, televised to great popular acclaim.

To set a good example Lee visits the United Nations in a horse drawn carriage. Public opinion in China is further outraged when their Prime Minister, while in New York City, is pelted with garbage by unemployed automotive workers. Although he escapes serious injury the Prime Minister returns to China in a huff.

Broadcasts of Lee's audacious demands to ban cars spark angry demonstrations and protests in Detroit. He is burnt in effigy as a threat to the jobs of millions of Americans.

Autoworkers boycott Chinese restaurants and products. They smash windows before being stopped by police. American automotive executives together with union officials demand the impeachment of US President, Ralph Nader. They are outraged by his sympathetic response to Lee's demands.

As the US Congress begins its hearings into Nader's impeachment Lee seeks the mediation efforts of the President of the Organization of Middle Eastern States, Yasser Arafat. Arafat meets in Kuwait with the royal families of the Persian Gulf. These emirs and sheikhs still have considerable wealth. Before the final seven days of their absolute rule the now chastened constitutional rulers wisely choose to invest in the growing solar energy business.

In Kuwait, Arafat attempts to develop a financial package that will restore harmony to global markets seriously shaken by boycotts between China and America. Surrounded by financial advisers, Arafat realises the solution to the economic crisis is to offer automotive companies a financial compensation package. This will allow the giant corporations to make more money while still accepting Lee's demands.

While attending to business Arafat also seeks spiritual advice. He has religious figures from around the world assemble in Kuwait. The Pope, the Grand Ayatollah of Iran, the Patriarch of the Eastern Orthodox Church, the Archbishop of Canterbury, the Tadaho of the Iroquois Confederacy and the Dalai Lama (to mention only a few) pray fervently for a solution to the impasse. The whirling dances of Sufi dervishes help break up more conventional ways of thinking.

Arafat is well positioned to serve as a mediator in this most serious global crisis since the end of dictatorships. He is by now the most senior and respected of democratic politicians and is able to broker difficult compromises. His connections delay Congressional hearings demanding Nader's impeachment for the "high crime and misdemeanours" of threatening the auto industry.

Kuwait inspires both spiritual leaders and investors by its quick transition from an oil to a financial centre. Here a comprehensive plan is developed to facilitate the dismantling of the automotive economy. The Arafat plan finances the needed technologies for Africa and Asia. Disused automotive factories will turn out solar-powered photovoltaic generators, cisterns, composting toilets, smokeless stoves and improved versions of animal-draft farming technology.

Most automotive executives and trade union officials are pleased with the Arafat brokered Kuwaiti deal. A minority however, passionately love their cars. They are out of reach of the arguments of reason. These diehards refuse to listen to the advantageous financial terms being offered. To counter their fundamentalist opposition Arafat with the help of Vanunu urges the assembled holy men and women to pray and have their faithful followers send e-mail, letters and faxes to the US Congress.

Hard-line auto lobbyists meet with the powerful Christian Coalition, a fundamentalist group still wielding considerable power in the US Congress. It demands that Nader's impeachment proceed because of the President's outrageous sell-out to foreign interests hostile to the realisation of the old American dream.

On the day the US Congress' Justice Committee is to begin impeach-ment hearings a massive hurricane devastates the US eastern seaboard. Despite the progress made in curbing greenhouse gas emissions the climate has not stabilized. The main barrier is the serious pollution still caused by automotive production, although the light-weight carbon fibre vehicles powered by fuel cells and hydrogen no longer emit any fumes.

With greenhouse gas emissions still running too high, damage from global warming continues. The year 2012 establishes a new record for destruction by extreme weather events. The considerable efforts of fundamentalist preachers fail to stem the hurricane's advance on Washington. At the same time the greatest wave of destruction yet unleashed hits the tornado alley of Oklahoma and the Texas Panhandle with massive floods and thunderstorms.

Much propaganda is made out of the fact that the offices of the Buffalo Commons Alliance, a small environmental group, remains untouched after devastation hits Tulsa's auto dealerships. A wave of tornadoes converts most of the cars of the bible belt into scrap metal.

The selectivity of the force of the hurricane weakens the resolve of the fundamentalists to impeach the President. Their office files are scattered by the strong winds. These documents blowing in the wind provide the answer to Nader's Congressional difficulties. They disclose damaging evidence of corrupt dealings between the Christian Coalition and the automotive industry. Evidence is also produced of a potential sex scandal which involves the Congressional Republican leadership. Nader uses the incriminating evidence to obtain the resignation of the Speaker of the House of Representatives.

A stirring State-of-the-Union Address by President Nader is held in the historic Philadelphia State House — which temporarily serves as a Congress hall while the hurricane-damaged Capitol building is undergoing repairs. In this historic setting the automotive conversion plan is accepted. The economic boom experienced by Americans from automotive conversion causes the Republicans to lose their Congressional majority.

After two years however, an antigreen backlash develops. In a bout of environmental enthusiasm the US Congress bans gas and electric powered lawn mowers. The Republicans gain considerable support by campaigning against this infringement on the freedoms of Americans. In their new Contract with America they proclaim that the right of the people to mow their lawns shall not be infringed. This provides a basis for a new Republican

Congressional majority. It overrides President Nader's veto and removes the ban on motor mowers.

The reversal of the lawn mower ban does not go down well however, in China. Here such polluters were banned seven years ago in an early bout of green democratic zeal. The stage is set for another serious international crisis in 2016. Lee is set to make further trouble by adding snowmobiles, and motor boats to his prohibition list.

Resolving Disputes Nonviolently in a Democratic World

As the world moves towards democratic peace there is neither the finality of an end of history nor the tumultuous conflict of a clash of civilizations. Debates over contentious issues continue to divide humanity. They increasingly are resolved through nonviolent means without the need of armies. Disputes over the continued use of cars and motor mowers however are typical of the conflicts that would characterize even the most successful and environmentally oriented systems of democratic world government.

Conflicts over luxuries which do considerable harm to the environment will not be easy to resolve. This Francis Fukuyama wisely understood by omitting them from his anticipated consumer paradise of universal free market democracy. These are luxuries which will never be affordable to the majority of humanity. Despite this they have become very much part of the normal life style for many families in what is termed the affluent First World, setting the stage for a bitter clash of comforts.

Disconcerting waves of difficult-to-regulate immigration can be set in motion by unequal access to private motorized travel. This could induce a sizeable minority in a largely carless country to move across the oceans to earn incomes high enough for the magical motorized luxuries which are not affordable at home. Such a clash of comforts would become a major administrative obstacle to a smoothly functioning world government.

Democratic investments in health and education can bring an American level of life expectancy but not its access to motorized comforts. Such are the challenges still to be faced in the democratic and sustainable peace achieved after abolishing petrotyranny.

NOTES

1. Freedom House Survey Team "Freedom in the World, 1997-98" (New York: Freedom House, 1998) pp.77-82; "Carlos Westendorp, Bosnia's Euro-Spanish viceroy", *The Economist*, September 5, 1998, p.52; "War of the Airwaves", *The Economist*, August 30, 1997, pp.37, 38.

2. Dietrich Fisher, "United Nations Reform: A Systems Approach", in Eric Fawcett and Hanna Newcombe ed., "United Nations Reform" (Toronto: Science for Peace, 1995) p.73.

3. Freedom House Survey Team, *loc. cit.*, p.279.

4. "Interfaith Conferences," *The Anglican Journal*, January 2000, pp.12-13.

5. Freedom House Survey Team, *loc. cit.*, pp.169-172.

6. Daniel Yergin, "The Prize" (New York: Simon & Schuster, 1991) pp.661-663.

7. Tracy C. Rembert, "Electric Currents", *E Magazine*, November/December, 1997, pp.29-35.

8. Robin Wright and Doyle McManus, "Flash-Points" (New York: Alfred A. Knopf, 1991) pp.87, 100.

9. Hanna Newcombe, "The Roots of Co-operation", in Hanna Newcombe edited, "Hopes and Fears" (Toronto: Science for Peace, 1992) p.150.

10. For practical proposals for democratic UN reform see, Dieter Heinrich, "A United Nations Parliamentary Assembly" in Eric Fawcett and Hanna Newcombe edited, *loc. cit.*, pp.95-100.

APPENDIX I
The Effects of Oil Price Changes

The relatively slow pace of democratization in the post-Cold-War world can be traced in part to the price of oil. While rising petroleum profits strengthen dictatorships, there is no simple relationship of oil price down, freedom up. One of the curses of oil is that its price fluctuations have effects that can undermine the best intentions of enlightened statesmen to democratize repressive societies.

Lower oil prices hurt dictatorships in many ways. In addition to weakening repressive militaries, they encourage a tendency to focus public outrage for poorer living conditions on a country's ruling elite. This helped sweep away repressive governments in Nigeria and Indonesia, hastening the demise of malevolent petrotyrannies. However, authoritarian movements seeking to discredit vulnerable governments in new and fragile democracies can manipulate popular rage. If the greatest dangers occur when despotic rulers are trying to reform, these risks are compounded when they suffer a sudden loss of petroleum revenue.

Reformist leaders of Algeria's ruling socialist Front Liberation Nationale (FLN) were cursed by low oil prices during their attempts to effect transitions to democratic rule. Lower oil prices, which fostered unpopular cuts in public spending on health care, social welfare and education, were a bonanza for Algeria's Islamic fundamentalists. These antidemocratic extremists reaped a political windfall of discontent.

Nigeria's Second Republic was weakened because its elected rulers had the misfortune of holding office when oil prices collapsed. This made them vulnerable to protests by Islamic fundamentalists and military elites.

Mikhail Gorbachev's visionary efforts to work co-operatively with the United States through the United Nations to secure a stable and environmentally sustainable democratic global peace were essentially destroyed by unstable oil prices. His opponents blamed his liberalization for hardships caused by the low oil price.

The beginning of the year 2000 sees a turbulent brew of possibilities that may follow from fluctuating oil prices. The new democracies of Nigeria and Indonesia are now blessed by an increase in oil prices. Algeria's democratizing government is also helped in its peace efforts to reach a compromise with the country's Islamic opposition by higher petroleum revenues. A sudden drop in the price of oil may wreak havoc on these difficult democratic transitions.

While some democratizing governments are helped by higher oil prices, increasing oil wealth is reducing pressures on the governments of Sudan and Angola to make democratic compromises for peace. In the Middle East the flood of oil wealth to repressive rulers will impede any advance toward democracy throughout the region. The new nationalist and authoritarian President of Russia, Vladimir Putin, benefits from a considerable oil windfall while manipulating a bloody war against the Chechens for electoral advantage.

The vast majority of democracies import most of their oil. They do not experience sporadic windfall petroprofits. Since 1973, the European Union and Japan have weakened the impact of petroleum price fluctuations on their economies through heavy oil taxes, which they lightened to counter recent OPEC-induced increases. This has eliminated petroleum shock on everything but these countries' national finances.

Some democratic states remain vulnerable to the OPEC cartel. In the absence of heavy petroleum taxation, Canada, the United States, Australia and New Zealand risk economic contraction through rising oil prices. The most pessimistic economic forecasts for the year 2000 are based on rising US interest rates in response to balance of payments problems and inflation caused by rising oil prices.

A sudden rise in oil price has played a role in the demise of some oil-poor dictatorships — see Chapter Thirteen, under the subheading "The Long Road to Democratic Peace in Europe."

APPENDIX II
STEPS TOWARD ABOLISHING PETROTYRANNY

ENERGY POLICY

1. Eliminating all subsidies to the fossil-fuel industry.
2. Eliminating tax breaks for the fossil-fuel industry, for example, for oil exploration.
3. Prohibiting as far as possible new investments in fuel exploration and development.
4. Eliminating gas flaring.
5. Working toward greater efficiencies from operating oil fields and pipelines.
6. Ratifying the Kyoto Agreement.
7. Investing more in renewable energy development so as to reduce costs .
8. Instituting land-use planning that will stop urban sprawl and reduce dependence on automotive transport.
9. Taxing and planning so as to discourage automotive transport and encourage public transit, rail freight, cycling and walking.
10. Promoting voluntary simplicity.
11. Encouraging organic farming, especially through public education.
12. Promoting energy conservation.
13. Using a carbon tax to offset any oil-price reduction.
14. Imposing deadlines for staged introduction of zero-emission vehicles.
15. Promoting awareness of natural alternatives to fossil-fuel based products.
16. Creating more public awareness of the problems of global warming, and encouraging appropriate public and private responses.
17. Discouraging and restricting the use of pesticides.
18. Planting more trees to improve urban microclimates.
19. Legislating the planting of trees along river banks for better water and soil conservation.

HUMAN RIGHTS

1. Curbing foreign investment in states that violate human rights.
2. Providing better terms for debt reduction to countries that are making progress in human rights.
3. Refusing to repudiate debt incurred by dictatorships until completion of democratic transitions.
4. Providing assistance for democratic opposition to oppression.
5. Giving truly unfavorable publicity to human-rights violations.
6. Assisting human-rights and environmental organizations in repressive nations and new democracies.
7. Assisting indigenous peoples to use their land rights to restrict fossil-fuel development.

John Bacher received his PhD in History from McMaster University in 1985. His dissertation "Keeping to the Marketplace: the Evolution of Canadian Housing Policy" was published by McGill/Queen's Press in 1991. He was a co-author of the first edition of "Get a Life." He has taught courses in Peace Studies at the University of Toronto and McMaster University and has published several papers in academic journals. In both his activist involvement and academic research he has stressed the reinforcing connections between peace, environmental protection and human rights, subjects he has written about for *The St. Catharines Standard*, *Peace Magazine*, *The Activist* and *Now Magazine*. Much of his work in the peace movement was devoted to assisting independent peace organizations and civil society in Eastern Europe and the USSR.

For eight years John was President of the Preservation of Agricultural Lands Society. For six years he served on a panel of a government regulatory body: the Ontario Drainage Tribunal. He is currently Chair of the Niagara River Restoration Council, and a member of the Niagara Free Wheelers, the Bruce Trail Association, the Peninsula Field Naturalists, the Niagara Falls Nature Club and the Artists' Environment Forum. He is a member of St. Barnabas Anglican parish church in St. Catharines.

INDEX

OTHER BOOKS FROM SCIENCE FOR PEACE

(With Dundurn Press)

Good Taxes: The Case for Taxing Currency Exchange and Other Financial Transactions, by Alex Michalos. 1997. 87 pp.

United Nations Reform: Looking Ahead after Fifty Years, edited by Eric Fawcett and Hanna Newcombe. 1995, 336 pp.

World Security: The New Challenge, edited by Carl Jacobsen, Morris Miller, Metta Spencer and Eric Tollefson. 1994. 282 pp.

(With Samuel Stevens)

Arctic Alternatives: Civility or Militarism in the Circumpolar North, edited by Franklyn Giffiths. 1992. 313 pp.

Unarmed Forces, edited by Graeme MacQueen. 1992. 129 pp.

Canada and the World: An Agenda for the Last Decade of the Millennium, by Anatol Rapoport and Anthony Rapoport. 1992. 127 pp.

Hopes and Fears: The Human Future, edited by Hanna Newcombe. 1992. 195 pp.

Disarmament's Missing Dimension: A UN Agency to Administer Multilateral Treaties, by The Markland Policy Group. 1990. 150 pp.

Accidental Nuclear War, edited by Derek Paul, Michael D. Intriligator and Paul Smoker. 1990. 169 pp.

A few older titles are still available from the Science for Peace office.

SECRETS *of the*

TEENAGE
BRAIN

SECOND EDITION

To my four adolescents, Jen, Scott, Rachel, and James.

Sheryl G. Feinstein

Foreword by Eric Jensen

SECRETS

of the

TEENAGE
BRAIN

Research-Based Strategies for
Reaching and Teaching Today's Adolescents

SECOND EDITION

CORWIN
A SAGE Company

For information:

Corwin
A SAGE Company
2455 Teller Road
Thousand Oaks, California 91320
(800) 233-9936
Fax: (800) 417-2466
www.corwinpress.com

SAGE India Pvt. Ltd.
B 1/I 1 Mohan Cooperative
    Industrial Area
Mathura Road, New Delhi 110 044
India

SAGE Ltd.
1 Oliver's Yard
55 City Road
London EC1Y 1SP
United Kingdom

SAGE Asia-Pacific Pte. Ltd.
33 Pekin Street #02-01
Far East Square
Singapore 048763

Printed in the United States of America

Library of Congress Cataloging-in-Publication Data

Feinstein, Sheryl.
Secrets of the teenage brain : research-based strategies for reaching and teaching today's adolescents/Sheryl G. Feinstein. — 2nd ed.
    p. cm.
Includes bibliographical references and index.
ISBN 978-1-4129-6266-7 (cloth)
ISBN 978-1-4129-6267-4 (pbk.)
    1. Teenagers–Education–United States. 2. Adolescent psychology–United States.
3. Learning. 4. Brain. I. Title.

LB1737.U6F418 2009
373.180973--dc22   2009019902

This book is printed on acid-free paper.

09   10   11   12   13   10   9   8   7   6   5   4   3   2   1

Acquisitions Editor:	Carol Chambers Collins
Editorial Assistant:	Brett Ory
Production Editor:	Amy Schroller
Copy Editor:	Cindy Long
Typesetter:	C&M Digitals (P) Ltd.
Proofreader:	Carole Quandt
Indexer:	Gloria Tierney
Cover Designer:	Michael Dubowe

Contents

Foreword

I am delighted to add my comments to this fabulous resource. Every teacher and parent can relate to the teen years because they've been there. As a teen growing up in the '60s, I was awkward, fearful, excited, risk taking, and cocky but mostly just happy to survive. My grades were all over the place; you would have thought I had multiple personalities attending school under assumed names—it was truly such a crazy time. I was delighted when Dr. Sheryl Feinstein suggested this book and even more so when it became part of my library. I am now pleased to announce that a second edition is being offered, updating everyone on the latest research and strategies for the teenage brain. As a former teenager, you'll relate to so much of this book. If you are the parent of teens, you'll really enjoy it!

When I was a teen, I needed structure but wanted independence. I loved doing risky things even though they rarely paid off. The teachers I had who really cared sure got my attention. For example, my sixth-grade and eighth-grade English teachers were very personable. As a result, I not only worked harder for them, they became role models for me. Years later, I ended up teaching middle school English. There's quite a bit of power in the appropriate role model at the right time in one's life!

What makes adolescents so different from the adults they would become and from the children they used to be? The list of various culprits we've pinpointed is a long one: hormones, rebellious nature, youthful exuberance, and plain old immaturity are among the favorites. No one expected, however, that the teen brain was keeping secrets—and big ones!

Who knew that the teen brain was still growing? Scientists have assumed until just recently that the brain was mostly finished growing in childhood and left it at that. New achievements in brain-imaging technology, especially functional MRIs, finally enabled neuroscientists to look inside the heads of teens and check it out. What they saw took everyone by surprise—the adolescent brain is a hotbed of activity. Even more shocking was the discovery that the brain keeps developing at least into the twenties.

These findings reveal a whole new perspective on the role of secondary education. Teens are neither "big children" practicing to be adults nor are they "adults with a smaller brain"! Rather, they bring different interests and expectations to the classroom. Educators are just starting to view them as a unique group. *Secrets of the Teenage Brain* investigates the neurological and biological changes that teenagers experience. In each chapter are new facts and research findings that topple assumptions we've held about teenagers as well as a comprehensive list of strategies teachers can use with adolescent students.

The second edition of *Secrets of the Teenage Brain* expands our knowledge on the teenage brain, including cutting-edge research and fresh strategies. Special features include technology and the brain, students with ADHD (attention-deficit/hyperactivity disorder), steroid use, and violence and aggression, giving new perspectives to contemporary issues. I must admit, one of my favorite additions to this book is the book club discussion questions. They are a wonderful way to bring educators together for meaningful dialogue; I can't wait for the conversation to begin.

Hopefully, you'll enjoy learning why teens act like they do; no matter what, you'll definitely see them in a new light when you are done! *Secrets of the Teenage Brain* will reveal the exciting answers to the tantalizing secrets that have eluded educators ever since teenagers have been going to school. As a mother of teens, the author, Dr. Feinstein, also brings quite a bit of firsthand knowledge to these pages. Her experience combined with science should reveal to you, well, the *Secrets of the Teenage Brain!*

—*Eric Jensen*

Acknowledgments

Corwin gratefully acknowledges the contributions of the following reviewers:

Barry Corbin
Professor of Education, School of Education
Acadia University
Wolfville, Nova Scotia, Canada

Judy Filkins
Math and Science Curriculum Coordinator
SAU 88 Lebanon School District
Lebanon, New Hampshire

Robert Sylwester
Emeritus Professor of Education
University of Oregon

Brigitte Tennis
Head Mistress and Seventh-Grade Teacher
Stella Schola Middle School
Redmond, Washington

Kathy Tritz-Rhodes
Principal
Marcus-Meriden-Cleghorn Schools
Marcus and Cleghorn, Iowa

About the Author

 **Sheryl G. Feinstein,** EdD, is an associate professor in the Education Department at Augustana College in Sioux Falls, South Dakota, where she teaches courses in educational psychology and adolescent development. She also serves as an educational consultant for an adolescent correctional facility in Minnesota. She has worked with adolescents as a public school teacher and as a K–12 curriculum coordinator; she has also served as director at an alternative secondary school. She is the author of numerous books, and during the 2007–2008 school year she was a Fulbright Scholar in Tanzania where she continued her research on adolescents. Contact her at sherylfeinstein@yahoo.com

Introduction

The halls swarm with kids dawdling, talking to friends, obviously in no particular hurry to get to class; a girl slumps in the corner by her locker, priming for a total, tearful meltdown; and two boys circle the lunchroom table, gearing up to lock fists in a knock-down, drag-out brawl. What's going on? What are they thinking? It may seem like a mystery at first, but by taking an extended glimpse at what's happening in the transitioning teenage brain we can better understand, educate, and support this mystifying creature.

Today's educators seek an informed, holistic approach to middle school and high school students. Concepts, such as cost-benefit analysis and calculating the circumference of the circle using pi, are systematically taught while the social and emotional needs of individuality and self-esteem are supported. Teachers strive to ensure that all developmental needs of their students' are valued and tended. At first, their charge of educating youth may seem daunting, but thanks to neuroscience, psychology, and education, the pieces of the puzzle are falling into place.

A second edition of *Secrets of the Teenage Brain* was written to nourish the inquiring and often overburdened minds of educators. Because the field of neuroscience is continuously and extensively emerging with new research, it was important to supplement the first edition with the latest cutting-edge research, fresh instructional strategies, and current insights into trends and topics. Technology and the brain, mirror neurons, and at-risk behaviors like cutting, violence, and aggression are just a few of the new topics included in the second edition. Perhaps most exciting is an educator's book club guide that has been added for colleagues wanting to discuss the trials, tribulations, and joys of teaching at the secondary level.

Secrets of the Teenage Brain, Second Edition, is a hands-on, teacher friendly book. The book is organized around chapters that help educators understand the key issues facing adolescents, including academics, emotional, social, and physical well-being. Each chapter is supported with a multitude of instructional strategies that can be modified and adapted to individual content areas. Only the imagination of the teacher is needed to transform each strategy into something that works in their classroom. Special "Secret Revealed" sections go into interesting stories and research that relate to the topic, adding frosting to the cake.

I hope you enjoy the read.

Teen Brain

Under Construction

Neuroscience has recently put forward the startling fact that teen brains resemble blueprints more than they resemble skyscrapers. Secondary educators who once considered a teenage mind an empty house that needed furnishings would do better to understand it as the framing of a house that still needs walls, wiring, and a roof.

Did you know that . . .

- The brain, not hormones, is to blame for the inexplicable behavior of teens
- Short-term memory increases by about thirty percent during adolescence
- The activities teens invest their time and energy in influence what activities they'll invest in as adults
- Teens are ruled far more by their emotions than by logic

A group of middle school boys was sitting around the lunch table telling "Yo' Mama" jokes. Everyone was having fun until one boy went too far; tempers started to flare. A boy at an adjoining table stepped in to avert the fight that threatened to brew. Before anyone knew it, a fight had erupted between two boys who hadn't been telling jokes in the first place! A teacher, Mr. Kenith, broke up the fight and asked them, "Why are you fighting?" Both boys answered, "I don't know." And they really didn't.

CATERPILLARS TO BUTTERFLIES

Teenage behavior—nothing is more unpredictable, volatile, or intriguing. Teens want more privacy on the computer and minimize the screen as soon as you enter the room. They cycle earnestly through the roles of vegetarian, stand-up comedian, and swing dancer. They streak around the block in subfreezing weather on New Year's Eve. The sweet boy who blushed and hid his head under a sofa pillow when the Victoria's Secret commercials came on now watches and comments on the models.

Common knowledge used to be that adolescence was a phase all kids went through and that adults should wait it out. Quips like "raging hormones" and "rebel without a clue" attempted to explain the erratic thought patterns and subsequent behavior of adolescents. In their frustration, teachers and parents pondered the question, "Why can't they act like adults?" The real explanation provides a remarkable answer: They can't act like adults because they don't think like adults. Neuroscience confirms what we've always thought—the adolescent brain is still under construction.

The implications of the transitioning state of the adolescent's brain are exciting and unsettling. It's a time of great vulnerability. Teenagers' brains are growing and changing by adding gray matter and pruning old synapses. Choices teens make during adolescence potentially affect their brains for the rest of their lives. For parents and teachers, this discovery can be disconcerting. They had a great deal of power and influence over preschool and elementary school brains. Parents could ensure that young children were not exposed to excessive television, videos, computer games, and other passive activities. Teachers could monitor the books students read in class, assign projects for kids to work on (during academic work and during free time), and design a curriculum that applied to every student. But adult influence is much less effective on adolescents; to a great degree, teenagers are the masters of their own destiny and determine the fate of their brains (Spinks, 2002).

Secret Revealed

Hormones are off the list of primary suspects! The teenagers-act-crazy-because-of-hormones theory is incomplete. Think of it this way: Adults have hormones in their bodies, too, yet manage to write memos and grade homework even while thinking about a hot date later that evening. Adolescents aren't victims of chemicals coursing through their veins and turning their fancies to thoughts of love or mayhem; if they have trouble sitting still in school and concentrating on their lesson plans, it's because their brains aren't finished yet! MRI scans performed by Dr. Jay Giedd (Giedd, Blumenthal, Jeffries, Rajapakse, et al., 1999) of the National Institute of Mental Health have revealed that rather than leaving childhood with a brain ready to take on the responsibilities of young adulthood, teens have to contend with a brain that is destroying old neural connections and building new ones. Instead of battening down the hatches to wait out some hormonal storm, teens are navigating a cerebral hurricane without a compass. This profound discovery will forever alter how educators and parents interpret the mysterious behaviors of adolescence.

Teenagers also notice the differences between their childhood days and their newfound adolescent interests. One girl said, "I go out more, hang out, talk on the phone." Another said, "I go to the mall, go to parties, dance, listen to music. . . . They're ways to have fun and spend more time with your friends." A middle school boy said simply, "I just chill." These are the same kids who, one year ago, were racing each other to the swings at recess, playing *Candy Land,* and letting Mom pick out their clothes.

POURING THE FOUNDATION

Understanding the complexity of how the brain grows during adolescence requires knowledge about how the brain is structured. It is composed of two types of cells, neurons and glial cells. Glial cells are the "glue" that binds cells together; they compose ninety percent of the cells in the brain. The other ten percent of brain cells are neurons, cells associated with learning. Neurons hold the secrets of the mind. They are the body's communicators and constantly strike up conversations all over the brain. They coordinate thoughts, ideas, and feelings at breakneck speeds. You can practically hear the neurons roar and rumble in a teenager's head as they fire, ignite, and spring into action!

Neurons are composed of a cell body, dendrites, and one axon. Dendrites, hairlike branches emerging from the plump cell body, receive information from other neurons. Every time an individual has a new experience or gains a bit of information, another connection is made. I once asked a group of middle school and high school students what they had learned in the last month. I was bombarded with responses: I started to drive, I learned how to wait tables, I found out about mono, I learned how to calculate interest, I learned what *jugar* means in Spanish. What a burst of dendrite growth in their minds! Creating dendrites is an exciting proposition to educators; we want our students' brains to teem with them. The more dendrite receptors there are, the better the brain cells' ability to network with one another. And good news—there is plenty of room around the neuron table. Although neurons average about one thousand dendrites, one neuron can have many, many more.

Learning would not occur if neurons were isolated from each other. Each cell's single axon is a long extension from the cell body that sends information to another neuron's dendrite. The space between a dendrite and an axon (where communication between neurons takes place) is called a synapse. Messages sprint from neuron to neuron via the synapses. When the proverbial lightbulb flashes over a student's head in a moment of sudden comprehension, the synapses go wild. Neurons spark and fire across this entire network of cells in the brain. As synapses are strengthened through use, memories are reinforced and the ability to communicate with other neurons increases (Dahl, 2003).

UPGRADING THE HARD DRIVE

When we think of learning and memory, the cortex is often the first part of the brain to come to mind, but the hippocampus is also involved in learning. This small horseshoe-shaped part of the brain is capable of neurogenesis, the ability to give birth to new neurons. The hippocampus stands in stark contrast to the rest of the brain, which remains infertile. To a large degree, the 100 billion neurons you are born with tend to be your entire slice of the pie. A thought-provoking study of learning done by researchers at the University of Colorado revealed that the cortex finds patterns, integrates information, and attempts to give structure to information (the important stuff); the hippocampus deals with facts and details (rote memory). From this it is inferred that the hippocampus memorizes and the cortex learns (O'Reilly & Rudy, 2000). Like the rest of the brain, the hippocampus creates new dendrites and synapses during adolescence, which increases short-term memory in teenagers. Instead of just five to seven bits of information, teens may now be able to remember seven to nine bits (Woolfolk, 2006). They are better positioned to memorize that wistful sonnet or crucial math theorem.

Figure 1.1   Human Brain

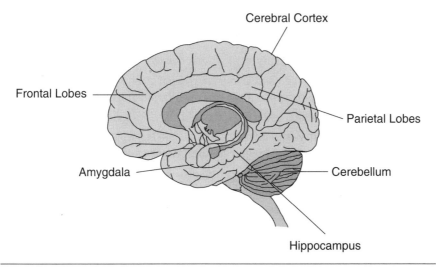

SOURCE: Adapted from Sousa, D. A. (2003), *How the Gifted Brain Learns,* p. 18.

Secret Revealed

Remember Piaget's theory of cognition and the information processing model from your Ed Psych classes? They both state that the quality of short-term memory increases when students enter the teenage years, but neither explained why. Dr. Paul Thompson from the UCLA Laboratory of Neuro Imaging put adolescents into an MRI scanner to image their brains and actually witnessed the brains growing in size and power! (Thompson et al., 2000) The formation of new gray and white matter—through dendrites, synapses, and myelination—enables teens to remember more and remember it better. Now, Ed Psych professors can support Piaget's theory and the information processing model with hard data. Finally, teachers in the field and in training have the whole story.

The hippocampus is slow to develop; in fact, there isn't much evidence of activity until about age three. (This probably explains why we have trouble remembering anything in infancy.) The hippocampus is associated with short-term memory—it helps us remember the name and phone number of the person we just met or the location of our favorite pizza place. It acts as a switchboard connecting short- and long-term memory and constantly communicates between the two. This dialogue linking the hippocampus and the cortex helps give meaning to new information (Schacter, 1996).

The cerebral cortex, or neocortex, is the wrinkled outer covering of the brain, the site of higher-level thinking and self-awareness. The most developed part of the human brain, the cerebral cortex allows us to problem solve, think critically, and make decisions. "No, I don't want a beer" or "Sure, I'll have a cigarette" are decisions made in the cortex. Students who say, "Math is my favorite subject," "I like Geography," or "I enjoy my creative writing class" are referring to the content that dwells in the cerebral cortex.

Most mental tasks require communication between both hemispheres of the brain. The corpus callosum acts as a bridge between the two sides, allowing information to cross with ease. Even uncomplicated activities, such as comprehending a joke or singing a song, are not confined to one hemisphere but, rather, require complex connections between both sides of the brain. The more bells and whistles a task has, the more you use the entire brain to complete it (Weissman & Banich, 2000). During adolescence, the corpus callosum increases in size by creating more dendrites and synapses. As the adolescent brain becomes capable of more complex tasks, the corpus callosum becomes larger and thicker, better able to handle the job. Scientists were amazed to discover its long maturation cycle—it continues growing into young adulthood (Keshavan et al., 2002).

A relationship has recently been established between the corpus callosum and self-awareness (the ability to monitor one's own thoughts). New neuroimaging technology has enabled researchers to study the process of self-awareness in the brain. The sense of self seems to be located in the right hemisphere of the brain, and the sense of others in the left (Kircher et al., 2001; Platek, Keenan, Gallup, & Mohammed, 2004). The strengthening corpus callosum enables teens to better understand themselves in relation to others—this budding awareness is part of what turns adolescents into adults.

USE IT OR LOSE IT

Two processes occur as the human brain develops. The first is an overproduction of dendrites and synapses—gray matter—that results in an overload of dendrites from the cell bodies. Dendrites and synapses are multiplying like crazy in the brain! The second process, the pruning (or elimination) of brain cells, follows this overproduction. Which neurons survive or die is determined by survival of the fittest. The brain selectively strengthens or prunes neurons based on activity. Synapses continually used will flourish; those that are not will wither away. It's "use it or lose it" in action.

This overproduction of neurons, dendrites, and synapses begins at birth and continues until a child is approximately three years old; at this age, the average child has many more synapses than an adult. Obviously, an amazing amount of activity occurs in the brain during this time. From the moment of birth, however, synapses and neurons that are not being used begin to be pruned. This process is very efficient, allowing the brain to invest in strengthening the synapses that the individual finds most necessary and important.

Figure 1.2 Significant Brain Changes Occur During Teenage Years

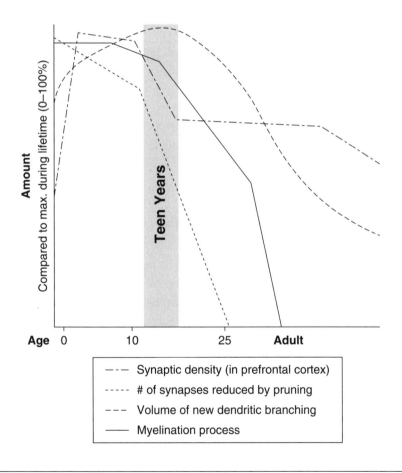

SOURCES: Bourgeois (2001); Huttenlocher and Dabholkar (1997); Sampaio and Truwit (2001).

This period of neural growth has become the focus of popular attention in education, sparking a great deal of excitement from early childhood educators and parents. Research suggests that, as a result of the creation of gray matter, we are biologically primed for learning in the early years. Some individuals have taken this information about the young child to the extreme, claiming that preschoolers who "snooze" will lose the opportunity to grow any more brain cells—ever. This dire prediction places tremendous pressure on preschool children and their parents to fill childhood with as many educational and enrichment activities as possible (Puckett, Marshall, & Davis, 1999).

Secret Revealed

Did you go to your high school reunion? Were you surprised that the "Class Clown" was a prosperous salesperson or that "Most Likely to Succeed" did? You shouldn't have been. The girl who spent all those science classes making students laugh when the teacher's back was turned built her brain around the ability to make customers enjoy themselves—and buy products. The boy who spent his time reading, thinking, organizing his notes, and acing projects and exams built into his brain the ability to develop and grow his own business. Any information teens use and learn in school will be hardwired into the brain's structure (good and bad), and anything they ignore will lose its priority. For parents and teachers of preschool children, this concept has been a no-brainer for quite some time. What no one realized until very recently was that teenage brains were still open to this kind of direction and input!

Such emphasis on the preschool brain has overshadowed the opportunities for growth and change in the brain during adolescence. This is known as *plasticity*. Brain plasticity refers to the brain's ability to change as it experiences fresh phenomenon and learns new information. In essence, it means the brain is on a continual course of rewiring in order to make sense of its environment. Amazingly, due to plasticity, changes occur in both the brain's physical structure and in the way it functions throughout our lifespan. This allows the sixty-year-old man to change his golf stroke or the forty-year-old woman to return to school for her master's degree. It also gives special assistance to those with a brain injury, helping them depend more on their remaining brain functions.

Plasticity has promising implications for teachers and students alike. For instance, as a teacher your original course of study may have been social studies, but due to hiring needs you find yourself teaching math. Being pragmatic you hone your math skills, enriching your brain. As a result, there will actually be more gray matter in your brain dealing with math; synapses are being generated. Even if you are not doing a dramatic switch of disciplines, education is an ever-changing field. Fortunately, our minds, and hopefully our spirits, are always up to the challenge. As for students, the same benefits apply; as they learn new information, their brain makes adjustments and grows (Doidges, 2007).

Neuroscience discovered that the brain remains quite malleable in cognitive and emotional development during adolescence and even into adulthood. In the early 1990s, Dr. Jay Giedd of the National Institute of Mental Health began doing MRIs on the brains of 145 healthy children from ages four to twenty-one. The participants selected for the study were scanned every two years to monitor possible anatomical changes occurring with maturation. He noted an undeniable overproduction of gray matter during adolescence (Giedd, Blumenthal, Jeffries, Castellanos, et al., 1999).

This overproduction gives teens the opportunity to excel in all kinds of areas; synapses spawn all over their brains. If teens do a lot of reading, they become better readers; if they are fond of and practice a lot of science, they will probably become scientists; kids who solve problems become great problem solvers. This is a neurological reason to involve adolescents in responsible activities and introduce them to all kinds of new experiences—teens who aren't involved in healthy activities may build their brains around the infamous sex, drugs, and rock 'n' roll! As Dr. Giedd said, "Teens are most likely to experiment with drugs and alcohol. I often show teens my data curve [and say], 'If you do this tonight, you may be affecting your brains not just this weekend but for the next eighty years of your life'" (Vedantam, 2001).

Just as important as the creation of additional gray matter to the adolescent is the process of pruning that follows. The use it or lose it theory pertains to adolescents as well as to ten-year-olds. The neural connections a teenager makes endure a lifetime, and unused connections are lost forever. If they aren't reading, doing science, or solving problems, the synapses for those activities will be pruned. It is hypothesized that pruning at this age permits the adolescent brain to organize its circuitry and refine its thinking processes (Thompson et al., 2000). It is a golden opportunity to build a better brain. It is also a golden opportunity to waste the brain's potential and water it down instead.

> The mother of a seventh-grade boy who was getting ready for his first dance said, "His dad and I just could not believe it. He prepped for hours. Lifted weights that afternoon and then went on the treadmill. He took a selection of shirts and jeans into the bathroom—he never does that. He's always particular with his hair, but this time he was overly particular."

> A supervisor at a middle school afterschool program said, "There's a group of sixth-grade girls really into boys. Two or three will follow a boy around for a day, take his pencil, that kind of thing. Eighth graders are more subtle. A boy and girl will sit close together, but if you look under the lunch table she'll have her leg over his."

Some scientists even speculate that adolescence is when people learn the mating ritual. Teenagers are very interested in the opposite sex and how to navigate this explosive social field. They commit an extensive amount of time and thought to mastering this particular learning opportunity. As luck would have it, hormones come into play at this very same time, inspiring a mating dance both painful and poetic. The chaos that ensues consumes the minds and lives of teens and everyone else they touch.

With all this restructuring, is it any wonder that the adolescent brain is at times unorganized, spontaneous, and prone to misinterpretations? They have a lot to adjust to. "I can literally stand right in front of my class and say that at 3:00 p.m. we are going to load the bus. The two kids right in front of me will come up one minute later and ask what time the bus will be loaded!" one teacher said. Eighth grader Jamiesha and her mother look at the world from different angles. "Mom tells me I'm supposed to be in at a certain time. I come in late 'cause I decided to go to my friend's house for a little while. She gets all mad. I don't get it." To Jamiesha, being late is no big deal. So what if she changed her plans an hour one way or the other! She came home, didn't she?

THE INFORMATION SUPER HIGHWAY

After synapses are generated in the brain, myelin—a fatty substance made of glial—is produced to insulate the neurons. Myelin covers the axons of neurons and enables information to travel efficiently. Myelinated tissue is referred to as white matter. The more extensive the myelination of axons, the faster information flows between the cells. At the same time, the ability to use symbolism, metaphors, and analogies increases in older adolescents. They are able to appreciate irony and sarcasm; their sense of humor becomes more sophisticated, and teachers often find themselves the objects of this increased capability (Santrock, 2003). The adolescent is ready to hypothesize, create abstractly, and comprehend complex math theorems. The rampant changes are dynamic and undeniable. The transition from the childhood brain to the adolescent brain is like paving a gravel road with asphalt; teens are on their way to becoming faster, sleeker thinking machines. Their steadfast memory, jaunty step, thinking processes, language skills, and emotions all benefit from this smoother ride.

Construction occurs throughout the teen brain. The parietal lobes (which process and desegregate sensory information like sights, sounds, and smells), temporal lobes (which process language and emotional behavior), occipital lobes (which processes visual information), cerebellum (which processes coordination and thinking skills), and hippocampus (seat of short-term memory) all benefit from the overproduction and pruning of synapses. Researchers at the UCLA Laboratory of Neuro Imaging discovered that the parietal lobes did not complete the creation of gray matter until about the age of twelve—and only then did they start pruning. Temporal lobes limped even further behind—they did not finish growing gray matter or begin the processes of pruning and myelination until the age of sixteen (Giedd, Blumenthal, Jeffries, Castellanos, et al., 1999)! In some areas, pruning and myelination follow even later.

The brain does not release myelin to all neurons at the same time but rather in stages. The timing of the release of myelin appears to be dependent upon the developmental age of the individual, environment, and genetics. One of the last parts of the brain to receive myelin is the frontal cortex, the area responsible for abstract thinking, language, and decision making (Fuster, 2002). As the brain's frontal lobes become myelinated during adolescence, teens develop the ability to hypothesize, look into the future, deduct, analyze, and logically reason.

Secret Revealed

 There was a time when me and my best friend since first grade got into a fight. She told someone a secret I'd told her. I told her she was a liar; she said I was being paranoid. So I hit her.

—Kenisha, eighth grade

Have you ever felt like hitting your boss because of something he or she said about you? Did you? Why not? No matter how infuriated or exasperated adults become with each other, logic and reason usually prevail. Adults choose their words carefully and try to calmly discuss problems instead of rolling up their shirtsleeves and taking it outside. No matter how

(Continued)

(Continued)

good it may feel to indulge in the wild emotions of the moment, adults think through the consequences and make decisions based on what might happen the next day and how their reactions affect things like income, family security, and personal relationships. Teens, however, are famous for not calmly assessing consequences and for making poor, on-the-spot decisions. Teens succumb to the temptation of hitting first and talking later.

In two separate studies, Dr. Deborah Yurgelun-Todd (Yurgelun-Todd, Killgore, & Young, 2002) of McLean Hospital and Dr. Elizabeth Sowell (Sowell, Thompson, Holmes, Jernigan, & Toga, 1999) of the UCLA Laboratory of Neuro Imaging found out why. Until the frontal lobes, the seat of language and reason, are completely formed, teens rely overmuch on their amygdala—the seat of emotion. Not only do the wild emotions get first say about what teens will do next, their ability to negotiate their way out of a tense moment by using carefully chosen, diplomatic language is fledgling at best. Fortunately, the adults and adult brains that are often at the receiving end of adolescent outbursts can understand what is happening and de-escalate confrontations when they do occur.

The frontal lobes are in charge of taming the beast within us, humanizing our nature, and making us be the best we can be. They have an interesting relationship with the amygdala, an organ that controls our often tumultuous array of emotions. Pleasure, anger, and fear all spring from this small but mighty structure located a few inches from the ears in the lower center of the brain. When confronted with information, the adolescent brain reacts quite differently than the adult brain. Adults rely more on the frontal lobes of their brain and less on the amygdala, and therefore respond logically to the input they receive. The adolescent, on the other hand, tends to rely more on the amygdala than the frontal lobes and responds emotionally to stimuli (Baird et al., 1999). This explains the poor decisions they make, like going shopping (instead of doing homework) or having unprotected sex, and their highly emotional responses to ordinary requests, such as remarks like "I hate you!" or "Don't tell me what to do!"

The frontal lobes are also the province of language. Frustrated teens answer frustrated adults with inarticulate expressions like "Whatever" and "I don't know." For years, educational psychologists have documented the vague and mumbled expressions of adolescents (Woolfolk, 2006), but it wasn't until recently that neuroscientists examined the phenomenon. Dr. Elizabeth Sowell examined language production in adolescents and found that there is a shift in function as brains mature (Sowell et al., 1999). Young adolescents have more difficulty generating words and expressing themselves than do older adolescents. By high school, teens start speaking in a more rational and logical manner.

MIRROR, MIRROR ON THE WALL

One of the most exciting new discoveries in neuroscience is that of mirror neurons. Evidence of mirror neurons was actually discovered in macaque monkeys during the mid-1990s, but not in humans until the early twenty-first century, when neuroimaging technology advanced to the point where studies could be done on humans. The very nature of mirror neurons is found in their name: Neuroscientists discovered that a network of neurons fired when they vicariously experienced something; it was as though another person's action was reflected in a mirror. The same parts of the human brain were activated in the observer as the neurons in the person doing the activity (Iacoboni, 2008; Sylwester, 2007).

Literally speaking, it means we actually experience another person's pain or joy. Early studies are suggesting that mirror neurons may help us understand how empathy, language, self-awareness, intentions, and altruism are developed. Individuals who have a burst of mirror neurons igniting in response to other's facial expressions are able to empathize with the sadness of failing a test or being rejected by a potential girlfriend and the happiness of scoring an A or getting that first date. These individuals develop a sense of caring, enabling them to share other's emotions and identify other's needs. In contrast, individuals with autism have few mirror neurons igniting in response to others, explaining their lack of social development. It may also add further support to  learning through observation and imitation, a theory that Albert Bandura, the psychologist, promoted (see Woolfolk, 2006). There are possibilities for every content area, so stay tuned for exciting discoveries and educational implications in this neuron neighborhood.

ADOLESCENCE: THE FINAL FRONTIER

Innovations in brain technology have led to discoveries that spark the interest of educators and provide rich possibilities for instruction and assessment. But like the crew of the starship *Enterprise*, teachers and parents must go where no one has gone before—into the uniqueness of the brain that spans the abyss between childhood and adulthood. Teenagers seem irresponsible and unreasonable only when they are compared to people older and younger. But viewed against the backdrop of the profound and rapid neurological and biological changes that are happening in their bodies, their behavior is much more understandable and logical.

Why do adolescents blurt out answers in class? Why do they fall asleep during third period? Why do they fight so bitterly over late homework assignments or missed points on a test? Take comfort in the fact that they do not plot their unruliness; they are just trying to cope in a school run and designed by adults from an adult perspective—adults with brains that are structured and that function in ways vastly different from their own. This book attempts to highlight the primary differences in teen and adult brains and behavior as well as offer suggestions for channeling these differences toward a more productive classroom, academically and emotionally.

Teen Cognition and Learning

Conventional wisdom about teenagers is wrong. Teenagers are not incoherent, clumsy, sex-crazed, unpredictable, irrational monsters who can't be reasoned with—they are intelligent creatures not yet accustomed to their (unevenly) burgeoning mental strengths and capabilities. Adolescence is a time of startling growth and streamlining in the brain, enabling teens to think abstractly, speak expressively, and move gracefully. Of course, they often use their newfound abilities to talk their way out of homework deadlines or concoct elaborate games to play behind teachers' backs, but it's a good start!

Did you know that . . .

- The teen brain is particularly susceptible to novelty
- ADHD is not caused by a bad student, bad parent, or bad teacher; the reason can be found in the brain
- The burst of growth in the frontal lobes means that teens overcomplicate problems, idealize the world, and say one thing while doing another
- The development of the parietal lobes helps teen athletes improve their pace and teen musicians improve their beat
- Physical movement helps the cerebellum develop, thereby helping teens improve their cognitive processing skills
- Feedback improves the brain's efficiency
- Teens crave structure and organization in spite of their attraction to novelty

The wacky and weird teenagers who filled the hallway of the high school transformed suddenly to zombies as they filed into their English class. With drooping shoulders and shuffling feet, they exchanged resigned looks and rolled their eyes knowingly at one another. They sat in the unbroken silence and waited for their student teacher to enter.

She entered the room in the same manner as her students—no welcoming smile, no friendly words. She went to the front of the class with a stiff, swift step and abruptly launched her fifty-minute lecture on punctuation. One boy leaned over to his neighbor and pleaded, "Kill me. Kill me now." The teacher lost everyone's attention by droning on and on about the various uses of the apostrophe. All around the room, students daydreamed and drifted to sleep.

ATTENTION-GETTING DEVICES

Our first objective as teachers is to capture students' attention. If we don't gain their attention, the chance that they'll learn anything is remote at best. The process of attention serves two primary purposes, the first of which is survival. The brain kept our ancestors safe by alerting them to possible hazards in their midst like strangers, thunder clouds, or wild animals. Fortunately, it is the rare occasion that survival is at stake in school. Instead, attention serves its second purpose—maintaining pleasurable feelings. The exotic girl with the pierced tongue, a double chocolate ice cream bar, and listening to rock music on the radio are pleasurable diversions for modern teenagers. So are funny stories, terrible tragedies, and the first snowfall.

The brain is bombarded with information from the senses. Everything we see, hear, touch, smell, and taste finds its way to the sensory receptors, from the clothes on your back to the beige walls of the room and the radio playing softly in the background. At the base of the brain is the brain stem, which controls involuntary actions like breathing, blood pressure, and heartbeats. Deep within the brain stem is the reticular formation, a system of neurons that gathers information from all of your senses and controls your awareness levels. Some awareness is at a conscious level (what you see and hear the teacher do and say) and some at an unconscious level (the color of the walls or the socks you are wearing). It would be impossible for the brain to consciously focus on each bit of data it receives. You may be oblivious to the feel of a baseball hat on your head while the cute girl beside you captures your full attention. Considering the immense amount of information the brain is capable of absorbing, from the spinach stuck in your teeth to the lint on your coat, we are fortunate to be able to forget most things. Otherwise, we'd overload.

Secret Revealed

No matter what you heard in the past, teens can be as interested in photosynthesis as the armpit squelches that come from the back of the classroom! The adolescent brain really does want to learn more about the world we live in and less about the student who enters the classroom to collect the attendance, but it values novelty and unpredictability. Not even a lecture and slide show about alien technology would hold your students' attention for long without these two elements!

Dr. Linda Spear (2000), a behavioral neuroscientist at Binghamton University, studies the teenage propensity for seeking novelty; she finds that the physical changes in the brain during adolescence significantly affect what appeals to teens. Fortunately, novelty and surprise can be planned for any lesson content. Instead of just lecturing about photosynthesis, work with plants and sunlamps. Instead of labeling anatomical charts, dissect a frog. Appeal directly to the teen brain's innate interest in the unexpected and enjoy a more productive classroom.

Ask a group of teenagers what they think about school and you probably won't be surprised by the answers: "Boring." "Stupid." "School sucks." Of course, friends, potential dates, lunchtime, and doodling don't bore them; the adolescent brain is fascinated by (and seeks out) novelty and emotion (Koepp et al., 1998; Spear, 2000). Sitting through classroom instruction that fails to include either is the real test of a teen's attention. Many teaching strategies and testing options have a great deal of difficulty keeping attention and arousing emotion. Worksheets require students to pay attention to something that evolution and instinct quite frankly say is irrelevant to life. Lecture, which can be an efficient way to deliver instruction, is often not emotionally charged. Objective tests, such as those in multiple-choice or true-false formats, rarely generate emotion and are extremely difficult to apply to real-world applications. Yet lecture and worksheets are dismayingly popular means of presenting content. We miss academic opportunities when we overuse strategies that neglect our emotional and cognitive constitution—two powerful memory builders.

Capturing students' attention by engaging them in feel-good experiences is good news for teachers and teens alike; everyone enjoys dwelling on the positive. People who know how to entertain an audience are almost always sure to get their educational messages across. Consider Simon, a spirited ninth grader who definitely captured his classmates' attention when he gave his presentation about a city in America. The students had already heard a dozen speeches about cities from Philadelphia to Portland

and waited politely for another colorless, note-card-heavy tale of yet another metropolis. Nonetheless, Simon strode confidently to the front of the room and began by telling the class to imagine themselves sitting in a lawn chair, gazing at mountains, and sipping a latte. "It was such a beautiful morning. Where could we be? Aspen? Salt Lake City? No, Mianus." In complete earnestness, he continued. "I suppose you're wondering what we can do for fun in Mianus, what people are like in Mianus. That's what I am here to tell you today." Every eye in the room was riveted on Simon, first in disbelief and then in hysterics. Needless to say, Simon had everyone's attention (even if he didn't have all the facts correct).

So did a physics teacher, Mr. Berndt. Mr. Berndt thrilled his students by entering their classroom one day on in-line skates. As if the novelty of skating in class weren't enough, he had brought skates for them to use, too! Soon everyone had taken turns pulling each other around the room to determine force and speed with two different masses. In a biology class, Mr. Gjornes (who is young and in exceptional shape) turned cartwheels to demonstrate the rotation of molecules. These were two classes during which no students daydreamed, no minds drifted, and every brain gave its attention to the teacher and the lesson; not only were the activities fun, they were content meaningful, too.

Attention-getting activities are not required to be amusing or participatory, however. Mr. Hoffman, a high school principal, explained how a guest speaker captivated the entire student body with a story about how his younger brother was killed by a drunk driver and finally revealed himself as the driver. The story had the students so riveted that they carried his message right into their other classes, relating his experiences to their own actions, past and future. The principal even received phone calls from parents explaining how this tale had transformed their teenagers.

Instructional Strategies

May I Have Your Attention Please?

You can only maintain student attention if you've already captured it. Introducing novelty is one way to do it, so is engaging the physical senses and arousing curiosity. Throw novelty at teens from all sides—vary the pace and tone of your voice, dress in bell-bottoms, circulate around the room, use colored chalk, bring flowers into the room, or add the scent of lemon. Incorporate all the senses in the learning adventure.

Mrs. Reynolds introduced a unit on poetry to her ninth-grade English students by speaking to the class in French. The look of amazement on students' faces made dusting off her high school French book worth the effort. Mr. Amundson strung lights around a bulletin board describing how the legislature passes a bill, literally lighting up the room (to use a sophomoric pun)! But teachers should not always be the performers. Encourage students to act in novel ways themselves. Change their seats or surprise them with a hands-on task. You could even video record them in action and have them analyze what snags their attention.

The flip side of keeping student attention is that they have an easier time watching and listening to you when there are fewer distractions in the room. Not that you should remove a single thing from the walls—but you should be aware of annoying or repetitive mannerisms you may have, such as habitual throat clearing or fidgeting with a necklace. You would hate to discover that a student chose to spend the entire period tallying how many times you tapped your pencil against the desk or said the word *okay*. This is not the attention we're striving for.

Things to Try

- Show a comic strip or a few minutes of a television cartoon to put a smile on their faces.
- Tell a riddle: How many teenagers does it take to screw in a light bulb? (One answer is one to screw in the bulb, one to hold the ladder, and one to order a pizza. You could have students take a minute or two to write their own punch lines, too.)
- Play a song from a popular CD and ask them about why they like it—inquiring about their interests will capture their attention.
- Show a video of a trendy commercial—it's the last thing they'll expect!
- Have every one of your students find a place at the board and start listing all the words that describe what they learned that week.
- Share a story from your own middle school or high school days. Students will connect with you on a personal level, and if told well, the story will draw emotion into the classroom.
- Bring in candy as a writing prompt. You could have students create metaphors for the candy out of class content while they munch and chew.
- Pass around clay, feathers, or pieces of packing foam; hands-on objects arouse curiosity and activate the tactile senses.
- Move the location of your desk periodically. In fact, move everything periodically. Change not just students' seats but also the actual desk arrangement a few times a year.
- Mix it up; occasionally have students stand up to deliver important information or respond to key ideas.
- Read a poem by Shel Silverstein or Emily Dickinson to set a mood and engage emotions.
- Start a service project for immigrant adolescents in your community. The opportunity to contribute directly toward helping a peer is meaningful, specific, and unique. The idea will pique their interest at the very least.
- Surprise them with a celebration for work well done. Make popcorn or roller-skate on the blacktop!

ATTENTION-DEFICIT/
HYPERACTIVITY DISORDER (ADHD)

The subject of attention has particular significance for students who have attention-deficit/hyperactivity disorder (ADHD). These students are a challenge to themselves, their parents, and their teachers. Known for being distracted, impulsive, and argumentative, they lack the very cornerstones of what is needed to succeed in the classroom.

Lack of focus is one of the major obstacles students with ADHD face; it negatively impacts every aspect of their lives: academics, friendships, extracurricular, and jobs. Teachers often hear the constant refrain "I don't know" to every question posed. Where is your homework? I don't know. Why are you wandering the room? I don't know. What are you talking to her for? I don't know. This frustrating chant manifests their inability to focus.

Hyperactivity is also associated with ADHD, causing these students and everyone around them grief. Continually wired, teachers often describe the behavior of students with ADHD as "he is literally bouncing off the wall," "he can't sit still, he blurts out answers," and "he doesn't listen, he never pays attention."

Recognizing cause and effect constitutes another challenge for the student with ADHD. While most teenagers are beginning to understand that if they turn their homework in on time they learn more, have better grades, and have less stress in their lives, the teen with ADHD misses the connection.

Hyperfocusing is also a featured attribute of students with ADHD. The activity that triggers hyperfocusing is usually one that requires quick, spontaneous responses. Computer games are the perfect vehicle for this ride. Once something has caught their attention and manages to keep their attention, they are not about to put on the brakes. Interrupting a student with ADHD when they are hyperfocusing is a sure recipe for a meltdown.

Brain differences are abundant between individuals with ADHD and those without. Brain size is about three to four percent smaller in teenagers with ADHD compared to their age-mates. Fortunately, the difference in brain size in no way impacts their intelligence. Other brain differences include the basal ganglia, a part of the brain associated with thinking and emotion, and the frontal lobes, the thoughtful, decision-making center of the brain. Both have reduced activity. This affects their ability to pay attention and control their emotions. Dopamine only adds fuel to the confusion. Dopamine transporters take on too much dopamine before they pass it between brain cells; this

Instructional Strategies

- Reduce distractions—seat them near the front of the room, clear their desks of objects, and keep their desks away from high traffic areas.
- Give directions one step at a time.
- Allow frequent participation and, if possible, movement.
- Break down objectives and assignments into small segments.
- Use computer-based instruction; it will draw their attention.
- Help their disorganized minds become organized by using planners and directly teaching study skills.
- If they act inappropriately and will not control themselves, remove them from the classroom.
- Reset your expectations: don't be shocked by explosive, unacceptable behavior.
- Stay calm, because they won't. Their lack of self-control means as adults we must have more control.
- Don't engage in an argument when they are out of control.
- Supply accurate information to parents and physicians as to behaviors seen in the classroom. Because of the behavior expectations in school, we are an important part of putting the puzzle together.

misstep further affects attention and impulse control (Bloom, Beal, & Kupfer, 2006).

THE FOREST OR THE TREES?

The frontal lobes are located in the front of the brain and are the largest part of the cortex. Positioned right behind the forehead, they are responsible for cognitive processing. Speaking, reading, writing, math, and music are all processed in the frontal lobes, along with the ability to analyze, apply, and evaluate. Secondary educators are constantly contemplating how to engage students in higher-order thinking, how to start their cognitive gears turning, and how to activate their frontal lobes. Fully under-standing the maturation process during adolescence paves the way for compatible instruction. Neuroscience has allowed us the opportunity to witness the dramatic changes in the frontal lobes between childhood, adolescence, and adulthood.

Figure 2.1   Human Brain

Frontal Lobe

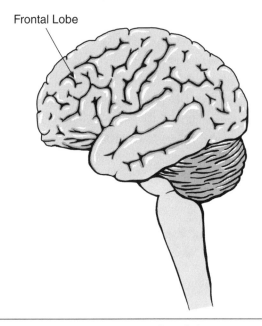

SOURCE: Adapted from Sousa, D. A. (2003), *How the Gifted Brain Learns*, p. 16.

Children look at the world very concretely. When visiting an elementary school, I overheard a group of kindergartners trying to decide who was older between a husband and wife. It was obvious to me at first glance that the husband was older, but the kindergartners gave it an interesting twist. Lety ended the discussion by announcing, in a tone denoting the obviousness of the statement, "She's taller, so she must be the oldest." The children in attendance agreed; Lety's logic apparent to everyone. Later that day, their teacher, Ms. Gibbons, gathered all her students at the front of the room and announced that it was Presidents' Day. "Whose birthdays do we celebrate on Presidents' Day?" she asked. No one responded, so Ms. Gibbons said, "One person is Abraham Lincoln." A hand immediately shot up from the back of the group and Micah hopefully inquired, "Did he bring cupcakes?" Innocent and sweet? Absolutely. But surviving in a concrete world has its limitations. Young children have no sense of the past: Abraham Lincoln is alive, butterflies don't come from caterpillars, and monsters really do live under the bed. Adult brains are necessary to guide and structure the lives of children; they need our fine-tuned frontal lobes to shelter them.

Secret Revealed

For years, adults have assumed that teenagers are self-absorbed, uncaring, and oblivious to the world around them. Meanwhile, teens have always been certain that they could solve all the world's problems if their stupid parents would only give them a chance. They would never allow the planet to become so polluted; they would never put an extra refrigerator in the garage when so many people are starving! If teens were in charge, all beaches would be clean and there'd be sports drinks for everyone. The world would be a better place.

As the frontal lobes mature, teens are increasingly capable of moral reasoning and idealism. Children's brains may think only in the concrete—Did I get as many cookies as she did?—but adolescence is when the brain's awareness and interest expands. Able to imagine the thoughts of another person and to appreciate the passage of time, teens suddenly become aware that they are not the only people in the world and that actions can have future consequences. They see the world not only as it is but how it could be.

The frontal lobes that distinguish men and women from boys and girls begin to mature during adolescence (Giedd, Blumenthal, Jeffries, Castellanos, et al., 1999). Young teenagers begin to think abstractly and become capable of pondering concepts that have little or no basis in concrete reality. Teens can consider hypothetical questions like "If there are millions of plants found in the rain forests, and if the majority of medicines that are discovered come from plants found in the rain forests, what implications does the deforestation of the rain forests have for our future?" They can embark on discussions ranging from civil rights to the death penalty. Teenagers can analyze, deduce, and make reflective decisions.

Educators know that secondary students need exposure to higher-level thinking skills, but the role of physical development cannot be overstated. It is the combination of biological maturation with thoughtful instructional strategies that creates a better brain. To compare teenagers to computers, we can expose teenagers to all the software we want, but until their "hard drives" are upgraded, it will have minimal impact (Epstein, 2001). "Software" that reinforces the acquisition of abstract thinking skills includes exploring various hypothetical questions, teaching broad concepts, and encouraging scientific reasoning and reflective decision making. Mostly, though, the best way to wait out this period of development is with patience and understanding. The great city of Rome wasn't built in a day, and neither is the teenage brain.

Neuroscientists and educational psychologists concur that not all teenagers develop the capacity for abstract thought at the same time. Concrete learning strategies are still needed at the middle school and high school level (Neimark, 1975). Pierre van Heile, who designed the model of geometric thought, did valuable research in teaching geometry at the high school level (Mason, 1998). He found that many older students still require concrete, hands-on material when initially studying geometry. Teacher expectations were that high school students could handle the complex and often-unfamiliar material without the support of hands-on activities. The result was student frustration and failure in this subject area.

Providing hands-on materials enabled students to quickly transition into abstract thought in geometry. This same premise is true in other areas of the curriculum. Shawna, a vivacious tenth grader, said, "My history teacher just lectures, which is not a good style for me. I daydream in that class. I try not to, but I always do. In biology class, my teacher has us doing things. One week we dissected fetal pigs. It smelled, but it made it easy to understand the parts of the body. I think I finally figured out the different ventricles in the heart." For Jason, a thoughtful boy of seventeen, concrete examples made all the difference in his understanding of upper level math. He commented, "I like my math class. We don't just do worksheets or listen to the teacher talk; we get to actually work with objects. Sometimes I need to see it to understand it."

BRUSH OFF OLD CLASSROOM FAVORITES

Some of the most traditional lesson elements are well researched and brain friendly. Robert Marzano (Marzano, Pickering, & Pollock, 2001) and his team at MCCREL (Mid-Continent Research for Education and Learning) have led educators to institute ten nonnegotiable strategies in their classrooms. Incorporating some of these following activities will give teens the chance to practice their burgeoning ability to think abstractly while still grounding them firmly in concrete facts and information.

1. *Ask students to write a summary of a lesson.* Despite its reputation, the act of summarizing requires students to delete, substitute, and retain knowledge as they analyze information. Sifting through information during and at the end of a lesson increases their understanding of it—and it doesn't always have to happen in paragraph form. Have students directly connect five concepts that they learned that day in class, write a newspaper headline for what was covered, make a prediction about what they'll learn in the next day's class, or bring technology into the forum; have

them text message a summary. Cell phones aren't a prerequisite (they just add to the ambiance); the text can be written on a sheet of paper.

2. *Identify similarities and differences.* The brain stores by similarity, but retrieves through differences. This is another simple activity that has been shown to increase academic achievement on standardized tests. Higher-order thinking is required to compare and classify information; students must analyze and evaluate information before they can categorize it. Venn diagrams, matrix, and charts add a supportive visual to the process.

Figure 2.2   Venn Diagram

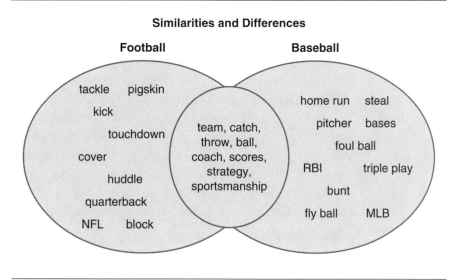

3. *Write metaphors and analogies.* Writing metaphors and analogies is an effective way to engage higher-order thinking skills. Imagine how many ways there are to fill in the blanks of the sentence: Adolescents are like _____ because _____. When given this assignment, one veteran teacher wrote, "Adolescents are like TV shows because sometimes you thoroughly enjoy them and other times you wonder who produced them." Students might enjoy filling in the blanks of a sentence like "The Internet is to _____ as the brain is to _____."

4. *Present material nonlinguistically.* Knowledge is stored in two ways, visually and linguistically. Incorporate both for optimal learning. Embracing graphic organizers, body movements, and multiple intelligences will form a firm foundation.

5. *Create and test a hypothesis.* Challenge students to apply their knowledge. Generating a hypothesis, a part of the inquiry process, helps

build a better brain. Examine water quality in school, healthy lifestyles of freshman versus seniors, or ways to make your school more Green. Amazingly, it does not matter if the answer is discovered; the journey is what matters, not the destination.

6. *Reinforce effort and provide recognition for accomplishments.* Make the connection between effort and achievement, show examples of people who overcame the odds, and inspire students to do the same. All the while, praise them for their effort and for taking that risk. Intrinsic, intrinsic, intrinsic—when it comes to recognition, replace the rewards of candy and stickers with feelings of accomplishment, and at the same time build a positive self-concept.

7. *Assign homework and provide practice.* Repeating skills helps them stick in memory. Refiring synapses strengthens the memory and makes it easier to recall; homework provides that memory-producing practice. Homework may take various forms: memorization (ribosomes, cytoplasm, proteins = Robots Can Produce), prep for the next day (read Chapter 2), understanding complex content (compare and contrast energy sources), and increasing speed (flash cards), all valuable avenues for practice. Difficulty in content and time spent on homework should increase with age; remember the fourteen-year-old brain does not have the same capabilities as the seventeen-year-old brain. Interestingly, parental assistance should be kept to a minimum; homework is no time for them to hover.

8. *Facilitate cooperative learning.* In the process, support positive interdependence. Keep the groups small and vary the composition; no one wants to always be in the "average" or the "at-risk" group. Webquests—inquiry-based Internet activities—add novelty to this first-class strategy.

9. *Set objectives and provide feedback.* Teacher objectives help set the direction of learning; when students personalize those objectives, ownership occurs. Long-term and short-term objectives, both have a place in the classroom. Feedback resets the direction of learning, immediate and specific is most effective.

10. *Start and reinforce lessons with cues, questions, and advance organizers.* Begin class on the right foot, jog their memory with questions and advance organizers. Focus on what's most important: Don't confuse the issue with trivia; they'll flounder sifting through the muck. While details may be the spice of life (goats in Morocco can climb trees), they shouldn't be the main course. Inspire students to analyze, instead of merely reacting to or describing a situation, by asking questions that force them to view a scenario in a new light. Try "How did you do that?" "What would you do differently next time?" "Why did you make that choice?" "What evidence

substantiates your conclusion?" and "What did you learn that you could apply in another class?" And remember to use wait time, the added return in quality answers is well worth your patience.

Instructional Strategies

I Think (and Solve and Inquire), Therefore I Learn

When choosing strategies, it is important to remember three things about the brain: It is capable of multiprocessing, it thrives on challenges, and it makes synapses when actively involved with learning. Instructional strategies that provide complex thinking skills and interaction provide opportunities for the brain to work more efficiently.

Take advantage of the adolescent's new ability to think abstractly by introducing a thinking curriculum into the classroom. Challenge students with assignments that promote higher-level thinking skills, such as problem-based learning, research projects, experimentation, inquiry, authentic data analysis, persuasive writing, presentations, dramas, composing music (even in a nonmusic class), and visual analysis. One day, have the students guess the legal consequences of keeping marijuana in their locker or painting graffiti or gang signs on the bathroom wall; the next day, invite a lawyer or police officer to the class to explain the actual consequences. Create a political comic book, look for a philosophy of life in popular songs, analyze a TV show or discuss hot topics like dating, parents, sex, drinking, drugs, friends, and work.

Things to Try

- Develop a new strategy for the football team or an election campaign for the candidate running for student counsel. Data mining information from the computer to solve these problems reinforces the positive use of technology.
- Think out loud for your students—verbally go through your thoughts as you decide on a topic for a writing assignment or solve a problem in trigonometry.
- Simulate a crime and investigate it; the continual popularity of this type of TV programming will grab the interest of wannabe detectives.
- Form pairs or small groups and put the students in charge. Let them teach their classmates; reciprocal teaching is one good formula for letting them shine.
- Rewrite a scene from Shakespeare against a modern day setting. Then, identify and explain similarities and differences between the two versions.
- Seek out members of the community: Interview employers about hiring adolescent workers, talk to the elderly for their historical perspective of an important event, or shadow a state legislator or city council member.

(Continued)

(Continued)

- Tap into the multiple intelligences of your students: Chart birth rates in the United States or on each continent, listen to and write about bird songs, invent a game, or visit a museum.
- View political debates on television and analyze them; watch fifteen minutes of local news and identify which issues are most likely to affect teenagers; write about contemporary concerns like forest fires, combating terrorism, stem cell research, or the use of steroids by athletes; or search the Internet to identify topics of immediate importance.
- Have students write and distribute a survey to their schoolmates (perhaps about the effect of sports programs on school spirit or academic achievement—something of significance in their lives), and collect and analyze the data.
- Develop a game of chance, like a lottery or raffle, for a charitable cause. Predict earnings and run a simulation of the game.
- Publish a class newspaper from a contemporary (what would biologists want to subscribe to?), historical (during World War I), or fictional perspective (what might Jane Eyre read?). Write engaging headlines and lead stories, draw comic strips, provide entertainment reviews, and include a financial page and advice column.
- Foreign language teachers: Have students study a country and collect information about it for the purpose of writing a tourist guide.
- Middle school teachers: Collaborate on a thematic unit. Host a Renaissance fair, sponsor an archeological dig, or investigate garbage in the community.

MAKING THE WORLD A BETTER PLACE

Abstract thought is not the only change observable in the adolescent as the frontal lobes bloom. With cognitive maturation emerges idealistic behavior; teenagers are finally able to understand the way the world works as well as envision the possibilities of an ideal place. During this stage, adolescents can become very critical of past generations (in particular, their parents' generation). In middle school, this behavior often manifests only in verbal statements—kids will talk a good game but rarely follow it up with action. For all of Jordan's arguments about the need to recycle and Kajia's concerns about the ways girls are portrayed in the media, fervent words are probably the most they will contribute to the cause. Expect even the most environmentally conscious thirteen-year-old to be assigned school ground cleanup duty for littering at least once!

As they enter high school, teens often turn idealism into activism. Older teenagers may become absorbed in service clubs that meet a variety of real-world needs, such as helping the elderly reset their clocks to daylight savings time, tutoring young children, or participating in a local walk-a-thon. Lars volunteers weekly at the local soup kitchen. He commented, "I feel really good, like I'm making a difference, helping out a lot of less-fortunate people." Mark teaches religious school to second and third graders. "I do it for community service and to help teach youth in my temple about Judaism. I enjoy it because I like working with the kids and I feel good about it because I give them a good role model. Even though they may not appreciate it or show it now, I think they'll remember my positive influence later."

But it is not uncommon for the young adolescent to be somewhat hypocritical in their idealistic behavior. They often have a difficult time practicing what they preach. David Elkind (1978) identified this characteristic as "adolescent hypocrisy" and linked it to intellectual immaturity, as opposed to a character flaw. In the context of brain development, their hypocritical behavior parallels the frontal lobe development and myelin enveloping the frontal lobes as the adolescence matures. The brain is not yet a smooth, paved road—there are still plenty of potholes, dirt paths, and back alleys to even out.

Anita spent hours telling her friends how important honesty was to her and how she would never lie to them. But when her mother asked her with whom she was going to the movies, she conveniently neglected to mention any of the boys' names. Lindsey, Kelsey, and Maggy all joined SALSA (Serve & Learn Student Association), a group committed to service. They talked excitedly about their first project, a highway cleanup south of town, sure that it was a chance to make a real difference in their community. The girls made detailed plans for the day: who would drive them there, what grubby clothes to wear, and what to put in their sack lunches. Yet Maggy's mother—who drove—was perplexed by their behavior. When asked how the day went, she replied, "The girls worked hard and had a lot of fun, but I don't understand teenagers. After picking up trash for two hours in the hot sun, we stopped for a snack; when they were finished eating, the girls left their candy wrappers on the ground! What were they thinking?"

Pseudostupidity is another educational psychology term that describes the transitioning adolescent brain (Elkind, 1978). With the development of the frontal lobes, teens are able to look at a problem from a number of perspectives. No longer is there just one correct answer; instead, they can imagine all kinds of possibilities. It sounds wonderful, but instead of simplifying their lives, it complicates them. Faced with a problem, they will think and think and think, unable to give any answer—not because it is too difficult to solve but because they have made the problem too complex. The answer may be right in front of their noses but they concentrate on every possible solution rather than an obvious one.

Mr. Armstrong, a middle school math teacher, assigned a simple assignment as homework. Students were to use toothpicks to show how one aspect of geometry (exponential growth) worked. All the assignment required was toothpicks, paper, and glue. What could be easier than doubling one toothpick to a group of two, the group of two to a group of four, four to eight, and so on? By doing the assignment, students would learn just how fast exponential growth took place. At 9:30 that evening, Mr. Armstrong received a phone call from a frantic parent whose sixth-grade son, Sam, was in tears. Sam was sure he needed to demonstrate the complexities of the geometric system to the hundredth degree; the family didn't have anywhere near enough toothpicks in the house, and the drugstore was closed. Somehow, in this student's mind, the project had become much more complex than what had been assigned.

Pseudostupidity also appears in social settings. A simple request to hang up a coat in the closet can set the adolescent mind running amuck: "Are they trying to control me? If I refuse am I just doing it because I think they are trying to control me when they aren't? What should I do?" Usually what a teenager does is get mad. An innocent remark becomes fuel for a teenage conflagration—or for a teenage anxiety attack: Amanda, a very likable teenager, was worried about making friends after her family moved to a new school district. One of her teachers reported that she went to extremes to get classmates to like her—brought them treats, agreed with everything they said, just wore herself out to get noticed—when all she really had to do was be herself.

Instructional Strategies

Walking the Walk: Countering Teenage Hypocrisy

The best way to counter teenage hypocrisy is to immerse them in the real world and in their community. Exposing adolescents to the way things really work and showing them real-life consequences to their behavior will help make the connection between well-intentioned words and meaningful actions.

- Have students research service agencies and volunteer in the community at soup kitchens or shelters, act as mentors to younger children, or participate in diversity projects.

- Encourage students to offer help on a local political campaign.
- Invite people from the community—an elderly veteran, a local artist, someone who trains Seeing Eye dogs, anyone of interest—to be guest speakers in your class.
- Enact historical or government simulations.
- Compare the experiences of characters on television or in books to the real lives of students.
- Take a trip to a city dump or landfill and talk about recycling and littering on your campus.
- Attend cyberschool—investigate controversial issues on the Internet and discuss how they impact your thinking. Stimulate the conversation further by figuring out solutions. Channel that adolescent energy into positive action.

Secret Revealed

 It may come as some surprise for parents to learn that teenagers aren't claiming the garage for rock band practice just to give them a headache. Research has discovered the real reason behind the sudden enthusiasm for this noisy pastime—the parietal lobes are in full bloom! Suddenly, kids who grumbled about practicing for weekly music lessons can't get enough of playing the guitar or singing into a microphone. Kids who grumbled when Saturday morning cartoons ended now "waste" the day shooting hoops or hitting a tennis ball against the front of the house.

The parietal lobes control our sense of spatial awareness and the fluidity of the body's movements. Teen brains are busy forming new neurons and cleaning up old synaptic connections, fine-tuning adolescents' control over their fingers, arms, and legs. Their interest in all things physical springs from the discovery that, for the first time, they can actually play that tricky chord pattern and predict where that fly ball is going to land. Practice finally is likely to make perfect—the extra effort pays off, and everything is so much more fun.

BACKSTAGE IN THE THEATER OF THE TEEN MIND

The parietal lobes are located at the top of the brain toward the back of each hemisphere. The front and back areas of the parietal lobes each have separate jobs. The front part receives messages from our senses, like pain, pressure, and temperature. Am I cold? Do I need a jacket? Are these pants too tight? Information from all over the body is sent here and then monitored. Not all areas of the body are represented equally, however; the lips and tongue are particularly sensitive to outside stimulus and have extensive network access to the parietal lobes. The back part of the parietal lobes is responsible for logic and spatial awareness and keeps track of where our fingers, feet, and head are in relation to our surroundings. They keep the rhythms of our motions going and help us avoid that clumsy misstep.

Figure 2.3 Human Brain

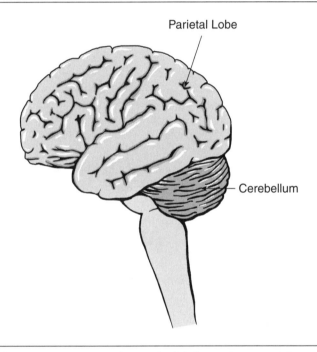

SOURCE: Adapted from Sousa, D. A. (2003), *How the Gifted Brain Learns*, p. 16.

Because early adolescence is when the parietal lobes create gray matter and prune extraneous neurons, it is a critical time for learning. As the parietal lobes mature, the ability to become proficient in sports and musical instruments is particularly enhanced. Caitlin, a track star, exudes enthusiasm as she completes the mile five seconds faster than her personal best. Wyatt practices the piano, playing with an ease and grace that is appreciated by everyone within earshot. Both of these individuals made huge strides in their capabilities during their teenage years.

We see this growth in athletics all the time. The junior varsity basketball team may have a tough time competing against the varsity team today, but the younger athletes keep practicing and learning the plays; next year, they'll be the ones playing varsity. Ninth-grade teachers are probably the most familiar with this transformation—their students go from confused, intimidated, and naïve in September to confident by May. The ninth-grade boy who spent the whole year with all his textbooks in his backpack (because he was too embarrassed to ask for help locating his locker) casually approaches the principal to discuss a class change in tenth grade.

"EVERY MOVE YOU MAKE, EVERY STEP YOU TAKE . . ."

The cerebellum, located at the back of the brain, looks like a head of cauliflower and has more neurons than any other area of the brain. It is another part of the brain associated with movement. It is particularly linked to balance, posture, and gross motor skills like riding a bike, jogging, or snapping your flip-flops. It does not reach maturation until young adulthood, and its greatest changes happen during adolescence. Although Sting, the lead singer of the band, Police, may not have been referring to the cerebellum with his lyrics, "every move you make, every step you take, I'll be watching you," they certainly apply—the cerebellum guides and modifies our every action! But neuroscience has recently revealed that the cerebellum is also involved in the coordination of cognitive processes. It actually makes thinking tasks easier. Just as it balances and guides our physical movement, it keeps our thought processes moving smoothly. The more complicated a task facing us, the larger the role the cerebellum plays in resolving it (Giedd, Blumenthal, Jeffries, Castellanos, et al., 1999).

Secret Revealed

Maybe we shouldn't have been making jokes about "dumb jocks" for all these years. Have you ever noticed how complicated a football playbook is? Could you memorize all those diagrams and recall them during the stress of competition? New research reveals that physical fitness might be what helps football players keep it in their heads! Dr. Jay Giedd (Giedd, Castellanos, Rajapakse, Vaituzis, & Rapoport, 1997), the neuroscientist from the National Institute of Mental Health (Remember him from Chapter 1?), also discovered that the

(Continued)

(Continued)

cerebellum, so long considered the "motor center" of the brain, plays a crucial role in coordinating thought processes and making decisions, too.

Teens need to move! Contradictory though it may seem, cutting PE and intramural sports is not the right way to improve academic programs at schools. A strong cerebellum is essential for efficient problem-solving skills and mental planning. Without regular physical activity, the teen brain gets the signal that the neurons in the cerebellum aren't as important as the neurons in other places (and less important neurons are in danger of being pruned). And without a strong and healthy cerebellum, that multistep math problem and reflective essay are much harder to do.

The cerebellum works in coordination with the motor cortex. When the cortex decides at a conscious level to move, it relays a message to the cerebellum. The cerebellum is connected by neurons to all the muscles in the body; it calculates which muscles are needed to enact the motion, sends them the message to move, and off you go! The cerebellum then continues to monitor and make adjustments to your movements. No wonder some people find it difficult to walk and chew gum at the same time! The combination requires the cerebellum to control two completely different sets of muscle groups.

Just as the abilities to play soccer, dance, or walk to school are guided by the cerebellum, so seem to be the thinking skills involved in planning a party, organizing a research paper, or making a reflective decision (Giedd, Blumenthal, Jeffries, Castellanos, et al., 1999). Your ability to read (although not your ability to comprehend) is stored in the cerebellum, as are song lyrics and lines from favorite movies ("Here's lookin' at you, kid") (Leonard, 1999). Like learning physical skills, the adolescent needs opportunities to practice cognitive processes in order to improve them. Teachers who involve students in thinking skills will help their students' cerebellums refine processing skills. Adolescents involved in bodily kinesthetic movement, whether taking part in a structured physical education class, participating in extracurricular activities, or playing musical instruments, will strengthen the neural connections in their adolescent cerebellum. Use it or lose it applies to the neurons in the cerebellum as much as the neurons in the cortex; they are all strengthened or sacrificed depending on usage.

Sadly, participation in all types of physical activity declines as children advance through school; maintaining moderate activity levels is a greater challenge for the adolescent than the child. As districts face financial challenges, physical education graduation requirements are being reduced throughout the country. For example, districts that once required one credit of physical education for graduation are now considering reducing the requirement to one-half credit. Although most schools still maintain afterschool sports programs and individual students exercise during their (ever-diminishing) free time, the lack of formal physical education classes will ultimately affect student cognition as well as coordination.

It is known that the adolescent who engages in challenging cognitive activities increases and strengthens the neurons involved in coordinating thinking skills (Giedd, Blumenthal, Jeffries, Castellanos, et al., 1999). Actively involving students with brain-compatible learning strategies, such as art or science projects, simulations, and problem-solving activities, will build better cerebellums than will forcing students into the roles of consistently passive recipients of knowledge. Elementary school teachers commonly use body movements to support learning, but secondary teachers aren't always comfortable with such techniques. Even though their students say things like "A math teacher had us move to learn a theorem—it was helpful," and "In our American Studies class, the teacher had guys act out the characters of different stories. I can still see how they did it!"

Interestingly, the cerebellum is the area of the brain that differs the most between teenage boys and girls. Cerebellums in adolescent boys are about fourteen percent larger than cerebellums in adolescent girls, and the difference remains through adulthood (Raz, Gunning-Dixon, Head, Williamson, & Acker, 2001). It is speculated that the difference between male and female cerebellum size is partially a result of human evolution—males were the ones tracking and hunting while females were the ones keeping the home fires burning. Because the cerebellum controlled the skills the males were using, they developed larger cerebellums. (In general, the size of any brain component is proportionate to the amount of processing it does.) Whether or not this supposition is true, a larger cerebellum may explain why the boys in your class like to be in motion (moving their legs and stretching their arms) and the girls don't mind sitting and listening. Boys and girls both benefit, however, from the cognitive skills that come from physical movement.

Instructional Strategies

Of Sound Mind and Body

An extensive study of the benefits of active learning was done in elementary and middle schools in Chicago. Classrooms that actively engaged students were compared to classrooms that viewed students as passive receptors, relying on drill and practice to increase learning. The results were impressive. Classrooms that had a great deal of interaction and didactic instruction saw dramatic increases in scores on the Iowa Test of Basic Skills in reading and math over a four-year period (Smith, Lee, & Newmann, 2001).

Active learning doesn't come without challenges: Limited class time, greater prep time, lack of materials, and of course the biggest challenge of all—the possibility that students won't engage, are some of the issues teachers face. Give yourself a break; remember that while creative methods of urging participation are great, simply mixing lecture and discussion creates an actively involved classroom. Whatever method you use to actively engage students, the payback in academic achievement is worth taking the risk.

Teachers come to the same conclusion informally all the time. Mr. Miller, a high school math teacher, was concerned that year after year his students had difficulty understanding the concept of slope. He decided to see if active learning in place of paper and pencil exercises would make a difference. "I had them measuring the slope on the school's handicapped accessible ramps, the football field, and the staircases. I know I had a lot of fun, and I think they did, too. The best news was that their tests showed they had a much better understanding of slope when all was said and done." Active learning works.

So incorporate movement into learning—sit less and move more. Enact simulations, play charades, and do energizers. Choreograph body movements to represent phenomena in nature or the emotions of a character in literature. Allow students to step into the psyche of a new character. Let them act out the experience of being a boring guest speaker, substitute teacher, or the teacher arguing with a student over a grade by stepping into another person's shoes. Compose a song. Create a collage, time capsule, or board game. Conduct a science experiment. Get out the cotton swabs, construction paper, marshmallows, and toothpicks and get busy!

Things to Try

- Have students create time capsules of their lives. "Bury" the collective contributions somewhere on campus (in a safe place) and open them a year or two later. Then, let students take their individual capsules home. The personal connection at both ends of the project will engage all students.
- Simulate a mock Congress. Having representatives from every state will involve every student. Students work individually to gather data but work collectively to present it.
- Make a board game about some lesson in a social studies, English, or math class. Have students exchange games and play them. Small groups of students will form naturally; designing the games is educational, but playing them is fun.

- Design a bumper sticker that reflects political views on an issue—this activity combines creativity with academic research. Have a contest with silly prizes for the best bumper stickers in a variety of categories, such as "Bumper Sticker that Will Fit on the Smallest Car."
- Tour and study historic buildings in your area. Not only will a field trip give students a sense of perspective about their community and times gone by, the novelty of the location will make a better background against which to remember new knowledge. The effort of walking through rooms or from building to building will engage the cerebellum.
- Create a collage from recycled materials. This hands-on project allows students to communicate their ideas about real-world issues while expressing themselves artistically.
- Create an advertisement for nutritional eating. Higher-level thinking is engaged as students analyze and decide what information is most important for consumers to know, what will grab their attention, and how to get the message across.
- Make a brochure of your life, school, or community. Who are you? What do you stand for? Choose an audience of peers, parents, teachers, or community. Ask students to discuss how their brochures could change to suit different audiences.
- Teach a lesson in television-talk-show or trivia-game-show format. Students can write questions and keep score. They can also take turns playing host and guests or game participants—and so can you!
- For physical education teachers: Have students design and implement a personal fitness program after assessing personal strength, endurance, and flexibility. Teens will practice setting goals, compete with themselves instead of each other (promoting camaraderie and cooperation), and benefit from improved physical health.
- Research a need in the community, hypothesize a solution, and propose it to the local school board. Not only would students have to think abstractly, they would also have the chance to offer their knowledge to the community. Making a real contribution is a motivator and a true self-esteem builder.

FEEDBACK: FOOD FOR LEARNING

The brain works via a system of checks and balances. It chooses its next cognitive move on the basis of what it just did (Bangert-Drowns, Kulik, Kulik, & Morgan, 1991). Feedback is required to clarify and correct the information we receive; it allows the brain to readjust and reevaluate what it thinks it knows. Feedback is best when it is corrective in nature, explaining what students did right and wrong. Positive feedback—which can include suggestions about how to improve or change—helps us cope with stress. Our adrenal system goes into overdrive when we are stressed; hearing the words "That's right," "Good job," or "Nice work" keeps us relaxed.

Secret Revealed

 It's time for teachers to reconsider everything they've thought about giving feedback to students. Teens don't crave feedback because they are insecure about their academic performance or needy for attention—they crave feedback because it helps them finish learning. Learning, the growth of new neurons and the creation of new synaptic connections, is the brain's response to stimulus. Stimulus, response, stimulus, response—responding to environmental stimulus is one of the basic life functions. Externally, we respond to rain by seeking shelter and to hot stoves by pulling our hand away. Internally, we respond to hunger by eating and to germs by activating the immune system—and by restructuring the brain according to knowledge we acquire.

Feedback is one form of stimulus. When the brain gets no stimulus of feedback, it has no reason to respond to information by learning. Feedback is especially important to teenagers because of the changes occurring in their brain. Without information about their performance, their brains won't know what neurons to grow or which ones to prune. Positive feedback actually releases serotonin into the brain, reinforcing feelings of calm and happiness. Feedback, in the classroom and in life, is one of the most important ways you can help teens turn their brains into efficient learning systems.

Feedback is especially important during adolescence, when the brain is undergoing so much building and pruning of synapses. Rarely do students understand things the first time they are presented; the brain learns through trial and error. As their brains take in new information, certain neurons are activated and certain neurons are not. Feedback is just as important as the original information sent to the brain because it completes the cycle of learning. Feedback helps teen brains decide which neurons to turn on and which to turn off, assisting the brain in making adjustments and correcting misinformation. The brain tries one combination and then another until the correct response is learned (and probably does more eliminating than increasing of neuron activity).

Feedback must be timely and specific to be of any use. Consider Lee, who was frustrated and disgusted with his English teacher. "The whole semester we only did one paper, at the beginning of the year, and we didn't get it back until finals. My paper just had one large B on the front—no other comments. It was really stupid. She hardly had anything to grade our writing on, and we never got a chance to improve." Worst-case scenario, sure, but returning work in an untimely fashion is a recurring theme in some classrooms. The assignment that is not returned to the student for weeks loses its impetus, as does the paper that receives only a letter grade with no follow-up comments (Marzano et al., 2001).

Multiple assessment strategies make the failure to grade and hand back assignments much more avoidable. Use a variety of formal and informal assessments to communicate with your students. Distribute slips of brown paper on which students can write questions about the "muddy waters" that obscure their comprehension of the content. Pass quickly around the room having each student contribute one thing they learned in class that day. Keep records on academic and nonacademic achievement, along with portfolios of student work (including photos or videos of work that can't be documented in other ways). At every stage, involve students in the process of their own evaluation and assessment.

Instructional Strategies

Fun With Feedback

Performance-based assessment counters teacher-made multiple-choice and standardized tests by assessing students during real-world activities, or at least as close to the real world as possible. It emphasizes doing (active participation) and it usually takes places over a long period of time—from a week to even a month. The teacher and students reflect on the work, noting its strengths and weaknesses. Such feedback helps the student strengthen synaptic connections. The possible tools are unlimited:

- Advertisements
- Advice columns
- Autobiographies
- Bedtime stories
- Book jackets
- Campaign speeches
- Data sheets
- Diary entries
- Dramatic presentations

- Editorial writings
- Encyclopedia entries
- Epilogues
- Experiments
- Fairy tales
- Films
- Greeting cards
- Nutrition charts
- Paintings
- Parodies

- Petitions
- Radio programs
- Sales pitches
- Scrapbooks
- Sculptures
- Sequels
- Simulations
- Speeches
- Superstitions
- Tributes
- TV commercials

(Continued)

(Continued)

Things to Try

- Before a new lesson, give students a short questionnaire to fill out, or conduct a brief discussion to determine their background knowledge. This formative assessment will help you determine where to start the lesson (and who might need extra attention during the unit).
- Pick an important term or concept from your daily lesson and have students list ideas associated with it. For example, students in a government class might list *Native American, reservation, self-determination, rights,* and *politics* for the word *sovereignty.* Then, have students compare their lists with a partner, noting what items are common to both lists and discussing the items that appear on one list but not the other.
- Distribute empty or partially completed outlines before a class lecture or during a video, and have students fill in the blanks as information is presented. This will focus their attention and help them identify important ideas.
- Have students create a memory matrix based on categories you assign. For instance, you could compare feudalism to mercantilism with the following categories: sources of wealth, generation of wealth, distribution of wealth, and population centers. Students will see immediately what important information they remember and what they need to keep studying.
- Assign a sixty-second paper on what you covered during that day's lesson. One minute is a very small amount of class time to invest in an assignment that will tell you at a glance if students understand the main points of your lesson or are simply focusing on minor and supporting ideas.
- Have students devise a pro-and-con grid for one concept they are learning. Listing advantages and disadvantages requires them to go beyond memorizing facts to analyzing information; it reinforces their decision-making skills.
- Use concept maps—drawings that show the connections between concepts and facts—for insight into how students are thinking about their own thinking.
- Make space in your room to store student portfolios. Annotated portfolios include artifacts from class along with explanations of the significance of the selections. (Often, the relevance of the artifact is explained in terms of classroom goals and content.)
- Let students generate test questions and answers. To write a good question, they must have an understanding of the material and the key points. The quality of their questions can help you assess their weaknesses. Returning these questions to students in the form of a practice test also makes them part of the process, removing them from the role of "innocent bystander" during assessment.

Many of these ideas are from the book *Classroom Assessment Techniques: A Handbook for College Teachers (2nd Edition)*, by Thomas A. Angelo and K. Patricia Cross (1998: Jossey-Bass).

ORGANIZATION ≠ OPPRESSION

The brain stores new information by identifying patterns in it. As it receives fresh material, the brain searches its established neural networks for a background against which it can comprehend the new knowledge. Anything familiar—sensory information (like a remembered scent), a pattern, a relationship—will serve as a connection to information already stored in the brain. If the brain finds nothing on which to build, it abandons the new information. Many study skills and instructional strategies are compatible with the brain's innate desire to decipher patterns. Disheartened middle and high school students make remarks about their homework like "I don't know where to start," "This stuff is so boring," and "One minute I know it, and the next I've forgotten it" because their brains have a difficult time tapping into these patterns.

Secret Revealed

Contrary to popular belief, teens aren't looking to pick fights with the adults in their lives. They aren't arguing about skipping breakfast and borrowing the car because they enjoy the verbal sparring. Parents and teachers who give brooding teens a wide berth to avoid provoking an outburst are going at it all the wrong way. They ought to be looking for ways to guide teenagers instead.

Sound shocking? Prepare yourself for this: Teenagers actually want and need guidance from adults about important life issues like education and work plans (Schneider & Younger, 1996). This emotional support from adults is imperative to adolescents' healthy development. Don't be fooled into backing off just because of a teen's show of resistance to your advice. What may appear to be oppositional behavior is often a desire for personal autonomy. Teens want to choose their own clothes, friends, and hobbies—these things demonstrate their independence and individuality. The search for autonomy is normal; it's the beginning step toward taking on adult responsibilities. Once the argument about homework ends, however, teens are very receptive to suggestions about choosing a college or how to act during a job interview.

Help teenagers access these patterns by providing models, organization, and structure to their lives. Every student needs a planner to track assignments; it's hard to accomplish something if you're not sure what you need to do. Hold young teens accountable for keeping their planners up-to-date, and they'll maintain the habit as they grow older. Teach them how to budget their time by deciding what to study and for how long, to take advantage of mental stamina by doing the hard or boring stuff first, to establish a context for studying by always working in the same place—and nag them to get off the Internet!

It's only fair that teachers and parents help teens establish order in their lives; we are the ones who expect them to achieve academically, participate in extracurricular activities, help with many of the household chores, and perhaps hold down a job. Students have never been busier. Many adolescents barely have time to grab a snack or change clothes between activities. They hold up their part of the bargain pretty well but do better when we provide study skills and the support to perfect them.

In class, cue them. Emphasize and repeat important information. Teach students different note-taking methods (Cornell–2-column, SQ3R, outlines, or your personal favorite) and have them practice one style until they can do it automatically while listening to a lecture. Remind them to review their notes within twenty-four hours to improve their retention (and save study time in the long run). The brain remembers images more easily than words, which makes graphic organizers, pictures, charts, and graphs effective tools for organizing patterns.

My personal favorite note-taking style is Double Column notes because they allow the students to encode the information in a variety of ways and are easily modified to meet different students' needs and purposes.

Figure 2.4   Double-Column Notes

Double-Column Notes

EVERY GOOD BOY DOES FINE

While we would prefer that all learning be meaningful, in the real world people need to memorize important information that is arbitrary and dull. In classroom situations, students can benefit from mnemonics, techniques for remembering information with images and words (Carney & Levin, 2000). For example, the names of the planets or the number of days in each month are more easily memorized with the help of a mnemonic. Rhymes and acronyms are two common strategies that can be fun for students learning by rote.

A teacher may provide mnemonics, but they are more meaningful when the students construct them. Younger children do better with auditory mnemonics, such as "When two vowels go a-walking, the first one does the talking." Adolescents, with their increased mental capacities, do well with visual or auditory mnemonics like the following examples (Wang & Thomas, 1995):

- PMAT: prophase, metaphase, anaphase, telophase—the four stages of cellular mitosis.
- I Am A Person: Indian, Arctic, Atlantic, Pacific—the four oceans of the world.
- Sober Physicists Don't Find Giraffes In Kitchens: the orbital names for electrons are S, P, D, F, G, I, K.
- Associate each school supply with a particular spot in your bedroom. Imagine your backpack with your desk, band music on the bed, and PE clothes in the drawer. Before leaving for school each morning, mentally walk around the room. Have you remembered all your items? Visualizing your dresser will cue you to bring your P. E. clothes if you've forgotten to pack them.
- To remember that Annapolis is the capital of Maryland, visualize two apples. For St. Paul, Minnesota, imagine a saint sipping a soda.
- To remember the twelve cranial nerves (for a brain-compatible teaching class, of course), just think of the rhyme, "On Old Olympus Towering Tops, A Finn And German Viewed Some Hops": the cranial nerves are the olfactory, optic, occulomotor, trochlear, trigeminal, abducens, facial, auditory, glossopharyngeal, vagus, spinal accessory, and hypoglossal!

Time-management and test-taking strategies also should be taught to teenagers. When students have a framework for remembering information and keeping track of their due dates on calendars, they are much better prepared to cope with the cognitive and structural chaos inside their heads.

Study skills help the brain organize and make connections. Students stop cold if they are overwhelmed by too much to learn in too little time, by not knowing where to start or by not having time to let information sink in. Study strategies can make the difference between academic success and meltdown. Share the following items with your students to help them take charge of their learning.

Effective Study Strategies

- Take notes. Whether you prefer KWL (What I KNOW, What I WANT to Know, and What I LEARNED), outline, or double columns, pick one and practice it until it becomes second nature.
- Tap into prior knowledge.
- Organize information in notebooks, on note cards, or in a computer.
- Budget study time. Schedule an hour or two each day at a desk in your bedroom or school library, wherever you want. Take a ten-minute brain break every fifty minutes and stick to the plan.
- Summarize in writing what you've learned at the end of each study session.
- Monitor your learning while you study; reflect on what needs more work and what you don't understand.
- Keep an assignment notebook. Break down large assignments into smaller tasks and cross items off your list as you complete them.
- Eliminate distractions, turn off the TV, stop instant messaging, and let voicemail collect your cell phone messages.
- Be positive—as they say, "Change your thoughts, change your life."
- Do the difficult material first, while you are still fresh.

Secret Revealed

Instant messaging, googling, and downloading songs while attempting to do homework—a good thing or a bad thing? David Meyer, a psychologist who directs the Brain, Cognition, and Action Laboratory at the University of Michigan (www.umich.edu/~bcalab) warns that each interruption requires time for the brain to readjust. A small math or language arts assignment that would normally take thirty minutes, will suddenly take two or three hours if multitasking is involved.

Surprisingly, the more divergent the task, the easier the work is for the brain. If we are trying to pet our dog while we do homework, the brain continues to operate smoothly; however, if we are trying to do two similar jobs with our brain, such as instant messaging and writing a composition, the brain gets stuck on pause.

Effective Test-Taking Strategies

The pressure to perform on tests is impacting the way teachers instruct, students learn, and parents fret. Providing students with added support in the art of test taking is a requirement for the twenty-first century.

- Test prep should begin on the first day of class (and no, I'm not kidding, high schoolers)—reviews, homework, readings, and attending class, are all important parts of the process. The best way to reduce anxiety is to be prepared.
- Identify your best test-studying strategies—do you study best alone or in a group, with flash cards or highlighting, or is a combination the best?
- Eat before a test; a fully performing brain needs the energy supply food provides.
- Quickly peruse the test when you first get it and catch the general gist.
- Stay positive during the test—if you start to feel anxious, breath deeply, or use other stress-reducing tactics.
- Do the easiest problems first (this is the opposite approach of study strategies, where the most difficult assignments are tackled first).
- Be sure to complete the items with the greatest point value. If something has to give, let it be the one-pointers.
- Students, create a mock test; this requires higher-level thinking and is a good way to review.

A BETTER DAY STUDENT TEACHING

"Good morning," the student teacher said to each student as the teenagers shuffled into class. She paused now and then to ask individual students about a dance recital the night before or to compliment them on the tiebreaking goal they scored at the game. The room filled with noisy chatter as the class took their seats. She began class by passing around an empty box and asking students to put something of no real

value in it (such as pencils, pieces of paper, or movie ticket stubs). As the box went around the room, she asked the students for examples of storytelling, perhaps from their own families. When the box returned to the front of the room, she told a story about how her great-grandmother had participated in the women's suffrage movement. She punctuated elements of her tale with props from the box—the class was riveted. Afterward, the teacher divided the class and the items from the box into four groups for a cooperative learning assignment. The students told and listened to each other's stories; the signal to clean up at the end of class caught them all by surprise.

The Social Brain

Science has demonstrated that emotions strongly impact learning. This is problematic because teens are still learning to balance and manage their emotions. They are also learning how to negotiate their place in the world, from maintaining friendships to practicing the mating dance.

Did you know that . . .

- Adolescence is when the brain begins to develop templates for adult relationships
- Teen emotions can easily cement lifelong memories or form powerful learning blocks
- Teens value adult influence even though they complain about it
- Teenagers will climb the moral ladder only as their frontal lobes develop
- Boy brains and girl brains really are different—it's not just socialization

Senior Prom—the ultimate spring mating ritual. Joseph stood on his porch, arms folded, his face a mixture of happiness and apprehension. His daughter, Sarah, was all dressed up in a full-length, midnight blue evening gown (advertised at the boutique as the "strapless wonder" for obvious reasons). Lex, her date, looked like Prince Charming in a black tuxedo with a white rose boutonniere. The couple cheerfully posed for pictures, waved good-bye, and dashed off in his car. Their anticipation of the night ahead of them was palpable. Joseph watched them drive out of sight and then turned to his wife and said, drolly, "They're all in heat." She agreed immediately.

LOVE ON THE BRAIN

Ashley, a bubbly fourteen-year-old, spends most of her time daydreaming about Andy. She watches his every move, wears clothes that are too risqué, and laughs a little too loud, all in hopes of catching his attention. Andy, busy doing his math, is totally oblivious to the fact that the mating dance is about to begin.

Teenagers are very eager to share their thoughts about the opposite sex. You have to prod them to discuss academic subjects, but words just flow when it comes to boyfriends and girlfriends. Boys are consumed with thoughts about girls and girls are consumed with thoughts about boys. Questions such as "Does she like me?" and "Will he ask me out?" hover constantly in their love-afflicted minds; questions about how to solve math equations with double variables are almost never entertained!

Most researchers agree that there are sensitive times for learning certain material. Although the concept of "critical periods" is controversial, clearly there are ideal times to learn to crawl, to talk, and to learn a foreign language (Puckett, Marshall, & Davis, 1999). A number of neuroscientists believe that adolescence is the ideal time to learn the mating ritual. Research by Dr. Martha McClintock shows that boys and girls have their first real crush at age ten (before puberty) and suggests that these crushes spring from connections in their brains that are made during this time (McClintock & Herdt, 1996). During adolescence, teenagers have the opportunity to become involved with their own sexuality and ultimately begin the search to find a mate. The low-slung jeans, pierced belly buttons beneath midriff tops, and macho, fly-by-the-seat-of-your-pants baggy jeans are all attempts to experiment with sexual attractiveness.

Secret Revealed

 To the bewilderment and frustration of teachers and parents, "hangin' around and talkin'" is one of teens' favorite pastimes. Given to their own devices, teenagers can spend a full afternoon mulling over how they will spend the afternoon only to suddenly realize the afternoon is over and it's time to start contemplating the evening. As adults we often view this as time lost, a pure and simple waste of an afternoon, but in actuality this idleness provides a meaningful period of problem solving. It is while they are hangin' and talkin' that they explore, negotiate, and make decisions.

The next time you see them engaged in something that appears to be unproductive during lunch or after school, leave them to their mystifying deliberations. Resist the temptation to offer suggestions (they won't be appreciated) and just walk away knowing they are constructing a new and improved brain.

THE LEVELS OF LOVE

Anthropologist Dr. Helen Fisher is enamored of the subject of love, in teens and adults alike. She speculates that there are different levels of love, each influenced by a different system in the brain (Fisher, Aron, Mashek, Li, & Brown, 2002). One level is lust—immediate sexual attraction for someone. In this stage, it is accurate to say we have sex on the brain. The male hormone, testosterone, is associated with increasing the sex  drive in both men and women. Because levels of testosterone surge through the teen body during puberty, it is no surprise that teenage thoughts and behaviors focus so often on sexual mates and desire.

Another stage of love is romantic love—think Romeo and Juliet. During this stage, we become obsessed with the person who is the object of our attention. We are unable to think of anyone or anything else. We want to be with this person day and night. This romp with romance can be witnessed in the all-consuming adolescent crush. One high school girl admitted that she spent about ninety percent of her time thinking about her boyfriend. A high school boy said, "I think about girls every three seconds, unless I'm playing Nintendo." Is it any wonder that most girls start dating at fourteen and most boys follow close on their heels six months to a year later? (A girl's interest in dating and being dated usually precedes a boy's for the mere fact that she hits puberty earlier.)

Younger teens are just getting their toes wet in the dating scene. They tend to gravitate toward people who enjoy the same things they do; having fun is usually their goal. When asked to describe his first date in eighth grade, an eleventh grader recalled, "We went to Jeff's house to watch a movie. There were about five of us there—two couples and an extra girl. I thought it was kind of awkward. I'm not sure who asked who out." Another boy said, "My first date was in the seventh grade. We went to the mall with another couple. I had fun. Bought the CD for the Aquabats. She asked me who they were and I said, 'They're awesome.' I can still remember the conversation." A teenage girl recalled, "My first date was in sixth grade. I went to the park with him and a group of kids. We swung on swings and went on the merry-go-round. We didn't talk much but it was fun." Older teens also want fun, but they are beginning to look for more intimacy on dates—someone with whom they can talk openly about their feelings and for whom they feel respect and affection. Of course, until adolescents figure out who they are and develop a self-identity, it's difficult for them to carry on a sustained relationship.

Dating serves a number of purposes for a teenager

- Provides a form of recreation
- Serves as a source of status and achievement
- Shows independence from the family
- Offers the opportunity to begin to experiment sexually

WHY LOVE FEELS SO GOOD

When we are in love, dopamine is released (and boy do we feel great). Dr. Marian Diamond said that a person in love "is often more creative, has more endurance, more energy and is more focused and less interested in the broad problems of society" (2000, para. 9). The only proof you'll probably need of the veracity of this statement is the memory of the first time you fell in love! And once we are in love, we want to experience this good feeling more and more. Love and pleasure are particularly affected by the chemical dopamine—the all-time feel-good neurotransmitter. At times it seems as if all pleasure is connected to dopamine and dopamine alone. Dopamine's effect on the mind has been compared to the effect of cocaine and other addictive drugs. Our brains interpret love and sex as a reward and actively search for the next fix.

Dopamine and adolescence make a spine-tingling combination. The teen brain seems to be particularly sensitive to dopamine levels and craves the euphoric thrill it brings (Spear, 2002). Curiously, many teenagers equate falling in love with taking a risk, which is another event that increases dopamine levels in the brain. "Hooking up" with that new boy or girl in your chemistry class is a surefire way to get a dopamine rush. Once teens figure that out, the race is on for a date and possible mate. Further complicating matters is the fact that teenagers' lives are filled with action, excitement, and danger—highly aroused states that make them particularly susceptible to falling in love. For some reason, if a teen (or anybody, actually) meets someone at an emotionally charged moment, such as at a football game or during a violent thunderstorm, the chances increase that they'll fall in love. Because teenagers look for novelty and excitement in their lives, they are at risk for finding love in all the wrong places.

As fate would have it, their brain structure increases love's compelling appeal. At University College London, Dr. Semir Zeki and Dr. Andreas Bartels scanned the brains of young adults who had fallen madly in love within the last six months or year and who were looking at photographs of their sweethearts (Bartels & Zeki, 2000). Four regions of the brain lit up like lights on a Christmas tree: the medial insula, which is associated with emotional interpretations—particularly visual ones; the anterior cingulate gyrus, a part of the brain involved in feelings of euphoria; and the putamen and the caudate nuclei, two tiny areas deep within the brain that are related to positive experiences and addiction. Furthermore, love highly stimulates the reticular formation (Diamond, 2000), which is a network in the central core of the brain stem responsible for gathering information from all over the body and for regulating sleep and arousal patterns. Within the reticular formation are neuron groups that run through the lower brain stem and up to the cerebellum, hypothalamus, thalamus, amygdala, and cerebral cortex.

Secret Revealed

 Stop and compare this piece of new information to what you've always thought: The brain, not the gonads, is what fills teenagers with lust. (Actually, it fills everybody with lust but teens in particular.) Adolescence is when the brain lays down the circuitry that will enable teens to later form adult sexual relationships and reproduce—the main prerogative of the species! Crushes and going steady are just practice, so teens will have it figured out when they are ready for parenthood.

Dr. Semir Zeki and Dr. Andreas Bartels, scientists at University College London, studied love and its expression with MRI technology. They discovered that areas of the brain involved in the feeling of euphoria, emotion, and addiction lit up when people gazed upon photographs of their beloved. Euphoria and addiction—no wonder the teen brain seeks to engage feelings of love over and over again. Add to the mix the fact that teens are still learning to regulate their emotions, and you've got a heady mix of the boy-and-girl-crazies in the classroom!

The more active the reticular formation, the more able we are to focus attention on things outside of us—like a romantic interest. If you see a boy you're attracted to, your amygdala registers pleasure, and your frontal lobes translate it as love. Adolescents have trouble dealing with romantic feelings not only because they have such strong sexual desires but also because their frontal lobes are not yet well developed enough to regulate them. They feel lust, so they make an inappropriate pass at a girl without pausing to think of her reaction. Until age and maturity enable adolescents to better control their desires and focus, learning and responsibility are much lower priorities in their brains.

Instructional Strategies

Sex Versus Social Studies

It's normal for students to be preoccupied with the opposite sex. Teachers need to accept this fact and get used to it because teens aren't in any hurry to change. Be tolerant of the strange (yet normal) habits and behaviors they exhibit in your classroom (at least, the nondisruptive ones). To attract the opposite sex, teens experiment with hair color, clothes, body piercing, and tattoos (maybe tattoos aren't that normal!). Breakups are traumatic; help them understand that intense feelings are to be expected and that it is acceptable to express them. However, the classroom is a place of learning first and foremost—not a venue to show off spaghetti straps or low-slung jeans. Set limits on sexually explicit clothes. Work with other teachers, parents, and administrators to regulate dress codes and determine what may and may not be worn to school.

Put students in mixed-sex groups to discuss academic issues. Boys and girls who interact in class find common ground that is not based on sex and learn to view each other as more than just future romantic partners. Positive adult role models and mentors are crucial guides for teens as they explore their sexuality. The media portrays casual sex as the rule, not the exception. Young girls in particular draw the conclusion that their sexuality is the most important way to validate themselves and attract a boy's attention. Important adults in their life can balance and channel a teen's energy into other social and academic endeavors. If businesspeople are too busy to act as mentors, ask young adults and college students, senior citizens, or homemakers to contribute. You can also introduce teenagers to books and magazines that don't focus on sex and relationships but rather on hobbies, sports, and educational interests.

A SENSE OF "ME"

Adolescents' romantic development parallels their cognitive and physical development. Cognitively, the adolescent is able to ponder the future and whip out sarcastic zingers; physically, breasts are budding and limbs are sprouting; and emotionally, a sense of morality and self-concept start to gel (Greenspan & Benderly, 1997).

Adolescence is the time to ponder the question, "Who am I?" Teenagers spend a great deal of time experimenting with various roles— how to look, who to hang out with, what hobbies to adopt—as they form an identity and define themselves as a person. Through constant changes of hairstyles, clothes, music preferences, dating partners, and social grouping, teenagers begin to understand who they are. This is a time-honored tradition of every generation. In the 1950s, teenagers greased their hair, wore leather jackets, and listened to Elvis Presley. In the 1960s, it was go-go boots, long hair, and the Beatles. Today, it's body piercing, crop tops, and Miley Cyrus. (This complements their parents' time-honored tradition of general disapproval and belief that the world was a better place when they were young!) As teens experiment with and identify who they are, they begin to form an image of their strengths and weaknesses.

Our self-concept is the way we view ourselves. "I love playing trumpet; I'm first chair in the band," "Biology is my favorite subject," and "I'm running-back on the varsity football team" are all statements made by students with high self-concepts. In contrast, Will sits at the back of the class, arms folded, silently daring the teacher to ask him a question. He lost interest in this class a long time ago. His reason? "I can't do math." Monica, who constantly talks to her neighbor and glances around the room, has a different reason: "This stuff is impossible to learn. I'm thinking about lunch instead." Both of these students exhibit signs of a low self-concept.

Secret Revealed

American culture has a long history of not trusting emotions. Instead of appreciating and respecting emotions, our culture tends to devalue them. It is assumed that emotions lead to poor decision making, hysteria, and ultimately chaos. This perspective is particularly pervasive in schools. There, emotions are avoided, not encouraged. They are considered a disruption to learning, not an enhancement. After all, how can teens be attentive and learn if they are emotionally wound up? Fortunately, new neuroscience technology is confirming

(Continued)

(Continued)

and legitimizing the dynamic role of emotion. Dr. Antonio Damasio (1994), a primary researcher in this field, has shown that emotions are a key part of cognitive processes.

For educators, this means rethinking the role of emotions and acknowledging emotions not as just a piece of life but rather as a critical part of learning and memory. The logical part of the brain might set goals like acing a serve in tennis or eating nutritionally, but it is the emotional part that makes us passionate about achieving them.

Self-concept is shaped by our past experiences. Positive experiences, such as earning an A in a challenging class, receiving a sincere compliment from a teacher, or having friends who save you a seat at lunch, help build a positive self-concept. Failing a class, being the brunt of a mean-spirited joke, or being humiliated in class reinforce a negative self-concept. All these experiences cause emotional reactions in the amygdala. The amygdala remembers pleasurable experiences and craves more. Likewise, it closes the gate to learning when a remembered emotion is anger or fear. In school, there is a strong correlation between a student's self-concept and academic achievement, motivation, and teacher and peer relationships; the combination puts them in either an upward spin or a downward spiral in school. Students with negative self-concepts are more at risk of dropping out of school, becoming pregnant, or using drugs—scary realities for too many adolescents (Ormrod, 2000).

When academic content is connected to a pleasant experience, we make a pleasant association. The next time we are in a similar situation, the amygdala remembers the pleasant feeling and opens the mental gate to learn more about that particular topic. The amygdala also remembers negative emotions connected to an experience or concept and will be hesitant to pass it on to working memory. If it feels good, we want to learn more; if it does not, we steer clear. We categorize things that make us feel good as our strengths and continue to work on them, further building a positive self-concept in this area. In this way, we continue to positively and negatively reinforce our self-concepts.

Comments like those made by Will and Monica are not-so-subtle clues to problems in math. Teachers react to this by repeating concepts, reteaching at a slower pace, or breaking a large assignment into small steps, but even such basic strategies do not guarantee a student will learn the information. An educator's time would be better spent focusing on a student's emotional feelings about the content. It's very difficult for concepts to override an emotion. Until the student's emotional disposition toward a topic changes, information has little chance of making it into memory. Emotional engagement leads to learning, which leads in yet another way to a positive self-concept.

Instructional Strategies

Engage Positive Emotions in the Classroom

Middle school students in a family and consumer science class were learning to sew. The teacher spent twenty minutes patiently showing everyone how to thread a bobbin. Finally, after lots of trial and error and some frustration, all the bobbins were threaded. To their dismay, the teacher next told the students to unthread and then rethread the bobbins. This time, all the bobbins were threaded within a few minutes, and everyone was ready to go. To accompany the sound of the sewing machines, the teacher put an Elvis CD on the stereo, and to the tune of "A Hunka' Hunka' Burnin' Love," she told a story of her visit to Graceland and her love of The King. Looking around the room, it was clear that everyone was having fun.

Our emotional experiences always matter when it comes to learning. They affect what we pay attention to, our motivation, reasoning strategies, and our ability to remember. Music can be a powerful memory and emotion builder. It enables us to make personal connections by expressing a variety of emotions, from love, hope, and triumph to fear, anxiety, and despair. It can instill unforgettable fear or create a sense of euphoria. Good manners and a pleasant demeanor evoke positive emotions, as do opportunities for peer interaction. Teachers who encourage healthy expressions of emotions will capitalize on the best of the baffling and boisterous teen outbursts.

Things to Try

- Share an emotional story like that of a Holocaust survivor or Lance Armstrong's victory over cancer and his subsequent triumphs in the Tour de France.
- Demonstrate your love of learning and enthusiasm for teaching. Not only will you bring emotion into the classroom, you will also act as a role model for lifelong learning.
- Teens find interactive technology like computer animation, multimedia software, or supervised chat rooms fun and exhilarating. Bring it into your lesson plans.
- Celebrate achievement in your class. Go roller-skating on the school blacktop after a week of standardized testing, or watch a movie at the culmination of a unit. Smile in class, be friendly, tell a joke, or play a game. Have fun!
- Show empathy for the problems students encounter by making comments like "I've made that same mistake" and "I can tell you're worried."

(Continued)

(Continued)

- Never ridicule a student's questions or comments. If one student verbally ambushes another, model appropriate behavior. Ask the attacking student to express only his or her thoughts instead of abusing another student's ideas.
- During seatwork, allow students to ask a friend or neighbor for help, or establish support groups of three or four students who can turn to each other for assistance.
- Explicitly teach social behaviors, covering everything from keeping your hands and feet to yourself to understanding trigger words for anger and how to diffuse it. Positive peer relationships and the skills to maintain them are particularly important at this age.
- Give students your full attention. Make eye contact, smile, actively listen, and inquire about their state of minds. Remark, "You've got an awfully big grin on your face. Did you get good news?" and "We missed you in class yesterday."
- Communicate honestly to students that you value them. The following comments let students know one adult believes they are important: "I like how you explained that," "I appreciate the effort you put into that project," and "Thank you for helping."
- Play soft music as students enter the room or in the background during an assignment. Music can set any mood and ties into almost any content area: Try "The Planets" by Gustav Holst during science or George Cohan's "Yankee Doodle Dandy" to introduce World War II. Students can also rewrite the lyrics to a song and perform it.

A MIND OF MY OWN

As adolescents begin to define their self-concept in more meaningful terms, they begin to think about who they are, what they believe in, and where their life is headed. The changes occurring within the adolescent are not happening in a vacuum. They adopt these roles not always for their own sake but because of the influence of the world around them. Parent and peer validation is very important to the formation of identity. The adolescent is emotionally dependent upon supportive parents and accepting peers.

Secret Revealed

Despite what you may have learned from books and movies, teens don't resist advice and guidelines purely to be ornery (well, not all the time). They are trying to express themselves as unique individuals and are struggling to distinguish their values and interests from other people's. "Question authority" is more than a smart-aleck attitude about following rules—it's an essential stage of a teenager's life!

Swedish scientist Dr. Lena Adamson (Adamson, Hartman, & Lyxell, 1999) specializes in adolescent self-concept formation. Her research team identified teens' need to balance their own wishes and desires in relation to the wishes and desires of others as the most influential factor in developing their own identity. Fitting in with the peer group is one way to strike a balance but so is opposing the adults they know! Ironically, Adamson's research shows that adults are also very important to teenagers as sources of knowledge and experience. (But try getting one to admit it!)

During this stage, adolescents begin to desire emotional autonomy and want to be more independent and self-sufficient. Be aware, there is a significant difference between the autonomy of a younger adolescent and an older adolescent. Seventeen- and eighteen-year-olds are about seventy percent more independent than twelve- and thirteen-year-olds. Perhaps stemming from an instinctive desire to perpetuate the species, teens search outside the family to friends and potential mates. As they gradually (or to the unsuspecting parent, abruptly) shift their interest from parents to their peers, teenagers can appear to be almost indifferent to adults. Mom is someone who puts supper on the table, and Dad keeps the car working—two gray shadows in their friend-filled lives. If asked to choose between spending a night at home with Mom and Dad or going over to a friend's house, the friend wins hands down.

As much as it may appear that teens don't need adults, however, they have a strong need to interact with positive adult role models (Adamson et al., 1999). In these relationships, teens prefer the team approach with all participants on equal footing. In a teen-perfect world, no parents tell them what to do, how to do it, or when. Instead, parents and adolescents make decisions together; if parents lay down the law, they always do so with a thoughtful explanation. Amazingly, that part of what they want is what they need. Teen brains are not satisfied with a "because I said so" response. Their developing frontal lobes prepare them to be involved in the decision-making process and they "get it" when adults explain their decisions.

At the same time that they have a compelling desire for their own space, they desperately want parental guidance and affirmation. Parents need to set limits, hold high expectations, and never let their teenagers see them sweat. It can be a ticklish balancing act for parents, but it is not as big a contradiction as it seems. Parents who use their control to guide the teen and elect to talk through problems when they happen (instead of resorting to other discipline techniques) tend to raise the happiest and healthiest adolescents.

Common Conflicts Between Teenagers and Parents

- Friends and dates
- Curfews
- Going out
- Going steady
- Hairstyles
- Clothes

- Where they are going
- Household chores
- Spending money responsibly
- Car
- Telephone

- School grades
- Homework
- Behavior at school
- Lack of respect for parents

Common Conflicts Between Teenagers and Teachers

- Unfinished work
- Bullying
- Tardiness
- Truancy
- Lying
- The question, "Why do I need to know this?"

- Vague directions
- Boring lessons
- Verbal threats of class failure
- Inconsistent limits, rules, and consequences
- Overreactions

- Failure to listen
- The question, "How many times do I have to tell you?"
- Bad attitude
- Disrespect for authority

CONSCIENCE AND CONSCIOUSNESS

"I'd cheat if I thought I wouldn't get caught." "She got to turn her paper in late! It's not fair!" "I was the one who left the candy wrapper on the music stand."

Moral development in adolescence aligns with cognitive development. As adolescents become able to think abstractly, they climb the moral ladder. Increasing reliance on their developing frontal lobes allows them to realize that moral rules help us maneuver and regulate society. They also learn that, although rules are important, people are more important. The maturing adolescent will change rules and make exceptions and realize

that it will not result in bedlam. Teens learn to take into account personal motivation for people's behavior and understand that it matters why somebody does something (Woolfolk, 2006). The black and white of the world open up first to shades of gray before blossoming into full color. As moral development progresses, adolescent decisions and choices become more rational and thoughtful.

Secret Revealed

 It's too simple to say that teenagers behave better in high school only because they want letters of recommendation for college applications. In fact, teens are in a profound state of moral development and are discovering a conscience! As their frontal lobes gain influence over their behaviors and decisions, they are increasingly aware of the value of social and moral rules and restraints, as well as of how their actions may hurt or help others. Moral development requires a sincere mix of logical and emotional intelligence.

A girl known for her catty remarks in junior high starts ignoring gossip and makes conversation about movies, books, or homework instead. A boy who was famous for his single-minded pursuit of straight A's decides not to cheat on the final exam and accepts the B for the semester grade. Teens begin to learn that silence is golden, not to kiss and tell, and to otherwise exercise discretion and restraint in all facets of social, academic, and personal life. They can imagine how it feels from someone else's point of view and they gain respect and desire for fairness.

As teens mature in their moral thinking, they understand that their lifestyle and culture are neither superior nor inferior to others. They develop a true respect for other ways of life and the value of diversity. Recognizing the importance of caring for others, granting and receiving forgiveness, being honest with themselves and others, and taking responsibility for their actions become a way of life—their lives are no longer just about them. Adolescents often develop an altruistic spirit and the desire to protect other people's rights with their own. Discussions that help students identify their personal values and encourage knowledge, involvement, and contributions to the community build character.

Instructional Strategies

Self-Concept and Moral Development

During adolescence, teenagers look inward with questions of "Who am I?" and "What am I worth?" These questions are best explored in an emotionally secure environment. Friends, family, and school form the foundation of that environment. To develop a sense of identity and self-esteem, adolescents look for acceptance and recognition from those people who

(Continued)

(Continued)

immediately influence them. Assuming that the school is a physically safe harbor, students are in a position to sift through the rubble in their brain and discover who they are.

Things to Try

- Recognize individual differences. Quality teachers adapt to students' preferred learning styles. Vary the nature, content, and rate of your instruction to appeal to different learners in turn by the minute, the day, or the semester—students' needs and available hours in the day will dictate these changes.
- Cultivate individual student passions and interests. Take time once a month to get to know your students' interests. Showing you value them adds positively to the classroom climate; knowing their interests helps you tailor the curriculum.
- Respect peer pressure. Research shows that its benefits outweigh the disadvantages (Arnett, 2001). Positive influence by friends discourages at-risk behavior and lends that all-important emotional support to troubled or despairing teens.
- Encourage students to look at social issues from a variety of perspectives. Rewrite Cinderella from a stepsister's point of view, act out skits about discrimination, and use the Internet to correspond with people worldwide, always being careful to go only to safe, appropriate sites.
- Let students know you respect and want to hear their opinions; allow them opportunities to speak. Also respect privacy—give them permission to pass if they don't want to share their thoughts on material of a sensitive nature.
- Establish cooperative learning groups and peer-buddy relationships to embed academics in a social setting.
- Teenagers are very social creatures. Social interactions need not always occur in academic settings; sometimes let them socialize just for the sake of it. Give students time to talk about their feelings in large- and small-group discussions.
- Experimentation is a part of identity formation, and adolescents are drawn to fads. They are also preoccupied with sex and spend a great deal of time thinking about each other. Have a sense of humor about it. Understanding these innate and compelling distractions will reduce your frustration levels!
- Present many models for career choices and other roles. Speakers, field trips, and job shadowing will open students' eyes to a world of possibilities.
- Build independence through choice and personal responsibility. Plan some events or assignments together as a class—it is an effective way to tap into individual interests and learning styles. Let them choose a topic to study, such as teenage runaways, drugs, or truancy, and design a performance assessment to complement it—create a video, give an oral report, or present an original brochure or scrapbook.

- Explore current social topics and help students discover where they stand on controversial issues through discussion, debate, and journaling. Participate in worthy causes like a local election, cross-age tutoring, or volunteering at a children's hospital.
- Prod adolescents to examine inconsistencies in their actions and values through friendly discussions. It is not uncommon for teenagers to expound on the value of honesty while boasting that they lied to their parents and attended a party (or for them to emphasize the importance of good nutrition while munching on French fries).
- Establish a caring classroom with moral standards by not tolerating cheating, stealing, or harming others.
- Start a class with "You don't know this about me, but. . . ." Build a relationship with your students; let them get to know you.
- Have students stand on a continuum of Agree and Disagree, and then reflect on why they took their stance.
- Provide class mentors for some students—relationship building leads to positive emotional feelings.
- Write an encouraging note to the athlete before the big game, to the musician before the semester concert, or to the student organizer before their annual service project. Never underestimate the power of your words.

Secret Revealed

Twelve thousand high school students were surveyed concerning their sense of belonging. Did they feel liked and valued at school, were they treated fairly by their teachers, were they loved and appreciated at home? Students who felt high levels of connecting and belonging suffered less stress and exhibited fewer at-risk behaviors, such as alcohol abuse, depression, and violence. A spirit of belonging not only makes us feel happy, it adds to our social and emotional well-being (National Longitudinal Study on Adolescent Health, 2008).

BOYS WILL BE BOYS . . .

Many educators and psychologists attribute to cultural and social factors the gender roles adolescents adopt. Society expects girls to be nurturing and soothing, so they are. Boys are expected to be self-reliant and independent, so they are. It's like all adolescents are acting out roles they learned in some secret Gender School—enrollment mandatory!

The most common examples used to prove society's role in gender preferences are the studies done in the areas of math and science. Boys and girls are equally proficient in these areas until their early teens, when girls begin to lag behind. Nationally, the result of this inequality is that boys outscored girls by forty-five points on the math portion of the SAT in 2006–2007. According to the National Assessment of Educational Progress (NAEP), a higher percentage of boys than girls are proficient in math and science at the eighth- and twelfth-grade levels, though the gap is narrowing. Furthermore, young women take far fewer "hard science" courses in postsecondary education (like physics, engineering, or computer science) than do young men. This disparity in math and science coursework ultimately limits girls' career options and (by extension) future income potential (*Title IX at 30*, 2002). However, girls continue to excel in writing, scoring eighteen points higher than boys at the twelfth-grade level and twenty points at the eighth-grade level (NAEP, 2002).

Discrimination prevailed as the foremost explanation for many years and impacted the decision in the famous 1967 John/Joan case of sexual reassignment (Diamond, 1997). Psychologist Dr. John Money decided to prove this theory in 1965 after a botched circumcision left one male identical twin without a penis. At the urging of psychologists, the infant John's parents allowed doctors to perform sexual reassignment surgery before he was two years old. If gender and gender roles were considered neutral at birth, there was no reason to believe that, with hormonal supplements, the child (newly christened "Joan") could not comfortably grow up female. Nurture would prevail over nature and the baby boy would adjust to life as a girl.

Although the child, his twin brother, and his classmates were never made aware of his birth as a male, he had many problems adjusting to life as a female. Joan fought like a boy, dressed like a boy, and played with dump trucks. When, at fifteen years of age, "Joan" was informed by "her" parents of what had happened, his reaction was of overwhelming relief. He finally understood his life of turmoil and attraction to girls and resumed a male identity immediately—with seemingly few problems, although he committed suicide in 2004 at the age of thirty-eight.

Dr. Milton Diamond, who did much of the later research refuting Money's conclusions from this case, stated, "If all these combined medical, surgical, and social efforts could not succeed in making a child accept a female gender identity, then maybe we really have to think that there is something important in the individual's biological make up; that we don't come to this world neutral; that we come to this world with some degree of maleness and femaleness which will transcend whatever the society wants to put into it" (as cited in Colapinto, 2000, pp. 174–175). Neuroscientists need to examine further the roles that the brain, puberty, and culture play in our gender behavior if they hope to gain a true understanding of it. For example, the brain seems be a powerful determinant of gender roles—as early as the sixth or seventh week of gestation, hormone levels rise in the fetal brain and remain high throughout gestation. This hormone wash contributes to sex differentiation and brain differentiation (Hiort & Holterhus, 2000; Kimura, 2002).

. . . AND GIRLS WILL BE GIRLS

Brain differences manifest between infant girls and boys shortly after birth. Baby girls look longer at visual stimuli than baby boys do and are also more sensitive to touch, odor, taste, and sound. Boys tend to be better at detecting slight movements in their field of vision and recognizing the passage of time (Kimura, 1992). These differences continue throughout childhood; boys are drawn to cars, blocks, and balls and girls to dolls and playhouses. Boys enjoy roughhousing and girls act out school. (Both, however, seem to enjoy equally the ever-popular "doctor"!)

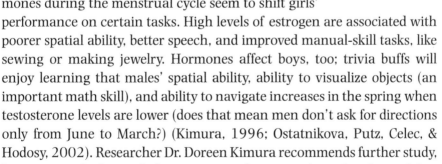

Gender differences become notably apparent with puberty. Puberty signals dramatic changes in the adolescent's body; estrogen levels increase in girls, and testosterone levels increase in boys; the primary and secondary sex characteristics develop, and first crushes unfold. The increase and decrease of hormones during the menstrual cycle seem to shift girls' performance on certain tasks. High levels of estrogen are associated with poorer spatial ability, better speech, and improved manual-skill tasks, like sewing or making jewelry. Hormones affect boys, too; trivia buffs will enjoy learning that males' spatial ability, ability to visualize objects (an important math skill), and ability to navigate increases in the spring when testosterone levels are lower (does that mean men don't ask for directions only from June to March?) (Kimura, 1996; Ostatnikova, Putz, Celec, & Hodosy, 2002). Researcher Dr. Doreen Kimura recommends further study, however, to find out if there is an evolutionary base for these ability changes during the springtime or if the results were just a fluke.

Research hints that estrogen may play a role in the development of the hippocampus during adolescence (McEwen, 2002). During this time, the hippocampus grows faster in girls than in boys because of the rising level of estrogen during puberty. Scientists speculate that the enlarged hippocampus enables girls to be savvy at coordinating complex social relationships. Girls can size up a social situation and know what to say and what not to say. They are sensitive to others and know when to give a compliment, when to lend emotional support, and when to give someone privacy. They listen well and communicate well, skills that were and are important to our survival.

Of course, there are some downsides to the priority girls give social relationships. Kelsey recounts the following story, "In middle school I was voted 'the most funny.' It was an honor. I was always trying to make the cool girls laugh; sometimes it was easier, sometimes harder. In my heart I always thought they were cooler than me. I remember doing such mean things to stay cool. A nerdy girl I was friends with, but only in German class, put her lunch bag on our lunch table. She thought it would be okay since we were 'friends.' When she went to get a drink I moved her bag to another table. She came back and quietly sat alone. Everyone laughed; I felt bad even then, but I had to publicly reject her to remain cool." Happily, this type of social behavior wanes as social and emotional development progresses.

Just as teenage girls have a more developed hippocampus, teenage boys have a larger amygdala. This helps explain their irritability, anger, and hostility. Binge drinking, driving at warp speeds, and picking a fight with their best friend are all built on illogical, split-second decision making. For instance, one middle school boy, enraged by a "bad" call, tackled his own mom, who was sitting on the sidelines. Needless to say, his coach, teammates, and fans were almost as surprised as his mother. Inappropriate behavior, you bet. Hard to explain, maybe not. The reason for this mystifying behavior can probably be found in his overactive amygdala. Fortunately, boys tend to grow out of this rowdy behavior by age nineteen.

A student teacher who was supervising an afterschool program said he was struck by how insensitive some of the boys could be. "One boy approached a table but it must have been the wrong table because another boy yelled, 'Get the hell out of here,' at him. I couldn't believe how mean he was." Rachel, a bubbly, fun-loving senior has the opposite viewpoint. "Guys are more laid back and girls are more high maintenance. They are way more self-conscious than guys. They care about what their friends will think of their decisions and they are way more dramatic. For instance, if a guy says to another guy, 'Your mom's hot,' he'll just laugh and mess around with him. But if he says it to a girl, she'll get all bent out of shape, say, 'You are so mean!' and try to punch him." Personally, I haven't found girls to be kinder and gentler than boys at this age, either. Research on the hippocampus's involvement with girls' social talents will be interesting to follow in this area.

YIN AND YANG

Most structures of the brain show no distinction between genders, but there are differences in the hypothalamus, cerebellum, white and gray matter, and the corpus callosum. Some scientists attribute these differences in the brain to evolution. It is thought that the early survival of the species depended on a division of labor; men were responsible for hunting, scavenging, and making and using weapons, and women for gathering food, tending small children and the home, preparing food, and making clothing. A specialization by gender could have allowed for a natural selection process that led to the current differences we see between the male and female brains.

Figure 3.1 Human Brain

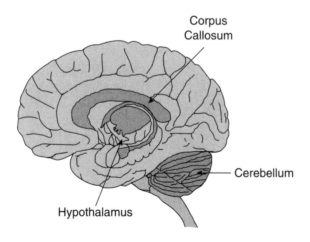

SOURCE: Adapted from Sousa, D. A. (2003), *How the Gifted Brain Learns*, p. 18.

The hypothalamus is the part of the brain responsible for emotions, sexual desire, and controlling the body's thermostat. It controls our biological rhythms. When we overheat, we sweat; when we get a chill, goose bumps appear; when we are thirsty, we get dry mouth—all these involuntary actions are controlled by the hypothalamus. It is involved in the "fight or flight" response and keeps us on our toes when we face danger. The hypothalamus also regulates the release of our sex hormones, maintaining them at low levels during childhood and increasing them during puberty (Kulin, 1991). The hypothalamus is larger and thicker in men than in women. It is hypothesized that this may account for the male's greater sexual desire and aggressive nature (Stoleru et al., 1999). Fifteen-year-old Seth characterizes this drive perfectly. "I love football," he says. "It gives me a chance to hit somebody and not get in any trouble. It's rough but exciting and I feel tough when I play."

Secret Revealed

 Gender differences are not limited to sex hormones—did you know that the male brain is about eight percent larger than the female brain? That the corpus callosum is larger in females than males? Or that males and females have different ratios of white to gray matter? A bigger brain, however, does not mean more brainpower; males and females perform equally well on intelligence tests. But the differences in brain structure do translate to differences in some cognitive abilities. Boys, in general, have a better spatial awareness; girls, in general, have better verbal skills. Some educators and political activists worry that these generalizations reinforce sexist stereotypes, such as boys can't express their feelings and girls are prone to gossip. Neuroscience, however, puts these fears to rest. Despite differences in how males and females process information, both sexes are capable of learning and remembering as much and as thoroughly. Savvy educators will use information about gender differences for perspective on adolescent behaviors, not to determine what to teach individual teenagers.

The male brain has a greater proportion of white matter than the female brain; the female brain has a greater proportion of gray matter than the male brain. It is speculated that the additional white matter enables men to transfer information easily to all regions of the brain, enhancing their spatial abilities and giving them an advantage in matters of navigation, mathematical problem solving, and aiming at targets (Gur et al., 2000; Yurgelun-Todd, Killgore, & Young, 2002). The abundance of gray matter found in the female brain might allow for more efficiency of thought processes and a greater ability to process information, which perhaps explains the female's strong language skills and the ability to juggle a number of activities at one time. During study hall, a high school girl writes a note to a friend, reviews her chemistry notes, makes a schedule for tennis practice, and flirts with the boy next to her with an ease that puts an efficiency expert to shame. Meanwhile, the high school boy at the next table is concentrating on only one thing: her.

The corpus callosum—the part of the brain that links the two hemispheres—allows information to be transferred back and forth between the left and right sides of the brain. It is another part of the brain that differs by gender. It is larger in females than in males, permitting better communication between the left and right hemispheres. This enhances the ability of women to use both sides of their brain. For instance, while performing verbal activities like chatting, reading, giving a speech, or gossiping, females activate both hemispheres and males activate primarily the left side of their brain—two routes to the same cognitive destination with no effect on either accuracy or speed (Shaywitz et al., 1995). As men age, the corpus callosum begins to shrink (there is almost no shrinkage in women). It was originally hypothesized that this could restrict communication between the two hemispheres, perhaps making it difficult to process information, but no evidence has been found to suggest that occurs. Men are at no cognitive disadvantage to women as they age (Yoder et al., 2001).

There are female professional athletes and male poets, of course—gender does not dictate individual careers or proclivities. It is interesting to note, however, some general brain differences between the sexes (James, 2007). Although the comparisons between the male and female brain suggest differences, they are only group tendencies and can't predict the individual strengths and weaknesses of a male or female.

Male Brain Advantages and Characteristics

- Performs well at visual spatial activities (visualizing sports positions and plays)
- Adept at aiming at stationary or moving targets (tossing paper into the wastebasket from their seats)
- Adept at throwing and intercepting projectiles (catching a basketball, football, or soccer ball)
- Navigates by distance, spatial cues, and time
- Adept at solving quantitative problems (understanding mean, median, mode, and standard deviation—on the first try)
- Achieves higher scores on multiple-choice tests

(Continued)

(Continued)

- Adept at imagining the rotation of an object
- Adept at manipulating an object in a new way (taking apart the classroom pencil sharpener)
- Exhibits more aggression
- Enjoys more rough-and-tumble play (tripping a friend, hurling his hat, or flipping his books)
- Excels in higher levels of math

Female Brain Advantages and Characteristics

- Demonstrates better verbal abilities (expressing feelings, depicting a social exchange accurately)
- Demonstrates higher ability for memory tasks
- Adept at generating synonyms
- Adept at naming colors (knows the differences between azure, teal, turquoise, navy, cornflower, and blue)
- Adept at listing items beginning with a certain letter
- Adept at organizing (planning a surprise party or pep rally)
- Excels on untimed tests and written tests
- Achieves higher grades in school
- Is more nurturing (first to volunteer to help the teacher)
- Is more attuned to details (has a cover page on everything, remembers the bibliography, adds graphics to computer presentations)
- Navigates by landmarks and experience
- Is more subdued (likes to read, listen, and write—often keeps a journal)
- Adept at interpreting emotions
- Is more intuitive (knows who will ask her to Homecoming)
- Recognizes inferences and hidden meanings (knows from a look or turn of a phrase when she is or is not welcome)
- Adept at language and writing skills (talking to friends, writing notes to friends)

Instructional Strategies

Gender-Sensitive Classrooms

Although neither is smarter than the other, boys and girls have different strengths and weaknesses in the classroom, both academic and behavioral. Choose materials in the classroom that portray traditional and nontraditional roles for males and females at home, work, and play. Provide positive role models for both genders. Discuss gender role bias in the media. Have high expectations for all students.

Don't overnurture girls—it encourages dependence. Instead, encourage girls to be active learners. Really involve them in hands-on activities; they tend to be more passive than their male classmates. Balance cooperative and competitive group work in your class; girls prefer cooperative work and boys enjoy the competition.

Boys are under unique pressures of their own, however. Supplement reading and writing activities with action—and let them read from computer screens (when applicable) instead of a book, if that is what they prefer. Right now, boys contribute to ninety percent of behavioral problems and represent eighty percent of ADHD (attention-deficit/hyperactivity disorder) cases in school. Help them out by letting them move and actively involve themselves in their learning—there is nothing wrong with motion in the classroom. The book *Real Boys* by William Pollack (1999) is one source of valuable insight and information about what it is like to be a boy.

Things to Try

- Define and discuss gender bias; constructing a definition gives added meaning to a concept. Use library or Internet resources to examine magazines, newspapers, posters, TV, movies, or music videos for evidence.
- Have students record for one week their personal interactions at school, home, work, and in social situations that counter gender stereotypes. One class period, bring out the lists and let the conversation begin.
- Debate the effects of gender on self-esteem and career opportunities. After the debate, have students research a career from Internet sources and discuss what they found.
- As a class, design a code of ethics that represents gender equity, and keep it posted in the room. Include tenets such as these: Don't interrupt each other, give equal amounts of help, and offer worthy feedback.
- Provide male and female role models: Tiger Woods and Mia Hamm are two famous athletes; Maya Angelou and Allen Ginsberg are two famous poets. Also, include young adult graduates from your high school and middle school who would be willing to meet your class and talk about their lives.
- Boys like competition. Play a trivia game about academic content, or host a contest for the best slogan that describes the current academic unit.
- Girls like cooperation. Don't grade on a competitive curve, and put students into same-sex groups to work sometimes.
- Do you call on boys more than girls? Are you sure? Divide your room into sections and make sure you call on a variety of students from each section throughout the day. Then make sure you're asking girls questions that tap into higher-level thinking and not just the easy, factual questions.
- Stress "safety" concerns as opposed to "dangers"—girls will often back off if they feel there is danger in an activity or lab.

(Continued)

(Continued)

- Encourage girls to become active in math and science extracurricular activities.
- Encourage an atmosphere of "effort leads to achievement." Girls tend to credit their achievements to luck rather than to their effort or ability.
- Examine your own biases as a teacher. Talk to an expert, watch a video, or read a book or an article about gender discrimination and bias in school. Discuss your views and findings with your colleagues.

COOLING OFF THE KIDS AFTER PROM

Sarah and Lex spent Prom wrapped in each other's arms, dancing to each slow dance and frequently sneaking out to the patio to be alone in the shadows. At midnight, the music stopped and the lights came on. Grinning, they hopped into Lex's car and drove off.

When they reached the school gymnasium, they pulled duffel bags with a change of clothes out of the trunk and joined the party that was

starting in the all-night "lock-in" inside. Sarah exchanged sexy high heels for canvas sneakers with as much relief as Lex pulled off his bowtie and threw on a sweatshirt. The Prom committee had advertised this event as a not-to-miss party, and it was already living up to its promise. Kids gorged on pizza and chips all night while they played silly games and danced to loud music. Local businesses had donated tee shirts and other prizes for contests and raffles; Sarah won a five-dollar gift card for a fast-food restaurant, but her best friend went home with a DVD player! The chaperoning parents and teachers kept each other awake and kept the junk food coming. This was one evening, at least, when students would worry more about what candy bar to have next than whether they were too high to drive or if they should go all the way.

Communication and the Unfinished Brain

Abrupt, mean-spirited comments or a subtle use of irony, symbolism, and sarcasm? No one is ever quite sure what words will come out of a teenager's mouth! The rapidly changing brain is responsible for the adolescent communication gaps and growth. Neuroscientists are finally able to help educators adjust to the highs and lows in teen dialogue.

Did you know that . . .

- Adolescence is when language ability and short-term memory improve
- The teen brain reacts emotionally instead of logically
- Music is a way to communicate information and emotion
- Teens experience emotions before they can verbally articulate them
- Teenage self-awareness and teenage self-consciousness go hand in hand
- Teens are more vulnerable to stress than adults are

It was May and time for the final band concert at the middle school. Proud parents, antsy brothers and sisters, and adoring grandparents filed into the auditorium with anticipation. The middle school musicians nervously took their places on the stage, arranged their music, and waited for their band director, Mrs. Hudson, to lift her baton and start the concert. The music filled the air, evidence enough of the students' hard work. They had practiced all semester and it showed; the concert went off without a hitch. After the concert, Mrs. Hudson headed for the band room where students were busy putting their instruments away. As soon as she entered the room, Katie rushed up to her, clearly shaken, and said, "Did you see how I tripped when I was going up on stage?" Mrs. Hudson assured her she hadn't noticed any stumble, nor did she think anyone in the audience noticed. Still, Katie was mortified, certain that everyone had seen her clumsiness.

PERENNIALLY TONGUE-TIED

As a mother of four teenagers, I can relate to the communication gap between our generations. My sixteen-year-old daughter pleads with me to let her stay out one extra hour and my thirteen-year-old son insists he doesn't need his coat—even though the temperature outside is below zero! These were the same children who once promised me they'd never act like their older siblings, with emotional flare-ups and temper tantrums. Why did they change so dramatically? Why are we not communicating?

The answer to this question can be found in the temporal lobes of an adolescent's brain. Located below the frontal lobes (right above the ears), the temporal lobes' primary function is to process auditory stimuli. Hearing, language, and auditory memory are all channeled through this part of the brain. Researchers at the UCLA Laboratory of Neuro Imaging found that the temporal lobes do not complete growing gray matter until the age of sixteen, and only then is the brain able to begin the pruning and myelination processes (Thompson et al., 2000)! Although the temporal lobes are delayed in development, once the process begins, they consistently have the highest growth rate of all areas in the brain.

Secret Revealed

No, teens aren't more articulate than children because they've learned lots more vocabulary words—their brains' language functions are maturing! At UCLA, Dr. Arthur Toga (Thompson et al., 2000) and his colleagues scanned preadolescents, adolescents, and adults and found striking differences in the myelination patterns of their frontal lobes. (Young adults had the most myelination.) More efficient frontal lobes mean a better control of the language; as teens grow up, they are able to communicate and understand elaborate, detailed, high-level information.

Book sales records show that children love whimsical, straightforward stories like *Harry Potter* and the adventures of the *Boxcar Children*. But the older kids get, the more complex the books and movies that they enjoy become. Spy novels and romance sagas show up during silent reading; teens stand in line at the theaters for suspense thrillers and crime dramas. They don't spend their free time playing tag anymore, either. Now they verbally engage with their friends on the telephone and in Internet chat sessions for hours, expressing and analyzing their thoughts, ideas, and feelings.

Wernicke's area, a region in the temporal lobes that is responsible for deciphering our native language and giving meaning to the spoken word, has received particular attention. In cooperation with Broca's area (a part of the brain in the frontal lobes that stores vocabulary, grammar, and syntax), Wernicke's area changes our thoughts into words. Language production is further delineated within these two areas of the brain. For instance, there is a section in the brain for nouns and verbs, with the nouns area further divided into sections for tools and animals. It was once believed that the Wernicke's and Broca's areas solely were responsible for language interpretation and communication—a belief that underestimated the complexities of the brain. Language is not restricted to these two areas; ninety-five percent of our verbal skills reside in the left hemisphere. When we speak, neurons fire all over the frontal cortex.

Figure 4.1   Human Brain: Side View

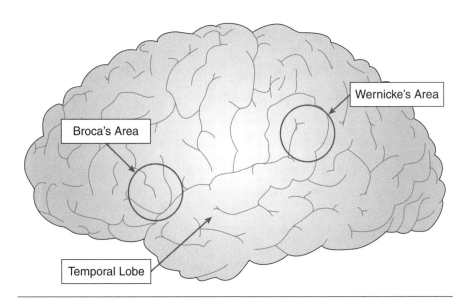

Adolescence is the time when the Wernicke's area begins to be fully connected by myelination in the corpus callosum, which allows communication between the two hemispheres. A number of subskills of most tasks require communication between both hemispheres of the brain. Even uncomplicated activities, such as word identification or singing a song, invoke complex connections between both sides of the brain. The more elaborate the task, the more we need to use both hemispheres, thereby exercising our brain to a fuller capacity (Weissman & Banich, 2000). Without the corpus callosum, the two hemispheres of your brain would not communicate at all. Although the corpus callosum is by no means disconnected before this myelination occurs, it has not yet reached its full potential.

The hippocampus is also located in the temporal lobes. It is the part of the brain that is responsible for short-term memory, primarily for remembering pesky facts and details. During adolescence, the hippocampus changes and develops with the rest of the brain. Finally, teenagers can take pride in how easy it is to memorize the Preamble to the Declaration of Independence and the introduction to the Constitution in an eighth-grade social studies class, or remember long lists of the bones of the human skeleton for a twelfth-grade anatomy lesson. Memorization is a snap—at least in the short term—with the power of the new and improved adolescent hippocampus. The combination of a surge of growth in the temporal lobes' language capabilities and the hippocampus's memory abilities during early adolescence also makes this a favorable time to improve native vocabulary and learn a second language, including sign language. (After puberty, the ability to acquire a second language is greatly diminished, although certainly possible.)

Older teenagers can take their burgeoning temporal lobes a step further. They can interpret, memorize, and comprehend sophisticated literature, such as a poem by T. S. Eliot:

Lines from *A Dedication to My Wife*

No peevish winter wind shall chill
No sullen tropic sun shall wither
The roses in the rose-garden which is ours and ours only.

To middle school students, the poem is about roses withstanding inclement weather. They understand the words literally. You say what you mean, and you mean what you say. Roses don't go by any other name in seventh grade. High school students, however, are able to view the roses as a metaphor for enduring love because they understand the symbolism. They understand that there is more than one meaning possible in a passage or in the spoken word. Sometimes people speak literally and sometimes they don't; you need to look below the surface of words to understand true meaning. And eleventh graders can.

Instructional Strategies

Knock, Knock. Who's There?

Where do belly buttons go to college? The Navel Academy.

Immature humor? You bet. Young middle school students will laugh at this joke, but high school students will disdain it. Teens' language skills become more sophisticated as the frontal lobes develop. The older adolescent is able to go beyond a literal meaning to the abstract. They understand subtlety. This increased language ability is one of the most exciting developments we see in school. Humor, sarcasm, irony, symbolism, and satire are an active part of the high school life.

Developing writing and speaking skills is a high priority in our schools. The gold standard for teaching writing emphasizes sentence structure, content, organization, voice, conventions, and word choice. Basic instruction begins in elementary school, where children are taught to structure a sentence or paragraph and make informal presentations. By middle school and high school, adolescents write fiction and nonfiction, news articles, analytical essays, and poetry. They speak in front of their peers in formal and informal situations. Campaigns for school elections, performance on job interviews, and lunchtime conversations reveal their new sophistication.

Journal, compose, and report. Writing prompts us to organize our thoughts and put our spoken and internal thoughts on paper. It is an effective source of ascertaining patterns and helping the brain unravel complex information. It guides our thinking and assists our thought processes. The more we write, the stronger those synapses become, and the better we are at expressing ourselves. Writing is now understood to be an interdisciplinary skill. Teens who practice writing and become skilled at it will develop and strengthen these synapses in their brain.

Things to Try

- Write across the curriculum. Have students keep learning logs as they read *The Scarlet Letter*, write detailed observations of plants exposed to differing degrees of light in biology, and record investigations into the school board's policymaking process for history or civics class.
- Instigate debates. Compel students to look at both sides of relevant issues and frame arguments to substantiate their view. Or for a change of pace, view and analyze political debates on television. (They're constantly broadcast, so take advantage of them.) Ask them to explore a subject in-depth. Assign position papers on opposing views of stem cell research, Alaskan oil, health insurance, or terrorism.
- Spend time brainstorming ideas for writing—how to combat writer's block, suggestions for topics, suggestions about technique, or strategies for revision—and post the list in the classroom.
- Organize student-led book clubs, either with books from the course or for personal reading. Allow them to meet during class time once a week or once a month.
- Teach note-taking skills. There are many different ways to help teenagers formulate their thoughts and ideas quickly into words on the page.

(Continued)

(Continued)

- Compare and contrast characters in literature, figures in history, and solutions to mathematical and scientific problems.
- Be creative about the kinds of writing assignments you give. Try original fairy tales, describing dreams and memories, biographies of real people who overcame great odds, stories to explain unusual images or photos of current events, the view through a pair of binoculars, or responses to thought-provoking quotes. What would your students say about this quote from Cliff Fadiman (n.d.): "My Faulkner, of course, is interested in making your mind rather than your flesh creep"?
- Analyze advertisements. How do they look? What are the models and actors wearing? What do they seem to care about? Is this a realistic portrayal of life? What information is missing?
- Trade that journal in for a blog—this interactive site creates a verbal picture of thoughts and experiences.
- Connect to online writing sites, such as fanfiction.com. Write a different ending, introduce a new character, add dialogue, or change the era—fast-forward it into the past or present.

SCHOOL OF ROCK

Is the song "Crazy Rap Lyrics" by Afroman music to your ears? Probably not, but how about "Honey Honey" by Abba? Two songs, from two different generations, with two different messages and melodies; but both can compel a group (albeit, different groups) to gyrate and shake it up baby. Adults, children, and teenagers all love music. Teenagers, in particular, spend a great deal of time listening, singing, and dancing to their favorite tunes. It calms them, energizes them, and reflects and creates their moods.

Neuroscientists are finding that music impacts both the academic and emotional well-being of teenagers. So what's happening in the brain when we hear that do re mi? Music enters the inner ear, where it begins to ignite numerous areas of the brain. First it travels to the brain stem, then on to the thalamus, and finally to the temporal lobes in both hemispheres of the brain. The various patterns of the beat engage neurons associated with emotions, experiences, and knowledge, allowing us to feel tranquil, invigorated, or just plain happy.

Instructional Strategies

The Positive Influence of Music

The simple act of listening to music seems to have a positive emotional and intellectual impact, but participating in making music takes everything to a higher level. Research points to active music involvement improving memory, visual-spatial relations (math and science), and self-esteem (Kluball, 2000). In fact, SAT scores in the verbal and math areas improve when music is involved (Americans for the Arts, 2006). It even acts as a protective agent; teenage musicians are less likely to use drugs or engage in other at-risk activities (Costa-Giomi, 1998).

The type of music doesn't seem to make a difference in teenager's academic achievement or put their emotional disposition at risk (depression, aggression), somewhat surprising news. All that matters is that the music is enjoyed. If it's enjoyed, it's a good thing. This finding has implications for concerns about heavy metal music. It seems adult worries are unwarranted; violent and sexual themes in heavy metal music are more a reflection of problems already in a teenager's life than a cause (Copley, 2008). However, music videos that combine music with pictures are a different story. They have a more powerful and detrimental influence.

Lyrics communicate information and blend with the melody, dynamics, and rhythm to express how we feel about information. The potential for learning through this medium is easy on the brain.

Things to Try

- Draw students' attention by starting the class with your own musical talent, such as Jack Black did in *School of Rock*.
- Play soft music as they enter the room to set the mood and quiet the inner beast.
- Create a rap song that reinforces a math theorem, or better yet, let the students create one.
- Bring in musical instruments from other cultures, or if you can't get your hands on the real thing, show visuals. This brings a rich context to the concepts being studied.
- Play music from different periods in history and countries to create an appreciation of our diverse world.
- Assign Internet searches of music and musical instruments as part of a research project.
- Use soothing music as background for journal writing or group work.
- Energize that lethargic mind partway through a lesson with blues, rock, pop, or rap.
- Create your own curriculum lyrics to "The Chicken Dance," and then sing and dance the period away.
- Take rap music (be careful to scrutinize for proper content prior to class) and analyze the message.
- Put the words to "We Didn't Start the Fire" by Billy Joel on an overhead to start a discussion on political responsibility.

Don't leave music in the lone territory of the music teacher; make it a part of your instruction. In the words of Bob Marley, "Music gonna teach dem a lesson."

Secret Revealed

 Skeptical about the impact of music in our schools? Groundbreaking and inspiring music research out of East Harlem's schools should change your mind. Eighty-seven percent of the student body there was performing below grade level in both reading and in math. It was a demoralizing and frustrating proposition for all concerned. In order to rectify the problem, administrators decided to reinstate their music program. After only eighteen months, seventy-one percent of the students were at grade level, an amazing accomplishment. Administrators attributed the success primarily to the music program (American Music Conference, 2007).

TEENAGER AHEAD! PROCEED WITH CAUTION

Sincerely trying to help a struggling student, Mrs. Andrews suggested that Tyler come in for extra help after school. The teenager, face red with shame, said to a friend, "She thinks I'm stupid." Beverly and her daughter, Tiffany, enjoyed their day shopping until Tiffany emerged from a dressing room wearing a skintight top. Beverly suggested that Tiffany try the same top in a larger size. Her daughter stared at her in disbelief, deeply insulted, and shrieked, "You think I'm fat! I hate you!" Mariko calls Julia to invite her to the mall, but Julia already has plans with Heather. Mariko is convinced that Julia no longer wants to be her friend.

Teenagers' rooms are messy, they forget to turn in their homework, and don't prepare for college entrance exams until the night before. They burst into tears, fly into rages, and then give you a hug for baking their favorite cookies, all in one afternoon. No wonder adults find their behavior inexplicable! Dr. Charles Nelson, a leader in the field of adolescent brain development and director of the Center for Neurobehavioral Development at the University of Minnesota, was interviewed on "Inside the Teenage Brain," a PBS *Frontline* program (Spinks, 2002). He said, "Teenagers—particularly when they're first becoming teenagers—have every reason to believe and to feel that no one understands them." He believes that teenagers often aren't paying attention, are unorganized, and are unable to multitask. He went on to suggest that they generally understand information quite differently than adults. They hear a disproportionate amount of criticism and rejection, and their reactions to statements that adults would classify as helpful or innocent are overly sensitive and exaggerated.

Figure 4.2   Human Brain

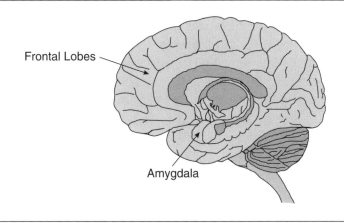

Frontal Lobes

Amygdala

SOURCE: Adapted from Sousa, D. A. (2003), *How the Gifted Brain Learns,* p. 18.

Studies are being conducted on the frontal lobes and amygdala of adolescents to better understand their bewildering behavior. The frontal lobes are the area of the cortex in charge of higher-level thinking skills. Their relationship with the amygdala, the center of emotions, is interesting. Either region could be in the "driver's seat" at any given moment. Do the logical, mature frontal lobes calmly maneuver down the road toward a responsible decision, or does the emotional amygdala floor the gas pedal for a quick joy ride? Even when the amygdala is not at the wheel, it carries on in the background like a jumpy backseat driver.

The amygdala is one inch long, shaped like an almond, and part of the unconscious brain. It is thought to be responsible for our actions when we feel threatened and signals a child to either respond to a bully by running away or fighting back—the "fight or flight" instinct (LeDoux, 2003). Even though the amygdala operates on a lower, more instinctive level as compared to the cortex, its influence should never be underestimated. Damage to the amygdala can be devastating to an individual. In the few reported cases of people who have had their amygdala removed or severely damaged, their quality of life suffered tremendously. Imagination, enthusiasm, and decision making are all drastically affected when the amygdala does not work at full capacity (Damasio, 1994).

Adults depend less on the amygdala than on the frontal lobes of their brain, so they respond rationally to information. Because the frontal lobes of the adult brain have completed their overproduction of synapses and the processes of pruning and myelination, they are ready and willing to take on the added responsibilities of reacting logically and reasonably. Adolescents, on the other hand, tend to rely more on the amygdala, which helps explain their emotional and impulsive behavior. Conversations such as the following are all-too-familiar results of this dependence: A parent makes what he believes is a factual observation to his teenage daughter and tells her, "Your hair is in your eyes." The teenager responds with, "You hate my hair! You've always hated my hair!" and leaves the room in tears (Davies & Rose, 1999).

The reliance on the amygdala goes beyond emotionally charged reactions; it affects how well teens can read body language and facial expressions, too. This ability to interpret someone's affection, agitation, or concern is a learned skill, not something inherently known. Teenagers have not yet mastered the art of body language. To adolescents, interpreting body language is like trying to decipher a foreign tongue. A teacher shakes his head in confusion, and the student explains it as "He hates me." A look of surprise is interpreted as a glare of anger. A teacher cracks a joke, and a teen takes it seriously and finds offense. These misunderstandings and misinterpretations are common occurrences behind much moodiness and temperamental behavior.

At McLean Hospital in Massachusetts, Deborah Yurgelun-Todd's team of researchers used MRI technology to view the brain responses of adults and teenagers as they viewed a series of photographs (Baird et al., 1999). The participants in the study were asked to identify the emotion on the face of a woman. Every adult was able to identify the emotion as fear, compared to only fifty percent of the adolescents. The other fifty percent of the adolescents confused the facial expression with shock or anger. On further inspection, the researchers noted that adolescents and adults used different parts of their brain when interpreting the photos. The adolescents relied on their amygdala, whereas the adults relied on their frontal lobes. At San Diego State University, neuroscientist Robert McGivern made an interesting discovery when he found that children going through puberty decreased in their ability to identify emotions by as much as twenty percent and did not resume normal levels until about age eighteen (McGivern, Andersen, Byrd, Mutter, & Reilly, 2002). Their lack of dependence on the frontal lobes, and subsequent lack of mature thought processes to regulate their emotions, provides insight into an adolescent's emotional state. The adolescent is much more apt to misread another's feelings and may confuse sadness with anger and surprise with fear. No wonder miscommunication is so rampant at this age!

Secret Revealed

 School must be an awfully boring place if teens are so fascinated by sensationalist gossip, right? Why else would they spread and exaggerate rumors about three students dying in a school bus accident that morning (when, in reality, the school bus was empty and the driver wasn't even hurt)? It turns out that a teenager's emotions are regulated by the highly excitable and passionate amygdala. Dr. Charles Nelson (Spinks, 2002), the Director of the Center of Neurobehavioral Development at the University of Minnesota, blames hysterical, knee-jerk overreactions to information on the "emotional lability" (read: instability) of the teenage brain. Adolescents change emotions by the nanosecond, regularly blow situations out of proportion, and find something to be self-conscious about at every turn. Hormones are partly to blame, but mostly he believes it is the still-maturing frontal cortex that is the root of the problem. Until it assumes full executive control of the brain's reactions, the teenage mind will be a volatile place.

This apparent obliviousness to the mental states of other people also stems from their newly developing frontal lobes. The teen's ability to understand themselves and others does increase (thanks to the over-production and pruning of synapses and the myelination of the frontal lobes and corpus callosum), but only with growing pains. The frontal lobes and corpus callosum, areas responsible for self-awareness, are maturing, true, but teens lack experience in operating them. Adolescents have trouble distinguishing between their own thoughts and the thoughts of others. They confuse the two. Teens are so busy thinking about themselves that they are sure everyone else is also concentrating on them full-time. Hence, they become more self-conscious. This egocentrism explains why they want to be dropped off five blocks from school, are devastated if laughed at in class, become hysterical over the appearance of a zit, and never, ever want to be seen at a movie with their parents. It's obvious to teens, disgraced as they are by their parents' outrageous behavior, that their peers will notice every embarrassment and make judgments that will linger beyond graduation. I still remember the day my oldest daughter and her friends asked me to duck down below the windows of the car as we passed a group of boys—even though I was the one driving! (The fact that I tried to accommodate them is even more amazing.)

The story doesn't stop there; observing others goes beyond perceptions and interpretations to actual imitation of words, dances, and problem solving. Mirror neurons give the brain the amazing ability to observe another with the sole intention of repeating their actions. Teenagers spend some time observing their parents and teachers for signals and clues, but not surprising they turn primarily to their peers for guidance. Friends are looked to for appropriate behavior, language, and empathy, and what they see they repeat. One could say it's a case of the blind leading the blind (Iacoboni, 2005).

This amazing gift has implications for learning and behavior in school. Instructional strategies such as science demonstrations, conflict resolution, role playing, and modeling math problems are reinforced through mirror neurons. It also lends credence to dealing with inappropriate behaviors quickly and efficiently to avoid imitation.

I simply told my daughter not to be late getting home.

There was no unkind thought, no accusation, just a statement. All of a sudden, we were in a big argument.

"You don't trust me," she screamed. "I always am being told what to do, nobody trusts me!" The hysteria continued.

Finally, with her hand on the door and her eyes flashing, she yelled, "Just shut the f— up!" Needless to say, that put an end to her evening with friends.

—*Veronica, mother of a teenager*

WHAT'S (REALLY) UP?

Adolescents' behavior is further complicated because they feel things before they can regulate or articulate them. They feel an emotion but lack the ability to express it in a socially appropriate way, amplifying the frustration between the adolescent and the people who share their world. Parents in particular are often exasperated by their teenager's behavior. They tell a son to clean his room and stop watching TV. He responds by continuing to watch TV. When his parents become angry, the adolescent is genuinely surprised; he hadn't processed the message as a command—it was more like a suggestion, a suggestion he chose not to take. He responds to their anger with a "Screw you." No discussion or reflection about why his parents might be annoyed, just a fiery retort. Something, clearly, has been lost in translation.

Secret Revealed

It's a classic scene—Lindsey sits in a restaurant pouring her heart out to Matt, who nods mutely, answers her questions with "Uh-huh," and then blurts out something about his brother's car. Immediately, she bursts into tears and stammers incoherently as she tries to explain why her feelings are hurt! No, he isn't insensitive and she isn't high-strung. So how could this conversation go so awry?

This is yet another manifestation of the amygdala's influence on the teen. Not only are the language regions of the brain still maturing in adolescents, they are directed by emotions. When Lindsey finds herself unable to state exactly what is on her mind, what would be mild frustration to an adult she experiences as psychic torture. Furthermore, adults are much better at holding their tongue; adolescents often say the first thing that comes to mind. In a few years, Matt will be able to tell Lindsey how his brother's car relates to her story, and she'll be able to make a joke instead of crying.

At school, Mr. Halstef assigned a writing project to ninth graders on the topic of their choice. They were to research something that interested them and write a five-page paper about it. What could be easier? Anything, it turned out. Students were frustrated and didn't understand what he wanted—they complained that it would never end! Mr. Halstef was frustrated with the quality of work he received. "It was so obvious that most of them had waited until a day or two before the due date to even start it!" he complained. But his teenage students were genuinely perplexed by what he wanted and how to organize it. They put off the dreaded task as long as possible and then did the best that they could. Not one student thought about doing the obvious and asking for clarification; they all trudged along in their own personal misery instead. Once again, the lack of maturation in the frontal lobes left teens prey to the effects of the amygdala (Paus et al., 1999).

Of course, sometimes a teen relying on the amygdala is the right person to communicate with another teen doing the same thing—logic isn't always the best answer among adolescents! Colleen, a freshman tennis player, was mercilessly attacked during games by her doubles partner. Her every shot was criticized, she was to blame for all lost points; the faultfinding went on and on. Understandably, Colleen was dejected and on the verge of quitting the team after only a few matches. She was tired of being verbally beat up but was shy and uncomfortable about confrontation. One of her friends and I intervened to discuss with her how she might best handle the situation.

My reasonable, adult advice was that Colleen should explain to her partner how her remarks were hurting Colleen's feelings and to ask her to please stop. My frontal lobes could clearly see why this girl's behavior was inappropriate and counterproductive to winning the match. Her friend's advice was more direct: "I'd just tell her to shut up." Amygdala versus frontal lobes. This match went to the teen-triggered amygdala. "Shut up" it was. Colleen tried out this succinct phrase the very next day. Her nemesis, shocked, made no more comments for the rest of the season.

Instructional Strategies

Discipline Versus Management

We talk, they listen. They talk, we listen. It's a simple concept: orderly classrooms where everyone can talk, think, and work. Who wouldn't want that? Many of our students demonstrate that they do want it—they have mastered self-control and cause no problems—but a disruptive minority of students will be insolent or even aggressive. Your best tactic for handling these outbursts is to look for signs of stress before defiant behavior erupts. Refusals to work, passing notes, slamming books, inattention, huffy voices, and heated gesticulations are all signs of a possible blowup. Circumventing negative behavior with positive discipline strategies will diffuse most potential explosions; when it doesn't, staying calm and acting decisively will help cool tempers down.

Ultimately the purpose of discipline is to develop self-control in our students. The most effective teachers expect that students are capable of high-level work and communicate that expectation to them—a very straightforward, effective strategy.

Things to Try

- Rather than threatening students who break rules, simply calmly enforce rules. Why prompt another emotional response?
- Track which rules are frequently broken, and rethink those rules and their consequences. Rules are meant to serve a purpose. When they don't, they need to be improved and reconstructed.
- Preempt destruction—desks too near walls and chalkboards become distractions and are prime opportunities for vandalism.
- Use nonverbal actions to redirect behavior. Move closer to a student, make eye contact, hand a noisy student another copy of the class assignment—they'll get the message.

- Create a student-centered classroom where students talk more than you do, creativity is valued, some lessons and assignments are planned together, and courtesy abounds. Setting a positive tone is one way to manage discipline problems proactively (before they even start).
- Ignore fleeting behavior that doesn't really affect others. Identify the difference between your personal peeves and real disruptions. Relationships, even between teachers and students, require give and take. Sometimes it's better to be personally annoyed or distracted if it benefits the dynamics of the group.
- Reprimand gently and in private when necessary. Confronting a student in front of the whole class is disruptive (and could come back to haunt you). Likewise, forcing a student to make a personal apology to you or the rest of the class is humiliating; it's doubtful the apology would be sincere anyway.
- Avoid telling students about your own youthful indiscretions. Rarely will it serve to create a personal bond and more likely will hamper your effect as a positive role model. It may also turn into student rationale for later misbehavior!
- Don't punish everyone for the mistakes of one or two students. Not only is it unfair, it usually results in the entire class being angry with one student and all of them mad at you.
- Don't assign extra work as a punishment. We want to encourage a love of learning, not discourage it!
- Anticipate and prevent problems by paying attention to your students. When a situation is about to sour, often a quiet, calm word will put everyone back on track.
- Speak calmly even when you don't feel calm. Your voice will set a tone and carry the message that you are in charge.
- Immediately involve parents in serious problems; describe an event or behavior with specific details and without commenting on a student's character or personality. This conveys the message that it is the behavior, not the teenager, that you find unacceptable.
- Schedule special student-teacher meetings to enhance communication. Taking time to talk individually to students conveys the message you care about them. It also enables you to build a personal relationship with your students, enhancing the possibility of meeting their needs more effectively and decreasing the chance you'll talk past each other.
- Clarify teacher expectations. Ease anxiety by making your classroom expectations clear to your students on the very first day and then be consistent. Students who understand exactly what behaviors are required from them have a better background against which to evaluate your comments and directions.
- Be careful not to set up fierce competition among students. If winning or losing becomes the top priority, the spirit of working in cooperation will be difficult to establish.

(Continued)

(Continued)

- Introduce athletes, scientists, and businesspeople who had frustrations and challenges in their life. Not only are they role models for handling problems, but they show the power of effort and positive risk taking.
- Encourage involvement in sports or extracurriculars. They are the perfect venue to learn how to negotiate on a committee or accept the bad call from the umpire.

CELL PHONES: CAN YOU HEAR ME NOW?

No one can deny that the age of cell phones is upon us. Everyone wants one, has one, or is wrestling to borrow one. They play an integral part in communication between Hayden, Ella, and Madison and everyone else in the teenager's life. Since they are rarely part of school life and fall more under home domain, a brief word here will suffice.

Most schools have taken a proactive stance and forbidden all cell phones in classrooms. The justification is clear; it opens the door to rampant and unabashed cheating. They make it all too easy and too tempting; after all, you just text a good buddy one row over, and you have your answer. To make it even more inviting, the new phones have Internet features that allow students to surf the Net if a buddy can't come up with the correct answer.

Perhaps just as aggravating is the potential for conversing with friends, letting Hannah know that Jabar is not taking her to the movies, but that Matt is willing to, or even worse, watching *The Dark Knight*—best Batman ever—instead of paying attention and participating in class. No wonder this was a no-brainer for educators.

The other concern with cell phones is the school parking lot. Combining cell phone talking with driving is an accident waiting to happen. Each activity (driving and phone use) draws heavily from different parts of the brain, requiring more multitasking than is humanly possible. The driver and anyone in their path are potentially at risk. In fact, driving abilities tumble so low that it has been compared to drunk driving (Just, Kellera, & Cynkara, 2008). Regrettably, most schools do not have the staff or money to regulate and monitor this effectively. However, some states are taking the initiative and creating legislation to prohibit the use of cell phone use while driving; this certainly helps out schools and everyone on the road.

ON THE VERGE

Stress. We work to avoid it, attempt to control it, and try to cope with it. Adolescent stress is usually associated with peers, grades, or family dynamics. Susan's mind goes blank during a final exam; she starts to sweat, her stomach hurts, her brain shuts down. Despite all her studying, she is now pumped and primed to fail the exam even though she knows the material perfectly. Micky hates lunch because it's the perfect time for Joe to pick on him. He hasn't eaten his dessert in a month. (Joe, in the meantime, has put on a few extra pounds.) Amanda is convinced that her geometry teacher's only goal is to track down and call on the unprepared; she doesn't hear a single word about equilateral triangles because she is too busy worrying that she'll be the next person to be called on. These are all common stress producers in an ordinary day on a school campus.

Let's face it—school can be a stressful place. Stress may occur between teacher and student, between student and student, or be brought into the classroom from sources outside the school. Students who are ignored by peers or who must babysit younger siblings and make dinner before starting homework show the same signs of stress as students who are intimidated by bullies or who are feeling threatened in other ways (Rice, 2002). Teachers who continually threaten students with detention, lower grades, or loss of privileges also contribute to a stressful atmosphere.

Secret Revealed

Teens aren't lazy procrastinators. The adolescent brain is very susceptible to stress, and they defensively avoid situations that cause it—like big projects. Have you ever heard yourself snap at a class of stressed-out teenagers when they complained to you about how much work they had to do before finals? "If you'd paid more attention during the semester you wouldn't be worried about exams now!" Try sympathy instead. You may think a history test is nothing compared to your spouse's cancer scare or the mortgage on your house, but a teen perceives it as proof that the sky is falling.

(Continued)

(Continued)

The stress hormone, cortisol, can interfere with memory retrieval because of its effects on the hippocampus. Even if they study, some teens can't remember information from the class as they are taking the test. Also, excess cortisol increases the likelihood a teen will make rash decisions, like trying to stay awake all night to study or blowing off a test by going out to a party the night before. Add to the mix all the emphasis placed these days on GPA, and the average adolescent has plenty of reason to be a nervous wreck.

Cortisol is the hormone most associated with stress. It is released from the adrenal glands during moments of physical, academic, emotional, or environmental danger, and it stays in the body a long time. Cortisol depresses immune system function, increasing the likelihood of illness. A prime time for adolescents to experience this particular side effect of prolonged stress is during end-of-semester tests when they are concerned about their grades, sleep deprived, and eating unhealthily and irregularly. They feel stress with a capital *S* and contract sore throats, colds, and worse. Great numbers of students become ill immediately following this stress-filled week. Scientists from the University of Wisconsin at Madison compared student immune systems before and during finals; they found that immune systems consistently functioned better when they were not under a great deal of stress, like when the student's exams were behind them (Davidson, Coe, Dolski, & Donzella, 1999). Girls are at particular risk for stress because of the hormone progesterone. Children and post-menopausal women have relatively low levels of progesterone, but with the onset of puberty, progesterone levels increase in girls. Progesterone allows cortisol to run rampant. Once the teenage girl becomes stressed, it takes a long time to de-stress.

Mrs. Bartrum, an eleventh-grade English teacher, commented, "Students are under so much stress during finals that it's painful to watch. Once I talked to the class about it and asked how we could reduce some of their stress. They began listing all of their various obligations and assignments; I must admit that even I felt overwhelmed! I ended up extending the timeline for one of my assignments. I felt better, and so did they."

Cortisol also affects the ability to remember and organize thoughts. Elevated levels of prolonged stress (one or two months) can harm cells in the hippocampus (the part of the brain responsible for short-term memory), further impacting a student's ability to retrieve information (Kim & Diamond, 2002). The inability to remember an answer on a test is often stress related. Students may be able to visualize the day and room in which they learned the material, hear the teacher's voice relaying the information but be unable to recall the specific fact. Often, once they finish the test and leave the classroom, stress levels diminish and the answer just pops into their head.

Cortisol in the system increases the likelihood of making rash decisions. Sometimes it is useful to make impromptu decisions before gathering all pertinent information, but it is not a practical habit. The teenager under a great deal of stress overreacts when he misses the shot in a basketball game or forgets to turn in a school assignment. A teenager from a low-income neighborhood doing poorly in academics may choose a more violent solution to a problem than a student who is not experiencing long-term stress. Additionally, psychiatrist Dr. Margaret Altemus from the Weill Cornell Medical Center in New York suggests that higher progesterone levels in girls seem to let cortisol run rampant in their brains, putting them more at risk for stress-related problems than boys (Lurie, 2003). Chapter 6, "The Risk-Taking Brain," further discusses stress and the heavy role it plays in depression and other at-risk behaviors.

Stress Producers for Teenagers

- Failing an exam
- Physical appearance
- Judgment or evaluation by others
- Unrealistic classroom demands
- The future
- Problems with peers
- Problems with a boyfriend or girlfriend
- Any situation that threatens self-esteem
- Disagreements with teachers, parents, or other adults
- Trying to pass between classes in four minutes while stopping at their lockers and visiting the bathroom
- Embarrassing them in front of their peers
- Only one type of assessment in a course
- Not allowing any class discussion
- The pop quiz

Instructional Strategies

Just Chill

Letizia stood in front of her seventh-grade language arts class giving a speech about Harriet Tubman. She spoke with confidence (despite the fact that speech assignments are undoubtedly stress inducing!). During her summation, however, Letizia informed the class that Harriet Tubman died of pneumonia in 1913. Unfortunately, she pronounced the *p* in pneumonia and the class began to laugh. Not surprisingly, Letizia froze in her tracks, completely unable to remember the rest of her speech.

(Continued)

(Continued)

Most people can remember reacting to such an incident in a highly emotional way. Rare is the individual who does not at one point succumb to the overpowering emotional control of the amygdala. If teachers reduce stress and emotional threat in the classroom and help students develop strategies to combat stress, students will learn more. Productive classes are safe and comfortable places.

Things to Try

- Assure students that they are not expected to give all or nothing. Make comments like "You don't have to be able to answer every question today correctly," "It's okay to review your notes in order to remember what we went over yesterday," and "I know talking in front of a group isn't easy."
- Ensure that students have the academic background needed to accomplish their assignments. Frustration and anger can be eliminated if students understand the task ahead and have the knowledge and skills necessary to complete the work.
- Use competition carefully; when there is competition, make sure everyone has a chance at some success.
- Be fair and consistent with evaluation and discipline. Knowing which behaviors are expected and acceptable and believing that equal offenses receive equal consequences reduces stress.
- Offer academic support outside of the classroom with homework helpers and tutors.
- Incorporate full body movement into your lessons with skits, plays, games, and celebrations.
- Before a test, public speaking, or other stressful situations, have students practice tightening and relaxing muscles. Contracted muscles limit blood circulation and oxygenation. Releasing tension from tight muscles allows the mind and body to relax so the brain can perform at its best.
- Look to Howard Gardner's theory of multiple intelligences (Armstrong, 2000). Varied instruction gives everyone a better chance of success by addressing individual preferences and learning needs. Students who may struggle to understand a concept presented in one fashion can take comfort in the fact that you will present it in a different way next.
- Have students rate and chart their personal stress on a scale of one to ten. Quantifying a level of stress can help put it in perspective. Set aside time to journal or talk about the stressors in their lives.
- Encourage students to "play" a favorite song in their heads as a relaxation technique.
- Show a movie of someone who handled a stressful situation well as an inspirational role model.

- Have students role-play appropriate behavior for handling future stress. This can act as a cue when they are in a real life anxiety-producing situation.
- Give students a few minutes to transition to your classroom and its required mind-set, especially if they are under a great deal of stress. A classmate's suicide, bomb threats, and severe illness create different needs in the classroom. Teachers are eager to secure control of the class and not waste a precious moment of teaching time and too often immediately assign a task to students or begin instruction. By giving students a moment at the beginning of class to settle into their new surroundings, their adjustment will be smoother.
- Refer students showing serious signs of stress to a counselor. Students need to realize they are not alone and can take advantage of the many services inside and outside the school that provide support and help.
- Start class with a review, particularly if students are showing signs of frustration.
- Take a break and focus on breathing techniques, one of the most powerful ways to self soothe. Concentrate on breathing for ten breaths, inhale through the nose and exhale through the mouth.
- Allow some choice in content or process; students want/need to do it their way once in a while.
- Incorporate writing: Have students write a letter of frustration and then tear it up; they'll love the chance to vent.

CALMING DOWN KATIE THE BAND STUDENT

Trying to convince Katie that her misstep went completely unnoticed would have been impossible—Katie was positive that everyone had seen it. Instead, Mrs. Hudson took a different approach to calm her down. "Even if anyone did see you stumble," she said, acknowledging Katie's concern before redirecting her attention, "I doubt they would remember." Mrs. Hudson shrugged it off casually. "You played great—that's what everyone noticed. I've never heard the French horns sound better. It was obvious how hard you all practiced. Didn't you hear the applause?" Katie nodded and smiled, pleased by the praise. She had heard the applause. Her mortification was forgotten.

Self-Concept Under Attack

Moodiness, schmoodiness. Adolescence is a time of great fluctuation in the levels of neurotransmitters, the chemical messengers in the axons of neurons that excite and inhibit behaviors. When levels of these chemicals go astray, teens face a variety of mental upheavals such as depression, eating disorders, and shifts in sleep habits.

Did you know that . . .

- Testosterone and estrogen are found all over the brain during puberty
- Deficits and excesses of serotonin—the "take it easy" neurotransmitter—contribute to teen depression and eating disorders
- Obesity may have a chemical origin (and that some overweight teens may not lack self-control)
- Melatonin changes the sleep patterns of teenagers

Eddie slammed Peter up against the lockers and began slugging him. Words like fatty, tank, and tubs stung in his ears; he hated Peter. The other seventh graders circled the two boys, not sure of what to do. One stunned observer said, "I couldn't believe it. Eddie was so mad and he did it right in school. But Peter deserved it—he's really mean." As things heated up, one of the coaches came along, broke up the fight, and marched both boys to the principal's office. Eddie's eyes stung with tears as he recounted the teasing that he'd been suffering. He felt bad enough about his size without having Peter call him names in front of everybody.

ON YOUR MARK, GET SET, PUBERTY!

Middle school students are on a roller-coaster ride that won't stop. Forget school—they're dealing with training bras, cracking voices, rampant acne, and underarm hair. They react to these developments with everything from joy and surprise to fear. Jenny's feet are too big for the tennis shoes she bought a month ago; Toby doesn't know if he should pluck the chest hair he found or let it grow. Puberty has found them!

Teachers are daily observers of the nonstop physical transformations of pubescence. A seventh-grade teacher remarked, "I can hardly stand to walk down the corridor during May because the body odor is so strong—I'll do anything to avoid it. We need to have that talk on hygiene again." One physical education teacher noted, "The girls are beating the boys at everything. They can jump farther, run faster. You'd think the boys would be upset but everybody seems oblivious to it."

Neuroscientists believe that the brain, in collaboration with hormones, masterminds the transformations of height, weight, and reproductive function that are the significant physical changes of puberty. Some researchers theorize that it is the pruning of synapses during early adolescence that sets puberty rolling. This rampant pruning prompts the hypothalamus, the part of the brain in charge of pain, pleasure, and sexual appetite, to fire off a message to the pituitary gland. When the pituitary gland receives the message, it increases the production of gonadotropin releasing hormone (GnRH) and then sets in motion an increased release of hormones—androgens in males and estrogen in females. These hormones trigger the further development of the primary sexual characteristics, the testes and ovaries, and secondary sexual characteristics, like breast development and the growth of pubic, facial, and body hair.

The primary sexual characteristics relate directly to reproduction; the testes and ovaries set into motion the processes of sperm production, ovulation, and menstruation. The secondary sexual characteristics are the overt physical changes that distinguish the adolescent from a child: pubic hair and underarm hair grow in both boys and girls; boys grow chest hair and facial hair; skin becomes rougher and more oily and sweat glands increase production, contributing to acne and body odor; voices deepen—especially in boys; bones become denser; boys develop an increased proportion of muscle to fat and wider shoulders; girls develop an increased proportion of fat to muscle, broader hips, a wider mouth with fuller lips, and breasts.

Girls enter puberty around ten or eleven years of age and complete their growth spurt by sixteen. In eighth grade, my own daughter grew six inches, gained fifteen pounds, and went from wearing a child's size twelve shoe to a ladies' size six. In one whirlwind of puberty, she changed from a little girl able to sit on her father's lap to a young woman buying acne cream, deodorant, and tampons. (Menstruation starts when girls have a minimum of seventeen percent body fat and a weight of 106 pounds; most girls meet these criteria in sixth grade; Brooks-Gunn & Paikoff, 1997). A mother of a teenage girl remembers the dramatic highs and lows that accompanied her daughter's period. "After a while, I began tracking her reactions and arguments. After three or four months, I showed them to her. It was the only way I could prove to her how her period was affecting her."

Secret Revealed

 Is puberty really a phenomenon of the brain more than the body? Hormones play an important role in the transformation from child to adult, but the brain sets it all in motion. Furthermore, testosterone and estrogen contribute to more than just development of body hair and deep voices—these sex steroids affect the structures of the brain, too.

Not only does the onset of puberty complicate teenagers' lives by radically changing their bodies as it changes their brains, the timing of puberty can have lasting effects on a teen's mental health, social environment, and attention span. Dr. Julia Graber (Graber, Lewinsohn, Seeley, & Brooks-Gunn, 1997), a professor of psychology at the University of Florida, studies how early and late bloomers handle the experience of puberty. Hardly surprising, being ahead or behind your peers is a mixed blessing. With early physical development often comes pressure to behave as a much older person; late-maturing teens are often not taken seriously by friends or adults. Being aware how the timing of puberty affects adolescents will help parents and teachers interact with them more meaningfully.

Boys don't start puberty until they are twelve or thirteen and don't finish their growth spurt until about age eighteen. Throughout the awkwardness of adolescence, girls are about two years ahead of the game. Nothing is a better indication of this lag of physical development than the excruciatingly awkward slow dance in a middle school cafeteria, with boys reaching up to put their arms around their partners' necks. One father of three teenagers said, "I first knew puberty was coming by the physical changes, the bras hanging in the bathroom, my son's cracking voice. They also became more combative—they'd buck the curfew and then argue about it. I don't remember how many times they said, 'I'll be home,' and then they weren't."

For a long time, we've known that androgens—the general class of male hormones—and estrogen are associated with the hypothalamus. Only now are we finding these hormones scattered all over the brain, including the cortex and cerebellum (Keefe, 2002). Hormones play an important role in the erratic behavior of teenagers by adding to the commotion of puberty. Testosterone and estrogen are the main culprits. Males and females produce both hormones, but the levels present in the body differ by gender. Males have about ten times as much testosterone (which is associated with sexual interest and aggression) as females; they are jolted by its release about ten times a day! Interestingly, testosterone levels in males have also been shown to rise when they are faced with a fight or are participating in a sporting event. Testosterone can be directed in positive or negative directions; professional athletes, ambitious politicians, and entrepreneurs have all been found to have high levels of estrogen.

Females have about ten times as much estrogen as males. Estrogen stimulates the development of female sexual characteristics and helps maintain the functioning of the uterus and vagina. Higher levels of estrogen have also been linked to girls being more receptive to boys' sexual advances (as compared to lower levels of estrogen). Still, hormones play only a small role in how girls demonstrate their sexuality. The environment, instead, seems to be the greatest determinant of a girl's potentially coy, provocative, spicy, flirtatious, modest, or unassertive behavior. Conversely, testosterone is directly tied to boys' sexuality (Hutchinson, 1995).

Androgens also affect females. Studies have been conducted on girls with congenital adrenal hyperplasia (CAH), a condition where female embryos are exposed to high levels of androgens for the majority of their gestation. Girls with CAH prefer "boy" toys (like guns and cars) to "girl" toys and games (like dolls and playing house). They are also more aggressive than girls with average amounts of androgens and are willing and, at times, eager to fight (Kreeger, 2002).

TRANSGENDER TEENAGERS

Bobbi is a fifteen-year-old girl trapped in a boy's body. She chooses to express her female identity in her dress and actions. She wears push up-bras, strappy sandals, and short skirts to school. Her makeup includes blush and mascara, and she's a member of the Girl's Club. Today Bobbi is feeling pretty good about herself, but that hasn't always been the case. A few years back, as puberty hit, she became very depressed, hating herself and her peers. She tried morphing herself into a male-female blended identity; it didn't work. Feelings of hopelessness and being lost permeated her mind. To add to her pain, kids would ask her hurtful questions like "Are you a boy or a girl?" Fortunately, through therapy, family support, and a few good friends, Bobbi has learned to accept herself just as she is.

Some of the most solid research has emerged connecting transgender with the brain. Transgender is the state of believing you were born in a body that does not match your true gender identity. A female feels she is trapped in the body of a man or vice versa. Now neuroscientists have found concrete evidence that supports these convictions. For example, transgender males have a significantly smaller hypothalamus, the part of the brain associated with sexual interest, than their heterosexual counterparts. This research may support why transgender individuals feel they really are trapped in the wrong body (Zhou, Hofman, Gooren, & Swaab, 1995).

Puberty holds painful challenges for these students. Identity formation, in particular, is difficult because they are conflicting in a very basic way with society's expectations. As a result depression often follows.

Suggestions for dealing with transgender students:

- Examine your own prejudices and bias; talk to a counselor if you think you will have difficulty treating this student in a way that will benefit their positive identity formation.
- Use the name they prefer and the desired pronoun, *he* or *she.*
- Provide private restrooms.
- Arrange a private locker room for physical education.
- Keep their biological gender confidential if they desire.
- Respect their clothing choices.
- Refer them to a counselor or other professional if needed.
- Suggest transgender support groups.
- Forbid harassment from their peers or other staff.

"DO THESE JEANS MAKE ME LOOK FAT?"

"Am I hot?" "Am I a dog?" Adolescents spend a lot of time in the mirror searching for answers to these questions. The physical and mental changes of puberty affect the way teenagers look at themselves. Body image is your perception of your body and the level of satisfaction (or dissatisfaction) you have with your looks. It is considered an important part of our self-esteem. It is estimated that about twenty-five percent of how much we like or dislike ourselves is determined by our physical appearance. Taken to the extreme, a poor body image coupled with immature coping skills and life stresses may even lead as far as the development of an eating disorder, depression, or suicide attempt.

The timing of puberty is key to how we view teens and how they view themselves. Late bloomers and early bloomers can have very different self-concepts. Consider Matt, an eighth grader with a mustache. To say he sticks out in a sea of hairless faces is an understatement. A fine baseball athlete, Matt is a skilled infielder and has a powerful swing. Early maturing boys have a distinct advantage over their peers because they embody everything our society values: masculinity, attractiveness, and competence. They have an athletic edge and are often chosen as leaders. Early maturing boys enjoy a positive body image (Alsaker, 1992), but as with most things, early onset of puberty has a downside: Society places high expectations on early maturing boys and pressures them to make lifelong decisions on things like career, religion, and political affiliation at an early age. As a result, they tend to be more somber and serious than their age-mates.

On the other hand, the late-maturing boys are routinely seen as less mature because of their childlike appearance—regardless of their actions. They look like children and are treated like children. Like a self-fulfilling prophecy, they live up to these expectations and behave immaturely. If given the choice, teachers and parents (and people in general) give them fewer important responsibilities; girls are less likely to view them as dating material, and they are typically the last people chosen for an athletic team, partly because they are seen as less capable (and possibly because they are still growing and developing coordination). Not surprisingly, they are less self-assured, more restless, more talkative, and less popular (Laitinen-Krispijn, Van der Ende, Hazebroek-Kampschreur, & Verhulst, 1999). Fortunately, they also feel few pressures to grow up fast and enjoy their teen years without the stresses of the adult world looming menacingly ahead of them.

David is a late-maturing boy on Matt's baseball team. Not only does he look much younger than his teammates, he is a staggering eight to ten inches shorter than they are! While it is often difficult from the bleachers to identify boys in their uniforms, parents always know where David is, when he is batting, and what position he's playing—he's the short one (fondly dubbed the "Mini-Me" of the team). Everybody likes David, but he isn't always taken seriously. He talks too much without saying enough and jumps up and down in a frenzy to get anyone's attention. His juvenile tactics mean he is usually ignored.

Late-maturing girls experience a prolonged childhood with few of the negative experiences of late-maturing boys. They physically develop about the same time the average boy does. They may have a few worries at the outset about acquiring full femininity, but once they physically catch up with their peers, they quickly come to terms with their newfound womanhood (Magnusson, Stattin, & Allen, 1986). Mary Pat didn't start her period until she turned fifteen, long after all of her friends. Relieved at the proof that nothing was wrong with her after all, she rode her bicycle to her friend's house shouting, "I'm a woman! I'm a woman!" the whole way.

Early maturing girls have the most difficult time adjusting to their rate of physical development. They can mature two to three years ahead of girls their age and five to six years ahead of boys. In the scheme of their lives, this is a big age difference. Furthermore, not only are their bodies growing quicker, so are their brains! They tend to be ahead of their peers in interests and abilities. Further complicating matters is the fact that these girls are treated as old as they look; many of these girls start hanging out with an older crowd of friends. Older boys lust after them, which leads to early sexual experimentation. They seek more independence from parental control and have more problems in school with grades and behavior. The laundry list goes on and on. They are more likely to smoke, drink alcohol, be depressed, or suffer from an eating disorder than their on-schedule peers (Kaltiala-Heino, Marttunen, Rantanen, & Rimpela, 2003). Although their brains and bodies are developing at turbo speed, they lack the life experience to deal with the above-age pressures. Fortunately, once they become comfortable with their bodies, they have the confidence and ability to responsibly enjoy their popularity in older adolescence.

In general, boys have more positive body images than girls. Girls tend to be very critical of their attributes and complain about hair being too curly, thighs too fat, and eyelashes too short. Girls usually think they are less attractive than they are. In contrast, boys rate themselves pretty well, wishing only to be a little more muscular (a wish that naturally comes true soon enough). The right friends (captain of the football team, president of the senior class, and homecoming queen) and appearance (usually elements of physical attractiveness such as having fine features, flowing hair, and a creamy complexion) also weigh into the mix. A sense of belonging and having friends further reinforces positive self-esteem (and vice versa). On a side note, appealing looks indirectly influence self-esteem because attractive people have a better chance of being accepted into a group of peers; they benefit from their good looks.

In both genders, however, body image is strongly tied to self-esteem. The more attractive teens believe they are and the more accepting they are of their looks, the higher their self-esteem—and vice versa. Adolescents' bodies are constantly changing, so it is easy for them to have a distorted image of themselves. If they sometimes feel like they are all arms, legs, and nose, it is because they often are.

Instructional Strategies

You're OK (But Am I OK?)

Most students enter puberty together and develop at the same rate. They are all beginning to sprout and bloom at about the same time. These students find comfort in numbers and feel normal (as normal as possible) because they are sharing this experience with their friends. Because the physical changes of puberty affect teen friendships, self-esteem, and (ultimately) academic achievement, the teacher who understands this process of transformation can better meet their school needs.

Things to Try

- Steer clear of calling attention to physical differences, particularly height or weight. The students who are shorter don't always want to stand in the front row. Don't allow nicknames based on physical characteristics such as "Shorty" or "Ribs."
- Work information on physical development into your subject area. Chart growth rates in math, journal about physical changes in English, examine how standards of attractiveness differ between developing and developed countries in social studies. The power of eating cauliflower and staying in motion are perfect topics for health, PE, and life and consumer science. Support the physical education program in your school.
- Furnish opportunities for group work and other social interaction. Independent work is fine (even essential to some parts of learning), but it is important to make students part of a group at times. It's reassuring to be one of many, especially when all their physical changes make teenagers feel like they are the only ones experiencing them.
- Give students models of successful adults who do not meet the standard body image. Abraham Lincoln was tall and scrawny, Stephen Hawking is in a wheelchair, and Queen Latifah and Oprah are overweight, but all are famous for their ideas and actions rather than their looks.
- Examine the media's role in physical expectations. Analyze popular TV shows, critique teen magazines, and discuss music videos.

- Compliment students on their abilities rather than their looks. Be a good role model—avoid criticizing your own body.
- Learn your school's policy of discussing physical concerns like menstruation and obesity with a student. If a student has a question, should the teacher respond or refer them to the nurse or guidance counselor?

"I HATE MYSELF, I HATE MYSELF."

Keith was a late bloomer, puberty didn't hit until late in his junior year of high school. During ninth and tenth grade, he was the butt of everyone's jokes and suffered merciless teasing, all because of his physical stature. Brad, an athlete and probably the last person anyone in the school would have expected, felt compassion for Keith and made a point of getting to know him. Brad said, "It seemed so ridiculous, he was getting picked on for something he had no control over." Years later, Keith told Brad that he had been considering suicide during high school, and the only thing that stopped him was Brad's friendship. The power of one cannot be denied.

As many as one in twelve teens suffer from clinical depression. Between 1990 and 2003 there was an actual decline in teen suicide, but alarmingly 2003–2004 saw an eight percent increase; it's the third leading cause of teen death, following motor vehicle accidents (#1) and homicide (#2). During high school, seventeen percent seriously consider ending their lives (Center for Disease Control and Prevention, 2007). Strangely, the method has changed; in the past, firearms were the weapon of choice for both boys and girls, but now girls are choosing hanging and suffocation. It is not  unusual for a teen to feel blue (in fact, teenagers have a more negative disposition than adults or children—this ends about age eighteen), but a constant lament of gloom, moodiness, and drooping energy is a sign of true depression. The causes of teen depression are complex. Most professionals believe depression is a combination of genetics, environment, and biology. A genetic link is suggested by the documentation of families with a history of this illness running through aunts, uncles, cousins, and parents. An environment of physical and mental abuse during childhood has been associated with depression. Academics, unrealistic family expectations, and problems with friends can also lead to feelings of rejection, which are related to depression—teens are subject to overreact to any and all of these situations, putting them at greater risk for depression. Getting kicked off the football team, breaking up with a boyfriend, or receiving a D in a class may signal the end of the world to a teen, that they have nothing left to live for and that the shame and pain of this humiliation is impossible to bear.

Secret Revealed

 It's not true that teens have nothing to complain about. No, they don't pay rent or buy food, and yes, they get to go to school and see their friends, but life is just as stressful to them as to adults. Breakups, sports losses, homework, and arguments with friends are just a few of the ordinary events that contribute to adolescent anxiety and depression. Even in a perfect life at a perfect school, however, a teenager would succumb to periods of depression—the teenage brain is vulnerable!

Serotonin, the neurotransmitter that makes us feel calm and at peace, is at a natural low during adolescence. Additionally, because the frontal lobes are in the process of maturing, the amygdala has more control over the brain of a teen than of an adult. As a result, the emotionally reactive, often negative amygdala gets more input than the calm, cool, collected cerebral cortex. To some teenagers, being subjected to the dramatic highs and lows of assessing everything as a possible threat makes it seem like everything in life is bad. With less calming serotonin and more negative impulses, life can be demoralizing and scary. No wonder rates of teen depression are dramatically high.

Then there's the role of biology. Researchers from the National Institute of Health studied the connection between puberty and depression. They found the rate of major depression correlates with how far along a child is in puberty as opposed to his or her chronological age. It seems that as we develop physically during puberty, the chances of depression increase (Walkup et al., 2001).

The teen years are marked by low levels of the neurotransmitter, serotonin. Serotonin manages a multitude of jobs in the body spanning from head to toe; it regulates temperature, blood pressure, blood clotting, immunity, pain, digestion, and sleep. It also plays an important role in our emotions as a calming agent. In the properly functioning brain, serotonin inhibits the firing of neurons, making us feel relaxed. It counteracts the emotional amygdala. The decrease of serotonin during adolescence is natural. During the pruning stage, serotonin neurons are selectively eliminated. This normal process does not cause problems for most teens.

But for the others . . . ? Two theories exist about why serotonin levels may cause depression in some teenagers: Either their brains are unable to properly use the serotonin that is there (they have enough serotonin but can't take advantage of it), or their levels of serotonin are so low that the brain is unable to run smoothly. These two educated hunches have spawned the use of medications with a serotonin base to treat depression, which has proven effective in some cases.

Figure 5.1   Human Brain

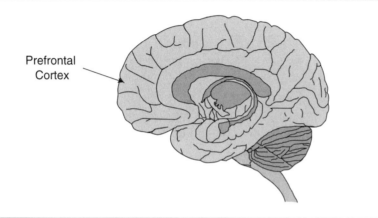

Prefrontal
Cortex

SOURCE: Adapted from Sousa, D. A. (2003), *How the Gifted Brain Learns*, p. 18.

But serotonin is not the only influence on feelings and emotions. The right prefrontal cortex is activated by negative feelings, and the left prefrontal cortex controls positive feelings. The two usually work in sync, keeping our emotions in balance. The left prefrontal cortex is the side that receives and filters emotional information from the amygdala. If the amygdala signals danger, the left prefrontal cortex processes the information and then relays its interpretation of the information back to the amygdala: "Yes, this is a problem" or "Calm down, everything's okay." If the left side decreases in activity (a sure sign it isn't working properly), the amygdala runs wild. Feelings of helplessness, despair, and anxiety run amok. This inactivity in the left prefrontal cortex results in the dominance of the right prefrontal cortex—the controller of negative feelings—and may explain why people with depression tend to remember negative memories rather than pleasant ones. As a person comes out of a depression, the activity in the left prefrontal cortex increases. Which is the cause and which is the effect is not known, but the link between depression and the left prefrontal cortex is clear.

Stress is also related to adolescent depression. Although school, friends, and family are all sources of potential support to teens, they are also potential stressors. Teenagers suffering from depression are more likely to drop out of school or start abusing drugs and alcohol. They are at high risk for committing suicide. Ignoring teenage depression and assuming that "they'll snap out of it" are mistakes no one can afford. Teachers are in the perfect position to spot two of the early warning signs: increased absenteeism and a drop in achievement (an A or B student may suddenly struggle to maintain Cs and Ds). The sooner an adolescent with depression is identified, the better. Letting teens know that there are people willing to help and educating them about the available support systems at their school and in their community can make a real difference in an adolescent's life.

Depression has more than emotional repercussions; it also affects the hippocampus, which influences short-term memory and our ability to process emotion and information. The hippocampus actually decreases in volume during episodes of chronic depression because its neurons wither and die. Fortunately, the hippocampus is resilient and grows new synaptic connections when the depression lifts (Thomas & Peterson, 2003).

WASTING AWAY

Shawna was a well-adjusted high school student, confident and well liked by her peers. Sophomore year she tried out for the cheerleading squad and made the team. It changed her social life overnight. "Suddenly I went from being accepted to being really popular. Everyone noticed what I was wearing and what I looked like. I liked the feeling, but I also felt a little uncomfortable, like it was all out of control. People were giving me a lot of attention, but I wasn't sure if they really liked me. Sometimes it seemed like they didn't even know me.

"With the extra cheerleading workouts I dropped about ten pounds, and I began to get more compliments. That's when my obsession with food began. I started to watch everything I ate. I wanted to lose weight, but then it got out of control. At one point I was barely eating, maybe having just a diet soda and a cigarette." When five-foot-six-inch Shawna dropped in weight to ninety-five pounds, she was hospitalized. After a six-week treatment program, she returned to school, quit cheerleading, and spent all her energy on regaining her health. Each morning she was weighed; if she had lost weight, she wasn't allowed to attend school that day. Shawna has since graduated from high school but still struggles to maintain a healthy lifestyle. If she follows the course of most recovering anorexics, she will likely struggle for the rest of her life to lead a normal existence in terms of food.

Perhaps up to ten percent of all Americans suffer from some kind of an eating disorder, of whom the vast majority afflicted are females (Spearing, 2001). Although this problem persists into adulthood, its origins are in adolescence. Eighty-sixty percent of adults with an eating disorder say it started before they were twenty years old. This is definitely a teenage problem (Paxton et al., 1991). Rates of anorexia nervosa and bulimia—two of the most common eating disorders—are on the rise with teenage girls in America. In fact, the numbers have doubled since 1960 (Ice, 2003). Anorexia and bulimia have the highest mortality rate of any mental illness—up to twenty percent of those afflicted die. Fortunately, this figure of twenty percent reflects relatively small numbers; only about one percent of the population is anorexic, and only three percent bulimic.

Anorexia nervosa is self-starvation characterized by excessive weight loss. Though people with anorexia avoid eating, they have an intense interest in food. It's not unusual for them to set a formal place for themselves at the dinner table, replete with place mat, silverware, and plate. Anyone walking into the dining room would think they were ready to sit down and enjoy a hearty meal. Instead, their meal would consist of a small amount of low-calorie food, which is cut into small pieces and slowly eaten. Symptoms of anorexia often include noticeable weight loss, the consumption of large amounts of water or noncaloric beverages, always feeling cold, and developing a fine downy hair over the entire body. Individuals with bulimia, in contrast, turn toward food to cope. They often eat large quantities of food, but with the help of purging, suppositories, and laxatives they are able to rid the body of unwanted calories. This cycle of binge eating and purging causes weight fluctuation. Symptoms of bulimia include deterioration of tooth enamel, chronic constipation, and depression. Complications from either of these eating disorders may include kidney failure, loss of menstruation, impaired thinking, and ultimately death.

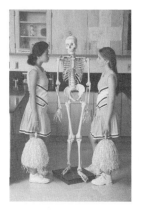

Secret Revealed

Teenagers with eating disorders are not necessarily gluttonous or vain. Pathological issues with body weight—manifested in anorexia nervosa or obesity—have significant impact on teens, partially due to changes in their brains. Serotonin and leptin are two brain chemicals currently under scrutiny for their contributions to obsessive eating behaviors. Twenty

(Continued)

(Continued)

percent of anorexic people die, making it the most lethal mental illness (Ice, 2003); eighty percent of teenagers who are obese will become adults who are obese and will then suffer from the myriad of health problems that accompany obesity, from heart disease and diabetes to muscular problems. Although it is certain that many other factors besides neurotransmitters contribute to the desire to over- or undereat, science is hoping that finding the causes in the brain will help heal teens with these conditions.

The media and societal expectations have taken the brunt of the blame for our obsession with weight. The message they send is simple: Unless you weigh one hundred pounds and wear size two jeans, you are not making the grade. Although this message is pervasive and harmful, neuroscientists believe that changes in the brain during puberty make their own contributions to eating disorders. Serotonin is thought to impact obsessive, anxious behavior (Barbarich, 2002); girls with eating disorders such as anorexia and bulimia have higher levels of serotonin than girls of average weight (Aguilera, Selgas, Codoceo, & Bajo, 2000). With the increased serotonin levels in these girls' brains, they become obsessed with their weight and with food. Complicating the situation is the fact that food contains elements necessary for the body to manufacture serotonin. By not eating, the body of an anorexic or bulimic is unable to produce serotonin. As these girls starve themselves, they reduce their serotonin levels. This eventually enables them to reduce their own obsessive behavior and feel calmer, but the price they pay is high—irregular heart rate, osteoporosis, kidney failure, and ultimately death can be the consequence of an eating disorder. It is estimated that three thousand young women die each year from eating disorders.

"WOULD YOU LIKE FRIES WITH THAT?"

Obesity is starting to be classified as another type of eating disorder, one as tied up in body-image issues as anorexia nervosa and bulimia are (Heller, 2003). For people suffering from obesity, food is an obsession with physical repercussions. Obesity has no gender bias; males and females are equally plagued. It's not easy to be obese in our thin-obsessed society. Adolescents with obesity deal with more teasing, fatigue, and lower self-esteem than their friends of normal weight—and the problems don't stop there. Adolescents are heavier than ever before, and we are beginning to see them contract Type 2 diabetes at an alarming rate. (Ninety percent of all cases of diabetes fall into the Type 2 category.) Individuals with diabetes either do not produce enough insulin to control their glucose levels or else their cells do not respond to the insulin in their bloodstream. Obesity is a major contributor to this disease because excess fat blocks insulin from moving glucose into the body's cells to give them energy. As adolescents who are obese enter adulthood, health issues such as heart disease and cancer develop at an alarming pace.

There is no doubt that obesity is a growing problem in the United States. The U.S. Department of Health and Human Services reported that fifteen percent of school-age children are overweight, triple what it was twenty years ago (Dietz, 2002). Health patterns established in adolescence are highly associated with obesity in adulthood—eighty percent of obese adolescents eventually become obese adults (Manisses, 2003). Traditionally we've looked at genetics, eating habits, exercise, and metabolism to understand the overweight body, but the time has come to look at the brain's role.

It takes ten minutes after eating for the brain of a person of normal weight to get the information that the stomach is full—the hormone leptin is released from fat cells and informs the brain that you've had enough to eat. The delay is longer in people who are obese. Research shows that individuals who are obese are not receiving signals to the brain that tell them to quit eating. Their brains don't seem to get the message. Researchers hypothesize that the message is not received in their brain because either leptin is being transported improperly or the brain is misinterpreting the information (Banks, 2003).

As a result of not getting the signal to stop eating, it is speculated that people who are obese go into a frenzy to get the signal moving to the brain. They eat more and more, hoping to produce a surge of leptin and send the necessary message to the brain. Their internal logic is correct—in the person who is normal weight, this eating would have the intended effect. Unfortunately, for the person who is overweight, the reverse happens. Obesity prevents the signal from getting to the brain, so their overeating is an act of futility. Now the vicious cycle has begun. The less leptin received by the brain, the more obese they become. They eat more in an attempt to break the brain's barrier to leptin and get the signal.

Nor do the brain differences between the obese and normal-weight person stop there. The U.S. Department of Energy's Brookhaven National Laboratory showed that obese people have fewer brain receptors for dopamine (a neurotransmitter that creates feelings of pleasure and calm) than normal-weight people. When a person eats, he or she is rewarded with a rush of feel-good dopamine. (We've all had that satisfied feeling after consuming a hearty meal.) Regrettably, the person who is obese has fewer dopamine receptors and so needs to overeat to release the same amount of dopamine. Much like the addict who anticipates the craved pleasure or the numbing that accompanies the drug, the person who is overweight craves food to achieve that satisfied feeling (Wang, Volkow, & Fowler, 2002).

The impending health factors are not the only problems. The teen with obesity worries about body image and social acceptance like any adolescent, but unlike normal-weight teens, teens with obesity may also worry that they don't "measure up" in adult society's eyes. Poor self-esteem and rejection can lead to depression; depression can negatively affect academic performance. The domino effect is irrefutable (Manisses, 2003). Just being overweight can indirectly start the toppling—the first to fall is body image, then self-esteem, followed by depression and difficulty in school.

Explanations for the rise in anorexia nervosa, bulimia, and depression are not forthcoming. It is possible that the rates are the same as they have always been but we keep better records or that the stigma associated with these diseases has lessened so more people seek treatment. Some people blame the changing standards of beauty and attractiveness in the media and the availability of cosmetic surgery for putting pressure on individuals to strive for unattainable perfection. Dr. Elizabeth Young, professor of psychiatry and research scientist at the University of Michigan Mental Health Research Institute, speculates that teenagers are under just as much pressure and feel just as much stress as their parents do (Lurie, 2003). They are juggling boyfriends and girlfriends, schoolwork, jobs, parents—all of which are complications to life and commonly considered sources of depression.

Instructional Strategies

Educate Teens About the Issues That Affect Them

Eating disorders and depression are the leading internal issues facing teens today, and all these conditions are on the rise at alarming rates. But why now? Why are today's teens more at risk for these dangers than the teens of fifty years ago? Obesity perhaps has the clearest explanation. The caloric intake of the average American has increased by twenty percent since 1982, and sugar intake has grown by twenty percent (Putnam, Allshouse, & Kantor, 2002). Physical activity is on the decline, and girls in particular become less active during adolescence. Teenagers watch more television than they used to—forty-three percent watch more than two hours a day! They also spend more time playing sedentary computer and video games. Trying to explain why eating disorders are on the rise may not solve the problem, but it does give us a place to start looking for answers.

Things to Try

- Involve teens with their peers. Healthy personal relationships improve self-esteem and are fun.
- Encourage students to participate in sports, find an afterschool job, or join extracurricular activities. If their minds are occupied with external activities, they will be less likely to focus on destructive internal issues.
- Focus on the positive in class. Wearing a smile actually helps your disposition and may directly contribute to a student's happy thoughts and good mood.
- Arrange help for students who are afflicted by depression or eating disorders. Refer them to the guidance counselor or proper school personnel.
- Greet students at the door each day, and get to know them as individuals. This personal attention may give an isolated teen a sense of belonging; friendly rapport with your students will put you in a better position to note changes in behavior that may signal depression.
- Internet Web sites can offer support for specific issues that teens face (of course discretion is advised).
- If a teen confesses an eating disorder, depression, or other problem, validate his or her feelings. You don't have to approve of the behavior, but you do need to acknowledge that it's okay to feel upset, overwhelmed, or depressed.
- Signs of depression or an eating disorder that persist longer than two weeks should be taken seriously.

THE NEED TO SLEEP

It's noon at my house, and two teenagers are curled up under the covers, snoozing away. "Never wake a baby or a teenager" is a rule I live by. And boy, do teenagers love to sleep! The complaints from parents about it sound so much alike. "My son will fight tooth and nail to watch another half hour of sports at night and then drags the next morning." "No matter what time she goes to sleep, Sandra cannot stay awake in church." "Going to bed early means 1:00 a.m.! They'll sleep as late as I let them and even then can't focus on what they are doing." "During their sports season, my teens are irritable, short-tempered, and disrespectful." It is not uncommon for adults to think teenagers are lazy. After all, sixteen-year-olds sleep until noon, walk around the house in a daze, and then shuffle into the shower—where they spend the next thirty minutes. What happened to the child who woke up early, hungry for a bowl of cereal, and eager to watch cartoons? In a word, puberty!

Puberty changes the sleep patterns of the adolescent. During puberty, the body secretes melatonin (a hormone associated with sleep) at a different time than during childhood or adulthood, significantly altering their  sleep cycle. This change causes the teenager to fall asleep much later at night and wake up later in the day. Children who fell asleep at 9:00 or 9:30 p.m. now find themselves wide-awake at midnight. Besides the change in sleep patterns, teenagers also need more sleep than adults do. It's thought the average adult needs eight and one-quarter hours of sleep, while the average teen needs nine and one-quarter hours. This change may be ascribed to the fact that the body is trying to encourage their sexual development—the hormones necessary for sexual development are mainly released while you sleep. (There is no proof, however, that losing sleep derails the release of these hormones; Carskadon, 2002.)

Teenagers themselves are painfully cognizant of their new sleeping and waking cycles. "In the summer I sleep way too much, and during the school year, not nearly enough. On weekends, I get up at noon and I'm still tired." "At night I never get tired and don't know how much sleep I need until the next morning. During marching band season, I have to get up at six in the morning every day. I'll reset my alarm for five more minutes and then reset it again until I have about five minutes before it's time to go! Sleep is the most important thing in my life." "During free time in class I lay my head down and sleep. If I could stay awake, I'd read or talk to a friend."

Secret Revealed

Although it certainly seems so, teens don't sleep in on Saturday morning just to shirk chores. Adolescence has completely altered their daily sleep and wake patterns! Dr. Mary Carskadon (2002) from Brown University has been studying teens and their sleep schedules and has discovered that they need more sleep than their parents but not as much as their younger siblings.

And not only do they need more sleep—they get sleepy later than ever. Even teens who try to go to bed early find themselves awake and restless until close to midnight. Complicating matters is the early start time of most secondary schools. Instead of being tucked into bed at 8:00 a.m., finishing up a dream, students are already on their way to their second class. That's hardly good for learning. It's not very good for teacher-student conflicts either—notice how snappy and touchy you get when you are tired. Imagine what a teenager (still learning to manage emotions) feels like!

Dr. Mary Carskadon from Brown University is an expert on understanding adolescent sleep patterns. She found that the majority of high school students were sleep deprived, resulting in twenty percent of high school students falling asleep in school. Perhaps even more interesting was that she found forcing them to go to bed earlier did not solve the problem (Carskadon, 2002). Not surprisingly, most high school students get less than eight hours of sleep and one-third get less than seven. School schedules only complicate the situation. Schools start early, some as early as 7:15 or 7:30 a.m. On the weekends, motivated by aggravation or misguided efforts to produce an industrious child, parents wake teenagers out of a sound sleep. This leaves them starting their day tired and run down. We have a flock of sleep-deprived individuals trying to maneuver their way through adolescence.

There are significant differences between those students who get enough sleep versus those who do not. Sleep deprivation makes it more difficult for most students to learn, remember, and think creatively. Research studies show that high school students not receiving enough sleep suffer in grades and overall school success. Emotions are also harder to control when adolescents are sleep deprived. Normal mood swings that accompany hormone changes increase, as do irritability and depression. The immune system is negatively affected, leaving a student at risk of catching a cold or developing a sore throat. Most disturbing is the increase in aggressive behavior in students who are sleep deprived (Carskadon, 2002).

Minnesotans have been particularly concerned about the impact of sleep on high school students. Many districts have moved their school start time from 7:20 to 8:30 a.m. Grades improved and discipline problems decreased at these schools with a later start time (Reiss, 1998). School systems, however, are reluctant to change school start times. Bus schedules and extracurricular activities make it a complicated venture. The best we can do is encourage teenagers to get plenty of sleep. Verbally acknowledging and reinforcing the fact that they actually do need more sleep then adults gives them "permission" to indulge their desire to sleep (after school, of course!).

If adolescents are tired, listless, and only thinking about their next nap, it is not easy to get their attention in school. Sleep impacts memory and creativity. That extensive list of defined biology terms and the fanciful memoir will both be of higher quality if the teenager does them when awake and refreshed. Likewise, sleep affects our emotions. When teens are tired, they are more likely to be irritable and have mood swings. The student who would amicably agree to work in a teacher-chosen group when well rested may become upset and even belligerent about it when tired.

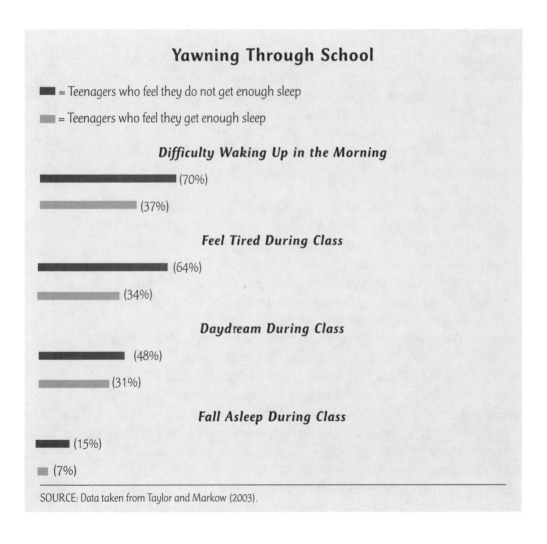

Yawning Through School

■■■ = Teenagers who feel they do not get enough sleep

▭▭ = Teenagers who feel they get enough sleep

Difficulty Waking Up in the Morning

(70%)

(37%)

Feel Tired During Class

(64%)

(34%)

Daydream During Class

(48%)

(31%)

Fall Asleep During Class

(15%)

(7%)

SOURCE: Data taken from Taylor and Markow (2003).

Instructional Strategies

Accommodate Sleep and Wake Patterns

Imagine all your students coming to class wide-awake—what a lovely dream! Sleep is one process that affects both behavior and achievement over which teachers have little or no control. No wonder we are so frustrated when we see a student sleeping through class time— teenagers and their parents are the only people with the power to change this situation. Your best bet for ameliorating student sleepiness is with a relentless informational campaign. Use school newsletters and parent-teacher conferences to educate them on the importance of sleep to the teenager, or take your message to the entire community by writing a letter to the editor or a small article for your local newspaper.

Things to Try

- Let indoors imitate outdoors as much as possible. Keep lights low in the evening and open a curtain in the morning. (Light helps reset the biological clock.)
- Introduce the issue of starting high school later to the school board. If biology and puberty do not seem like sufficient reasons, remind them that the change of schedule could also help reduce teenage crime and pregnancy—rates of each peak between the hours of 3:30 and 5:00 p.m., when teens are often without supervision. (*After School for America's Teens*, 2001)
- Encourage parents to allow teens to sleep until at least 9:00 a.m. on weekends and later if possible.
- Educate teenagers on the importance of sleep to their physical well-being. Design a two- or three-day unit on the importance of sleep, or assign a research paper or project on this topic. Knowledge is power; most teens probably walk around too tired to wonder why their energy is so low and would be relieved to have an answer for it.
- Stay away from stimulants such as caffeine and nicotine because they interfere with the body's natural sleep processes.
- Avoid stimulating activities before bed, such as heavy studying or computer games. Energizing activities arouse the brain, making it difficult to prepare the body for a good night's sleep. But do exercise during the day; a minimum of thirty minutes per day will help tire you out and prepare you for a good night's sleep.
- Eliminate late-night arguments. Encourage parents to save it until morning. Confrontation raises the heart rate and blood pressure, which also stimulates the brain and makes it more difficult to fall asleep.
- Start a worry book—unload all your worries into a worry book and then let your mind relax. This will reduce adrenaline production.

(Continued)

(Continued)

- Create a sleeping habit—wake up and go to sleep at similar times each day (this recommendation is made with the realization that most teens like to burn the midnight oil on weekends—and so it may not be a realistic option).
- Don't sleep with a pet—they are frequently sleep disturbers.
- Resist the temptation to look at the clock (It's 2:00 a.m. and I'm not asleep—aaaaah!); seeing the time tends to create more anxiety.
- Keep the temperature cool, no higher than sixty-eight degrees for optimal sleeping.

HELPING EDDIE HANDLE HIS AGGRESSION

The principal spoke to Eddie and Peter separately about the fight. With both boys he calmly discussed the motivation for the fight and suggested appropriate ways to handle their anger. "Next time," he gently chided Eddie, "find a teacher or just walk away." Eddie nodded the whole time. He already knew he should respond to teasing without fighting, but cracks about his weight hit too close to home.

Mr. Wyatt, Eddie's teacher, wasn't really surprised that Peter's taunts finally had this effect. When Eddie resumed classes, Mr. Wyatt took him aside a few moments during lunch to talk not about the fight but about starting a club. The two of them had something in common, he said—they were both collectors. Eddie collected stamps, he collected American memorabilia . . . did he know any other collectors who would like to join? The project caught Eddie's interest and he started asking around. Within a month, he'd rallied enough interest to organize one. Focusing on the club's activities gave him more to think about than his weight; Peter's name-calling lost its sting after a while. Later, when Mr. Wyatt and Eddie talked about walking for thirty minutes a day instead of spending the time watching television, Eddie took the advice as wisdom rather than as an insult.

The Risk-Taking Brain

The teen years have always been risk-taking years but not because adolescence is boring. Teenagers don't drive too fast and smoke cigarettes behind the gym out of youthful exuberance. Neuroscientists are shedding light on the brain's significant role in reckless behaviors, suggesting that mistakes teens make now can have lasting physiological effects.

Did you know that . . .

- Teens are very susceptible to the dopamine rushes that come with taking risks
- Teens have trouble anticipating the consequences of their behavior because they rely more on the emotional amygdala than the rational frontal lobes
- Teens are extremely vulnerable to addiction and that adolescent addictions are harder to break
- Violent video games reinforce violent behavior in boys
- Cutting releases endorphins into the body, creating feelings of pleasure

With much enthusiasm, eighth-grader Scott detailed how he, his father, and his uncle took mountain bikes down Vail Pass, a trail with an extremely steep grade. Scott felt excited and confident as they approached the top of the path. His uncle planned to pace his descent at twenty-five miles an hour and had brought a speedometer to control it. Scott rolled his eyes and told his father how weird and dorky that was.

Scott set a fast pace for his own ride down the mountain and found it fun. "I thought I could handle it because it was paved and well traveled," he said. "A lot of people ride this trail. So could I." He rapidly picked up speed and took a curve too quickly. His bike skidded and he was thrown over the handlebars, arms and legs flailing. The result? Bloody elbows and knees, a serious case of road rash, and a very bruised ego.

The rest of his ride down the mountain was uneventful. "I was cautious. I took slow turns, slow everything. I got nervous when someone passed me. I kept thinking, at least I'm OK, no broken bones." When asked if he was surprised that he had fallen, he said, "I didn't really think it would happen."

RISKY BUSINESS

We know a lot about what makes a teenager an "at-risk" teenager; poverty, violence, substance abuse, neglect, and sexual assault just begin the list. Adolescents living under these conditions have a greater chance of dropping out of school, becoming pregnant, or turning to drugs. Even the "safe" end of the at-risk continuum includes smoking a cigarette, sipping a beer, and driving too fast—tantalizing and dicey adventures for the teenager.

The statistics are alarming:

- Seventeen percent of high school students seriously consider suicide; it's the third leading cause of death among teenagers (Center for Disease Control and Prevention, 2007).
- Seventy-seven percent of the calls to the National Runaway Switchboard (2008) are females, and the primary reason they give for running away is family dynamics.
- Nearly twelve percent of teenagers have used an illicit drug in the past month (compared to just over eight percent of the national population) (U.S. Department of Health and Human Services, 2002).
- Nearly fifty percent of high school seniors drink alcohol at least once a month (Johnston, O'Malley, & Bachman, 2003).
- About twenty-five percent of males are arrested before the age of eighteen (Ortiz, 2003).

Fortunately, not all teens face deprivation and abuse—most experience the world as a safe and secure place. But the changes brewing in the adolescent brain put them all at risk for making unhealthy decisions with somber consequences. Teenagers, in general, travel a dangerous road; reflecting back on your own adolescence will possibly evoke some ill thought out decisions and activities.

TECHNOLOGY MEETS THE TEENAGE BRAIN

"I swear at the computer game." "I want to karate chop my littler brother." "I'd like to punch somebody." These are all quotes from teens expressing their feelings while playing violent video games. As surprising as their remarks are, the real surprise came when I went into a classroom and asked who played violent video games, and three-quarters of the class unashamedly raised their hands.

There is no doubt that teenagers love video games; ninety percent play them regularly. They are the new generation's recreation of choice. As is true in so many things in life, there is an upside and a downside to this pastime.

Torkel Klingberg (Fernandez & Klingberg, 2006) found the upside. He conducted an intriguing study involving memory training through computer games. His research showed that some computer games were able to increase attention and reduce hyperactivity in middle schoolers with ADHD (attention-deficit/hyperactivity disorder). The more the game simulated real life, the more effectively it strengthened attention. To add further excitement to his discovery, memory and creativity also improved.

The downside to this technology comes in the form of violent video games. They are a prime example of an element introduced into the environment that counters everything the teen brain is working to overcome. Teenagers are trying to become more reflective and exhibit fewer knee-jerk reactions, but computer games play on their reflexive responses, encouraging them to make faster and faster decisions. Quickly they learn that blasting and exploding their way to the next level is the way to win.

There is no doubt the lack of impulse control is computer-game induced—frontal lobes actually become less active while playing violent video games and continue to remain so for a period of time. In addition, higher levels of testosterone are released into the system, further agitating the amygdala. The emotional amygdala is reinforced, and the reflective frontal lobes are neglected. The teen is now ripe to take this behavior out of the computer and into the classroom.

Neuroscientists also found that older adolescents who frequently played violent video games had less empathy. When shown real-life violent crimes, they underreacted. In effect, they become numb to others' pain and bloodshed.

Mirror neurons, the neurons that allow us to learn from observation, bring an interesting piece to the puzzle on violent video games. Cutting-edge research conducted by Marco Iacoboni (2008) led to speculation that playing violent video games (and watching violent movies) influenced imitative violence. The teenager who "kills" for hours on a video game is then more likely to become violent in real life. Frighteningly, in this context, neuroscientists found that individuals were often unaware and powerless when it came to producing or inhibiting the automatic imitations found in mirror neurons; it was beyond their control. The more subjects observed, the more they imitated. Hence, extensive playing of violent video games may put teenagers (and children and adults) at risk for aggressive and cruel violence.

In addition, Iacoboni's research team found that what a person brings to the game is more important than the game content. An adolescent who has a sense of what normal behavior is will recognize unhealthy behavior and not want to imitate it. Conversely, an adolescent who has experienced violence and aggression in life may view the violence in video games as normal behavior (Iacoboni, 2008).

Cell phones are another source of concern. Initially, the combination of driving and cell phone chats were thought to be brain possible. The multitasking required by this twosome calls for different parts of the brain to ignite, something the brain finds easy to do compared to two similar tasks. (For instance, it's simpler for the brain to listen to music and read than it is to write and speak at the same time.) However, researchers found that driving abilities were reduced by thirty-seven percent when talking on a cell phone, making it more likely to not stop at the red light and more likely to swerve into the next lane (Spice, 2008). Indeed, there seem to be limits on how far we can stretch the brain's multitasking abilities. Dangerous and deadly, cell phone use and driving are not brain compatible.

The Internet is another source of technology with multiple positive and negative possibilities. In one short decade, the Internet has redefined the term friendship. Web sites like My Space and Facebook enable teens to recover their long-lost friends, share thoughts instantaneously (no reflection necessary, discretion to the wind), and then back up their comments with personal pictures to ensure everyone has a visual. Teenagers are flocking to them like bees to honey; in their mind it's the perfect blend of friendship and technology. (Personally, thanks to his Facebook I just found out my son and his girlfriend broke up—he's now registered as "single.")

Surfing the Internet makes it possible for them to connect with chat rooms and blogs that share their common interests and activities 24/7. The support and camaraderie they find add to their social and emotional development. The adolescent fighting bulimia, the athlete considering steroids, or the student who just had a fight with a teacher can find a soul mate any day, anytime. Used properly, this type of technology can enrich lives and act as a techno safety-net.

The Internet also supplies us with a huge amount of information; for educators, this means the library doors expand the globe, increasing the growth of dendrites and synaptic connections. This has created a boon of knowledge, a school dream come true. As educators we walk the tightrope of enthusiastically embedding technology into our classrooms while vigilantly monitoring it's every click. This visionary technology, for all its promise, can cause loss of reputation, safety, and job. Cyberstalkers are eager to prey on the young and naïve. Teens too frequently disclose personal information that puts them at risk for becoming someone's victim. School and parental supervision are necessary for children and teenagers in this ever-expanding techno-world.

Instructional Strategies

Things to Try: Technology Rules!

- Collaboratively set up rules for working on computers at school. Rules might include the following:

    o Don't alter the hard or soft drive.
    o Stay on your assignment; computer work must be related to schoolwork.
    o Do not surf the Internet or check e-mail unless you have permission.
    o Print only the pages necessary—be Green.
    o Cite the URLs used for assignments; remember copyright laws.
    o Don't eat or drink near computers.
    o Share computer time with your peers, and limit your time if someone is waiting.
    o Report any problems (malfunctions, inappropriate sites) to the teacher.

- Allow all students access to technology. Be sensitive to homework that requires a computer—students may not have home access.
- Directly instruct students on how to determine if a source is credible or not. Then let them select a topic related to your content and send them surfing to find two legitimate and two shady sources.

(Continued)

(Continued)

- Discuss cybercrimes such as downloading games and music, hacking, and plagiarism. Then draw connections between the real world and the cyberworld; for example, pose these questions: Is it legal to go into a store and take a DVD without paying for it? Does this differ from downloading music without paying?
- Give students the benefit of the doubt at the outset; many don't realize that downloading and hacking are illegal. Consider it an honest mistake; then set up the expectation that now that they know better, they will do better.
- Permit pairs to work on computers; this becomes a true learning trifecta: socializing, subject content, and technology.

Secret Revealed

Neuroscientists compared the brains of individuals playing Nintendo with those doing simple arithmetic problems. Considering the flash and flair found in Nintendo, they expected to find the same kind of dynamic drama going on in the brain. Instead, they found the computer game stimulated a few meager areas of the brain, primarily vision and movement, while the basic arithmetic problems engaged the frontal lobes in both hemispheres of the brain.

CUTTING

Katie appears to be an average middle schooler; her father is a physician and her mom stays at home to care for the family, but in Katie's words, "my mom has issues." When Mom is in one of her ugly moods, it is not uncommon for her to call Katie a "whore," "worthless," and "stupid." Needless to say, their relationship is dysfunctional. During eighth grade, Katie began hanging out with older kids; she liked their company, and they seemed to have a lot in common. One night she went to a party; drinking was involved and before the night was over, she had been sexually assaulted by multiple boys; that's when she began cutting. With every cut, a little pressure was relieved; in her words, "It's a way to cope."

It has been said that boys explode and girls implode. Cutting, along with eating disorders and depression, is one of the chosen forms for teenage girls to implode. This form of self-harm is particularly prevalent in young adolescents. It stems primarily from environmental issues that exist outside the school walls. Sexual and physical abuse and neglect are the primary culprits, but the brain also plays a role.

Every cut acts as reinforcement for further cutting. As girls cut themselves, endorphins are released into their body, generating feelings of satisfaction and calming their wounded soul. At the same time, serotonin, the great pacifier, is not effectively used in their brains (Schwarz, 2006).

Cutting tends to occur during young adolescence, making middle school teachers the first line of defense. Be on the lookout for girls who always wears long sleeves to school, no matter how hot the weather. Once identified, these girls need to learn alternative, healthy coping skills with the help of professional counselors.

VIOLENCE AND AGGRESSION

The gym was reduced to a barroom brawl; punches were thrown, lips were split, and eyes were swollen shut. It was the ultimate fight: football players against wrestlers. No one knew how it started, and no one cared. It took ten teachers and three administrators to end the chaos. Once things calmed down, one of the rebels, Bruno, had the following to say, "The fight was between football players and wrestlers; it didn't matter who he was, if he was a football player, I was punching him. It was out of control."

Violence and aggression increase during the teenage years, particularly for males. The environment plays a large role in explaining this turbulent behavior, as does the search for autonomy (parents have less control than in childhood), but the brain is also a culprit. Neuroscientists are adding to the body of knowledge provided by psychologists and sociologists on this confrontational and cantankerous behavior during adolescence.

Serotonin levels have been linked to aggression and violence. Unfortunately for the teen, levels of serotonin in the prefrontal cortex are especially low, reducing its ability to control the emotional amygdala. There are also lower levels of glucose metabolism, an energy source, in the prefrontal cortex and higher levels in the amygdala, hippocampus, thalamus, and other emotional areas of the brain. As a result, we find less energy in the decision-making, logical part of the brain and more energy in the emotional areas of the brain (Dahl, 2003). Not the balance needed for healthy choices.

Secret Revealed

Teens are acutely susceptible to stress, peer pressure, and other negative forces. Controlling their lives is a struggle for most of them, and for some, violence becomes their means of taking charge. Interestingly, teens begin showing violence toward others around the age of sixteen, but as the brain develops they seem to grow out of it. If they haven't committed a violent crime by nineteen, they probably won't.

The uniqueness of the adolescent brain propelled Laurence Steinberg, a Temple University psychology professor, to prepare the legal brief for the U.S. Supreme Court from the American Psychological Association (Beckman, 2004). A case was made to differentiate juvenile criminals from adult criminals. In essence, they successfully argued that juveniles' brains are not fully developed (this does not mean they aren't responsible for their actions).

WHY NICE KIDS DO STUPID THINGS

Andy is fourteen years old and taller than most of his classmates. He is a quintessential class leader, liked by students and teachers equally. It is not uncommon for a group of kids to gather around Andy's desk as he tells funny stories about football practice—he can make anyone laugh and puts everyone at ease. He knows how to handle his popularity and is a responsible person. Still, he has some serious lapses of judgment. Last week, for instance, he was caught driving without an adult in the car. When asked why he was driving without a license or training, he simply replied, "I don't know."

Why do nice kids do stupid things? This is not a rhetorical question—adults want an answer. How can we explain the crazy behavior of teens and their decisions to try things even a child wouldn't risk? Blame their inherent cravings for novelty. Teen brains are drawn to rowdy and foolhardy acts, more so than children or adult brains. Novelty, especially when attached to the thrill of danger, is very attractive to adolescents because it produces intense feelings of pleasure that tempt even cautious and prudent teens to engage in dangerous experimentation. In the brain, novelty stimulates dopamine, which makes you feel good. It is believed the same neurons are affected by novelty as those affected by drugs such as cocaine. Reckless behavior provides the same rush. To complicate matters, levels of serotonin (the calming neurotransmitter) seem to decline during adolescence, further jeopardizing their stability and the likelihood of impulsive behavior (Chugani et al., 1999).

Secret Revealed

When two teenage drivers race along the road, darting through traffic in order to get ahead of each other, it's not because they think they are still on the sports field. They are doing it partly because of the risk and danger involved—risk and danger reward the brain because they trigger the very pleasurable dopamine. At this stage of life, risk and danger are fun!

Adolescents' attraction to novelty is in part responsible for their reckless behavior. Most educators think of novelty only in terms of livening up the classroom, but teens look for it in every facet of life. No wonder they flock to amusement parks to ride roller coasters and free-falling attractions—high speeds, fast corners, and turning upside down are not usually experienced on the school bus. When life seems too predictable, wild excitement can seem like a perfectly reasonable pursuit.

Neuroscience is shedding light on the wild side of the adolescent brain, too. Findings suggest the volatility of adolescent behavior is, in part, caused by the lack of emotional regulation in the frontal cortex (Spinks, 2002). Furthermore, the frontal lobes are not always functioning fully in teenagers, which suggests that they do not think through the potential consequences of the impulsive behaviors prompted by their amygdalas.

This imbalance between amygdala and frontal-lobe control in their brains may explain their minor and major at-risk behaviors, from arguing over a homework assignment to drug experimentation and unprotected sex. Think of a teacher-student confrontation. In each person, the frontal lobes consciously and logically analyze the information from the event, evaluate it, and decide upon a reaction (Siegel, 2001). Perhaps the frontal lobes in the adult and the adolescent identify accompanying emotions as fear and anger. The teacher, with fully developed frontal lobes, will probably get the mental signal to calm down because fighting with a student is inappropriate. The teenage student, however, is at the mercy of the amygdala and will likely react explosively by accusing the teacher of unfairness, calling the class stupid, or slamming books around.

Interestingly, increases in testosterone levels in males during puberty cause an enlarged growth in the amygdala. As a result, boys' amygdalas are much bigger than girls' (Giedd, Castellanos, Rajapakse, Vaituzis, & Rapoport, 1997). This proportional difference is thought to explain aggressiveness and greater at-risk behavior by boys. Still, this does not mean that all boys experience increased aggression just because their testosterone levels rise. Whether a boy reacts reflectively or impulsively to aggression depends on his disposition (Sylwester, 2000).

BAD THINGS HAPPEN TO OTHER PEOPLE

With her dark, curly hair swept neatly into a scrunchie on top of her head, tennis racket in hand, and shy demeanor, Jennifer hardly looked the risk-taking type. As she put it, "I'm generally a good kid."

But Saturday night, she and a friend sneaked out of the house to walk to an all-night convenience store. As teenage luck would have it, her dad walked past her closed bedroom door and noticed a slight draft. Curious, he gently knocked. There was no answer. After numerous attempts to awaken his daughter, he opened the door and discovered the empty bedroom and open window. When Jennifer returned, her father, in a tone mixed with anger and relief, asked simply, "Why?" Her response? "We wanted to. It seemed fun. Nothing was going to happen—it was just two blocks away." When reminded that her mother had specifically forbidden them to walk to the convenience store after dark, she said, "I thought Mom was being pointless and overprotective."

The teen brain is unaccustomed to relying on its frontal lobes. There are still lots of rough edges to smooth out before it becomes a fine-tuned thinking machine. Synapses are generating, pruning is liquidating cells, myelin is spreading—the changes literally boggle the mind. One of these rough edges is teens' belief that they are indestructible. As adolescents adjust to the frontal lobes' new capabilities of abstract thinking, symbolism, and logical reasoning, they become totally absorbed with themselves—naturally assuming that everyone else is, too! The next conclusion that adolescents draw is that they are pretty darn special. (Why else would everyone be so interested?) From their sense of their own uniqueness comes the frustration and loneliness of believing that no one could possibly understand them. With a condescending tone and a perfectly straight face, they can tell their parents, "You don't know what it's like to be in love!"

This belief in their unique place in the world promotes the belief they are invulnerable and nothing can hurt them, which leads them to take chances. They can walk alone at night without tempting fate. They can drive drunk, have unprotected sex, and experiment with drugs and face no serious consequences. Bad things happen to other people, not them (Rice & Dolgin, 2002). Their inability to determine the consequences of their behavior contributes to their mistaken view that they are indestructible. It also gives them permission to take risks because they don't fully comprehend the ramifications of the choices they make.

Instructional Strategies

Mr. Toad's Wild Ride

Three middle school boys were running down the street with a computer chair. One would sit on the chair while the other two pushed him down a hill—backwards. Mystified, I observed them for a few minutes before asking them what they were doing. One boy spoke up for the group and said, "We were bored. There's nothing better to do and it's really fun when the chair flips."

I, an adult, stood perplexed by their behavior. The hazards were obvious to me and certainly not worth the second or two of excitement riding a chair down the street provided! None of my friends would think it was fun. Even small children would think it was a harebrained, dangerous idea. But these boys decided, without hesitation, that it was perfectly safe. Teens seem to go out of their way to find thrills and chills. If you can bring the emotions of riding a roller coaster into your classroom, students will find learning (if not exactly thrilling) very exciting.

Things to Try

- Place less emphasis on textbooks and more on projects. Take away sedentary seat time and actively involve them in learning.
- Individualize the members of your class rather than always treating them as a group. Get to know each student's abilities, talents, and interests. Knowing who your students are and what they like is a first step in offering a curriculum that they can relate to and get enthused about.
- Play up problem-solving skills. Don't provide all the answers—let students discover solutions. The process of solving problems is what is important anyway, not necessarily having the correct answer. The ability to think abstractly, engage in reflective thought, hone critical reasoning skills, and develop alternative solutions to frustrating situations will create challenges and allow teens to take the risk of being original.
- Teach a thinking curriculum—content and process. Process will help students learn how to make decisions. Being skilled at a process is as powerful as having knowledge.
- Give students plenty of opportunities for success. Victory is a thrilling sensation, especially after a serious challenge. You don't always have to pit students against each other—pit cooperative groups against a difficult problem or help individual students master a task they've been struggling with.
- Encourage reasonable risk taking. Ask students to try something they've never done before, like inventing a game, composing and performing a song, learning a new sport, or designing a cartoon.
- Advocate involvement in extracurricular activities. An encouraging word can make the difference between taking the risk of personal involvement and sitting on the sidelines.

(Continued)

(Continued)

- Support afterschool programs for middle school students who are unsupervised after school. Middle school (and high school!) students left totally alone on a daily basis for long periods of time make poor choices. Adult supervision is a much-needed and well-deserved safety net.
- Scaffold, create that firm foundation for learning. Start with the concrete and get creative: Show a clip of modern dancers, and have students identify the geometric shapes in their movements.
- Encourage participation in sports. Running for the touchdown, kicking the winning goal, or securing the final match—it's hard to beat sports for healthy risk taking. In sports, effort is rewarded by achieving goals and gaining recognition, motivating the athlete to continue. Dopamine is in high swing, reinforcing every thrill. Additionally, preliminary research shows that participation in sports may reduce other types of risk-taking behavior (Bloom, Beal, & Kupfer, 2006).
- Rethink your school discipline policy; is punishment overused? In some schools, students are given detention for going to the restroom during class (it doesn't matter that your period just started), for not having their bottom completely on their chair, and for not having a pen in class (ignoring the fact that the pen ran out of ink while taking class notes). If this sounds like your school, it's time to reconsider the rules.

DECISIONS, DECISIONS

Adolescents face difficult decisions every day: to smoke or not to smoke, who to date, when to do homework, and where to go with friends. Research by educational psychologists parallels the information neuroscience reveals: Young adolescents demonstrate a lack of thought when they make decisions. Making decisions is a complicated process that involves searching for options, tapping into prior knowledge, problem solving, creativity, and evaluation. It's unrealistic to expect teenagers to organize information and make decisions with the same skill level as an adult.

A significant difference has been found between the ability of young adolescents and older adolescents to make decisions. For instance, when young adolescents consider careers, they may choose to be a professional athlete, movie star, or rock musician. To them, no career choice is

Three boys were arrested for breaking curfew. When the officer couldn't reach any of their parents, he told them they could make one phone call. Half an hour later a man showed up at the police station. The officer asked, "Are you their lawyer?" The man said, "No, I'm delivering the pizza they ordered."

—One teacher's joke about teenagers

unrealistic or impossible. It's simple—make a decision based on what interests you: "I want to be a lawyer, politician, chiropractor, or fashion designer." The increased brainpower of later adolescence, however, identifies more options, consults more experts, and anticipates future consequences of decisions (Friedman & Mann, 1993). Older adolescents weigh their personal interests with their values and capabilities, thereby making more realistic decisions: "I decided to be a biologist because I saw a pamphlet on it and it seemed fun. I'd done well in biology classes and thought they were interesting."

Secret Revealed

Why should teenagers worry? Parents and teachers already worry too much about what they're up to, so they don't bother. Actually, teens forge blindly ahead with whatever they want to do because they can't imagine all the things that could go wrong with the same clarity as an adult. Adolescents live for the moment and are under the notion that they are indestructible: They are not accustomed to letting their rational frontal lobes control their decisions. The excitable amygdala is having fun, so they go along. Until they learn to put emotional impulses in context and develop a sense of how the world affects them, teens are oblivious to the dangers that accompany jumping off the roof into the swimming pool (as well as to the problems of choosing a college based on where their girlfriend is going).

Teens tend to focus on the immediate future—right now—when they make choices. This is a severe limitation on the quality of their decisions—decisions they may have to live with for a week, month, or even a lifetime. Teachers, parents, and mentors can soften the potential blows of poor decision making by allowing teenagers to make age-appropriate decisions but structuring the larger, life-impacting decisions for them. For instance, choosing where they want to apply for a job, decorating their bedroom, and (in most cases) deciding what friends to hang around with are all age-appropriate decisions. Deciding to stay out all night, ditching school, or experimenting with drugs have long-lasting repercussions.

Friends carry a lot of influence when adolescents have to make decisions. If their friends think something is a good idea, teens are easily persuaded that it is. Sometimes their friends direct them down a solid path to a worthy decision. But beware. A teenager's well-intentioned friends are still teenagers themselves! They don't have the life experience to always make thoughtful decisions. And unpredictable teenage emotions complicate any matter; a teenager in a good mood will ignore a snotty remark, but that same teen in a bad mood might think starting a fight is the best response. Adolescents can benefit from direct instruction on the decision-making process. Peers and the emotion of the moment are powerful influences at the point of making decisions; having a backup plan to rely on can make the difference between teenage fun and teenage disaster.

**Directly teach
decision-making skills**

- Make a goal.
- Identify obstacles to realizing the goal.
- Find alternatives for overcoming each obstacle.
- Rank the alternatives.
- Choose the best alternative.

TEENS IN TROUBLE

October, 2003, in Sioux Falls, SD: A high school senior is charged and booked for possession of drugs and resisting arrest.

May, 2003, in Northbrook, IL: Twelfth-grade girls haze younger classmates by covering them in feces and hitting and kicking them.

October, 2002, in Virginia and Washington, DC: A sixteen-year-old boy and his surrogate father embark upon a sharp-shooting spree, leaving ten people dead in less than three weeks.

Sometimes adolescents make bad decisions that break not just school rules but also the law. These stories make headlines too often to be ignored. Adolescent crime is particularly unsettling; we see teens as children in many ways and have a difficult time comprehending how a child could commit an act so egregious. Much controversy surrounds the question of the legal culpability of minors. Advocates for adolescents agree that they should be held responsible for their actions, but not to the same degree as adults. They argue that the dramatic hormonal, emotional, and physical brain changes occurring during adolescence would benefit from a corrective, as opposed to punitive, stance (or sentence). No one thinks that teenagers are exempt from criminal sanctions, but many people wonder if incarceration is truly a solution. Our current juvenile correction programs have high recidivism rates, particularly at the larger facilities—once an adolescent enters the correctional system, it is difficult to break out.

GROUP IDENTITY

Teenagers want to be liked by their peers and be part of a group. Not only does belonging serve as a form of social validation (it is a benchmark against which they can measure themselves), it has the added bonus of being fun. Members of groups often share the qualities of age, race, and socioeconomic status, and among younger teens, they are of the same sex. These groups, the social cliques so often portrayed in movies and on television, take on distinct personalities: the preppies, the motorheads, the jocks, the nerds, the activists . . . the list goes on and on.

School is the perfect staging area for teenage groups. Because kids are required to attend school, they can always count on finding friends to eat lunch with, sit next to in class, or gossip with in the hallways. Within these gregarious groups are even tighter alliances; teens (as do adults) find a few people with whom they are extremely close—people they can count on for help and loyalty. From "She won't talk behind my back when I leave practice" and "I know he'll stand up for me in a fight" to "He'll bring home my schoolwork when I get sick," these intimate relationships form the foundation for positive self-esteem and social adjustment.

Gangs are the antithesis of friendly peer groups, although teens join them for many of the same reasons that their peers hang with the chess club or form an arts group: companionship, protection, and fun. Ironically, gangs reflect the positive cultural values of courage, heroism, masculinity, and physical strength; gang members express these values, however, through illegal and particularly violent acts. They provide security and protection to fellow members, but in antisocial ways—gangs directly challenge family, school, and police. A positive classroom environment can go a long way toward fulfilling the sense of belonging that so many students seek in dangerous places. From establishing a warm and inclusive classroom dynamic to building opportunities for productive social interaction into their lesson plans, teachers can make a difference in a lonely student's life.

Instructional Strategies

Working With At-Risk Kids

Derrick seems to cause problems wherever he goes. He purposely pushes other students in the hallways and instigates fights. Twice he's been suspended from school for fighting; one more incident and he'll be expelled. He is rude and defiant to teachers. He typically comes to class

(Continued)

(Continued)

late, sits at the back of the room, and falls asleep. He is belligerent and does not hesitate to yell profanities. He refuses to participate in class activities, doesn't complete assignments, and resists all efforts by the teachers to give help. He seems to be counting the days until he can drop out of school.

In the best-case scenario, students like Derrick are at risk of failing to take full advantage of the benefits of a high school education and in the worst-case scenario of dropping out altogether. Without a high school diploma, the adult workforce is one long, dead-end road. "Stay in school" isn't just a public service announcement cliché; it is an economic lifeline.

Things to Try

- Identify "at-risk" students as soon as possible. Early intervention plays a key role in setting them on the right track to academic success.
- Create a sense of hope by acknowledging that all students have a right to participate, and establish a community of fairness with clear rules that apply to everyone equally.
- Set clear, consistent boundaries. Involve students in determining class rules and consequences.
- Develop students' feelings of security with their peers. Promote noncompetitive group activities, and set challenges that are positive. Make sure that leader and supporting roles rotate among the students. Within group activities, help students concentrate on their similarities rather than their differences. (Just committing to work together on a project lays the foundation for one set of experiences they can share.)
- By concentrating on students' assets, you'll be able to better see and teach to their potential. Find ways for them to use their unique backgrounds to make positive contributions to the class. Helping others builds self-esteem; helping to build self-esteem and providing a caring environment are two effective ways to serve at-risk kids.
- Teach life skills like cooking, balancing a checkbook, or filling out a job application. Possessing the skills needed to maneuver through life reinforces a teen's sense of self-sufficiency and self-esteem.
- Vary your instruction by teaching to a range of learning styles and multiple intelligences. Include multicultural content. Let students know that you value all the classes taught at the school, from art and PE to music and community service opportunities.
- Ask students to assess (with a ten-point scale or simple rubric) how they feel at the beginning and end of the day. Discuss ways to cope with feelings.
- Have students write a personal mission statement to stimulate their thinking and help them set goals. Setting goals can make the difference between dropping out of school or walking across the auditorium to pick up a diploma.
- Do not eliminate repetitive practice, but do reduce it. Drill and routine can seem boring and meaningless; you'll lose student engagement eventually.
- Do keep unsupervised seatwork to a minimum. Adolescents too easily become distracted. They lack self-control and will benefit from your guidance.

- Do not rely on tracking—tracking is particularly damaging to low-achieving students because it has been abused too often to evoke confidence in its benefits. Rather than educating students more effectively, it has tended to merely separate them from each other. Offering help before or after school or arranging for a tutor or a mentor are better ways to provide academic assistance.

- Alter the assessment landscape with portfolio assessments, self-examination journals, and creative artwork.
- Encourage students to attend conflict-resolution and anger-management classes to increase their coping skills. Some schools offer these classes during the school day in an attempt to better serve their students; more options are probably offered through the community.
- Facilitate their involvement in extracurricular programs, community service, and after-school jobs. Not only do they provide opportunities to belong and succeed outside of academics, but they also allow the teenager to put their problem-solving skills to work in meaningful ways.
- Ask your school board, administrators, counselors, and fellow teachers if all students have the opportunity to take college prep courses. If the answer is no, consider it the perfect opportunity to become active in a worthy cause.

IT'S HARD TO JUST SAY NO

Walk into any hospital emergency room and you'll see some patients suffering from life-threatening conditions, like heart attacks or strokes, and other patients sporting relatively minor cuts and bruises. Everyone needs help, but for some patients, it's a matter of life or death. The same is true of adolescents—any teen is vulnerable to the temptation of having a drink or smoking a cigarette, but they aren't all equally at risk of becoming addicted to alcohol or nicotine.

Words like *adventurous, novelty seeker,* and *impulsive* are used to profile people with the highest risk of developing addictions (to anything), according to Dr. Alan Leshner, the director of the National Institute on Drug Abuse, who was interviewed on the NPR (National Public Radio) program *Gray Matters: Alcohol, Drugs and the Brain* (Kirchner & Gunther, 2000). These words also describe an adolescent! Is it any wonder that so many teens are at such a high risk for addiction? At the same time, it would be unfair to say all teenagers are "at-risk"—most are just transitioning between childhood and adulthood, trying to form an identity while facing childhood insecurities. It's a complex time of life.

The environment, genetics, and stages of brain development all make their contributions to the development of addictions. One of the more dra-

matic sociocultural studies was of Vietnam veterans in the late 1960s and early 1970s (Kirchner & Gunther, 2000). An unusually high number of soldiers were returning home addicted to heroin; eleven percent were using heroin on a regular basis—an alarming figure by anyone's account. The army was greatly concerned; this drug use threatened not only the military but also the stability of our homeland as these soldiers returned to their normal places in society. Curiously, within one year of returning to their normal lives, ninety-nine percent of the veterans that had been addicted were no longer using heroin. Once they were removed from the war environment, they found no reason to use the drug. A wartime Vietnam was perhaps more tolerable within the haze of a drug-induced cloud; the peacetime United States could be endured and even enjoyed with mental faculties intact. On an ordinary scale, teenagers who belong to certain groups of friends may find more "reasons" to indulge in alcohol and drug use than do teenagers who belong to a more sensible (or protective) crowd.

The genetic connection to alcoholism is also well researched. A few years ago, scientists excitedly believed they had identified an actual alcoholism gene (this was later disproved); the current genetic explanation is much more complex. It is now thought that a combination of genes creates a predisposition for alcoholism. Interestingly, individuals with a family history of alcoholism are less sensitive to the effects of alcohol. In other words, they can hold their liquor. A genetic predisposition to alcohol is only a predisposition, however. You may be at greater risk of developing a behavior, but you have a choice about your destiny. To drink or not to drink? Some people who are genetically predisposed never become alcoholics. The ones who do become alcoholics fight an uphill battle for recovery.

THE "DEADLY PLEASURE"

Approximately fifty percent of high school seniors drink once a month, more than a third of eighth graders have been drunk one or more times, and girls are particularly susceptible to alcohol addiction (Johnston et al., 2003). Alcohol kills brain cells, impairs the decision-making process, and spurs impulsive behavior. Girls put themselves in unsafe sexual situations, boys recklessly speed while driving, and both escape to the pleasant stupor found within a bottle of beer rather than addressing the problems that arise from living in the world. Habitual drinking begins as a voluntary activity within our control. Once we are hooked, however, the habit is unyielding and ruthless. Thoughts of alcohol permeate your consciousness. One recovering alcoholic admitted, "I thought about drinking constantly. I even dreamed about it."

Teenage drinking is a constant and clear problem (White, 2003), partly because alcohol modifies the brain. Typically, we feel a natural high when we hand in an excruciatingly long research paper or successfully give a speech in front of the class. Alcohol short-circuits the brain's ability to generate the natural high and leaves the brain demanding more alcohol for itself instead. (Alcohol is such an easy way to trigger the high that some people start to rely on it as a shortcut.) Research confirms the power of pleasurable experiences. Experiments in the 1950s and 1960s found that rats were so motivated by pleasure that they were willing to scamper across a hot griddle, run themselves to exhaustion, or go without food in order to press a lever that was connected to electrodes stimulating the pleasure area of their brain. Although humans may not be willing to walk across hot coals or starve to death for pleasure, it is a powerful motivator. A middle school principal told the story of a girl who always seemed to have a bad attitude in school; she put forth little effort academically or socially. One day her teacher casually complimented her on the pretty sweater she was wearing. For the next week the girl wore that same sweater every day to school. A simple compliment meant more to the girl than the teacher had ever dreamed.

ON SHAKY GROUND

Andrew Chambers, MD, at Yale School of Medicine believes that although society and genetics play a role in alcoholism, they fail to fully explain it. He was a member of a research team at Yale that studied the role of the brain, especially the adolescent brain, in the development of this disease. Using magnetic resonance imaging (MRI) technology, he found that adolescents are particularly susceptible to addictions like alcohol, nicotine, and drugs. The very regions that are rapidly changing within a teenager's brain—the frontal lobes and hippocampus—are also the ones associated with addiction. This fact may explain the rapid onset and endurance of addictions that begin in adolescence (Chambers, Taylor, & Potenza, 2003).

Secret Revealed

Why are teenage parties always represented with cigarette smoke in the air and alcohol flowing from kegs? Many assume that teens are impatient for the onset of adulthood and enjoy some of the privileges a few years early. Adults consider adolescents' binges as an unfortunate phase that will pass when they graduate from high school and college and can legally enjoy those substances. The work of Dr. Aaron White (2003) at Duke University, however, reveals that the rapid changes occurring in the adolescent brain—susceptibility to the rewards of dopamine, a decrease in serotonin levels, a disrupted sleeping cycle, and an attraction to danger—render teens vulnerable to addiction.

Not only are teens attracted to the altered states that accompany substance use, they are also in danger of building a dependence on the substance into the circuitry of their brain! An adult who drinks heavily may take five to fifteen years to become fully dependent on alcohol, but the adolescent may become addicted in less than eighteen months (Bloom, Beal, & Kupfer, 2006). Sadly, for many adolescents who succumb to the temptation of nicotine, alcohol, and other drugs, the developing processes in their brains will make it very easy to become addicted and very hard to kick the habit when they are older.

The adolescent hippocampus is especially sensitive to the adverse effects of alcohol (De Bellis et al., 2000). Alcohol interferes with new memories (rather than long-term, stored memories) by selectively shutting down the activity of cells it comes into contact with. In the best of circumstances it is easy to forget the name of people you just met, but under the influence of alcohol, you may not only forget their names but also forget even meeting them! The more you drink, the more the hippocampal circuitry is disrupted. Teenagers who drink suffer in cognitive performance—especially memory (Brown, Tapert, Granholm, & Delis, 2000). That history exam or list of Spanish vocabulary words is much more difficult to recall for teens who live life under the influence. Binge drinking (often defined as five drinks in a row for men and four for women) may result in a complete blackout with absolutely no memory of the event. In fact, memory may be affected for up to a month after a single binge-drinking episode. The hippocampus is generally very resilient—when drinking stops, it usually returns to normal cell structure and size—but MRIs show the hippocampus is smaller in adolescents who abuse alcohol on a regular basis. Preliminary research shows that if this brain structure is continually exposed to alcohol, it will suffer permanent damage (Uekermann, Daum, Schlebusch, Wiebel, & Trenckmann, 2003).

Alcohol also disrupts the workings of the prefrontal cortex, which is instrumental in making good decisions. Even if judgment and physical coordination are impaired, drunk teenagers still believe they are in control. From this perspective, those few shots of tequila have nothing to do with the ability to drive home (Lyvers, 2000). Alcohol also tends to reduce inhibitions in the subcortical regions of the brain that are responsible for sex, eating, and the "fight or flight" response, like the basal ganglia and cerebellum (both involved in movement) and the hypothalamus and amygdala (Zhu, Volkow, Ma, Fowler, & Wang, 2004). After a few too many drinks, the mild-mannered boy becomes irate if someone looks at his girlfriend or steps on his feet. The usually reserved girl sheds her clothes and skinny dips with strangers. Mary, a sophomore, remembers a time when a group of drunk guys decided to beat up a boy because they thought he was a loser; they were so drunk, they attacked one of their own friends. None of these things would happen under normal circumstances, but alcohol changes the rules of the game.

A HARD HABIT TO BREAK

As was explained in Chapter 4, "Communication and the Unfinished Brain," preliminary research points to the teenage brain being particularly sensitive to stress, which puts them at further risk for alcohol and drug abuse (substance abuse). Alcohol is a depressant that interferes with glutamate, the neurotransmitter that keeps us alert. Teens under a great deal of stress may turn to alcohol to reduce anxiety and tension because as they drink, they relax. If they drink enough, they will fall asleep.

Remember that the feelings of pleasure triggered by dopamine can be addictive. Some scientists believe that the alcoholic's brain doesn't release dopamine in normal amounts with the effect that there is a reduced feeling of natural pleasure; drinking more and more alcohol is required to reach the "stoned" zone (Volkow, Fowler, Wang, & Goldstein, 2002). Others believe that dopamine receptors in the brain do not function correctly, rendering the individual more vulnerable to addiction (Dagher et al., 2001). In either case, by drinking larger quantities, alcoholics can achieve extreme pleasure and so are seduced into drinking more and more.

The problem of addiction doesn't stop with alcohol. Nicotine is another legal drug chosen by teenagers. Just like the adolescent susceptibility to alcohol, people who begin smoking in their teens are particularly vulnerable to nicotine addiction because the region of the brain that governs impulse and motivation is not fully formed. Not only that, because of neural development and plasticity, a still-growing brain sculpts itself around the nicotine addiction, hard-wiring addiction into its very structure. Ninety percent of smokers had their first cigarette before the age of twenty-one; five percent of eighth graders and nearly twenty percent of high school seniors smoke regularly (*Adolescent Smoking Statistics*, 2003). Tobacco smoking, associated with lung cancer, cardiovascular disease, and emphysema, is the single largest identifiable cause of death in the United States. Perhaps this is because nicotine is one of the most addictive substances on earth—it causes dopamine to spike in the body and feeds the brain a steady stream of satisfaction afterward.

The teen brain is susceptible to other addictions, too, like cocaine, crack, marijuana, and heroin. Heroin use is at its highest in twenty-five years; ecstasy use nearly doubled from six percent of the population in 1996 to eleven percent in 2000. Like many aspects of technology, drug manufacturing has improved; drugs produced now are of a higher grade and more powerful than they used to be. Because of the changes occurring in the brain during adolescence, teens who use drugs risk permanently damaging their brains (Chambers et al., 2003).

Marco Iacoboni's (2008) groundbreaking research on mirror neurons has important implications. He specifically conducted research on smokers and found that when past smokers observed someone smoking, mirror neurons were automatically activated. They struck the lighter, inhaled the smoke, and then exhaled—vicariously enjoying every puff. This put them at greater risk of a smoking relapse. Iacoboni speculates that this has consequences for all addictive substances: alcohol, cocaine, and meth. The social nature of teenagers puts them particularly at risk when trying to break an addiction. They may find it intolerable to break the habit while at the same time remaining in the company of friends that have the bad habit.

Secret Revealed

"It was the summer after sixth grade; we were at the back of the city swimming pool, where a lot of bad things went down. Somebody that smoked let us all take a puff. I didn't really want to, but I did want to try." Obviously, this sixth grader, almost seventh grader, has mixed feelings about smoking, but push comes to shove and she gave it a try, a pretty typical choice for her age.

Warning for pregnant women: Smoking during pregnancy seems to rewire the infant brain making their future teenager susceptible to cigarette addiction. Teenagers whose mothers smoked during pregnancy showed signs of addiction after just five cigarettes. And for the skeptics in the crowd, these mothers did not smoke after pregnancy, eliminating the chance of it being the result of role modeling.

Instructional Strategies

Drugs, Alcohol, and Sex Education

As fourteen-year-old Amanda says, "It's not like when you're little and you think there's going to be this person in an alley saying, 'Do you wanna smoke?' It's so casual. A friend is smoking and they just say, 'Oh, would you like one?' It makes it easier and harder to say no." Antismoking and drinking programs have been met with mixed reviews. Even if they have increased public awareness to the problem, their impact on curbing drug or tobacco use is constantly up for debate. There is no simple solution to combating addiction and substance abuse in teens (or for that matter, eliminating risky behavior), but that doesn't mean schools shouldn't try.

Things to Try

- Encourage resilience by providing opportunities for meaningful participation. Once students have gained a skill, give them chances to use it. Act like a coach rather than a teacher, and let students work. If one attempt fails, encourage them to try again until they reach success.

- Introduce students to mentors. Gary Sykes, an expert on mentoring, pointed out that "a personality, rather than a technique, a skill or knowledge, was most important in touching the lives of students" (Taylor-Dunlop & Norton, 1997, p. 275). Someone with life experience can help teens expand their horizons and put possibilities like college, jobs, and extracurricular activities on their radar screen. Mentors can also encourage adolescents to pursue their goals, examine their belief system, listen to troubles and triumphs, and offer opportunities to assume responsibility. Whether a mentor is an older adolescent, a caring member from the community, or a recovered addict, he or she can still lend a hand. Despite their skepticism of adults and their ways, teens consider them very important.

- Develop character by having teens examine the people in their lives who inspire them, someone they want to emulate, a hero. Barack Obama? Hillary Clinton? Their teacher? Role models are examples we live by; watching how one person adapts to challenges in life gives guidance to how we can tackle the problems in our own.

(Continued)

(Continued)

- Bond, bond, and bond. Teens need to feel like they belong, and they need adults in their life who are interested in their well-being. Do as much as you can to reassure them that you want them to succeed and are willing to help.
- Divorcing parents, romantic breakups, and added responsibilities outside of school (like contributing to family finances and babysitting younger siblings) all contribute to stress in students' lives. Be aware of these important life changes and be sensitive to requests from students for accommodations. Feeling overwhelmed and powerless to cope with sudden changes is one reason many teens turn to drugs, alcohol, or reckless behavior in the first place.
- There are also many support groups on the Web; once checked out by a responsible adult, they can give twenty-four-hour-a-day support.

SCOTT THE MOUNTAIN BIKER: THE NEXT RIDE

Last week, Scott and his friend John hit a local bike trail. The two boys picked up speed and passed cyclist after cyclist on the path. With their heads down, they pushed forward harder and harder. No sooner had they whisked by a pair of "slowpokes" than came two other riders barreling from the opposite direction. The hair rose on their necks as they narrowly avoided a collision. "We made it!" John called, laughing and darting ahead at breakneck speed. But Scott slowed down with thoughts whirling in his mind. He'd already had one too-close-for-comfort call on his bicycle. Then he remembered a checklist his teacher had given them about staying safe and avoiding accidents. Pedaling more thoughtfully, he mentally checked off items on the list as he pedaled more carefully to catch up with his friend.

Reaching and Teaching Today's Adolescents— Tomorrow!

Our new understanding of the teenage brain and its unique characteristics should be reflected in how we run our schools and our classrooms. Now that educators and scientists are aware of what really drives teen cognition and behavior, middle schools and high schools need to reexamine how they are structured and how they can better help their adolescent population.

Make school a place that . . .

- Eases the transition from child brain to adolescent brain and appeals to teenagers' innate interest in the world around them
- Feels more like a community than an institution and nurtures teens' burgeoning sense of empathy and compassion
- Allows teens to explore and develop a self-identity and express themselves as individuals
- Provides the support and structure teens need to productively channel and invest their energy and enthusiasm

A Montreal community was drowning in poverty. More than a third of its residents were homeless or unemployed throughout their lifetime. The situation was grim. Social scientists had tracked the neighborhood for generations searching for an explanation for the high levels of violence and the low levels of education. In hopes of breaking the poverty cycle, they searched for common threads among the small number to reach middle class and found one: Miss A, a first-grade teacher. Miss A was a teacher who constantly reinforced the idea that school was important and could improve their lives, who spent extra time helping students who needed it, and who believed absolutely that every student was capable of learning. Amazingly, not one of Miss A's former students was homeless or unemployed. This one teacher made a life-altering difference to each and every one of her students (Fallon, 2002; Pedersen, Faucher, & Eaton, 1978). Her life and work is eloquent proof that teachers do matter to students and really can affect their lives.

TEACHERS MATTER

Working with adolescents can be both frustrating and rewarding. Teachers are dedicated to meeting the unique needs of the teenage brain but often find their efforts to tailor their curriculum unproductive. It's not easy to design a course that appeals to the unpredictable teen personality—they are simultaneously restless, self-conscious, impatient, and idealistic. The power of the primitive amygdala is partly to blame; adolescence is when the frontal lobes are just beginning to assert themselves and myelin just starting to coat the areas of the brain that improve higher-level reasoning and abstract thought. Teens aren't quite in full control of their rational faculties!

Educators are not innocent bystanders merely witnessing this transformation of the teenage brain. We either promote neural growth or stunt it depending on the kind of classrooms we set up. Our job is to figure out how to create classrooms that will foster learning, support emotional and social growth in our students' brains, and ease the transition from childhood to adulthood. However daunting this task appears at first glance, it is nonetheless very doable upon closer inspection. Teens come to school wanting to learn, wanting to form relationships with classmates and faculty, wanting the chance to express themselves as individuals, and wanting (however secretly) the guidance and advice teachers and administrators can give them. To meet these desires, all we have to do is adjust our schedules and routines in small ways that will nonetheless make a huge difference in the effectiveness of educational programs.

MAINTAINING THE DESIRE TO LEARN

In the last decade, a lot of time and money has been spent on determining what students need to learn. State governments have created the long lists of standards that give form to our curriculum. Their enthusiasm perhaps has taken them so far that students' personal interests—a very important part of the equation—have been overlooked. When we take student interest into consideration, we help guarantee that the standardized content can be applied to real life. This interplay between knowledge and application is critical to motivating students.

Just because the teen brain is becoming mature enough to understand the value of having information that may not be immediately appealing doesn't mean that everything a teen learns has to be presented in a dry and abstract manner. Too often we hear teenagers expressing their skepticism of academic content with a perplexed "Why do I need to know this?" (As one senior boy resignedly said, "The only thing I'm ever going to need calculus for is another math class.") Relevance is the key to gaining student attention and prompting motivation. Relating content to real life is imperative for learning to occur. It's difficult for students to find meaning and purpose from worksheets. Filling in the blanks with measurement units and matching fraction questions and answers can seem pointless; however, you'd be hard-pressed to find a student who isn't intrigued about applying these same skills to plan and build instrument storage cabinets for the band room or a gazebo for the school campus.

Despite observations to the contrary, teenagers are passionate beings. It is evident in their enthusiasm for sports, music, technology, and friends. The student who is bored by Marco Polo's travels to China may have memorized everything there is to know about the history of Middle Earth (the hobbit stuff); the student who skips math class may have spent the weekend programming computer software to enhance the play of a favorite video game; the student who spaces out in English class may have planned an elaborate surprise birthday party for a friend, complete with handmade invitations and party favors. These passions can be brought into the classroom if you sustain teens' natural curiosity.

Another Perspective

Adolescents are not merely proto-adults getting ready to enter the workforce. Rather, they're cognitive, physical, social, emotional, and spiritual beings. Students come to school to learn and grow; they prefer to be active participants in the process rather than passive recipients of knowledge. Their engagement is strengthened when they are involved in activities that stress thinking about what they are doing (as opposed to mimicking a technique or reciting information by rote). The development of abstract thinking skills and the analytical and

(Continued)

(Continued)

physical coordination skills made possible by the maturing frontal lobes, parietal lobes, and cerebellum means that teens are more capable than ever of understanding meaty, detailed information at greater depth. Provide opportunities for them to enjoy it!

Tap into adolescent interests by shifting your instructional strategies and content to appeal to your students, and you'll have a classroom full of self-motivated learners. Be adventurous; incorporate topics like animals, oceanography, basketball, World War I, chemicals, movies, politics, and finances into your prescribed curriculum. Besides, if students already have interesting background knowledge when they embark upon a new unit or lesson, their personal mastery of that subject doesn't seem like an arbitrary or remote possibility.

Students who believe that they have the chance to be successful are intrinsically motivated to learn; students who constantly face failure and criticism quickly define themselves as inadequate (Brendtro, Brokenleg, & Van Bockern, 2002). An educator's task is to curb feelings of inadequacy and promote a sense of mastery in our students. Because the brain is naturally social and collaborative, providing opportunities for personal interaction will engage students in the learning process and give them incentive to keep participating.

Offering choices to students is a wonderful way to encourage them to develop ownership of their learning. Identifying subtopics within a required unit is just one way to give students options. For instance, if you were studying communities, you could give students the choice of researching local government, hospitals, cemeteries, senior citizen centers, newspapers, or transportation. Not only will the variety motivate students to study an issue because it personally interests them, they will get practice making decisions and taking responsibility for the time they spend in your classroom. Like a sponge, the brain can soak up the material it encounters and still thirst for more.

Secret Revealed

A few years ago, neuroscientists found monkeys' brain signals could control a robotic arm reaching for objects and grasping for food. The world was amazed. This research has now been expanded, taking a particularly exciting tangent. Duke University (2008) studied the ability of a monkey's brain in the United States to control a robot's actions in Japan.

Electrodes were attached to the monkey's brain as he walked backward and forward on a treadmill. All the time, the electrodes were collecting information from the neurons. Researchers recorded the brain activity, made speculations concerning the pattern of the movements, and forwarded the commands to the robot. The robot walked.

The implications of this study reach beyond the ability to fascinate us. Researchers hope this discovery will lead to robotic leg braces for severely paralyzed people, allowing them to walk again and forever change their lives.

ADOLESCENTS ARE NOT ALL ALIKE

A recent visit to a middle school presented this all-too-familiar scene: A frustrated sixth grader stood with his head against his locker, staring into space, exhausted by his attempts to open the combination lock. According to the sympathetic, eighth-grade witness, he'd been standing like that for half an hour. It is easy for adults to forget what an anxious time these years can be!

Like high school students, middle school students struggle with puberty, the desire for independence, peer influence, and their interest in love and dating. Unlike high school students, they are struggling with a fundamental change in the way they are educated at the very same time. Middle school students go from being part of an established group with a single teacher in an elementary classroom to one of many students with a mix of teachers in a variety of classrooms. To top this off, they also suffer the loss of status as they go from being the top dogs at elementary school to occupying the lowest rung of the social ladder at middle school. No wonder these students and their parents pass more than a few sleepless nights in the days leading up to the change.

A smooth transition from elementary to secondary school cannot be made with one ceremonial tour of the building. The switch is better managed with a gradual exposure to the complex environment of lockers, hallways, and multiple teachers (versus the self-contained classroom and personalized cubbyholes to store class materials). Visiting the middle school well before school starts helps. Students need chances to find classrooms and practice opening a locker—that universal nemesis—with the full support of teachers, administrators, and other school staff. Query parents, administrators, and other teachers about ways to better accommodate new students at middle school

(or even high school!). Relieving incoming students from the stress of imagined terrors awaiting them on a new campus will benefit everyone during the first few weeks of the school year.

Realize, too, that middle school students have different needs than high school students. Great differences exist in the brains of older and younger adolescents. Older adolescents have a better reliance on their frontal lobes; they are more logical and less emotional, make better decisions, and think abstractly with ease. Younger adolescents are more reactionary, impulsive, and curious and are still trying to figure themselves out. Exploratory programs at the middle school level are an excellent way to expose them to a range of academic subjects like foreign languages, personal finance, music composition, and creative writing and to interests such as technology, student government, community service, and art as well as to recreational pastimes like intramural sports and clubs.

Wondering and seeking information helps them form their identity.

Still, middle school students welcome some familiar vestiges of their elementary school days. Interdisciplinary team teaching, or assigning a core of teachers to the same group of students, not only offers some of the security of a smaller group of classmates within a larger school setting, but it allows for much academic flexibility. When teams are in place, thematic units are possible. Teachers are often criticized for curriculum that is a mile wide and an inch thick; thematic units allow in-depth study, with richer learning. Thematic units do much more than integrate subjects—they encourage young teens to seek answers, dream, struggle, argue, and love the act of learning. A thematic unit on rivers, for example, provides chances to measure water levels, track animals, journal, determine power sources, research the history of the river, design maps and graphs, study local ecology, and maybe incorporate some travel. In-depth study of a subject requires a great deal of cooperation and work from the interdisciplinary team teachers, but despite its initial messiness, the effort pays off in the long run.

Middle schools can offer added support to young teens and their families by providing an afterschool program. The majority of adolescents have mothers and fathers who work outside the home, and the time gap between parents' schedules and school schedules can amount to more than twenty hours per week of unsupervised time. Afterschool programs provide safety for these kids and the communities they live in as well as a fun place to socialize with friends and enjoy some unstructured time after a day of school. But they don't have to be supervised parties; some programs use the time to teach kids the skills usually taught in organizations like 4-H and Girl Scouts. As a result, students develop a sense of self and build social relationships. The positive social and emotional effects of an afterschool program spill into other aspects of the middle school student's life, including academic performance.

Making It Work

Adolescence is when the brain starts to "think outside the body" and see the world from a broader perspective. Teens value novel experiences and appreciate the chance to exert their new cognitive and abstract thinking skills. Teachers and school administrators often perceive teens' goals to be at variance with their curriculum requirements and testing obligations, but student interests do not have to be suppressed in favor of instructional efficiency.

Federal and state legislation have put so many requirements on our school! How can we teach to proficiency on all these academic topics and still have time to incorporate students' personal interests?

Exploring students' personal interests by combining them with content leads to proficiency and achievement. Actively involving them in real-world projects, role-playing situations, writing, and physical activities will engage their brains, tap into their new cognitive strengths, and interest them in the next lesson.

If I hear "Why do I need to know this?" or "I'm never going to use this!" one more time, I'll scream. How can I help my students see the importance of what they are learning?

As frustrating as they can be, these exasperating questions really are legitimate concerns. The teen brain is so full of stimulus here and changes there, all of which are hard enough to keep track of. Teens want to be sure that teachers aren't wasting their time when their lives are already complicated. Help students see the connection between what they are learning and how to apply it to their lives by giving them real-world context for the subjects they study. If they can see how it will immediately benefit them to know something, you bet they'll pay attention! If you can't easily make a connection between academic concepts and practical application, investigate why those concepts are in the curriculum.

(Continued)

(Continued)

Middle school students start the year eager and optimistic about changing classes and learning "older" subjects, but by the end of the year they are listless and bored. What can we do to maintain their curiosity and expand their horizons?

Young teens are still learning where their interests lie. Choosing one elective class at the beginning of the semester is not enough opportunity to explore all the things that are out there! Chances to explore new turf within the classes they have—and through intramural clubs and activities—open their eyes to exciting possibilities. The more they learn about themselves, the more they'll want to know. We also need to be aware of what we are emphasizing. Scientists and psychologists have worried that our middle schools require too much multitasking and quick decision making. These tasks are emphasized at the expense of skills such as planning and reflection, important lifelong skills (Bloom, Beal, & Kupfer, 2006).

Those poor sixth graders who start school here! The look of fear on their faces is so pathetic. If they weren't so scared, I think some of them might actually enjoy the experience of middle school. Is there any way to make the transition easier?

Have you gone to elementary schools to ask fifth graders what makes them nervous about middle school? Addressing the specific fears and anxieties about what awaits them at their new school will go a long way to ease the transition. Recruit seventh and eighth graders to act as "buddies" for new sixth graders so students start the year with an older and wiser friend on campus. Invite parents to visit the school and learn what routines are in place (like how to handle absences or what kind of food the cafeteria offers). If students don't feel like complete strangers to the student body and the school system, they might actually anticipate (rather than dread) the change.

THE SPIRIT OF BELONGING

Belonging is a basic human need. Young children find belonging when they have someone to hold them, feed them, protect them, and otherwise assure them that the world is a safe and caring place. For adolescents, a sense of belonging comes with friends and family they can depend on and who respect, support, and validate them. Unfortunately, too many students live in the world without feeling like they belong there; they experience a world where neither the home nor community nor school meets their needs. Some desperate students form bonds with gangs or cults rather than live a life of loneliness and isolation. Although schools cannot completely fill the gap left by absent or disengaged parents, teachers have within their power the ability to make the six or seven hours students spend there warm and friendly.

But read the responses of a group of high school students asked to describe their school! "It's all about the worksheets—fill in the blanks or busy work." "There are a lot of rules. The teacher talks and we just sit; it's a long day." "Even the good kids get in trouble sometimes." These first impressions are harsh. Too many students regard school as an obligation, some unpleasant reality. Teachers are frustrated, too. We've all seen students who are physically, but not psychologically, present in the classroom. We spend the class talking, doing, and encouraging, but students are barely there, staring into space, oblivious to any and all of our efforts. They equate learning with negative feelings and have no plans to invest in the experience. To make matters more challenging, the abundance of testing and documentation that is required by state and federal mandates often overshadows the job of teaching. How can we meet the external dictates while still fostering the emotional and social growth of our students?

A supportive classroom environment starts with the teacher-student relationship. Make personal connections in small, sincere ways. Talk informally with your students, attend their extracurricular activities, and single out a few when you cross the lunchroom, and they will receive your message that you care about them. They appreciate it. One student commented, "Mr. Halsted always said 'hi' to us; even if we were far away, he'd yell our name and say 'hi.'" Another student said, "Mrs. Sorenson told funny stores about herself, like the first time she went skiing. Everyone there had perfect matching gear and she was dressed in blue ski pants, pink hat, red jacket, and brown mittens. She didn't know how to stop and crashed into a group of skiers all decked out in color-coordinated ski gear!" No wonder these students enjoy their teachers—Mr. Halsted and Mrs. Sorenson are considerate and fun loving.

Since teenagers face such pressure inside and outside of school, a caring teacher-student relationship is a protective factor against their stress-filled lives. If teachers can't completely protect their students from experiencing stress (and they can't), they can at least not add to it. Stress hurts. Mild forms of classroom stress come from teachers who are too controlling. "They always think they're right," one student said about such teachers. "You can't discuss anything with them. You tell them they missed a step and they say, 'No. The subject is closed.'" Higher levels of stress from constant yelling or threats like "At this rate you'll never graduate" not only negatively impact the individual student but the class as a whole. Students who may not be able to escape physically from stressful classrooms do so mentally. If they feel powerless or at the mercy of others, they may become aggressive or submissive just to cope.

In fact, creating a sense of belonging will reduce student stress. Teachers who give students a voice, pay attention to their interests, and make themselves available and approachable run less stressful classrooms. Accommodate students in this way by conferring with them and asking for their input—what do they think is a reasonable way to approach this assignment or that classroom rule? Each semester, give students one or two "late tickets" for assignments to turn in after a deadline without any penalties (the mere fact of knowing they could turn in an assignment late reduces anxiety). Set up an e-mail account for corresponding with students and check it regularly (even put assignments on a Web page). Finally, remind students when important events or deadlines are forthcoming—that common courtesy would be appreciated by anyone.

DEVELOPING A CONSCIENCE

Human beings find safety and comfort within the boundaries of a caring community, but accepting these benefits obligates the individual to give back to the community in return. Codes of ethics and morality exist to address the needs of communities to have an agreed-upon set of values and customs that makes living within a group as beneficial to everyone as possible. Moral character, however, does not develop naturally—it has to be encouraged and challenged. Teenagers, as members of many communities, deserve schools that promote moral sensitivity and character. These ideas can be taught through character education, sensitivity training, moral dilemmas, and community service or can be embedded in the curriculum. Morality and ethics discussions help students see their place in a larger community and understand the positive and negative consequences of their actions. Having students consider relevant questions, like whether or not truancy should be punished with suspension or whether one student should turn in another for cheating, are good starting places that can be accommodated in any class. School and life experiences that support moral character foster individuals with high self-esteem who are capable and willing to give back to others.

Teaching morality can be a dicey business. Take the character education programs at the middle school level—some teachers and students find them very meaningful, but others criticize them for having a "flavor of the week" approach (if it's Wednesday, it must be "Respect" day). High school moral education is often a free-for-all by individual teachers with no schoolwide efforts. Sure, values and cooperation are taught pervasively, but too indirectly. A concerted plan for moral education is necessary to real progress in this skill.

Moral education begins with realizing the importance and power of communication. It's through communication that we relay our thoughts and begin to understand someone else's. Understanding how other people's words affect you and how your words affect them increases our sensitivity. The eleventh grader who says, "That is the stupidest thing I've ever heard," "Who cares?" or "Do you ever shut up?" may be expressing an honest response but needs to know how that choice of words affects her peers.

Knowing that we have a variety of choices available when we make decisions and then making the correct choice advances us up the moral ladder. It isn't until we develop abstract thought that we realize the multitude of possibilities and the probable consequences of most situations. Making decisions is more than deciding "What works for me?" Mature and sensitive people take into account the effect their behavior has on others. Adolescents are finally in a position to understand that they have options about what actions to take. Teenagers start to realize that they can control what they do in advance of an event: "I'm going to drink at the party," "I'm going to the party, but I'm not going to drink," or "I'm not going to the party; I'll find something else to do." They ponder how their choices will affect themselves and their friends, teachers, and parents before making a decision.

Another Perspective

Teenagers who always choose the party or the television program over dinner with family or algebra homework need to be challenged in their thoughts—what's really important and why? Morally motivated individuals are capable of prioritizing personal values such as school, friends, work, and pleasures. Setting priorities lets us reflect on what is important and what is peripheral to our lives. Teenagers who only value partying until dawn, using the TV clicker adeptly, and ordering fast food efficiently are going to face some serious disadvantages when they embark upon adult moral terrain. If they are unable to engage in the normal give-and-take of personal interactions while still under the protection of their parents and teachers, how are they going to navigate through life when they have job responsibilities and landlords?

Individuals with moral character live up to the strength of their convictions. They are able to persist in the face of fatigue, discouragement, or distractions. This takes work. Too often it's easier to go along with the crowd instead of taking a stand or fighting the good fight because it seems like too much effort to bother. To overcome challenges, we set goals and exhibit self-discipline. And age has nothing to do with the ability to instill positive change. Teenagers start charity drives, do community fundraising, and take up the cause of political candidates. Their actions belie their moral convictions.

THROUGH ANOTHER'S EYES

As adolescents begin to see from the perspectives of other people, they acquire empathy. From empathy develops altruistic behavior. A spirit of generosity is based in unselfish and giving behavior. Children are egocentric by nature—it's beyond their mental capabilities to realize that other people have different feelings and experiences. They perceive the world by how it affects them; if they are happy, everyone must be happy! Adopting an alternate perspective is the first step towards becoming less egocentric. Seeing the world through another person's eyes enhances your ability to be empathetic. As the adolescent brain develops, the world broadens and teens are able to look at matters from the perspective of others (Brendtro et al., 2002; Woolfolk, 2006).

Service learning is an effective way for teenagers to develop a spirit of generosity. More than just volunteering, service learning invigorates the traditional classroom by incorporating students' educational backgrounds into service. Students profit from the feelings of empathy and altruism they develop through this experience, and the community profits from their meaningful contributions (Witmer & Anderson, 1994). High school students who mentor at a middle school afterschool program or track water levels for a local environmental agency benefit themselves and others.

Classrooms that nurture a spirit of generosity and encourage morality create an atmosphere where all individuals know they are worthy because everyone is needed to sustain and enrich the community. As individuals grow, the group is strengthened. The aim is for all to reach their full potential, not just a select few. Only in this way will all benefit and will the group flourish. Altruistic behavior may begin in the classroom, but it expands to the community, family, future coworkers, and possibly the nation. Adolescents who learn how to make contributions to the world around them will live satisfying lives and come that much closer to self-actualization.

Making It Work

The brain's instinct is to flock to social groups, and teens are usually enthusiastic about the chance to pal around with each other, especially during class. Teamwork and community involvement also help adolescents learn to appreciate the strengths and talents other people possess, as well as instill in them a sense of pride when they can lend their strengths and talents to help another person. Focus their attention and energy on ways they can contribute and you'll find yourself in a class of willing participants.

Besides the fact that they live within the same school boundaries, my students are too diverse to make a community. Some work after school, some play sports, some are just biding time until graduation. . . . They have nothing in common outside of school.

No matter what teenagers spend their free time doing, they all need and want a place to belong. The fact that they spend seven or eight hours a day together is sufficient reason to make school a community in which everyone is an important member. They share classrooms, lunch yards, and other school facilities—they have plenty of commonalities to act as starting points for them to develop new interests together.

I have great students, but if I spent time every day talking to them, we'd never get any work done!

Teachers are the focal point of the classroom community, not because they have the most authority but because the teacher is the one constant in a class that may have students transferring in and out as schedules change or families move. It takes only a few minutes a day for a teacher to greet students at the door and ask individual students about personal milestones or struggles. A smile every day to the class and a kind word to an individual student once in a while go a long way toward making teens feel as though they are valued within the community.

Once teens start talking to each other, it's hard to get them to stop! Won't mixing socialization and academics be too much of a distraction in class?

Socializing is an important part of adolescence. Teenagers are compelled to seek out each other's company. Combining socialization with academics will probably reduce their distractibility during class time because the opportunity to interact constructively has been provided for them. Cooperative groups, peer tutoring, and support teams are just a few ways to meet their need to socialize and your need to deliver content.

(Continued)

(Continued)

I am a moral person, but I have no business foisting my beliefs on anyone else. Besides, shouldn't public schools stay out of the morality business?

Morality is not solely the province of religion. Giving adolescents the tools to make thoughtful decisions, communicate effectively, understand other people's viewpoints, respect diversity, and actively contribute to the world they live in is an obligation of every adult in their lives. Moral development in school is as useful as cognitive development, and teens will benefit from it just as much.

LENDING A HELPING HAND

Puberty and adolescence can be a very lonely time for some teenagers. Their bodies and brains are changing so rapidly that they often do not know if they are coming or going. They surprise themselves by what they say and often overreact to what other people say to them. More than a few adolescents become so unsettled that they develop an unhealthy fixation on themselves and their problems. They appreciate the attention and assistance a concerned adult can give them, but they desperately need the company of peers, too—peers who can empathize with them because they are also in a state of rapid biological and cognitive change.

Another Perspective

The success of a peer-tutoring program depends on how it is presented to participating teens. Enforce the idea that it is a partnership with no passive roles. The tutor is not the person doing all the work—the tutee must be willing to express his or her thoughts on the subject, ask questions, and take risks. If peers don't communicate their feelings and ideas about the subject matter, then there is no way of knowing if knowledge is being shared and developed.

With sufficient preparation and the right attitude, adolescents can benefit from peer-tutoring relationships in ways that would not be achieved in an adult tutor relationship. Interaction is more balanced and lively between peers, which contributes to positive emotions. Because peer tutoring usually occurs on campus—within a class period, during study hall, or before and after school—it takes place in a familiar environment. Finally, it's far more likely that a tutee will get the chance to return the favor later by tutoring a peer tutor in another subject. Both participants benefit.

Frequently, putting aside one's own problems to help other people with theirs is therapeutic. Peer tutoring—one student helping another student (at the same grade level) with a skill or concept—is one particularly useful arrangement for teenagers struggling with this stage of life. Not only have successful peer-tutoring programs been found to improve the tutee's academics, social interactions, classroom discipline, and peer relations but also to benefit the other individuals involved (Thomas, 1993; Kalkowski, 1995).

The enjoyment tutors find while helping a peer is obvious: They get to be a font of knowledge and information, which builds confidence; and they reap the internal benefits of altruism. The tutee is perhaps in a more precarious position. On the one hand, some students find it difficult to accept help from anyone, especially from someone their age. On the other hand, the tutee benefits from personalized attention in an era when schools are overcrowded and teachers are overextended. A peer-tutoring program, formal or informal, that is structured to put everyone at some point in the roles of tutee and tutor (after all, everyone has some expertise to share) is much more likely to be welcomed by students. It is even better if the teacher or adviser spends time at the beginning training students on how to be successful tutors; one class period is usually sufficient. A mind-set in which students relate to each other and understand that it is important for everyone to learn makes peer tutoring a rewarding experience for all participants.

TO EACH HIS OWN

Another way to help adolescents confused by the changes they experience is to acknowledge that the changes are happening. Yes, it's normal to hang out with a new group of friends; yes, it's normal to change your mind about what you want to do in the future. By adolescence, each teen has a unique set of background experiences, personal interests, aptitudes, and curiosities that combine to create an environment of many different individual needs. Even the most rigid standards of curriculum can be expanded to address this diversity of learning needs and desires. Furthermore, the use of cooperative learning groups allows students to teach each other. With more "instructors" in the classroom, content delivery and performance will be that much more diverse.

Differentiated instruction is one method of reaching a multitude of interests at once. It is based on two premises: (1) There are multiple paths to learning for different abilities. (2) Every brain is unique. Content is presented in ways that address personal interests and different styles of learning. Teachers can differentiate instruction through the content choices, delivery processes, learning products and outcomes, and individual learning styles. Furthermore, varying experiences help student brains remember what they've learned. Problem-solving assignments give students multiple ways to arrive at the same solution. Cooperative learning groups, hands-on and student-centered activities, and flexible scheduling are all ways to address students' questions, focus on real life, actively engage learning, and emphasize collaboration and community between peers.

MEANINGFUL ASSESSMENT

"I did not get along well with my French teacher, so I was surprised when I was chosen to take a prestigious exam; it was an honor. I had to go everyday for two weeks for tutoring before the exam. I had to be there on time—exactly. I kept dreaming about it every night; it just kept running through my mind. I woke up once, thought it was time to take the test, woke up my mom, she showered, we ate breakfast, and then realized it was still dark outside—it was 4:00 a.m. It was so stressful!"

As teens' interests and passions develop, so do their talents. Discovering an aptitude for a certain skill or task frequently encourages a student to apply it in other ways—like with an enthusiastic demonstration to the teacher! Teens practically burst with excitement when they finally solve a problem or comprehend an idea that has been eluding them. They are eager and proud to show off their newfound knowledge. Many classrooms, however, have no provisions for incorporating these spontaneous demonstrations into formal assessments.

The responsibility of educating our youth is filled with more and more objectives and guidelines, and the proof required of schools and teachers is overwhelmingly in the form of standardized tests. Politicians and administrators emphasize assessment with the best of intentions—to improve education in our schools—but their insistence on evaluating students by statistics and numbers has forced educators to concentrate on memorized facts and to define students by test scores. Not to mention the fact that divergent, creative thinking goes out the window in favor of the one correct answer required in standardized tests. The ability to think divergently, to problem solve, would serve them better in real life.

One teacher commented, "There is more emphasis on finding out what students don't know than what they do know." This overemphasis on traditional assessment establishes an atmosphere of stress and competition within the classroom. The message to work against one another, as opposed to working with each other, is the one most heard by students (and it is heard loudly). Although some students thrive in this competitive atmosphere, many develop feelings of inferiority.

The focus on assessment needs to shift from who made the grade and who did not to making good decisions in the best interest of our students. Meaningful assessment accounts for individual differences in style, attitudes, and interests. Ongoing records, discussions, anecdotal notes, portfolio entries, conferences, and observations are all means by which we can informally assess students and develop a picture of their individual progress. Formal assessments, often the preferred way to determine what students have learned, can take the traditional form of a paper-and-pencil test, or they can include personalized, performance-based assessments in the form of portfolios, presentations, projects, science experiments, written reports, and short investigations. Before selecting any type of assessment, consider your purpose and the student you are assessing, and match that to an appropriate assessment tool.

Although multiple-choice tests are quick to grade (and therefore cheap!) and easy to compare against students from other districts or other nations, they are not the best way to get a complete picture of what a student has accomplished during a course. Furthermore, they are mentally exhausting and minimally inspiring. Learning where your score falls against the national percentile is not nearly as rewarding as hearing the applause for giving a great oral presentation or seeing your annotated diagram of how space dust becomes a solar system hanging in the front office.

Making It Work

The physical and mental experience of adolescence is trying enough, even without the stress of succeeding in a school where uniformity is the primary experience. When students are asked to excel at the same subjects and demonstrate knowledge in the same way, is it any wonder that some teens criticize themselves as never being able to fit in? Offering variety in content, instruction style, and assessment methods reinforces the idea that teens don't have to be the same. Rather than worrying about whether their term papers are as good as everyone else's, teens—given the freedom to pursue their interests and talents—focus instead on what they are good at.

I feel like my students are completely overtested, but I have no control over the federal and district mandates that require the testing. What can I do to ensure that what we are testing is meaningful to the students?

Students do take a lot of tests these days, but assessments have potential to help students and teachers. Change the way you perceive them. Explain to students that testing is just another form

(Continued)

(Continued)

of feedback that helps them see what they did correctly and what they need to fix. Use your class scores to identify points of mastery and holes in the group's knowledge when you design your lesson plans.

How can I meet the individual needs of my students and at the same time deal with a classroom full of thirty students?

Although no one will tell you it is easy to individualize curriculum to meet students' personal interest and academic levels, the payoff is tremendous. Differentiated instruction and teaching to the multiple intelligences helps every student reach his or her potential. But you don't have to write several different lesson plans for each day of class—build flexibility into your instruction. Offer students choices about how they would like to present work or about what subtopics they'd like to study more.

My students hate cooperative groups and so do I. One or two people end up doing all the work, and the other kids in the group get credit for them. Why should I waste any more class time with them?

Working cooperatively in groups doesn't come naturally to teens—you will have to teach them how. But using cooperative groups in the classroom doesn't come naturally to teachers. It's a skill that needs to be learned and practiced. If there are no staff development opportunities available for you to learn how to structure and manage a cooperative group, find a book about it. Many titles are available that address cooperative learning in a variety of situations; *Cooperative Learning* by Spencer Kagan (1994) is an excellent start.

In general, start with small groups doing short assignments (perhaps pairs of students analyzing a poem). Gradually expand to more complex projects and larger groups. Diversity within the groups promotes a better exchange of ideas (and therefore better learning); sometimes mix boys and girls and high achievers and low achievers to achieve a heterogeneous mix. If your first attempt at using cooperative groups in your classroom is less than successful, don't give up. Most things worthwhile don't come easy.

FRIENDLY ADULTS

Peer interaction is not enough to help teenagers become healthy adults. Even the nicest friends are subject to the upheaval of the teen brain, too! Left alone, responsible teenagers frequently engage in risky activities for the simple reason that it seemed like a good idea at the time. Running an idea by an adult first often averts disaster. It's not that easy, however, for some students to find adults to talk to. Parents often work two jobs, neighbors often don't know each other, and teachers and administrators are stretched thin at crowded schools. Chances to interact with adults on a personal level are usually hit or miss. Some students are fortunate enough to have a relationship with a coach or extracurricular adviser, but many are not. Time scheduled during the school day for students to share their interests and concerns with dedicated adults will support their social and emotional growth.

An advisory program can be a veritable lifeline. It guarantees the opportunity for a student to interact meaningfully with peers and an adult. It also creates a sense of belonging in the classroom. More than a reincarnation of the traditional homeroom class (where nothing happened but taking attendance and making announcements), advisory programs build close relationships between students and adults. Relatively small groups of students, ideally fewer than twenty, are assigned during one period to a caring teacher, administrator, or other staff member to form a safe haven in which advisers and advisees communicate abut issues near and dear to the teenage heart. Topics of discussion may range from becoming an oceanographer or a nurse to why your mother makes you wear a coat or do chores. Programs like this contribute to a better school climate and develop student self-concept (Coleman, 1996).

Another Perspective

Even though the definition of family is changing, one thing is not—students need their parents or guardians involved in their life. Caring teachers, coaches, and mentors can enhance the security families provide, but they can never replace it. You may have to extend special efforts to involve some families in school activities. Single parents, grandparents acting as parents, and guardians are often struggling with issues that the traditional family does not face. Shortage of time and financial strains may further impact any family's ability to interact with the school. Immigrant parents may have limited experiences in classrooms and find schools foreboding and unwelcoming places. Illiteracy or the inability to speak English may prompt further separation. Unconditional acceptance and realistic expectations will foster their involvement.

Mentoring programs that introduce caring adults in the community to teenagers serve many of the same purposes as advisory programs, although they are not centered in the classroom. Mentoring is a one-on-one relationship between an adult and teen based on trust. The teen learns to rely on a mentor as a constant presence in his or her life. Their commitment to each other is long term; rather than a semester or school year, mentor friendships can last a lifetime. Because mentors are usually older and more experienced than the mentee, they guide and nurture the adolescent's growth, giving structure to the tumultuous teenage life.

Mentors provide support in a variety of ways to the teenager. They care just as much about band practice and Friday-night parties as academic achievement. ("Finally!" you can hear teenagers sigh in collective relief, "somebody cares about the same things we care about!") This caring adult provides a friendly forum for examining and communicating thoughts and views. Opinions like "I think we should lower the drinking age" and indignant questions like "Why can't we drive at fifteen?" are bantered in a casual atmosphere. The typical adult (parents or teachers) may be tempted to use these openings for a lecture on what the teen should and shouldn't do—the choices are clear, after all, to them. The savvy mentor knows that it is far more productive to withhold judgment and encourage the teen to explore their thoughts with a responsible adult rather than limiting such discussions to their age-mates. Mentors, like teachers, also serve as important academic role models. They can demonstrate professional skills, such as how to be an effective writer or researcher, or personal skills, such as how to be a gracious winner or loser.

READY, SET, GOAL

As adults, it's easy to understand why students need to understand this or memorize that. Communicating the reason to teenagers is where the challenge comes. Secondary education—splintered across many subjects and rampant with rules about what classes to take when and requirements for graduation—can be so overwhelming that success seems unattainable. Goals, which motivate people to act, are a way to connect the student with the curriculum. Goals also direct our attention to what we still need to accomplish to achieve our desires. Teenagers become engaged in learning when they see a practical application for a course. Showing them how learning algebra will help them finance a car or how writing with correct grammar will help them get a job (to pay for the car loan!) will increase their motivation to succeed.

Goals are motivators because they are personal challenges. (Objectives that are too easy to accomplish have little meaning.) Difficult, but not impossible, goals inspire us to work just a little harder and more creatively to achieve them. If something in our strategy for reaching a difficult goal goes awry, we devise alternate strategies to succeed. If we want to make the varsity dance team and don't, we try for the junior varsity team or work harder in other dance classes. On the other hand, aspirations that are unreachable are very easy to abandon. Many middle schools and high schools actively teach and promote reasonable goal setting. One school district has students write their goals for each course and share them with their parents at conferences. Not only does the writing of goals give students some direction for success in a course, the goals serve as an excellent communication tool between school and home.

Setting goals also grounds students in realism. If they can say, "I want a high school diploma" or "I plan to paint houses when I finish school," most likely those things will happen. Sadly, many adolescents don't understand what goals are and answer the question "What are your goals for after high school?" with responses like "Skateboarding," "Modeling," "Either be a scientist or beautician," and "Play for the NFL" (this from a boy who had never joined the football team!). Not that skateboarding and modeling aren't possible careers—but if the only plans they've made to attain them are to assume that they will be discovered by talent scouts while walking down the street, they are not likely to realize these dreams. A student who can't decide between scientist and beautician has made no differentiation between the educational demands and requirements of the two careers. Students need goals that are realistic and attainable, not fantasies, and we should teach our students how to create them.

Setting short-term goals reduces the likelihood that students will become distracted by other goals. A seventh-grade teacher who only promotes setting goals for how to live life after college will find that students have trouble staying focused on events so far away. It has been said that to the middle school mind the future is 3:00 p.m., or whatever time they get out of school. Even high school seems like a lifetime away. (Hardly a coincidence, a sense of time and future doesn't develop until about age fifteen or sixteen, when the frontal lobes take on more responsibility.) Work with students to establish goals that are worth accomplishing (personally meaningful), and follow up with their progress.

Ways to Practice Setting Goals

- Project completion timelines
- Explore careers
- Establish study habits
- Prioritize amounts and types of social involvement
- Personalize unit goals
- Share goals with friends
- Brainstorm ways to achieve goals

Goals to Set

- Apply to college
- Solo in chorus
- Earn a part in a play
- Achieve in sports
- Attain an advanced seat in band or orchestra
- Run for class office for extracurricular activities
- Accumulate volunteer hours
- Choose a behavior to improve
- Commit to beneficial exercise habits
- Eat healthier

Making It Work

Apprenticeships are as old as industry itself. The best way to learn to be a silversmith is to train with one. Learning to be an adult is no different. Teens who are left to their own devices or who spend most of their time in the company of friends enter adulthood without the same wisdom and perspective that many of their peers have. Schools need to give teens the chance to interact with adults as individuals so they can thrive and eventually make productive contributions to society.

More than seventy percent of the students at our school qualify for free or reduced lunch, and the majority are from single-parent homes. What meaningful support could we possibly offer to these adolescents?

Time during the day to discuss life's triumphs and difficulties, like during an advisory period, goes some distance toward supplementing the attention they get from their family. Advisers are also in a position to identify kids who might be at risk so that they can get the immediate intervention that they need. Establishing a relationship with a mentor also gives the student the chance to interact with an adult who does not need his or her help as a babysitter or wage earner—during the time they spend together, the teen is free to meet his or her own needs first.

Parents in our neighborhood are just so busy.
How can we get them involved if they don't have the time?

Most parents come to open house, and many are willing to help but don't know how. Take the initiative and communicate—through a school Web site or with a newsletter—specific ways they can participate. Besides chaperoning field trips, businesspeople can open their office to student interns, and crafty parents can help make costumes for the drama department; other parents can staff homework centers or act as translators for parents who may not speak English well. Identify what you would like from parents and then ask for it.

How can I teach goal setting when class time is
already filled trying to get through all the standards?

Goal setting isn't something you spend a day or week on and then hope students do it themselves for the rest of the year. Goal setting should be incorporated into every single lesson plan of every subject. It takes mere seconds to do. Ask students to write down what they hope to accomplish during a science project, or ask them to make a checkoff list for tasks they need to complete before finishing a term paper. Teachers already have students keep assignment books and homework logs—goals are just another element to include.

Conclusion

Secrets of the Teenage Brain—Revealed!

No one has a more challenging job than teachers and school administrators who work with teens on a daily basis. Until recently, we've had only our personal experiences and our preservice college classes to guide us down the rocky path of instructing adolescents (and we've done amazingly well). Now, discoveries about the brain and how it changes provide clues to help us solve the mystery about why teenagers behave the way they do. Even information that confirms what we already suspected sheds light on the motivations and desires of these students.

Any book on education risks overwhelming the reader. Idea after idea is put forth—far too many to implement at once. So start small. Take from this book one or two suggestions that have the most meaning for you, and work them into your classroom routine. That way you won't bury yourself in unrealistic expectations but will rather grow new dendrites in your own brain as you strive to make your classroom adolescent friendly.

Adolescence is a pivotal time in a person's development. The changes teens experience determine much about who they are—their work ethic, interests, self-esteem, morality—and who they will become. This, in turn, shapes our society; teachers play a critical role in determining the kinds of people who will lead us into the future. Educating teenagers is not an easy job, but it is a rewarding one. As the world becomes "smaller" and our activities more global, teachers quite literally are changing the world— one teenager at a time.

In Summary

CHAPTER 1. TEEN BRAIN: UNDER CONSTRUCTION

Teen brains resemble blueprints more than they resemble skyscrapers. Instead of thinking about a teenage mind as an empty house that needs furnishings, understand it as the framing of a house that still needs walls, wiring, and a roof.

You've learned that . . .

- The brain, not hormones, is to blame for the inexplicable behavior of teens
- Short-term memory increases by about thirty percent during adolescence
- The activities teens invest their time and energy in influence what activities they'll invest in as adults
- Teens are ruled far more by their emotions than by logic

CHAPTER 2. TEEN COGNITION AND LEARNING

Teenagers are not incoherent, clumsy, sex-crazed, unpredictable, irrational monsters who can't be reasoned with—they are intelligent creatures not yet accustomed to their (unevenly) burgeoning mental strengths and capabilities. Adolescence is a time of startling growth and streamlining in the brain, enabling teens to think abstractly, speak expressively, and move gracefully.

You've learned that . . .

- The teen brain is particularly susceptible to novelty
- The burst of growth in the frontal lobes means that teens overcomplicate problems, idealize the world, and say one thing while doing another

- The development of the parietal lobes helps teen athletes improve their pace and teen musicians improve their beat
- Physical movement helps the cerebellum develop, thereby helping teens improve their cognitive processing skills
- Feedback improves the brain's efficiency
- Teens crave structure and organization in spite of their attraction to novelty
- Brains of individuals with ADHD differ from those without it

CHAPTER 3. THE SOCIAL BRAIN

Emotions strongly impact learning, which is problematic because teens are still learning how to balance and manage their emotions. They are also learning how to negotiate their place in the world, from maintaining friendships to practicing the mating dance.

You've learned that . . .

- Adolescence is when the brain begins to develop templates for adult relationships
- Teen emotions can easily cement lifelong memories or form powerful learning blocks
- Teenagers value adult influence even though they complain about it
- Teens will climb the moral ladder only as their frontal lobes develop
- Boy brains and girl brains really are different—it's not just socialization

CHAPTER 4. COMMUNICATION AND THE UNFINISHED BRAIN

The rapidly changing brain is responsible for the adolescent communication gaps and growth. Neuroscientists are finally able to help educators adjust to the highs and lows of teen dialogue.

You've learned that . . .

- Adolescence is when language ability and short-term memory improve
- The teen brain relies more on the amygdala than on the frontal lobes, setting the stage for emotional outbursts
- Teens experience emotions before they can verbally articulate them

- Teenage self-awareness and teenage self-consciousness go hand in hand
- Teens are more vulnerable to stress than adults are

CHAPTER 5. SELF-CONCEPT UNDER ATTACK

Adolescence is a time of great fluctuation in the levels of neurotransmitters, the chemical messengers in the axons of neurons that excite and inhibit behaviors. When levels of these chemicals go astray, teens face a variety of mental upheavals such as depression, eating disorders, and shifts in sleep habits.

You've learned that . . .

- Testosterone and estrogen are found all over the brain during puberty
- Deficits and excesses of serotonin—the "take it easy" neurotransmitter—contribute to teen depression and eating disorders
- Obesity may have a chemical origin (and that some overweight teens may not lack self-control)
- Melatonin changes the sleep patterns of teenagers
- Transgender has its roots in the brain, not in the genitals

CHAPTER 6. THE RISK-TAKING BRAIN

The adolescent brain plays a significant role in reckless teen behaviors, and some mistakes (not all) teens make now can have lasting physiological effects.

You've learned that . . .

- Teens are very susceptible to the dopamine rushes that come with taking risks
- Teens have trouble anticipating the consequences of their behavior because they rely more on the emotional amygdala than the rational frontal lobes
- Teens are extremely vulnerable to addiction and adolescent addictions are harder to break
- Technology can rewire the brain
- Cutting is a pleasurable, but unhealthy, habit
- Violence and aggression decrease with age

CHAPTER 7. REACHING AND TEACHING TODAY'S ADOLESCENTS—TOMORROW!

Knowledge about the teenage brain and its unique characteristics should be reflected in how we run our schools and our classrooms. Middle schools and high schools need to reexamine how they are structured and how they can better help their adolescent population.

Make school a place that . . .

- Eases the transition from child brain to adolescent brain and appeals to teenagers' innate interest in the world around them
- Feels more like a community than an institution and nurtures teens' burgeoning sense of empathy and compassion
- Allows teens to explore and develop a self-identity and to express themselves as individuals
- Provides the support and structure teens need to productively channel and invest their energy and enthusiasm

Book Club
Discussion Questions

Congratulations on undertaking a book club study of *Secrets of the Teenage Brain*. Your desire to participate in a book club is a sure sign you are committed to the profession of teaching and have a desire to share information, common experiences, and strategies with your colleagues.

If your book club is just starting out, you may find the answers to the following questions helpful in ensuring that it runs smoothly:

1. Who will mediate? Will one person be designated the leader, or will you alternate the responsibility at each gathering?

2. Will you use a structured set of questions, semistructured (additional questions will be honored as they arise), or totally unstructured?

3. Will communication be casual, with people offering when they choose, or more formal, with each person responding in turn to the discussion question? (Some groups start with a general group discussion and then devote the last ten minutes to those who have not shared.)

4. Will you review the book in its entirety or divide it into one or two chapter segments? Whatever you choose, be sure to give enough time for everyone to complete the reading.

5. Do you plan to meet monthly, bimonthly, or once a semester? Do you want to have a set time each month, or will one person be in charge of arranging a convenient time to meet?

6. Consider online discussion groups if you can't find a group at your school.

7. Bring treats and have fun!

CHAPTER 1. TEEN BRAIN: UNDER CONSTRUCTION

1. What are some common, and not so common, adolescent behaviors you see in the classroom and outside the classroom?

2. What surprised you most in this chapter?

3. Choose the four most valuable points in this chapter. How will they impact you and your teaching?

4. What have you learned or experienced in the last two months that grew dendrites in your brain?

5. How are your students growing dendrites in and out of your classroom? Are they properly preparing their brain for the adult world?

6. Do you think there is an appropriate balance between academics and other experiences and activities in your students' lives?

7. What vicarious experiences increased your ability to be empathetic as a teacher?

8. Are you a role model for your students: Do you demonstrate empathy and a desire to understand the intentions of others? If so, in what ways?

9. What is one question you have after reading this chapter?

CHAPTER 2. TEEN COGNITION AND LEARNING

1. How do you gain students' attention in your class? What ways do you find most effective? What is one novel strategy you will try?

2. Create a simile for the statement, "Teaching is like _____ because _____." (Group leaders may want to bring objects from their classroom or home to fill in the first blank. Pass out a flash drive, magic marker, puzzle piece, or clay so that each person has a different object.) For instance, Teaching is like *a puzzle piece* because _____, or Teaching is like *clay* because _____.

3. What new instructional strategies from this chapter will you incorporate into your teaching? Will you make adaptations to the strategy?

4. What is one new way you can include multiple intelligences in your classroom?

5. Refer to the heading "Making the World a Better Place." What examples of *pseudostupidity* and *teenage hypocrisy* have you seen in your classroom? How could you handle those situations in the future?

6. What is the status of physical education at your school? What changes if any, are needed?

7. How frequently do students actively participate in your class? What methods do you use to engage students in your classroom?

8. Share one fun or favorite mnemonic device.

9. How do you give feedback to your students' work, and how do they respond to your feedback?

10. What are some methods to assess your students that do not discourage them?

11. What role should schools play in teaching study and test strategies? What do you plan to do in your classroom?

12. What is something new you learned about students with ADHD?

13. What strategies have you found to be most effective when working with students with ADHD? Is there a new strategy you will try?

CHAPTER 3. THE SOCIAL BRAIN

1. Telling stories is a favorite way to connect with students. What stories have you and your students shared, and what have been the effects?

2. Share a time you felt a natural dopamine rush.

3. How might you bring emotion into your classroom?

4. What are your views about expressing a sense of humor in the classroom?

5. Take the following identity inventory:
   a. My career is _____.
   b. My political stance is _____ (conservative, liberal, apathetic, moderate).
   c. My spirituality is _____ (Lutheran, Baptist, Muslim, Jew, agnostic, no formal religion).

    d. My personality is _____ (choose a few descriptors: fun, depressed, introverted, excited, bossy).

    e. My sexuality is _____ (heterosexual, homosexual, bisexual).

    f. My interests include _____ (choose a few: hobbies, sports, music).

    g. Intellectually I am _____ (academic, non-intellectual, middle of the road).

    h. My body image is _____ (I constantly criticize myself; I'm gorgeous; I may not be gorgeous, but I'm satisfied with myself).

    i. My ethnic or cultural affiliation is _____.

    j. I am (circle one) married, single, cohabitating.

In a nutshell these responses represent your identity. In what way (or ways) is your school or classroom supporting the identity formation of your students in each of these categories?

6. Discuss the cheating policy at your school or in your classroom. How does it fit with what we know about the brain and adolescent development?

7. Should moral behavior be taught in the school? If so, around what parameters?

8. Analyze the way gender is portrayed in televisions shows, movies, and magazines. Does your school add or detract from traditional gender role identification?

9. Discuss possible gender biases you have. Do you tend to prefer working with one gender over the other? If so, why?

10. Have you found strategies that meet the unique needs of girls? Of boys?

CHAPTER 4. COMMUNICATION AND THE UNFINISHED BRAIN

1. What do you see as the central message of this chapter? How does it resonate with you and your students?

2. How do you incorporate writing and speaking skills into your classroom? What is the best thing about including them, and what is most frustrating?

3. Discuss teenager misunderstandings you have witnessed. How might you help to calm them down or reduce them in the future?

4. What stressors do you perceive your students have? Do they prevent them from moving ahead with their learning?

5. What can you do to help relieve your students' stress levels?

6. What stressors do you have that prevent you from taking risks in your life as a teacher?

7. From your experience, what words of wisdom would you like to share with someone entering—or in—the education profession?

CHAPTER 5. SELF-CONCEPT UNDER ATTACK

1. In your opinion, what is the value of bringing information about puberty into your teaching? Is there content that you are uncomfortable incorporating into your subject area?

2. What ways have you found to value students' uniqueness?

3. How comfortable with your own body image are you? In what way does it impact your students?

4. How can you combat media messages about body image for girls? For boys?

5. Early bloomers and late bloomers: what are ways to help them feel more comfortable in their own bodies?

6. Share a story of a student who has faced an eating disorder. What role should the school play?

7. Discuss examples of students who have exhibited sleep deprivation. How did it impact their learning and their behavior? What can you do as a teacher to support good sleep habits?

CHAPTER 6. THE RISK-TAKING BRAIN

1. In what ways do you facilitate positive risk taking with your students?

2. How do you define "difficult students" in your own teaching experiences?

3. How successful have you been in your efforts to deal with difficult students? What are some ideal ways to deal with them? What would you do differently?

4. List positive and negative contributions to education and life from technology. What are your views on how to control the negative impact?

5. How do you incorporate technology into your classroom? Do you believe it enriches or hinders learning?

6. Reread the passage on "Group Identity." Put the passage into your own words as it relates to your students.

7. Are schools and communities too strict with our teenagers? What role has the media played in sensationalizing teenage problems?

8. Compare and contrast veteran– and beginning–teachers' views on at-risk students. Are there differences? If so, speculate as to why.

CHAPTER 7. REACHING AND TEACHING TODAY'S ADOLESCENTS—TOMORROW!

1. What are the most common academic interests of your students? How do you nourish their interests?

2. How do you encourage diverse students to work together?

3. What are your views about creating a sense of belonging in the classroom? What are the challenges? What are the workable strategies?

4. How do you ensure that students find your subject area meaningful?

5. In what ways do you and your colleagues support the transition between elementary school and middle school *or* middle school and high school? What is your opinion of current transition-support services? What changes would you recommend?

6. Who has been a mentor to you as a student or teacher? In what way has this person affected your views of yourself and your practices as a teacher?

7. What do you perceive to be the qualities of a good mentor?

8. What challenges do you face dealing with students' parents? How might relationships be strengthened?

9. List three strengths your school has in easing the evolution from child brain to adolescent brain and three areas where there is work to be done.

10. Will you change your teaching as a result of what you've read in this book? Why or why not?

Glossary of Brain Terms

amygdala. An almond-shaped area of the brain located deep in the temporal lobes that processes and remembers emotions; it is part of the limbic system.

axon. A long extension coming from a neuron that sends information to other neurons.

basal ganglia. A group of neural structures in the brain that controls voluntary movement (along with the cerebellum) and is involved with cognition and emotion.

brain. Located in the skull, it is the main part of the central nervous system and contains gray and white matter. It controls mental processes and physical movements; it also manages emotions, consciousness, and memory.

Broca's area. Associated with creating language, it is responsible for speech production and language processing. It is located in the left hemisphere of the frontal lobe and works in conjunction with Wernicke's area.

cell body. It contains the neuron's nucleus.

cerebellum. The part of the brain in control of voluntary motor movement (works in combination with the basal ganglia), balance, and muscle tone. Located at the lower back of the brain.

cerebral hemispheres. The two symmetrical halves of the brain, referred to as the right hemisphere and the left hemisphere.

cingulate system. Detects emotional meaning and allows a person to shift thoughts and ideas. It is part of the limbic system.

cognition. Process of thinking.

corpus callosum. A network of neurons that connects the left and right hemispheres of the brain and allows communication between them.

cortex (cerebral cortex). Outer layer of gray matter that covers the cerebral hemispheres.

cortisol. The primary stress hormone. It is released with the "fight or flight" reaction.

dendrite. Branch that emerges from a neuron. Receives messages from other cell bodies; one neuron may possess thousands of dendrites.

dopamine. A neurotransmitter in the brain associated with pleasure, movement, and sexual desire.

EEG (electroencephalography). Technology that studies electrical currents in the brain.

endorphins. Opiate-like hormones that give a sense of well-being and euphoria and reduce pain.

epinephrine. A hormone released when individuals experience pain or fear. It stimulates the heart and opens up the lungs. It is also known as adrenaline and is initially released as part of the "fight or flight" response.

estrogen. A female hormone produced by the ovaries; involved with menstruation, breast development, and pregnancy.

fMRI Scans (functional magnetic resonance imaging). Technology that examines the functions of the brain.

frontal lobes. The executive function of the brain resides here. It is involved in decision making, language, problem solving, planning, and controlling sense of self. It is located in the front of each hemisphere of the brain, behind the forehead.

glial cells. Brain cells that digest dead neurons, create myelin, and provide nutritional support to neurons. They are not capable of transmitting nerve impulses. Glial cells make up ninety percent of the brain's cells.

gray matter. Refers to the nerve cell bodies and dendrites in the brain.

hippocampus. Plays a key role in memory processing and helps regulate emotion.

hypothalamus. Regulates the pituitary gland and is part of the brain in control of pain, pleasure, hunger, thirst, and sexual desire.

leptin. A hormone that regulates metabolism, often associated with fat cells and appetite.

limbic system. A group of interconnected structures in the brain involved in emotion, motivation, and the sense of smell. Structures involved include the amygdala, hypothalamus, and hippocampus.

melatonin. A hormone released by the brain to cause and regulate the sleep-wake cycle.

mirror neurons. A neuron that fires both when it does an act and when it observes the act being done by another.

myelination. Fatty substance that insulates and protects neurons so they can communicate more efficiently.

neuroscience. The study of the nervous system and the brain.

neuron. A brain cell that sends and receives information to and from the brain and the *central nervous system.* It consists of dendrites, an axon, and a cell body. Neurons make up ten percent of the brain's cells.

norepinephrine. A hormone and a neurotransmitter that increases heart rate and blood pressure, it releases energy.

occipital lobe. In charge of visual processing in the brain. Located at the back of each cerebral hemisphere.

oxytocin. A hormone that creates feelings of bonding and trust and is involved in reproduction.

parietal lobes. A part of the brain associated with touch, temperature, and pain; located behind the frontal lobes at the top of the brain.

PET scan (positron-emission tomography scan). A three-dimensional view of the brain that allows neuroscientists to observe the structure and functions in the brain.

plasticity. The ability of the brain to reorganize itself as it gains information and has new experiences. It allows the brain to prune weak synapses and develop strong synapses.

pruning. Elimination of weak and ineffective synaptic connections in the brain.

serotonin. A neurotransmitter that regulates mood, it acts as a calming agent.

synaptic connection. The space that connects one neuron to another.

temporal lobes. A part of the brain involved with visual and verbal memory; located on each side of the brain, right above the ears.

testosterone. A male sex hormone produced by the testes; it is the strongest of the male hormones and is required for sperm production and secondary sexual characteristics, such as facial hair and a deeper voice.

Wernicke's area. Important in language development and works with Broca's area. Involved in recognizing and processing words that are spoken; located at the back of the temporal lobes on the left hemisphere.

white matter. Myelinated neurons in the cortex.

Bibliography

Adamson, L., Hartman, S. G., & Lyxell, B. (1999). Adolescent identity—a qualitative approach: Self-concept, existential questions and adult contacts. *Scandinavian Journal of Psychology, 40*(1), 21–31.

Adolescent smoking statistics. (2003). Retrieved from www.lungusa.org/site/c.dvLUK9O0E/b.39868/k.AFBF/Adolescent_Smoking_Statistics.htm

After school for America's teens: A national survey of teen attitudes and behaviors in the hours after school (An executive summary report by the YMCA of the USA). (2001). Retrieved March 26, 2004, fromwww.drugpolicy.org/library/bibliography/afterschool

Aguilera, A., Sanchez-Tomero J. A., & Selgas, R. (2007). Brain activation in uremic anorexia. *Journal of Renal Nutrition, 17*(1), 57–61. Retrieved from www.ncbi.nlm.nih.gov/pubmed/17198934

Aguilera, A., Selgas, R., Codoceo, R., & Bajo, A. (2000). Uremic anorexia: A consequence of persistently high brain serotonin levels? The tryptophan/serotonin disorder hypothesis. *Peritoneal Dialysis International, 20*(6), 810–816.

Alsaker, F. D. (1992). Pubertal timing, overweight, and psychological adjustment. *Journal of Early Adolescence, 12,* 396–419.

American Music Conference. (2007). *Music and the brain.* Available at www.amcmusic.com/musiceducation/social.htm Retrieved January 7, 2008.

Americans for the Arts. (2006). *Arts students outperform non-arts students on SAT: Average points better on SAT by arts students* [Data file]. Retrieved January 7, 2008, from www.artsusa.org/pdf/get_involved/advocacy/research/2007/SAT.pdf

Angelo, T., & Cross, K. P. (1998). *Classroom assessment techniques: A handbook for college teachers* (2nd ed.). San Francisco: Jossey-Bass.

Armstrong, T. (2000). *Multiple intelligences in the classroom* (2nd ed.). Alexandria, VA: Association for Supervision and Curriculum Development.

Arnett, J. J. (2001). *Adolescence and emerging adulthood: A cultural approach.* Upper Saddle River, NJ: Prentice Hall.

Aron, A., Fisher, H., Mashek, D. J., Strong, G., Li, H., & Brown, L. (2005). Reward, motivation, and emotion systems associated with early-stage intense romantic love. *Journal of Neurophysiology, 94*(1), 327–337.

Atallah, H. E., Frank, J. J., & O'Reilly, R. C. (2004). Hippocampus, cortex, and basal ganglia: Insights from computational models of complementary learning systems. *Neurobiology of Learning and Memory, 82*(3), 253–267.

Ausubel, D. P. (1968). *Educational psychology: A cognitive view.* New York: Holt, Rinehart & Winston.

Baird, A. A., Gruber, S. A., Fein, D. A., Maas, L. C., Steingard, R. J., Renshaw, P. F., et al. (1999). Functional magnetic resonance imaging of facial affect recognition in children and adolescents. *Journal of the American Academy of Child and Adolescent Psychiatry, 38*(2), 195–199.

Bangert-Drowns, R., Kulik, C. C., Kulik, J. A., & Morgan, M. (1991). The instructional effect of feedback in test-like events. *Review of Educational Research, 61*(2), 213–238.

Banks, W. A. (2003). Is obesity a disease of the blood-brain barrier? Physiological, pathological, and evolutionary considerations. *Current Pharmaceutical Design, 9*(10), 801–809.

Banks, W. A. (2008). The blood-brain barrier as a cause of obesity. *Current Pharmaceutical Design, 14*(16), 1606–1614.

Barbarich, N. (2002). Is there a common mechanism of serotonin dysregulation in anorexia nervosa and obsessive compulsive disorder? *Eating and Weight Disorders, 7*(3), 221–231.

Bartels, A., & Zeki, S. (2000). The neural basis of romantic love. *Neuroreport, 11*(17), 3829–3834.

Beckman, M. (2004, July 30). Neuroscience, crime, culpability, and the adolescent brain. *Science, 305*(5684), 595–599.

Benes, F., Turtle, M., Khan, Y., & Farol, P. (1994). Myelination of a key relay zone in the hippocampal formation occurs in the human brain during childhood, adolescence, and adulthood. *Archives of General Psychiatry, 51*(6), 477–484.

Blood, A. J., & Zatorre, R. J. (2001). Intensely pleasurable responses to music correlate with activity in brain regions implicated in reward and emotion. *Proceedings of the National Academy of Sciences, USA, 98*(20), 11818–11823.

Bloom, F. E., Beal, M. F., & Kupfer, D. J. (Eds.). (2006). *The Dana guide to brain health.* Available from www.dana.org

Bourgeois, J. P. (2001). Synaptogenesis in the neocortex of the newborn: The ultimate frontier of individuation? In C. A. Nelson & M. Luciana (Eds.), *Handbook of developmental cognitive neuroscience* (pp. 23–34). Cambridge: MIT Press.

Bourgeois, J. P. (2005). Brain synaptogenesis and epigenesist. *Medical Science (Paris), 21*(4), 428–433.

Brandt, R. (1999). Educators need to know about the human brain. *Phi Delta Kappan, 81*(3), 235–238.

Brandt, R. (2000). On teaching brains to think: A conversation with Robert Sylwester. *Educational Leadership, 57*(7), 72–75.

Bremner, J. D., Narayan, M., Anderson, E. R., Staib, L. H., Miller, H. L., & Charney, D. S. (2000). Hippocampal volume reduction in major depression. *American Journal of Psychiatry, 157*(1), 115–118.

Brendtro, L., Brokenleg, M., & Van Bockern, S. (2002). *Reclaiming youth at risk: Our hope for the future.* Bloomington, IN: National Education Service.

Breur, J. (1999). In search of . . . brain-based education. *Phi Delta Kappan, 80*(9), 648–657.

Brooks-Gunn, J., & Paikoff, R. (1997). Sexuality and developmental transitions during adolescence. In J. Schulenberg, J. L. Maggs, & K. Hurrelmann (Eds.), *Health risks and developmental transitions during adolescence* (pp. 190–219). New York: Cambridge University Press.

Brown, S. A., Tapert, S. F., Granholm, E., & Delis, D. C. (2000). Neurocognitive functioning of adolescents: Effects of protracted alcohol use. *Alcoholism, Clinical and Experimental Research, 24*(2), 164–171.

Brownell, S. (1999, August 9). Anorexia's roots in the brain. *U.S. News & World Report*, pp. 52–53.

Brownlee, S., Hotinski, R., Pailthorp, B., Ragan, E., & Wong, K. (1999, August 9). Inside the teen brain. *U.S. News & World Report*, pp. 44–54.

Buchel, C., Coull, J. T., & Friston, K. J. (1999, March 5). The predictive value of changes in effective connectivity for human learning. *Science, 283*(5407), 1538–1541.

Buis, J. N., & Thompson, D. N. (1989). Imaginary audience and personal fable: A brief review. *Adolescence, 24*(96), 773–781.

Caine, R. N., & Caine, G. (1990). Understanding a brain-based approach to learning and teaching. *Educational Leadership, 48*(2), 66–70.

Carney, R. N., & Levin, J. R. (2000). Mnemonic instruction, with a focus on transfer. *Journal of Educational Psychology, 92*(4), 783–790.

Carney, R. N., & Levin, J. R. (2008). Conquering mnemonophobia, with help from three practical measures of memory and application. *Teaching of Psychology, 35*(3), 176–183.

Carskadon, M. (Ed.). (2002). *Adolescent sleep patterns: Biological, social, and psychological influences.* New York: Cambridge University Press.

Center for Disease Control and Prevention. (2007). *Suicide trends among youths and young adults aged 10–24 years—United States, 1990–2004.* Retrieved September 3, 2008, from www.cdc.gov/mmwr/preview/mmwrhtml/mm5635a2.htm

Chambers, R. A., Taylor, J. R., & Potenza, M. N. (2003). Developmental neurocircuitry of motivation in adolescence: A critical period of addiction vulnerability. *American Journal of Psychiatry, 160*(6), 1041–1052.

Chugani, D. C., Muzik, O., Behen, M., Rothermel, R., Janisse, J. J., Lee, J., et al. (1999). Developmental changes in brain serotonin synthesis capacity in autistic and nonautistic children. *Annals of Neurology, 45*(3), 287–295.

Colapinto, J. (2000). *As nature made him: The boy who was raised as a girl.* New York: HarperCollins.

Coleman, O. D. (1996). An analysis of the perceptions of senior and junior students regarding the effectiveness of academic advisement in a teacher education program (Doctoral dissertation, Illinois State University, 1996). *Dissertation Abstracts International, 57*(06), 2441.

Compton, R. J. (2003). The interface between emotion and attention: A review of evidence from psychology and neuroscience. *Behavioral and Cognitive Neuroscience Reviews, 2*(2), 115–129.

Copley, J. (2008). *Psychology of heavy metal music: Effects on mood, aggression, suicide, drug use and intelligence.* Available from www.psychology.suite101.com/article.cfm/psychology_of_heavy_metal_music Retrieved January 4, 2009

Costa-Giomi, E. (1998, April). *The McGill Piano Project: Effects of three years of piano instruction on children's cognitive abilities, academic achievement, and self-esteem.* Paper presented at the meeting of the Music Educators National Conference, Phoenix, AZ.

Dagher, A., Bleicher, C., Aston, J. A., Gunn, R. N., Clarke, P. B., & Cumming, P. (2001). Reduced dopamine D1 receptor binding in the ventral striatum of cigarette smokers. *Synapse, 42*(1), 48–53.

Dahl, R. E. (2003). Beyond raging hormones: The tinderbox in the teenage brain. *Cerebrum: The Dana Forum on Brain Science, 5*(3), 7–22.

Dahl, R. E. (2008). Biological, developmental, and neurobehavioral factors relevant to adolescent driving risks. *American Journal of Preventive Medicine, 35* (3, Suppl. 1), S278–S284.

Damasio, A. (1994). *Descartes' error: Emotion, reason, and the human brain.* New York: Putnam.

D'Arcangelo, M. (2000). How does the brain develop? A conversation with Steven Petersen. *Educational Leadership, 58*(3), 68–71.

Davidson, R. J., Coe, C. C., Dolski, I., & Donzella, B. (1999). Individual differences in prefrontal activation asymmetry predict natural killer cell activity at rest and in response to challenge. *Brain Behavior and Immunity, 13*(2), 93–108.

Davidson, R. J., Putnam, K. M., & Larson, C. L. (2000, January 15). Dysfunction in the neural circuitry of emotion regulation: A possible prelude to violence. *Science, 289*(5479), 591–594.

Davies, P. L., & Rose, J. D. (1999). Assessment of cognitive development in adolescents by means of neuropsychological tasks. *Developmental Neuropsychology, 15*(2), 227–248.

De Bellis, M. D., Clark, D. B., Beers, S. R., Soloff, P. H., Boring, A. M., Hall, J., et al. (2000). Hippocampal volume in adolescent-onset alcohol use disorders. *American Journal of Psychiatry, 157*(5), 737–744.

De Bellis, M. D., Keshavan, M. S., Beers, S. R., Hall, J., Frustaci, K., Masalehdan, A., et al. (2001). Sex differences in brain maturation during childhood and adolescence. *Cerebral Cortex, 11*(6), 552–557.

Diamond, M. (1997). Sexual identity and sexual orientation in children with traumatized or ambiguous genitalia. *Journal of Sex Research, 34*(2), 199–211.

Diamond, M. C. (1988). *Enriching heredity: The impact of the environment on the anatomy of the brain.* New York: Free Press.

Diamond, M. C. (2000). *My search for love and wisdom in the brain.* Retrieved from www.newhorizons.org/neuro/diamond_wisdom.htm

Dietz, W. H. (2002). *CDC's role in combating the obesity epidemic before the Senate Committee on Health, Education, Labor and Pensions.* Retrieved from www.hhs.gov/asl/testify/t020521a.html

Doidges, N. (2007). *The brain that changes itself: Stories of personal triumph from the frontiers of brain science.* New York: Penguin.

Duke University Health System. (2008). *Monkey's thoughts make robot walk from across the globe.* Retrieved from www.dukehealth.org/HealthLibrary/News/10218

Dwek, L. B. (2002, July). Finding depression. *Psychology Today, 35*(4), 23.

Elkind, D. (1978). Understanding the young adolescent. *Adolescence, 13,* 127–134.

Epstein, H. T. (2001). An outline of the role of brain in human cognitive development. *Brain and Cognition, 45*(1), 44–51.

Fadiman, C. (n.d.). *Brainy Quote.* Retrieved April 20, 2009 from www.brainyquote.com/quotes/quotes/c/clifffadim165601.html

Fallon, D. (2002, March 19). *The amazing Miss A and why we should care about her.* Keynote speaker address at the Conversation between Foundation Officers and College and University Presidents, New York.

Feinstein, S. (2003). A case for middle school after-school programs in rural America. *Middle School Journal, 34*(3), 32–37.

Feinstein, S. (Ed.). (2006). *The Praeger handbook of learning and the brain.* Westport, CT: Praeger.

Feinstein, S. (2007). *Teaching the at-risk teenage brain.* Lanham, MD: Rowman & Littlefield.

Fernandez, A. (Interviewer), & Klingberg, T. (Interviewee). (2006). *Working memory training and RoboMemo: Interview with Dr. Torkel Klingberg.* Retrieved from www.sharpbrains.com/blog/2006/09/25/working-memory-training-and-robomemo-interview-with-dr-torkel-klingberg

Fishback, S. J. (1999). Learning and the brain. *Adult Learning, 10*(2), 18–22.

Fisher, H. E., Aron, A., Mashek, D., Li, H., & Brown, L. L. (2002). Defining the brain systems of lust, romantic attraction, and attachment. *Archives of Sexual Behavior, 31*(5), 413–419.

Flannery, D., Rowe, D., & Gulley, B. (1993). Impact of pubertal status, timing, and age on adolescent sexual experience and delinquency. *Journal of Adolescent Research, 8*(1), 21–40.

Friedman, I. A., & Mann, L. (1993). Coping patterns in adolescent decision making: An Israeli-Australian comparison. *Journal of Adolescence, 16*(2), 187–199.

Fuster, J. M. (2002). Frontal lobe and cognitive development. *Journal of Neurocytology, 31*(3–5), 373–385.

Gazzaniga, M. S., Bogen, J. E., & Sperry, R. W. (1962). Some functional effects of sectioning the cerebral commissures in man. *Proceedings of the National Academy of Sciences, USA, 48,* 1765–1769.

Giedd, J., Blumenthal, J., Jeffries, N. O., Castellanos, F., Liu, H., Zijdenbos, A., et al. (1999). Brain development during childhood and adolescence: A longitudinal MRI study. *Nature Neuroscience, 2*(10), 861–863.

Giedd, J., Blumenthal, J., Jeffries, N. O., Rajapakse, J., Vaituzis, A., Liu, H., et al. (1999). Development of the human corpus callosum during childhood and adolescence: A longitudinal MRI study. *Progress in Neuro-Psychopharmacology & Biological Psychiatry, 23*(4), 571–588.

Giedd, J. N., Castellanos, F. X., Rajapakse, J. C., Vaituzis, A. C., & Rapoport, J. L. (1997). Sexual dimorphism of the developing human brain. *Progress in Neuro-Psychopharmacology & Biological Psychiatry, 21*(8), 1185–1201.

Given, B. K. (2000). Theaters of the mind. *Educational Leadership, 58*(3), 72–75.

Goleman, D. (1995). *Emotional intelligence.* New York: Bantam Books.

Graber, J. A., Lewinsohn, P. M., Seeley, J. R., & Brooks-Gunn, J. (1997). Is psychopathology associated with the timing of pubertal development? *Journal of the American Academy of Child and Adolescent Psychiatry, 36*(12), 1768–1776.

Graham-Rowe, D. (2002, October 16). Teen angst rooted in busy brain. *New Scientist, 176*(2365), 16.

Greene, J. M., Ennett, S. T., & Ringwalt, C. L. (1999). Prevalence and correlates of survival sex among runaway and homeless youth. *American Journal of Public Health, 89*(9), 1406–1409.

Greenspan, S., & Benderly, B. L. (1997). *The growth of the mind and the endangered origins of intelligence.* Reading, MA: Perseus.

Gur, R. C., Alsop, D., Glahn, D., Petty, R., Swanson, C. L., Maldjian, J. A., et al. (2000). An fMRI study of sex differences in regional activation to a verbal and a spatial task. *Brain and Language, 74*(2), 157–170.

Gur, R. C., Gunning-Dixon, F., Bilker, W. B., & Gur, R. E. (2002). Sex differences in temporo-limbic and frontal brain volumes of healthy adults. *Cerebral Cortex, 12*(9), 998–1003.

Hardiman, M. (2001). Connecting brain research with dimensions of learning. *Educational Leadership, 59*(3), 52–55.

Healy, J. (1990). *Endangered minds: Why our children don't think.* New York: Simon & Schuster.

Heller, T. (2003). *Eating disorders: A handbook for teens, families, and teachers.* Jefferson, NC: McFarland.

Hennessy, J. W., King, M. G., McClure, T. A., & Levine, S. (1977). Uncertainty, as defined by the contingency between environmental events, and the adreno-cortical response of the rat to electric shock. *Journal of Comparative and Physiological Psychology, 91*(6), 1447–1460.

Henningsen, M. (1996). *Attachment disorder: Theory, parenting, and therapy.* Retrieved from www.attachmentdisorder.net/Treatment_Links.htm

Hiort, O., & Holterhus, P. M. (2000). The molecular basis of male sexual differentiation. *European Journal of Endocrinology, 142*(2), 101–110.

Hotz, R. (1998, June 25). Rebels with a cause: Studies of adolescents' brains find possible physiological basis for turbulent teenage emotions. *Los Angeles Times,* p. B2.

Houdart, R. (1994). [Consciousness]. *Encephale, 20*(2), 159–168.

Howard, P. (1994). *The owner's manual for the brain: Everyday applications from mind-brain research.* Austin, TX: Leornian Press.

Hutchinson K. A. (1995). Androgens and sexuality. *American Journal of Medicine, 98*(1A), 111S–115S.

Huttenlocher, P. R., & Dabholkar, A. S. (1997). Regional differences in synapto-genesis in human cerebral cortex. *Journal of Comparative Neurology, 387*(2), 167–178.

Iacoboni, M. (2005). Understanding others: imitation, language, empathy. In S. Hurley & N. Chater (Eds.), *Perspectives on imitation: From cognitive neuro-science to social science* (pp. 11–55). Cambridge: MIT Press.

Iacoboni, M. (2008). *Mirroring people: The new science of how we connect with others.* New York: Farrar, Straus, & Giroux.

Ice, S. (2003). *Statistics.* Available from www.eatingdisorderscoalition.org

Jacobs, B., Schall, M., & Scheibel, A. B. (1993). A quantitative dendritic analysis of Wernicke's area in humans. II. Gender, hemispheric, and environmental factors. *Journal of Comparative Neurology, 327*(1), 97–111.

James, A. (2007). *Teaching the male brain: How boys think, feel, and learn in school.* Thousand Oaks, CA: Corwin.

Johnston, L. D., O'Malley, P. M., & Bachman, J. G. (2003). *Table 2: Trends in annual and 30-day prevalence of use of various drugs for eighth, tenth, and twelfth graders* [Data file]. Available from www.monitoringthefuture.org/data/03data.html# 2003data-drugs

Just, M. A., Kellera, T. A., & Cynkara, J. (2008). Listening to cell phones impairs driving, study. *Brain Research.* Retrieved January 4, 2009, from www.medicalnewstoday.com/articles/99696.php

Kagan, S. (1994). *Cooperative learning.* San Juan Capistrano, CA: Kagan Cooperative Learning.

Kalkowski, P. (1995). *School improvement research series: Peer and cross-age tutoring* (Close-up No. 18). Retrieved from www.nwrel.org/scpd/sirs/9/c018.html

Kaltiala-Heino, R., Marttunen, M., Rantanen, P., & Rimpela, M. (2003). Early puberty is associated with mental health problems in middle adolescence. *Social Science and Medicine, 57*(6), 1055–1064.

Keefe, D. L. (2002). Sex hormones and neural mechanisms. *Archives of Sexual Behavior, 31*(5), 401–403.

Kempermann, G., & Gage, F. H. (1999, May). New nerve cells for the adult brain. *Scientific American, 280*(5), 48–53.

Keshavan, M. S., Diwadkar, V. A., De Bellis, M., Dick, E., Kotwal, R., Rosenberg, D. R., et al. (2002). Development of the corpus callosum in childhood, adolescence and early adulthood. *Life Sciences, 70*(16), 1909–1922.

Kim, J. J., & Diamond, D. M. (2002). The stressed hippocampus, synaptic plasticity, and lost memories. *Nature Reviews: Neuroscience, 3*(6), 453–462.

Kimura, D. (1992, September). Sex differences in the brain. *Scientific American, 267*(3), 118–125.

Kimura, D. (1996). Sex, sexual orientation and sex hormones influence human cognitive function. *Current Opinion in Neurobiology, 6,* 259–263.

Kimura, D. (2002). Sex hormones influence human cognitive patterns. *Neuroendocrinology Letters, 23*(Suppl. 4), 67–77.

Kircher, T. T., Senior, C., Phillips, M. L., Rabe-Hesketh, S., Benson, P. J., Bullmore, E. T., et al. (2001). Recognizing one's own face. *Cognition, 78*(1), B1–B15.

Kirchner, M. B., & Gunther, N. (Producers). (2000). Alcohol, drugs and the brain [Radio series episode]. In *Gray Matters.* Joint production of Public Radio International and Dana Alliance for Brain Initiatives.

Kluball, J. L. (2000). The relationship of instrumental music instruction and academic achievement for the senior class of 2000 at Lee County High School (Doctoral dissertation, University of Sarasota, 2000). *Dissertation Abstracts International 61*(11), 4320A.

Koepp, M. J., Gunn, R. N., Lawrence, A. D., Cunningham, V. J., Dagher, A., Jones, T., et al. (1998, May 21). Evidence for striatal dopamine release during a video game. *Nature, 393*(6682), 266–268.

Koff, E., Rierdan, J., & Stubbs, M. L. (1990). Gender, body image, and self-concept in early adolescence. *Journal of Early Adolescence, 10,* 56–68.

Kohn, A. (1993). *Punished by rewards: The trouble with gold stars, incentive plans, A's, praise, and other bribes.* Boston: Houghton Mifflin.

Kreeger, K. (2002). Deciphering how the sexes think: It's not necessarily about who is better at what, but why the sexes process some stimuli in dissimilar ways. *The Scientist, 16*(2), 28–29.

Kulin, H. (1991). Puberty, endocrine changes. In R. M. Lerner, A. C. Petersen, & J. Brooks-Gunn (Eds.), *Encyclopedia of adolescence* (Vol. 2, pp. 897–899). New York: Garland.

Laitinen-Krispijn, S., Van der Ende, J., Hazebroek-Kampschreur, A. A., & Verhulst, F. C. (1999). Pubertal maturation and the development of behavioural and emotional problems in early adolescence. *Acta Psychiatrica Scandinavica, 99*(1), 16–25.

LeDoux, J. (1996). *The emotional brain: The mysterious underpinning of emotional life.* New York: Simon & Schuster.

LeDoux, J. (2003). The emotional brain, fear, and the amygdala. *Cellular and Molecular Neurobiology, 23*(4–5), 727–738.

LeDoux, J. (2007). The amygdala. *Current Biology, 17*(20), 868–874.

Leonard, J. (1999, May). The sorcerer's apprentice: Unlocking the secrets of the brain's basement. *Harvard Magazine, 101*(5), 56–62.

Lerner, R. M., Delaney, M., Hess, L. E., Jovanovic, J. D., & von Eye, A. (1990). Early adolescent physical attractiveness and academic competence. *Journal of Early Adolescence, 10,* 4–20.

Levy, J. (1983). Research synthesis on right and left hemispheres: We think with both sides of the brain. *Educational Leadership, 40*(4), 66–71.

Lurie, K. (2003, November 4). *Teen stress.* Retrieved from www.sciencentral.com/articles/view.php3?language=english&type=&article_id=218392097

Lyvers, M. (2000). Cognition, emotion and the alcohol-aggression relationship: Comment on Giancola. *Experimental and Clinical Psychopharmacology, 8*(4), 607–608, 612–617.

Magnusson, D., Stattin, H., & Allen, V. (1986). Differential maturation among girls and its relation to social adjustment: A longitudinal perspective. In P. Baltes, D. Featherman, & R. Lerner (Eds.), *Life-span development and behavior* (Vol. 7, pp. 135–172). Hillsdale, NJ: Erlbaum.

Manisses Communications Group. (2003, May). What you should know about obesity in children and adolescents. *Brown University Child and Adolescent Behavior Letter, 19*(5), SI(2).

Marano, H. (2003, July). The new sex scorecard. *Psychology Today, 36*(4), 38–46.

Marzano, R., Pickering, D., & Pollock, J. (2001). *Classroom instruction that works: Research-based strategies for increasing student achievement.* Alexandria, VA: Association for Supervision and Curriculum Development.

Mason, M. (1998). *The van Hiele levels of geometric understanding.* Retrieved April 26, 2009, from www.coe.tamu.edu/~rcapraro/Graduate_Courses/EDCI%20624%20625/EDCI%20624%20CD/literature/van%20Hiele%20Levels.pdf

McBride, D., Barrett, S. P., Kelly, J. T., Aw, A., & Dagher, A. (2006). Effects of expectancy and abstinence on the neural response to smoking cues in cigarette smokers: An fMRI study. *Neuropsychopharmacology, 31*(12), 2728–2738.

McClintock, M. K., & Herdt, G. (1996). Rethinking puberty: The development of sexual attraction. *Current Directions in Psychological Science, 5*(6), 178–183.

McCluckey, K., & Mays, A. (2003). *Mentoring for talent development.* Sioux Falls, SD: Reclaiming Youth International.

McEwen, B. (1999). Development of the cerebral cortex: XIII. Stress and brain development: II. *Journal of the American Academy of Child and Adolescent Psychiatry, 38*(1), 101–103.

McEwen, B. (2002). Estrogen actions throughout the brain. *Recent Progress in Hormone Research, 57,* 357–84.

McGivern, R. F., Andersen, J., Byrd, D., Mutter, K. L., & Reilly, J. (2002). Cognitive efficiency on a match to sample task decreases at the onset of puberty in children. *Brain and Cognition, 50*(1), 73–89.

National Assessment of Educational Progress. (2002). Retrieved from www.nces.ed.gov/naep3/

National Longitudinal Study on Adolescent Health, 1994–2002. (2008). Retrieved from http://dx.doi.org/10.3886/ICPSR21600

National Institute of Mental Health. (2000, September). *Depression in children and adolescents: A fact sheet for physicians.* Retrieved from www.nimh.nih.gov/publicat/depchildresfact.cfm

National Runaway Switchboard. (2008). *National statistics.* Retrieved April 24, 2009, from www.1800runaway.org/news_events/call_stats.html

Neimark, E. D. (1975). Intellectual development during adolescence. In F. D. Horowitz (Ed.), *Review of child development research* (Vol. 4, pp. 541–594). Chicago: University of Chicago Press.

Nichols, M. (1996, January 22). Boys, girls and brainpower: The sexes differ in more than appearance. *Maclean's, 109*(4), 49.

O'Reilly, R. C., & Fran, M. J. (2006). Making working memory work: A computational model of learning in the prefrontal cortex and basal ganglia. *Neural Computation, 18*(2), 283–328.

O'Reilly, R. C., & Rudy, J. W. (2000). Computational principles of learning in the neocortex and hippocampus. *Hippocampus, 10*(4), 389–397.

Ormrod, J. E. (2000). *Educational psychology: Developing learners* (3rd ed.). Upper Saddle River, NJ: Merrill.

Ortiz, A. (2003). *Adolescent brain development and legal culpability.* Retrieved from www.abanet.org/crimjust/juvjus/resources.html#brain

Ostatnikova, D., Putz, Z., Celec, P., & Hodosy, J. (2002). May testosterone levels and their fluctuations influence cognitive performance in humans? *Scripta Medica (BRNO), 75*(5), 245–254.

Paus, T., Zijdenbos, A., Worsley, K., Collins, D. L., Blumenthal, J., Giedd, J. N., et al. (1999, March 19). Structural maturation of neural pathways in children and adolescents: In vivo study. *Science, 283*(5409), 1908–1911.

Paxton, S., Wertheim, E., Gibbons, K., Szmukler, G., Hillier, L., & Petrovoch, J. (1991). Body image satisfaction, dieting beliefs, and weight loss behaviors in adolescent girls and boys. *Journal of Youth and Adolescence, 20*(3), 361–379.

Pedersen, E., Faucher, T. A., & Eaton, W. W. (1978). A new perspective on the effects of first-grade teachers on children's subsequent adult status. *Harvard Educational Review, 48*(1), 1–31.

Perina, K. (2002, May). Mood swing: How feelings help and hurt. *Psychology Today, 35*(3), 17–18.

Piaget, J. (1970). *The science of education and the psychology of the child* (D. Coltman, Trans.). New York: Orion Press. (Original work published 1969)

Pipher, M. (1994). *Reviving Ophelia: Saving the selves of adolescent girls.* New York: Putnam.

Platek, S. M., Keenan, J. P., Gallup, G. G., Jr., & Mohammed, F. B. (2004). Where am I? The neurological correlates of self and other. *Brain Research: Cognitive Brain Research, 19*(2), 114–122.

Platek, S. M., Wathne, K., Tierney, N. G., & Thomson, J. W. (2008). Neural correlates of self-face recognition: An effect-location meta-analysis. *Brain Research, 1232*, 173–184.

Pollack, W. (1999). *Real boys: Rescuing our sons from the myths of boyhood.* New York: Henry Holt.

Puckett, M., Marshall, C., & Davis, R. (1999). Examining the emergence of brain development research: The promises and the perils. *Childhood Education, 76*(1), 8–12.

Putnam, J., Allshouse, J., & Kantor, L. S. (2002). U.S. per capita food supply trends: More calories, refined carbohydrates and fats. *FoodReview (A Publication of the Economic Research Service, USDA), 25*(3), 2–15.

Rapoport, J., Giedd, J., Blumenthal, J., Hamburger, S., Jeffries, N., Fernandez, T., et al. (1999). Progressive cortical change during adolescence in childhood onset schizophrenia. A longitudinal magnetic resonance imaging study. *Archives of General Psychiatry, 56*(7), 649–654.

Raz, N., Gunning-Dixon, F., Head, D., Williamson, A., & Acker, J. D. (2001). Age and sex differences in the cerebellum and ventral pons: A prospective MR study of healthy adults. *American Journal of Neuroradiology, 22*(6), 1161–1167.

Reiss, T. (1998). Wake-up call on kids' biological clocks. *NEA Today, 16*(6), 19–20.

Restak, R. (1994). *Receptors.* New York: Bantam Books.

Rice, P., & Dolgin, K. G. (2002). *Adolescent: Development, relationships, and culture* (10th ed.). Needham Heights, MA: Allyn & Bacon.

Saigh, P. A., Yaslik, A. E., Oberfield, R. A., Halamandaris, P. V., & Bremner, J. D. (2006). The intellectual performance of traumatized children and adolescents with or without posttraumatic stress disorder. *Journal of Abnormal Psychology, 115*(2), 332–340.

Sampaio, R. C., & Truwit, C. L. (2001). Myelination in the developing brain. In C. A. Nelson & M. Luciana (Eds.), *Handbook of developmental cognitive neuroscience* (pp. 35–44). Cambridge: MIT Press.

Santrock, J. W. (2003). *Adolescence* (9th ed.). Boston: McGraw-Hill.

Schacter, D. L. (1996). *Searching for memory: The brain, the mind, and the past.* New York: Basic Books.

Schiller, D., Ley, I., Niv, Y., LeDoux, J. E., & Phelps, E. A. (2008). From fear to safety and back: Reversal of fear in the human brain. *Journal of Neuroscience, 28*(45), 11517–11525.

Schneider, B. H., & Younger, A. J. (1996). Adolescent-parent attachment and adolescents' relations with their peers. *Youth and Society, 28*(1), 95–108.

Schwarz, J. (2006). *Researchers find physiological markers for cutting, other self-harming behaviors by teenage girls.* Retrieved from www.uwnews.org/article.asp?articleID=25024

Shaywitz, B. A., Shaywitz, S. E., Pugh, K. R., Constable, R. T., Skudlarski, P., Fulbright, R. K., et al. (1995, February 16). Sex differences in the functional organization of the brain for language. *Nature, 373*(6515), 607–609.

Siegel, D. J. (2001). Memory: An overview, with emphasis on developmental, interpersonal, and neurobiological aspects. *Journal of the American Academy of Child and Adolescent Psychiatry, 40*(9), 997–1011.

Siegel, D. J. (2006). An interpersonal neurobiology approach to psychotherapy: Awareness, mirror neurons, and neural plasticity in the development of well-being. *Psychiatric Annals, 36*(4), 248–256.

Smilkstein, R. (2003). *We're born to learn: Using the brain's natural learning process to create today's curriculum.* Thousand Oaks, CA: Corwin.

Smith, J. B., Lee, V. E., & Newmann, F. M. (2001). *Instruction and achievement in Chicago elementary schools.* Chicago: Consortium on Chicago School Research.

Sousa, D. (1998). Brain research can help principals reform secondary schools. *NASSP Bulletin, 82*(598), 21–28.

Sousa, D. (2001). *How the brain learns: A classroom teacher's guide* (2nd ed.). Thousand Oaks, CA: Corwin.

Sousa, D. A. (2003). *How the gifted brain learns.* Thousand Oaks, CA: Corwin.

Sowell, E. R., Thompson, P. M., Holmes, C. J., Jernigan, T. L., & Toga, A. W. (1999). In vivo evidence for post-adolescent brain maturation in frontal and striatal regions. *Nature Neuroscience, 2*(10), 859–861.

Spear, L. P. (2000). The adolescent brain and age-related behavioral manifestations. *Neuroscience and Biobehavioral Reviews, 24*(4), 417–463.

Spear, L. P. (2002, March). The adolescent brain and the college drinker: Biological basis of propensity to use and misuse alcohol. *Journal of Studies on Alcohol,* (Suppl. 14), 71–81.

Spearing, M. (2001). *Eating disorders: Facts about eating disorders and the search for solutions* (National Institute of Health Publication No. 01–4901). Retrieved from www.nimh.nih.gov/Publicat/eatingdisorders.cfm

Spice, B. (2008). *Carnegie Mellon study shows just listening to cell phones significantly impairs drivers.* Pittsburgh, PA: Carnegie Mellon.

Spinks, S. (Writer & Director). (2002, January 31). Inside the teenage brain (Program No. 2011). [Television broadcast]. In D. Fanning (Executive Producer), *Frontline.* Boston: WGBH.

Sprenger, M. (1999). *Learning and memory: The brain in action.* Alexandria, VA: Association for Supervision and Curriculum Development.

Squire, L. R., & Kandel, E. R. (2000). *Memory: From mind to molecules.* New York: Scientific American Library.

Stoleru, S., Gregoire, M. C., Gerard, D., Decety, J., Lafarge, E., Cinotti, L., et al. (1999). Neuroanatomical correlates of visually evoked sexual arousal in human males. *Archives of Sexual Behavior, 28*(1), 1–21.

Strauch, B. (2003). *The primal teen: What the new discoveries about the teenage brain tell us about our kids.* New York: Doubleday.

Sylwester, R. (2000). *A biological brain in a cultural classroom: Applying biological research to classroom management.* Thousand Oaks, CA: Corwin.

Sylwester, R. (2001). Unconscious emotions, conscious feelings, and curricular challenges. *New Horizons Online Journal, 6*(3). Available from www.newhorizons.org/journal/journa129.htm

Sylwester, R. (2007). *The adolescent brain: Reaching for autonomy.* Thousand Oaks, CA: Corwin.

Taylor, H., & Markow, D. (2003). Many high school students do not get enough sleep—and their performance suffers. *Harris Poll #24.* Retrieved from www.harrisinteractive.com/harris_poll/index.asp?PID=372

Taylor-Dunlop, K., & Norton, M. (1997). Out of the mouths of babes: Voices of at risk adolescents. *The Clearing House, 70*(5), 274–278.

Teenage brain: A work in progress (NIH Publication No. 01–4929). (2001). Retrieved from www.nimh.nih.gov/publicat/teenbrain.cfm_

Thomas, R. (1993, February). *Cross-age and peer tutoring* (Report No. EDO-CS-93–01). Retrieved from www.indiana.edu/~reading/ieo/digests/d78.html

Thomas, R. M., & Peterson, D. A. (2003). A neurogenic theory of depression gains momentum. *Molecular Interventions, 3*(8), 441–444.

Thompson, P. M., Giedd, J. N., Woods, R. P., MacDonald, D., Evans, A. C., & Toga, A. W. (2000, March 9). Growth patterns in the developing brain detected by using continuum mechanical tensor maps. *Nature, 404*(6774), 190–193.

Title IX at 30: Report card on gender equity (2002, June). A report of the National Coalition for Women and Girls in Education. Retrieved from www.ncwge.org/pubs.htm

Udry, J. R. (1990). Hormonal and social determinants of adolescent sexual initiation. In J. Bancroft & J. M. Reinisch (Eds.), *Adolescence and Puberty* (pp. 70–87). New York: Oxford University Press.

Uekermann, J., Daum, I., Schlebusch, P., & Trenckmann, U. (2005). Processing of affective stimuli in alcoholism. *Cortex, 41*(2), 189–194.

Uekermann, J., Daum, I., Schlebusch, P., Wiebel, B., & Trenckmann, U. (2003). Depression and cognitive functioning in alcoholism. *Addiction, 98*(11), 1521–1529.

U.S. Department of Education. (2001). Societal support for learning: Parental involvement in schools (Indicator No. 54). In *The Condition of Education 2001* (Report No. NCES 2001–072, p. 93). Retrieved from http://nces.ed.gov/pubs2001/2001072.pdf

U.S. Department of Health and Human Services. (2002). *National Survey on Drug Use and Health.* Available from http://oas.samhsa.gov/nhsda/2k2nsduh/Overview/2k2Overview.htm#

Vedantam, S. (2001, June 3). Are teens just wired that way? Researchers theorize brain changes are linked to behavior. *Washington Post,* p. A1.

Volkow, N. D., Fowler, J. S., Wang, G. J., & Goldstein, R. Z. (2002). Role of dopamine, the frontal cortex and memory circuits in drug addiction: Insight from imaging studies. *Neurobiology of Learning and Memory, 78*(3), 610–624.

Volkow, N. D., Fowler, J. S., Wang, G. J., Swanson, J. M., & Telang, F. (2007). Dopamine in drug abuse and addiction: Results of imaging studies and treatment implications. *Archives of Nuerology. 64*(11), 1575–1579.

Wade, T. J., Cairney, J., & Pevalin, D. J. (2002). Emergence of gender differences in depression during adolescence: National panel results from three countries. *Journal of the American Academy of Child and Adolescent Psychiatry, 41*(2), 190–198.

Walkup, J. T., Labellarte, M. J., Riddle, M. A., Pine, D. S., Greenhill, L., Klein, R., et al. (2001). Fluvoxamine for the treatment of anxiety disorders in children and adolescents. *New England Journal of Medicine, 344,* 1279–1285.

Wang, A., & Thomas, M. (1995). Effects of keywords on long-term retention: Help or hindrance? *Journal of Educational Psychology, 87,* 468–475.

Wang, G. J., Volkow, N. D., & Fowler, J. S. (2002). The role of dopamine in motivation for food in humans: Implications for obesity. *Expert Opinion on Therapeutic Targets, 6*(5), 601–609.

Weissman, D. H., & Banich, M. T. (2000). The cerebral hemispheres cooperate to perform complex but not simple tasks. *Neuropsychology, 14*(1), 41–59.

White, A. M. (2003). Substance use and adolescent brain development: An overview of recent findings with a focus on alcohol. *Youth Studies Australia, 22,* 39–45.

White, A. M., & Swartzwelder, H. S. (2005). Age-related effects of alcohol on memory and memory-related brain function in adolescents and adults. *Recent Developments in Alcohol, 17,* 161–176.

Windle, M., Spear, L. P., Fuligni, A. J., Angold, A., Brown, J. D., Pine, D., et al. (2008). Transitions into underage and problem drinking: Developmental processes and mechanisms between 10 and 15 years of age. *Pediatrics* (Suppl. 4), 274–289.

Wingert, P., & Kantrowitz, B. (2002, October 7). Young and depressed. *Newsweek,* pp. 53–61.

Witmer, J. T., & Anderson, C. S. (1994). *How to establish a high school service learning program.* Alexandria, VA: Association for Supervision and Curriculum Development.

Wolfe, P. (2001). *Brain matters: Translating research into classroom practice.* Alexandria, VA: Association for Supervision and Curriculum Development.

Woolfolk, A. (2006). *Educational Psychology* (10th ed.). Needham Heights, MA: Allyn & Bacon.

Yoder, C. Y., Weitzen, S., Pickle, L. W., Grant, B., Herrmann, D., & Schnitzer, S. B. (2001). Cognitive functioning in the last year of life as a function of age, gender, and race. *Experimental Aging Research, 27*(3), 241–256.

Yurgelun-Todd, D. A., Killgore, W. D., & Young, A. D. (2002). Sex differences in cerebral tissue volume and cognitive performance during adolescence. *Psychological Reports, 91*(3, Pt. 1), 743–757.

Zeng, L., Leplow, B., Holl, D., & Mehdorn, M. (2003). Quantification of human spatial behavior in an open field-locomotor maze. *Perceptual and Motor Skills, 3*(Pt. 1), 917–935.

Zhou, J. N., Hofman, M. A., Gooren, L. J., & Swaab, D. F. (1995, November). A sex difference in the human brain and its relation to transsexuality. *Nature, 378,* 68–70.

Zhu, W., Volkow, N. D., Ma, Y., Fowler, J. S., & Wang, G. J. (2004). Relationship between ethanol-induced changes in brain regional metabolism and its motor, behavioural and cognitive effects. *Alcohol and Alcoholism, 39*(1), 53–58.

Index

CORWIN

A SAGE Company

The Corwin logo—a raven striding across an open book—represents the union of courage and learning. Corwin is committed to improving education for all learners by publishing books and other professional development resources for those serving the field of PreK–12 education. By providing practical, hands-on materials, Corwin continues to carry out the promise of its motto: **"Helping Educators Do Their Work Better."**